The Bennetts

The Bennetts

AN ACTING FAMILY

Brian Kellow

THE UNIVERSITY PRESS OF KENTUCKY

Publication of this volume was made possible in part by a grant from the National Endowment for the Humanities.

Scholarly publisher for the Commonwealth,
serving Bellarmine University, Berea College, Centre
College of Kentucky, Eastern Kentucky University,
The Filson Historical Society, Georgetown College,
Kentucky Historical Society, Kentucky State University,
Morehead State University, Murray State University,
Northern Kentucky University, Transylvania University,
University of Kentucky, University of Louisville,
and Western Kentucky University.

Editorial and Sales Offices: The University Press of Kentucky
663 South Limestone Street, Lexington, Kentucky 40508-4008
www.kentuckypress.com

05 06 07 08 5 4 3 2

Frontispiece: The Bennetts at home:
Constance, Mabel, Joan, Richard, Barbara. (Photofest)

Library of Congress Cataloging-in-Publication Data

Kellow, Brian.
The Bennetts : an acting family / Brian Kellow.
p. cm.
Includes bibliographical references and index.
ISBN 0-8131-2329-1 (alk. paper)
1. Bennett, Richard, 1873-1944. 2. Bennett, Constance, 1904-1965.
3. Bennett, Joan, 1910- 4. Bennett, Barbara, 1906-1958. 5. Actors—United States—Biography. I. Title.
PN2285.K42 2004
791.4302'8'092273—dc22

2004020805

This book is printed on acid-free recycled paper meeting the requirements of the American National Standard for Permanence in Paper for Printed Library Materials.

Manufactured in the United States of America.

Member of the Association of
American University Presses

For Erik Dahl

Contents

Preface

When I was a student at Oregon State University, the English Department sponsored an every-Friday-night International Film Series. There I first encountered many marvelous foreign-language films of the period, including *Bread and Chocolate, Spirit of the Beehive, Jonah Who Will Be 25 in the Year 2000,* and *Seven Beauties.* But occasionally the department's interpretation of "international" was opened up slightly, to include films of European-born directors working in Hollywood, such as Billy Wilder and Ernst Lubitsch. And one chilly Friday night in October 1978, the film shown was Fritz Lang's *The Woman in the Window.* I became entranced with the movie on the spot, and ultimately it led me to many of the other glorious examples of 1940s film noir, including Lang's startling *Scarlet Street* and Max Ophuls's remarkable *The Reckless Moment,* both of which boasted the same leading lady, Joan Bennett.

Ten years later, by this time launched on a career in journalism, I met Joan Bennett at her home in Scarsdale, New York. My encounter with her was memorable as well as slightly disappointing. She was courteous and charming, but fuzzy on details of her glamorous past, and she seemed apologetically conscious of this. Nevertheless, I was always aware that I was in the presence of a star: although she gave me very little information, her few deep-toned observations, mysterious silences, and long, slow drags on her Carltons somehow made a potent impression on me. I sensed that there was a great deal in what she wasn't saying, and I decided to find out about it on my own. In the back of my mind was the vague notion that if what I discovered seemed interesting enough, I might try to undertake a book about the entire family. As it turned out, it was, and I did.

By the time I began my research in earnest in 1998, I had already read two books that were to be of the utmost importance to me. The first was *The Bennett Playbill,* Joan's own history of her family, written with actress-author-director Lois Kibbee and published in 1970. It has proven a very useful guide to the Bennett family history. Matthew Bernstein's admirable biography of Joan's third husband, *Walter Wanger: Hollywood Independent,* surely one of the most painstakingly researched studies of exactly how films get made, was also a welcome anchor as I began work on my book.

At numerous archives, my queries were placed in capable and trustworthy hands. For information on Richard Bennett's early life, I am indebted to Martha Wright of the Indiana State Historical Society and Patricia Al-Wahaili of the Indiana State Library.

I spent a fascinating week at the State Historical Society of Wisconsin, where Walter Wanger's papers are housed; there I received an enthusiastic reception from Maxine Ducey and her staff. I also owe deepest thanks to the staffs of the Film and Television Archives at the University of California at Los Angeles, the Lincoln Center Library for the Performing Arts, the Library of Congress, the Lilly Library at Indiana University, the Sterling Library at Yale University, and the motion picture department of The George Eastman House. Thanks also to Barbara Hall of the Academy of Motion Picture Arts and Sciences, Annette Fern of the Harvard Theater Collection, Martin Jacobs of the Museum of the City of New York, Steve Wilson and the staff of the Harry Ransom Humanities Research Collection at the University of Texas at Austin (in particular, my research proxy, Bill Fagelson), Sean D. Noel of the Howard Gotlieb Archival Research Center at Boston University, Stephen Reynolds of the Duke of York's Theatre, and Raymond Wemmlinger of the Hampden/Booth Theater Library of The Players. Special thanks to Ned Comstock of the University of Southern California Cinema and Television Archive. Ned did many special favors for me, including dredging up materials from USC's Warner

Bros. archive and tracking down financial reports from Constance Bennett's RKO years.

I was unprepared for the generosity extended to me by many well-respected writers on film. Donald Spoto was among the first to encourage me to write about the Bennett family. I am also indebted to Jeanine Basinger, James Harvey, Roy Moseley, Robert Osborne, Barry Paris, Sam Staggs, James Watters, and most of all to Ronald L. Bowers, who spent many hours recalling his close friendship with Joan Bennett. Ron also telephoned me with numerous leads and ideas, and lent me many out-of-print volumes from his vast collection of cinema books. His enthusiasm for Hollywood's golden age is boundless. Thanks also to Howard and Ron Mandelbaum of Photofest, Jerry Ohlinger, and Bill Sprague, for providing me with a copy of Barbara Bennett's hard-to-find film *Syncopation,* and to Tom Toth, for sharing his print of Constance's silent hit *Sally, Irene and Mary.*

For help in negotiating the legal maze regarding Philip Plant's estate, I owe deep thanks to Jackie Zeppieri of the New London, Connecticut, Probate Court, and Helen Falvey and Alice Schroeder of the Groton, Connecticut, Probate Court; Ms. Schroeder was particularly helpful in laying hands on depositions related to Constance Bennett's 1943 battle with Mae Hayward.

Given the fact that so many individuals that Constance and Joan Bennett worked with are deceased, it was crucial that I secure the cooperation of surviving family members. Here I was extremely lucky. The book would not have materialized without the participation of Joan's eldest daughter, Diana Anderson, who was enthused about the project from the beginning and lent unfailing support. On two different occasions, she opened up her home to me while I was in Los Angeles on fact-finding missions. Together we spent hours talking about all the Bennetts; Diana's shrewd perceptions and strong family feeling helped immeasurably in creating the backbone of the book. I am also delighted to have had the contributions of all five of her children: Amanda Anderson, Timothy Anderson, Cynthia Anderson Barker, Lisa Anderson, and Felix Werner.

I met Constance's son, Peter Plant, at a birthday party for Diana in New York in 1997. Over the years, Peter had spoken about his mother with only a handful of writers, and then only on very limited topics. Once I described my concept of the book to him, however, he gave me his fullest cooperation. I came to admire his honesty, humor, fairness, and precision; his answers to my questions were always carefully weighed and scrupulously considered, and together we made our way through some of the more baffling episodes in his mother's life. That I was able to earn his trust means a great deal to me.

I am also pleased to have secured the participation of Constance's two daughters, Lorinda Roland and Gyl Roland, both of whom gave generously of their time—Lorinda at her artist hideaway on Orcas Island, Washington, and Gyl at her Los Angeles apartment. Their perspectives contrasted sharply with one another, but in the end, both were tremendously helpful in putting together a portrait of their complex mother.

Thanks, also, to Joan's second daughter, Melinda Markey, who spoke with me by telephone from her home in South Carolina. I am also grateful to Joan's two youngest daughters, Stephanie Wanger Guest and Shelley Wanger, who met with me several times in New York.

Michael Downey is the oldest and only surviving child of Barbara Bennett and Morton Downey. From the outset, Michael made it clear that he guarded his privacy zealously and that his participation would be quite limited. Once we connected, however, he was willing to share his memories, and I am happy that he was.

I met with David Wilde, Joan's fourth husband, several times at his home in Scarsdale, New York. Sadly, David did not live to see the book reach publication; overcome by depression and declining health, he committed suicide late in 2001.

Deepest thanks to the many other people who took the time to speak with me: Iris Adrian, Hartney Arthur, Nancy Barrett, Mary Cooper, Arlene Dahl, Tony de Santis, Carmen DiRigo, Edward Downey, Keir Dullea, Alice Faye, John Frankenheimer, James Fraser, Penny Fuller, Henry Garson, Janet Fox Goldsmith, Louise Gore,

James Graves, Jane Greer, Peter Haskell, Helen Hayes, Charles Hollerith, Marsha Hunt, Alexandra Iles, Salome Jens, Marta Eggerth Kiepura, Jack Klugman, Susan Kohner, Florence Kriendler, Paula Laurence, June Lockhart, Patricia Coulter McElroy, Ellie and Victor Morrison, Julian Myers, Patricia O'Connell, Neva Patterson, Jim Pierson, Donald Pippin, Vera Hruba Ralston, Charles Nelson Reilly, Hilda Rolfe, Kathryn Leigh Scott, Daniel Selznick, Harvey Silbert, Erica Silverman, Penny Singleton, Anne Slater, Peggy Sobel, Jan Sterling, Risë Stevens, Gloria Stuart, William Studer, Bazey Tankersley, Audrey Totter, Marie Wallace, Robert Wallsten, Arthur Whitelaw, Victoria Wilson, William Windom, Teresa Wright, and Jane Wyatt. Of all those I interviewed, I am especially indebted to Joan's good friend Richard Stack. As the book progressed, I leaned heavily on Richard, and always welcomed his insights and points of view. He has in turn become a great friend of mine.

Four colleagues at *Opera News* were of enormous help. F. Paul Driscoll, the magazine's editor-in-chief, was a valued resource throughout the writing. He possesses an astonishing command of film and theater history, and as the book progressed, he was never too busy to discuss a point that was perplexing me at any given moment. Elizabeth Diggans, *Opera News*'s associate art director and an inveterate film-lover, lent welcome humor and encouragement along the way. Assistant editor Betsy Mingo helped me with much of the research—always thoroughly, always promptly. Art director Gregory Downer generously provided my jacket photo.

Many of the Bennett family's films I viewed with my good friends Tracy Turner and Arlo McKinnon, who offered insightful comments and, as always, good company. Other friends who helped in a variety of ways include Patricia Adams, Sara Charlton, Craig Haladay, Jessica and Omus Hirshbein, James M. Keller, Brenda Lewis, John Manis, Eric Myers, Karen Kriendler Nelson, David Niedenthal, Rebecca Paller, Monica Parks, Brooks Peters, Cynthia Peterson, Fred Plotkin, Robert Sandla, Helen Sheehy, and James Whitson.

I was delighted by the highly professional treatment my book received from the staff of the University Press of Kentucky. Ken Cherry was enthusiastic about the project from the beginning. And working with Leila Salisbury and David Cobb has been pure pleasure.

I would like to express my deepest gratitude to Joel Honig, who died in September 2003 and whose absence is sorely felt. For years, dozens of authors enjoyed the benefit of Joel's adroit editing, impeccable research skills, and depths of arcane knowledge. He was a busy freelance copy editor (including a nineteen-year association with Charles Scribner's Sons), and always he labored to make the books he was entrusted with as good as they possibly could be. He was a superb writer himself; for many years, I had the pleasure of working as his editor at *Opera News*. With *The Bennetts,* the tables were turned, and Joel played his role with relentless brilliance, always pressing me to go further, to make the story of the Bennetts more incisive, illuminating, and alive.

I am lucky to have the sustaining presence in my life of my family. My parents, Jack and Marjorie Kellow, and my brother and sister-in-law, Barry and Kami Kellow, have always encouraged my writing pursuits and my interest in the performing arts, and I am grateful.

Most of all, I was blessed to have Bill Braun by my side throughout my work on the book. He endured watching many old movies that he easily could have done without, always asking, in vain, if tonight's selection might be in color. He didn't complain while I neglected house and yard to concentrate on research, brought me back to earth when I panicked over deadlines, and endured my need for solitude as I bore down on the final chapters.

Prologue

"There are only three great actors still alive in America today," Richard Bennett told a reporter in the early 1930s. "Maude Adams, Feodor Chaliapin, and Lionel Barrymore. Four if you count me!" Bennett could afford to be immodest—at the time he made that comment, he had racked up a record of achievement that few other actors could match. Along with John Barrymore, he was probably the most important American-born stage actor of his generation. Bennett's stardom had slightly preceded Barrymore's and would outlast it by several years. Yet by the mid-1920s, when Bennett had reached the zenith of his acting career, he believed that the most glorious era in the American theater had come and gone. To him, the stage was haunted by ghosts: Joseph Jefferson, who had trouped around the country for decades treating audiences to his classic portrayal of Rip Van Winkle, died in 1905. The noble, dark-eyed tragedian Edwin Booth, the most celebrated Hamlet of his day, had been dead since 1893. Charles F. Coghlan, Lester Wallack, Nat Goodwin, and Edward Harrigan and Tony Hart, and dozens of other actors whose work had been an inspiration to Bennett, had long since faded from the scene.

Richard Bennett's own stage debut had come in 1891, and although he might have had every good reason to feel nostalgic for the great stars of the period, the plays themselves were often best forgotten. While Shakespeare, in the hands of actors such as E.H. Sothern, Julia Marlowe, Viola Allen, and Otis Skinner, was a staple on the New York stage to a degree that seems unimaginable to us now, it was creaking melodrama, often running to five acts or more, that provided much of the meat of the American theater scene.

Because so few of the great stars of the last years of the nineteenth century and the first decade of the twentieth have left any permanent record of their work, we are forced to rely chiefly on written accounts from the period to gain any sense at all of what they were like onstage. These tell us, among other things, that it was an age of great personalities, in which player dominated playwright. Many stars became so identified with a single role that their demanding and unimaginative public refused to accept them in anything else. James O'Neill, father of Eugene, once a promising young actor, made such a success in an 1883 production of *The Count of Monte Cristo* that he became essentially a one-trick pony, doomed to play the same role over and over for the remainder of his career. Phoebe Davies played the role of Anna Moore in Lottie Blair Parker and Joseph R. Grismer's rip-roaring 1898 melodrama *Way Down East* some four thousand times during the course of her career. And Bennett's own father-in-law, Lewis Morrison, played Mephistopheles in *Faust,* virtually without a break, from 1885 until his death in 1906.

Many of the leading stars of this period performed in a florid, heart-on-sleeve style perhaps most accurately described as "heroic," relying on richly individual personalities, charm, and highly cultivated voices. Joseph Jefferson, one critic commented, "could have recited the alphabet in a way to make his hearers shed sympathetic tears." They were out to please the public first, last, and always. (Critics, at this time, were of fairly little importance in determining the fate of a play; only later would they ascend to positions of power. One reason Richard Bennett scorned critics during his peak years was because he remembered the early days when they had not mattered so much.)

Whatever the caliber of these performers, one condition did make theirs a golden period: they had unprecedented opportunities to perform. By the mid-1890s, New York boasted thirty-nine legitimate theaters. By 1900, the number of theaters spread out over the entire nation totaled approximately five thousand. No matter how modest their condition, these theaters added immeasurably to the cultural life of both small and large towns. In those days, the road was an integral part of the theater. Both major stars and third-rate stock players traveled the length and breadth of the country. It was a bountiful era, and in his old age Richard Bennett was consumed by nostalgia for it. Writing about those long-gone days in his unpublished memoirs, from the perspective of an elderly man whose career had nearly reached its end, he insisted that he could "count on five fingers even the near-greats of today. They are not artists . . . nor nearer art than photography is to oil paintings."

This is a curious statement, and perhaps it can be attributed to nothing more than an actor's bitterness over his failing powers and fading fame. Certainly the 1920s was one of the most remarkable decades the American theater has ever known, and the one in which Richard Bennett reached his peak. True, the rapid growth of the film industry had reduced the sheer quantity of stage productions available. By the time D.W. Griffith's immensely successful *The Birth of a Nation* was released in 1915, over six thousand nickelodeons were operating around the country, while the number of professional playhouses had shrunk to something under fifteen hundred. Nevertheless, Broadway in the 1920s was a thriving industry. Exciting and innovative plays would take the theater in thrilling new directions, and the decade's leading stars did not make only occasional appearances—they were constant, returning one season after another, providing the real backbone of Broadway.

If Richard Bennett regarded this embarrassment of riches as a time of artistic bankruptcy, he was slighting some of his own brilliant contributions to the theater—something he surely never would have intended to do. Although he had appeared in many important plays during the first two decades of the century, the 1920s was a vintage period for him. Beginning with O'Neill's *Beyond the Horizon* in 1920, Bennett set forth on a series of successes that gave him ample opportunity to display his acting prowess as never before. In 1921, he starred as Andrew Lane in Gilbert Emery's *The Hero,* a searing drama set in the aftermath of World War I. There was Leonid Andreyev's *He Who Gets Slapped* in 1922, a highly imaginative and lyrical work produced by the Theatre Guild, one of the most enterprising new organizations of the day. While visiting New

York, Konstantin Stanislavsky attended a performance of *He* and proclaimed Richard Bennett the finest American actor he had ever seen. The following year brought Gerald Du Maurier's *The Dancers,* in which Bennett scored another success as Tony, the Canadian saloonkeeper who inherits an English title. In 1924, Bennett starred as Tony Patucci, the Italian-American vineyard owner in the Theatre Guild's production of Sidney Howard's *They Knew What They Wanted,* a work that challenged audiences' ideas of acceptable morality. Of lesser literary quality, but a success with audiences, was Charles Beahan and Garrett Fort's *Jarnegan* (1928), a sensational exposé of Hollywood, in which Richard's youngest daughter, Joan, was introduced to Broadway.

It was an impressive string of achievements, and by the end of the 1920s, few in the profession would have doubted that Richard Bennett would one day take his place among the theater's immortals. Yet by 1930, his glory days were behind him, and only a handful of stage appearances lay in his future. In 1931, he settled in Hollywood, where two of his three daughters, Constance and Joan, were carving out successful movie careers. (At the time, Constance was billed as Hollywood's highest-paid actress, commanding $30,000 a week.) Richard went to work in a series of mostly forgettable films. Although he grandly referred to his time in Hollywood as his "noble experiment in the sun-drenched hills," few of his movies gave him any reason to be proud. He was dismayed to see how quickly Broadway would forget about him, how capably the theater could continue in his absence. Good riddance, he claimed. "My God," he had said only in the mid-1920s, when his middle daughter Barbara was attracting attention as an exhibition ballroom dancer, "the day may come when I'll be known as the father of the Bennett girls. It would damn well serve me right!" Speaking of *Bought!,* a mediocre 1931 movie he made with Constance, he said, defensively, "I wouldn't give up my part in this picture for anything on Broadway." In fact, he missed the stage desperately. Like an impulsive lover, he had turned his back on the world that had meant so much to him, and eventually seemed unable to return to it. No show business fame can fade quite so quickly as theatrical stardom, and year by year, Richard saw his own stunning achievements recede into a dimly remembered past.

In the end, Richard Bennett failed to take his place among the immortals of the stage. Theater histories that devote ample space to the accomplishments of the Barrymores, Paul Robeson, and Laurette Taylor often sum up Richard's career in a footnote, or omit mention of him altogether. By 1940, he was largely forgotten, financially dependent on family and friends, living a sadly reduced existence in southern California. His prediction had come true: to the extent that he was remembered at all, it was as the father of movie stars Constance and Joan Bennett. No doubt he did not feel that such a fate "served him right" at all. It must have seemed an unjust end for someone who had given so much to the theater, and gotten so much in return.

Chapter One

1870–1900

Long before he was famous for being the father of Constance and Joan Bennett, Richard Bennett had been famous for the intensity of his stage performances, his heavy drinking, his brushes with the law, his long-winded curtain speeches, and perhaps most of all, for his incendiary temper. He unleashed it freely and often, until it became part of theater legend. It was an age of outsized theatrical personalities, and Richard Bennett often crossed the line between going too far—and farther. Perhaps he believed, as one journalist noted, that any good actor should behave as if the curtain had never gone down. He had an egalitarian approach to picking fights: he feuded with his wives, his daughters, his producers and directors, his leading ladies, with playwrights, politicians, servants, stagehands, and most famously of all, with critics and audiences. The sources of his outbursts included a quest for perfection, contempt for laziness and complacency, an almost adolescent love of creating chaos for its own sake, and a bitter disappointment, suffered his whole life through, that not everyone felt things as intensely as he did.

About Bennett's temper, one thing at least is clear. It was not something that he suddenly acquired as an accoutrement of theatrical stardom; it was present from early childhood. Throughout his years in the theater, the facts of Richard's birth were jumbled and often contradictory. For reasons of his own, he took pains to obscure his birthplace as well as his birth date. Many official biographies list him as having been born in Deacon's Mills (as the town of

Deacon was known locally), Indiana, on May 21, 1872, while some put his birth as occurring exactly one year later. In several sources, his birthplace is alternatively identified as Hoover, Bennett's Switch, and Bennett's Mills. Joan Bennett's 1970 autobiography, *The Bennett Playbill*, further confuses matters; she states that her father's birthplace was "Bennett's Switch, which is located near Kokomo and Logansport on the banks of the Wabash River." (Bennett's Switch is not on the Wabash.)

In Indiana, birth certificates are unavailable for any date preceding 1880, but the matter is somewhat clarified by the 1870 census schedule, which lists Richard's parents, George Washington Bennett and Eliza Leonora Bennett, as residing in Deer Creek Township, a tiny village in the southwest corner of Cass County, Indiana. Their eldest child, Clarence Charles William Henry Richard Bennett, is stated as having been born in May 1870—most likely on the 21st. (Richard would be known as Clarence until sometime after he was ten years old.) Certainly many actors play fast and loose with the truth about their birth dates, and it is easy to understand why Richard would remove a few years in the hope of extending the period in which he could be considered for romantic leading-man roles. But why lie about where he was born, if he were merely going to substitute one small Indiana town for another? In any case, he probably taught his oldest daughter a trick or two in this respect: throughout her film and stage career, Constance was extremely skilled at fooling the press about her age—and numerous other things.

Deer Creek was initially part of the thirty-square-mile Miami Indian reservation. Settled in the late 1830s, its population grew very little over the next few decades. By the mid-1880s, there were only fifteen people in town. Richard's father, George Bennett, owned and operated a sawmill, like the three generations of Bennetts before him. According to Richard, George carried on another family tradition: he was a circuit rider, an unordained, itinerant preacher who traveled on horseback from town to town, proclaiming the glory of God and the rewards of salvation that lay in wait for any sinner, no matter how far gone. This particular family tradition died with George Bennett's generation. Although he was made to attend church regularly as a child, Richard harbored a deep-seated mistrust of all religions for most of his adult life.

Four years after Richard's arrival, his mother gave birth to a daughter, Ina Blanche. When Richard was still quite young, the family moved to Kokomo, the principal town of Howard County, along the Peru and Indianapolis Rivers. As a child, he was short for his age, and extremely thin, but far from fragile. He was wild and energetic, and spent most of his time outdoors, swimming, riding ponies, roller-skating on the course between the Union and Main Street bridges, and raiding the plentiful berry patches owned by a local judge. By the time he neared school age, he had developed into something of a holy terror, not unlike the willful Georgie in his fellow Hoosier Booth Tarkington's *The Magnificent Ambersons.* "Tip," as Richard's family nicknamed him, was constantly getting into trouble; for a small boy, he exhibited uncommonly violent behavior. At six, he hurled a kitten against a fence because it had bitten him. At seven, he kicked an elderly neighbor in the shins because she denounced him as the "meanest boy in town." That same year, he slaughtered his pet goat because it charged his mother and sister. At eight, he was temporarily thrown out of school for writing obscenities on the schoolhouse fence. At least one of his teachers thought him emotionally disturbed, and throughout his life he exhibited all manner of bizarre behavior. These childhood incidents, strung together, suggest an intriguing pattern: a boy who has already defined himself as some kind of avenger, wildly striking back to wound those who have threatened him or the ones he loves.

Apart from his parents and sister, one person Tip adored and felt enormously protective of was his Grandmother Bennett, a devout Catholic whose peaceful, orderly life was constantly disrupted by her young grandson. From an early age, Tip exhibited a pleasing singing voice. Although his grandmother tried to persuade him to pursue private organ and voice lessons, he wanted no part of music, thinking it unmanly.

Tip's aggressive nature continued throughout high school. One day, as he and his father were crossing the town square, George reprimanded his son for swearing. Suddenly, Tip struck out at him, furiously pounding him in the face with his fists. That incident drew the attention of a friend of George Bennett's, Sam Carson, a big, lumbering bear of a man who had once had a career as a prize-fighter. Carson decided that he should take Tip to live with him at his farm some miles away, where he would put him through a kind of training program, building up his frail body and teaching him how to fight like a professional. Also, it was approaching time to harvest the cornfields, and Carson could always use an extra hand, no matter how young. George Bennett readily agreed; probably the entire family was grateful to have a reprieve from Tip's stormy moods.

Not long after Tip had joined their household, Sam Carson and his niece Mary, a pretty blonde girl, went into the parlor after dinner. Carson enjoyed listening to music in the evening, and his daughter, a competent organist with a pleasant alto voice, began to play and sing "I Know That My Redeemer Liveth" from Handel's *Messiah*. Sam joined in, and after a while, the warm family scene began to make Tip feel homesick. Afraid he was going to cry, he joined in the singing. After they had sung "Little Brown Church in the Vale" and "The Old Oaken Bucket," Sam complimented Tip on his voice and suggested that he continue to work at singing, as it would be a good method of building up his lungs. Sam stressed that while it was important for a boy to become physically strong and learn how to use his fists, it was also important to cultivate other interests, to develop a keen mind to accompany a hard, muscular body.

After some months at the Carson farm, Tip began to put on pounds and gain energy; now he could run a long distance without even getting winded. Sam Carson had put together a makeshift gymnasium in the loft over the granary in the barn, where he intended to teach Tip the elements of boxing. He also promised to coach the boy in jujitsu and wrestling, hoping it would not only "make a man" out of him but also help him gain a greater understanding of people who were not as physically strong as he was. Sam was concerned that Tip had developed, at such an early age, into a reckless bully who would take on anyone in any circumstances. Sam explained patiently to Tip that he had no sense of fair play, that "we got to learn you to keep your temper no matter what comes."

Sam Carson was in many ways the strong father figure that Tip had always needed. George Bennett's soul-saving missions had kept him away from home for long periods; more crucially, he seems to have possessed some of the same arrogance and self-absorption that his son would display throughout his life. George Bennett was a local constable, and in 1881 he was deputized by the Cass County sheriff to aid in the capture of a Dr. Henry C. Cole, Kokomo's mayor. It ranks as one of the notorious incidents in Kokomo's history. According to local historian Ned Booher, Kokomo had by the early 1880s acquired a reputation as a lawless town. Henry C. Cole, a Kentucky native, had assumed the office of mayor and announced his plans to clean up the town—but Cole himself was reported to have an unsavory past that included robbery, arson, and murder. The most popular version of the story has it that Cole had plotted to rob and burn one of the town's biggest flour mills. When he arrived at the mill, armed with a pair of .38 caliber Smith & Wesson revolvers, a group of lawmen was waiting. A skirmish ensued, and the shot that killed Cole was fired by George Washington Bennett. Whatever the details of the case, George seems to have persuaded his son that he singlehandedly took care of the entire gang of outlaws headed by Cole.

In 1885, the Bennetts moved to Logansport, a prosperous town of around fifteen thousand along the Wabash. It was in many respects a move up for the family: Logansport boasted handsome, well-built homes, excellent public schools, numerous churches, even a normal college and an opera house—a far cry from uncivilized Kokomo. The town had built its reputation on manufacturing—everything from flour and paper to furniture and leather goods. For a time Tip dabbled at learning the tailoring trade, but never took it too seriously. George did little to encourage him, certain that Tip would take over the family mill business. As Tip matured and began to show signs of restlessness, George decided that it might be best for him to strike out on his own. Once he got a taste of the world, he would no doubt come running back home in no time. Soon, George had arranged a job for Tip at a clothing store in Indianapolis, run by a couple named Perry and Emily Packet. By this time, Tip was becoming an extremely handsome young man, with a strong, masculine jaw, compelling, deep-set blue-gray eyes, and an expressive mouth. His burgeoning physical maturity had a definite impact on his apprenticeship, for he later claimed that Mrs. Packet provided him with his first sexual encounter. But even more important, Mr. Packet, unaware of his wife's relationship with his young charge, offered to take Tip to New York to initiate him into the buying end of the business.

Nothing in Richard's cornbelt background had prepared him for his first glimpse of New York City. The dramatic skyline, the multitude of ships, the great rush of horse-drawn trucks, hansom cabs, streetcars with their conductors in spit-and-polished uniforms, the street vendors hawking their goods on pushcarts—for the teen-aged boy from Indiana, it seemed nearly impossible to take in. For several days, Tip made the rounds with the Packets, selecting merchandise from wholesale houses and the model dressmaking establishments such as Redfern, Ltd., the Madison Square salon owned by John Redfern, who was later appointed dressmaker to Queen Victoria. At night, while Mr. Packet collapsed into a hot bath and had dinner in his room, Tip was expected to escort Mrs. Packet to the theater.

One evening, he and Mrs. Packet took in a performance of *Rip Van Winkle* starring Joseph Jefferson. After they had returned to their Murray Hill hotel, Mrs. Packet posed a startling question: had Tip ever thought of becoming an actor? When the young man expressed astonishment at such an idea, Mrs. Packet responded that in the short time she had known him, she had come to believe that it was the ideal profession for him.

In his memoirs, Richard gives an account of what happened next. The truth of his story is doubtful—though it would account for one of the most bizarre episodes of his early life. He claims that Emily Packet told him that she was carrying his child. Mr. Packet would have to be told about it, since they had not been intimate for some time, and thus it was impossible for her to construct the fantasy that he was the child's father. She was spared the embarrassment of her confession when Mr. Packet suffered a heart attack on the return trip to Indianapolis ("an act of Divine Providence," Richard later called it) and died soon after. A few months later, she gave birth to a son, and only days afterward died of peritonitis. When Tip learned of the news, he was so overcome with shock, grief, and remorse that he succumbed to complete physical and emotional trauma. He passed into a semicomatose state, unable to speak. Nearly two years later, he returned to full consciousness in a hospital in Buffalo, New York, unable to remember a single thing that had happened in the interim.

Throughout his life, Richard had a wild imagination, and his account of this period virtually begs to be taken for a slightly deranged fantasy. The details, taken all together, are too much to believe: the convenient deaths of both Packets just as things had become impossibly complicated, Richard's own inability to account for two years in his life. More to the point, Indianapolis city directories from 1879 to 1890 show no Packet listed, and no obituaries are recorded for them. The truth may be simple: Richard wrote his memoirs in the mid-1930s, when he was finding it nearly impossible to get work and was financially dependent on his daughters. Perhaps the strange episode of the Packets was included merely to lure a publisher.

Although Tip possessed a restless, curious nature, George Bennett never questioned that his son would eventually enter the family business. When Tip reached his late teens, George lost no time in setting him up as night watchman at the family-owned mill in Logansport. From the beginning, Tip loathed the job. It is difficult to imagine a less appropriate task for someone of his extroverted qualities. George was adamant that he continue, learning the business from the ground up, but Tip had other ideas: after all, Chicago, city of opportunity, was only 116 miles away. One day, he announced that he was going to make his own way on the open road. He went home, packed his things, and, despite pleadings from his mother and denouncements from his father, left Logansport behind.

For the next couple of years, Tip roamed around the Midwest, picking up jobs wherever he could find them. It was a hardscrabble life, and there were many nights when he went without eating or had to find makeshift sleeping arrangements, but he exulted in his newfound freedom. For a time he worked as a dishwasher in a Chicago restaurant. Once, when he was down and out, he was picked up by the managers of a touring medicine show and traveled with them for a time. On the street corners of town after town, Richard sang in a quartet, danced, or performed short sketches. Once a crowd had gathered, his boss would move in for the kill, volunteering to extract a tooth from a "stooge" planted in the crowd. The extraction was bogus, of course—the stooge would have the tooth planted on his tongue—but the crowd would be assured that it was painless, provided that a few drops of Hamlin's Wizard Oil were applied. Then they would be given the precious chance to buy a bottle of it for only fifty cents.

The medicine show eventually wound down, and by early 1891 Tip had fallen back on his routine of working at odd jobs. One night he ventured into a local playhouse to see the latest touring attraction. After the performance, he joined two of the actors for a night of heavy drinking on the town. One month later, he ran into them while visiting a burlesque house in Chicago. They were in town playing in *The Limited Mail,* an action-packed melodrama by Elmer E. Vance. This was a company of the "ten, twent', thirt'" variety—the term for cut-rate touring shows that played both small towns and large cities, charging an admission fee ranging from ten to thirty cents. Although their repertory was shoddy compared with the productions Tip would have seen during his purported visit to New York with the Packets, he went to see the show a second time. Afterward, while backstage visiting his friends, he met the rest of the cast and the show's manager. Richard's friends, who had been impressed with his impromptu bursts of singing during their recent night on the town, recommended him to the manager. By the time he left Haviland's Theatre that night, he had been engaged to run props, play a few minor roles, and sing in the onstage quartet—all at a salary of twenty dollars a week.

On May 10, 1891, shortly before his twenty-first birthday, Richard Bennett—"Tip" was now part of his past—made his first professional appearance on the stage, in a small part in *The Limited Mail,* at Chicago's Standard Theater. But he found his stint as property man loathsome because, as he put it, "a property man is a laborer socially beneath the dignity of the artists." *The Limited Mail* set out on a rough-and-ready tour of one-night stands at spots along the Union Pacific, including Reno, Virginia City, and Carson City, Nevada, and Cheyenne, Wyoming. The general circumstances were primitive. Much of the audience was made up of local ranchers who poured into town on horseback or in spring wagons, carrying kerosene lamps to light their way. Even the poorest country folk considered the traveling shows enough of an occasion to turn up in their Sunday best. Guns, of course, had to be checked at the door. (Later on, Edna Ferber would characterize this breed of audience in her 1926 novel, *Show Boat.*)

The tour made its way to Los Angeles, then a town with one main street and surrounded by acres of oat and bean ranches. After finishing up its run, the play moved back to Chicago, then on to a string of one-night stands throughout Indiana. When an actor suddenly dropped out, the management asked Richard Bennett to take over the leading role of the train conductor, and after a quick rehearsal he opened in Fort Wayne. It was not regarded as a momentous occasion by other members of the cast, who felt that Richard had rushed through the play pell-mell, with little thought about how he shared scenes with the other actors. Nevertheless, he continued in the part through Logansport, Kokomo, Muncie, and Anderson. Wherever he went, he received a valuable boost of publicity from the local newspapers, which proudly pointed out that the leading man was a Hoosier.

By November, he made it to New York, at the Niblo's Garden, at the time the city's oldest theater. He was thrilled to be back in the city that had made such a staggering impression on him a few years earlier. After the tour ended, Richard returned to Chicago, much more secure financially than he had been when he left. All in all, he had been on the road with *The Limited Mail* for fifty-four weeks. He had emerged successfully from his first theatrical experience and looked forward to enjoying a good long rest while he contemplated his next move. But he had barely gotten off the stage before he was desperate to get back on. "From the time you first cast in your lot with Thespis to the moment when the curtain goes down on your final performance," he recalled, " you are under a baptism and your illusions are in a constant state of being shattered. . . . Yet I know of few who would depart from its romance. Its fascination holds as nothing else, no other profession, can."

A few days after his return to Chicago, George Bennett came to visit, sure that now that Richard had some money put away, he would return to Indiana to take over the mill business. But Richard had other plans, and no amount of parental cautioning or cajoling would change that.

With his father back in Indiana, Richard tried to figure out what to do next. He missed the camaraderie of the *Limited Mail* company, and longed to dig into another part. Before long, he received an offer to join the company of another melodrama, *The Railroad Ticket,* headed for the West Coast. During this tour, Richard began to revise his after-hours habits. He was less inclined to go out drinking, and instead began returning to his hotel room to settle in with a book. Though he had read very little, he soon discovered an unbridled passion for books and went on a self-imposed culture binge, reading everything he could get his hands on. Wherever he traveled, he carried a dictionary and a *Roget's Thesaurus* with him.

A few months later, when the tour of *The Railroad Ticket* had ended, Richard concluded that the life of the ten, twent', thirt' circuit, playing mostly one-nighters in smaller towns, was a dead end. He made his way back to New York, but was unable to secure work in the theater. With his nest egg vanishing, he took a bartending job in a joint on Houston Street. One day he spotted a newspaper advertisement for the American Academy of Dramatic Art, where his acting ambitions could be legitimized and where he might further his career. He was far too low on funds to afford the tuition that the Academy charged, so he devised a plan. The Academy offered courses in classic dancing but none in show dancing. Since the American musical comedy was becoming an ever-more significant part of the theater scene, Richard offered to teach a class in theatrical dance, in exchange for free acting instruction. As proof of his abilities, he demonstrated a buck-and-wing, waltz clog, and soft-shoe. Present at his audition was Gustave Frohman, the fast-talking producer who, with his brothers Daniel and Charles, had become a major force on the New York theatrical scene in the 1880s. Frohman was so impressed with Richard's dancing ability and bright, energetic nature that he offered to help him find work. But Richard was adamant that he wanted to put dancing behind him permanently. "I want to be an actor," he told Frohman, "not just one of those hams you see hanging around, but one whom managers look up to!"

Frohman went home and thought the matter over. The following afternoon, he and Richard boarded the train from Grand Central bound for Chicago. Richard was afraid his money would run out, but there was some comfort in knowing that Frohman had arranged a job for him, in the Chicago company of Brandon Thomas's *Charley's Aunt*. This was something different for him: a rollicking farce about a college student, in need of a chaperone, who persuades a friend to pass himself off as his aunt. In one scene, Richard was to enter carrying a shaded lamp, which he was to put on top of a piano. At two consecutive performances, the shade slipped off the lamp, eliciting a huge laugh from the audience. But Frohman was pleased and decided to give him a larger part. Richard learned the role quickly, and Frohman subsequently helped him to get a job as a bellhop at the Palace Hotel. For twenty-five dollars a month and a room, he worked the graveyard shift, from midnight to 6 A.M. After a few hours' rest, he reported to the theater for acting lessons from *Charley's Aunt*'s director. After resting a bit more, he would report to work for the evening performance. Delighted with Richard's progress, Frohman arranged for him to go on the road in *Charley's Aunt.* "Here I was again," Richard would recall, "up to my neck in one-night stands. But what did I care? I was with a Frohman show, and being put through my dramatic paces every day."

In 1896, after a few more jobs in stock, Richard made an appointment to see the producer Abraham Lincoln Erlanger. A crass, vain, self-important bully, Erlanger cared much less about the theater than he did about consolidating power. In that year, along with six other managers, including his partner, attorney Marc Klaw, he formed the infamous Theater Syndicate. Originally, the Syndicate's aims were not unreasonable: it sought to organize road shows, which for years had suffered from the chaotic and haphazard way in which they were assembled. Through the practice of block booking, the Syndicate soon amassed immense power and became a dangerous monopoly, and Erlanger ran his business with the ruthlessness of a Mafia don. The Syndicate would lease major theaters, and essentially get paid twice: once by the theater's owners for bringing them a play to fill the house, and again by independent play producers for securing a playing space. The men who ran the Syndicate made enemies of some of the theater's biggest names by decreeing that no star actor could have a successful career without being part of it. If actors refused to sign a long-term contract with the Syndicate, they would find it very difficult to get work, either in New York or on the road. Players such as Richard Mansfield, Mrs. Minnie Maddern Fiske, and Sarah Bernhardt turned their backs on the Syndicate, and attracted huge crowds by playing in local burlesque houses and tents. Eventually, the Syndicate was done in by the combined forces of Sam, Lee, and Jacob Shubert, who went on to form a powerful monopoly of their own. But from the 1890s through the early part of the new century, Klaw, Erlanger, and company were riding high.

Richard's first appearance for Erlanger came in a musical show, *The Round of Pleasure,* which opened on Broadway in May 1897 at the Knickerbocker Theatre and ran throughout the summer. When Richard had signed to do the play, Erlanger had taken out an option for his future services. During the run of *The Round of Pleasure,* Erlanger was approached by Charles Frohman, who was searching for a juvenile lead for his new production, *The Proper Caper,* and thought that Richard Bennett might do. Evidently Erlanger failed to see the same potential in the young actor, as he willingly dropped his option.

Unlike Erlanger, Frohman had an abiding love for the theater and its people. As long as his breed of producer existed, star actors' lives were reasonably secure. Helen Hayes once observed that actors during the early part of the twentieth century "had a double responsibility. If a play was not good, the audience would still come to see *you.* And *you* had to make up the difference between the bad and the good play. You felt a responsibility to those people, your public. [Later on,] actors got freed of the producers who enslaved us, and they enslaved us by coddling us and giving us an audience and promoting us. That's how actors are developed into great stars, and they develop their public."

Throughout his career, Charles Frohman was just such a producer. Born in 1860 in Sandusky, Ohio, Frohman came to New York when he was a young man. He immediately went to work for the *New York Tribune,* which also employed his brother Daniel, before going into business as a producer of plays. Although in the beginning Daniel produced a tonier line of plays than his brother, Charles soon distinguished himself, both as a gambler and a sound businessman. Occasionally his productions pulled themselves together at the eleventh hour. Legend had it that, once, a foreign theatrical troupe he was presenting docked in New York at 7:30 in the evening and made it onstage in Brooklyn exactly one hour later. But whatever his methods, Charles Frohman quickly became a force to be reckoned with. In one season, he employed 792 actors in twenty-five different stage productions.

Frohman always cultivated a low profile. James M. Barrie, whose *Peter Pan* gave Frohman one of his hardiest successes, once observed that many actors had appeared in Frohman's productions without ever exchanging a word with him. Always shy and elusive, he was known to dart into alleyways when he saw one of his contract stars approaching on the street. Frohman's only passion was the theater. He read plays all day long, even while he was taking his meals. He seldom had a reserve of ready cash, for the simple reason that he perpetually dumped the proceeds from one play into the production of another. When choosing a play, he operated primarily on gut instinct. “A play that has vitality in it will sooner or later get on the stage,” he once said. “It keeps itself alive until the opportunity. I read a play. As I read it, I can see the characters and action in pantomime. That’s a good test. . . . I could not give or analyze my reasons why I choose it. It is instinctive, and that is some of the fascination of the work.” (As Richard matured as an actor, he would choose plays in a similarly intuitive way.)

Frohman’s stable of stars included Maude Adams, Blanche Bates, Viola Allen, Julia Marlowe, Otis Skinner, John Drew, Julia Sanderson, and Ethel Barrymore. Many of the stars of the time seem to have succeeded on two levels: they had riveting stage presence, yet they were also capable of suggesting great intimacy with the audience, to make each person in the theater feel that they were playing to him and to no one else. Both these qualities were needed to carry the sentimental plays that the public never seemed to tire of. To be included in Frohman’s select group of actors marked an enormous step forward for Richard; it was an association that would endure for seventeen years.

When *The Proper Caper* opened at Hoyt’s Theater on West Twenty-fourth Street, Richard wasn’t much noticed, but his next part under Frohman’s aegis represented a real breakthrough for him: the role of Dick Beach in *The White Heather,* a melodrama by Cecil Raleigh and Henry Hamilton that opened at the Academy of Music on Fourteenth Street and Irving Place on January 24, 1898, and ran the entire season. After *The White Heather,* Richard found that he didn’t have to wait long for offers of work.

In the summer months, Richard often toured in stock engagements, and it was on one of these tours in 1901, while playing at Bush’s Theater in San Francisco, that he met a dark-haired, brown-eyed beauty named Grena Heller. He was thirty-one (at the time, quite well along for a man who had never been married). Grena was only seventeen, and had already studied piano, theory and composition, both in her native San Francisco and in France. After a brief courtship, they were married.

Within the year, Richard's life on the road had become an obstacle that their marriage could not withstand, and soon they were separated, although they didn't file for divorce until 1903. Reference to this early marriage was omitted from many of Richard's official publicity materials, and he scarcely, if ever, mentioned her in the presence of his three children.

Later in life, Grena Bennett had a successful career as a music critic for the *New York American* (later the *Journal-American*), a post she took on when she was only twenty-two. As a critic, she gave first-class coverage of events in New York, as well as abroad. She was an advocate of the American singer and seldom missed the opportunity to sail to Italy whenever American artists were performing major roles in the leading opera houses there.

Grena was a person of great spirit and resourcefulness, even if she didn't always hold to the strictest journalistic standards. Once, in 1943, she was assigned to cover Ezio Pinza's Metropolitan Opera performances of *Les Contes d'Hoffmann.* Unfortunately, she became ill and was unable to attend the performance, so she secretly asked her close friend Marta Eggerth, the noted Hungarian soprano, to go in her place. "After each act I had to call her," remembered Eggerth, "and it was wonderful, except for Pinza, who made very bad errors. He did not get good applause; it was not a success with the audience. Now, if I were a critic, I simply could not write anything negative, so I had told her it was wonderful and gorgeous. And she got in the biggest trouble, because all of the other newspaper reviews were bad except for her review in the *Journal-American*! She said, 'Marta—never again. It was your debut as a critic, and your good-bye.'"

It was easy for Richard to blame the collapse of his marriage on the rigors of touring. But there was another, more important reason. In September of 1900, he had gone into Charles Frohman's production of *A Royal Family,* by Captain Robert Marshall. In the supporting cast was another seventeen-year-old girl, Mabel Adrienne Morrison.

Chapter Two

1900–1904

From the time they met during rehearsals of *A Royal Family,* Mabel Morrison was one woman Richard Bennett consistently failed to dominate. No doubt this first-generation actor was somewhat intimidated by Mabel's distinguished theatrical pedigree. Her father, Lewis Morrison, was one of the most successful actor-managers of his time. Morrison had practically made a career out of touring in one role—Mephistopheles in his own production of *Faust*—and he had long been one of Richard's idols. Mabel's mother, Rose Wood, was one of the most prominent actresses of the 1880s. Rose had enjoyed her first success touring with stock companies in the midwestern and southern United States and had appeared with her husband at the Walnut Street Theater in Philadelphia. But it was as a leading lady at New York's famed Wallack's Theatre that she found stardom, in roles such as Lydia Languish in Richard Sheridan's *The Rivals*.

Rose's side of the family could boast of having had actors in several preceding generations. Her father, William F. Wood, was one of the most skilled pantomimists of his day. A derivative of the classic Italian commedia dell'arte, pantomime was a thriving art form in the early nineteenth century, a lively combination of song, dance, pratfalls, and biting topical satire, often aimed at leading public figures. Eventually, the material of pantomime moved onto higher moral ground, and here William F. Wood found fame in dramas such as *The Cherokee Chief and His Poor Dog Tray* and

The Dumb Man of Manchester. Rose's grandfather, William Wodin (later changed to "Wood") was a Welshman who traveled to England, where in the waning days of the eighteenth century he became a strolling player—an actor who moved from town to town, performing in whatever space might be available, whether it was country inn or country fair.

Mabel was not the only member of her generation to continue the family tradition. Her older sister, Rosabel, had gone on the stage while still in her teens, achieving particular distinction in 1885 as Marguerite in her father's production of *Faust.* A graceful and willowy dark-haired beauty, Rosabel was later praised by one newspaper critic as one of the theater's outstanding interpreters of the doomed Marguerite.

Rosabel soon took on additional duties. Rose Wood and Lewis Morrison were divorced in 1890. While Lewis found himself another wife, actress Florence Roberts, the collapse of the marriage triggered a latent streak of emotional instability in Rose. She began to withdraw more and more, leaving Rosabel in charge of her younger siblings—Mabel and Victor Jago. Lewis, away on tour and busy with his new wife, provided unstinting financial support but little else. Rose's bouts of depression would grow worse as time went on, and she would finish out her life as a virtual shut-in.

Perhaps it was the loss of anything resembling a stable home environment that made Mabel so eager to set out on a career of her own. She had made her professional debut at an even earlier age than Rosabel—in 1896, when she was thirteen, in the secondary part of Anita in an adaptation of Prosper Merimée's *Carmen,* with Rosabel in the title role. Despite Mabel's impatience to launch her acting career, it seems that there was little rivalry between the sisters. Increasingly, Lewis Morrison's frequent absences and Rose Wood's gradual withdrawal from the mainstream of life assigned Rosabel to the role of surrogate mother to her two younger siblings. For Mabel, this fragmented family life gave rise to a fierce desire for independence. For the youngest child, Victor, the chaos of his parents' life left him with a distaste for the acting profession;

he would be the only Morrison of his generation to turn his back on the theater, opting instead for a military career.

Mabel's performance in *Carmen* struck her father as so promising that once the tour closed, he began to coach her in the role of Juliet. He reasoned that, unlike many actresses who attempted it, she would be the correct age to play Shakespeare's heroine. Her subsequent success in the part cemented her father's belief in her abilities, and for the next few years he included her in the extensive national tours of his own company, in which her greatest triumph came with Rosabel's old part, Marguerite in *Faust.*

Although she was not under personal contract to Charles Frohman, Mabel had appeared in several of his productions by the time she joined the cast of *A Royal Family.* Like her sister, Rosabel, Mab, as the family called her, was striking. Sloe-eyed and with a broad nose and a good firm jaw, she was the kind of woman once described as handsome. She wore clothes with great style and favored bright, exotic colors that made her look, according to one reporter, "like a flag flying." Her temperament was essentially serene, but her surface coolness masked a formidable strength of will. Her warm, cello-like voice and natural aristocratic bearing made her steadily employable in any plays that featured "well-bred" female characters. "Born in the theater and of it," Richard remembered, "with no small opinion of her ideas, she was much given to having her own way in all things. . . . She was smart. And talk! I could listen to her for hours, watching the fire spring into her brown eyes when she was enthused over some book or hero."

All of these qualities contributed to Mabel's popularity with men. During the run of *A Royal Family,* Richard had plenty of opportunity to observe the parade of stage-door Johnnies who came calling for her in their hansom cabs. Richard judged that she was "socially bent," with "a definite leaning toward the Uptown Blue Book." When Richard asked her why she seemed to favor him over all her other prospective beaus, her reply caught him off guard.

"You are the first person I've ever met who cared nothing for anything or anybody. I don't think you'd care if the world blew up!" These were exactly the words that Mabel's suitor longed to hear. One evening, after a performance, Mabel introduced Richard to her father. One might have expected that the rising young actor would put on at least a show of humility when coming face to face with the celebrated Lewis Morrison. But there was no chance of that.

"I'm glad to meet you, Mr. Morrison," said Richard as he stuck out his hand. "I have always wanted to meet you, one of the great artists of our day. Think of being the confrere of people like Booth, Jefferson, Modjeska, Neilson, Rehan . . . the giants of our theater! . . . I wish I could have more opportunity to study their technique. Go to the theater now. What do you see? A lot of namby-pambies . . . the spawn of bricklayers and scavengers . . . We have today, in our leading positions, a lot of airy, fairy Lillians!"

First impressions notwithstanding, Richard was invited out to the Morrisons' country house near Peekskill, New York, on the following Sunday. The estate was sizeable, and as Richard drove up in a hired team he saw immaculately trimmed hedges and graveled walks, with young people playing croquet near the carriage house, others shooting on the archery field. Mabel looked lovely and pristine in a crisp white dress, and Richard knew at once that he really was in love with her. "I had never seen anything so beautiful in such a perfect setting," he remembered. He could not have anticipated what happened later that day. While presiding over tea on the verandah, Lewis Morrison took it upon himself to announce Mabel and Richard's engagement. "Here I was, hooked high and dry," said Richard. "I gulped the scalding tea and never noticed it was hot."

Mabel's intended chose not to debate the matter of the wedding, only the details of where and when it would be. Rather than have a private ceremony at the Morrison farm, as Lewis Morrison had hoped, Mabel and Richard decided to elope and were married by a justice of the peace in New Jersey on November 8, 1903.

After a brief honeymoon in Europe, the newlyweds returned to New York. Richard was preparing to go on tour with a play he had recently performed with success in New York, Augustus Thomas's *The Other Girl*. Because his weekly salary had been raised to $150, while Mabel's was a mere $45, Richard suggested it would be less costly for her to forgo the tour and stay at home. If they were touring together, she would expect to stay in more comfortable and expensive hotels along the way; he could stay in cheaper places, and thus they could save a good deal of money. What he hadn't reckoned on was Mabel's steely determination to continue her career, married or not. To top if off, she had been offered a contract to support Annie Russell in Jerome K. Jerome's *Miss Hobbs.* Richard was livid. A woman belonged at home—but Mabel thought otherwise. She had just begun to make progress in the theater, and she was not about to walk out on a promising career and sit at home, waiting for her husband to return from one of his lengthy tours. A terrible row ensued, and Richard stormed out and moved into a boarding house. Because he had crisscrossed the country for years with his own wife, Lewis Morrison did not share his son-in-law's view. Having encouraged Mabel to pursue acting in the first place, Lewis saw no reason for her to give it up merely because she had married an arrogant, hidebound man who had yet to make his own mark in the theater. After giving the matter some thought, Lewis decided to pay Richard a visit.

The meeting did not go well. Any good will that Richard might have built up with his new father-in-law vanished, as their discussion degenerated into a frenzy of name-calling. "If all you married my daughter for is to make a slave of her," railed Morrison, "make her old through bearing children while you prance around the country preening yourself like a turkey cock, then you are not fit to be a husband!"

Richard returned the volley, telling Lewis that he was in no position to pass judgment. After all, Mabel had repeatedly told Richard that her father had always put career before family. The argument grew more and more incendiary until Lewis brought it to an end by punching Richard in the nose.

Mabel and Richard managed to settle their differences temporarily, and all was serene for a while—until *The Other Girl* commenced its tour in March 1904. In Baltimore, the play's leading lady, Elsie de Wolfe, fell ill with bronchitis. There was no understudy—in those days, road productions often did without them—and Mabel, sensing that this might be her big chance, asked Richard to use his influence with Charles Frohman to let her go on in de Wolfe's place. Richard telephoned Frohman, who agreed. This was not at all what Richard wanted to hear. A part this good might put Mabel over in a big way and dash any hopes of keeping her at home. So he decided to lie, to tell Mabel that Frohman was in Boston and couldn't be reached.

Just then, they were interrupted by the stage manager, who showed them the telegram he had just received from Frohman. It read, "PUT MORRISON IN DE WOLFE'S PART. . . . FROHMAN."

Mabel was enraged. "Liar!" she screamed, and ordered Richard out of the room. When he returned, several hours later, her bags were gone. The hotel clerk told Richard that Mabel had checked out and left no forwarding address. Richard hastened to the nearest bar, where he consumed one bourbon after another. When he arrived at the theater, there was a note waiting from Mabel: "All I ask of you is to stay away from me. I won't grieve if it's forever."

Still reeling from too many drinks, Richard managed to stagger through that night's performance. After the curtain came down, the stage manager approached him. Mabel's performance, he said, had been unsatisfactory, and he was going to send for the regular understudy from the New York company until Elsie de Wolfe recovered. Richard realized that this development would do nothing to repair the damage he had done, and argued that Mabel be permitted to continue. "It's no use, Dick," said the stage manager. "She'd ruin our next week's business in Philadelphia."

Once she was fired, Mabel packed up and returned to New York, to begin rehearsals for *Miss Hobbs*. When Richard finally reached her on the telephone at the Morrison home in Peekskill, he got an icy reception: "I will not say that I do not care for you. . . . But you have your own idea and I have mine. You stand between me and success. I am tired of living in reflected glory. I never want to see you again." And she hung up.

As the tour continued, Richard wrote daily to try to appease

Mabel. She answered him with silence. By October 1904, he was convinced that the battle had been lost and that he would have to get along without her. As the tour was about to end, he decided to seek out Mabel and divorce her for desertion. He was just about to leave for New York when a telegram arrived: "PLEASE COME TO FLAT B AT 457 WEST 123 STREET NEW YORK IMMEDIATELY."

When he reached the apartment, a red-headed Irish maid answered the door. Richard was attempting to explain who he was and why he'd come when he heard a baby crying in the next room. There, in a bed behind a screen, lay Mabel. Richard knelt by the bed, kissing Mabel again and again, and after a few moments they had forgiven each other and admitted that their behavior had been willful and thoughtless. Only then did Richard ask if he had a son or a daughter.

"I knew you'd want a boy . . . but it's a girl, dear," replied Mabel. "She seems to have your spirit, though."

Mabel's pregnancy had been a little under two months along when she was fired from *The Other Girl.* Once a doctor confirmed her condition, she had kept it a secret from Richard, not knowing whether or not she wanted to remain married to him. Once the baby arrived, however, Mabel decided that the burden of raising a child on her own was too much, and sent for her errant husband.

Richard leaned over and looked into the bassinet. His newborn daughter was red-faced, screaming away with her fists clenched. She was carrying on so ferociously that Richard at first thought something might be wrong with her, but Mabel assured him, "She is her father's own daughter. . . . She wants attention, dear."

Richard moved into the apartment with Mabel and their new daughter, whom they named Constance Campbell Bennett. The choice of "Campbell" was a nod to Mabel's grandmother, Sarah Campbell. The wife of William F. Wood, Sarah had been a successful actress and dancer in her own right. Before she was old enough to have any say in the matter, Constance Bennett was being pointed toward an actor's life.

Chapter Three

1904–1914

Throughout her career, Constance Bennett delighted in confusing the public, friends, and even family about the exact year of her birth. She carried it to extremes, as if it were somehow a point of honor. After they had both become successful Hollywood stars, Joan often remarked that Constance had started out the oldest sister, moved into middle position, and wound up the youngest.

In an effort to publicize her tempestuous nature, Constance always claimed to have been born during a thunderstorm, and it is true that New York was hit with heavy rains the day she was born, October 22, 1904, five days before the opening of the city's subway system. She was an energetic, robust, and healthy baby. As her first summer arrived, Richard and Mabel decided to remove their nine-month-old daughter from the stifling heat in New York, and rented a cottage on a Staten Island beach. Constance spent much of her time outside and immediately took to the sunshine and fresh air.

Richard had little difficulty finding work, going from one play to another, continually polishing his technique. Then, unexpectedly, Mabel stepped out of the reflected glory that she had lived in for most of her professional life. She was selected to portray the Indian girl Nat-u-ritch in Edwin Milton Royle's *The Squaw Man*. It was one of the colorful, romantic, outdoor dramas of the period that found favor with audiences: Jim Carston, an English aristocrat, flees his country after becoming involved in a scandal. He sails to America, where he settles out west and promptly makes an enemy of the vicious desperado Cash Hawkins (played by future silent film star William S. Hart). Just as Hawkins is about to kill Jim, Nat-u-ritch, daughter of an Indian chief, shoots him. Overcome by gratitude, Jim marries Nat-u-ritch and she bears him a son. When she realizes that she stands in the way of Jim returning to England and claiming an Earldom, she commits suicide. *The Squaw Man* opened at Wallack's Theatre, where Mabel's mother, Rose, had enjoyed so many of her successes. The *New York Times* reported that the characters were "never burlesque, even in the comedy scenes, and the play runs through its four acts without a drag. . . . Miss Mabel Morrison as a squaw—a difficult and trying role—won immediate recognition." *The Squaw Man* was one of the big hits of the season, running for 222 performances. It would be revived in road productions for years to come, and later made into an important silent film by Cecil B. DeMille and Oscar Apfel.

Having a personal triumph of her own meant that Mabel was for the time being much easier to live with. Nevertheless, the notion of his wife having a career was far from settled in Richard's mind, and he was no doubt delighted when, a few months into the run of *The Squaw Man,* she discovered that she was pregnant again. Eventually Mabel was forced to give notice, and she settled down to await the baby's arrival. She missed going to the theater every night, but she felt a definite satisfaction that her point had been made: namely, that she had no intention of abandoning the stage. Surely, now that she had made a hit in *The Squaw Man,* there would be more offers, and better ones.

Meanwhile, Frohman had a hot property lined up for Richard, Charles Klein's *The Lion and the Mouse.* A biting comedy-drama, it hinted at the sort of changes that would gradually reshape the American theater. The plot concerns a spirited young woman (played by Grace Elliston) whose father, a respectable judge (Walter Allen), has been discredited professionally by a wealthy magnate (Edmund Breese). The woman, under an assumed name, strikes up a relationship with the millionaire's son (Richard) and infiltrates the household for the purpose of laying hands on the papers that will clear her father's name. *The Lion and the Mouse* was one of a number of "problem plays" that were cropping up sporadically in New York—plays in which a conventional love story might be wrapped up in some trenchant observations about the social, political, or economic realities of modern life.

Although Richard had the third part in *The Lion and the Mouse,* Frohman felt it would give an important boost to his career. The producer believed passionately in the script, and he urged Richard to remember that he was surrounding him with a good cast. "You always want to take that into consideration," Frohman cautioned him. "No matter how good your part is, if you are in a bad play with a poor cast, just throw the whole thing aside." Frohman's judgment turned out to be excellent, and the critics heaped praise on the play. Charles W. Collins of the *Chicago Tribune* found it "a new kind of play . . . with the inevitable love story based on expositions of questions which are compelling the American people to think." *The Lion and the Mouse* was one of the runaway successes of the 1905–1906 season, lasting for 586 performances, over twice as long as David Belasco's big hit, *The Girl of the Golden West.* With Mabel appearing in *The Squaw Man,* the Bennetts had a two-hit household, and it was one of the happiest times of their marriage.

By the time he acted in *The Lion and the Mouse,* Richard had developed a specific method of working that he would employ throughout his stage career. He would go through the play learning all the other roles before attempting to memorize his own lines. He edged into his characterization very slowly, as if he were afraid that he might misjudge some facet of it and not be able to correct his mistakes. Gradually, his performance revealed itself to him and to his fellow actors. More than anything, Richard believed that the theater had the potential to depict reality, and this conviction helped him develop his signature style: a fresh naturalism, underscored by the power and presence that he had taken from the earlier generation of actors he admired—the Keans and Jeffersons and Marlowes.

During the run of *The Lion and the Mouse,* the Bennetts moved briefly to an apartment at 1020 Longwood Avenue in the Bronx.

They didn't stay long. Certain that *The Lion and the Mouse* would prove equally popular in London, Frohman arranged for a production at the Duke of York's Theatre with several members of the New York company, Richard included. At this point, Richard became overconfident. Since Mabel was pregnant again, he wanted to see her comfortably settled, and rented a pleasant house in St. John's Wood. The family sailed for England in the spring of 1906 on the S.S. *Baltic,* and Constance took her first steps on board the ship.

The London experience was a grave disappointment. When *The Lion and the Mouse* opened at the Duke of York's Theatre in May 1906, the English critics flayed it. The *Times of London* sneered, "Mr. Richard Bennett, in the rather thankless part of Jefferson, is one of the neat, round-faced boys with sweet expressions whom America often send us." At the end of three weeks, the company was notified that the play would close. Having paid three months' rent in advance on the house in St. John's Wood, Richard was devastated. He complained so bitterly that the play's company manager arranged to have him reimbursed for the house rental.

The Bennetts sailed back to New York. With the new baby on the way, the apartment on Longwood Avenue would be much too small. They set about looking for a house to buy, and found one in Fort Lee, New Jersey, just across the Hudson River from Manhattan. The house was in a section known as Palisade, a newly developed enclave of Fort Lee, made up of a post office, school, and little more than a dozen houses. The southernmost section of Fort Lee, Palisade adjoined Cliffside Park and the Palisades Amusement Park. Later, in their official biographies, Richard and his daughters would refer to this residence as being in "Palisade, New Jersey," which is a little like substituting Park Slope for Brooklyn. No doubt Palisade was chosen because it sounded more glamorous than Fort Lee.

The Bennetts moved into their new home at 1074 Dearborn Road, which they christened "Benn-Morr," on July 23, 1906. The month of August brought a number of changes to the family's life. On August 13, Richard and Mabel's second child, Barbara Jane

Bennett, was born, at the house in Palisade. Five days later, Lewis Morrison died, following complications from stomach surgery. On the advice of the physician who delivered Barbara, Richard didn't tell Mabel about her father's death for a few days, and managed to keep the newspapers and telegrams of condolence away from her until she had gained back some of her strength.

The third major event was the opening of Richard's new play, Henry Arthur Jones's *The Hypocrites,* at the Hudson Theatre on August 30. His leading lady was Doris Keane, then near the beginning of an important starring career. For his performance as a man engaged to a rich girl who gets a poor girl pregnant, and then tries to wriggle out of his responsibility, the *New York Times* wrote, "Richard Bennett merits more praise than time or space will permit. . . ."

The next few months passed calmly enough. By the time Barbara was weaned, however, Richard and Mabel faced another stormy period in their marriage. Months of enforced inactivity had only strengthened Mabel's determination to continue with her stage career as soon as she was able. Having learned nothing from his previous battles with his wife over her career, Richard once again stated his objections. He had hoped that after Barbara's arrival, Mabel would resign herself to being a housewife and mother. Since that was not yet the case, perhaps yet another baby would do the trick. Much as he loved Barbara, he longed for a son; if Mabel were to become pregnant again, he might get his wish. So he began a campaign to persuade her that pursuing a career made her an unfit mother and that she had no business continuing to act; her place was at home with her babies.

Generally, Mabel was not given to great emotional displays; if she had been, it is doubtful that her marriage to Richard could have survived for a single year. But she was far from being a pushover. When Richard attempted to use his repertoire of intimidation tricks, her response was a quiet aggression that could become downright unnerving. In this particular instance, she coolly reminded him of her family's 120 years in the theater, and insisted that she was not about to abandon her calling to stay at home and play house. They found themselves at another impasse, and Richard decided to seek counsel from Charles Frohman. The producer brought him up short by telling him that he felt Mabel had a bright future in the theater, and went so far as to suggest that she join the touring company of *The Hypocrites,* playing the role created by Doris Keane. Hearing his mentor assume the voice of reason finally led Richard to acquiesce, provided that they take Constance and Barbara along with them.

By this time, the enormous difference in the girls' personalities was becoming apparent. Constance, once she had learned to talk, did so unceasingly. A headstrong, energetic tomboy, she showed a marked degree of independence at an early age. She hated being fawned over by adults, even her parents, and would frequently squirm out of an enveloping embrace and skitter away "with the affection of a cockroach," as Richard observed. While Constance seemed to throw tantrums for the pure satisfaction of it, Barbara was shy and introverted, and much easier to handle.

The tour of *The Hypocrites* proved a trying time for both Richard and Mabel. Richard was still uncomfortable with the idea of his wife traveling with him. His resentment of her career ambitions was one issue, but there were other complications: Mabel's presence on tour made it difficult for him to go on drinking sprees and arrange liaisons with other women, two of his greatest pleasures in being on the road. As the tour wore on, tension between the couple built once more. Richard began to imagine that Mabel's quiet wilfulness was robbing him of all his natural rights as a husband and father. It seemed to him that he possessed no authority whatsoever in household matters, and he even began to entertain the paranoid fantasy that Constance and Barbara had fixed on their mother as the emotional center of their lives, regarding him as a mere interloper.

Richard continued appearing in plays at a steady rate. His status as a Frohman leading man guaranteed him a certain job security, but he was starting to feel restless. He simply wasn't advancing at the rate he had once hoped. In June 1907, he was back in London at the Duke of York's Theatre, appearing with Grace George in a revival of Victorien Sardou's comedy *Divorçons,* which proved altogether a happier experience than *The Lion and the Mouse* the previous year. Richard then appeared in a play called *Twenty Days in the Shade,* which played for sixty-four performances. He didn't want to do his next play, Cicely Hamilton's *Diana of Dobson's,* starring Carlotta Neilson. He loathed his role of a "silly-assed Englishman." Rehearsals were difficult, with the director correcting Richard on every move, every line reading. Richard noticed that Charles Frohman was breaking his usual pattern of being an invisible presence during the rehearsal period; the producer frequently showed up at the theater, and seemed to be studying Richard carefully. A week after *Diana of Dobson's* opened, Richard experienced a first: he was fired.

He flew into a panic. It was the middle of the season, and with most of the other big plays already cast, he had no idea how he was going to support his family. Frohman sent for him, and when Richard reported to his office, the producer told him that he had a new part lined up for him. As he passed the contract to Richard, he hinted that it was the choice role of the season and would automatically elevate him to stardom. There had been some opposition to Richard playing the part, but Frohman assured him that everything would be all right; Richard should go home, read the contract, sign it, and—above all—not worry.

Richard did as he was told, but he was troubled that the contract mysteriously avoided mentioning a specific role. Weeks went by, and he came no closer to learning which part he had committed to play. He took Mabel, Constance, and Barbara to Peaks Island, Maine, for part of the summer. One day, Mabel rushed up, holding a copy of the *New York Times.* In it was an item announcing that Richard would be Maude Adams's leading man in her next play, J.M. Barrie's *What Every Woman Knows.* Frohman had already sent the play on a lengthy U.S. tour, with Hilda Trevelyan and Gerald Du Maurier. Now that it was ready for Broadway, he decided to relaunch it as a deluxe vehicle for Adams.

Richard could scarcely believe his good fortune as rehearsals began in October 1908. Frohman prescribed an unusual method of rehearsing his casts: there was no initial reading; the actors simply milled about the stage, scripts in hand, prompted only by occasional suggestions from the stage manager, until the play slowly began to take shape for them. "It was worse than army drill," Richard observed, " . . . you just moved about until the light of comprehension burst forth upon you." Maude Adams didn't appear until the fourth day of rehearsals. Never before had he worked with a star of her magnitude. Watching her step onto the stage and hearing the warm sincerity of her greeting to the company, Richard knew in an instant that he had reached a high-water mark. "A small-town, midwest country boy," he recalled, " . . . sans education, except such as I had gleaned from my choice of reading . . . now the leading man of Maude Adams, America's greatest box-office draw, under the management of the great Charles Frohman. It was almost too much to believe."

By the time she appeared in *What Every Woman Knows*, Maude Adams was already the most celebrated actress in America. At the time, it was estimated that she played each year to approximately a half million people, and earned twice the salary of Pres. Theodore Roosevelt. Petite and serene-looking, she was far from beautiful, yet her fame had far outdistanced many of her more glamorous contemporaries. Her mother, Annie Adams, had been a leading lady in stock companies throughout the United States, and Maude had made her first stage appearance when she was only nine months old, in *The Lost Child*. She made her adult debut at fifteen, and four years later was engaged to support John Drew in a string of plays, including *The Masked Ball* and *The Bauble Shop*. One evening, a young Scot visiting the United States caught her opposite Drew in a performance of *Rosemary* and was so taken by her subtle charm and poetic grace that he set about dramatizing his novel *The Little Minister* for her. The play opened at the Empire Theatre in 1897, and Adams, in the role of Lady Babbie, suddenly found herself an important star. James M. Barrie figured in her career from then on. In 1905, his *Peter Pan* became her most successful vehicle ever.

However textured her characterizations were, Adams usually conveyed a plainness and gentleness onstage; in this respect, Helen Hayes was probably her natural successor. One writer observed of

Adams, "Probably it is true that her art is limited in scope. Horror and the notes of tragedy she does not awaken. She has no grasp of the fierce elemental passions of animal sex. To depict those things does not interest her. The fountain head of her personality is nun-like and virginal."

What Every Woman Knows is the story of Maggie, a plain Scottish girl whose brothers long to see her married. The play's most memorable speech comes early in the first act. When asked by one of the other characters, "What is charm, exactly, Maggie?" Maggie replies:

> Oh, it's—it's a sort of bloom on a woman. If you have it, you don't need anything else; and if you don't have it, it doesn't much matter what else you have. Some women, the few, have charm for all; and most have charm for one. But some have charm for none.

Maggie sees herself as one who has "charm for none." But her brothers strike a bargain with an ambitious but poor young man named John Shand: if he will marry Maggie, they will finance his education to the tune of £300. Both Maggie and John agree to the arrangement. Six years go by, and John has completed his schooling and run successfully for Parliament—and become arrogant and self-absorbed in the process. Maggie tells him that he need not be bound by his promise, and he nearly leaves her for a glamorous rival. But in the end, he realizes that he will not be half the man he can be without Maggie at his side. As she explains to him, "It's nothing unusual I've done, John. Every man who is high up loves to think that he has done it all himself, and the wife smiles, and lets it go at that. It's our only joke. Every woman knows that."

For most of the actors in *What Every Woman Knows,* mastering the Scottish accents that the play required proved a daunting challenge. After several days of rehearsal, Richard found that most of the actors' lines were so unintelligible that he couldn't recognize his cues. He sprang into action, searching the piers around the Brooklyn Bridge until he found a longshoreman who was a native

Scot. He took him to a nearby bar and bought him one drink after another, listening to every nuance of the man's speech until he felt he had mastered the tricky dialect. It was still much too guttural, and he knew that the audience would never be able to comprehend it, so he began to spend long hours talking with a Scottish actor in the cast named David Torrence, who had attended the University of Edinburgh and had only a moderate, upper-class accent. Richard practiced crossing the two dialects in various combinations until he finally came up with a sound that made him feel right as John Shand.

As rehearsals progressed, *What Every Woman Knows* was developing into much more than a vehicle for Maude Adams. Richard's characterization was probing, intelligent, and beautifully observed. His rich, deep voice had developed to the point where he could project it effortlessly, making it heard in every corner of the theater. Over the years, he had slowly learned one of the things that so many actors find difficult: how to listen. In rehearsals for *What Every Woman Knows,* it was clear that Richard had mastered the art of listening. His performances had always born the mark of his own naturally fiery personality, but as John Shand, his lyric quality was balanced by a greater sense of realism than he had ever shown before. Many of his most beautiful moments were silent ones.

When the play opened at the Empire Theatre on December 23, 1908, it immediately became the hit of the season. Richard was singled out for praise by all the major critics. The *New York Times* wrote, "The triumph of the night was unquestionably Mr. Bennett's. His Shand is a perfectly studied and delivered characterization. Its humor is irresistible. It has vigor, force, bluntness—all the qualities, in fact, which Mr. Barrie apparently seeks to show." (The same critic found that Adams was occasionally "overwrought almost to the point of hysteria.") Maggie's "charm" speech was the season's most-quoted piece of dialogue. The play even inspired a popular song, "What Every Woman Knows," written by Walter Pulitzer and Eden E. Grenville.

When *What Every Woman Knows* closed temporarily in the spring of 1909, Richard was still uneasy about the situation at home. He felt that he had not spent enough time with Constance and

Barbara to establish a sound relationship with them, and he thought that Mabel had indulged them terribly, causing them to become lazy and self-centered. Because he was home with them so little, they frequently talked back to him or ignored him altogether. Now that he was a bona fide Broadway star, he began to exert his will at home more than he had in the past. He persuaded Mabel to join her brother Victor on a trip to Europe, so that he could enjoy some time alone with the girls. During Mabel's two-month sojourn, Richard finally took the opportunity to break his daughters of some of the bad habits they had developed. Constance, being much more willful and headstrong than Barbara, posed a greater challenge. When she couldn't get her way, Constance was given to shutting herself up in her bedroom and banging her head on the floor repeatedly. But after two months of orders barked at her day and night, even she began to show a degree of respect for him. At last, he made his presence felt as head of the household. His time alone with the girls produced enduring results with Constance. For most of her life she would feel a profound attachment to her father. Barbara continued to be fearful of his brazen, egocentric personality, but Constance was alternately unfazed and delighted by it.

After Mabel's return from Europe, Richard went to Los Angeles for a season with Oliver Morosco's stock company. It was a golden time for stock companies in California: the silent movie industry was taking off, and struggling actors had discovered that playing in stock made an excellent springboard for getting into motion pictures. Richard's fellow actors at Morosco that season included three future movie names: Charles Ruggles, Harold Lloyd, and Fay Bainter. In the fall of 1909, he returned to New York, where *What Every Woman Knows* was picking up again after the summer layoff. Just as rehearsals were beginning, Mabel told Richard that she was expecting another child. Certain that this time Mabel would give birth to a son, Richard chose the name John—after John Shand.

Once again he was disappointed. On February 27, 1910, Joan Geraldine Bennett was born at home in New Jersey. Richard, who was appearing in *What Every Woman Knows* in Bangor, Maine, left the company after a Saturday night performance, took an overnight train to New York, and made it to Palisade by Sunday morning. It was a brief meeting; he had to leave almost immediately for the play's Chicago opening, after which the company would travel to the West Coast. It was nearly five months before he was able to return home for his second glimpse of Joan: "She was lying in her baby carriage on the verandah, looking as beautiful as the rose in the sun, at which she was cooing. She has always been that little rosebud since."

Richard's sadness at leaving the new baby behind was somewhat alleviated by the success of *What Every Woman Knows* on the road. It played to capacity houses at every stop on its long national tour. Professionally, Richard was flying high, but he was rapidly growing dissatisfied with his costar. Adams was constantly looking for little things that would improve the play—and Richard's performance. Richard found her incessant tinkering annoying, and relations between them cooled as the tour progressed. In 1911, Adams starred in the title role of Edmond Rostand's *Chantecler,* in which all the characters were barnyard animals. The part had been intended for Otis Skinner until Adams usurped it for herself. Richard sent her a telegram: "I CONGRATULATE YOU ON THE REALIZATION OF YOUR FONDEST AMBITION. AT LAST YOU ARE YOUR OWN LEADING MAN." In the last years of his life, Richard would speak disparagingly of Adams, calling her "a very much overrated actress," entirely dependent on Frohman's judgment, and saying that when he died, she hadn't the means or knowhow to continue acting. (In fact, Adams did retire from the stage a few years after Frohman's death, returning only for two isolated engagements much later on.)

For *The Deep Purple,* a melodrama by Paul Armstrong and Wilson Mizner, Frohman lent Richard to producer George C. Tyler. Rehearsals were hectic. The playwrights had heated battles both with Tyler and each other, and scene after scene was rewritten wholesale each day. At the end of three weeks, the script had metamorphosed into "a rather lively, moving melodrama" after its opening at the Lyric Theatre in January 1911.

The Deep Purple not only marked Richard Bennett's twentieth year in the theater but also, in a sense, was a benchmark in his career. Ever since *What Every Woman Knows,* he had been an established Frohman star, a favorite with critics, and a box-office draw. It was only natural, then, that he would now begin to exert some degree of control over the kind of plays in which he appeared, rather than merely accepting whatever role was offered him.

Although he had received only a bare-bones education back home in Indiana, Richard possessed a drive and intellectual curiosity that grew in intensity each year. He continued to read voraciously; his beloved dictionary and thesaurus always within arm's reach. As he went from play to play, he had formed the opinion that the theater might have the potential to do more than entertain. It might also be used as a means of reaching out to the public and educating them on subjects normally considered taboo.

Richard's attitude toward sex had always been colored by what would now be regarded as a double standard. He believed that sex was intended essentially for the pleasure of men, who by nature were driven to satisfy their appetite; women had to get used to the idea that the men they married would indulge in an occasional affair. Women, on the other hand, were held to a strict Victorian code of ethics. While there is no indication that Mabel was ever unfaithful to him, she hardly conformed to his idea of the submissive, dutiful wife and mother—but clearly, her rebellious, individualistic streak was also part of what drew Richard to her.

Given these unenlightened attitudes, it is surprising that Richard should have been so taken with Eugene Brieux's *Damaged Goods,* and that he should have made such a mighty effort to see that it reached the stage. Throughout his life, Brieux was a crusading playwright. "My idea is very simple," he once told an interviewer. "I love life, movement, joy. I want to see life and joy everywhere, and attack everything that kills joy and life. I want to see healthy men, women, and children, and must combat the conditions that make for misery and unhappiness."

Damaged Goods was a study of the crippling effects of congenital syphilis. The play had come to Richard's attention during the summer of 1911. Staged in Paris, as *Les Avariés,* it had been banned. For years, George Bernard Shaw had championed the play in London, but had made no progress whatsoever. In the preface to the published version of the play, Shaw railed against the "stupid people" who contributed to the conspiracy of silence that had led to the rise of syphilis and other dreaded social diseases. Shaw attacked them for their belief that the theater was not the proper place to raise such issues. "When asked, 'What, then, is the proper place?'" he wrote, "they plead that the proper place is out of hearing of the general public: that is, not in a school, not in a church, not in a newspaper, not in a public meeting, but in medical textbooks which are read only by medical students. . . . One hardly knows whether to laugh or cry at such perverse stupidity."

In 1913, syphilis was indeed an explosive subject for a play. There had been little progress in the public's acceptance of it as material for an evening in the theater since 1881, when Henrik Ibsen published his masterpiece *Ghosts*. Although Ibsen never mentions the disease by name, the play's published version was denounced in the press as a work that had no place in any decent Christian home. The book failed to run through its original printing of ten thousand copies, and no theater in Sweden, Norway, or Denmark would produce it. *Ghosts* finally received its world premiere in Chicago—but for years the taint of scandal prevented it from entering the mainstream repertory.

From the moment he finished reading *Damaged Goods,* Richard became convinced that it was no less than his civic duty to see that it got onstage in the United States. The play concerns the fate of a young man, George Dupont, whose happy future is threatened when he contracts syphilis from a prostitute. His doctor urges him to postpone his impending marriage by as much as three to four years, until he has undergone treatment. But George, unable to accept the truth, opts for a second opinion, from a quack who gives him a clean bill of health. He marries, but the first doctor's prediction proves correct—in no time, George passes the disease on to his wife, Henriette. In the end, the couple's tragedy is magnified when they learn that the disease has been passed on to their child. The second act, in which George confronts the prostitute, who reveals that she purposely infected him out of spite for "respectable" men like himself, is intensely dramatic; elsewhere, *Damaged Goods* reads a bit like a medical school lecture. Characteristic is the doctor's speech to Loches, Henriette's father, about the desperate need for the facts of syphilis to be disseminated to the public:

> . . . . All that is needed is for people to understand the nature of disease better. It would soon become the custom for a man who proposed for a girl's hand to add to the other things for which he is asked a medical statement of bodily fitness, which would make it certain that he did not bring plague into the family with him. It would be perfectly simple. Once it was the custom, the man would go to his doctor for a certificate of health before he could sign the register—just as now, before he can be married in church, he goes to his priest for a certificate that he has confessed.

No doubt the script of *Damaged Goods* appealed to Richard in part because so much of it sounded remarkably like his own rants on any of a number of social issues, from the necessity of birth control to the oppressive and willful ignorance of many leading churches. All his life, Richard was hostile toward organized religion, blaming church leaders for impeding social progress in America. For some time, Richard had felt the urgent need for a more progressive view of sex education, that legislators had to push through laws that would protect the majority of the population from being infected with syphilis.

Not that he didn't have every right to be concerned about the public's attitude toward sexually transmitted diseases. Syphilis had emerged as a significant public health problem in the United States, but public discussion of venereal disease was practically nonexistent. The Wasserman test, the standard means of monitoring the blood for venereal disease, had been developed in 1906, and salvarsan, known as Dr. Ehrlich's "magic bullet," had been introduced in 1910. But not until 1935 would any American state—

Connecticut—require both men and women to pass a blood test before being granted a marriage license.

Immediately, Richard took the *Damaged Goods* script to Charles Frohman, who told him that the play didn't have a chance of being produced and to do himself the favor of forgetting about it as quickly as possible. But Richard didn't give up. *Damaged Goods* was not just another routine farce or melodrama; it was the kind of play he had been looking for, something with a strong social message that would shake the listless Broadway audiences out of their complacency. He decided to direct, as well as star as George Dupont. House payments and the cost of raising three young daughters left him little in the way of disposable income, but he managed to come up with five hundred dollars for a year's option on the Brieux play. He went down the list of possible producers, but not one of them would consider taking on *Damaged Goods.* Wherever he went, he talked up the play, to no avail. Even Mabel regarded the play as a lost cause, and tried to dissuade her husband from spending any more time on it. But the growing wall of opposition only made him twice as determined to get *Damaged Goods* on its feet.

In time, Sam Harris, the well-known producer, asked Richard to accompany him to Bridgeport, Connecticut, where *Stop, Thief!,* a new farce he was producing with his partner George M. Cohan, was being tried out, none too successfully. Richard had the right kind of electricity to make the play a hit, and Harris asked him to consider taking over the leading role of Jack Doogan. Richard thought that *Stop, Thief!* was pretty bad, but finally, he cut a deal with Harris. He would star in *Stop, Thief!* at the Gaiety Theatre in New York, provided that Harris let him use the theater for a special matinee of *Damaged Goods.*

Richard snatched up the opportunity, and went to work on *Stop, Thief!,* but the play wasn't coming off because the laughs were being sledge-hammered home to the audience. A farce succeeds, he explained to the creative team, only when the characters seem unaware that anything funny is happening. After a few weeks of rehearsal, a largely rewritten *Stop, Thief!* opened at the Gaiety and became one of the hits of the season. Because he had put in so much work on the script, Richard received one percent of the gross, most of which he put aside for the projected production of *Damaged Goods*.

But there were further obstacles. When Harris offered the Gaiety to Richard, he had not read the Brieux play. When a member of his staff told him the story, he promptly reneged on the deal. Still, Richard wasn't discouraged. He worked fiendishly on the play's script, commissioning three separate translations, then making his own adaptation. He also began to assemble his company—no easy task, since nearly all of the actors who read the script turned it down flat, preferring not to risk their reputations on such a controversial work. He had managed to secure Wilton Lackaye for the role of the doctor, a calculated move on Richard's part: Lackaye was a man of distinction whose personal reputation was beyond reproach, and Richard figured that his participation would count as a kind of seal of approval in some quarters. Slowly, he assembled the rest of the cast. For the key role of Laura, the syphilitic prostitute, who spoke some of the play's most shocking lines, Richard rehearsed a number of actresses, all of whom departed quickly. He finally decided to simplify matters by casting Mabel in the part. "For once," Joan later commented, "Father was glad he'd married an actress and accepted her gratefully." There was still no theater, so the members of the company began to rehearse in any space they could find. Richard even begged the management of several leading hotels to rent him space for one performance—but again, there were no takers.

Along the way, Richard had met Dr. Frederick Robertson, editor and publisher of the *Medical Review of Reviews*. Looking to boost his magazine's circulation, Robertson asked Richard to let him scoop all the other newspapers and magazines with the details, once they were known, of the premiere of *Damaged Goods*. After toying with the idea for some months, Richard devised a plan: *Damaged Goods* would be presented under the auspices of the *Medical Review of Reviews*, with a committee of sponsors selected from the medical profession and the church. With such respectable backing, any problems with the police or the censors could no doubt be avoided. In order to gain admission, one had to become a member of the Society of the Medical Review, which cost five dollars. A membership card would ensure a seat at *Damaged Goods*. Finally, a mutual acquaintance arranged for Richard to meet with John D. Rockefeller Jr. After looking over the script, Rockefeller was impressed. "I think you are doing something worthwhile," he told Richard, and he agreed to lend his name as one of the play's sponsors.

Rumors of the forthcoming production had some persuasive effect on the New York theater community, and at the eleventh hour the management of the Fulton Theatre nervously agreed to rent the house for a single performance. The premiere had received the protection of Mayor William J. Gaynor; still, every possible precaution was taken. Advertisements reassured the public that *Damaged Goods* contained "no scene to provoke scandal or arouse disgust, nor is there in it any obscene word, and it may be witnessed by everyone, unless we must believe that folly and ignorance are necessary conditions of female virtue." By opening night, March 14, 1913, *Damaged Goods* had become a cause célèbre and there was not a seat to be had. Doctors, politicians, social leaders, and some of the most important producers and stars on Broadway filed through the doors of the Fulton not knowing exactly what to expect. In the end, every newspaper in New York had taken out membership in the Society of the Medical Review, thus ensuring maximum press coverage.

Although a few critics complained that *Damaged Goods* was less a play than persuasive propaganda, most of the notices were excellent. Richard felt vindicated, but he didn't stop there. He took the play to the National Theater in Washington, D.C., where it was given a special matinee performance. This time, there were over twice as many ticket requests as there were available seats. Unable to argue with such success, the management of the Fulton Theatre in New York took *Damaged Goods* for its regular night bill; it played out the season, racking up a total of sixty-six performances. In the fall of 1913, *Damaged Goods* went on the road, drawing long lines at the box office in town after town before returning to Broadway in December 1913. During the play's two-season tour, the girls joined their parents, accompanied by a governess, on their first cross-country family trip. Although they traveled by train for longer stretches, Richard insisted on driving the shorter distances, and bought himself a roomy new Locomobile.

In Chicago, the play ran into censorship difficulties. The company was forced to cut some of the racier dialogue, and Mayor Carter Harrison Jr. decreed that only those over eighteen would be allowed to see the play. In a brazen public relations stunt, Richard promptly trotted out his three daughters to share his curtain call as proof that he was a respectable family man, not a leering degenerate, and that he didn't give a damn about the mayor's eighteen-or-over ruling. The Chicago reviews were disappointing. Given that *Damaged Goods* depicted George Dupont entering into marriage with full knowledge of the risk to himself and others, the *Chicago Tribune*'s Percy Hammond felt that the play provided "as much a sermon on imbecility as on poison in the blood." He did, however, admit that "the play is fortified by the excellent acting of Mr. Bennett," and also praised Mabel's "vivid" portrayal of the prostitute. But the thumbs-down notices affected the box office, and the scheduled run of three weeks diminished to two.

The Chicago engagement was significant for another reason. It was there that Richard began railing at his audiences in a series of incendiary curtain speeches—something that soon would become his trademark. His rhetoric was notable for its florid language. "I do not feel that I am an inspired or divine Messiah sent to reform the world," he bellowed after one performance of *Damaged Goods*, "but I intend to behave as though I were. Some day, when millions owe me clean veins and clean hearts and a birthright realized, my children's children may see monuments to their ancestor, whose generation afflicted him with criticism from flat-head ignorami, annoyance from beer-soaked censors with the mental breadth of cockroaches, and managers who value a dollar above an epoch!"

If he had failed to win over his harshest critics, he was amply rewarded by a long succession of accolades from many of the nation's political and religious leaders. "The more we have of *Damaged Goods* on the stage the less damaged goods we will have in actual life," proclaimed Connecticut congressman Thomas L. Reilly. Dr. Newell Dwight Hillis, pastor of the Plymouth Church in Brooklyn, wrote to Richard, "It is not too much to say that you have changed the thinking of the people of our country as to the social evil. . . . You have done a work for which your generation owes you an immeasurable debt of gratitude."

Damaged Goods marked another turning point for Richard as well. Fueled by the success of his efforts in *Damaged Goods,* he now began increasingly to see himself as a crusader. Throughout his life, he would strive to propel America into the twentieth century, lecturing, haranguing, and writing letters to newspaper editors on public issues that concerned him deeply. Like most crusaders, he would eventually take on a note of arrogance and self-congratulatory smugness. Nevertheless, he deserved every word of praise heaped on him for his perseverance in bringing *Damaged Goods* to the American public. More than twenty years later, he would write, "I had fought a ten-year battle in eighteen months. My hair had started to turn gray, my nervous system was impaired by the strain, but I was happier than ever before or since."

Chapter Four

1914–1920

With *Damaged Goods,* Richard had overturned conventional notions about what American theatrical audiences would accept. For his next Broadway vehicle, he chose another Brieux play, *Maternity.* Although it too dealt with a risky subject—legalized abortion—it made its way to the stage with few obstacles. Again, Richard produced and starred, and again there was a good part for Mabel—or Adrienne, as she now called herself professionally, having decided to use her middle name because two other Mabel Morrisons had turned up on the New York stage. But in spite of its shocking theme, the play failed to coalesce, and its run at the Princess Theater was brief.

By now, Richard was free of his contract with Charles Frohman. It had been a fruitful seventeen-year association, but Richard had been stung by Frohman's refusal to present *Damaged Goods,* and his respect for his mentor diminished as a result. Then, too, *Damaged Goods* had given him a boost of confidence. If he could manage to get such a controversial play produced against staggering odds, why not press further in the same direction? In Europe, the First World War had been raging since the summer of 1914, and Richard anticipated that such calamitous events were sure to bring about a greater demand for serious plays. If he were to strike out on his own, he might be able to leave behind the fluffy comedies and purple melodramas that had made up the bulk of his assignments for Frohman. Richard's obsession with improving himself showed no sign of flagging; he wanted to drink in all of life, to rise to the absolute top of his profession.

By this time, the movies, only a little more than a decade old, were becoming America's favorite form of entertainment. In the spring of 1915, the American-Mutual Film Company engaged Richard to direct, write, and star in a screen version of *Damaged Goods*. Although Joan recalled that neither of her parents ever regarded the movies "with anything but polite tolerance and contempt," Richard was delighted to be able to put his pet project on film, and even more delighted that American-Mutual had given him complete creative control. It was shot in San Francisco and Los Angeles that summer, and provided the Bennetts with a double screen debut: Mabel was signed to recreate the role of Laura.

The film version of *Damaged Goods* appears to be lost, but reviews indicate that it went even further than the play, showing shocking close-ups of patients, scarred and paralyzed, suffering from advanced stages of syphilis. *Variety* praised the film for providing "a ray of hope for the syphilitic" and singled out Richard for his "creditable performance of a rather difficult character." *Damaged Goods* was a solid box-office success, and American-Mutual was so pleased that it persuaded Richard to make another film geared to raise social consciousness, *The Valley of Decision*. The topic was birth control, but the movie was a condemnation, not an endorsement. Joan later commented that only sheer perverseness made Richard, with his strong views on the necessity of birth control, agree to make this prolife preachment. *The Valley of Decision* was shot in Santa Barbara, and this time around, the entire family was involved in the filming: Mabel played the female lead, and Constance, Barbara, and Joan all made their film debuts in an allegorical prologue called "The Shadowland of Souls Unborn." Wearing absurd Grecian outfits, the girls were directed by their father to dance, in Joan's words, "like refugees from a number three company of Isadora Duncan."

By now, Constance was ten, Barbara eight, and Joan five. Their screen debut was more a matter of convenience on Richard's part than anything else. Neither Richard nor Mabel had done much to prod their children toward the theater. For one thing, they were far too young. For another, Mabel still had ambivalent feelings about her own unsettled childhood, and wanted to be sure that her daughters had a secure and comfortable home environment. Despite her own busy schedule, and Richard's frequent dalliances with other women, she tried her best to provide them with it. Mabel wanted her girls to grow into proper, polite, well-dressed young ladies. She praised them frequently, but stopped short of spoiling them, and always encouraged their growing signs of independence.

Already, Mabel's own acting ambitions were beginning to fade. Like most young hopefuls, her heart was originally set on stardom, and her parents' eminence had no doubt done a great deal to fuel her fantasies. But for most actors, there is a turning point, when they realize that stardom is no longer realistically within their grasp. It is then that most settle for becoming steady, working actors. Mabel's turning point seems to have come around 1915. Richard's constant attempts to thwart her ambitions had no doubt taken their toll, and the more she looked around her, her first priority seemed to be to provide her children with a home life that was as serene and natural as possible. Above all, she hoped it would provide them with a solid base for the future—preferably as sensible, well-married women.

But with two parents so deeply rooted in the theater, it was naive to think that the girls would resist the lure of the stage forever. At this point, the only one who showed any real enthusiasm was Constance, the eldest. In 1914, the Bennetts moved temporarily into the Hotel Ansonia, a Manhattan residence hotel popular with actors and musicians, on the corner of Seventy-third Street and Broadway. While there, Constance got her hands on a sheet of Ansonia stationery and wrote herself a letter:

> Dear Miss Bennett,
>
> Won't you come over to the Liberty Theatre and try a new leading part, and I wouldn't get any Body else. We have a Starr part for you called The Kidnapped Child it

is a great part and just your tipe. Please come if your Mother will let you—

Yours very truly,
Douglas Fairbanks

Mabel admired her daughter's ingenuity. But for the time being, Constance remained at Miss Chandor's School, at 137 East Sixty-second Street, just off Park Avenue. Mabel had selected Miss Chandor's because of its reputation as one of the city's more successful college prep schools—although as a student, Constance was never very serious or disciplined.

In 1915, the Bennetts embarked on one of the happiest times of their lives when they left the house in Palisade (it did not burn down, as Joan stated in her memoirs) and purchased a spacious home at 179 Park Hill Avenue in Yonkers, just north of New York City. Living in Park Hill meant a forty-five-minute rail commute into the city, but the inconvenience was worth it. The entire family loved the spacious, tapestry brick Georgian house, with great sloping lawns where the girls could run and play, and plenty of gardening space for Richard to grow flowers and vegetables. He also had a field day furnishing the house by ransacking the antique shops in and around New York. While Richard spent hours stripping, sanding, refinishing, and painting furniture, Mabel brought a keen decorator's eye to all the rooms. She was especially pleased with the paintings and photographs of her ancestors that she arranged not long after they moved in. Once he saw it, Richard lost no time in fixing up a display of his own press clippings on an adjacent wall. For the four years that the Bennetts would occupy the Park Hill house, Richard seemed more contented than ever. "Father at home," Joan remembered, "was Father at his very best."

In their great orchestral work, *Knoxville: Summer of 1915,* Samuel Barber and James Agee pay tribute to a gentle, sleepy American way of life that had existed before the country thrust itself into World War I. Perhaps no other work of art so poignantly captures this insular world where traditional values still prevailed, of people sitting on their porches, "rocking gently and talking gently." Barber and Agee recalled a graceful era on the verge of disappearing. In this sense, Richard's belief in *Damaged Goods,* his conviction that audiences could handle more mature themes, had been remarkably prescient. For in 1914, the beginning of war in Europe would force America into wholesale reinvention. What most people in power had believed would be a brief war—the Germans had predicted victory in forty-two days—quickly degenerated into a bloody stalemate. Throughout its history, the United States had struggled to remain aloof from hostilities between major European powers, and during the first years of World War I the country desperately tried to maintain this policy. Comforted by Pres. Woodrow Wilson's persistent position of neutrality, the United States benefited economically from the war while avoiding participation in it. The country's vast reserves of steel, coal, and other products suddenly were in great demand abroad, and the result was a staggering economic boom, in which a factory worker could see his piddling weekly salary multiply nearly ten times over.

The first major step toward U.S. entry into the war was the sinking of the *Lusitania* in May 1915. For some time, the presence of German submarines had made transatlantic crossings a risky proposition, but the loss of 128 American lives (among them, Charles Frohman) on the *Lusitania* was a grave shock to the public. Meanwhile, the conflict in Europe was one of unprecedented horror. By the end of the first year of the war, the number of French casualties reportedly edged toward 1 million. On July 1, 1917, the first day of the bloody Battle of the Somme, twenty thousand men were killed. Faced with such grim statistics, and with the great number of German attacks on unarmed ships, Wilson could not remain neutral forever. On April 2, 1917, he asked Congress for a declaration of war.

Poorly trained, often without benefit of weapons or uniforms, American soldiers entered the war with little idea of what lay in store for them. According to historian Robert H. Zieger, 31 percent of U.S. Army inductees were functionally illiterate. In an attempt to boost support for this decidedly unpopular war, Wilson created the Committee on Public Information, designed to persuade a skeptical and fearful American public that this was a war worth fighting.

The mood of the theater was changing accordingly. All around the country, the Little Theater movement was taking hold, ready to provide a challenge to the commercial pablum offered on Broadway. These enterprising companies sought out plays dealing with urgent social issues, plays meant to shake audiences out of their complacency. The Provincetown Players, a dynamic group on Cape Cod that later moved to Greenwich Village, launched the early plays of Eugene O'Neill in New York. Another influential group was the Washington Square Players, which in its short life presented important works by Chekhov, Zoe Akins, and O'Neill.

Richard watched the rise of these groups with great interest, although for the time being he was too big a star to be expected to join them. Instead, he did what he could for the war effort. One of his many projects was a benefit production of *A Midsummer Night's Dream* staged in the backyard at Park Hill in July 1917. Thirteen-year-old Constance played Titania; Barbara, eleven, was Mustardseed; and seven-year-old Joan was Peaseblossom. It was attended by many notables of the theater, including Florenz Ziegfeld and Billie Burke.

By now, Constance had graduated from Miss Chandor's School and moved on to Oaksmere, Mrs. Merrill's Boarding School for Girls in Mamaroneck, Westchester County. Although the school was only eleven years old at the time Constance enrolled, it was already among the highest-priced private schools in the area, described in one handbook as "patronized by those who spend freely." Isabella Starr, the school's dean, was known for her high standards and exacting methods, and at Oaksmere, Constance met a regimen even more formidable than the one Richard had tried to impose.

Fueled by her dissatisfaction with school life, Constance continued to beseech her parents to allow her to go on the stage. In 1918, Mabel finally relented. She had committed to appear in a production of the sixteenth-century morality play *Everyman*, staged by an avant-garde company on Grand Street known as the Neighborhood Players. Mabel took the role of Knowledge, and Constance appeared as the White Angel. Joan remembered that Richard turned up for opening night and declared that Constance played the part "like a Roman senator, but she looked beautiful, and he was 'damn proud.'"

Although Richard often held forth about the sanctity of domestic life, for him, it was more of a concept to be revered than a reality to be honored. Consistently, he failed to square his love of his family with the pleasures of his acting career. Arrogant as ever, he took no great pains to hide his affairs, and when Mabel inevitably found out about them, their battles were long and intense.

Only four or five years earlier, when he had been a matinee idol, Mabel had been able to shrug off his womanizing more easily. Now, he was not only as handsome as ever, but one of New York's most respected actors. There were women everywhere—actresses, producer's secretaries, fans—all too willing to demonstrate the depth of their admiration for him, and Richard seldom did much to resist. Joan felt that Richard breathed sex appeal "like a hot wind. The female 'oh's' and 'ah's' trailed him wherever he went, and his matinees were mobbed by flushed, agreeable ladies who fairly quivered in his presence."

Mabel decided that fewer temptations might be placed in Richard's path if the family moved into the city, where she could keep a closer watch over him. She was wrong, of course. Richard was an unrepentant womanizer, with little more control over his impulses than a kleptomaniac. Nevertheless, Mabel forced the issue. If the family were to move back to the city, she might be able to spend adequate time at home with the girls, keep an eye on Richard, and still find an occasional play to do. Richard hated to surrender his double life as cosmopolitan roué and hearth-loving country squire, but finally he gave in. Late in the spring of 1918, the Bennetts left Park Hill and moved into an elegant, four-story house at 22 West Eighth Street, near Washington Square in Greenwich Village. In those days, Fifth Avenue still ran through the middle of Washington Square Park, which Joan remembered as "a long patch of shaded green . . . where families strolled casually on Sundays, and children played in freedom around an organ-grinder." From the start, the girls loved the understated elegance of the house, with its high ceilings, shiny, wooden-pegged floors, and gleaming brass fixtures.

Richard's success in *Damaged Goods* had fed his view of himself as a crusader for high moral and ethical standards; he was now playing the same part at home, often with turbulent results. Richard was a conundrum: He believed in the emancipation of women, but he was stunned when Mabel took up smoking and bobbed her hair. He felt that family life was practically sacred, yet he believed in birth control, perhaps because he wanted to insure that his own affairs had no serious consequences. He saw himself as a free thinker always eager to campaign against injustices of any kind, but in fact he was a deeply prejudiced man with a particular animosity toward Jews. (He gave his benefactor Charles Frohman the ultimate backhanded compliment, calling him "the grandest, squarest Jew in the theater.") He wanted to set the rules, both in the theater and at home, and did not hesitate to play judge, jury, and executioner. The more successful his career, the more erratic his behavior.

Shortly after moving into the house on Eighth Street, Richard staged a terrifying domestic episode that would haunt the girls for years. One evening, Constance, by now thirteen, broke one of the cardinal rules of the house by coming home late. Barbara and Joan, roused from their sleep by the sound of angry voices, crept to the top of the stairway. Downstairs, Richard and Constance were in the midst of a violent argument, with Mabel vainly attempting to calm them both down. As the shouting escalated, Constance flew upstairs to Barbara and Joan's room and dived under a bed. Richard rushed in, pointing a gun at the girls and demanding that they all line up against the wall. Screaming that either the family would conform to his expectations or there wouldn't be any family, he wondered aloud if it wouldn't be better to eliminate all three girls on the spot rather than permit them to carry on in their lazy, undisciplined ways. Even Constance was too terrified to move or speak. Finally, Richard could sustain his anger no longer and imploded.

He broke down in tears as Mabel led him out of the room. Possibly he was drunk. Possibly it was mostly an exercise in melodramatic self-indulgence. Certainly it seems that Richard had already begun to nurse the suspicion that his daughters had the potential to betray him.

These blind rages intimidated both Barbara and Joan, who clung to Mabel for security and calm. Only Constance was able to stand off against him. She watched closely as he freely exerted his will with no thought of the consequences, even as his mercurial temperament chipped away at his marriage. Constance watched and she learned. As she entered her mid-teens, she was more willful than ever, and cared only about having her own way. Despite the episode with the gun, the rules of the house meant little to her. She was an intensely feminine teenager, pretty and trim, who wanted to be out with her friends as much as possible.

The family allegiances had already taken shape, and over the years they varied remarkably little. It was a complicated pattern of crisscrossing loyalties: while Constance retained a powerful identification with her father, Richard made little attempt to hide his preference for Joan. And while Constance was Mabel's favorite, Joan was a mother's girl from the outset. Sandwiched between her sisters was Barbara, loved and encouraged but the favorite of neither parent. As a child, Barbara suffered extreme mood swings. Although she seemed essentially placid and gentle, she would burst into a wild tantrum without warning, and Mabel would have great difficulty calming her down. It is likely that this sudden, inexplicable loss of equilibrium must have struck Mabel as a reprise of her own mother's fragile emotional condition. (Rose Wood, by this time, was nearly a complete recluse, living in suburban Tenafly, New Jersey.)

By now, Barbara and Joan had followed Constance into Miss Chandor's School. Actress Jane Wyatt, then a student at Miss Chapin's School on East Fifty-seventh Street, recalled riding the bus to school with Barbara and Joan. "They always sat in the front seat," she remembered, "and no matter how hard my sister and I tried to get that seat, they always beat us to it. Of course, we knew who they were. Everyone did, because their father was Richard Bennett, and he was a terribly popular and handsome man."

In September 1918, Richard had another hit in Roland West and Carlyle Moore's *The Unknown Purple.* It had a fantastic plot: Richard played Peter Marchmont, a kindly, struggling inventor who discovers a method of converting ultraviolet rays that renders him invisible. He is so consumed by his experiment that he fails to see that his wife is neglecting their child while carrying on an affair with a family friend. Eventually, the wife and her lover arrange to have Peter jailed on a phony charge. When Peter is released from jail, he uses his secret invention to make himself invisible and exact his revenge.

It sounds like preposterous stuff, but evidently it was persuasive: The *New York Times* found it "skillfully motivated and constructed." Although Richard suffered the handicap of not being seen for many of the play's most thrilling moments, the *Times* thought it was an indication of his artistry that he nevertheless managed to dominate the play, and called his performance "a real triumph of imaginative impersonation." George Jean Nathan, in *Smart Set,* found that *The Unknown Purple* "surpasses in ingenuity the majority of Grand Guignol melopieces." It had one of the best runs of the year, 273 performances.

Once he was free of *The Unknown Purple,* Richard took another stab at the movies. The picture was called *The End of the Road,* and he was drawn to it because it was a return to the subject matter of *Damaged Goods*—a plea for the public to wake up and face the threat of venereal disease. The film was backed by the American Social Hygiene Association, and it was shown as part of the national campaign of the Social Hygiene Division of the War Department Commission Training Camp Activities, which hoped to curb the spread of syphilis and gonorrhea that had plagued uninitiated American war veterans returning from overseas. It is an oddly structured movie, so intent on getting across its message (often in graphic visual terms) that it never builds any dramatic momentum. It focuses on two young women. Mary (Claire Adams) is going into nurses training, while Vera (Joyce Fair) has been encouraged by her mother to think there is nothing more important than snagging a rich man. Mary goes to work for Philip Bell (Richard), a brilliant surgeon who longs to enlighten the masses about the dangers of venereal disease. One of his saddest cases is a young woman who has contracted gonorrhea thanks to her husband's "excursion on the primrose path," and whose little boy has been born blind. Dr. Bell warns her that "the ignorance, prudery, and false standards of our fathers are more to blame than your husband."

Trying to honor her mother's wishes, Vera is kept by a wealthy man, who walks out on her after infecting her with syphilis. She goes to Dr. Bell for help, and he shows her some of the extreme cases in the hospital's syphilis ward, warning her of the necessity of early treatment. Eventually, Mary's boyfriend, about to enlist in the war, attempts to persuade her to sleep with him before he sails overseas, but Mary declines and winds up in the much safer arms of Dr. Bell.

While much of *The End of the Road* was filmed at Famous Players studios in New York, several of its shocking hospital sequences were shot at the women's wards on Blackwell's Island, New York. These scenes repulsed some reviewers and terrified many patrons, but not enough to prevent the film from becoming a commercial success.

On December 19, 1919, Richard opened at the Playhouse, on West Forty-eighth Street, in *For the Defense* by Elmer Rice, a young playwright who would one day win acclaim for his expressionistic satire *The Adding Machine* (1923) and his realistic urban drama *Street Scene* (1929). *For the Defense,* an unusual suspense drama tinged with elements of the occult, marked a significant early success for Rice. The *New York Times* found that "in a season of many murder mysteries, it takes high rank." In the role of District Attorney Christopher Armstrong, Richard had already led the Rice play on a successful pre–New York tour around the United States, with Mabel cast in a supporting role. The producer of *For the Defense* was John D. Williams, an enterprising man who had been around the New York theater scene long enough to form the opinion that there was a potential audience for serious modern drama.

Very soon, he would help Richard into his most fertile period as an actor.

By the 1920s, the motion picture was badly damaging the business of road companies, but in New York the theater was thriving. The number of plays on the stage would climb gradually throughout the decade, reaching its apex in 1927–1928, when 268 productions opened. It was a time, unimaginable to us now, of overcrowding. There were simply not enough theaters to accommodate the number of plays awaiting production.

Best of all, this boom market coincided with the rise of the modern theater—plays informed by the growing complexity of contemporary life that dealt with adult themes. The ravages of World War I had left many Americans in a state of profound uncertainty about the future. The English novelist Ivy Compton-Burnett once remarked that in Britain, the war entered every home. In the end, the Empire suffered the loss of 942,135 1ives. And while the United States had not sustained losses to compare with France (1,386,000) and Russia (around 1,700,000), 116,516 American men and women had perished.

The armistice did not usher in a jubilant period in American life. There was little sense that the war had helped remedy great wrongs. Now that the fighting was over and almost 120,000 Americans had been sacrificed, the "war to end all wars" was seen as a tragic exercise in opportunism in which Germany had attempted to gain political influence to match its military might. There was peace but little satisfaction among Woodrow Wilson's "great and peaceful people."

Adding to the feeling of betrayal and confusion were the miserable conditions of the immediate postwar years. The escalating national debt, aggravated by the influx of millions of poverty-stricken Europeans and the isolationist policies of Pres. Warren G. Harding's administration, led to an ugly period of constriction and repression, with xenophobia at an all-time high. It was not uncommon, in many small American towns, for citizens with German names to be forced to kneel down and kiss the sidewalk. The Bolshevik Revolution had fueled a national Red Scare, and American Socialists were under particularly heavy fire, having openly opposed America's entry into the war. Socialist leaders were routinely arrested for no just cause, and labor unions became suspect by definition. The Industrial Workers of the World, one of the shining hopes of improving wretched working conditions when it was organized in 1905, saw some two thousand of its members arrested—mostly because they were tainted with the brush of liberalism. A 1925 amendment proposing strict regulation of child labor was attacked as radical and died in Congress. According to labor historian Joseph G. Rayback, overall union membership declined by around two hundred thousand between 1924 and 1930.

Even more disturbing was the growing power and influence of the Ku Klux Klan. Membership had been on the rise after the spectacular box-office success in 1915 of D.W. Griffith's *The Birth of a Nation,* in which the Klan is portrayed as a heroic force in a post–Civil War South overrun by carpetbaggers and renegade slaves. America's involvement in the Great War provided the Klan with the greatest recruiting poster it had ever had: any and all aliens, not just blacks, were now branded as enemies of the people. In 1920, the Klan organized a system for soliciting new members, and in a few short years the KKK was some 2 million strong.

It was in many respects one of the most dispiriting and regressive periods in recent American history, yet it had a galvanizing effect on the theater. Although a star system still existed on Broadway, new plays began to take on a more political and subversive nature. One of the most important events during this time was the formation, in 1919, of the Theatre Guild, which aimed to have a serious impact on New York theater life by presenting works of greater literary and intellectual substance than the standard Broadway fare offered. New York was also visited by groups such as Konstantin Stanislavsky's Moscow Art Theatre and the Comedie Française, further expanding the horizons of mainstream Broadway theatergoers.

Only a few years into the 1920s, the country was in the bloom of a new prosperity. Good times had increased the number of independent producers by a considerable degree, which turned out to be a very good thing for the theater. These producers were a new breed, more willing to take a chance on unusual subject matter than their commercially conservative predecessors had been. There was some concern in New York that the motion picture business, looking to turn successful plays into even more successful films, was exerting too much financial control over more legitimate theaters. But the infusion of movie money benefited the New York theater much more than it harmed it, since the sunnier economic climate meant that any commercial failures could be more easily cushioned. As the decade progressed, the musty melodramas of the Belasco years, with their emphasis on spectacle and local color, vanished from the stage, to be replaced by a new breed of serious plays that probed deeper into previously accepted truths and conventions, that questioned the nature and value of authority, war, romance, and prosperity.

The year 1921 brought Ferenc Molnar's *Liliom,* a delicate piece about a ne'er-do-well who dies but is given the chance to return to earth to witness the fate of his surviving wife and child. Clemence Dane's *A Bill of Divorcement* dealt with a family crippled by hereditary mental illness. The next year, 1922, introduced audiences to Luigi Pirandello's *Six Characters in Search of an Author,* a work that challenged standard ideas about the boundaries between reality and fiction. In 1923, John Galsworthy's *Windows* showed a family of idealists intruded upon by the real world. The Maxwell Anderson–Laurence Stallings play *What Price Glory?* (1924) gave World War I a bracing, unromantic treatment. One of the era's big hits was Michael Arlen's *The Green Hat,* which cast Katharine Cornell as a woman whose husband commits suicide on their wedding night rather than admit he is infected with syphilis. In *The Vortex* (1925), Noël Coward offered a complex mother-son relationship; in that same year, John Howard Lawson's *Processional,* a kind of jazz symphony of American life done in a style that didn't resemble conventional narrative, roused heated debate between conservatives and modernists. Among the more striking works of

1926 were *The Captive,* a portrait of an unhappy lesbian, *Juno and the Paycock,* a shattering comedy-drama about the Irish civil war, and Maxwell Anderson's *Saturday's Children,* a moving portrait of the struggles of young marrieds living in the slums. Many of the great comedies of the 1920s also revealed a serious undercurrent, notably Ben Hecht and Charles MacArthur's *The Front Page,* a raucous comedy given weight by its sobering view of the irresponsibility of the American press. Perhaps the strongest indication of changing times came in 1927 with Jerome Kern and Oscar Hammerstein's *Show Boat.* Who could have imagined that miscegenation would ever be the subject of a musical?

This thrilling period in the theater came at a time when Richard had reached the peak of his powers. Up until now, his own tastes and ambitions had seemed to develop at a rate too fast for Broadway to accommodate. Now, the theater's new maturity provided him with the most artistically fulfilling period of his life. The play that marked a giant step forward for him was Eugene O'Neill's *Beyond the Horizon.* Since *What Every Woman Knows,* Richard had enjoyed a reputation as an actor to be reckoned with, yet it had been some time—not since *Damaged Goods*—that he had appeared in a play that provided him with the kind of creative challenge he craved.

Like many plays, this one had a difficult gestation, but Richard proved a capable midwife, much as he had with *Damaged Goods.* Even a thumbnail history of *Beyond the Horizon* serves as compelling evidence that Richard influenced the development of the American theater far more than it influenced him.

In 1919, John D. Williams, the producer of *For the Defense,* spent five hundred dollars to option *Beyond the Horizon.* For the past four years, O'Neill had put in a brilliant apprenticeship with the enterprising Provincetown Players, which had produced many of his exciting and original one-acters. But *Beyond the Horizon* was O'Neill's first full-length drama, and he had his sights set on a Broadway production.

One day during the run of *For the Defense,* Richard was meeting with Williams and spotted a copy of *Beyond the Horizon* on the producer's desk. Williams had not yet taken any steps toward seeing the play into production. Although he believed that *Beyond the Horizon* was an important play that deserved to be seen, he was worried that its raw power might prove too much for Broadway audiences. The producer had another, more convenient excuse for not moving ahead with the play. In 1912, Actors' Equity Association had been formed, largely as a reaction to the harsh methods of the Theatrical Syndicate. By 1919, the standard contract had come up for renewal, and negotiations had broken down over the minimum number of weekly paid performances. In August 1919, the actors went out on strike, effectively crippling the season. But by December of 1919, the strike had been resolved and Broadway was in full bloom once more. In fact, with so many long-term hits in place, not a single theater was available.

Richard picked up the manuscript of *Beyond the Horizon* and began to read. After only a few pages, he recognized that this unvarnished tragedy was unlike anything attempted before. Immediately, he demanded that Williams cast him as the young hero, Robert Mayo. (At the time, it seemed far from ideal casting: Robert Mayo is twenty-three when the play opens. In 1919, Richard was forty-seven.)

A rambling drama centering on two brothers, Robert and Andrew Mayo, *Beyond the Horizon* had an unusual plot: on the eve of fulfilling his lifelong ambition to see the world, Robert realizes that he is in love with Ruth, his brother's sweetheart. He abandons his ambitions to travel and settles down to run the family farm. Andrew, to whom home and hearth mean everything, reacts by running away on the steamer that was supposed to carry Robert off to a life of adventure. Soon enough, both brothers realize they have made the wrong choices. Robert possesses no knack at all for running the farm; the property soon falls to ruins and his family is destitute. Ruth's love for him has turned to contempt, and their child dies. Andrew fares no better—his choice of a life on the road has left him empty and unfulfilled. There is no last-act resolution for either Mayo brother; at the end of the play, Robert, broken and defeated, dies of tuberculosis.

Richard was so enthusiastic about the play that he quickly

thought up a solution for the lack of a theater. Why not open the new play at the Morosco, where *For the Defense* had now moved, under special circumstances? Richard proposed a schedule of matinee performances on Mondays, Tuesdays, Wednesdays, and Fridays only. He told Williams that any good actor was certain to feel as strongly about *Beyond the Horizon* as he had, and that he could easily persuade several of the cast members of *For the Defense* to rehearse the new play during the day. Williams would scarcely have to lift a finger; Richard would arrange it all.

To play Andrew and Ruth, Richard signed up Edward Arnold and Helen MacKellar, both of whom were appearing in a popular play called *The Storm*. As he promised, several other key roles were filled by the actors in *For the Defense*: George Riddell, Mar Jeffrey, and, as Ruth's self-pitying, mean-spirited mother, character actress Louise Closser Hale. Rehearsing all day and appearing elsewhere at night proved taxing for the actors, but Richard's passionate belief in the play drove them onward. In a short time, the entire cast was sure that they were working on something of great importance.

The only one who wasn't happy was O'Neill. He complained about the cheap production values Williams had opted for, and he was uneasy about the casting of Richard. O'Neill had envisioned John Barrymore in the role, and he feared that Richard, twenty-four years older than the character he was portraying, would throw the entire play off balance. He was also upset when Williams suggested extensive cuts throughout the play. No doubt the producer's instincts were correct, since the final published version of *Beyond the Horizon,* while containing much of the potent language of O'Neill's later masterpieces, is frequently clumsy and overburdened. In *Anna Christie,* the coal barge captain Chris Christopherson evokes "that old debbil sea" enough times to vex the most patient members of the audience. Similarly, at the beginning of *Beyond the Horizon,* Robert Mayo's expressions of his wanderlust are awkward and overemphasized: "Supposing I was to tell you that it's just Beauty that's calling me, the beauty of the far off and unknown, the mystery and spell of the East which lures me in the books I've read, the need of the freedom of great wide spaces, the joy of wandering on and on—in quest of the secret which is hidden over there, beyond the horizon?" And later, when Robert confesses his desires to Ruth: "I got to know all the different kinds of sunsets by heart. And all those sunsets took place over there—(He points) beyond the horizon. So gradually I came to believe that all the wonders of the world happened on the other side of those hills. There was the home of the good fairies who performed beautiful miracles. I believed in fairies then. (With a smile) Perhaps I still do believe in them."

O'Neill was not about to cut his play down to size without a fight. Richard, however, was on Williams's side; he perceived that New York audiences would not accept this misshapen tragedy unless it were pruned substantially. In mid-January of 1920, following a performance of *For the Defense,* Richard and Mabel invited O'Neill to their home on Eighth Street. After preparing a midnight supper of scrambled eggs, Mabel retired and Richard invited O'Neill to step into his study. "Do you like absinthe?" he inquired of his guest. He knew the answer, of course, having taken the trouble to find out. O'Neill replied that he did, for all the good it did him these days. Prohibition had been in effect for a year, and there wasn't any authentic Pernod available in the United States. Richard quickly produced a bottle from one of the fifty cases that he had stashed away in his house. The two men sat down, poured themselves a drink, and began to go through the play line by line. By the time they stopped working at 7:30 that morning, Richard had gotten O'Neill to agree to all of his suggested cuts, even securing his initials in the margin next to each excision. Richard later claimed that "there was not a line changed or a line added to my version."

Rehearsals were shaky at first. O'Neill remained convinced that Williams was a shoddy producer who wanted to throw together his play as cheaply as possible. "I'm sick of *Beyond,*" he wrote to his wife, "and convinced that I must forget it. In my judgment there won't be an ounce of Fame or a cent of money in it for us. All I want to do is get done with it and throw the script into the deep blue sea. I'd never go near a rehearsal if I didn't have to—and

I'll certainly never see a performance. Those people will never—can never—be my Robert, Ruth, and Andy. . . ."

O'Neill, of course, did wind up attending the rehearsals, and at the second one he found himself locked in combat with Richard over his highly emotional interpretation of Robert. O'Neill refused to back down, and in the end Richard listened to reason and played it O'Neill's way, telling the young playwright, "Let's have a few more fights and this play'll pick up 100 percent." In time, O'Neill even admitted that the cuts he and Richard had made resulted in a "much more thrilling" play.

And it became clear to O'Neill that, despite his age, Richard was beautifully cast as Robert. Early on, he used his lyrical style to show Robert's romantic yearnings. In the scene in which Robert decides to stay at home and marry Ruth, he was the picture of youthful passion, yet he also indicated the self-doubt that lurked beneath the surface, foreshadowing the tragic turn the play takes in the second act. He used his great, sad eyes to register the air of defeat that haunts Robert, and his depiction of Robert's death rattle was chillingly realistic—for many in the company, almost unbearably painful to watch.

On February 3, 1920, the first of *Beyond the Horizon*'s special matinee performances took place at the Morosco. O'Neill cringed as the curtain rose to reveal Homer S. Saint-Gaudens's cheap, literal-minded settings. Once the performance got under way, however, it is unlikely that many in the audience paid the least attention to the scenery. They sat in stunned silence, absorbed in a searing drama that unfolded without a conventional plot, without abject moralizing, without a happy ending that would send them home reassured that such terrible things couldn't happen to decent people. O'Neill, watching the audience leave the theater in silence, was sure that his first Broadway effort had missed the mark. The reviews the following morning, however, were glowing. The *New York Times* judged that "the fare available for the New York theatergoer is immeasurably richer and more substantial" because of *Beyond the Horizon*. The *Times* also observed that "as the homebound wanderer, Richard Bennett plays with fine eloquence, imagination and finesse—a performance people will remember. . . ." The *New York Evening World* observed, "Richard Bennett realizes the hapless dreamer with understanding, rare imagination, and tender sympathy." Several critics made a point of mentioning Richard's fearless handling of Robert's death scene; many in the audience found it difficult to believe he had been acting.

Quickly, *Beyond the Horizon* became the play that all serious theatergoers in New York had to see. When *For the Defense*'s box office began to flag, Williams closed it and *Beyond the Horizon* was switched to regular evening performances, first at the Criterion, and then at the Little Theatre, where it ran through the season, closing on June 26 after 111 performances. But of much greater significance than the play's commercial success was the landmark status it soon attained. By offering a new kind of drama, O'Neill helped to shape a new kind of audience, one that eventually would welcome Sidney Howard, Sidney Kingsley, Robert E. Sherwood, George Kelly, Maxwell Anderson, and, later on, Tennessee Williams and Arthur Miller.

The success of *Beyond the Horizon* marked yet another turning point in Richard's career. For the past ten years, he had crusaded to build the theater into more than a purveyor of solid, wholesome entertainment. He had believed that if only audiences would put aside their pursuit of mindless entertainment and strive to engage their intellects, the result would be better theater for everyone. Partly, this was just Richard brandishing his famous ego. But there is little question that he earnestly believed that if the theater were permitted to stagnate, there was no chance it could survive.

Chapter Five

1920–1924

In the summer of 1920, after two years in Greenwich Village, the Bennetts moved to a large apartment at 950 Park Avenue, at Eighty-second Street. It was the grandest address they had had up to that time, and as tangible a sign as any of Richard's increasing professional stature. Barbara and Joan were enrolled in Miss Hopkins's School for Girls, just a few blocks away on East Eightieth Street. The year before, Constance had graduated from Miss Merrill's—"a cause for relief on both sides," Joan remembered—and Mabel decided that the next logical step would be for her to attend a first-class finishing school abroad. She selected Madame Balsam's in Paris. Although Constance did little to encourage her, Mabel had not given up the idea that her daughters would be given every social advantage possible. More than anything, she wanted them to make suitable marriages. In the face of Richard's bizarre behavior and their continued squabbles and separations, Mabel had begun to think that she might have done well to marry a different sort of man, someone faithful and reliable. By now, Mabel was approaching thirty-seven, and her career was losing momentum while her husband's celebrity grew with each play. Stardom was no longer a possibility for her, and few opportunities would exist for an actress approaching forty. The theater was changing, and Mabel was not entirely sure that she could change with it. (Director George Cukor, who saw her several times in her prime, felt that she was a not a first-rate talent, being too mannered and actressy.) At this point, she derived more satisfaction from being a mother than an actress, anyway. Eventually, she might leave acting behind altogether and move into some other profession.

In the meantime, there was Constance's future to attend to. Nearly sixteen, a ravishing, reed-thin blonde with a sharp wit and adventurous personality, Constance seemed uncertain about what she wanted to do professionally. She showed talent as an artist and took up sketching briefly, but quickly abandoned it. Mabel was more concerned about her personal future anyway, and in the fall of 1920 she arranged for Constance to make her society debut in Washington, D.C., after sailing home from France. Richard, touring with *Beyond the Horizon,* was apoplectic at the thought of his daughter undergoing such a mindless ritual. He railed at Mabel via letter and telephone, but to no avail. In any case, he was having his own difficulties. *Beyond the Horizon* was not doing well on the road. It had been well-received in Chicago, but in Boston and Baltimore it played to half-empty houses. The apathy of the Boston public gave Richard the opportunity to hold forth on one of his favorite topics, the ignorance of the Catholic Church. "Catholic communities are, and have always been, poor theatrical centers," he complained, and he gave a series of vitriolic interviews in which he ranted about the stupidity and closed-mindedness of those in "the hinterland." Despite his attempts to light a fire at the box office, *Beyond the Horizon* limped through the remainder of its tour.

Back in New York, Richard decided that if the theater insisted on rejecting what he had to offer, he would simply go elsewhere. He contacted Adolph Zukor, then head of Paramount Pictures, and told him that he wanted to study moviemaking techniques—this time, from behind the camera. Zukor handed him a five-year contract with six-month options, calling for his participation in a broad range of duties, including screenwriting, casting, and location scouting.

Once in Hollywood, Richard found himself surrounded by Paramount's impressive collection of first-class talent, including Cecil B. DeMille, Gloria Swanson, Fatty Arbuckle, Jack Holt, and Wallace Reid. He did serve as technical director on a few pictures, including

R.S.V.P. and *The Barnstormer* (both released in 1921), but he very quickly realized that Hollywood was not for him. He detested the decision-by-committee attitude that prevailed, and his tactless comments in script conferences quickly earned him a string of enemies. It is likely that his strong streak of anti-Semitism made him uncomfortable in the presence of the predominantly Jewish studio moguls. At the end of six months, he went to Jesse Lasky, the studio's vice president and chief executive, and requested a release from his contract, which Lasky willingly granted. Richard did, however, emerge with his respect for Adolph Zukor intact. "The shiftiest manipulator in pictures," he called Zukor, "the longest-surviving and noblest Roman of them all."

So he returned to New York. Though the heartland might have been in the grip of xenophobia, still grasping for an irretrievable past when Victorian values dominated, in New York the mood was bright, and the young, smart set was moving headlong into what seemed a bountiful future. America, after the war, was a nation eager to shed its skin, and in no time at all it did. The country that had staggered into the war carrying an enormous backlog of debt was now operating from a new position of strength as a creditor nation. Suddenly, New York, with dozens of skyscrapers shooting up, was the most glamorous boom town in history.

As consumerism flourished, advertising became a driving force in American life, and "Madison Avenue" entered the public consciousness, just as "Wall Street" did—abstractions to most Americans, but potent abstractions, packed with meaning. The most gifted chronicler of the period, F. Scott Fitzgerald, once remarked that life had little to offer except youth, and in the 1920s the place where American youth gravitated in great numbers was the city. Urban populations swelled throughout the decade, and New York was the most enticing destination of all.

It was the beginning of what Fitzgerald called "the greatest, gaudiest spree in history." And one of the strongest symbols of the new era was the 1920s woman. After decades of struggling, women won the right to vote in 1920. Inhibitions dropped as hemlines rose. For the first time, it was acceptable for women to live on their own, and to expand their employment possibilities beyond the traditional categories of nursing, teaching, and secretarial work. Women crowded dance halls, drank bootleg liquor at parties and in speakeasies, and smoked in public without a second thought.

Constance, whose motor had always run a little fast for the times, suddenly found that the times had caught up with her. In many ways, she represented the perfect flowering of the flapper era. She smoked. She attended all-night parties, football games, and Ivy League proms. She liked young men and wasn't afraid to admit it (in the new sexual candor of the times she had no reason to be). She fell short of the flapper ideal in one respect only: she hated the taste of liquor. She was confident and tough, and she possessed the arrogance of youth. Had he known her, Fitzgerald could have had her in mind when he created the cool, self-possessed Jordan Baker in *The Great Gatsby,* with her "pleasing contemptuous expression." Constance's clashes with Richard became more frequent; he objected to her habit of staying out all night with her string of handsome and socially prominent beaus. And he was incensed when, on June 6, 1921, not yet seventeen, she married one of them.

Chester Hirst Moorehead was a bright and promising young pre-law student at the University of Virginia. He had known Constance for only a couple of months, and it is likely that getting married was her idea, probably more as a means of exasperating her parents than anything else. The young couple eloped to Greenwich, Connecticut, where they were married by a justice of the peace. Richard, performing a season of summer stock in Los Angeles, was safely out of the way, but Mabel, once notified, sped to Greenwich immediately and dragged Constance home before the couple had had a chance to enjoy one night of their honeymoon. Once their plans were foiled, Constance and Moorehead apparently had little contact with one another. Mabel immediately put a safe distance between them by hustling Constance off to Europe until the affair quieted down. Moorehead returned to his law studies. Two years later, the marriage was annulled. In time, the whole matter faded into family history as just another of Constance's caprices. Although in later years the press routinely mentioned her episode as a runaway bride, she seldom spoke of it. Little more was heard of Chester Moorehead until December 12, 1945, when he committed suicide in a Chicago hotel room at age forty-two. A photograph of Constance was found in his room.

Once Richard returned to New York, he took Constance in hand. Her problem, he had decided, was that she suffered from undirected and undisciplined talent and energy. Surely if she could find some meaningful occupation she would rid herself of her reckless habits. To Richard, it only made sense that she enter the acting profession as soon as possible. After all, she had grown up in the theater and had the advantage of knowing its people and customs. She was beautiful and had an excellent figure and a distinctive, husky voice. Why not try the stage and see if she liked it? But Constance wanted no part of it. She relished her flapper lifestyle, and saw no point in giving it up for an eight-a-week grind. But Richard persisted, and finally Constance permitted him to help her land small parts in a couple of silent films produced by his friend Lewis J. Selznick.

By this time, Selznick, father of future Hollywood giants David and Myron, was near the end of a career notable for its spectacular highs and lows. His own company had already gone under, done in partly by his reckless gambling and spending. In a last-ditch effort to salvage his career, he had gone into partnership with former rival Adolph Zukor to form Select Pictures Corporation, which specialized in minor, low-budget silent films. Constance played small parts in two of these, *Reckless Youth* and *Evidence,* both released in 1922. Immediately afterward, she was cast in a third film, *What's Wrong with the Women?,* appropriately, as a fast-living flapper. The star of *What's Wrong with the Women?* was popular actor Rod LaRocque, which guaranteed the film's box-office success. Constance registered positively, although she couldn't have cared less. To her, acting was an easy means of ready cash, nothing more, and she refused to consider it as a career possibility.

Richard was disappointed. Mabel was delighted.

Richard's next play of significance was Gilbert Emery's *The Hero.* Like *Beyond the Horizon,* it is a story of two brothers with crisscrossing fates, and another example of the Broadway theater's move toward more serious themes and naturalistic dialogue. It opened at the Longacre in March 1921 for a limited run of four matinee performances, but Sam Harris thought so highly of it that he decided to present it in a regular run at the Belmont. Richard played Andrew Lane, a mild-mannered insurance salesman who spent the war years at home, working to make a decent home for his wife, son, and widowed mother. Andrew's brother, Oswald (played by Robert Ames), served overseas. As the play opens, word has come that Oswald, thought to be missing in action, will be coming home to rejoin the family. Oswald, it turns out, has always been something of a bad seed with a criminal streak, but military service seems to have changed him. He returns home a much-decorated hero. Everyone is impressed with his war record, especially his doting mother and Hester, Andrew's wife, who finds herself deeply attracted to him. But Oswald has not changed at all. At heart he is still a sociopath, which he demonstrates by seducing the young Belgian refugee living in the Lane household and later making off with a stash of money that Andrew had been collecting for the local church. Just as Oswald is about to skip town with the cash, the nearby schoolhouse catches fire. Oswald rushes in and manages to save little Andy, Andrew and Hester's son, but dies himself. Hester, who knows of Oswald's theft, says nothing about it to Andrew, who concludes, "I'm just old Andy, I am. But Os—Os was a hero."

The role of Andrew Lane was a decided change of pace for Richard. Much less showy than most of the parts he played, it provided him with an opportunity to create a complex and delicately shaded character study. Richard admired the way that the playwright examined the nature of heroism from more than one angle: Oswald, the conventional type of hero, was seen in contrast to Andrew, the drab, ordinary brother who stayed behind and struggled to hold his family together. Richard believed that not every soldier who returned a conquering hero deserved the acclaim heaped on him; he suspected that many of them had gone overseas seeking honor and glory, and not necessarily out of a sense of patriotic duty. He believed that the part of Andrew spoke for the millions who had remained behind, reading the newspaper accounts of the war's heroes and being forced to explain again and again why they weren't out fighting the Kaiser.

The Hero opened at the Belmont Theatre on September 5, 1921. In a season that included O'Neill's *Anna Christie* and W. Somerset Maugham's *The Circle,* it earned some of the best notices of the year. "It is a drama marked by astonishing courage and sincerity," said the *New York Evening Telegram.* "No serious admirer of the stage can afford to miss it." Alexander Woollcott in the *New York Times* called it "an uncommonly nourishing play, interesting all the way through and admirably staged" and praised Richard's work as "artful and intelligent." But the play's highly textured and ironic portrait of a war hero was still a risky proposition in 1921. Many veterans of the Great War complained loudly about *The Hero,* causing it to close after eighty performances. In his curtain speeches, Richard thanked the management for permitting him to appear in another solid American drama. Had it been written by Ibsen, he insisted, it would have been recognized as a classic.

In his personal life, Richard may have considered himself a defender of tradition, but as an actor he consistently sought the new and unusual—even the experimental. He had little interest in performing Shakespeare or works of the classical theater, simply because he didn't think that his generation of American actors performed them particularly well. "When I see a man now trying to do Shakespeare," he wrote, "I immediately underrate the great bard. Shakespeare had design and form . . . just as great paintings have. . . . Why in the name of God actors all get the itch for the classics, at some time in their careers . . . an itch which, if not cured, carries them into the realm of atrophied hams . . . I cannot understand."

As the 1920s progressed, Richard continued searching for fresh acting challenges. In 1922, he was given the kind of opportunity he craved when Theresa Helburn, executive director of the Theatre Guild, asked him to play the title role in the Guild's forthcoming production of Leonid Andreyev's *He Who Gets Slapped*.

The Russian-born Andreyev had long been one of the most controversial figures in the theater, a playwright who eschewed the plot-driven "well-made" plays of Alexandre Dumas and Victorien Sardou in favor of a more cerebral approach. At this time, there was a kind of mass production of "well-made" plays both in London's West End and on Broadway. Many of these were star vehicles, well-oiled machines in which situations were neatly set up and just as neatly resolved. A bit too neatly—for there was a fine line between good craftsmanship and formula. A fictional example of the opening of a typical "well-made" play: the curtain rises to reveal the drawing room of an elegant English country house. A pair of maids chat about the preparations for that evening's party. A telephone rings, and one of the maids answers it. A handsome young woman, in a dressing gown of saffron-colored silk, appears at the top of the stairs, to a huge ovation, and calls down, "Who is it, Nora?" (Maids in "well-made" plays always seemed to be called Nora.) It is the lady's ne'er-do-well younger brother, absent from the family home for some years, ever since he lost his position with the bank for reasons that have never been entirely clear. He has been living abroad, and now he is telephoning from Victoria Station, announcing that he will be arriving that very evening to spend a fortnight. The lady of the house rings off and retreats to her room, visibly distressed. The maids speculate on what her brother's arrival may mean.

It was exactly the sort of thing that Andreyev rebelled against. "Life has withdrawn itself into the inner recesses of the soul," he once wrote, "whereas the theater has paused at the threshold of those new and profound psychological experiences and intellectual striving—the struggle of man's thoughts with man—and has never thrown open the door that leads to them." Such a point of view was bound to appeal to Richard, who himself had grown weary of the predictable sitdrams being forced on Broadway audiences.

He Who Gets Slapped is a complex and poetic statement of

Andreyev's belief in theater as an intellectual exercise. The play depicts a motley group of performers in a French circus. Into their midst comes a mysterious gentleman who appears to be an aristocrat. He has been permanently disillusioned by the machinations of his faithless wife and the man he once believed to be his best friend. The stranger asks to be allowed to join the circus troupe as He—a white-faced, idiotically grinning clown whose sole function is to be slapped, over and over, by every other member of the company. He quickly becomes one of the circus's most popular attractions. At the same time, He becomes enamored of Consuelo, the young bareback rider. Consuelo's father, Count Mancini, is trying to restore the family fortune by marrying her off to a raffish baron, but He, who believes Consuelo to be the personification of an innocence he had forgotten existed, tries to dissuade her from going through with it. In the end, Consuelo refuses to listen. Rather than see her ruined, He shares a poisoned drink with her.

Despite Andreyev's objections to conventional dramatic models, *He* was undeniably Sophoclean in its portrayal of individuals in the grip of fate; each of the characters, in a different way, is doomed to a life of misery. It was a biting, sardonic tragedy, not the sort of thing that the New York public was accustomed to seeing. Although she believed in the play's artistic merit, Theresa Helburn was concerned that its sharpness and complexity might fail to attract an audience.

"What do you care?" Richard snapped. "You are running a theater for art's sake. *I'm* the one who will be taking the chance—I need the money!"

He Who Gets Slapped went into a three-week rehearsal period over the Christmas holidays in late 1921. Others in the cast included Margalo Gillmore, near the beginning of what would become a distinguished career, as Consuelo, and Helen Westley as Zinida, the fiery and jealous lion tamer. The play's English translation was by Gregory Zilboorg, who later gained fame as the psychoanalyst of many notable New Yorkers, George Gershwin among them. Richard judged *He* "a great play," but once rehearsals began, he didn't seem entirely sure what it was about. Zilboorg took

Richard aside and attempted to elucidate the play's meaning, but succeeded only in confusing him. The play was essentially a dark meditation on the cruelty and unfairness of life, but Richard, with the complicity of stage director Robert Milton, felt compelled to give it more of an emotional core: he conceived of He as a character with his heart on his sleeve, one with whom the audience could form immediate identification. Slowly, the play became less a bitter allegory and more a heartrending study of one lost, pathetic soul. Both Helburn and the Guild's codirector, Lawrence Langner, were concerned that Andreyev's meaning was being distorted by their headstrong star. But they had to admit that his results were impressive. In Richard's hands, He became a Christlike figure of universal suffering. "That was the way he saw it," remembered Theresa Helburn, adding, "Of course, given half a chance, any actor will leap at the chance to play Christ. And, as a rule, when he does so you are lost." Richard silenced Helburn and Langner's objections by saying with casual confidence, "Don't worry, children, it will run."

He Who Gets Slapped opened at the Garrick Theater on January 9, 1922. Alexander Woollcott in the *New York Times* judged that "the Theatre Guild emerged, flushed and triumphant, last night from the most daring of all its encounters with plays." He went on to praise the work for being "alive in its every moment and abrim with color and beauty." Woollcott also found Richard's characterization as He done "with his customary artfulness and understanding . . . an admirable and a strengthening performance." There was also much praise for the settings of Lee Simonson, which managed to suggest great spaciousness. *He* chalked up 308 performances in New York, and Richard's first outing for the Guild provided them with "the biggest hit since Eva LeGallienne put over *Liliom* for them." The demand for tickets was so great that the company soon had to abandon the Garrick and move to the more capacious Fulton Theatre. Richard had been right all along, and his instincts made the play "much more successful than it had any right to be." Richard couldn't help gloating that this was the second time he had been instrumental in reviving the fortunes of the Fulton Theatre, the other being *Damaged Goods*.

The following season, while *He* was rapidly making a fortune for the Theatre Guild, Konstantin Stanislavsky and the Moscow Art Players made their first visit to New York with a repertory that included *The Cherry Orchard, Three Sisters,* and an adaptation of *The Brothers Karamazov.* The New York theater world was intrigued by Stanislavsky's revolutionary acting concepts, including "sense memory"—the creation of an onstage emotion by calling up a specific episode from one's own past. There were many, however, who believed that such techniques held as many traps as rewards for the actor—a tendency toward self-indulgence being the most dangerous one.

As an actor, Richard relied most on his own powers of imagination. He was such a creature of instinct that it is difficult to think that he would have approved of any sort of analytical "method," no matter how spectacular the results. In any case, he seemed unimpressed when Stanislavsky paid tribute to him backstage after a performance of *He.* Undone by Richard's interpretation, Stanislavsky proclaimed him the greatest living actor in the United States, and threw himself into his arms, kissing him. For Richard, who suspected Stanislavsky of being "a Russian fairy," the incident was a source of more embarrassment than pride.

Neither Barbara nor Joan seemed inclined to give Constance a run for her money as the resident hellion of 950 Park Avenue. Joan was a quiet girl who clung to her mother and was diligent about her studies. Her main obstacle in life was her poor eyesight, which required her to wear thick, unflattering glasses that made her self-conscious. During rehearsals of *He Who Gets Slapped,* Margalo Gillmore had plenty of opportunity to observe Joan, who came to the theater after school to wait until her father could take her home. Gillmore remembered her as slightly overweight, with a poor complexion, shy, and awkward. "That poor girl," Gillmore used to think, watching Joan pore over her schoolbooks. "And Constance is one of the most glamorous girls in New York."

Barbara had evolved into a dark-haired, long-legged teenager who on the surface seemed nearly as poised as Constance—and just as uninterested in an acting career. But Barbara's extreme emotionalism and odd, introverted tendencies were still ever present. Frequently she became sullen and withdrawn, and neither Richard's bullying nor Mabel's pleading could bring her out of it. Her capacity for being wounded was tremendous, and in 1922 an episode took place that shook the entire family.

One of the people Barbara most adored was Antoinette Glover, the wife of the distinguished Spanish stage and film actor Pedro de Cordoba. The de Cordobas had appeared with Mabel and Constance in the Greenwich Village production of *Everyman* in 1918, and were often guests in the Bennett home. In 1921, Antoinette Glover died quite unexpectedly. Barbara was devastated. She shut herself up in her room, refused to eat, and grew thinner and weaker by the day.

Antoinette Glover and her husband were devout Catholics, and perhaps in an attempt to create some sort of spiritual connection with them, Barbara began to study Catholicism with obsessive fervor. Richard was enraged—the Catholic Church's disapproving response to many of his greatest triumphs, particularly *Damaged Goods, Maternity,* and *Beyond the Horizon,* had only exacerbated his intolerance for any form of organized religion, and when Barbara announced that she planned to enter a convent, he became apoplectic. Under no circumstances was any child living under his roof to consider any form of religious vocation. He carried on so violently that he hardly noticed Barbara withdrawing into herself once more.

Once Richard had quieted down, Mabel quietly took stock of the situation. She knew that Barbara's behavior was not the sort of thing normally encountered in a healthy fifteen-year-old girl. After weeks of failing to pull her out of her depression, Mabel sent Barbara out to Los Angeles to spend some time with her good friend Molly Anderson, wife of Gilbert M. "Bronco Billy" Anderson, the screen's first cowboy star.

Weeks went by and Barbara showed no progress. Finally, in an attempt to induce her to eat, "Aunt" Molly hit on the idea of giving her a glass of sherry before lunch and dinner. Much to Molly's relief, the sherry had a noticeably relaxing effect, and Barbara was able to manage a bit of food. Slowly her strength returned, and in time her morale improved to the point that Mrs. Anderson felt confident sending her, shaky but stable, back to New York. Once she was home, there was no further discussion about her entering a convent.

As always, Richard believed that the answer to all his daughters' problems was stricter discipline. Before long, Barbara was enrolled in the summer session of the Denishawn Dancing School at Mariarden, a camp near Petersborough, New Hampshire. To Richard, the only practical means of taming Constance's wild streak and pulling Barbara out of herself was to give them both a push in the direction of the theater, where a little hard work would no doubt force them to come to their senses.

Years later, Joan speculated that Barbara's spiritual leanings had been "intense and sincere," and that Richard's interference had been a great mistake. It is naive, however, to suppose that she would have led a serene and happy life, free of inner turmoil, had she entered a convent. Although there is no existing medical diagnosis for the instability that would haunt Barbara throughout her life, her episodes of despair may have signaled some form of clinical depression. But in the 1920s, precious little was known about mental illness. Episodes like Barbara's were often dismissed as passing melancholia, and given no more serious treatment than the common cold.

Initially, however, fifteen-year-old Barbara seemed happy enough at Denishawn. The school had been founded by Ted Shawn and his wife, Ruth St. Denis, in New York City and Los Angeles. Its Manhattan studios, at 344 West Seventy-second Street, soon became a leading center of modern dance in the country, offering courses in basic technique, creative dance, dramatic gesture, and music visualization. Many of its alumni, most notably Martha Graham and Doris Humphrey, would become vital forces in the dance world. Actors seeking greater command of physical movement also flocked to Denishawn. Lillian Gish, who studied there during her apprenticeship under D.W. Griffith, remembered that her regimen at Denishawn left her with a body "as trained and responsive as that of a dancer or an athlete."

The summer sessions at Mariarden lasted from the beginning of July to late August, and emphasized work in drama and classic dancing. From time to time, Mabel and Pedro de Cordoba had offered their talents at Mariarden classes, a connection that Barbara found reassuring. Also, Mariarden's location—250 acres of cool, wooded countryside in New Hampshire—gave her a welcome change from the oppressive summers in New York. Although she liked it all well enough to return in the summer of 1923, she thought little of most of the other pupils, many of whom came from solid midwestern families and had nothing in common with her. Not long into the summer session, however, she did find a fellow student she liked. Her name was Louise Brooks. She also hailed from the Midwest—Kansas, precisely—but she wasn't like the others: she was pretty, she could dance, and she showed an independent streak. Barbara found some of her eccentricities appealing, particularly her habit of eating enormous wedges of apple pie for breakfast. Barbara chose to overlook Louise's gaucherie and her twangy Kansas accent, and the two girls joined forces to disrupt the staid atmosphere that prevailed at Mariarden.

This involved, mostly, boys, whom they invited to their cabin in defiance of the 9 P.M. curfew. Barbara and Louise demanded cigarettes and applejack, but gave nothing in return other than a string of "blue" songs and jokes that Barbara had picked up along the line. Louise's favorite was:

> In Fairy Town,
> In Fairy Town,
> They don't go up,
> They all go down.
> Even the chief of police is queer
> Oops, my dear! Listen here!
> The elevators there, they say,
> They don't go up, just the other way.

Holy Bejesus, there's lots of Paresis
In Fairy Town!

Once Mariarden let out at the end of the summer, the two girls continued their friendship in New York. There, Louise was treated to an up-close view of the Bennett household. There was plenty for her to observe, for the strain on Richard and Mabel's marriage was becoming close to unbearable—for Mabel, at least. Earlier in the summer they had gone to Rome, where Richard supported Barbara LaMarr in *The Eternal City*, an adaptation of Hall Caine's popular novel, produced by Samuel Goldwyn. The Bennetts had taken Joan along, and Richard wangled her a bit part as a pageboy. Once they returned to New York, tensions between Richard and Mabel were evident even to an occasional visitor such as Louise Brooks. Richard, Brooks recalled, took his first glass of whiskey in the morning before getting dressed, and she felt that Mabel looked "worn and unhappy . . . uncared for and unloved." Eventually, both Richard and Mabel had to face the fact that all attempts at maintaining peace had failed. On September 30, 1923, they separated.

Since the family was no longer to be together, keeping the big Park Avenue apartment was impractical. Richard and Barbara moved to 168 West Fifty-eighth Street, while Mabel and Constance found an apartment at 126 East Fifty-fourth Street. The press gave plenty of coverage to the breakup, which soon became known as "the six-block separation." Both parties took pains to put a civilized face on the arrangement; Richard pronounced it "a wonderful success" and intimated that it in no way foreshadowed the end of their marriage. Mabel was more candid: "Mr. Bennett, you see, is a genius. At any rate, persons regard him as a genius, and I suppose that geniuses should be—what should I say—perhaps 'segregated' would do as well as another word."

The breakup of the family was hardest on Joan, who by now was a boarding student at St. Margaret's Academy in Waterbury, Connecticut. She came down to New York on weekends and divided her time between the two households. Although Mabel had considered leaving Richard at several earlier junctures, she had delayed doing so largely out of concern for the girls' well-being. By the time the rift finally occurred, Constance was nearly nineteen, and Barbara seventeen, but Joan was only thirteen, and not yet mature enough to absorb fully such a drastic change in her life. As she grew older, Joan would develop an almost insatiable craving for stability, a compulsive need to create order around her.

Barbara had a convenient distraction from all the turmoil—a part in Richard's new play, Viola Tree and Gerald Du Maurier's *The Dancers*. The play was intended to be a potent study of the reckless lifestyle spawned by the Jazz Age. It had been a major success in London, but when it opened at the Broadhurst Theater on October 17, 1923, John Corbin of the *New York Times* wasn't sure why. Corbin felt that *The Dancers* failed to develop into "a coherent and finely articulated play." Still, Richard's marquee value meant there was enough public interest to sustain a healthy run.

Barbara's small role as Nellie, a dance hall girl, went mostly unnoticed by the press, but Richard was delighted that he had finally persuaded one of his daughters to appear on Broadway. For Barbara, it was a hand-me-down debut. Richard had initially offered the role to Constance, who declined it because she didn't want to be hemmed in, in case the play had a long run. No matter that Barbara was second choice; Richard immediately predicted great things for her, ignoring that she had accepted the offer only because she was at loose ends and needed a job. She was no more ambitious than Constance, and Richard soon found out that she could be just as much trouble. One night, Barbara stayed out very late with Pat Somerset, an actor in *The Dancers*. Mabel joined the hysterical Richard at the Fifty-eighth Street apartment, where together they waited for the tardy couple to return. When they did, Richard laced into Somerset with a walking cane. When a policeman showed up to investigate the disturbance, Richard took a swing at him, too, before being taken away to the Midtown Precinct. For the time being, Barbara moved in with Mabel and Constance on Fifty-fourth Street.

It was a happy move, for now that Barbara was beyond Richard's reach, she and Louise Brooks could continue their escapades unchecked. They both attracted several wealthy admirers who took great pleasure in showering them with expensive clothes and jewels. Louise later claimed that during this period Barbara had attracted the attentions of William Rhinelander Stewart, the New York socialite once described as "the beau ideal of the twentieth century." Handsome and always elegantly attired, Stewart was endowed with impeccable manners and a keen wit, qualities that helped make him one of Manhattan society's most sought-after escorts. But he was more than just a bon vivant. Stewart was also a clever businessman who held an executive position with one of the city's leading insurance brokerage firms, John C. Paige & Co. Many of New York's most prominent society beauties maneuvered to be seen in his company, and for Barbara to snare him, however unofficially, was a great coup. Not long into their friendship, Stewart gave Barbara a square-cut emerald ring, which she lost one evening while swimming with Louise in Long Island Sound. According to Louise, Barbara replaced it with a fake, evidently undetected by Stewart. "Truly," said Louise, "ours was a heartless racket."

Constance, in the meantime, had found a wealthy beau of her own. On her way to a Yale football game, she met Philip Morgan Plant, scion of one of America's wealthiest and most socially prominent families. The foundation of the Plant fortune was laid by Philip's grandfather, Henry Bradley Plant, who had risen to power as a railroad magnate in pre–Civil War days. As an officer of the Adams Express Company, he had gained control of all of the firm's southern routes during the war, and his appearance of absolute neutrality enabled him to become one of the few northerners to remain in the South during the outbreak of fighting. As a result, he flourished, but also incurred the suspicions of many colleagues, who judged him a blatant opportunist. Eventually, Plant purchased so many railroad lines that it became necessary to found the Plant Investment Company, which united his holdings while seeking to expand and develop railroads elsewhere. Later, he acquired successful steamship lines as well as a long string of elegant and expensive hotels.

Henry Plant's son, Morton Freeman Plant, was born in 1852 on the family estate in Groton, Connecticut. He assumed the presidency of the Plant Investment Company when his father died in 1899, but was better known as a champion yachtsman and philanthropist than as a hard-driving businessman. His love of the sea and penchant for yachting earned him the title of "Commodore." Over the years, Morton established himself as a beloved citizen of Groton. He paved many town roads at his own expense, gave Groton $25,000 to construct its town hall, which still stands today, and opened the spectacular Griswold Hotel, which became a favorite spot of the international set. In 1904, he built Brantford House, a thirty-one-room mansion with seventeen Italian marble fireplaces and thirty-foot ceilings. Among the beneficiaries of his generosity was the Connecticut College for Women and New London's Lawrence Hospital, to which he provided $100,000 in his will.

Morton F. Plant had one son, Henry Plant II, by his first wife, Nellie Capron, a Baltimore socialite who died in 1913. When the Commodore was in his early sixties, he made the acquaintance of Mae Caldwell Manwaring, an attractive woman thirty years his junior, with neither wealth nor social position. What she did have was ambition. When Morton Plant met her, she was married to Seldon B. Manwaring, who managed a small restaurant in Waterford, Connecticut, near New London. Mae, or Maisie, as she liked to be called, worked there as a waitress. In 1901, she and Manwaring had had a son, Philip.

Maisie's charm and beauty captivated Morton Plant, and in 1914 Maisie suddenly divorced Manwaring and married the Commodore. The Plant family was scandalized. Their inner circle had been invaded by a common gold digger and an ex hash-slinger at that. Some members of the family would refer to her as "that barmaid." The Plant's Manhattan residence was a vast mansion at 653 Fifth Avenue, just down the street from the Vanderbilt's magnificent home, and designed to resemble a Renaissance palazzo. In 1917, Plant reportedly traded it to Cartier, the jewelry firm, in exchange for two strands of Oriental pearls valued at around $1,500,000. Cartier's main New York store is still in that mansion at Fifty-second Street and Fifth Avenue.

Few people expected Plant's marriage to Maisie Manwaring

to endure, and it didn't. In 1918, Plant died of pneumonia, leaving an estate of over $32 million—a staggering amount of money for the time. Maisie had not been idle during her four-year marriage. After divorcing Manwaring, she retained custody of her son and persuaded Plant to adopt the boy. Philip Morgan Plant inherited a substantial amount outright from his stepfather; in addition, a trust fund was set up, with amounts to be paid to Philip every five years until his fortieth birthday. The Widow Plant might have taken *her* inheritance and faded from public view—but Maisie's work was not yet done. In 1919, she made another advantageous marriage, to the prominent attorney William Hayward, father of Leland Hayward, who would become one of the entertainment industry's most successful agents and producers. "That barmaid" had done very well for herself.

From the moment that Philip Plant and Constance began seeing one another, Maisie made no secret of her disapproval. It was a time when the cream of society still harbored great suspicion of actors' values and morals. Offstage consequences were sometimes abrupt: Jane Wyatt, who went on to star in Hollywood films such as *Lost Horizon* (1937) and *None but the Lonely Heart* (1944), was dropped from the Social Register when she announced her intention of becoming an actress.

Maisie had additional reason to be suspicious of Constance: she of all people knew a social climber when she saw one. Maisie and Philip had an exceptionally close mother-son relationship, for he was mindful of how well she had looked after his interests. He was devoted to her, and when they were in New York he often took her out dancing all night. She had enormous potential to drive a wedge between Philip and any young woman, but typically, Constance made no attempt to ingratiate herself with Maisie. Then again, Constance and Philip quarreled so frequently that it was far from a sure thing that their relationship would ever lead to marriage. They were engaged several times, but one of them always broke it off for one reason or other.

Perhaps because he had assimilated some of his adoptive family's snobbery toward actors, Philip was opposed from the beginning to Constance's entering into her parents' profession. That seemed to be all the encouragement she needed. In the fall of 1923, Richard escorted Constance to the Actors' Equity Ball. Also in attendance was Hollywood producer Samuel Goldwyn. After his company, Goldwyn Pictures, in partnership with Edgar Selwyn, had failed and been folded into Metro-Goldwyn-Mayer, Goldwyn had vowed never again to go into business with a partner. He had recently set himself up as an independent producer, and now his company, Samuel Goldwyn Productions, was seeking top-quality properties that would make first-class motion pictures. One of Goldwyn's recent acquisitions was Joseph Hergesheimer's best-selling novel *Cytherea,* and when he was introduced to Constance at the Equity Ball, Goldwyn thought that she might be right for a key supporting role. He arranged a screen test for her, and, delighted with the results, offered a contract. Richard was pleased; it wasn't the stage, but it seemed a good enough opportunity. Perhaps if it went well, Constance would finally settle down to the business of becoming an actress. Mabel had seen enough of Hollywood to feel strongly that it was no place for a girl to be on her own. She protested loud and long, but Constance paid no attention and headed west.

She breezed through her first major assignment. When *Cytherea* was released in May 1925, most of the press notices focused on the stars: Lewis Stone, as a philandering husband, and Irene Rich, as his betrayed wife. But Constance's appearance did not pass unnoticed, and she enjoyed the experience enough to be talked into appearing in a cheap ten-reel serial called *Into the Net,* for Pathé, but she claimed not to be interested in signing a long-term contract with any studio. The main reason she had appeared in *Cytherea* was to thwart Philip Plant. There was another reason as well: Barbara had already appeared onstage with Richard, and Constance now had reason to consider her younger sister a potential rival. No doubt she relished an opportunity to overshadow her.

In the fall of 1924, Richard was reunited with the Theatre Guild for a new play, Sidney Howard's *They Knew What They Wanted.* It was a comedy-drama set in the wine country north of San Francisco, among the Italian-Swiss colony of grape farmers, whom Howard dubbed "the honest, God-fearing, thrifty people who find themselves by the odd turn of law and circumstance, the most amusing and picturesque of prohibition criminals." Richard was cast as Tony, an aging Napa Valley vintner who proposes by mail to Amy (Pauline Lord), a pretty young waitress he has spotted in an Italian café. But Tony worries that he is too old and homely for Amy to accept him, and sends her a picture of his handsome, strapping hired man Joe instead. On his way to meet Amy's train, Tony has an accident and breaks both his legs. Amy arrives at the vineyard and is immediately attracted to Joe; three months later, she discovers that she is pregnant by him. When she confesses to Tony, the unexpected happens: he asks her to stay, and agrees to raise the child as his own.

In 1924, this denouement was powerful stuff. A decade earlier, the play might well have ended with Tony casting Amy out into the snow, à la Anna Moore in *Way Down East.* For Howard to offer such a casual and tolerant view of adultery was in its way quite revolutionary, yet another sign that the American theater was catching up to the tempo of modern life, and that audiences were accepting plays that didn't cloak their themes in conventional, middle-class respectability. In a newspaper interview, Pauline Lord, the gifted actress who played Amy, observed that Howard "never points a moral; he never stands pointing the way to heaven like a signpost. But the meaning is there, always, if you want to look for it."

Like O'Neill, Howard sought to depict the fateful missteps of ordinary, working-class people, to show the pain waiting to burst through the surface of everyday life. His work expressed disdain for the slick conventions of the Broadway stage, but Howard's writing was leaner, less doggedly "poetic." When it opened at the Garrick Theater on November 24, 1924, Heywood Broun of the *New York World* wrote that *They Knew What They Wanted* "belongs among the best of all American comedies." In the *New York Sun,* Alexander Woollcott called it "a cheerful, intuitive, understanding contribution to the Comédie Humaine. . . ."

Tony's Italian accent and the chance to use crutches as props provided an acting binge for Richard. Too much so, perhaps. This time around, the critics were divided in their response to his performance. Although Heywood Broun found him "magnificent," *Theatre* magazine felt that he was "by turns comic and pathetic, but he pulls the heart up by the roots every time he speaks. He over-stresses the character." Production stills from the play indicate that the *Theatre* critic was on to something. Under excessively heavy makeup, Richard always seems to be smiling too broadly, as if determined to make Tony not just a character but a symbol—a kindly simpleton for the ages. He had sought to make a powerful statement with his Christlike portrayal in *He Who Gets Slapped,* but Andreyev's elliptical text supported such a transcendent approach. *They Knew What They Wanted,* on the other hand, was a realistic, earthy comedy, and on many nights the play seemed in danger of collapsing under the weight of Richard's performance.

They Knew What They Wanted settled in for a long run (192 performances in all), but Richard had difficulty enjoying the play's success. He had been surprisingly sanguine about his separation from Mabel a little over a year earlier, because he believed that eventually they would reconcile. But it was becoming clear that reuniting was the furthest thing from Mabel's mind. Richard missed her desperately and longed to be under the same roof with all his daughters once again, and his state of isolation made him more and more distraught. His drinking binges intensified. For the first time, his personal unhappiness spilled over into his professional life. Any minor incident was enough to send him into a tirade, and behavior that had once seemed colorful now looked unprofessional, if not downright demented. During one performance, he became incensed because the theater's steam pipes were banging. Five minutes into the play, he ordered the curtain rung down, announcing that he would resume only when the engineers fixed the problem. On at least two other occasions he disrupted the second act, when Tony, recuperating from his leg injuries, is confined to a cot. Richard had a habit of falling asleep, which left Pauline Lord stranded onstage, waiting for him to give her a cue. At one performance, she grew so angry that she stormed off the stage.

But the worst debacle of the play's run occurred in June 1925. The play was still enjoying packed houses, but Richard was more miserable than ever. That spring, Mabel had finally taken the step of entering divorce proceedings against him. Richard begged her to reconsider, but she refused to listen, ignoring his florid love letters. In April, Mabel issued her final decree, charging Richard with misconduct.

The weeks that followed were agonizing for Richard. He had come to the end of the most satisfying chapter in his life, with no clear view of his future. He sank deeper and deeper into anger and regret, and by June his mental state had deteriorated to the point that he felt unable to continue with *They Knew What They Wanted.* After a Saturday night performance, he packed a bag and headed by train for Montreal. Richard had wired the Guild that he was in need of a three-day rest, and he stayed away through the Monday and Tuesday night performances. His understudy, Francis Verdi, took over the role, and on Wednesday, when Richard returned to his apartment at 41 East Fiftieth Street, he found a letter from the Guild charging him with breach of contract. That same day, he showed up at the theater for the matinee performance, naively assuming that he would be allowed to resume playing Tony. But Francis Verdi had no intention of relinquishing such a plum role just because the prodigal star had decided to come home. A tremendous row broke out as the two actors struggled to get into Tony's costume.

"Who owns Tony's pants, Dick?" Verdi demanded, "You or the Theatre Guild?" Richard was momentarily flummoxed, and Verdi seized the moment to wrest the costume away from him and race onto the stage. Verdi's moment of glory was brief; by the end of the week, the Guild had hired Leo Carillo as Richard's permanent replacement. Richard protested, but Lawrence Langner and Theresa Helburn had had enough. The New York press was all over the story: Richard's caprices were one thing, but this time he had endangered the entire run of the play, and most observers felt that such a lapse of professionalism demanded severe punishment. Although he lodged a complaint with Actors' Equity, he never again played Tony in New York. The blow to his pride was enormous. Deep down, he knew he was wrong, just as he knew that being fired in such a public way might do harm to his career. As it happened, he was right.

Chapter Six

1925–1927

By mid-1925, Richard had reached the peak of his career, while his two oldest daughters were just beginning to make their presence known. Despite, or because of, Philip Plant's continued objections, Constance seemed at last to have settled on an acting career. Since *Cytherea,* she had gone from one film to another, appearing in a total of seven productions in 1925. One that has survived is *The Goose Woman,* a fascinating study of a broken-down ex-opera star (played by Louise Dresser). Once the discovery of the age, the singer had sacrificed her career for motherhood twenty years earlier. Now, she is barely getting by on a run-down farm where she raises geese. There is a startling scene in which the ex-diva's son Gerald accidentally breaks the last surviving recording of her voice. The titles read: "And to think I had to pay for you with my God-given talent! . . . You changed me from a nightingale into a frog. It's your fault, and I hate you!" Dresser dominates the film, but Constance has plenty of screen time as the ambitious young stage actress Gerald loves. In all her scenes, she comes across as a natural presence with keen instincts for the camera. She is especially adept in the scene in which she rushes off stage, sees Gerald waiting in the wings, and casually tosses her prop "baby" at the property man while rushing into Gerald's arms.

The same qualities are evident in *Married?*, a dull drama in which she plays a young woman pressured into an arranged marriage in order to hang on to her family's fortune. Although the plot made few demands of her, it is difficult to believe she had not been appearing before a camera for years. She is quick and assured; already she knows how to use her eyes effectively, and the square jaw and expressive mouth she inherited from Richard further contribute to her strong screen presence.

By far the most important film Constance released in 1925 was MGM's *Sally, Irene and Mary,* the story of three young women in search of romance and fortune that Hollywood would remake again and again, with different twists and variations. Here, the three women are chorus girls, played by Constance, Sally O'Neill, and MGM's new discovery, Joan Crawford. Constance was Sally, the toughest and most worldly of the trio, and her confident characterization impressed MGM's studio chief Louis B. Mayer enough for him to offer her a seven-year contract. Constance vexed him by agreeing to sign only after securing his promise that she could make films for other studios as well.

Only a few years later, MGM had become so powerful that it is doubtful that even an actress as strong-willed as Constance could have wangled a nonexclusive contract. But in 1925, MGM was in its infancy. It had been formed the previous year by the merger of three companies: Metro Pictures, Goldwyn Pictures, and the Louis B. Mayer Company, with Mayer as its vice president and general manager, and Irving G. Thalberg as vice president and supervisor of production. It might have seemed a good omen for Constance that MGM's inaugural production was the screen version of *He Who Gets Slapped,* with Lon Chaney in Richard's old role. By 1925, thanks in large part to Thalberg's creative genius, MGM had announced itself as a major force in Hollywood, with four films on the *New York Times*'s ten-best list: *The Big Parade, The Unholy Three, The Merry Widow,* and *Ben-Hur*—all great commercial hits as well.

The movie business had grown big—bigger than almost anyone would have dared to imagine ten years earlier. The nickelodeon was already a forgotten relic; by 1925, there were well over fifteen thousand movie theaters in the United States, and only eleven of these seated fewer than one hundred. Rudolph Valentino, Gloria Swanson, Mary Pickford, Norma Talmadge, Colleen Moore, and

Tom Mix were among the biggest box-office stars. Mayer, always looking for new faces, had screened several of Constance's films and felt she had the potential for major stardom. (From the beginning, Mayer, much more than Thalberg, was her champion.) After *Sally, Irene and Mary* became a hit, many columnists anticipated big things ahead for Constance.

And suddenly the first stage of Constance's film career came to an end. By mid-1925, Constance and Philip Plant appeared to have parted once and for all. In the spring, it had been announced that Plant would marry socialite Judith Smith of New York City. But a few weeks later, he and Constance tried for yet another reunion, and before long Smith faded from the picture. Evidently Plant's arguments had finally been persuasive: Constance soon informed Mayer that she would marry Plant in the fall and that her fiancé insisted that she not continue in pictures. She would have to break her MGM contract, but Mayer was surprisingly agreeable and wished her well, adding that if she ever changed her mind and wanted to rejoin the MGM roster, he would insist on exclusivity.

On November 3, 1925, Constance Bennett and Philip Plant were married at the Pickwick Arms Hotel in Greenwich, Connecticut, by the same justice of the peace who had united her four years before to Chester Moorehead. The couple then spent a lengthy honeymoon in Palm Beach. Mabel and Richard's reactions ran true to form. Mabel was delighted that her oldest daughter was married off (and married well) and seemed disinclined ever to go near the stage again.

Richard was livid. As a self-made man, he was suspicious of anyone who had had wealth and social position handed to him. He found Philip callow and superficial, and would have been much happier if Constance had married a fellow actor, as her mother had had the good sense to do. On the groom's side, Mae Hayward was horrified that her son had gone through with the marriage. Quietly, she resolved to keep a close watch on her new daughter-in-law.

Philip maintained homes in Paris, Biarritz, and the Swiss Alps, and when the couple returned from their honeymoon in Florida, they decided to take an extensive trip abroad. The night that they sailed from New York, Richard came to see them off. By the time he arrived, Philip was already holed up in their suite, very drunk. Constance, frantic and embarrassed, asked her father what she should do. The only advice Richard gave her was not to blow her nose all over the deck.

There was a musical-chairs rhythm to the Bennett sisters' professional lives during this period. A few years earlier, Barbara had stepped forward in *The Dancers,* just as Constance had temporarily given up acting. Now that Constance seemed once again to have turned her back on show business, Barbara moved into a higher gear. Maurice Mouvet, the famous exhibition dancer, had chosen her to be his new partner. Born in Brooklyn, Maurice—he had become so popular that he was known professionally only by his first name—had appeared in top night spots around the world, as well as in Broadway musicals. He had received a command invitation to dance before King Edward VII and had also performed before the tsar and tsarina of Russia.

Maurice once complained that the most taxing part of his career was the search for a suitable dancing partner—then training her and keeping her; most of them had a habit of leaving him flat to get married. Maurice was a harsh disciplinarian, a tyrant who demanded perfection in every detail. The qualities in a partner he most prized were spontaneity, grace, and individuality. Several women who danced opposite him were unable to withstand the strain of his rigorous rehearsals, but two of the long-term survivors were Florence Walton, who danced with him for nine years (their popularity rivaled that of Vernon and Irene Castle) and Leonora Hughes, who hung on from 1919 to 1924.

After Hughes defected, Maurice auditioned 250 girls. Most of them, he noted, "kicked and Charlestoned all over my floor with characteristic American vigor and acrobatic skill—but little grace." Eventually, he found his way to Barbara. With her slender figure and dark, bobbed hair, she was lovelier and more poised than most of the girls he had seen. There was just one problem: Maurice judged that, despite her Denishawn training, Barbara knew very little about proper dancing technique. But she showed potential, so Maurice took her on. He briefly put her through her paces in New York, and in April 1925 they sailed for Europe, where they were to open at the famous Paris club Jardin De Ma Soeur.

Rehearsals took place in Davosplatz, Switzerland, and Barbara soon began to wilt under the intensity of Maurice's demands. She had been even less prepared than he had thought, and he drove her hard to be sure she would be ready in time for the Paris opening on June 5. Barbara's self-esteem, fragile at best, was shattered. She became convinced that she would prove an embarrassment to Maurice, and her nerves, combined with physical exhaustion, pushed her to the edge. She telephoned Mabel and told her that she was going to commit suicide rather than risk the humiliation of an unsuccessful opening. Mabel immediately sailed for Europe.

All Barbara needed, Joan later recalled, was Mabel's soothing presence. Clearly, she needed much more than that. For her to threaten suicide over her inability to please her dancing partner was a signal, had anyone been paying attention, that she was in desperate need of help. But no one in the family seemed able to recognize Barbara's emotional fragility for what it was. Mabel's loving kindness simply calmed her down enough to open at Jardin De Ma Soeur as scheduled.

No sooner was one fire put out than another one began. Compared with her two sisters, Joan had led an utterly placid existence. Certainly she seemed the most uncharacteristic Bennett of all—quiet and diligent, almost complacent. Part of the reason for her low-boil personality was her growing inferiority complex. Shy, somewhat awkward, and struggling with her crippling nearsightedness, she felt there was no way she could ever pose a threat to Constance or Barbara. She seemed further isolated because of her complete lack of interest in the theatrical world that the rest of the family inhabited. The actors and directors and playwrights who had traipsed in and out of the Bennett home for as long as Joan could remember radiated flash and glamour—qualities that seemed alien to this repressed fifteen year old.

But the Bennett spirit was there, and soon it made its presence felt. Joan's first real sign of independence came in the summer of 1925. She had finished two years at St. Margaret's Academy, where she had been a good student and participated in the glee club, song competitions, and the hockey team, but she was feeling restless. Her parents' divorce had disturbed her deeply, and she longed to break away from the familiar surroundings that had grown oppressive. Her world had been rearranged, but she had not adjusted to it, so why not make a fresh start in a new place? Both Constance and Barbara had attended finishing schools abroad, and Joan persuaded her mother that she was ready to follow in her sisters' footsteps. Mabel gave in and enrolled her at Le Lierre, a prominent Paris finishing school. At St. Margaret's, Joan had conjugated enough French verbs that the prospect of completing her education abroad didn't seem too daunting.

In June 1925, accompanied by a chaperone, Mabel's close friend Countess Ina Bubna, Joan sailed for France on the *Homeric.* Constance came to see her off, and quickly spotted an acquaintance, John Fox, who also was sailing on the *Homeric.* She introduced him to Joan and prevailed on him to help her look after her luggage.

Fox was a strapping, handsome man in his mid-twenties. He came from a prominent Seattle family whose fortune had been made in the lumber business. Instead of following in his father's footsteps, however, John Fox—Jack to his friends—had ambitions to become a theatrical producer. Because he was a rebel, it shouldn't have surprised his family that he would pursue the sixteen-year-old daughter of a Broadway actor, and from the start he and Joan were attracted to one another and paid no heed to their ten-year age difference. That first evening on the *Homeric,* a shipboard romance began.

Fox was not bound for Paris; he was going to London, where he was scheduled to produce a new musical comedy. Some weeks earlier, Mabel had sailed for London to visit friends, and Joan bypassed Paris for London, where she reasoned she could stay with her ever-indulgent mother and see as much of Fox as possible. It was her first serious romance, and Joan was certain that once Mabel saw how much they meant to each other, she would lend her support.

But Mabel wasn't happy at all. She thought that Jack Fox was much too old for her teenage daughter, and made no attempt to hide her displeasure. She was relieved when late August rolled around and Joan left for Paris, where she would surely become absorbed in school and forget all about her objectionable suitor.

Mabel was wrong. Joan wanted to be where Jack was. On top of that, Le Lierre was not at all to her liking. "There was something cold and forbidding about it," Joan later wrote, "and it seemed even more so because it was almost deserted. Since I'd arrived before the term started, there was no one at school except for a few staff members and two girls my own age, neither of whom spoke English."

Once the fall term got under way, Jack Fox was a frequent weekend visitor to Le Lierre. He escorted Joan to a number of Paris's top night spots, including Jardin De Ma Soeur, where Barbara and Maurice were still packing them in nightly. The contrast of her gloomy school days and her romantic weekends with Jack soon proved too much for Joan, and one night she sneaked out of the school and scrambled over the wall. She was free, but she didn't have anywhere to go, and after a few hours of wandering around Paris she checked into a hotel.

The authorities at Le Lierre immediately notified Mabel, but she was powerless to do anything. Jack Fox had gone to Paris, collected Joan, and spirited her off to London, where she stayed with a friend of the Fox family. Richard might have admired Joan's unexpected display of independence—he didn't see why a finishing school was necessary, anyway—but Mabel was enraged and lost no time enrolling Joan at another school, L'Hermitage, in Versailles. Joan arrived for winter term, and much to Mabel's relief she fell in love with the school's elegant setting. The students lived in a chateau surrounded by magnificent gardens. All conversations were conducted in French, and she relished the twice-weekly trips to Paris's Opéra Comique and the frequent visits to the Palais Garnier, home of the Paris Opera. She finished out the term contentedly, largely because Jack continued to make frequent weekend visits.

Joan was not the only woman in the family to embark on a shipboard romance that year. The previous April, while sailing to Paris to see Barbara through her difficulties with Maurice, Mabel had met an attractive British literary agent named Eric Seabrooke Pinker. That summer, while visiting London, Mabel saw a good deal of him. Joan had met him before entering Le Lierre, and could see him as a potential substitute for their father. As a result, she decided she disliked him and refused to give him a fair chance. To Joan, Eric was "pompous," which Richard was not, and "overbearing," which Richard inarguably was. In time, Constance and Barbara came to share her opinion of Eric. The girls' maternal first cousin, Victor Morrison, met Pinker on numerous occasions and found it difficult to understand their enmity toward him. "He treated Auntie Mab like a queen," Morrison recalled, "and she was in love with him, obviously. And yet the girls didn't care for him. Eric was good, and their own father was an S.O.B.! I think Joan was the type who thought the family should stay together, come what may. She should have been more understanding." But Mabel seemed unconcerned about her daughters' reaction. Having suffered the humiliation of Richard's outbursts and infidelities for years, she reveled in the companionship of someone who seemed to think only of her.

By this time, Constance and Philip Plant were spending most of their time in Paris, where they had quickly become part of the international circuit. They were at the vortex, witnessing many of the most thrilling events in Paris of the time, including Charles Lindbergh's landing after his history-making flight across the Atlantic. Paris was then the liberal center of Europe, but Constance and Philip had no real interest in the creative life that had sprung up in the bars and cafés of Montparnasse. To Constance, the best reason for being in Paris was the brilliant world of European café society, which she found much more intoxicating than the New York theater.

Throughout 1925, Maurice and Barbara's stormy partnership

endured—just barely. Maurice's nerves were even more inflamed than usual. He was suffering from tuberculosis, which would eventually lead to his death in 1927, when he was only in his late thirties. But his deteriorating condition made him more determined than ever to achieve perfection, and he continued to drive Barbara mercilessly. Finally Barbara had had enough. In early December 1925, in the midst of an engagement at the Club Lido, Maurice and Barbara announced that they were separating because they were temperamentally unsuited. Barbara stayed on at the Club Lido with a new partner, William Reardon. Maurice took up with Eleanora Ambrose, and together they had a great success and eventually got married. In later interviews, Maurice was dismissive of his partnership with Barbara, referring to her as his "one find not stolen by Cupid," and claiming that he had chosen her only out of desperation, certain all along that she lacked the talent and discipline to be successful.

Barbara continued dancing around town with William Reardon, seemingly relieved that Maurice was out of her life. She was going through another period of intense emotional torment, but this time the source was unrequited love. At the annual Actors' Equity Ball the previous autumn, Richard and Mabel had introduced Barbara to Richard Barthelmess, the handsome, dark-eyed Hollywood actor who had become one of the most popular stars of the 1920s. In D.W. Griffith's *Way Down East* (1920), he was the hero who saved Lillian Gish as she was gliding down the river on the ice floes. After her breakup with Maurice, Barbara went to Los Angeles to fulfill a dancing engagement and also, her friends thought, to be near Barthelmess. The actor was also attracted to her, but was troubled by her mercurial behavior. Uncertain whether he should continue seeing her, Barthelmess consulted with his good friend Ronald Colman, who had seen enough of Barbara to caution Barthelmess about getting too deeply involved. Barthelmess took Colman's advice to heart and slowly withdrew from the relationship. Barbara fell into another deep depression. This time, Mabel was appearing in New York, as Gertrude in Basil Sydney's modern-dress production of *Hamlet,* and was unable to be with her to pick up the pieces. One night, toward the end of March 1926, Barbara came home to her Hollywood apartment and swallowed part of a bottle of antiseptic. She was rushed to the hospital, treated, and released. She claimed that she had mistaken the antiseptic for a bottle of cough medicine, but the press preferred to think that she had attempted suicide out of love for Barthelmess, and the story received wide newspaper coverage. Barbara seemed unconcerned about the bad publicity and returned to New York to contemplate her next move.

Meanwhile, Joan finished out her term at L'Hermitage, eager for the new life that awaited her once school was out: Jack Fox had asked her to marry him. On the surface, it was easy to see why Joan felt she had met the man of her dreams. Jack Fox was handsome, cultivated, and well-off, with an admirable streak of independence in his preference for the stage over the family lumber business. But he had one crippling flaw. Mabel had spotted it immediately, and soon Joan could not ignore it. He was an alcoholic—specifically, a binge drinker. He might not touch liquor for weeks at a time; then, on a particular evening, one drink would lead to many. By June 1926, Mabel was back in London, continuing her romance with Eric Pinker. After completing her studies at L'Hermitage, Joan joined her. It was probably the first time that they had seriously quarreled. The age difference was one matter, but Jack's excessive drinking was quite another—and Mabel knew how miserable life could be with a man who drank too much.

For once, she and Richard, touring on the West Coast, were in full agreement about something. He railed at his favorite daughter over the telephone, insisting that Fox was not the right man for her, but Joan would not change her mind. Of the three sisters, she remained the least reconciled to the collapse of Richard and Mabel's marriage. She saw Jack as her escape from her chaotic family existence, and she was determined that he wasn't going to slip away from her. She craved stability and a serene domestic routine, and she was sure that whatever bad habits Jack might possess would disappear once he was forced to shoulder the responsibilities of married life. At sixteen, she felt more than ready for any obstacle that might lie in her path. Surely it couldn't be worse than the past few years.

Mabel and Richard finally saw that it was pointless to argue, and they reluctantly gave Joan their blessing—and the money for a first-class trousseau: dresses and traveling suits from Maison de Blanc in London, hats from Clarice in Paris. Two days before the ceremony, an extravagant party in Joan's honor was thrown at London's Café de Paris. And on September 15, 1926, Jack Fox and Joan Bennett were married at St. Luke's Church, Chelsea. Constance and Philip came to London especially to attend the wedding, and the other guests were drawn from British aristocratic and theatrical circles. Joan was not as pleased to welcome one of the other guests: Eric Pinker. Mabel, wearing black—a statement?—escorted her daughter down the aisle. Joan recalled that she was "scared stiff" and spent most of the ceremony in tears, but she looked lovely in spite of it. She carried white orchids and lily of the valley and wore an ivory satin dress designed by Lanvin, a Juliet cap of rosepoint lace and orange blossom, a tulle veil she designed herself, and a train with a spray of orange blossoms.

After a champagne reception, the couple traveled in a Rolls-Royce to Victoria Station, where they boarded a train to Dover. They sailed on to Calais, then made their way to Paris, where they stayed at the Ritz Hotel. While there, they went to the opening of the nightclub Le Perroquet, and were joined by Constance and Philip. The two young married sisters tried to enjoy themselves as their husbands knocked back one drink after another. Two days later, they boarded the train to Venice, where they stayed at the Excelsior Palace. Venice in the fall made an enchanting backdrop for a honeymoon, and Jack and Joan spent a romantic week exploring The Doge's Palace, the Piazza San Marco, and the city's labyrinth of canals before returning to London on September 29.

They moved into Jack's house at 22 Carlyle Square, but Joan's blissful mood didn't last long. Once back in London, Jack's drinking binges continued unabated, and his attempts to crash into the theater had come to practically nothing. In a short time, Joan delivered an ultimatum: Jack would have to stop drinking altogether or she would leave him. And since the years living under Richard's roof had convinced her that a life in the theater spelled chaos, she made a further demand—Jack would have to give up his ambitions to be a producer and return with her to New York to find steady employment. Grudgingly, he agreed, and early in 1927 the newlyweds sailed for home.

Jack found a job with the New York Stock Exchange. It was rather demeaning work compared with what he had hoped for, but his salary allowed them to take up residence at the Shoreham Hotel, where, Joan remembered, "life was serene and happy again"—for a time.

Chapter Seven

1927–1929

Jack Fox's job with the Stock Exchange was short-lived. One night he told Joan that a hot theatrical prospect awaited him in London, the kind of opportunity he had been waiting for and that was guaranteed to launch him successfully in the business at last. Joan was skeptical, but at the last minute weakened and let him go, while she traveled to Los Angeles, where Jack's parents were now living. Life with the Foxes was anything but merry. Joan found them "the Western distributors for Babbitry, ultraconservative types who offered no room at all for high spirits and fun." One good thing came out of her time in California: she made two new friends. Marge Kelley was a sharp, funny young woman pursuing work in Hollywood, mostly as an extra. Marge's husband had a weakness for liquor, so the two women had much to talk about. Another woman who became a close confidante of Joan's was Muriel Reilly. At the time, Muriel was married to an assistant director of the Keystone Kops films; later on, she would marry Manhattan socialite Ben Finney and move to New York. A lively, unpretentious, high-spirited Irish-American girl, Muriel would remain one of Joan's closest friends for more than sixty years.

Two months after he had left for London, Jack came to Los Angeles. As Joan had feared, his theatrical prospects had come to nothing. He seemed to have spent his time abroad on a steady binge. He looked weary, years older, and much heavier. Jack managed to persuade her to return with him to London. It seemed a pleasant alternative to life with his parents, and Joan agreed. Shortly after they had moved back into 22 Carlyle Square, Joan learned that she was pregnant. As happy as she was at the thought of having a baby, she was worried about Jack's ability to take on the responsibility of a family. Mabel was appalled that she would even consider having a baby with such a no-account husband, and tried repeatedly to talk her into having an abortion—but Joan refused to consider it.

Impending fatherhood affected Jack's drinking habits only in one way: the binges became more frequent. His weakness for drink had developed into full-blown, chronic alcoholism, and even a hint of liquor in a dessert or sauce was enough to set him off. Joan left him for a time, then came back home, telling him that if he didn't stop drinking altogether she would file for divorce. Life would be more manageable in the United States, she decided, where, once the baby arrived, she would at least be closer to family and friends. They returned to Los Angeles and rented a small house in Hollywood. Jack found a job and promised that he would stay sober once and for all, and Joan tried her best to believe him. But after only one year, her marriage had settled into a pattern, unraveling and knitting itself back together and unraveling all over again, and it was hard for her to be very optimistic.

Mabel's prospects, on the other hand, looked like a sure thing. Her relationship with Eric Pinker had deepened into one of great trust and affection. And suddenly it seemed as if it would open a whole new career for her as well. Eric's father had long dreamed of opening a New York branch of his literary agency, to be managed by Eric. As plans for a New York office fell slowly into place, Mabel suggested to him that the agency might consider representing playwrights as well as novelists and nonfiction writers. Because Eric knew little about the theatrical world, Mabel persuaded him to let her try her hand at it. Instinct told her that this new line of work might be exactly what she had been looking for. As she aged, work in the theater was increasingly hard to come by, to the point that she had given serious thought to leaving it all behind. Her last appearance had been in the 1925 modern-dress production of *Ham-*

let at the Booth Theater. Two months into the run, she had broken her ankle onstage and had had to withdraw.

From the beginning, she loved being a play broker. In a short time, she sold her first property to the Shubert Brothers, and when the New York branch of the Pinker agency opened in 1927, numerous playwrights were clamoring for her to represent them. It was a good time to be a playwright. With more plays opening on Broadway than ever before, Mabel lost little time in accumulating a tony client list. The agency's future seemed promising, and on June 19, 1927, she and Eric brought their partnership full circle when they were married at Marie Sterner's art gallery in Manhattan. Of Mabel's daughters, only Barbara was in attendance.

Mabel and Eric spent weekdays in the city and weekends at their peaceful retreat in Old Lyme, Connecticut. Mabel seemed delighted with her new life. "She was beautiful and full of enthusiasm, enthusiasm for everything," recalled Victor Morrison. "We would go up to their home often, and they would play poker after dinner. She was very enthusiastic about her poker playing. She was always very aware of her nieces and nephews. A thoroughly fun, enjoyable person."

Stung by Mabel's remarriage, Richard responded by rushing into what he called "the most disastrous thing of my life." Only a few weeks later, on July 11, he married Aimee Raisch Hastings, a young socialite who had fallen in love with the theater—and with him. He had met her the year before while appearing in Los Angeles in a play called *Creoles*, in which she played a bit part. Richard renewed acquaintance with her when he did a brief West Coast tour of *They Knew What They Wanted*, his feud with the Theatre Guild having cooled off for the moment. It was Richard at his most perverse, marrying Aimee while pining for Mabel—and Aimee was in every way the antithesis of Mabel: shrill, quarrelsome, shallow, grasping. Although she pretended to dote on Richard, it was his position in the theater that excited her most. He may also have married her out of boredom. Since being forced to leave the cast of *They Knew What They Wanted*, he had had trouble finding another script that captured his imagination. He appeared on the West

Coast in both *Creoles* and Willard Mack's *The Dove,* but didn't come into New York with either of them, and later termed this particular season "more of an endurance test than any display of talent."

For the rest of 1927, Joan was occupied with preparations for her baby's arrival. Jack had known she wasn't kidding when she had delivered her no-drinking ultimatum, and he managed to stay sober until the middle of February 1928, when he suddenly took off on a two-day drinking binge. By the time he returned, Joan was in labor. On February 20, 1928, she gave birth to a daughter, Adrienne Ralston Fox, at Good Samaritan Hospital in Los Angeles.

Joan was delighted that Adrienne was healthy and thriving, but it wasn't an entirely happy time. Joan's excitement at being a mother was undercut by her growing awareness that she and Jack were in deep financial difficulty. Jack's string of short-term jobs had fizzled out, and he was drinking heavily again. The Fox family cut off all financial support, but Richard and Mabel pitched in, helping with the rent and hospital bills. On more than one occasion, however, Jack intercepted their checks in the mailbox and cashed them to buy liquor. Now that Joan was fighting not only for her own survival but for her daughter's as well, her arguments with Jack became more and more heated. Her plan to escape the instability of her own family's world had been a dismal failure. Mabel and Richard had been right after all: marrying Jack had been a grave mistake. Finally, she resorted to placing Jack under a restraining order. He violated it almost immediately, breaking into the house and angrily confronting her, frightening her to the extent that she called the police and had him jailed for ten days.

Her marriage was over, and the tranquil existence that she had imagined for herself had gone up in smoke. A quick household accounting confirmed what she already knew—she would have to find a job immediately. Although she had once considered a career as an interior decorator, she had no experience and no practical training in anything. One remote possibility, as a stopgap measure only, was acting. Much as she hated the idea, she *was* living in Hollywood, and Marge Kelley had assured her that with her looks and figure she might have a chance of landing some small parts in films. She wouldn't have to do it for long, and it might give her enough to get by on until she had landed a real job. So she made the rounds of studios, but the only jobs she got were low-paying stints as an extra. Her adult screen debut—as an extra—took place in 1928's *The Divine Lady,* starring Corrine Griffith, which won Frank Lloyd the Academy Award for Best Director. That same year, Joan also appeared in a tiny role in Pathé's *Power,* starring Alan Hale.

But such meager assignments didn't provide nearly enough to sustain herself and the baby, and she continued to scour Los Angeles for a decent job. All the while, she had accepted intermittent financial support from her parents without revealing how bad things really were; she hadn't even had the nerve to tell them that she and Jack had separated. One night in the spring of 1928, while she was out, Richard, who was appearing in Kenyon Nicholson's *The Barker* in San Francisco, telephoned and spoke to the baby's nurse. With a little coaxing, she blurted out that Jack was no longer living at home and that Joan was broke. Ever the protective father, Richard turned up in Los Angeles, as Joan recalled, "waving a gun and threatening to shoot the father of my child unless I got a divorce."

Fortunately, he also offered a more rational solution in the form of a steady job. *Jarnegan,* a new play by Charles Beahan and Garrett Fort, based on a novel by Jim Tully, was set to go into rehearsal in mid-summer for a September opening at Broadway's Longacre Theater on West Forty-eighth Street. There was a crucial string attached: no divorce, no job. It might have been unfair manipulation on Richard's part, but in her heart Joan knew the marriage was over and that she had to think of her baby's future above everything else. In no position to argue, she filed for divorce in California. Since she didn't even have the money to pay for the train fare east, she was forced to sell her furniture. Knowing that the pressure on her in New York would be so intense that she would not be able to care for the baby properly, Richard insisted that she leave Adrienne in Los Angeles with the nurse. After enlisting Marge Kelley to check on them every day, Joan reluctantly agreed.

Back in New York, Richard had taken the script out of the playwrights' hands and was busily rewriting it to show Joan off to best advantage. *Jarnegan* gave Richard a choice role as Jim Jarnegan, a coarse, hot-tempered roughneck who has put an unsavory past behind him and has become a top movie director. Jarnegan is disgusted with everything around him: lecherous producers, amoral starlets, gin-soaked actresses. His protégé is an innocent young woman named Daisy Carol (played by Joan), whom he tries to prevent being corrupted by Hollywood. But he fails. Daisy Carol is seduced, becomes pregnant, and dies as a result of a botched abortion. When Jarnegan realizes that the whole town is blaming him for her downfall, he tracks down the guilty man. In a blazing final scene, set at a big Hollywood party, Jarnegan exposes Daisy's seducer and angrily denounces the entire movie colony.

Richard felt that the part of the hard-drinking, foul-mouthed Jarnegan gave him his best chance in years. But the original script had little counterpoint—*many* of the characters were hard-drinking and foul-mouthed. So Richard's intention was that Daisy Carol should come off as utterly simple and graceful, in contrast with the scenery-chewing going on around her. She would become the eye of the hurricane, and audiences would be bound to focus on her.

But shortly after rehearsals began, Richard found that it wasn't turning out the way he'd planned. Joan had moved in with him for the run of *Jarnegan,* and at night Richard coached her endlessly in the part of Daisy Carol. Joan's voice was tiny and indistinct, and Richard spent hours showing her how to speak up and project using her diaphragm so as not to injure her vocal cords. It also bothered him that her interpretation seemed to grow more excessive with each passing day. One day, at rehearsal, he observed that she was being coached by everyone in sight: the playwrights, the company manager, even the press agent, and most of all by the director, Ira Hards.

"Mr. Hards," Richard snapped, "I explained to you before

rehearsals the way in which I wanted the part of Daisy to come over the footlights."

Hards tried to placate him, a quarrel ensued, and Richard fired the director on the spot. He took over directing duties himself for a few days, until the talented playwright-director George Abbott was available to lend a hand. Only in his early thirties, Abbott had already earned a reputation for staging heavy-breathing dramas like *Broadway* and *Chicago*. Abbott sat through one rehearsal and pronounced, "The girl's the best thing in the show—build up her part." In due time, another scene for Joan was added.

At home, Richard worked hard to make Joan understand that the part should play itself.

"Don't hamstring it with a lot of fool ideas about putting over the part," he insisted. Let the part unfold naturally. She should try to make every member of the audience feel that she was imparting a confidence to him and him alone.

Jarnegan opened on September 24, 1928. It fared better than most plays that year. With a total of 224 productions opening, the 1928–1929 season was one of the most prolific in recent memory. Unfortunately, few of the 224 had staying power. With the opening of *The Jazz Singer* in October 1927, talking pictures had announced themselves as a force to be reckoned with, at a fraction of the price of a Broadway ticket. Hollywood rushed headlong into the sound era, making even greater inroads on the theater audience. But the quality of plays being offered was also to blame. Burns Mantle, among others, believed that the prosperity of the 1920s had attracted many inexperienced and inept producers without taste or judgment. Hollywood money bankrolled stage productions for the sole purpose of having tailor-made material for the screen—and traditional Broadway standards, it was felt, were far ahead of those set by the movie business.

On *Jarnegan*'s opening night, Richard was terrified on Joan's behalf, while she was "completely nerveless, and just too inexperienced to know any better." She spent the moments before her second-act entrance polishing off an ice cream sundae. The reviews for *Jarnegan* were mixed, but the play's shock value guaranteed it a modestly successful run. In a way, Richard's scheme that all the actors except Joan should perform at high pitch backfired: the *New York Times* found that "In his playing he achieved the externals of an excellent performance, without actually giving one. He had color, strength and vigor, but he used them to cover a hollow shell of a characterization." The same critic thought that "His daughter, Joan, as the unfortunate Daisy Carol, was attractive and believable." In the *New York World,* St. John Ervine thought that the play's shortcomings presented "immense technical difficulties" for Richard, but that even he "cannot engage our attention by merely repeating the word 'hell' every ten seconds." Ervine also wrote that Joan "played with a pleasing clumsiness that exactly suited the character," while the *New York American* found that she "took a difficult part . . . and made the most of it."

"Joan made the grade—and how!" Richard later boasted. Her success in it filled him with enormous pride. With Constance gallivanting in Europe with Philip Plant and Barbara as uncertain as ever about what she wanted to do, all his ambitions were now centered on Joan. Best of all, she had proved herself in the theater, where she belonged, not in the movies, which he still regarded as a second-class art form.

For Joan, the most important aspect of her success in *Jarnegan* was that it allowed her to send for her infant daughter, Adrienne, and nurse. Once they arrived in New York, Joan rented a small apartment and settled in for *Jarnegan*'s 136-performance run. The time passed pleasantly. Joan had embarked on a romance with theater critic George Jean Nathan. On the surface, it might have seemed that this alliance would have pleased Richard. In his essays in *The Smart Set* and *American Mercury,* Nathan was one of the most passionate advocates of the thinking man's theater; early on, before it was fashionable, he had championed the works of Eugene O'Neill. But Richard regarded Nathan as one of the most destructive and ignorant critics around, and he tried unsuccessfully to prevent Joan from continuing with the romance.

First and foremost on Joan's mind was what to do once the run of *Jarnegan* ended. There were a couple of inquiries from the

West Coast. By now, nearly every studio in Hollywood—MGM was a notable exception—was sold on the inevitability of talking pictures, and they were spending a fortune having the theater chains they owned rewired to accommodate sound films. When the voices of silent screen idols Vilma Banky, John Gilbert, and numerous other stars proved uncongenial to the new technology, there was a rush to sign up stage-trained actors who would be able to make a smooth adjustment to microphone technique. Often an actor with an uncertain future on Broadway and only a handful of plays under his belt found himself the object of the studios' bidding wars. Spencer Tracy, Katharine Hepburn, Humphrey Bogart, Bette Davis, Barbara Stanwyck, and Claudette Colbert were a few of the struggling stage actors who would soon find themselves pulling into Pasadena on the Super Chief, ogling the vast acres of orange groves and contemplating a brighter future.

Joan made a couple of movie tests, one for Fox Studios and one for Famous Players–Lasky. Neither one impressed the studio bosses, and though Walter Wanger, Jesse Lasky's general manager of production, found Joan "very sweet," he felt she would "never photograph." Neither failure set her back much. If Hollywood wasn't interested, Broadway was. Not long after *Jarnegan*'s closing was announced, she was signed for *Hot Bed,* a new drama by a talented young playwright named Paul Osborn. The fact that Osborn was one of Mabel's clients at Pinker-Morrison didn't hurt Joan's chances of being cast.

One night during the end of *Jarnegan*'s run, Joan was paid a visit by Joseph Schenck, chairman of the board of United Artists Pictures, and his right-hand man, John Considine Jr. United Artists had been established in 1919 by three important stars, Mary Pickford, Douglas Fairbanks, and Charles Chaplin, and one important director, D.W. Griffith, as a company that would distribute their own independently made films, thus bypassing the major studios and allowing themselves to keep a much heftier percentage of the profits. But all that had been ten years ago. By now, with the arrival of sound, the careers of the four founding members had slipped, and United Artists was gradually evolving into a distribution wing for a wide cross-section of independent producers. One of the independents who had been releasing through UA was Samuel Goldwyn, who was now preparing Ronald Colman's first talkie, a thriller about a debonair army officer turned private eye called *Bulldog Drummond.* His immediate task at hand was finding a suitable leading lady for Colman. Having produced *The Eternal City,* which starred Richard, and subsequently given Constance her break in *Cytherea,* Goldwyn thought that lightning might strike a third time, and suggested to Schenck and Considine that they take a look at Joan. Schenck and Considine liked what they saw. Not only was Joan blonde and beautiful, there was something in her relaxed and natural presence that made them think she might take to the camera well. They offered a test, and were surprised when Joan turned them down. "I figured that if a studio wanted an actress badly enough, they'd sign her first and then do everything possible to make her look good," she recalled. Her gamble paid off. In a short time, she had withdrawn from the cast of *Hot Bed* and signed a five-year contract with United Artists.

Richard was adamant that Joan remain in New York, where he thought she had a great future. But Mabel felt it was in her best interests to go to California, and so signed the necessary papers as her legal guardian. Richard grumbled that United Artists' offer—five hundred dollars a week, over three times what she made in *Jarnegan*—was "good but not gorgeous," and was eager to step in to negotiate her contract, but Joan quietly insisted on handling all the details herself. In the early months of 1929, she was bound for Hollywood. When she insisted that the studio pay for a separate compartment for Adrienne and the nurse, United Artists complained that they weren't hiring her baby for pictures.

Joan took an apartment in the Beverly Wilshire Hotel and prepared for the filming on *Bulldog Drummond,* which began in late January 1929. She was nervous not only about playing her first important part in films, but about the new sound technique. Also, her poor eyesight was a handicap—making her way around the stage had been relatively simple, but now she had to contend with complicated lighting and camera angles and hitting her marks.

Fortunately, there was a lengthy rehearsal period before shooting began, and her fellow actors in the film did their best to put her at ease. Playing the villainess was actress and socialite Lilyan Tashman, who took a sisterly interest in Joan. And there was Ronald Colman. Only a few years earlier, Joan had been just another enthralled fan as she sat through Colman's big romantic pictures costarring Vilma Banky. Now she could scarcely believe that she herself was playing love scenes with him. His smooth, confident manner and instinctive understanding of microphone technique left little doubt that his future in sound films would be even bigger than his career in silents. He also took Joan aside and gave her pointers on how to keep her head turned toward the camera and stay in her light. Off-camera, they also began a short-lived romance which soon ran its course, with no bitterness on either side.

With her turned up-nose, marcelled hair, and striking figure, Joan certainly made an attractive leading lady. But Samuel Goldwyn wasn't pleased. After he viewed the early rushes, he told Joan that her performance was shaping up to be a disappointment. Perhaps thinking that he could get results by intimidation, he complained that she didn't measure up to Constance. As Joan later wrote, "it wasn't a particularly ego-building time."

It's easy to understand Goldwyn's concerns. Phyllis, a standard detective story lady-in-distress, isn't much of a part, and Joan is noticeably uncomfortable before the camera. In her first scene, in which she shows up at a gloomy English inn to seek Drummond's help in rescuing her imprisoned uncle, she pitches her performance too high. Like many actors of the time adapting to new and unfamiliar technology, she often speaks too emphatically for the microphone, and early on, when she's playing a scene with the dapper Colman, their dialogue seesaws back and forth in a jarring *forte/piano* dance. She settles down as the film progresses, however, and halfway through there is a lovely, quiet exchange in which Phyllis admits to Drummond that she is falling for him. The sequence is shot partly in close-up, and Joan reveals a gentle, spontaneous quality that is the high point of her performance—a fleeting but clear hint that she might be star material after all.

Despite the inadequacies of her performance, *Bulldog Drummond* was a lucky film for Joan, pulling in big grosses and earning an Academy Award nomination for the Best Picture of 1929. United Artists wasn't entirely sure what to make of its new leading lady, so they put her into *Three Live Ghosts,* a weak comedy starring Robert Montgomery. Joan observed that "That one didn't win me any acting awards either." United Artists agreed, and dropped their option on her future services.

With time on her hands, she decided to try her luck in the theater again, in a new play by William DuBois called *The Pirate.* Its star was Doris Keane, whose fame rested on her great success fifteen years before in Edward Sheldon's *Romance,* about the bittersweet love affair between a famous opera star and a rector. *Romance* had been an enormous hit on two continents; Keane never again had a success come close to equaling it. By 1929, she was nearing forty and desperate to make audiences forget about *Romance. The Pirate* gave her a lively role as a lady cutthroat who sails the Spanish Main. Joan looked forward to acting with Keane; Richard had appeared with the actress in *The Hypocrites* and held her in high regard. But *The Pirate* was an unhappy experience for everyone. It opened in Santa Barbara before moving to the Belasco Theater in Los Angeles. Apparently Joan had forgotten the lessons Richard had taught her in *Jarnegan,* for the *New York Times* commented that she "defeated her natural pulchritude by raucously shouting almost every line." The *Times* correctly predicted that the play would never make it to New York, and it turned out to be Doris Keane's farewell to the stage.

Joan wasn't the only one in the family experiencing rough sledding in the theater. Richard took *Jarnegan* on tour, with Elaine Temple in Joan's part—although he was so taken with the publicity value of father-daughter casting that he insisted on leaving Joan's name in the program. The play's rough language was met with resistance by many out-of-town audiences, and business in Boston was particularly bad. When the Boston censors demanded extensive cuts in the script, Richard fired up his curtain speeches, lashing out at what he considered the most provincial of American cities.

He told a reporter, "I wouldn't play that damn place if they gave me Bunker Hill Monument, threw in the Copley-Plaza, and called out the National Guard to meet me at the Back Bay Station. . . . Boston? Why, it's the most hypocritical, the most interfering, the most mendacious, the most immoral, the most bigoted place you'll find in a lifetime of trouping!"

When *The Pirate* folded, Joan began seeking more film work, this time on a freelance basis. *Bulldog Drummond*'s success had opened doors for her, and Warner Bros. soon cast her in *Disraeli,* with George Arliss in the title role as the British prime minister. Few studios had been as adept as Warners at recruiting actors from the New York stage, and Arliss was one of the recent "prestige" additions to their roster. *Disraeli,* a valentine to the dignified grandeur of Victorian England, had been a big Broadway hit for him in 1911. Under Alfred E. Green's direction, the film shows the early talkie drama at its creakiest. Because of the limitations of sound recording at this time, the camera is merely planted in one place for much of the time. Despite its references to Gladstone and the khedive of Egypt, the film is less a biography than a carefully wrought drawing room suspense drama pitting the crafty Disraeli against a cunning female spy (played by British character actress Doris Lloyd). Joan, cast as Lady Clarissa, Disraeli's protégé, looks stunning in the period costumes, and her performance has charm and spirit—a considerable improvement on her previous screen work. Richard Watts in the *New York Herald Tribune* wrote, "Joan Bennett, who must get tired of hearing it, is exquisite-looking, and in addition, believable." Despite film historian David Shipman's assessment that Arliss's idea of acting "consisted of twitching watery eyes to express cuteness—called for, it seems, at all times—and moving his mouth like a ventriloquist's dummy," *Disraeli* earned him an Academy Award as 1929's Best Actor. Its commercial success provided Joan with another career boost. She settled in, thinking that she liked Hollywood much more than she had anticipated. Perhaps she might stay for a while.

Chapter Eight

1929–1930

On January 20, 1929, Sarah Savina Armstrong, a twenty-eight-year-old Belfast housemaid, checked into London's Royal Free Hospital. The following day, she gave birth to a robust and beautiful boy, whom she named Dennis Arthur Armstrong. The baby's father was Arthur Hewitt, an English laborer, whom Miss Armstrong had met early in 1928. Both parents were of slender means. More than once, Hewitt promised to marry Miss Armstrong, but nothing came of it. Neither of them was in a position to support a child.

The mother's recovery was slow. Released from the hospital, she took the child and went to live at a YWCA in the Aberdeen Park section of London. While pregnant, she had stayed for a time with her sister, Lilian Nicholson. But Mrs. Nicholson was married and very concerned about maintaining her respectability; she declined to let Sarah and her baby recuperate at her home. Sarah Armstrong soon suffered a breakdown in health and placed her son temporarily with a London County Council–licensed foster mother. But she was told that the best thing in the long run would be to put Dennis up for adoption.

In September 1929, Sarah Armstrong applied to the National Adoption Society in Baker Street. On January 9, 1930, she signed an agreement with the Society allowing them to place Dennis with a mother who was in a position to bring him up properly. Sarah Armstrong recovered her health and began to prepare for a nursing career. It would be several years before she would have any idea what had happened to her child.

By early 1929, while Joan was in Hollywood filming *Bulldog Drummond,* Constance knew that her marriage to Philip Plant was doomed. He was drinking as heavily as ever, and she had long since wearied of his promises to stop. Her marriage had followed the pattern set by their courtship: high times punctuated by explosive fights and separations. Constance had relished her adventures in café society, but the drinking and nightlife that was so much a part of that world proved too great a temptation for Philip. Eventually, it was no longer realistic for Constance to participate in it and expect Philip to remain sober.

They parted company. Philip moved into the exclusive Lancaster Hotel on the rue de Berri, while Constance moved to the Hôtel d'Iéna. On April 19, they signed a separation agreement. In it, both parties clearly stated that their marriage had produced no children. Constance stayed on in Paris through the spring. One of her close friends during this time was another resident of the Hôtel d'Iéna, Rita Kaufman Lowe, an American woman with a small boy, Albert, around five years old. Constance appeared to dote on Albert, and spent evening after evening in Lowe's apartment, playing with him. She seemed downright wistful when she explained to Lowe how much she loved children, that she had never had one of her own, and that she desperately wanted one. Now that she and Philip were on the brink of a divorce, her chances of becoming a mother seemed more remote than ever.

There was another reason for Constance's eagerness to separate from Philip. She was entranced by someone else. When it came to divorcing their husbands, Mabel Morrison's daughters hardly ever followed her example. Mabel left Richard because she sought peace, stability, and a new and productive path for herself. Constance, Barbara, and Joan almost always left one man because they had found another.

During their years in Paris, Plant and Constance had occasionally found themselves in the company of Gloria Swanson and her husband, Henri, Marquis de la Falaise de la Coudraye. At Paramount Pictures, Swanson had risen to become one of the world's great box-office attractions in films such as *Male and Female* (1919), *Don't Change Your Husband* (1920), and *Zaza* (1923). In 1924, while still under contract to Paramount, she had gone to France to film *Madame Sans-Gêne,* Victorien Sardou's play about a French washerwoman elevated to nobility by Napoleon. For a major Hollywood star to appear in a European film was highly irregular. It was an extravagant production with, aside from Swanson, an all-French cast, to be filmed entirely on French locations.

As the first American star to appear in a French film, Swanson was expected to attend numerous official ceremonies. Paramount, concerned that she might flounder on foreign soil, decided that she needed someone to act as interpreter and general factotum, and selected Henri de la Falaise for the job. At the time, Falaise was a handsome, broad-shouldered man in his late twenties, with slicked-back blonde hair, gentle blue eyes, and an elegant mustache. Swanson recalled him as "every inch the aristocrat, in perfectly tailored clothes, the kind of dapper person who wore well-chosen suede gloves and carried a walking stick as if it were second nature to do so." Falaise was not entirely French; on his mother's side, he was descended from the Hennessys of County Cork, Ireland, who had made a sizeable fortune distilling cognac. Falaise was not only a man of culture, but of courage and character as well. During World War I, he had been awarded the Croix de Guerre for his bravery in the trenches.

Unfortunately, he shared the fate of many of the noblemen that Europe was riddled with at this time. Although he possessed an imposing ancestral home in Brittany, he had no money whatsoever, and currently was reduced to working at a routine job with an insurance firm. Swanson was unconcerned about his shaky financial condition. Falaise had other things, namely impeccable breeding and social connections that guaranteed her a seamless entry into Parisian social circles.

Throughout the shooting of *Madame Sans-Gêne,* Swanson relied heavily on Falaise to guide her through the diplomatic minefields of Paris. Whenever she was presented with an award or medal, Falaise coached her on exactly the right thing to say. "If French officialdom fell in love with me during those months," Swanson confessed, "it was largely because of Henri's flawless choreography." After years of suffering competitive cutthroats in Hollywood, Swanson was delighted to have discovered a man of such nobility and refinement. She was also passionately attracted to him. In January 1925 they were married.

Falaise expressed an interest in becoming a film producer, but Swanson thought him entirely too gentle and pliable to survive in such a brutal atmosphere. She was right. He was far too dignified to be effective in contract negotiations, and she arranged for him to be assigned a task where his sophistication and manners could be an asset: the translation and distribution of her films abroad.

Falaise received enormous exposure in the American press when he and Swanson sailed to the United States after *Madame Sans-Gêne* had finished filming. They subsequently crossed the country in a private train arranged by Paramount. At every stop, the train was mobbed by fans. It was a golden time in Swanson's life. Both her personal and professional lives were at their apex. She loved Falaise deeply, and she reveled in her relatively meaningless title, the Marquise de la Falaise de la Coudraye. Swanson would look back on this marriage with great affection, while her daughter, Gloria Day, would remember the Marquis as her favorite of her mother's six husbands.

After stormy marriages to actor Wallace Beery and restaurateur Herbert K. Somborn, Swanson believed she had finally made an ideal match. But in 1927, only two years after her marriage to Falaise, she met Joseph P. Kennedy. The Boston financier had entered the movie business in 1926 when he purchased a distribution company called Film Booking Office and began turning out cheap cowboy pictures. That same year, Swanson's Paramount contract expired. The company offered her $14,000 a week to renew, but United Artists had been courting her with promises of a lucrative deal and greater artistic control than Paramount or any other studio could guarantee. More than anything, Swanson wanted a film that would bear her personal stamp, one that would ensure her place in movie immortality, as United Artists' *The Gold Rush* in 1925 had ensured Charlie Chaplin's. So she turned down Paramount's offer and founded her own production company. Unfortunately, she soon found that as an independent businesswoman she was in over her head. Her debts were mounting by the week when she met Joseph Kennedy.

Until he met Swanson, the movies Kennedy produced had all been profitable but undistinguished. With Swanson, he made a bid to enter the big time. He took over her company, eliminating much of the deadweight personnel that she had surrounded herself with. She repaid him in the best way she knew how, by becoming his lover. In the long run, however, Swanson's own instincts about her career proved superior to Kennedy's. Before they met, he had been one of several producers who had signed a telegram to United Artists' Joseph M. Schenck, arguing that Swanson's new film, *Sadie Thompson,* was so racy that it would undermine the public's confidence in the moral judgment of Hollywood. He was dead wrong—*Sadie Thompson* turned out to be one of the most successful pictures of Swanson's career. Kennedy, on the other hand, persuaded Swanson to star in Erich von Stroheim's *Queen Kelly,* a bizarre mess that the actress walked out on after $600,000 had been spent on it. The debacle stung her badly, and she later judged Kennedy to be "a classic example of that person in the arts with lots of brains and drive but little taste or talent."

Swanson's affair with Kennedy would prove more potent than their short-lived professional collaboration, which lasted only three years altogether. Swanson, however, held to a double standard where extramarital affairs were concerned. In 1928, she didn't bat an eye when Kennedy, who had recently become chairman of the Pathé Exchange, arranged to have Falaise sent to Paris to watch over the studio's European interests. When he took over Pathé, Kennedy began searching for fresh talent to fill out his studio roster. Swanson recommended Constance, whom she had seen in *Sally, Irene and*

Mary and thought quite promising. Kennedy immediately sent Falaise to inquire about Constance's availability. Falaise's charms were not lost on Constance, and the affair blossomed as she took steps to extricate herself from her marriage to Plant.

Swanson's business associates had informed her of the rumors of Constance's involvement with Falaise. In the fall of 1929, the affair was brought home to Swanson in a way that she never forgot and never forgave. While staying in Paris at the Ritz Hotel, Swanson received a letter addressed to the Marquise de la Falaise de la Coudraye. When she had finished reading it, it seemed clear to her what she was supposed to think had happened. The sender of the letter had mistakenly addressed the letter to the Marquise when she had clearly intended it for the Marquis. It was a love letter from Constance to Henri.

A mistake? Swanson herself surely doubted that it was. Thanks to her finishing-school education, Constance had excellent command of French—Joan always claimed that it was much better than her own—and it is unlikely that she would have made such an elemental blunder. It seems much more credible as a classic Constance maneuver: by "misaddressing" the letter, she guaranteed that Swanson would find out about the affair. Soon afterward, Swanson received a letter from Falaise. "The fire has burnt the beautiful temple of our love," he wrote. "We thought that it was built of marble, and we wake up to find it has crumbled like the dust of clay. Little can be saved out of the burning ashes. But let's try and preserve our sweet friendship, our regard for each other, our decency!" Falaise's dignity and tact did little to cool Swanson's anger. She immediately filed divorce proceedings against him—just as Constance had known she would.

Constance's impending divorce from Philip presented one major complication—it cut her off from the Plant fortune. There was money to be made in Hollywood, but she would have to get busy while she was still young and beautiful, a marketable commodity. Now that Constance had exchanged the wealthy Plant for the impoverished Falaise, she decided to take a third run at a movie career, and no doubt she treasured the irony that Gloria Swanson was responsible for it. She was now signed with Pathé, and in the summer of 1929 she returned to the United States to resume her career.

Right away, she reported to work for her first film for Pathé, *This Thing Called Love,* a comedy costarring Edmund Lowe. She was paid a total salary of $14,500—the first money she had earned in some time. Sound films proved no difficulty for Constance, for she took to the microphone beautifully. When *This Thing Called Love* was released in December 1929, the *New York Times* praised her "agreeable, easy manner of talking."

On December 5, she and Philip signed a divorce decree in Nice, where Constance had taken up residence at a villa on the Avenue Valrose. Like the separation agreement, the divorce decree states that their marriage was childless. Despite reports that Constance received a cash settlement of over $500,000, records indicate that what she got was an outright settlement of $25,000, plus $700 monthly support payments for life. To anyone else, it might have seemed an ample amount.

On December 29, Constance traveled to London, where she checked in at the Mayfair Hotel. She stayed over New Year's, and departed on January 7. A little over two weeks later, on January 29, Constance quietly arrived in New York with a small child. She was evasive when asked whether or not it was hers, and many in Hollywood certainly had no idea that she had a child at the time she filmed *This Thing Called Love.* (Later she said that she and her closest professional associates felt that having a baby would not mesh well with her glamour-girl image, and thought it best to keep it a secret.) Constance stayed in New York for a while, and a nurse traveled by train with the baby to Los Angeles.

If Constance's behavior regarding her child puzzled or worried Mabel, she kept her concerns to herself. Publicly, she professed to be delighted that at last Constance had what she had wanted for so long, a child of her own. It was a wonderful thing, Mabel insisted, for she had always known that Constance had a great mothering heart.

The talkies also provided an unexpected opportunity for Barbara. In the fall of 1928, while Joan was appearing in *Jarnegan,* Barbara was filming a leading role in one of the first full-length sound musicals. Warner had introduced the sound era's first musical, Al Jolson's *The Singing Fool,* in 1928. When it earned $5.5 million at the box office, Hollywood studio executives got the message and scrambled to rewire their theater chains. For a time, the movies eased themselves into the sound era—intermittent talking sequences were dropped into a number of silent films to make them appear less dinosaur-like to the public. As *The Jazz Singer* and *The Singing Fool* proved, there was a tremendous potential market for musicals, but the technology was crude and uncertain; microphones had to be hidden at odd places around the set, resulting in a peculiar imbalance of sound, and elaborate song-and-dance sequences had to be shot from a distance, with the camera rooted in one place. But it didn't matter much to the public. The screen musical was uncharted territory, and audiences lined up for virtually anything that sang and danced.

Barbara's picture was called *Syncopation,* and it holds a historic spot for a number of reasons. It was the result of the shrewd machinations of Joseph Kennedy, who had been closely monitoring the technological changes in the movie industry. He had obtained the use of the Radio Corporation of America's sound system, Photophone, for all his Film Booking Office productions. But even though Kennedy was making a fortune from filmmaking ventures, he wasn't satisfied. He reasoned that he could never become a true force in Hollywood unless he owned a chain of theaters to show his films. For some time he had been eyeing the more than seven hundred vaudeville houses owned by the Keith-Albee-Orpheum circuit. With the rise of radio and talking films, the heyday of vaudeville was passing, and in May 1928 he purchased the chain for $4.2 million and set about having the theaters converted to sound. Later that year, he merged FBO into Keith-Albee-Orpheum, and called the company RKO Radio. The new studio's very first production was *Syncopation.*

Syncopation was filmed in New York City, at the Cosmopolitan Studios on upper Park Avenue. What plot there was involved Benny (Bobby Watson) and Flo (Barbara), a dance team that breaks up because of Flo's social aspirations. Most reviewers weren't impressed with *Syncopation*'s acting, story, or musical values, but none of that mattered. An all-singing and dancing musical was big news in 1929, and when *Syncopation* opened in New York in March of that year, it broke records. Seen today, *Syncopation* is fairly creaky, but Barbara's husky speaking voice (she sounds a great deal like Constance) and finishing school accent (all broad *A*s) help her register on camera. Yet she seems rather diffident. Most young actresses in films of this period try too hard to make an impression, almost begging us to like them. Barbara is clearly not one of them; she's more like a girl in a high school play who's slightly embarrassed to be onstage in front of her friends. In the dance sequences, she seems supple and willing, although they're difficult to judge, since they are necessarily shot from a distance.

Syncopation has one good song, "I'll Always Be in Love with You." It is sung by an affable, moon-faced Irish-American tenor named Morton Downey, who would benefit most from the movie's success. Born and raised in Wallingford, Connecticut, Downey had come up the hard way. Lean years as a newshawk and song plugger were alleviated in 1919 when he was engaged as a soloist with Paul Whiteman's orchestra for seventy dollars a week. He gained a following for his impassioned renditions of sentimental Irish numbers, such as "Mother Machree" and "Molly Malone." After a few years, he left the Whiteman band and became a favorite with the international set in Palm Beach and at some of the top clubs in London, Paris, Biarritz, and Berlin. One performance quickly became show business legend: one evening, when the Prince of Wales heard Downey perform at London's Café de Paris, he wound up asking him to sing Rodgers and Hart's "You Took Advantage of Me" eleven times.

Syncopation was Downey's first film, and he had been cast in it through the influence of Joseph Kennedy, a close friend for the past five or six years. Although he was overweight and had a plain, almost homely, Irish country boy face, he had a reputation as a ladykiller who had "made every chorus girl in every chorus line." Barbara fell for him immediately. On January 28, 1929, after *Syncopation* had wrapped, they were married at Saint Patrick's Cathedral in New York.

In some ways, Downey was not unlike another rising Irish-American singer, Bing Crosby. He was genial and easygoing, patient and considerate where his colleagues were concerned, and kind and generous to his fans—always willing to accept a compliment, shake a hand, sign an autograph. This was the Morton Downey that Barbara fell in love with, and for a while it was the only image of him she perceived. The Bennett sisters' cousin, Victor Morrison, found Downey "a typical, old-fashioned Irishman" who wanted Barbara "to be subservient, a typical Irish housewife." Certainly he didn't want Barbara to continue with her career. That was fine with her, for whatever ambitions she had were quickly running out of steam. She was in love with Downey, and wanted only to be a good wife and mother. In addition to being a rising star with a bright future ahead of him, he was Catholic, which made Barbara feel that her adolescent spiritual yearnings had been vindicated. She had survived the chaos of her family life and found the anchor she had always sought.

Later in 1929, she made another movie musical with Morton, *Mother's Boy,* for Pathé, now under Joe Kennedy's control. *Mother's Boy* was so bad that during the premiere Morton got up and walked out. Morton made two more forgettable pictures, and Barbara made one, in 1930, *Love Among the Millionaires,* an attempt to revive the sagging career of Clara Bow. Cast in a small part as a kind-hearted socialite, Barbara neither sang nor danced, and seemed more blasé than ever. Once filming was finished, she and Morton left Los Angeles for New York, where Morton opened his own nightclub, Delmonico's. But there was another reason Morton wanted to be in New York. He had felt for some time that his real future lay in radio, then in the midst of its glory years. Morton consulted with his friend Joe Kennedy, and later in 1930 his act was broadcast from Delmonico's over WABC, then the Columbia Broadcasting System's New York station. The response was tremendous, and soon he was being heard four times a week.

Most of Morton's family was still in Wallingford, Connecticut. He and Barbara bought a farm, some distance away, on the outskirts of Greenwich. It was a beautiful spot, and they both settled in happily. While Mabel reserved judgment on Morton, Richard seemed pleased with his daughter's match. He was occupied with the road company for *Jarnegan* during the early months of their marriage, and didn't actually meet his new son-in-law until October 1929, while Morton was appearing at the Palace Theater. Comedienne Beatrice Lillie, also appearing on the bill, called Richard up out of the audience for a very public introduction. After seeing the messy consequences of Constance and Joan marrying men from privileged backgrounds, Richard seemed to put some degree of trust in Barbara's choice of a husband. Morton was self-made, and Richard was probably alluding to him shortly thereafter when he told a journalist, "Here's what I ask 'em. How far could this one or that one . . . whoever the chap may be . . . get without money? And how far would he really want to get? That's ambition. If the girls can satisfy themselves that the lad who is hovering around could get somewhere without an inherited bank roll behind him . . . then I say go to it."

Barbara was delighted to leave show business behind, and the Downey family was delighted with Morton's choice of a wife. Edward Downey, Morton's youngest brother, remembered Barbara as "very pleasant, warm, and friendly." Those close to her observed that Barbara seemed finally to have found the happiness and contentment that had always eluded her. She had embarked on a performing career only out of necessity, and now she could put it behind her. She and Morton planned to have a large family, she told a reporter: "I'll not be satisfied until I have nine children."

Chapter Nine

1930–1931

While Constance and Joan flourished in Hollywood, Richard wandered around New York, complaining to anyone who would listen that Broadway was in its death throes. The Depression had unquestionably caused business to decline. A total of 239 productions in 1929–1930 fell to 187 the following season, and the numbers would keep dropping throughout the decade. Despite such crippling economic conditions, Broadway in the 1930s produced a wide range of remarkable work, proof that art can blossom even in the toughest of times. Unquestionably, the Depression had the effect of winnowing out struggling actors, those who were difficult to cast. With changing tastes and times, many aging character actors who had specialized in "well-bred" parts in costume dramas and drawing-room comedies found Broadway's atmosphere uncongenial and sped to Hollywood, where producers welcomed them with fat contracts for steady employment. No doubt Mabel, observing all this activity, was relieved that she had left the theater when she did. Both the Pinker-Morrison agency and the Pinker-Morrison marriage were thriving, and if her daughters insisted on making their livings as actresses, she was at least relieved that they were in Hollywood, where the money was.

Given the country's general financial condition, the years 1930–1931 were grim ones to be a struggling actor in New York. Yet author Eudora Welty, who spent that year in Manhattan attending Columbia University, recalled that the theater season was "like the year of a comet." That was the year of Noël Coward's sublime adult comedy *Private Lives,* and of Alfred Lunt and Lynn Fontanne in Maxwell Anderson's *Elizabeth the Queen,* Katharine Cornell in Rudolf Besier's *The Barretts of Wimpole Street,* and Nazimova and Alice Brady in O'Neill's *Mourning Becomes Electra.* The revolutionary spirit that had generated so much exciting stage work in the 1920s was still alive in the 1930s, and the first few years of the decade, despite a decrease in audiences and an increase in boarded-up theaters, offered a wealth of fine and important plays.

Driven partly by the growing popularity of socialism among New York's impoverished actors, writers, and artists, the 1930s saw the rise of a number of enterprising theatrical institutions. One of the most important was the Group Theater, which included Harold Clurman, Cheryl Crawford, and Lee Strasberg, all former members of the Theatre Guild, who felt that the Guild had sold out to commercial interests and abandoned its responsibilities to provide honest, provocative plays. It was the decade of the Federal Theatre Project, which grew out of the Works Progress Administration, aimed to replenish some of the jobs that had been wiped out by the Depression. The Project aimed to produce hard-hitting works free of commercial concerns, and for much of its short life it succeeded. Their efforts ranged from The Living Newspaper, in which some of the most pressing news stories of the day were given documentary-style treatment onstage, to an all-black *Macbeth* set in Haiti.

Perhaps the Broadway community was unwilling to forget the damage Richard had done to *They Knew What They Wanted* five years earlier, for he failed to land a job in any of the top plays of the 1930–1931 season. The best he could turn up was Lawton Campbell's *Solid South,* which toured the Midwest in the spring and summer of 1930 before opening in New York at the Lyceum Theatre in October. It was a comedy short on subtlety, but that didn't matter to Richard. The role of Major Follonsby, a bombastic, hot-tempered southerner whose family fortune was lost in the Civil War, was a ham actor's dream. And that was the problem. Only a few years earlier, Richard had been a model of the actor's actor, who nearly always forged a profound emotional connection with the part he was playing. But the heavy drinking and other excesses of his personal life had spilled over into his life onstage. He no longer cared so much about serving the play; chewing the scenery had become an end in itself.

The script of *Solid South* centered on the impoverished Major Follonsby's refusal to accept the changes that had overtaken the South since the end of the war. Even as his mansion crumbles around him, he upholds the old Confederate traditions, and desperately tries to foil a pair of Yankees intent on courting his widowed daughter-in-law and his young granddaughter. There was a good deal of Richard in Major Follonsby, who during the course of the play guzzles mint juleps, brandishes a pistol, and rails against everyone from Jews to Virginians. At one point, he learns that his Yankee enemies want to buy his mansion, tear it down, and build a factory in its place. "Progress. Bah!" bellows the Major. "It is nothing but pollution. As long as I live that place shall be dedicated to Beauty. No smokestack shall ever take the place of those stately columns. No merciless machinery shall ever defy the peace of my father's mansion. . . . We of the South will never surrender our glory and grandeur to you!"

The ingenue role of the Major's granddaughter, Bam, was played in the Broadway run by a young Bette Davis, then serving her acting apprenticeship on the New York stage. *Solid South* would be her final Broadway appearance before she departed for Hollywood and a contract with Universal Pictures.

Davis had signed on for *Solid South* with some trepidation. She had heard all the stories about Richard's wild temperament, and she wasn't disappointed when she met him at the theater ten days before the New York opening.

"So!" said Richard as he looked her over. "You're one of those actresses who think all they need are eyes to act. My daughters are the same."

Davis coolly replied that if she didn't please him she would be happy to leave immediately. Richard was delighted with this young ingenue's burst of spirit. "You'll do," he laughed.

Solid South opened on October 14, 1930, to mixed notices. Brooks Atkinson in the *New York Times* sneered that it possessed "enough mountbankery to make it palatable for unprincipled theatregoing." "It is amusing stuff, much of it," offered Burns Mantle in the *New York Daily News,* "but rather a wasted effort . . . so much that could be made truthful and revealing . . . is traded for laughs." Most of the critics' attitude toward Richard ranged from lenient to indulgent. "Mr. Bennett's blustering old fool may not be a faithful likeness of any living human, but it is consistently far-fetched and continuously good fun," wrote Mantle. "Mr. Bennett makes the Major a likable old duffer," admitted the *New Yorker,* "and the part gives him a chance to expand and boom and thunder in the old-style theatrical manner—which he loves." Others were not so kind. Stark Young in the *New Republic* spoke of "excessive actoralities," and Percy Hammond, now of the *New York Herald Tribune,* wrote, "I predict that ere his Lyceum engagement ends he will be tying tin cans to the tails of the critics and chasing them into their alley lairs . . . I believe his acting as Major Follonsby in *Solid South* is as shoddy an impersonation as a fine player could give." To Richard, these reviews were an insult, and he played out his frustrations onstage. Davis recalled that there was "a surprise and a tantrum every performance." One evening, faced with a particularly stony-faced crowd, Richard broke character, stormed down to the footlights, and said, "I guess I'll have to tell this audience a dirty story to get them to laugh." He also gave a few of his fiery curtain speeches, but the days when this could help him build a line at the box office were long gone. *Solid South* closed after thirty-one performances, and Richard took the play on tour while considering his next move.

Throughout 1929, the movie industry had hedged its bets regarding the arrival of sound. Although the major studios were rewiring their theaters, many films were prepared in both silent and talking versions, both to accommodate the theaters that had not yet been converted and as a precaution, in the event that the new technology turned out to be no more than a passing fad. But by 1930, the studios' dance was over—talkies were the future and silents already seemed part of a quaint and distant past.

The stakes were higher than ever now. Despite the Depression, people were desperate to see talking pictures, good, bad, or indifferent. In 1930, over $732 million was taken in at the box office; weekly attendance was around 90 million—up 65 million from 1920. In this climate, distribution had become an intensely complex and competitive racket, and the studios with solid theater chains—MGM, Paramount, Warners, Fox—left the others in the dust. Pathé, without a single theater to its name, was on shaky financial ground.

Pathé had entered the sound era short on female talent. Its most valuable properties were Ann Harding and Broadway star Ina Claire, who never took to films and would soon return to the stage. After reading Constance's notices for *This Thing Called Love,* Pathé was optimistic that they had gotten hold of an actress with box-office potential. Now, more than ever, the studio needed a hit, so it must have stung them when they loaned Constance out for two pictures that both turned out to be huge moneymakers. The first was *Son of the Gods,* at Warner Bros., opposite Barbara's old flame, Richard Barthelmess. It was a clunky story of a well-born young man who cannot get ahead in society because everyone thinks he has Chinese blood. Bad as it was, it grossed $1,416,000 worldwide.

The next film was more significant. Constance was sent over to Fox for *Common Clay.* In the beginning, no one had expected much of it. It was based on a play by Cleves Kinkead that had been a hit on Broadway for Jane Cowl back in 1915, but Fox shrewdly updated it so it might appeal to Depression audiences. Constance was cast as Ellen Neal, a fast-and-loose girl who makes her living as a hostess in a speakeasy. When the speakeasy is raided by the police and Ellen has to appear in court, she begins to rethink her future and takes what seems to be a respectable job, as a maid in the household of the Fullertons, one of New York's leading families. A maid's uniform does nothing to diminish Ellen's appeal for men, and soon enough she has to leave her job because the

Fullertons' good-looking son Hugh (Lew Ayres) has gotten her pregnant. But life for a single mother is almost insupportable, and Ellen seeks out the Fullertons' attorney, asking that Hugh marry her and give her baby his name. The horrified Fullertons refuse to have anything to do with her, so she hauls them into court. On the witness stand, her mother (played superbly by Beryl Mercer) blurts out the confession that Ellen is not really her daughter after all; she is the illegitimate child of an old friend and a socially prominent New York gentleman, and when the gentleman refused to marry Mrs. Neal's friend, she committed suicide and Mrs. Neal raised the baby as her own. Ellen's natural father is none other than the judge (Hale Hamilton) who is hearing the case. In a big, dramatic speech—the script's equivalent of an 11:00 number—Ellen tells the "respectable" judge and the Fullertons exactly what she thinks of them and people like them.

Despite its soap opera excesses, *Common Clay* had a tough modern streak that would make it the blueprint for a new screen genre, the "confession" picture. The label is lifted from the confession magazines so popular with women at the time—the "I Kept My Love-Child a Secret for Ten Years" brand of romance fiction. But it can also be seen to reflect the more literal, religious definition of the word: the admission of one's sins as a way of finding redemption. The deprivation that Americans had experienced even this early in the Depression made audiences—female audiences particularly—responsive to a movie heroine like Ellen Neal. For Ellen is a woman born without advantages, no money, education, or "respectable" background. She must get along as best she can, by working in a speakeasy, which only makes her a social outcast. And when she gives up the fancy gowns and fast-lane glamour of speakeasy life to work as the Fullertons' maid, she becomes an even worse kind of social outcast—an unwed mother. *Common Clay* takes great pains to point out the seemingly unbridgeable gap between the haves and have-nots, but in the end Ellen's own grit and integrity lead her to redemption—and a happy ending. After her outburst in the courtroom, Hugh Fullerton realizes that she is not the easy make that he originally took her for, but a woman of rare virtue, and he humbly asks her to marry him. Ellen, still deeply in love with him despite everything that has happened, accepts his proposal.

It's an ending that no doubt makes feminists squirm. A more sobering and satisfying conclusion might have been to show Ellen leaving the courtroom with her head held high, brimming with confidence and satisfaction for having exposed the Fullertons as the hypocrites that they are. But the ending that screenwriter Jules Furthman has provided is actually much less smug and more adult: Ellen accepts Hugh despite his shabby treatment of her; her lover is not the gallant and shining knight she once took him for, but she wants him anyway. Although Ellen is the prototype for the dozens of "confession" heroines that followed, she differs from them in one important respect. Despite her past as a "B" girl, she is pure of heart. She is not motivated by money, she simply wants to do the right thing for her baby.

The stars of the early talkies were either holdovers from the silent era, like Ronald Colman, Greta Garbo, and Joan Crawford, or émigrés from the theater, like George Arliss and Ruth Chatterton. But the success of *Common Clay* made Constance the first Hollywood-bred actress to become a major star in the sound era. With her husky speaking voice and elegant finishing-school speech, sound was ideal for her, and she for it.

Constance made two more pictures in 1930. The first was again on loan-out to Warner Bros.: *Three Faces East,* a spy drama that represents the early talkies at their sluggish worst. Like many films of the period, it is based on a dusty old play—the movies had no qualms about filming works that had long become dinosaurs in the theater. Constance's shapeless, overplayed performance was a step back for her; throughout the film, she shows none of the brittle self-possession that had made her work in *Common Clay* stand out. Much better was *Sin Takes a Holiday,* back at Pathé, a comedy about a marriage of convenience that blossoms into true love. Both *Three Faces East* and *Sin Takes a Holiday* were big, big hits.

By this time, Constance's old employer, MGM, had seen enough of her progress to decide that it wanted a piece of the action. In 1931, Louis B. Mayer borrowed Constance for *The Easiest Way.* Again it was based on a musty play—this one dated back to 1909, and had been something of a scandal at the time. In MGM's updating, the character Constance plays, Laura Murdock, is a kind of post-flapper coming face to face with the grim realities of the 1930s, a woman who craves luxury and isn't terribly concerned about how she gets it. When we first see her, she is a pretty but drab young girl who lives in a slum with her down-and-out family. Laura dreams of having beautiful clothes and a deluxe apartment, and finally decides to take matters into her own hands. She rises from department store clerk to fashion model, and eventually ends up being kept by Willard Brockton (Adolphe Menjou), a powerful advertising executive. Laura has made a devil's bargain: she has plenty of beautiful clothes and a posh Park Avenue residence, but she does not seem particularly happy and it is clear that she is denied any real sexual satisfaction. There are also family tensions. Her mother (Clara Blandick), horrified by how she has gotten her money, refuses to see her. And when Laura goes to visit her hardworking housewife sister Peg (Anita Page) and offers her a beautiful new dress, she is foiled by Peg's Babbity husband, Nick (Clark Gable), who tells her, "My wife don't need the cast-offs of a woman like you."

But soon Ellen is offered a chance for redemption in the form of Johnny Madison (Robert Montgomery), an ambitious young newspaper reporter. Laura and Johnny fall in love, and initially Johnny seems a cut above the men usually encountered in "confession" films. He knows all about Laura's past and doesn't care, even going so far as to admit that he's been pretty wild himself. Before he is called away on a story assignment, Laura accepts his proposal of marriage, and they promise to be true to each other during the months of their separation. Laura leaves Brockton, but Johnny's absence turns out to be longer than he'd anticipated, and Laura finds her promise hard to keep. Even after hocking some of the furs that Brockton gave her, she is unable to keep up the rent on her shabbily furnished room. After weeks have gone by with no word from Johnny, she assumes he has forgotten about her and returns to her life with Brockton. As it turns out, Johnny's cables simply didn't get delivered to the right place, and he unexpectedly returns to New York. They arrange to meet, although now Laura isn't at all sure that she deserves him. She is put straight by her good friend Effie (vividly played by Marjorie Rambeau, who had been a prominent stage star during Richard's heyday). Effie is also a kept woman, noticeably older and more beaten-up than Laura. Having been left high and dry because her married lover has fallen seriously ill and made no provision for her, Effie tells her friend to hang on to Johnny at any cost:

> EFFIE: If you lost out now, it won't be long till you're picking up men in speakeasies. You've got to grab your happiness now.
>
> LAURA (wearily): Oh, how can I?
>
> EFFIE: Why, Laura—a pretty girl like you is just prey for men. They cater to our vanity. They make us think they love us—well, they don't. They don't love anything but themselves and their own selfish pleasures.
>
> LAURA: But what can I do?
>
> EFFIE: Use your brain! Why, this life isn't a romance for girls like us. It's a game, with the men holding all the trumps. They like to look upon us as some animals they're proud to own.

Laura decides to come clean with Johnny and hope for the best. He is appalled, and walks out on her. Laura leaves Brockton. Now she is truly alone and destitute. At the end of the film, wandering through the snow on Christmas Eve, she finds her way to her sister's house. Through the window, Laura sees the fire roaring in the fireplace and the family trimming the tree—the life of respectability that has eluded her because she had the nerve to try to be mistress of her own fate.

The Easiest Way is in many ways a textbook example of the woman's soap opera of this period. As always, there is a sharp contrast between the two men in the heroine's life. There's the man who keeps the heroine—older, urbane, faintly unpleasant, and not at all virile—and the man whom she really loves—young, attractive, honest, hard-working, self-made. Like most of its companion films, *The Easiest Way* has more twists of fate than a Dreiser novel, notably the botched delivery of Johnny's cables. There's no illegitimate baby this time around, but there is another element that is much more interesting: a touch of hypocrisy in Laura's character, an indication that, unlike Ellen in *Common Clay,* she buys into the whole system. This comes out in a memorable scene between Laura and Effie. Laura has left Brockton and is struggling to make ends meet, while Effie is still riding high, courtesy of her married lover. Laura nervously asks her friend to loan her a hundred dollars, and gets an angry response:

> Effie: So that's it, huh? Well, if that ain't the nerve? Ain't we the little goody-goody? You know how I get my money—the same way that you got everything you ever had!
>
> Laura: But I didn't mean . . .
>
> Effie: No, but you're willing to accept my money to pay your debts, and all the time thinking that you're too good to do what I did to get it! You make me sick!

These excerpts from the script do much to explain the candle-in-the-wind nature of Laura and the many other movie heroines like her. Laura's position is too precarious for her ever to articulate a real point of view. The other characters are always explaining something to Laura, or imploring her, or reviling her. In her own way, she is as passive and helpless a heroine as someone out of a Samuel Richardson novel. Even at the beginning of the film, before she starts her climb up the ladder, she seems to have the feeling that it's all utterly hopeless.

Nevertheless, the strength and appeal of Constance's personality made Laura very real and sympathetic to 1931 audiences, and *The Easiest Way* was another hit, proving that *Common Clay* had not just been a fluke. The fallen woman was nothing new to the screen. The silent era had been riddled with women "in trouble," but the treatment of them had necessarily been more melodramatic, less "modern." Sound gave the fallen woman, literally, a voice. She could now express her longings and regrets in an urgent, personal way that the silents simply didn't allow for. In some ways, things hadn't changed so much. Like Lillian Gish's Anna Moore in D.W. Griffith's *Way Down East* (1920), Constance's Laura Murdock winds up wandering through the snow. But Anna is rescued by her true love. Laura's rescue is much less of a sure thing, although there is a faint hint at the end that her journalist boyfriend may forgive her—in time.

The Easiest Way, in particular, appealed to two opposite sides of the female moviegoer's nature. On one hand, there were probably few working-class American women in 1931 who couldn't identify with Laura Murdock's quest for a life of luxury. Constance's ravishing appearances in the film's René Hubert gowns provided justification enough for this dream. On the other hand, when Laura falls on hard times, they could feel that their own lives had been vindicated; they had the smug pleasure of seeing easy virtue go unrewarded. The idea that those who aspire to riches and luxury needed in some way to be punished is an abiding convention of women's fiction and women's films. It was in place long before Constance made *The Easiest Way* (one thinks of the novels of Fannie Hurst), and it was around decades later, when Jacqueline Susann used it as the foundation for her best-selling novels in the 1960s. Susann understood this female audience perhaps better than anyone else. "They want to press their noses against the windows of other people's houses," she said, "and get a look at the parties they'll never be invited to, the dresses they'll never get to wear. . . . But here's the catch. All the people they envy in my books, the ones who are glamorous, or beautiful, or rich . . . they have to suffer, see, because that way the people who read me can get off the subway and go home feeling better about their own crappy lives, and luckier than the people they've been reading about."

In the early 1930s, Pathé understood this, too, and while Constance was making *The Easiest Way* at MGM, her home studio was preparing two more scripts dealing with fallen women. By this time, in fact, Pathé was no longer Pathé. On January 29, 1931, the studio had been merged into RKO. The original plan was to keep RKO-Pathé as a separate imprint within RKO, and for a time Constance's films for the studio bore the banner, "An RKO-Pathé Picture"—the pre-title logo a crowing rooster perched on top of the globe. The crowing was premature. By the following year, RKO-Pathé had vanished, and the company was subsequently known as RKO-Radio.

The first script the studio had ready for Constance was *Born to Love,* which combined elements of *Common Clay* (unwed mother) and *The Easiest Way* (true love versus wealth and security). *Born to Love* opens in London during an air raid in World War I. Red Cross nurse Doris Kendall (Constance) meets Barry Craig (Joel McCrea), a flier on seven days' leave. They fall passionately in love, and he returns to the front with Doris's promise that she will marry him when the war is over. But after Doris receives a letter telling her that Barry has been killed in action, she receives a marriage proposal from the elegant Sir Wilfred Drake (Paul Cavanagh). Doris tells him she is carrying Barry's baby, but Sir Wilfred gallantly offers to marry her anyway and raise the child as his own—no one need know the truth. When Barry turns out not to be dead, Doris arranges a meeting with him, but is determined to do the honorable thing and stick by her child and the man who has given him a name. Sir Wilfred, however, suspects that she is still in love with Barry, and in one of the picture's big emotional scenes, he confronts her. Doris admits that he is right, that she loves Barry "with all my heart, with all my soul, with all my body!" to which Sir Wilfred responds in disgust, "With all . . . your . . . *body*!" He gives Doris her freedom, but at a high price: she must surrender their child to him. The justice awards Sir Wilfred custody ("In my experience, the English are wiser if they marry women who are, well . . . English") and Barry returns to America. Doris rents a cheap, squalid room and searches for work. One day, she goes to Sir Wilfred to visit their son. Sir Wilfred is strangely evasive. Doris rushes upstairs to the child's room, carrying a gift of a stuffed animal. We see the outline of her figure and the shadow of the crib. She leans over the crib and screams. The child is dead.

Born to Love transmits a couple of intriguing messages. One is that true love, genuine passion, can never be suppressed in an attempt to gain security. But the film also seems to imply that Doris might have been better off as a single mother, raising the baby on her own; the child's death seems to be her punishment for marrying a man she does not love. The doors are double-locked behind these women: sexual freedom brings unwanted pregnancy and social censure, but sexual hypocrisy, a denial of the self, leads to other kinds of misery.

Born to Love makes few demands on Constance as an actress, but as always, she is glamorous and confident, and her personal sheen holds the film together. Joel McCrea had been in films only for a couple of years and hadn't yet hit his stride; his line readings are often stiff and awkward, especially when he is trying to convey burning passion. *Born to Love* was his first lead, and it launched him on the path to an important starring career. He owed it all to Constance. Along with Gilbert Roland and Ray Milland, McCrea had tested for the part of Barry Craig, and assumed his chances of getting it were minimal. But one evening, at a house party at William Randolph Hearst's ranch in San Simeon, Constance ran all of the leading-man tests for *Born to Love.* McCrea, also Hearst's guest for the weekend, was certain that Gilbert Roland would be selected, and was startled the next morning to learn that Constance had chosen him over the others. It's easy to see why McCrea appealed to Constance: he was stunningly handsome, 6'2" and broad-shouldered, with an easygoing, masculine charm and a warm, appealing sense of humor. All of the Bennett sisters had a tendency to go after the men they were attracted to, and Constance, always the most sexually aggressive of the three, lost no time closing in on McCrea. Henri, after all, was in Europe occupied with Pathé business. She could hardly be expected to sit at home alone.

Soon, the Hollywood press was running frequent column items on Constance's romance with McCrea. "She was supposed to be a bitch," McCrea remembered. "She was supposed to be tough on the set. She was tough on deals because she was a shrewd businesswoman. . . . But she was just doggone nice to me."

Born to Love was a big grosser for RKO-Pathé—$649,000 in all—and Constance and McCrea were reteamed immediately for *The Common Law.* This time around, Constance was cast as Valerie West, a beautiful young girl on the loose in Paris. Valerie finds work as a model for John Neville Jr. (McCrea), an American painter from a socially prominent family who has set himself up in a Left Bank studio. It's love from the start, pre-Production Code style: when Valerie poses nude for him, John tells her, "You know, you should never wear clothes." But when John finds out that Valerie has a past as a kept woman, he denounces her: "And I was going to ask you to be my wife . . . (with disgust) . . . *my wife*!" Later, they are reunited, but John still considers Valerie too tainted to qualify as wife material. Soon John is summoned home by his overbearing socialite sister (Hedda Hopper) on the pretext that their father is ill. Valerie accompanies him, but John makes her tell his family that she arrived on another ship, which she reluctantly does. John's sister suspects the truth, however, and launches a campaign to humiliate Valerie into returning to Paris alone. Eventually, John realizes that the only way to make life equitable for Valerie is to do the right thing and marry her.

On the surface, *The Common Law* is just another melodramatic women's film of the period, yet it also serves as a kind of road map to the sexual hypocrisies that prevailed at the time. Valerie's body is her principal means of survival—both when she is kept by her wealthy lover and when she gets the job posing in the nude for John. But either way, Valerie is the loser. John feels compelled to punish her by rejecting her when he finds out about her past. Yet when they are reunited, the punishment doesn't stop: John denies her a legal marriage as a way of perpetually reminding her what a bad girl she's been, and how she doesn't really deserve him.

The sexual charge between Constance and McCrea was much stronger than it had been in *Born to Love,* and was no doubt one of the things that helped make *The Common Law* one of RKO's biggest hits of the year. All told, it grossed an impressive $713,000, bringing in a tidy profit of $150,000. The box-office performance of *Sin Takes a Holiday, Born to Love,* and *The Common Law* earned Constance RKO's gratitude, especially since the company was facing such monumental financial struggles. By this time, full-length talkies had been in existence for four years, and their novelty was coming to an end. As a unit that had been formed only earlier that year, RKO-Pathé might have had the excuse of finding its sea legs, but the studio as a whole was in no better shape. For some time, rumors had circulated that both William LeBaron and Charles R. Rogers, production chiefs of RKO and RKO-Pathé respectively, would soon be replaced. In order to survive competition from the other major studios, all of which had been around longer, RKO was going to have to have both hits and quality productions. At the moment, it had neither.

With the studio predicting that losses for 1931 might climb as high as $5 million, Constance had already perceived that it might become increasingly difficult to have her way about a number of things. The success of her films had made her the queen of RKO, and as royalty, she saw no reason why she should be made to suffer because of the studio's bad management. In 1929, she had signed a contract with Pathé running until 1934; following the success of *Sin Takes a Holiday,* it had been renegotiated in the fall of 1930. After May 1931, her salary was to rise from $2,750 to $5,000 weekly, going up in small annual increments until it sealed off at $7,000 a week in 1934, when the contract was due to expire. She was also guaranteed a ten-week vacation. But after *Born to Love* and *The Common Law* had taken off at the box office, Constance considered her RKO salary a pittance. Since she was obviously so important to the studio, she reasoned that she deserved a much bigger cut.

In the meantime, she had retained as her agent Myron Selznick, the older son of Lewis Selznick, who had started her on her movie career back in the early 1920s. After failing to make his mark as an independent producer, Myron had become an agent in 1928, and was already considered the most aggressive and hard-nosed flesh peddler in the business—and the one who produced the best financial results. In tandem with Myron, Constance proceeded to work out a deal with Warner Bros. that marked the birth of her reputation as Hollywood's most hard-headed businesswoman.

Warner Bros. was in a tight spot: its fast growth in the late 1920s had been undercut by the Depression, and its earnings had declined from a 1928–1929 high of $973,000 to $435,000 in 1931. The studio was short on top-grossing stars, and Darryl F. Zanuck, Warners' vice president in charge of production, reasoned that borrowing Constance for a couple of modestly budgeted films could generate big profits.

In January 1931, Constance signed an agreement with Warner Bros. calling for her to star in two films over a ten-week period at a salary of $30,000 a week. It was a staggering figure—even during the most orgiastic days of the silent era, a popular star like Tom Mix had pulled down no more than $20,000 a week. But for a star to command such an amount in the midst of the Depression was unheard of.

Or should have been, perhaps. Once the Warners contract was signed, the Hollywood trade papers blasted headlines about the $30,000-a-week star. Although she probably didn't care one way or the other, it would have been naive of Constance to assume that many in the competitive movie industry would not resent her for bringing off such a spectacular financial coup. Immediately rumors began circulating that she had strong-armed Warners into paying both Myron Selznick's commission and her personal income tax on the contracted amount.

Popular as she was with audiences, many of the actors and crew members who had worked with her felt differently. Reports had begun to filter out of RKO that her mercurial demands regarding sets, costumes, lighting, and script changes were causing costly delays. She was not very cooperative regarding interviews—in particular, fan magazine writers in the know were annoyed by her refusal to discuss her son, or permit him to be photographed—and several leading columnists had begun to carp. "That the business of suffering and persecution should be undertaken by Constance Bennett has its ironic side," wrote Elinor Hughes in the *Boston*

Herald. "Aside from the fact that much of the unhappiness experienced by the unfortunate ladies portrayed by Constance is needless and only piled on for purposes of effect, the spectator finds it very difficult at times to forget how eminently capable is this young lady of looking after her own interests. When she wanders disconsolately into a pawnbroker's shop or looks wistfully at a group around a Christmas tree, one thinks of the hard bargains she has driven with the studios . . . and of the arrogance she displays toward the players with whom she works."

Once Constance's deal with Warners was made public, Pathé sprang into action. Vice Pres. Lewis Innerarity fired off letters to both Constance and the Warners studio informing them that Constance's contract was to make pictures for Pathé and no other studio. Only days later, however, Pathé was swallowed up by RKO, and the opposition to Constance's on-the-side dealings with Warners appears to have run out of steam. It is unlikely that in any event Pathé would have won: the studio's contract with Constance allowed for ten weeks' vacation period, during which time she would be taken off salary; it did not stipulate that she was not allowed to make films for any other company during this time. What Constance had done was deceptively simple as well as legally binding: she would work, for $30,000 a week, during her vacation time.

The first film under the Warners deal was *Bought!,* and it demonstrated that Darryl F. Zanuck, Warners' production chief, had closely observed the successful formula of Constance's RKO-Pathé films. In *Bought!,* she was again a girl of the slums, Stephany Dale, who is sick of watching what a life of poverty has done to her hard-working seamstress mother. Stephany is shocked when her mother informs her that she is illegitimate, that Stephany's father was "common," leading her to run out on him. When her mother dies suddenly, Stephany is determined to make something of herself. She takes a job modeling for a wholesaler (a fellow model describes her ambition as "Park Avenue or nothing"), she reads Aldous Huxley and Michael Arlen novels to improve her mind, and fabricates a tony background for herself. She falls for an aspiring writer (Ben Lyon) but, with her eye still on Park Avenue, allows herself to be seduced in the moonlight by a rich boy (Ray Milland), who rejects her when he discovers her background. In what by now had become an obligatory scene in a Constance Bennett picture, she confesses to the writer that she is no longer a virgin, causing him to denounce her as "a mass of deception" and walk out, only to return to her later. (Constance's films would have us believe that no man in 1930s America was able to conceive of marrying a woman who wasn't a virgin.)

For Constance, *Bought!* was memorable for a reason other than her weekly paycheck: Richard Bennett was cast in the film as David Meyer, the elderly man who turns out to be her father. Fed up with the lack of interesting roles offered him on Broadway, and running desperately short on cash—Aimee Raisch Hastings had turned out to be not only quarrelsome but expensive to support—he had come out to Hollywood early in 1931. So far the move had been profitable, as he had found work in three films: *Five and Ten* for MGM, *Arrowsmith* for Samuel Goldwyn, and *Bought!* He came off best in *Arrowsmith,* Sinclair Lewis's story of a brilliant doctor's lifelong struggle to live by a strong code of ethics. Ronald Colman and Helen Hayes headed the cast, and it was respectfully reviewed, not an enormous popular success but one of the big prestige pictures of the year. Richard's performance as the crusading Swedish doctor who encourages Colman to follow his principles was called "sterling" by the *Motion Picture Herald.*

The money was welcome, but he was also, in proper parental fashion, delighted with Constance's success. Perhaps her pictures weren't much, but the women of America were flocking to see them. Greta Garbo's talkie debut in *Anna Christie* (1930) had made her a critic's pet, Joan Crawford was slightly higher in the box-office polls, and fat, lumpy Marie Dressler held a stronger place in the audience's hearts—but for most women moviegoers, it was Constance who epitomized Hollywood glamour and sophistication. In three short years, she had become one of the most powerful women in the industry, and she did it on the strength of her own brains and wit, her guile and stubbornness.

Constance was burning bright while Richard had begun a slow

fade. The irony of his situation could hardly have escaped him: the idealistic rebel who had struggled to push the theater in new directions having now accepted the role of character-actor-for-hire. Whatever he said in interviews at the time, he still regarded Hollywood as the enemy, and now he was financially dependent on the industry that had posed such a threat to his beloved Broadway. But alcohol and the advancing years had done their worst, and he was simply too tired to pass up the economic rewards offered by film. Still smarting from the past six seesaw years in New York, Richard must at least have been pleased that Hollywood enabled Constance to restore some of the family luster.

By the fall of 1931, she also decided to anchor her tumultuous private life. Her affair with Joel McCrea had continued since the filming of *Born to Love,* and although there was a tremendous sexual attraction between them, even Constance had to admit that they were far from an ideal match, as he was a man of simple tastes and background who had a more traditional view of marriage. McCrea later recalled that she half-heartedly suggested marriage, but that he hadn't thought it was a good idea, and anyway, he didn't think she was especially serious. They parted friends, and when Henri de la Falaise returned to Hollywood from one of his extensive European jaunts for the studio, he joined Constance at her rented house at 903 North Roxbury Drive in Beverly Hills.

It seems unlikely that Henri could have been fooled into thinking that Constance had been faithful to him during his absence, but their affection was genuine and sincere. On November 22, 1931, in a private ceremony held at the Beverly Hills home of director George Fitzmaurice, Constance and Falaise were married. Joan was her matron of honor, and Richard, who approved of Constance's third husband far more than he had the previous two, gave the bride away. Constance had a handsome and dignified new husband, and although his title had little currency, she reveled in being described in the newspapers as the new Marquise de la Falaise de la Coudraye. She also delighted in having succeeded Gloria Swanson, both at the box office and in bed. (Joan tactfully remembered that the rivalry between them was "an authentic one, not something contrived by the press.")

Constance and Falaise traveled by train to New York for a lengthy honeymoon. At several stops, enormous crowds gathered, eager for a glimpse of Hollywood's highest-paid actress. They were disappointed. Throughout her career, Constance did her best to dodge fans, reporters, and photographers, a practice which had already earned her a reputation as one of the most high-handed of stars. Joan Crawford might claim that she slavishly answered every fan letter because she owed her success to the ticket-buying public, but Constance felt she owed her own success to no one. Growing up as the daughter of Richard Bennett might have been an advantage, but she and she alone was responsible for it. Her belief in herself appeared justified, and she seemed to know exactly what she wanted, which was, she told a reporter, "to earn a million dollars by my own efforts. I want to be rich not for the luxury that wealth brings but for the independence it affords. I want to live in France. I have no desire to grow old acting in motion pictures. I look on my profession as a business and I give it my best efforts, but I don't want to give it my entire life."

Constance's dazzling success in the early 1930s made it impossible for the time being for Joan to be considered as anything other than the younger sister of a great movie star. Those who worked with her or met her socially often preferred Joan to Constance, who could be haughty and aggressive. Louise Brooks recalled, "Among the Hollywood detestables, even I was no match for Constance, who could sit across from me at the dinner table at Marion Davies's beach house and never acknowledge my existence with so much as an icy nod." Joan was much more pleasant—although she was undeniably reserved. George Cukor, one of the Broadway stage directors who had traveled to Hollywood with the coming of sound, saw Joan frequently during her early years in the movie industry, and found her somewhat difficult to get to know. To Cukor, there was something mildly disconcerting about her. She could seem slightly aloof, even tough. (Cukor had similar reactions to both Constance and Barbara.)

Joan was a far cry from the typically gregarious, eager-to-please Hollywood ingenue. She never sought to be the center of attention, as Constance did. She was quiet and polite, but the element of reserve that Cukor noted offended some people. Perhaps her eyesight was a factor—although she wore glasses in the privacy of her home, she never wore them in public because they were considered unglamorous. She had a peculiar habit of shaking her head slightly, as if she were trying to clear up her vision. But even if Joan struck some people as distant, she was happy in Hollywood from the beginning. She had rented an apartment at the Chateau de Fleur, and lost no time in turning it into a pleasantly comfortable home for herself and Adrienne (now renamed Diana, and known to family and friends by the nickname "Ditty"). She loved the climate, the endless variety of flowers in full bloom, the sweet, clean air decades before Los Angeles was blighted by smog. Her movie salary, although paltry compared with Constance's earnings, permitted her to maintain a small household staff and invest in a wardrobe befitting a rising Hollywood actress. Most of all, she enjoyed the social life that the movie industry offered, and like Constance, she was invited everywhere. One of the people who helped introduce her to Hollywood's social set was her *Bulldog Drummond* costar, Lilyan Tashman, one of the movie industry's leading hostesses—a woman who once, just before giving a dinner party, had her dining room repainted dark blue because the original color clashed with her gold hair. Tashman was a powerful friend to have in Hollywood, and she had immediately taken a liking to Joan, whom she nicknamed "Snoopy" because of her terrible myopia—during filming, she couldn't see a prop until she was nearly on top of it.

Since acting was still principally a means of supporting herself and Diana, Joan took the roles that were offered her. Unlike Constance, she did not aggressively pursue better and better deals, and consequently, her career rose at a much slower rate. Throughout 1930, she was assigned standard leading-lady parts in a number of inconsequential films, among them a musical, *Puttin' on the Ritz,* starring Harry Richman as a song-and-dance man who attempts to crash society. The movie musical was still young enough not to have set a rigorous standard for itself, and became a vehicle for all kinds of stars, including Joan Crawford, Janet Gaynor, and Clara Bow, regardless of their singing and dancing ability. *Puttin' on the Ritz* gave Joan her turn. In a toneless alto, she sang the now-forgotten Irving Berlin song "With You," a performance painful enough to ensure that she would not be flooded with offers for more musicals.

Later in 1930, she received a much more appropriate assignment, a leading role in Warner Bros.' *Moby Dick,* starring John Barrymore. Barrymore had already filmed the Herman Melville novel four years earlier as *The Sea Beast,* opposite his future wife, Dolores Costello, and it had given him one of the big successes of his rather patchy movie career. In both versions, the introduction of a love interest as the motivating force behind Captain Ahab's sea excursions was pure Hollywood. Since Barrymore's passion for Costello had ignited the screen in *The Sea Beast,* Joan had a hard act to follow, and she was doomed to fail. As the girl, Faith, she has charm and spirit, but there is little chemistry between her and Barrymore, and since the picture is weighted more toward romance than action, it falls flat. Because she knew all too well of Barrymore's alcoholism—years earlier, Richard had been one of his steady drinking companions—Joan was apprehensive about starting *Moby Dick*. Her fears were unwarranted. Dolores Costello was pregnant, and Barrymore was sober and serene throughout the filming. If the final result was a disappointment to those involved in it, there was consolation in that it turned out to be one of Warners' big films of the year, grossing $789,000.

Although she had no trouble finding jobs as a freelance actress, Joan decided that it would be to her benefit to sign a long-term contract with a major studio. The advantages were obvious—with a weekly paycheck, regardless of whether she worked in a movie or not, she wouldn't have to worry about balancing the fat with the lean. Also, a studio would have a vested interest in her and would work to build her career by developing appropriate vehicles for her—or so she thought. And so, in mid-1930, she signed with Fox Films.

The company had been founded by William Fox, one of the archetypal self-made movie moguls who had survived a squalid childhood on New York's Lower East Side to become a successful player in the movie distribution racket early in the century. By the 1920s, he was head of one of Hollywood's most powerful studios, but by the early 1930s Fox Films' best days seemed to be behind it. It had several important stars under contract, namely Janet Gaynor, Charles Farrell, and Will Rogers, but apart from a few isolated hits, Fox had fallen into the habit of cranking out mostly unmemorable films.

The Fox contract had been partially engineered by John Considine Jr., one of the producers who had come backstage during *Jarnegan* to discuss *Bulldog Drummond* with her. Considine's father had headed one of the nation's leading theater chains, the Sullivan and Considine Circuit, and after getting his start in that business, John Jr. had gone on to become a general manager at United Artists, then an associate producer at Fox. Sometime after she arrived in Hollywood, Joan began seeing Considine regularly—or as regularly as circumstances allowed. Considine was handsome and very masculine, with a slightly wild streak—at the same time he was dating Joan, Considine had been carrying on a longtime romance with Carmen Pantages, the daughter of Alexander Pantages, owner of the famous chain of movie theaters. Early in 1930, they had broken off their nearly year-long engagement, and when Joan began seeing him, he assured her that he was a free man.

Although never given to emotional extremes—she left that to the others in her family—she suddenly found herself in the midst of heated, passionate arguments with John. Usually, the topic was his sporadic relationship with Carmen Pantages. But Joan found that the more elusive Considine was, the more possessive she became. With a determination that seemed to rival Constance's, she set her mind on getting him—and keeping him.

Chapter Ten

1931–1932

Joan's years as a contract actress with Fox Films were busy and prolific. She worked steadily, both for the studio and on loan-out, but it is doubtful whether any young actress was ever stuck with such a miserable run of films. In the next two years, she would complete ten pictures, nearly all of them worthless. Fox tried her out as everything from an accused murderess (*The Trial of Vivienne Ware,* 1932) to a backwoods tomboy named Salomy Jane in *Wild Girl* (1932). Unfortunately, it cannot be said that Joan rose above her material. In most of these films, her line readings are wooden and she seems physically inert, her hands forever clasped in front of her. There are two exceptions, and not coincidentally, her costar in both films is Spencer Tracy.

She Wanted a Millionaire began shooting in the summer of 1931. It was an inconsequential melodrama that cast Joan as an ambitious girl from a small town in Missouri who dreams of landing a rich husband. Tracy played the good-natured train conductor who is sweet on her. Although Tracy had been doing his apprenticeship on the New York stage when Joan was appearing in *Jarnegan,* she had never met him until *She Wanted a Millionaire* began production. They liked each other immediately. She loved Tracy's teasing wit and thought it was funny that this actor, who usually played blue-collar types, should be so particular about the way he dressed. Each morning, he arrived at the studio impeccably turned out in elegantly tailored suits. Joan also found Tracy's approach to acting mesmerizing. Everything he did seemed natural and simple, he could strike just the right emotional chord without straining. After two years of playing scenes with some of Hollywood's typically lacquered leading men, Joan found Tracy's style refreshing, and she herself began to give a more relaxed performance.

Shooting on *She Wanted a Millionaire* proceeded uneventfully until July 28, when the company was on location in the Stone Canyon section of Bel Air, then open country. Joan was riding a horse named Gilda Grey up the bridle path to the location site. The animal was in an agitated state, and when a camera car unexpectedly came speeding down the hill, Gilda Grey panicked and bucked, and Joan was hurled through the air, crashing into a tree. She was taken by ambulance to Cedars of Lebanon Hospital, where it was revealed that she had a broken hip and three broken lumbar vertebrae. The following morning, an operation was performed by Dr. Ellis Jones, one of Los Angeles's leading orthopedic surgeons. Joan was expected to make a complete recovery, but she would not be able to return to work for four months at least. With only eight days left to film, production on *She Wanted a Millionaire* was suspended.

The family rallied immediately. Richard made repeated visits to Cedars of Lebanon, and Mabel and Barbara flew to Los Angeles from New York to be at her side. For about nine weeks, Joan remained in a spica plaster body cast, fortified with a wooden frame that looked, one reporter noted, like the stocks that Puritans built. A horizontal rod was placed between her legs to help speed the knitting of bones. Every attempt was made to make her feel at home. The hospital room was decorated in peach and green, two of her favorite colors, and Fox's Winfield Sheehan arranged to have a portable sound device and a projector installed in her room, so she could screen movies. (One of them was *Bought!,* which Richard watched with her.) She kept a diary, answered fan letters, and gave Morton Downey a plug by telling the press that she listened to him sing on the radio every day. Her recovery also permitted her to reflect on the situation with John Considine. Mabel didn't like what she had heard about the relationship, and she took advantage of

Joan's weakened condition to counsel her that a second bad marriage was the last thing she needed. Considine sent flowers and telegrams week after week, but Joan, who had heard from Marge Kelley and other friends that he and Carmen Pantages were still an item, thought it best for the time being to keep him at bay.

By mid-September, she had recovered sufficiently to attend the Pacific Southwest Annual Tennis Tournament in Los Angeles in a wheelchair. A few days later, Cedars of Lebanon finally released her. She checked into the Town House, an apartment hotel on Wilshire Boulevard, which had been outfitted with a hospital bed. Mabel stayed with her for a time, making sure that John Considine's frantic telephone calls were refused by the hotel switchboard. By early October, Joan was able to maneuver around her apartment on crutches. She had spent so much time in the body cast that essentially she had to learn to walk all over again.

During her hospital stay, Joan had received a string of get-well letters from Gene Markey, a screenwriter she remembered meeting earlier at a dinner party at Constance's home. The witty and fanciful tone of the letters delighted her, and later in the fall, once she was up to receiving visitors, Gene began to drop by the Town House frequently. After the chaos of her relationships with Jack Fox and John Considine, both Mabel and Richard were delighted to see their youngest daughter keeping company with Gene.

Born in Jackson, Michigan, Gene Markey graduated from Dartmouth in 1918. His skill at drawing led him to enter the Art Institute of Chicago, where he claimed that he "studied painting and learned nothing." After that, he embarked on a writing career. His novels, including *The Dark Island* and *The Road to Rouen,* may not have added much to contemporary literature—they were marked by a fey and precious quality—but one of them, *Stepping Out,* was sold to the movies and filmed as *Syncopation,* which served as Barbara's screen debut. Gene himself got to Hollywood in the late 1920s and quickly racked up several screenwriting credits, including *As You Desire Me* (1932), with Greta Garbo. He also became a popular extra man in Hollywood society, where his polished charm and wit graced many a dinner table. Although not extraordinarily handsome, he had the sort of suave, yacht club looks that passed for it in the 1930s. He was kind and thoughtful and flattered Joan with attention. His was not a towering intellect—he was a bit too entranced with Hollywood social life and had a facile, let-me-get-out-of-these-wet-things-and-into-a-dry-martini streak. But after her erratic, year-long relationship with Considine, Gene seemed a good bet. Perhaps she wasn't madly in love with him, as she had been with Fox and Considine, but he appealed to her need for stability.

Best of all, he and three-year-old Diana hit it off immediately. Once Joan was reasonably ambulatory, her doctor suggested a recuperative cruise through the Panama Canal. While she was away, in October and early November 1931, Gene looked in on Diana on a daily basis. He had a remarkable ability to enter into the world of a child, and he spent hours with the girl, creating a fairytale world just for the two of them. "He was my playmate," remembered Diana Anderson. "We would spend hours pretending to be Mr. and Mrs. Grasshopper. He was very kind and very sweet." Joan returned from her cruise in mid-November, and completed her work in *She Wanted a Millionaire*. Just before Christmas, it was announced in the press that she and Gene were engaged.

On March 12, 1932, Joan married Gene Markey at a small private ceremony at the Town House. The hotel's ballroom was decorated with peach blossoms and gardenias, and Joan wore a white turban, a hip-length jacket edged with white fox fur, and a blouse of Alençon lace. Gene's good friend Alan Clayton was best man, and Constance was the matron of honor. She was the only family member in attendance, as Richard was appearing in Santa Barbara in *Cyrano de Bergerac*. Joan was given away by C. Gardner Sullivan, a close friend and talented screenwriter. Mabel was also absent, since her mother, Rose Wood, had died at her home in Tenafly, New Jersey, only three days earlier. Guests included Henri de la Falaise, Marion Davies and William Randolph Hearst, Mr. and Mrs. Neil McCarthy, Mr. and Mrs. Reginald Denny, and Sally Eilers and her husband, cowboy actor Hoot Gibson. The couple immediately left for a honeymoon in northern California.

Upon her return, Joan had to face the fact that her association with Fox was getting her nowhere fast. Most of her films embarrassed her, particularly when she compared them with Constance's huge popular successes and Richard's stunning achievements in the theater. Years later, when asked how she felt she had stacked up to Constance, Joan replied quietly, "Well, I thought she was much better than I was." After three years in Hollywood, she was once again questioning whether or not she had any real talent, whether she might be tarnishing the Bennett name. And suddenly she was cast in her first good movie role.

Spencer Tracy had been just as unhappy as Joan with his Fox assignments. Frequently, they would get together at the Brown Derby to discuss the lack of good material. Their mutual dissatisfaction drew them closer together, and when Tracy happened on a script entitled *Pier 13,* he thought it might be an answer to their problems. It was a sharp comedy about the bumpy romance between a waterfront cop and a tough-talking, gum-chewing restaurant cashier. Fox had planned it as a vehicle for Sally Eilers and James Dunn, but once Tracy got hold of the script, he persuaded the studio to reassign it to Joan and himself.

The filming of *Pier 13,* which was soon retitled *Me and My Gal,* was pure pleasure for Joan. She was fascinated by Tracy's disdain for rehearsal. He always came to the set with his lines letter-perfect and saw no real reason to rehearse, fearing it would rob his performance of spontaneity. If he had to endure anything more than a basic rehearsal for the cameraman's benefit, he would complain, "Bore, bore, bore." Under Raoul Walsh's direction, both stars gave two of their most charming early performances. Again, Joan responded to Tracy's style, so natural that it almost resembled improvisation, and her portrayal of Helen, the wisecracking tough girl, surprised everyone who had pigeonholed her as a poker-faced leading lady. Tracy's confidence in *Me and My Gal* was vindicated by the reviews. The *Motion Picture Herald* thought Joan "a sheer delight," and the *New York Herald-Tribune* judged that "[She] has seldom been better than she is here."

Me and My Gal marked the beginning of a distinct pattern

that would run throughout Joan's career. Given a good director, such as Raoul Walsh, she responded with a fine performance. But if she was stuck with an indifferent script and a director who was no more than a traffic cop, her performance could be clumsy and inert. She never took over a movie; she lacked the natural magnetism and spark that allowed Constance to dominate her pictures. This malleable quality would work in Joan's favor years later, when some of Hollywood's most celebrated European directors would take her in hand, shaping performances that ideally suited their films. But for much of the 1930s, Joan's lack of assertiveness meant that she was stuck playing bland ingenue parts.

The success of *Me and My Gal* had come too late to help her at Fox. The studio was no longer interested in building her into a major star, and after they threw her into a minor film with James Dunn, *Arizona to Broadway* (1933), she and the studio parted company. Fox was in deep financial trouble by this time, and with good reason. For the past two years, MGM, Paramount, Warners, and RKO had left the studio in the dust when it came to developing stars and purchasing top properties. Executives at Fox had hoped that Joan might have the makings of a major box-office personality; now, they felt that they had given her more than enough chances and should cut their losses. Counting United Artists, two major studios had dropped her. Still, Joan didn't mind leaving Fox. She had been unhappy with them ever since their refusal to loan her to RKO to play John Barrymore's daughter in *A Bill of Divorcement,* which went to Katharine Hepburn. After losing out on such a coveted part, Joan lost all confidence that Fox would do anything to help her, and she decided to try her luck once more as a freelance actress.

Joan's future looked shaky, and she couldn't help comparing herself to Constance, who was still riding high as 1932 began. The "confession" films Constance had turned out for the past two years had become such big business that other studios were preparing variations on them. In Columbia's *Ten Cents a Dance* (1931), Barbara Stanwyck played a world-weary dance hall girl who pulls a reverse of the usual pattern in Constance's movies: she spurns the kindly rich man who really loves her for a man of her own station, who turns out to be a bum. At MGM, Joan Crawford had a big hit in *Possessed* (1931), playing a factory girl who becomes an "investment" for magnate Clark Gable, only to be considered a liability when he decides to run for governor. Constance's heroines tended to be more candid and less apologetic about their lowly origins than Crawford's; in *Possessed,* Crawford admits that after all the fancy perfume and elegant jewelry that Gable had thrown at her, she's still "a factory girl, smelling of sweat and glue. Common—that's what I am—common! And I like it!"

With the market so glutted, Constance was concerned that the "confession" formula might wear thin, and was delighted when her next film was a decided change of pace. *Lady with a Past* was a comedy, Constance's first since *This Thing Called Love* three years before. Its chief strength was a wry script by Horace Jackson, about a klutzy rich girl, Venice Muir (Constance) who has no success with men. She doesn't fit in at all in New York, and is forever talking to herself about her miserable predicament. "I talk so much to myself," she observes, "that I'm all worn out when I meet people." She decides that her life is too free of scandal for her to be of interest to anyone, so she hires a friend (Ben Lyon) to be "a kind of gigolo." Together they go to Paris, where he introduces her to all kinds of men and she quickly becomes a popular *femme du monde.*

Lady with a Past had more bite and wit than most of Constance's assignments, and she responded with a subtle comic performance. Once again, she was exquisitely gowned and photographed, cementing her image as the screen's most sophisticated actress. But there was something else this time around. In *Lady with a Past,* she has a special glow. In her past films, she had exhibited a kind of toughness that made her seem a somewhat synthetic personality—but in *Lady with a Past,* she is relaxed and luminous, as if the opportunity to play the bungling Venice, forever unsure of herself, had released a certain warmth that she had never before fully revealed.

The reviews were good—the *New York Times* judged the film

"bright and entertaining" and Constance's work in it "excellent"—but in 1932 business at the box office was continuing to fall off. *Lady with a Past* drew well—but not well enough to cover its hefty $541,000 production cost. All told, it lost $141,000, which came as a sharp blow after so many successive hits. The high production cost, it would seem, was largely attributable to Constance. Again, there were rumors of delays and overruns caused by her capricious demands. She was particularly exacting about lighting and camera angles and sometimes demanded that a key crew member be replaced. Such behavior was still possible in Hollywood before the technicians' unions emerged as a collective power. If the columnists insisted on calling her Hollywood's highest-paid actress, Constance intended to use every bit of the authority her position granted her. Early on in her film career, RKO's new star Katharine Hepburn was upbraided for her arrogant behavior by costume designer Walter Plunkett. "From the way you are starting," said Plunkett, "you'll soon be a worse bitch than Constance Bennett."

Constance continued to regard the movie industry with barely concealed contempt. In more than one interview, she observed that she found Hollywood painful even in small doses. She was routinely uncooperative with the press, and they were particularly piqued when she barred nearly all photographers from her wedding to Henri Falaise. She seemed not to grasp the idea that if she snubbed them, they might not support her when her career inevitably ran out of steam.

One thing that the press was extremely curious about was the presence of her son. After more than two years of keeping him under her roof, she refrained from mentioning him in interviews, and many did not even know that his name was Peter Plant. But several of Hollywood's more resourceful reporters were aware of his existence, and speculated whether his father was Philip Plant, Henri de la Falaise—or someone else entirely.

To several of the people closest to her, Constance maintained that Peter was Philip's son. To others, she claimed that he was the illegitimate son of an English cousin on the Morrison side whom she had adopted. She had reasons, she believed, for camouflaging the truth: she was afraid that Mrs. Hayward, who still exerted a powerful influence over her son, might goad Philip into taking legal action to gain custody of the boy, and adopted status might be a safeguard against such action. Even Constance, with all her Hollywood money, was not the slightest match for the resources of the Plant estate. So she continued her subterfuge regarding Peter's identity.

One legitimate source of her anxiety that Peter's existence might become public knowledge came in March 1932, with the kidnapping and murder of the Lindbergh baby. The crime so horrified Constance that she ordered bars put on the windows of Peter's bedroom and had a sophisticated alarm system installed. Peter would often wake up in the middle of the night to find members of the Los Angeles police department standing at the foot of his bed, making sure he was alright.

In January 1932, Constance took a step to further her contention that Peter was adopted, in the event that the Plants sought his custody. Her gambit was to secure a British passport in Los Angeles that included an Immigration Identification Card admitting him under the British quota for 1931–1932. She added "adopted" to the document in her own handwriting. One thing is fairly clear: Henri, who had repeatedly stated that he had no desire to have children of his own, wanted no part of her plan—whatever it shaped up to be. Some believed that Constance really did feel the need to fortify her position where the Plants were concerned. Others put it down to her love of confusing the press and public.

In 1931, there were changes at RKO that would benefit Constance. In New York, at the Radio Corporation of America, David Sarnoff had had enough of the studio's poor performance, and removed William LeBaron as studio chief. A strong candidate to replace him was David O. Selznick, the younger son of Lewis Selznick, who had been toiling at Paramount for the past three years as an associate director. More than anything, David Selznick wanted to form his own independent production company, but with the major studios dominating the action in Hollywood in the early 1930s, he had made no progress. He did, however, have a couple of distinct advantages: an intense level of creative energy and a taste in story material that was much more sophisticated than that of the average producer. David Sarnoff decided that Selznick might be the man to pull RKO out of its doldrums, and in November 1931 hired him as vice president in charge of production. Selznick's early months on the job were spent reviewing projects on RKO's production schedule, cutting the deadweight on the staff, and engaging new talent. One of the people he signed up first was George Cukor, whom he had known at Paramount. He admired Cukor's highly cultivated tastes and felt that he could be a major asset to RKO's stable of directors. And the first film that Selznick turned Cukor loose on was a Constance Bennett vehicle, *The Truth About Hollywood.*

The new film was based on a magazine story by Adela Rogers St. John dealing with rising and falling careers in the movie industry, and it in turn had several background sources from real life. One was Marshall Neilan, a silent film director whose career was destroyed by alcoholism. Another was silent star Colleen Moore, whose popularity in the 1920s contrasted with the drunken downfall of her husband, John McCormick, an executive with First National Pictures. In 1937, the original story would be pumped up into a more romantic and emotional film, *A Star Is Born,* with Janet Gaynor and Fredric March in the leads. Hollywood liked it so much that it was remade every couple of decades: with Judy Garland and James Mason in 1954, and with Barbra Streisand and Kris Kristofferson in 1976. (In the last one, the pop music industry stands in for Hollywood.)

There had been films about Hollywood for years—most of them farces, like *Merton of the Movies* (1924) or *Show People* (1928) with Marion Davies. But Selznick longed to make a serious work about the machinations of the film industry and the fleeting nature of success. More than anything, he wanted *The Truth About Hollywood* to give a realistic inside look at the business of making movies, and to that end, the team of screenwriters took much of their dialogue straight from their own experiences on movie sets, giving certain parts of the film a kind of docudrama feeling. Initially, *The Truth About Hollywood* was earmarked for Clara Bow—perhaps Selznick detected publicity value in the irony that Bow, whose career had declined with the advent of the sound era, would be cast as a rising Hollywood hopeful. But as the script was developed—to the dismay of RKO's sales department, which felt that films about Hollywood had no chance—Bow was out, and Constance was in.

Selznick was delighted with the switch. Constance was Myron Selznick's client, after all, so in a sense, the film, now retitled *What Price Hollywood?,* would keep things in the family. But there were other reasons that Selznick was happy to promote Constance's career. Despite his year-long marriage to Louis B. Mayer's daughter Irene, he was a compulsive womanizer, equally fond of actresses and secretaries. Constance had caught his eye the moment he arrived at RKO. She was sophisticated, worldly, and flirtatious, and made no bones about her love of men; it was rumored that she was no more faithful to Falaise than David was to Irene. David and Constance were often thrown together at Hollywood's infamous high-stakes poker games, where Constance was one of the only women good enough to join the table, and where she routinely fleeced David and the other moguls. David delighted in her company, and after looking over some of RKO's top stars—the patrician Ann Harding and the devout and virtuous Irene Dunne—perhaps he figured that he might have a better chance with Constance.

It's a shame that time has reduced *What Price Hollywood?* to a footnote in movie history, because it is more compelling and believable than any of the later *A Star Is Born* productions. It details the rise of Mary Evans (Constance), a sassy Brown Derby waitress who longs to be a movie star. A chance meeting with the maverick, alcoholic director Maximilian Carey (Lowell Sherman) puts her on the path to fame, and soon she is billed in lights as "Mary Evans, America's Pal." In the meantime, Carey drinks himself out of a career. Mary feels responsible for the man who gave her her break, and when Carey disappears on a bender, she is determined to find and take care of him. Eventually she does, but Carey realizes he cannot ask her to assume responsibility for him, and, in the film's most breathtaking sequence, he shoots himself in her guest bedroom.

What Price Hollywood? is distinguished from later reworkings by its sharp, satiric view of Hollywood life. From the moment we see Maximilian Carey stagger drunk into the Brown Derby on the night of a big Hollywood premiere, the picture's attitude toward the movie industry makes itself felt. It isn't exactly contempt that we feel as much as the folly of taking it seriously. The lesson of *What Price Hollywood?* is that Hollywood fame is inconstant; even the biggest stars can't control the whims of the public. This is particularly evident when Mary is interviewed by a gushing, prying lady fan-magazine writer, and in the scene where the circumstances of Carey's death turn Mary herself into a pariah overnight. Reporters storm her house demanding to know why Carey shot himself in her home. Were they lovers? The headlines do their worst, and she watches helplessly as her career evaporates as quickly as it rose.

What Price Hollywood? wisely stops short of concocting a romance between Mary Evans and Maximilian Carey; instead, she falls for a rich playboy (Neil Hamilton) who wants nothing to do with the movie business. This is the only part of the film that is badly written, and it does erode some of the good will built up in the earlier sections. Still, the fact that Mary and Carey never become lovers (there is a suggestion that Carey is gay—he is never seen in a clinch with a woman and, despite his success, seems something of an outsider in Hollywood) seems an unusually astute stroke on the part of the screenwriters. Despite their mutual affection, Mary's relationship with Carey is purely professional. And this somehow makes the whole situation more convincing. When Carey begins to slide down the drain, Mary's guilt is bound up in what she owes him professionally; we are spared the romantic soap opera dimension of her watching the tragic demise of the man she loves.

This is one way in which *What Price Hollywood?* surpasses its remakes. In the 1937 and 1954 versions of *A Star Is Born,* the talented young Esther Blodgett (Janet Gaynor and Judy Garland, respectively) falls in love with the dissipated, alcoholic actor Norman Maine (Fredric March and James Mason). But we may have trouble accepting the idea that any girl with healthy ambitions would run the risk of marrying a man who was bound to complicate her life and distract her from pursuing stardom. In the end, Norman Maine, realizing that his career is finished and he will only be a burden to Esther, makes the ultimate sacrifice of swimming gallantly out to sea. The later versions of the story stagger under the weight of their souped-up emotionalism. We feel the somewhat self-conscious nobility that pervades Norman Maine's decision to end it all, while Max Carey's suicide scene in *What Price Hollywood?* simply makes us experience the agony of a man at the end of his rope.

The movie is dotted with references to Constance's own career. The press's animosity toward Mary Evans because she refuses to have her small son photographed relates to Constance's own anxiety about Peter. There is an in-joke during the scene with Mary, Max Carey, and several others at an informal poolside story conference: the producer suggests that the script of Mary's new picture should depict her having a baby, and Mary responds, "I can't have a baby in *every* picture!"

Until *What Price Hollywood?,* Constance's directors had been run-of-the-mill members of the studio ranks who served mostly as traffic cops, keeping the storyline moving and the star in focus at all times. Suddenly, in George Cukor, she had a director of taste and wit and imagination. Cukor saw potential in her that had never been unleashed, and he rehearsed her carefully, working to downplay the synthetic qualities in her personality and help her sketch a believable, sympathetic character. She liked Cukor—throughout her life, she would have a natural affinity for gay men—and more important, she trusted him. Cukor felt a certain bond with her as well. He had been a great admirer of Richard's during his heyday, and he took pride in guiding the actor's eldest daughter through her first really challenging part. There are times, in Constance's big emotional scenes, when her performance is keyed a little too high, but all in all, her Mary Evans is warm and witty and sincere, and she holds her own with the brilliant Lowell Sherman, who brings a consistently surprising spin to his lines. She herself regarded *What Price Hollywood?* as the best film of her career.

Now that Constance was at her peak, she would presumably exercise more discretion in choosing her vehicles. But she followed *What Price Hollywood?* with a quick detour to Warners for the second film of her $30,000-a-week contract, *Two Against the World,* a weak drama about a society family rocked by scandal. She grabbed the money and ran back to RKO, where she had picked out her next vehicle: *Rockabye,* a screenplay by Jane Murfin about a Broadway stage star, on the verge of adopting a child, who is forced to give up the baby because of some of her unsavory past associations. She attempts to start over with a handsome young playwright (Joel McCrea, again), but when his estranged wife turns out to be pregnant and wants him back, she has no choice but to let him go. Selznick was skeptical about the material, but Constance was insistent, and George Fitzmaurice was signed to direct.

Rockabye turned out to be a setback for everyone involved. After a disastrous preview, RKO decided to reshoot much of the film, and Constance demanded that Cukor be assigned to it. Even Cukor, working straight through eighteen days and nights, couldn't save it. He later recalled that "the story was frankly rather crappy to begin with." The film has only two high points. Near the middle, Constance sings a jaunty song, "Till the Right Man Comes My Way," in a crowded speakeasy. And in a later scene, she takes McCrea back to her apartment to make him breakfast. In the kitchen, they engage in a little rough foreplay: he pushes her, she slaps him, over and over again, with gathering force, until they both wind up rolling on the floor in a passionate embrace while the scrambled eggs burn on the stove. Aside from those two provocative moments, *Rockabye* was the worst sound film Constance had made. When it was released, it was greeted with thumbs-down reviews and was a colossal box-office flop. Had the time already passed, Selznick wondered, when the public would buy Constance in anything?

Constance didn't mind if her films lost money. By now, she was eager to spend less time in California and more in France. Whenever her schedule permitted, she and Falaise stayed in Paris, in a spacious apartment on the rue Balzac, just off the Champs-

Elysées. Falaise also had a chateau in Brittany, and they spent many pleasant weekends there, going on picnics and fishing trips. It was, temporarily, a serene and pleasant interlude in Constance's hectic life.

Chapter Eleven

1933–1935

Early in 1932, Joan had rented a two-story, white stucco, Spanish-style house at 1121 Tower Road, in Benedict Canyon, and Gene joined her there. Diana, who had never known her own father, was delighted to have Gene in her life and immediately took to calling him Daddy. Every night, when Diana was ready for bed, Gene drew a series of cartoons for her, making up the story as he went along, to be continued the next evening. The entire family loved the pleasant country atmosphere of Tower Road, and Joan lost no time in decorating the house in her favorite shades of yellow, blue, and green.

Gene's work as a Hollywood screenwriter continued, and although he couldn't come close to matching Joan's salary, being regarded by the Hollywood community as Joan Bennett's husband didn't seem to bother him in the least. Gene's quiet confidence and even-keel personality kept insecurities at bay. He seemed a good match for Joan in other ways, too. He was a perfectionist who appreciated the luxurious elements of life; if the Markeys were giving a dinner party, Gene oversaw every last detail until everything was exactly the way he wanted it. Joan thought that he loved Hollywood society a bit too much. Although she enjoyed giving parties and going to them, she was able to view the movie community from a healthy distance. Gene, who possessed at least a latent strain of social ambition, reveled in every bit of it, and Joan was amused as she watched him plunge into party life with great enthusiasm. Joan's marriage to Gene also ushered in a new period of closeness and harmony with her own family. Now that Constance and Henri de la Falaise were settled into their home on Roxbury Drive, the two couples saw each other fairly often. And Richard, at last, had two sons-in-law who pleased him. Despite his skepticism over Henri's title, he found him warm and down to earth, and he called Gene "one of the finest boys in the world."

After her marriage, Joan dutifully worked out her Fox contract. Already, Joan had won the admiration of crews and fellow cast members for her punctuality and willingness to take direction. Every morning she was ready on the set with her lines learned perfectly, and she was gaining a reputation for never flubbing a take. If she had suggestions about a particular costume or the way she was being lit, she made them tactfully. As a result, she was much more popular with studio personnel than Constance ever had been, and fan magazines regularly ran stories on the remarkable difference between the two sisters—one divalike, the other demure.

After Joan broke with Fox, she was inactive for a spell. Now that she was without a long-term contract, she was waiting for just the right role to come along, something that would let her demonstrate her ability. Over at RKO, David Selznick was supervising the production of a film based on Louisa May Alcott's *Little Women.* Directed by George Cukor, it was planned as one of the studio's major releases of 1933. Both Selznick and Cukor were concerned that the Alcott story might be too saccharine for Depression-audience tastes, and the script underwent numerous revisions, all of them rejected, until the husband-and-wife writing team of Victor and Sarah Y. Heerman came up with a version that pleased everyone. The Heermans' adaptation wasn't quaint or fussy; there was plenty of humor to balance the pathos, and all of the characters had the breath of life.

Casting was a drawn-out and involved affair. Katharine Hepburn, who had made a successful movie debut in Cukor's *A Bill of Divorcement* the previous year, was set for the starring role of Jo, the tomboy who longs to be a writer. (The role was originally intended for Constance, whose position at RKO Hepburn had usurped; Hepburn even won an Oscar for *Morning Glory,* another project tailored for Constance.) Frances Dee, an up-and-coming actress married to Constance's ex-lover, Joel McCrea, was ideal as Meg, the eldest. A young, unknown actress named Jean Parker was cast as the fragile Beth, and character actress Spring Byington played the March girls' devoted, long-suffering Marmee.

The part of Amy, the spoiled, self-centered youngest sister, was the film's comedy role. It could have been filled acceptably by any of a dozen Hollywood ingenues, but Cukor was looking for an unusual casting angle. One night, he met Joan at a party. On other occasions, her aloofness had put him off slightly, but on this particular night she was slightly tipsy and very funny. He saw a spirited, mischievous streak in her that he had never noticed before, and he promptly cast her as Amy.

Cukor rehearsed the cast carefully before shooting began, often acting out the individual roles in considerable detail to show exactly the effects he wanted in each scene. It was an unusually happy company—each of the actresses was pleased with her role and trusted the director implicitly. When a scene was ready to be shot, Cukor would call out, "Come on, you little bitches! We're ready for you!"

Katharine Hepburn led the cast in style. Each afternoon, she would serve a hearty tea, with delicious homemade food provided by her maid. For Joan, there was only one problem: she was pregnant. She had known of it before filming began, but kept quiet for fear of losing such a plum part. Now, as shooting progressed, her condition was becoming impossible to hide. A few weeks into production, Joan finally confessed her condition to Cukor and the others. Since it was too late to replace her—as she had calculated—Walter Plunkett's costumes were merely let out and she was photographed from the chest up.

The miracle of *Little Women* is that it keeps cloying sentiment to a minimum. Cukor's attention to detail paid off, for seldom had there been such excellent ensemble work in a Hollywood film. The camaraderie on the set produced a wonderful dynamic on film: the four March girls, squabbling away at each other or bravely awaiting the return of their father, are entirely believable as a family. On the surface, Joan might seem like the odd woman out—with her blonde ringlets and regular features, she looks more Hollywood than do Hepburn, Dee, and Parker—but her Amy adds considerably to the mood of the film. Whether ruining Jo's performance of the melodrama "The Black Tower" by refusing to faint dramatically, or mangling the English language ("fastidious" for "fascinating," "satirical" for "sarcastic"), or grudgingly sharing her Christmas breakfast with a poor family up the street, her performance is the film's comic high point.

Little Women became one of the year's most celebrated movies. At the time, most films played first-run theaters for a week and only occasionally were held over. Big studios, like MGM, counted on this, producing an annual schedule of fifty-two pictures, one for each week of the year. But *Little Women* beat the odds, running for four weeks at its initial engagement at the Radio City Music Hall. The reviews were stellar, and Joan was not overlooked: "She looks like a child in the early scenes and wears a grace and dignity in the latter ones that is most becoming to her," said Kate Cameron in the *New York Daily News*. "Joan Bennett's Amy is so far beyond anything she has done before that she seems like a new person," wrote Regina Crewe of the *New York American*.

For the rest of her life, *Little Women* remained one of Joan's happiest experiences in films. "She took me to the studio to see the picture," remembered Diana Anderson. "I remember not wanting to go. But she made me go and see it. I think she was rather proud of it." With *Little Women* a worldwide success, Joan could relax a bit. She had appeared in an important film that made her feel she had done something, finally, to live up to the Bennett name. She settled in and waited for the baby to be born. Gene wasn't entirely sure he wanted to be a father—perhaps he was afraid it might interfere with his social life—but Joan was certain that once the baby arrived, he would love it as much as he loved Diana.

George Cukor was a miracle man, both Constance and Joan agreed. They had long talks about how he had guided them through *What*

Price Hollywood? and *Little Women.* He was virtually the only film director throughout Constance's career who would earn her respect and devotion, and she was delighted to work with him again on her first 1933 release, *Our Betters,* a film version of the W. Somerset Maugham play. It seemed an ideal vehicle for Constance, a wry drawing room comedy about an American heiress who thumbs her nose at English aristocracy when she finds out what a bounder her titled husband is. Unfortunately, Cukor brought to the material none of the visual wit and imagination he had showed in *What Price Hollywood?,* and the result was static and lifeless. It was her second flop in a row, and RKO nervously reacted by setting her up in what seemed a sure thing, a reteaming with Joel McCrea in *Bed of Roses.*

In most ways, it was a rehash of her earlier pictures with McCrea. Again Constance played a fallen woman, Lorry Evans, who tries to clean up her act to please her true love. This time around, though, her character was much less virtuous than usual—an out-and-out hooker and con artist who steals money from the nice guy (McCrea) who falls for her, then runs off to New Orleans, where she is kept by a wealthy publisher. What separates *Bed of Roses* from some of Constance's other soapy vehicles is its potent streak of bawdy comedy. The film takes a much more casual attitude toward sinning than *The Easiest Way* or *Born to Love*: Lorry is a tough, merry tart who doesn't stop to question her morals until fairly late in the film. Constance comes across as a more teasing, sexually aggressive personality than any of her previous films allowed her to be—the *New York Times* found that her acting made her role "much more interesting than it might have been in less talented hands"—but it wasn't enough to make *Bed of Roses* a hit.

RKO had another film ready for her, a World War I romantic spy drama called *After Tonight.* The script was poor, but she had other reasons to look forward to making it. In the supporting cast of *Our Betters* there had been a young Mexican actor named Gilbert Roland. He had been around Hollywood for years, and he was already something of a legend—not as an actor, but as a ladies' man.

Gilbert Roland was born Luis Antonio Démaso de Alonso in Chihuahua, Mexico. His father was a matador—not a particularly important one—who instructed his sons in the art of bullfighting. To Luis, his father represented the ultimate in masculine glamour. The boy was entranced by the way he swaggered into a room, by his fondness for wine and cigars. Luis was determined to be a torero himself, but instead he fell in love with the silent screen, and set his heart on an acting career. In the wake of the Mexican Revolution, the family moved to El Paso, and later Luis made his way to California, where he lived a hand-to-mouth existence as a three-dollar-a-day movie extra. Times grew so tough that he was forced to take a job as a dishwasher at a joint in Catalina. With the rise of Rudolph Valentino, Latin lovers had become very big in Hollywood, and eventually Luis was discovered by an agent, Ivan Kahn, who talked him up to the studios. He changed his name, inspired by his two favorite movie stars, John Gilbert (whom he resembled) and Ruth Roland. He played his first major role in 1925, and after making a hit as a Valentino type in *The Blonde Saint,* he signed a long-term contract with Joseph M. Schenck at United Artists. In 1927, he played opposite Schenck's wife, the popular silent star Norma Talmadge, in *Camille,* and Talmadge quickly joined the long list of Hollywood women who had fallen for him. At the time, perhaps no man in the movies was quite as dazzling as Gilbert. He was six feet tall and broad shouldered, with curly, blue-black hair, a sensual mouth, and soulful dark eyes. Some of Hollywood's handsomest men were also Hollywood's biggest fops, but not Roland, who was widely known to be one of the most potent and insatiable lovers around. Sexual drive was one of the principal ways that Hollywood's most powerful men defined themselves. No secretary was safe from David O. Selznick's advances, and Darryl F. Zanuck's afternoon liaisons in his office were already part of Hollywood legend. But word around town was that no actor was capable of generating quite as much heat as Gilbert Roland.

By the time Gilbert worked with her, Norma Talmadge's eleven-year marriage to Joseph Schenck had already run into serious trouble. Even so, Gilbert's decision to sleep with the boss's wife

Richard Bennett, the matinee idol. (Photofest)

Thc Bcnnetts at home: Constance, Mabel, Joan, Richard, Barbara. (Photofest)

Social and civic leaders hailed Eugene Brieux's *Damaged Goods* as a ground-breaking play—and Richard lost no time in publicizing the fact. (© Museum of the City of New York)

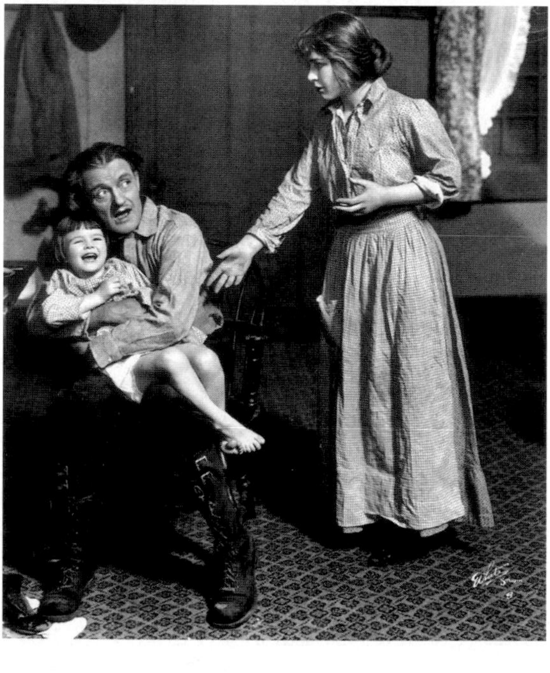

Richard as the tormented failure Robert Mayo in O'Neill's *Beyond the Horizon*, with Elfin Finn and Helen MacKellar. (© Museum of the City of New York)

Portrait of Richard as Tony in Sidney Howard's *They Knew What They Wanted* (1924). (© Museum of the City of New York)

Richard visiting the set of Constance's first big hit, *Sally, Irene and Mary* (1925), directed by Edmond Goulding (right). (Photofest)

Barbara, at the beginning of her brief career. (Wisconsin Center for Film and Theater Research, Image WCFTR-2296)

Mabel (left) bids farewell to Barbara, en route to Paris aboard the *Homeric* in 1924. (Photofest)

Philip Plant, Constance's second husband. (Courtesy of Peter Bennett Plant)

Joan's stage debut with Richard in *Jarnegan,* 1928. (Photofest)

Above, Constance with Lew Ayres in *Common Clay* (1930), which established her screen niche as an unwed mother. (Wisconsin Center for Film and Theater Research, Image WCFTR-2295) *Below,* Mabel visits Joan at her rented Malibu beach house in 1930. (Wisconsin Center for Film and Theater Research, Image WCFTR-2301)

Constance with Adolphe Menjou in *The Easiest Way* (1931), an old stage hit dusted off for the talkies. (Author's collection)

Constance and her third husband, Henri Falaise, the Marquis de la Coudraye. (Photofest)

Above, Barbara and Morton Downey returning from Europe, 1933. (Associated Press/Photofest) *Below,* Joan's "rebound" romance with screenwriter-producer Gene Markey turned into her least volatile marriage. (ACME/Photofest)

Above, Morton Downey, Barbara, and Joan at Hollywood's Brown Derby. (Wide World Photos/Photofest) *Below,* The Markey family, Diana, Joan, Gene, and Melinda, en route to New York. (Wide World Photos/Photofest)

Above, Constance and Richard in their only joint screen appearance, 1931's *Bought!* (Wisconsin Center for Film and Theater Research, Image WCFTR-2294) *Below,* Joan as a tough-talking waitress in *Me and My Gal* (1932), with Spencer Tracy, who became a lifelong friend. (Photofest)

Richard's farewell to Broadway: the guilt-ridden Judge Gaunt in Maxwell Anderson's *Winterset* (1935). (Vadamm Studio/Photofest)

Mid-1930s portrait of Constance, the human coat hanger. (Author's collection)

Above, Gregory LaCava directing Joan in the breakdown sequence in *Private Worlds* (1935). (Photofest) *Below,* Constance's most famous role: the ghostly Marion Kerby in *Topper* (1937), with Roland Young. (Wisconsin Center for Film and Theater Research, Image WCFTR-2292)

Constance playing bezique on the set of *Service de Luxe* (1938). (Photofest)

Joan in love, with Walter Wanger at the La Conga nightclub. (ACME/ Photofest)

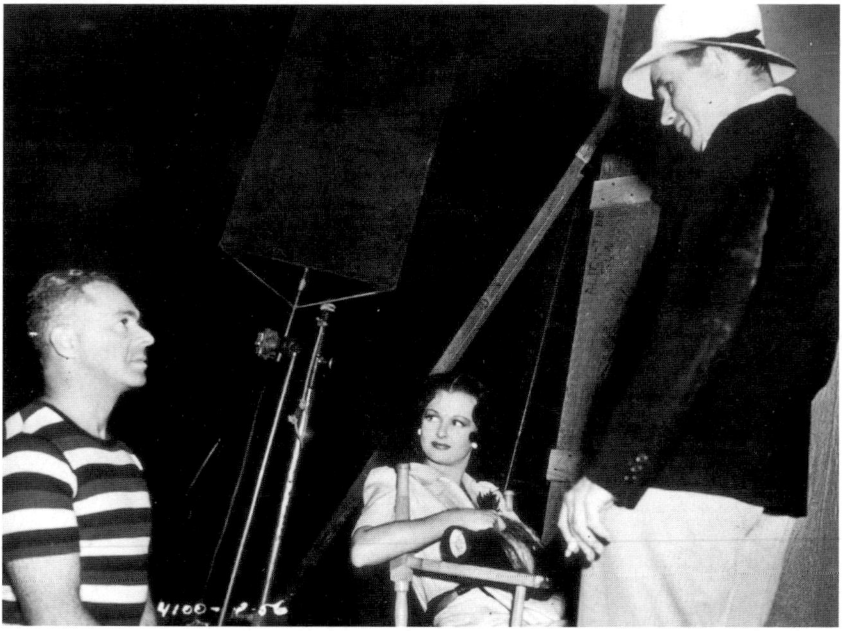

Above, Joan turned brunette in *Trade Winds* (1938), produced by Walter Wanger (left) and directed by Tay Garnett (right). (Wisconsin Center for Film and Theater Research, Image WCFTR-2300) *Below,* By 1935, Constance was carrying on a heated affair with Gilbert Roland. (Wide World Photos/Photofest)

The Wangers in 1940, at a Hollywood party with Claudette Colbert. (Photofest)

Joan being coached in Cockney dialect on the set of *Man Hunt* (1941), her first picture with Fritz Lang. (Photofest)

was incredibly reckless. Schenck was a proud man, and even if he and Talmadge were separated, the role of cuckold didn't suit him. He set out to undermine Gilbert with the murderous efficiency of a Mafia don, and put out the word to his producer colleagues that Gilbert was to be blacklisted. After having filmed three pictures in 1927, Gilbert made only one in 1928. (The rumor persisted for years that Schenck, not satisfied with having denied him work, had him castrated. Silent star Colleen Moore recalled, "One story that spread like wildfire was that Joe had engaged thugs who had not only beat up Gilbert Roland but castrated him as well. When the story reached Gilbert, he went down to the Hollywood Athletic Club on a day when the pool was filled with men—all of them naked, as was the Club's custom. Gilbert came out, stood around a while, and dived in."

Roland had reached the nadir of his career when *Camille* came into his life once more. This time it was a Los Angeles stage production, opposite Jane Cowl, and its success lifted him from Schenck's blacklist. By 1933, his performing life was back on track, and so was his social life. His affair with Talmadge had not survived the ordeal with Schenck, and although Gilbert would always refer to her as the one great love of his life, he was now looking elsewhere. During the filming of *Our Betters,* he found what he was looking for in Constance.

Apart from his love of classical music and opera, Gilbert was not a man of tremendous depth. In the movies, he most often played cardboard lovers, and in life he played much the same role. There was a somewhat stiff, studied, and actorish element in his personality that sometimes made him seem uncomfortable in ordinary social situations. Peter Plant felt that it was a long drop from Henri de la Falaise to Gilbert Roland, whom he found shallow. "He was not a bad man—not at all," remembered Peter, "but someone of no character at all." But it hardly mattered, since Constance hadn't picked him for character. In Gilbert, she had found someone as sexually driven as herself. "My mother was attracted to elegance, number one," said Constance and Gilbert's youngest daughter, Gyl Roland. "And number two, just plain old sensuality. My father was a perfect example of that. You don't get more suave and sensual than he. And I understand that they had a very torrid relationship." Gilbert and Constance's courtship grew more heated by the day, only to be interrupted in April 1933 when Gilbert sailed to Honolulu to make a film. He and Constance exchanged passionate letters during his long absence, and when he returned, they resumed their affair. It was easy, since Henri Falaise was still in Europe for long periods of time. In any case, coming from a sophisticated, continental background, he could hardly have expected Constance to remain faithful to him.

The chemistry between Constance and Gilbert was vividly present on the screen as well. Unfortunately, it was virtually the only sign of life in *After Tonight,* and it was Constance's third flop in a row. Her RKO contract had now expired, and neither she nor the studio saw any reason to renew it. Her great champion had been David Selznick , but after revitalizing the studio with hits such as *King Kong* and *Little Women,* he had moved on to MGM. Constance's decline at RKO had coincided with the rise of Katharine Hepburn. The long-suffering heroines of most of Constance's movies already seemed old-hat compared with the ambitious, independent women that Hepburn played. Surprisingly, Constance didn't seem to resent her rival at all, and for the rest of her life Hepburn would remain one of the actresses she most admired.

Ultimately, Constance had to take responsibility for the sharp decline of her film career. Her whims and temperament had pushed many of her films over budget; even a popular picture like *What Price Hollywood?* had cost so much that it lost $50,000. She was still applauded for her shrewdness in cutting lucrative business deals, but her careless judgment of scripts had put her career in serious jeopardy. Such a swift fall from grace would have undone most actresses, but Constance seemed unfazed by it. It was hard for her to take movies too seriously, and she was hardly the type to lie awake at night agonizing about whether her career was slipping. For her, acting was principally the best means she knew of supporting her expensive tastes, and she moved out of her RKO dressing room with no regrets and no worries. In no time, she had another contract in hand, this one with Twentieth Century Pictures, headed by Darryl F. Zanuck.

All of Hollywood's top production executives were gamblers, with shrewd instincts about actors and properties, and about what would and would not go over with the public. Zanuck was no exception, but he was more than just a businessman. He had something else that many of his colleagues lacked: a strong belief in the intelligence of the moviegoing public. His daily memos reveal his constant concern for credibility, above all else, in the films he produced. Zanuck had been a writer first, the author of adventure tales which he wound up selling to Warner Bros. in the early 1920s. In 1922, the studio hired him to grind out stories for its successful Rin-Tin-Tin movies, and eventually he graduated to bigger pictures, becoming the studio's production chief in 1929. Zanuck's background as a writer was his greatest tool as a producer, for he knew instinctively how to break down scripts and repair what was wrong with them. He was also a genius in the cutting process, where he showed an acute sense of those points which needed to be eliminated or amplified.

By 1933, the ever-worsening Depression posed an ominous threat to the studios. The financial institutions that lent the studios money were severely crippled, and after Franklin D. Roosevelt closed down the banks in March, the moguls met and decided to institute an eight-week, 50 percent salary cut for all studio employees earning more than fifty dollars a week. At MGM, the employees fell in line with no trouble at all—anything to please their beloved father figure, Louis B. Mayer—but other studios soon found that their employees lacked such unswerving loyalty. IATSE, the union that represented electricians and movie theater technicians, including projectionists, refused to consider such a sacrifice. Eventually, the decision was made to restrict the cuts to top stars and executives, but several actors—Constance, among them—showed their contempt by announcing that they would go off salary altogether rather than accept such demeaning cuts. At Warners, the cuts were put into effect, much to Zanuck's objection, and when he went over his bosses' heads by announcing that all reductions would be restored,

Warners countered with an announcement: not only would the cuts remain, they would be extended from eight weeks to nine. Zanuck, deeply angered and humiliated, immediately submitted his resignation. Soon he formed his own company with Joseph Schenck, Twentieth Century Pictures. They didn't have a studio—instead, they leased space on Samuel Goldwyn's lot—but from the beginning, they turned out quality films that did well at the box office.

In 1934, Constance starred in two of them. *Moulin Rouge,* a lively comedy, gave her a dual role as both halves of a stage sister act. In her throaty, Dietrich-style voice, she sang "Coffee in the Morning, Kisses at Night" and "Boulevard of Broken Dreams." She is exceptionally good in the film, pointing up the difference between the two sisters in subtle ways. It was a sly performance that gave plenty of indication that comedy, not soap opera, was the direction in which she should continue. Zanuck apparently thought so, because he promptly cast her in *The Affairs of Cellini,* about the romantic exploits of the sixteenth-century Florentine artist (played by Fredric March). Constance was funny and elegant as the frustrated Duchess of Florence, married to the woman-chasing Duke (Frank Morgan, whose performance earned him an Academy Award nomination). In 1934, in view of the rising number of violent gangster films, sexy Mae West comedies, and other "questionable" genres, the Motion Picture Producers and Distributors of America had launched the Production Code, geared to ensure that no American film would present any view of life that might be seen as morally objectionable. Specifically, the Code decreed that the audience should never be called upon to sympathize with criminals or other wrongdoers. The head of MPPDA, Will H. Hays, and Joseph I. Breen, director of the Code Administration, were ever-vigilant. All scripts had to be submitted to them for approval, and their objections frequently led to extensive revisions, dilutions, and delays. If a film was not judged to meet the Code's standard, the seal of approval was denied; as a result, Hays and Breen wielded enormous power over the moguls, who might have privately detested them but almost always fell in line.

Since sex was the main subject of *The Affairs of Cellini,* it immediately came under the censors' scrutiny. Early reports from J.I. Breen found that it possessed "a definite connotation of gross vulgarity" and that the characters played by Constance and Frank Morgan were "libidinous persons who engage in promiscuous sexuality." In the end, Zanuck and director Gregory LaCava tidied the film up to the point that the Hays Office gave it the go-ahead, and it enjoyed a successful run. Still, *The Affairs of Cellini* did little to help Constance's career. For the first time in years, she was not the focal point of a film, and the press and public perceived it as a Fredric March picture, not a Constance Bennett picture.

Zanuck was on the brink of merging Twentieth Century with Fox, and Constance was not one of the stars who made the transition to the new company. She had what seemed a much better offer, from MGM. It was the Tiffany of studios, where most actors dreamed of working, the studio with more stars than there were in heaven—which was part of the problem. RKO might have been down-at-the-heels compared with MGM, but at RKO Constance had been the studio queen. At MGM, she was only part of a crowd that included Greta Garbo, Joan Crawford, Myrna Loy, Jeanette MacDonald, Jean Harlow, and Helen Hayes.

Then there was Norma Shearer. Married to the studio's brilliant young production chief, Irving Thalberg, Shearer was an oddity among female stars: broad-featured, cross-eyed, and with a peculiarly limited talent, she had managed to persuade the moviegoing public that she was both a great beauty and a great actress. Because of Thalberg, her power at MGM was tremendous. Constance joined the studio roster in 1934, the same year that her good friend Marion Davies left it—forced out by Louis B. Mayer. Columnists wondered how Shearer would welcome Constance into the MGM "family," and weren't surprised when the two women had little to do with each other. Thalberg was never especially high on Constance, and in the end, MGM was a kind of stopping-off point in her career. She made only two films there, and both hastened her decline.

Outcast Lady, which Thalberg oversaw closely, had originally been intended for his wife. The title was Hollywoodese for *The*

Green Hat, the successful and scandalous novel by Michael Arlen, which he turned into a play in 1925, giving Katharine Cornell one of her most popular successes. In the 1920s, *The Green Hat* had been the last word in adult entertainment. It dealt with Iris March, a hard-luck woman who is prevented from marrying Napier, the true love of her life. Instead, she marries a wastrel who tells her on their wedding night that he has contracted venereal disease. Iris's horrified reaction leads him to throw himself out the window, and rather than ruin her husband's reputation by telling the truth, Iris nobly pretends that it was her own tainted condition that led him to kill himself. She keeps this secret for years, as she drifts from one man to the next, and she is a badly soiled dove by the time she is finally reunited with Napier. At last, she sleeps with him, but he is engaged to a respectable girl, and there is nothing left for Iris but to bear his illegitimate child—who dies—and to contract septic poisoning before taking matters into her own hands and ending her suffering by driving her sports car into a tree.

On one hand, it is easy to see how MGM thought *The Green Hat* would be a natural for Constance, since it is a kind of throwback to her earlier melodramas. But the studio failed to grasp that the public had tired of her in this sort of part, and *The Green Hat* turned out to be a headache from the start. MGM was prevented from using the original title, since the Hays Office felt that the scandalous source material should be kept a secret from the public. (This had also been a problem during the pre-Code era, when MGM starred Greta Garbo in a silent version of the story, and was forced to retitle it *A Woman of Affairs.*) This time around, Thalberg agreed to change the title to *Outcast Lady,* but the Hays Office was not appeased. Now it wasn't venereal disease that prompted Iris's husband to commit suicide but the fact that he had served a term in prison for committing an unnamed crime.

Once the picture was submitted to Breen for inspection, he insisted that all references to Iris and Napier's affair, as well as to the birth and death of their baby, be eliminated. This meant heavy rewriting and costly retakes, and when *Outcast Lady* was finished, it wasn't about much of anything. The *New York Times* observed that "The gallantry of Iris March has become the self-conscious and rather stubborn nobility of a silly woman," and further felt that Constance's "irradiations have the tendency to obscure poor, sad, futile Iris."

Trying to reverse the hex of *Outcast Lady,* MGM teamed Constance with Clark Gable, in a contemporary newspaper story, *After Office Hours.* Only four years earlier, when they had worked together in *The Easiest Way,* she had been one of the nation's top box-office stars, and he was just coming up through the studio ranks. Now he was MGM's top male star, and the winner of the 1934 Best Actor Academy Award for *It Happened One Night,* and Constance was a fading actress who needed a break by playing opposite him. She didn't get it with *After Office Hours,* a contrived, tedious story that reduced her to playing straight woman to Gable.

What happened? How was it possible that as shrewd a businesswoman as Constance Bennett had allowed her career to spin so hopelessly out of control? Few things can kill off a career as quickly as typecasting, and unquestionably, the repetitive content of Constance's pictures accelerated her fall from grace. In their own way, her films were nearly as risqué as Mae West's, and both of them had rough sledding after the Production Code came into being and studios began developing more wholesome images for their female stars.

Economics also had something to do with it. In the early 1930s, Constance's glamour and sophistication had been a powerful antidote for a legion of admiring American women seeking diversion from the bleakness of their own lives. But as the Depression deepened, and the hope of recovery seemed ever more remote, Constance's publicity as one of the screen's biggest wage-earners began to work against her. By the mid-1930s, her extravagant lifestyle seemed a gross example of Hollywood waste. As columnists sniped about the extravagance of an earlier era, her fans began to desert her.

Ultimately, the blame for Constance's swift decline rests with Constance herself. A hard, unyielding quality at the core of her personality had gradually made its presence felt. Her fans, after all, longed to think that beneath the brittle sophistication there was a woman of heart and soul—and somehow, she had failed to persuade them that this was true. In spite of her charm, her husky voice, her beauty and grace of movement, her adept way with a line, she was not a particularly nuanced actress. Only in *Lady with a Past* and *What Price Hollywood?* had she suggested any hidden depth. The essential quality that she lacked was humanity, something that less talented actresses—Norma Shearer, for example—had in greater supply. Claudette Colbert could be every bit as wry and elegant as Constance, but she had something else, a generosity of spirit. There was something in Constance's work that did not resonate deeply with the public over time. Years later, Louise Brooks astutely summed up the problem: ". . . beauty, great acting ability, and a lovely voice could not compensate for the lack of the one attribute without which the rest did not matter: she did not have that generosity, that love for her audience, which makes a true star."

Mayer and Thalberg batted around other story possibilities, but both had come to the conclusion that MGM was not the right place for Constance. Constance, never able to remain in a place where she wasn't wanted, didn't argue. She was nearly thirty-one, and probably she more than anyone else thought it was hilarious that the publicity tag "The World's Highest-Paid Actress" belonged to a woman who was out of work.

Chapter Twelve

1934–1937

When he first came to Hollywood in 1931, Richard had tried to give the impression that filmmaking would fill the void left in his creative life after he had turned his back on Broadway. By 1934, he could no longer preserve this illusion, for himself or anyone else. With the exception of *Arrowsmith* and *If I Had a Million,* a 1932 all-star comedy for Paramount, none of his movies was anything to be proud of, and he had wearied of the life of a Hollywood character actor. Regardless of the money, he loathed sitting around the set waiting for a shot to be set up, and he couldn't help but think back to his glory days in New York, when he had been the driving force behind *Damaged Goods, Beyond the Horizon,* and *He Who Gets Slapped.* Once he had simultaneously functioned as star, director, and stage manager. Now he simply tried to remember his few lines, hit his marks, and do as he was told.

By early 1934, he was sixty-three, and time was catching up with him. His great shock of hair had gone white, and gradually, illness was interfering with his work in films. The year before, a bad case of pneumonia had forced him to bow out of Paramount's *Song of Songs,* starring Marlene Dietrich. He had been slow to recover, and tired and listless once he was able to return to work. The columnists who still remembered his great days as a stage star continued to treat him with respect; both Louella Parsons and Hedda Hopper frequently devoted a few lines to him. But the sad truth was that many of the younger cast and crew members didn't quite seem to know who he was, and treated him as just another crotchety character actor. He was the father of Constance and Joan Bennett, and nothing more, and he didn't like it at all.

He had high hopes when Samuel Goldwyn requested him for his screen version of Emile Zola's novel *Nana*. He was cast as Gaston Greiner, the elderly impresario who becomes infatuated with the sultry title courtesan, played by Goldwyn's latest discovery, the German actress Anna Sten, soon to be known as "Goldwyn's folly." Sten did not take with American audiences at all, and the film itself, while no disgrace, turned out to be sluggish and ordinary. But it is one of Richard's best pieces of screen work. The pain reflected in his sad, deep-set eyes when Nana finally walks out on him provides the picture's emotional peak.

And then there was no work. If Richard couldn't make headlines as an actor, he would make them as an irate husband. His marriage to Aimee was approaching the seven-year mark, but everyone close to them knew that it could not continue much longer. Inactivity was not compatible with Richard's restless, intellectually curious nature, and his frustrations and rages were often taken out against his silly young wife. Joan had predicted that Richard would not be able to suffer a well-meaning dilettante like Aimee for long, and she was right. He now viewed Aimee as the shallow and superficial woman she was, and in his mind he connected her with his own drop from Olympic heights, conveniently forgetting that he had rushed into the marriage as a way of spiting Mabel. For her part, Aimee had grown more petulant as Richard's reputation in the entertainment world grew ever distant. When they married, Aimee imagined a glamorous and exciting life as the wife of one of America's greatest actors. But the spotlight that Richard formerly occupied had been gradually turned on other actors, and now Aimee found herself saddled with an ailing old man with an uncertain future. Their arguments, always heated, grew downright violent. In early April 1934 they separated. Aimee said that "seven years have proved conclusively we are unsuited to each other. We should never have been married." Richard gave his own side of the matter to reporters. He dismissed the separation as "a case of nerves" on

Aimee's part; there was no question of divorce, since he knew that Aimee "will be sending for me if she stays away a couple of months."

"RICHARD BENNETT BEAT HER, HIS SECOND WIFE CHARGES," blared newspaper headlines on April 16, 1934. Aimee had indeed sworn out a complaint against Richard in Beverly Hills Police Court, charging him with battery. She showed up in court with a bruised nose and a bad cut over one eye, claiming that Richard had threatened her with a pistol, struck her across the nose with it, and stabbed her in the face with a fingernail file. There was some confusion about her testimony; her attorneys later admitted that it was their initial understanding that Aimee had injured herself while packing up her belongings after she and Richard had agreed on a separation. The warrant could not be served because Richard's current residence, at 60 Ocean Way in Santa Monica, lay outside Beverly Hills' jurisdiction. Aimee dropped the charges, but by May she had filed a divorce action, again accusing him of physical abuse, and adding that she had caught him in his bedroom with his secretary. Aimee demanded a substantial community-property settlement—she valued it at $75,000—plus $3,000 a month for separate maintenance, $5,000 for legal fees, and $1,000 for court costs. It was a staggering amount, quite beyond Richard's means. In any case, Aimee had one immediate problem in pursuing the divorce: Richard could not be found.

For a few days, process servers searched for Aimee's errant husband and turned up nothing. Then she received a telegram at her apartment at the Beverly Wilshire Hotel: "DARLING. CAN'T YOU FIND SOME PLACE IN YOUR HEART TO ADJUDICATE THIS CUL DE SAC. I LOVE YOU. DICK." The telegram had been sent from Phoenix, and soon enough Richard was located. He claimed that he had made a quick trip to Arizona to inspect some polo ponies he was thinking of buying. When a reporter told him the details of Aimee's request for a settlement, Richard replied, "I'd rather pay the President's salary than what she's asking." He admitted that he did not mention the suit in his message to her, adding, "But it was a very nice telegram, wasn't it?" Now that he knew of the suit, he promised to return to Hollywood immediately.

But he did not. He was already in a legal jam, as he had been ordered not to leave California jurisdiction until a property settlement had been made. Now he compounded his difficulties by fleeing Arizona and driving east across the country. His destination was Barbara and Morton's forty-nine-acre Connecticut farm. What he planned to do there was anybody's guess—but he had a high time on his flight from justice, traveling in disguise and registering at hotels under the name of some of the characters he had played onstage. He arrived at the Downey home early in the morning, spent a few days there, then slipped up to Montreal and fled to England aboard *The Empress of Britain*.

Richard's fleeting visit disrupted Barbara's serene retirement from show business. She was busy with her growing family: she and Morton had two sons, Michael, a three-year-old child they claimed to have adopted in Ireland, and a boy of their own, Sean, born on December 8, 1932, who with his dark hair and fair skin favored both of his parents. (Michael's origins remain something of a mystery. Edward Downey admitted, "We never had any idea where Michael came from.") By the time Richard had taken temporary shelter with her, Barbara was expecting a third child in December. She seemed happy, although when Richard pumped her for information, she admitted that Morton's frequent absences were beginning to take their toll. (Morton was enormously successful by this time, pulling down a sizeable salary at CBS Radio, and he continued to make frequent tours across the United States and throughout Europe.) Still successfully eluding Aimee and her army of process servers, Richard sneaked back into the United States in November for a quick visit with Barbara. In order to be closer to her gynecologist, she had temporarily moved into the apartment that she and Morton kept at Manhattan's Ritz Towers on Fifty-seventh Street and Park Avenue. Richard delighted in walking the streets of New York without being recognized, and after a couple of weeks he sailed back to England. Had he stayed only a couple more weeks, he could have been present for the birth of Barbara and Morton's first daughter, Lorelle Ann, on November 18, 1934.

With his London cronies, over glasses of Scotch and pints of ale, Richard reveled in his new freedom and laughed at how successfully he had thwarted Aimee. Privately, though, he was concerned that there was little money coming in. Since *Nana,* he had made only one picture, *This Woman Is Mine,* a love story set against a circus background, produced in England by Pathé-Vogue. It led to no further offers, and as the new year came and went, Richard wondered where his next job was coming from.

In mid-February 1935, while visiting the home of actor John Loder in Hertfordshire, Richard was thrown from a horse. X-rays revealed that he had punctured a lung, fractured a collarbone, and broken two ribs, and he was sent to recuperate at a nursing home. Word was sent out to his daughters, but since Constance and Joan were both occupied in Hollywood, Barbara was elected the family delegate. She sailed for England, arriving in Southampton on February 21, and drove to Hertfordshire the following day. Given his age and weakened condition, doctors were pessimistic at first, but in a surprisingly short time Richard passed out of grave danger. Barbara remained with him at the nursing home until his recovery seemed a sure thing, then returned to Connecticut and her two boys and three-month-old daughter.

Slowly, Richard fought his way back to health. On his sickbed, his money worries continued to plague him. Two pictures and a play, *The Red Cat,* had been in the offing when his accident occurred—although he hadn't yet figured out how he was going to return to work in the United States with Aimee's suit hanging over his head. On March 23, 1935, he wrote to Constance, "Conka—I've had a hell of a time. They thought I was a goner. I think I should come home to recuperate which will take two months." He went on to propose that if Constance and her attorney, Neil McCarthy, put their heads together, they might arrange a substantial enough pay-off to Aimee so that Richard would not have to make the costly monthly alimony payments. If Constance could hand Aimee some of her much-publicized earnings, he could repay her at his leisure. "You are very definitely popular over here—where [I] once hoped to enhance your value—the order is now reversed."

Three weeks later, he contacted Constance again: "Did you

get in touch with Neil? I'm going mad in this proud country. They proposed that you lend me $15,000 to square this matter. I don't want my kids to square anything for me. I think the best thing is for me to come back and take the rap. Let the County of San Jose keep me in their jail house—because I will never work again if I have to pay her [Aimee]."

Richard returned quietly to New York, where the divorce case dragged on, with attorneys for both sides haggling back and forth. To buy himself time with Aimee, he declared voluntary bankruptcy, and by summer, with no money coming in, his situation was desperate. By now, he was living in Greenwich with Barbara and Morton, whose money was tied up in investments, a thriving farm, and a growing family. Barbara suggested that perhaps Constance was in the best position to help him. He swallowed his pride once more and wrote to Constance, asking her to endorse a note for $5,000. Constance, having helped out Mabel years earlier by paying bills for Barbara's doctors and Joan's education—which, she pointed out, had been Richard's responsibility—was reluctant to hand over the money until her business manager returned from vacation. She was also irritated that Barbara had volunteered her as Richard's financial savior, and from this point on, relations between the two sisters, which had never been close, grew increasingly strained. In a vitriolic letter to Richard, she pointed out that "no matter how large a fortune one is supposed to have, if it is wisely invested, it is not always as easy as one may assume to put one's hands on ready cash, particularly when one has a couple of hundred thousand dollars invested in pictures, and a like some [*sic*] in real estate." It pained her to see Aimee getting a bigger settlement than Mabel, who after all had been married to him for years and borne him three children. "However," she concluded, "one considers the latest settlement to 'MADAM' to be cheap at twice the price to get rid of her, and slightly add, even though very slightly, to the dignity of the name of 'BENNETT.'"

As the summer progressed, Richard stayed on with Barbara and Morton, and infuriated them both by inviting a woman he'd become attached to in London, a dancer named Peg DeBeer, to visit him for a week in Greenwich. Three weeks later, when DeBeer showed no sign of leaving, Barbara pressed him on the matter. Richard admitted that he had asked DeBeer to stay on well into the fall. Richard had told her that he was paying the Downeys weekly room and board for the duration of her stay—just so she would feel more at home. "He knows damned well that even if he offered to pay it, I wouldn't accept," Barbara wrote to Joan, "and anyhow, what the hell would he pay with—cigar coupons?"

Late in August, while still making the Downeys' life miserable in Connecticut, Richard wired Constance and Joan in California and asked them each for a loan. He asked Joan for $2,000, sending as security a diamond ring that he had bought several years earlier, claiming it was worth $5,000. (Barbara later told Joan that he had tried to sell it the week before and could raise a top price of only $500.) Joan did not reply immediately, and Richard's response to her, like many of the letters and telegrams he sent at this point, suggests that he might have made a magnificent King Lear.

"Dear Joan, Do your cheeks turn red when you think of answering me? For the first time in my life, I have asked you and Constance for a favor which will settle forever all obligations to Angela [Aimee]. I have whittled the amount from ten thousand to two. I have not asked anything more of Constance 'cause I do not care to be mixed up with anyone so ungrateful. If you think I am not embarrassed to come to either of you for this help believe me I have never felt in my life as I do now. . . ."

There is no record of Joan's answer, but on August 27, Constance wrote once more to Richard, enclosing his note which she had endorsed for $5,000, and a few more words of recrimination: "Believe it or not, even though I am supposed to have money which grows in trees, I too have a pretty big family that depends on ME for every BIT of their livelyhood [*sic*]. As I have no one on whom I can depend to help out, it is up to me. I must BUDGET things now to protect the future, and because of budgeting and careful investing, I have not large sums of money at any hour I want to call upon them.

"This money that is being sent is not (as you warned in your telegram) being sent so that I may retain my future peace of mind, but as a token of my forgiveness to you. . . ."

And then, unexpectedly, Richard was offered a job. Guthrie McClintic, for several years one of the most important directors on Broadway, was about to stage Maxwell Anderson's new play, *Winterset,* another of his experiments in blank verse like *Mary of Scotland* and *Elizabeth the Queen*—but this time, with a contemporary setting. Based on the Sacco-Vanzetti case, *Winterset* centers on young Mio Romagna, who wanders into an East Side slum neighborhood in search of evidence that will clear his father, who was executed for a crime he did not commit. McClintic asked Richard to play the part of Judge Gaunt, unhinged by his guilt over having sentenced an innocent man to death.

Richard was immediately taken with the part, which would be one of the most taxing of his career. That McClintic had such faith in him is a testament to the brilliance of Richard's past achievements, for by now his memory was beginning to fail him, and the prospect of memorizing the lengthy blank verse speeches was daunting. Anderson's lofty philosophizing—he considered the theater "a religious institution devoted to the exaltation of the spirit of man"—found a kindred soul in Richard. The actor was also fascinated by the play's rich, layered dialogue, which he felt had been in short supply in the American theater. With renewed enthusiasm and optimism, he set to work learning the role of Judge Gaunt.

One of the most fascinating dimensions of the judge's character is his refusal to admit that he erred in sending Mio's father to the gallows. Throughout the play, Judge Gaunt drifts in and out of rational thought, clinging pathetically to the belief that he was innocent of any wrongdoing. In the second act, he tells Mio:

> But my madness
> is only this—that I would fain back
> on a life well spent—without one stain—one breath
> of stain to flaw the glass—not in men's minds
> nor in my own. I take my God as witness
> I meant to earn that clearness, and believe

> that I have earned it. Yet my name is clouded
> with the blackest, fiercest scandal of our age
> that's touched a judge. What I can do to wipe
> that smutch from my fame I will. I think you know
> how deeply I've been hated, for no cause
> that I can find there. Can it not be—and I ask this
> quite honestly—that the great injustice lies
> on your side and not mine?

Richard admired McClintic's way of working. At the first reading, McClintic smoked, chewed gum, broke the legs off chairs by leaning back on them—did everything, in Richard's view, to distract the actors from the fact that they were about "to embark on the troubled waters of reading a very fine play by a very intelligent author." Richard found him "the finest directorial mind I have ever encountered in the theater . . . keen, sensitive to every nuance of dramatic value, coupled with a world of tolerance."

Richard's excitement was infectious, and the younger cast members were properly worshipful. Richard often held court after rehearsals, offering his thoughts on how the play was progressing, and regaling them with anecdotes of many of his past successes. One of his favorites in the company was the young Burgess Meredith, who played Mio Romagna. On opening night at the Martin Beck Theater, September 25, 1935, Richard could barely contain his enthusiasm, showing up at Meredith's East Side apartment and shouting out, "Awake and sing! The hour has come! *Winterset* opens tonight!"

Richard drove, or rather sped, Meredith to the theater, swearing at other drivers and sideswiping a trailer along the way. Meredith was unsure how *Winterset* would go over with the public, and by the time he made his entrance, his nerves were raw. He settled down by the second act, but as he was approaching his big confrontation with Judge Gaunt, he noticed that Richard seemed nervous and unsteady. "But then," remembered Meredith, "he found the pace, the rhythm, the center of meaning. In one giddy moment he stopped again and we were stretched on the rack of a long, unused pause.

But he went on. Each word stronger, calmer, more certain . . . until we found a reality we had never found before. We lost ourselves in the excitement, the discovery. It was a redemptive moment, and that doesn't happen often."

The morning after the opening, Brooks Atkinson in the *New York Times* hailed *Winterset* as "a brilliant work of art." He called Anderson's poetry "as hard as iron and as sharp as steel," and praised the entire cast. But his warmest words were reserved for the old lion: "As the judge whose mind has cracked under the strain of conscience, Richard Bennett gives a memorable performance—gentle in manner, kindly in tone, pathetically broken in mental process." *Winterset* became the dramatic success of the season, winning the first New York Drama Critics Circle Award as Best Play.

It was a happy time, all too brief. As the run continued, Richard fell back on some of his old tricks. His performances were highly inconsistent: he was still drinking heavily, which further impaired his already shaky memory, and often Judge Gaunt's lengthy speeches slipped out of his grasp. At some performances he was riveting, full of the old fire and lyricism. At others he was unfocused and tentative. As always, any disturbance was enough to throw him off. One night, after an epidemic of coughing in the audience had lasted for the entire first act and half of the second, Richard did a long, slow meltdown. At the end of his big scene in the second act, when police officers arrive to cart off the Judge, Richard spoke his line as written: "All right, gentlemen, I'll go with you." Then, without any change in inflection, he added, "And I'll stop at the corner drugstore and buy twelve packages of cough drops for those chuckleheads out in the audience!"

Four months into the run of *Winterset,* Richard fell ill with double pneumonia. Since he had never fully regained his strength after his riding accident in England earlier in the year, his illness hit him hard. He became too debilitated to perform, and one Saturday night following a performance, he collapsed. He was taken to his apartment in the Hotel Whitby, and later to Harbor Hospital on Madison Avenue. The newspapers reported that he was believed to be suffering from an incurable, nameless illness. It quickly became clear to him and to Guthrie McClintic that he would have to withdraw from the cast of *Winterset.*

Barbara, who by now had given birth to a fourth child, Anthony, telephoned Constance and Joan, telling them that she feared Richard didn't have long to live. They both flew from California immediately, and Barbara met them at Newark Airport. But shortly after their arrival Richard began to rally, and as the weeks passed, he fought his way back to a condition that was far from healthy, but at least stable. By early May 1936, he felt well enough to sail for Rio de Janeiro for a long rest. He stayed for several months, working on his memoirs. The book, once he had finished it, was pure Richard: arrogant, quixotic, filled with self-delusions, confused, inaccurate memories, and pathetic attempts to justify his bouts of irrational behavior. No doubt money alone motivated him to write it. He sent it to Scribner's, hoping that the great editor of his day, Maxwell Perkins, would publish it. But no offer was ever made, and eventually Richard put the book away and forgot about it.

For most Hollywood actresses in the studio era, competition was a way of life. Whether it was by threat, barter, scheme, or sexual politics, they knew how to get their way. The Bennett sisters, on the other hand, found this aspect of Hollywood distasteful. For Constance, the game was how to make the most money in the least amount of time, but she wasn't temperamentally suited to hustling the best parts in the best pictures. She found the whole thing exhausting and demeaning; she felt that producers should be chasing her down, not vice versa. Joan never developed a killer career instinct, either, but after the success of *Little Women* she did have modest hopes that better parts might await her. She was in luck. One of the people who had been impressed with her performance as Amy was the producer Walter Wanger.

If there was a common link among the leading Hollywood moguls, it was that most of them sprang from lower-class, immigrant families who had known great poverty. Louis B. Mayer was an ex-junkman, Samuel Goldwyn had gotten his start in a glove factory, William Fox was a former coat liner for S. Cohen and Son of New York, Harry Cohn a former song plugger and pool hustler, Jack Warner a butcher's son. Walter Wanger was one of the few executives who came from a privileged background. He was born in San Francisco in 1894, the son of a prominent clothing manufacturer, and was educated expensively in the United States and the Institute Sillig in Vevey, Switzerland. In 1912, Wanger entered Dartmouth College, where he became an enthusiastic participant in dramatics—so enthusiastic that his grades suffered. According to Wanger's biographer, Matthew Bernstein, he "refused to buckle down to the discipline of an ordinary student," and was forced to leave at the end of his freshman year. He was readmitted, but remained an undisciplined student and left Dartmouth without a degree in 1915. He didn't mind much; more than anything, he wanted a career in the theater, and he soon landed a job working for Elizabeth Marbury, a producing agent. After a year with her, he struck out on his own as an independent producer with *'Ception Shoals*, starring Alla Nazimova, which had a modestly successful run on Broadway early in 1917.

By this time, the United States was at war, and later in 1917 Wanger received a lieutenant's commission in the Army Signal Corps. After he completed training as a pilot at the Massachusetts Institute of Technology, he was shipped overseas and put in several stints in France and Italy, where he proved that he had no talent at all for flying; Joan later recalled that he "cracked up the first five planes assigned to him." He was transferred to intelligence, and was soon assigned to the Rome office of the Committee on Public Information, supervising newsreels and a short propaganda film showing Americans mobilizing for war.

After returning from Europe in 1919, Wanger was ready to resume his theatrical career. Instead, he had a chance meeting with Jesse Lasky, vice president in charge of production at Famous Players–Lasky, then the world's dominant movie company. Lasky was impressed with Wanger's knowledge of the New York theater scene and hired him as general manager of film production, scouting and developing Broadway plays with big screen potential. His greatest success came when he goaded Lasky into buying Edith Hull's *The Sheik,* which as a vehicle for Rudolph Valentino made sex the movie's most profitable commodity of the early 1920s. After a year, Wanger left Lasky and sailed for England, where he produced plays and took a three-month lease on London's Royal Opera House, which had temporarily suspended its performances of ballet and opera in the wake of the war. Wanger outfitted it as a first-class movie theater, determined, according to Bernstein, to sell "the appeal of the movies to the city's social elite." He produced the first U.S. tour of the famous *Charlot's Revue,* starring Gertrude Lawrence and Jack Buchanan, after which Jesse Lasky coaxed him back to his old job at the studio. His second period at Famous Players-Lasky (which later became Paramount Pictures) was altogether more substantial. Wanger stayed with the studio until 1931, helping to introduce Claudette Colbert, Miriam Hopkins, Tallulah Bankhead, and the Marx Brothers. During his two-year stint at Columbia Pictures, he sought to move the studio in the direction of contemporary social drama, but by 1933 he tired of Columbia's bargain-basement production methods and moved on to the plush environment of MGM, where Louis B. Mayer and Irving Thalberg made him an associate producer. At MGM, he supervised four 1933 releases, including Garbo's great success, *Queen Christina.*

By this time, Wanger had tired of being just another producer rattling around in an enormous factory. Frustrated by the big studios' political machinations and interferences, he set himself up as an independent producer with his own company, Walter Wanger Productions, Inc. He had just completed his first picture under his own banner, *The President Vanishes,* an indictment of capitalism, when Paramount, nervous about the film's political content, ordered drastic cuts. Despite some good reviews, the film did not recoup its cost. But its failure only strengthened Wanger's resolve to succeed with another serious topic.

In 1934, he began production on one of his most ambitious projects, *Private Worlds,* based on a popular novel by Phyllis Bottome. Most of Wanger's colleagues thought he was doomed to fail with this one, since it dealt with mental illness, a topic that

Hollywood had previously avoided. Richard's 1919 film, *The End of the Road,* had shown some painful scenes of syphilis patients suffering from severe brain damage, and psychopaths were a regular component of horror films, but insanity had never been the central subject of a Hollywood picture. In *Private Worlds,* Wanger set out to give the topic the treatment he felt it deserved. For the leads, he secured Claudette Colbert and, in his U.S. film debut, Charles Boyer. There was also a key role that Wanger felt Joan could handle, and he called her in an for an interview. He warned her that it wasn't the biggest part in the picture, but advised her that it might give her career a boost. Joan quietly listened to Wanger's sales pitch, and signed on for the film.

Private Worlds opens at Brentwood Hospital, a respected mental institution thrown into upheaval by political infighting and opposing ideas about proper methods of treatment. The stern matron (Esther Dale) favors a disciplinary approach, dosing the patients with castor oil and throwing them into solitary confinement; the progressive view is represented by Dr. Jane Everest (Colbert) and Dr. Alec Macgregor (Joel McCrea). Dr. Everest's soothing, maternal tones can calm the most violent patient in a matter of minutes, while Dr. Macgregor's counseling sessions sound a bit like excerpts from *Ask Ann Landers*. "The only way we conquer life is to fight back," he tells a troubled inmate early in the film. "When life hits you, you hit right back. Life's just a bully."

But the patients' suffering is only window dressing. The film's real focus is on the personal problems of the staff. Dr. Everest is repressed, terrified of sexual commitment since the death of her lover years earlier, while Dr. Macgregor is a victim of his own frustrated ambition. When he is passed over for the post of hospital superintendent in favor of an outsider, Dr. Monet (Boyer), Macgregor takes his revenge by jumping into an affair with Monet's shady sister (Helen Vinson). The film hammers home the message that everyone has the potential to tumble off the narrow path of sanity. Dr. Everest points out that the doctors differ from the inmates "only in one respect: they've gone so far into their private worlds they're unable to come back."

The question of insanity within sane people is most fully developed in the character of Dr. Macgregor's wife, Sally (Joan). Because she cannot share Alec's professional life as Dr. Everest does, Sally constantly worries that he will get tired of her. When he takes up with Dr. Monet's sister, Sally is overwhelmed by feelings of inadequacy. She becomes obsessed with one of the hospital's most hopeless cases, a young girl named Carrie Flint. Sally becomes convinced that if she can manage to help Carrie, she will win Alec back. Her plan fails miserably: when Sally invites Carrie to tea, the girl goes to pieces and has to be taken away. Left alone in the house during a driving rainstorm, Sally suffers a complete breakdown and tumbles down a flight of stairs, nearly killing herself.

Joan had gone through a spell of inactivity before filming began on *Private Worlds*. On her twenty-fourth birthday, February 27, 1934, she gave birth to a second daughter, Melinda. She was delighted to have another child—and especially happy that Diana would not have to grow up alone. Although Diana had been baptized at the All Saints' Episcopal Church in Beverly Hills, Melinda was baptized in the Church of the Good Shepherd, since Gene was a lifelong Catholic.

By the time production on *Private Worlds* began, Joan was eager to get back to work. She relished the part of Sally Macgregor, later calling it "the first really challenging and the most dramatic role I'd played up to that time." True enough, but she didn't play it particularly well. In the crucial early scenes, in which Sally's instability is supposed to manifest itself slowly, her performance doesn't build—she doesn't seem disturbed at all, just faintly glum, like a schoolgirl who always gets picked last for the hockey team. Much has been written about the breakdown sequence—through the racket of a thunderstorm, Sally hears voices calling her name. Gregory LaCava used it as a rough sketch for a much more effective scene with Andrea Leeds in *Stage Door* two years later—but Joan's performance is not sufficiently nuanced to make it truly chilling. Andre Sennwald, in the *New York Times*, took her to task, calling her "of almost no assistance in the highly promising role of the doctor's wife." But most other critics disagreed. *Variety* found her "at her dramatic best," and the *New York American* praised her for providing "the terrifying climax to the drama." The *Hollywood Reporter* called her "nothing short of amazing in her work. Miss Bennett goes temporarily insane before your eyes in a scene that will chill you to the marrow. She's beautiful, she's sweet, she's thoroughly feminine, and emerges as an actress." Joan also received special praise from the American Medical Association, which felt that she had captured Sally's hallucinations in precise detail.

In the end, *Private Worlds* lost money, but it was one of the year's most prestigious films. "That picture was a big help," recalled Joel McCrea. "It helped everybody." For Joan, it helped her to redefine her potential as an actress; perhaps now better offers would come her way. What she got instead was a bland leading-lady part in Bing Crosby's new musical at Paramount, *Mississippi.* Based on a story by Booth Tarkington, with a score by Richard Rodgers and Lorenz Hart (including "It's Easy to Remember"), it was a cobbled-together story of love and chivalry in the Deep South. Shooting, which began in the fall of 1934, was held up for some time while costar W.C. Fields completed his scenes in *David Copperfield* at MGM. Joan pocketed $15,625 for her work in *Mississippi,* and was immediately thrown into another Crosby vehicle, *Two for Tonight,* which occupied her for nearly twelve weeks in 1935. Publicly, she described Crosby as a relaxed and charming colleague; privately, she found him taciturn and remote. *Two for Tonight* had even less to offer than *Mississippi,* but it was significant for another reason. With it, she launched her new, personal contract with Walter Wanger. Her reviews for *Private Worlds* persuaded him that he had been right about her dramatic potential, and he added her to his stable of actors, which also included Sylvia Sidney and Henry Fonda.

Clearly, there were other reasons for Wanger's interest. His style, once his films were in production, was distinctly laissez-faire. He was not a producer in the vein of David O. Selznick, hovering around the set all day and interfering with the director at every turn. But during the filming of *Private Worlds,* Wanger turned up on the set only when one of Joan's scenes was being shot. Joan was aware that Wanger was married—since 1919, to one of New York's great beauties, an ex–*Ziegfeld Follies* girl named Justine Johnston—but she also had heard the rumors that it was an open marriage, and that Walter was a serious womanizer. In any case, she found him attractive. He was only of average height, but he was undeniably handsome, with a full head of dark hair and compelling green eyes. When she spoke, he seemed to be listening intently, hanging on every word. He was kind and sympathetic, spoke French and German fluently, and was passionately interested in both the classics and modern literature—none of them qualities associated with most Hollywood producers. He was an independent thinker, a maverick, and this appealed to her enormously; she knew that no other producer would have taken a chance on a risky project like *Private Worlds*. For the time being, she would place the direction of her career in his obviously capable hands.

Now, more than ever, Joan had to think of the future. In her most candid private moments, she had to admit to herself that her life with Gene Markey was not all that she had hoped it would be. Perhaps by permitting herself to be caught on the rebound from John Considine, she had programmed her marriage to Gene to fail. But she couldn't deny that some of his personal traits—his extreme fastidiousness, his too-obvious delight in shallow Hollywood social life—were beginning to wear on her nerves. Then, too, she was still the principal breadwinner at Tower Road. Gene's screenwriting career had been reasonably steady, but not very lucrative, and he had yet to claim one important film among his credits. His latest efforts included *Midnight Mary* with Loretta Young and *Fashions of 1934* with Bette Davis—both examples of the inconsequential fluff that had marked his writing career from the beginning. Whatever her father's failings, he had risen to the top of his profession and been a good provider, qualities that Joan had always sought in a husband. Kind and thoughtful though Gene was, she suspected him of being little more than a dilettante. Wanger, with his sophisticated tastes in literature and art, and his impressive list of movie credits, struck her as having altogether more substance.

For the rest of 1935 and into 1936, Joan worked steadily in a string of films that did nothing to further her career: *She Couldn't Take It* with George Raft, *The Man Who Broke the Bank at Monte Carlo* with Ronald Colman, an early "disaster" movie, *Thirteen Hours by Air,* and *Two in a Crowd,* a racetrack comedy with Joel McCrea. Again, she was frustrated by the growing sense that she was merely marking time. By now she had been in Hollywood for seven years, and although she was a recognizable leading lady with a growing public, real stardom had been elusive. The responsibilities of being a Bennett still hung over her head. Deep down, she longed to do something more substantial than Bing Crosby musicals, but the old fears that she really wasn't good enough always resurfaced.

By the mid-1930s, the studios' financial troubles had passed the crisis stage, and both audience attendance and the number of features being produced annually were up. She told herself that what really mattered most was that she had steady employment, that she didn't lack for anything and was able to provide a comfortable and stable home for Diana and Melinda. If her career hadn't reached the level she had hoped for, her social life was thriving. This, in particular, made Gene very happy. The Markeys attended parties constantly and frequently gave formal dinners. Among their regular guests were producer Arthur Hornblow Jr. and his wife, Leonora, director Alexander Hall, Edmund Lowe and Sally Eilers, Claudette Colbert and her husband, Dr. Joel Pressman, Frances Dee and Joel McCrea, and Constance and Henri de la Falaise.

Despite her growing interest in Wanger, Joan took the step, in the summer of 1936, of legally changing Diana's surname from Fox to Markey. She wanted the girls to grow up as real sisters, she claimed, to share everything, including their family name. Her decision prompted a few rumblings from Jack Fox. Since his divorce from Joan, he had remarried twice, his drinking had grown worse, and he had fallen on very hard times. He had not seen Diana since Joan left California for New York and *Jarnegan,* and had been unable to keep up his support payments; occasionally, he sent a letter to Tower Road asking for a loan. In the end, he was unable to pose any serious obstacle to the name change, and Diana Fox became Diana Markey.

At the beginning of her contract term, Wanger had been loaning Joan out to other studios, but by mid-1936 he had a picture of his own ready for her. A blend of screwball comedy and crime drama called *Big Brown Eyes,* it teamed her for the first time with Cary Grant, who was nearing the end of an unfulfilling contract with Paramount and had not yet emerged as a major star. *Big Brown Eyes* reunited Joan with director Raoul Walsh, who had helped her through a similar wisecracking part in *Me and My Gal.* In *Big Brown Eyes,* Joan plays a cynical, smart-mouthed manicurist who helps her policeman beau (Grant) foil a crime ring. It was an inconsequential film, but again, Walsh used the tough side of Joan's personality to advantage, and her performance is sharp and funny. Paramount was so happy with the results that later in 1936 she was reteamed with Grant for another comedy, *Wedding Present,* but it turned out very badly and they never again made a film together.

By now, Joan and Wanger had become romantically involved. Joan was deliriously happy. She listened to Wanger's plans to make serious and important pictures—he was realistic enough to know that he would have to turn out a certain number of lightweight crowd-pleasers to finance the work he really wanted to do. Everything about him intrigued her, his liberal political views, which coincided with her own, his sophisticated tastes in literature, his elegance and breeding and sartorial splendor. Among Hollywood's crass, money-grubbing producers, he seemed a man of taste and refinement. She listened for hours as he reiterated his belief that the motion picture industry had a mission to provide audiences with strong, adult entertainment—a mission in which, for the most part, it had failed. For Wanger, American films could be a powerful vehicle for social change, and they should reflect something of the tensions and conflicts of everyday life. In his view, the ravages of the Depression had been underrepresented in Hollywood films, and the rise of fascism and mounting tensions in Europe had barely been addressed at all. For the most part, he maintained, Hollywood had closed its eyes to realism. One had only to look at the work of European film directors to see how far behind American movies lagged in depicting everyday life onscreen. He yearned to make films with deeper, darker themes, convinced that if Hollywood continued to grind out mindless fluff, the entire motion picture industry was doomed to fail.

It is surprising, then, that Wanger's next picture for Joan, *Vogues of 1938,* was a fluffy musical. Released in 1937, it was Joan's first Technicolor film, and she had never looked so beautiful onscreen. It was a lavish comedy, with songs thrown in, about a headstrong socialite (Joan) who ditches her rich fiancé for a job as a model in a house of couture. The new Technicolor process was still crude, but the previous year Wanger had enjoyed great success with it in an outdoor drama called *Trail of the Lonesome Pine,* and he reasoned that it should do wonders for a film set in the fashion industry. *Vogues of 1938* grossed a whopping $1,089,956, but not quite enough to cover its high production cost, and it wound up losing money. Still, as a vehicle for Joan, it was an undeniable success. For the first time since the early Fox days, she was the picture's focal point, not just its leading lady; she was exquisitely photographed by Ray Rehnahan, and dominated the film with her sharp, tongue-in-cheek performance. *Vogues of 1938* was a crucial step toward becoming a star in her own right—and a testament to Wanger's growing attachment to her.

Throughout the film's production, Joan's romance with Wanger had flourished. Actress Penny Singleton, cast in a supporting role, remembered only one thing about it: "Love was in the air. That much was obvious to all of us."

Chapter Thirteen

1937–1940

Following her departure from MGM, Constance waited around for another decent contract offer to materialize. When none did, she signed a two-picture deal with Gaumont-British, a studio known for its Alfred Hitchcock thrillers and Jessie Matthews musicals. The first film was a World War I drama called *Everything Is Thunder,* adapted from a novel by J.B. Hardy; the second was being developed under the working title *The Hawk*. Constance was to receive a salary of $55,000 for each picture—a swift drop from her asking price a couple of years earlier—plus 10 percent of the U.S. gross. Once production began on *Everything Is Thunder,* Constance found that she was not to be paid in advance after all, as she had requested, but by the week. By filming's end, she had received only $35,000. There was more bad news. *The Hawk,* Gaumont-British now decided, was not to be made after all. Constance sued the company for breach of contract—$65,000 worth—and won. The case brought her lots of publicity, but what she needed was a good movie, particularly after *Everything Is Thunder* turned out to be another dud. In mid-1936 she was called back to Hollywood by her old friend Darryl Zanuck, whose Twentieth Century Pictures had now merged with Fox. Zanuck was preparing a romantic drama for the new studio called *Ladies in Love,* about three beautiful young women trying to snare rich husbands. On paper, it looked like a big picture, with an all-star cast including Loretta Young, Janet Gaynor, Don Ameche, and Tyrone Power, but it was done in by a witless, meandering script.

Both Constance and Joan had inherited their parents' fierce work ethic; throughout their entire careers, inactivity made them restless and irritable. Constance tried not to let her professional stagnation bother her, but privately she was itching to get back to work. It was not easy for her to adjust to life as a Hollywood also-ran, particularly when little sister Joan seemed to be getting all the work she could handle. There had been talk of pairing Constance with William Powell in the comedy *My Man Godfrey,* but the film's director, Gregory LaCava, had suffered her caprices in *Bed of Roses* and *The Affairs of Cellini* and refused to work with her again. Carole Lombard got the part, and the film was one of the great successes of the year.

Constance's dry spell ended with a call from producer Hal Roach. Having established his career with silent comedies starring Harold Lloyd, Roach had more recently been responsible for a string of Laurel and Hardy hits. His new project was more ambitious—the screen version of Thorne Smith's comic novel *Topper.* Roach thought that Constance might be right for the feminine lead, and offered a salary of $40,000. It was less than she was accustomed to, but because it was such a good script, she accepted at once. *Topper* was a biting, irreverent comedy about a feckless, fast-living couple, George and Marion Kerby, whose biggest problem is finding out where the next perfect martini is coming from. One morning, while speeding home after a long night of club-hopping, they crash their roadster into a tree and are instantly killed. But they come back as ghosts, invading the life of their neighbor Cosmo Topper, helping him to throw off his strait-jacketed Westchester lifestyle and embrace life wholeheartedly.

In the early 1930s, Constance had embodied the tensions of urban women caught in the grip of the Depression, whose only hope of escaping poverty was to shackle themselves to rich men. But Hollywood could not sustain such a pessimistic view forever. As the decade reached its halfway mark, a lighter mood began to prevail, and screwball comedy became an antidote to the sentiment that Hollywood had been pouring out by the bucketload. By this time, the message of Franklin Roosevelt's New Deal had gotten through: Americans could cling, however vaguely, to the hope that the hardships wrought by the Depression wouldn't last forever. This feeling was very strong in Hollywood, and it is tempting to imagine that the rise of screwball comedy was the studios' way of celebrating their emergence from the dire financial predicament of only a few years earlier.

In the confession pictures, the rich had been shown as callous, manipulative, inhumane, self-protective, the real cause of the suffering of the defenseless poor. But now this view seemed unsophisticated. The screwball comedies humanized the rich by burlesquing them, portraying them as a bunch of unruly, undisciplined children. By showing the upper classes to be wildly irresponsible, even addled, these films permitted audiences to take a more indulgent view of them—they could shake off their resentment and laugh at them. And as they went home, they could console themselves with the thought that they possessed things that the rich didn't—stability and common sense, for instance.

Topper was a pivotal film in Cary Grant's career. His performance as George Kerby fully revealed his comedic talents for the first time and started him on the road to his brilliant work in *The Awful Truth, Bringing Up Baby, The Philadelphia Story,* and *His Girl Friday*. But it is Constance who lingers in the memory long after we've seen the film. There was a lot of Marion in Constance—the delight in playing games for their own sake, the cool-headed certainty that she would come out on top, the habit of saying whatever was on her mind, the love of indulging herself without regard for the consequences. It is both her most vivid and most relaxed screen performance. She looks ravishing—still the human coat hanger—and her graceful movements, more liquid than ever, are ideal for the ghostly Marion. She quite literally seems to melt out of one scene and flow into the next (while Grant is too solid, too flesh-and-blood to be entirely convincing as a spirit). But the film itself lets them down about two-thirds of the way through. Although Norman Z. McLeod's direction is swift and assured, there isn't enough invention in the Erich Hatch–Jack Jevne script to sustain us to the end, and it becomes a one-joke movie: yet another scene of the Kerbys wreaking havoc on the hapless Topper. (This is something of a problem in Smith's novel as well. It has a slightly undigested quality, as if he never stopped to refine any of his comic situations.) But it hardly matters, the film is a fine showcase for the personalities of Constance and Grant, who carried it to enormous success in 1937. The critics didn't just praise Constance's work, they took up her cause. Hollywood was chided for not having taken advantage of her comic talents sooner. Decades later, when *Topper* was a popular attraction in revival houses, Pauline Kael wrote, "For those who don't know why Constance Bennett was a big movie star, her provocative, teasing Marion Kerby should provide the answer." Marion was the best role of Constance's career, and her reincarnation as a glamorous comedienne was 1937's biggest comeback story. Hal Roach, delighted with *Topper*'s success, was having another comedy prepared for her, to go into production as soon as possible.

By this time, Constance's marriage to Henri Falaise, who was still occupied with business affairs in Europe, had reached a plateau. His work in the film industry had not added up to much, although he did produce a feature-length documentary about Bali called *Legong: Dance of the Virgins,* released in 1935. Constance's romance with Gilbert Roland had continued in fits and starts and by now was an open secret in Hollywood. As early as 1933, the year that they met, the *Hollywood Reporter* had spotted them dining unchaperoned and took it as a signal that their romance was out in the open. They made headlines from time to time, notably in a bizarre incident on July 15, 1935, when a private plane lost its engine and nosedived, grazing Constance and Gilbert's car as they were driving down Roosevelt Highway, near Malibu Beach. No doubt Falaise knew of the romance, but he seemed unemotional and unconcerned as his marriage continued to decline.

By mid-fall of 1937, the new Hal Roach film, *Merrily We Live,* was ready to go into production. It was another screwball comedy, thrown together by Roach expressly to capitalize on Constance's success in *Topper,* and he showed his appreciation by giving her a slight pay raise: $50,000 for a ten-week guarantee. *Merrily We Live* was a breathless farce about a down-and-out writer (Brian Aherne) who goes to work as a butler in the home of a lunatic rich family, and eventually teaches the spoiled oldest daughter (Constance) the meaning of love. It was a blatant knockoff of *My Man Godfrey,* but it had hilarious patches, many of them courtesy of Billie Burke as Constance's sublimely deranged mother. Norman Z. McLeod was again the director, and Constance led the cast with another shrewd comic performance, proving that *Topper* had set her on the right path. *Merrily We Live* wrapped on January 8, 1938, and when it was released two months later, the *New York Daily Mirror* found it "the most exhilarating light comedy of the season." The *New York Daily News* wrote, "Constance Bennett, who proved to be a top-notch comedienne in *Topper,* plays the leading feminine role in the current comedy for all it is worth."

Just as *Topper* and *Merrily We Live* had re-established Constance in Hollywood, screwball comedy seemed to have run its course. With the spread of tensions in Europe, other producers began to echo Walter Wanger's plea for pictures that presented a more sobering and realistic view of the world. Suddenly, the high-living, irresponsible heiresses that Constance had played began to seem anachronistic. Her temperamental reputation had caught up with her, and few producers seemed willing to follow Hal Roach's lead and take a chance on her. Without a major studio behind her, she had to snatch what was offered, and what was offered wasn't very good: *Service de Luxe,* a thin comedy with Vincent Price; *Topper*'s inevitable sequel, *Topper Takes a Trip*; and *Tail Spin,* a drama about women flyers, with Constance as the haughtiest of the group. Alice Faye, who starred with her in *Tail Spin,* remembered, "There was a scene where she had to slap me. Usually you just fake the slap, but she really let me have it—and she had a hand like a whip!" Constance campaigned long and hard for the part of Lady Edwina Esketh in Twentieth Century–Fox's *The Rains Came,* knowing that it would give her career another burst of energy, but had to face the hard news that her friend Darryl Zanuck thought Myrna Loy more suitable.

Constance had an urgent need to keep working, even in inferior films. In 1937, she had purchased a sizeable lot on Carolwood

Drive in Holmby Hills, an exclusive neighborhood just north of Sunset Boulevard. Soon construction on a house began. Designed by architect James E. Dolena, who had created homes for William Powell, Walt Disney, and George Cukor, it was a spectacular house in the French Normandy style, with a white brick exterior and arched windows. Interior decoration was taken over by ex–silent film star William Haines, who outfitted the house with immense mirrors, finely detailed scenic panels, Louis XVI furniture, and vivid Chinese wallpaper. Constance supervised the installation of semi-formal gardens, with great white oaks, fully grown, brought in and planted around the house. She was delighted with the finished product, which she dubbed her "Hollywood-French" castle. In no time she set about entertaining on a grand scale. At one memorable party, she had the backyard transformed into a tented dance floor, bordered with chicken wire adorned with holly and gardenias. Glenn Miller and his orchestra were hired to play for the evening; the guest list included Marlene Dietrich and Noël Coward.

Her move to a home of her own was misleading in one sense, for her personal life was anything but settled. She was still conducting a passionate affair with Gilbert Roland, punctuated by interludes in Paris with Henri. On numerous occasions, she risked seeing Gilbert while Henri was in Los Angeles. Beginning in the mid-1930s, Constance rented a beach house in Santa Monica. To Gilbert, it seemed impossible that Henri did not know of his wife's infidelity, yet he seemed unconcerned about it. Once, Gilbert even accompanied Constance and Henri to a casino in Agnua Caliente. While Gilbert and Constance stayed up all night playing baccarat, Henri retired early, without the slightest display of jealousy. Gilbert kept anticipating a confrontation with Henri, but none ever materialized.

By this time, Constance had grown slightly more tolerant of publicity for Peter. She was proud of her son, who was growing up to be a bright, energetic, self-reliant young man who had cultivated a serious interest in photography and horses, having already won several trophies and ribbons riding in horse shows. For several years now, Philip Plant had recognized Peter as his son. Whenever

Constance was on the East Coast, a visit with Philip was arranged, and when Philip came to California, he always dropped in at Carolwood Drive. He was faithful about remembering Peter on birthdays and holidays, and often sent him postcards and letters, inquiring about his studies and his horsemanship successes in proper fatherly fashion. As time went on, Constance's fears about the threat posed by the Plant family appeared to be unfounded.

On October 8, Richard was finally divorced from Aimee. Los Angeles Superior Court Judge Charles Burnell awarded Aimee $50,000 in insurance policies, and an additional $10,000 in real estate. Aimee's attorneys had managed to build a compelling case around Richard's alleged physical abuse, and on the day that the court pronounced the divorce final, the ex–Mrs. Bennett continued her field day with the press. She complained that Richard performed his roles "very realistically, even off the stage. If he decides to play a role using a gun or a dagger, he carries it through to the end—and I have scars to show the results." Richard, in New York at the time, didn't contest the decision and, for once, had little to say for the record.

By now, Richard's financial condition was desperate. He had taken an apartment at the Westover Hotel on West Seventy-second Street, but his stay there was anything but restful. In December, the hotel's elevator door closed on his thumb, badly mangling it. He was in considerable pain for weeks afterward, and promptly filed a $100,000 lawsuit against the hotel's management. That he chose to magnify such a trivial incident is an indication of how empty his life had become. There seemed to be no decent parts available for him on Broadway, and most of his old friends had deserted the city. He knew that since his withdrawal from *Winterset,* many in the theater community whispered that he was no longer reliable, and inactivity was taking its toll.

Finally, in late 1937, he was offered what seemed an ideal opportunity to return to Broadway in grand style. The play was Paul Osborn's *On Borrowed Time*. Its director was the gifted young

Joshua Logan, making his Broadway debut. Logan had seen Richard in several of his previous successes, and thought he would be perfect for the role of Gramps, a feisty old man who finds himself summoned by Death. But Gramps isn't ready to go, as it turns out, and he chases Death up a tree while stalling for time. Richard was delighted with both the play and the part—not a supporting role, like Judge Gaunt, but a real star turn. Logan was quick to perceive how easily Gramps might become a crotchety, cornpone character out of low comedy, and he became convinced that Richard was the only actor who could give the part the kind of nobility called for in Osborn's script. The young director also was aware of Richard's difficulties with *Winterset,* but he had his heart set on him and decided to take the gamble.

In rehearsal, Richard felt his way through the part tentatively, hardly ever giving a full-out performance. Logan was patient and, at first, not especially worried. He figured that the character hadn't fully taken shape in Richard's imagination, and until it did, he would continue to mark his way through rehearsals. But as the days passed, it became clear that Richard was afraid to let go of his script. Many of Gramps's lines were maddeningly similar, and without the script in front of him, Richard frequently grew confused.

By the time the play opened at the Shubert Theatre in New Haven in January 1938, the part continued to elude Richard's grasp. A prompter was stationed at each side of the stage, but this only rattled him further. Once, when both prompters fed him the same line simultaneously, he shouted, "One at a time! One at a time!" The audience showed its support by breaking into applause, but as the evening wore on, Richard dropped more and more lines. When his performance came into focus, he was "vitally touching, virile, and funny," Logan recalled. Desperate to salvage the situation, the director thought of taping lines at various points around the stage. But the backers demanded that Richard be replaced before the play went into New York, and Dudley Digges took over the part. When *On Borrowed Time* opened at the Longacre on February 3, 1938, the critics proclaimed it one of the season's best plays. Robert Benchley compared it favorably with Thornton Wilder's *Our Town,* which opened the following night, and felt that Digges gave "one of the best performances of his career, making swearing, mild lechery, and even dying all major virtues."

Richard read the reviews with a heavy heart. The ignominy of being fired from a play that had become one of Broadway's biggest hits was almost more than he could bear. Deep down, he knew that the chances that he would ever again appear on the New York stage were slim to none. Still, he refused to take responsibility for his failure, insisting that he couldn't concentrate on his lines because of the pain he endured from the accident at the Westover.

The suit against the hotel seemed as much a panicked bid for cash as an attempt to see justice done, for only a month after his dismissal from *On Borrowed Time,* Richard's financial predicament threatened to become desperate. He temporarily moved in with friends in West Hartford, Connecticut, while trying to map out a plan for survival. Finally, he swallowed his pride and in mid-1938 wrote a letter to Constance, asking that she and Joan contribute three hundred dollars a month to his upkeep and offering to send a note for each payment. "I want a return of some of that bread I have cast upon the water," he wrote. "You girls could make me very happy at no expense to yourselves, and you know very well you would get it back." Otherwise, he predicted, he might have to present himself to the Actors' Home in New Jersey as a charity case.

On top of everything else, there was his own deteriorating health to contend with. In March he had all of his upper teeth removed, and a few weeks later a medical examination in Hartford revealed that he was suffering from an enlarged heart and liver, mild arteriosclerosis, and hemochromatosis, which indicated a combination of cirrhosis of the liver and diabetes. He wrote frequently to Constance, requesting loans, always taking care to remind her that the fame and financial success she had enjoyed would not last forever: "How are you going to feel at the age of sixty-seven when all of the toadies who are now making a sucker [*sic*] find you with no bank account?" It was now time for his daughters to start repaying him for the help he had given them in both their professional and personal lives; he had bent over backward "to make forsaken Joan's life more bearable. I rid her of Fox and started her career as I rid you of Mooreshead [*sic*]—lying cheating and faking to do so but what the hell did that matter? It was one of my kids I was fighting for—Did I warn you against that beggar on horseback Plant? I have never guided you wrongly or failed you. . . . Ah but this is all so cheap—sounds like a below stairs argument. . . . You were mine up to our public deliverance. . . . Those adorable years are mine alone to carry into eternity."

Constance replied promptly, although she made no promise that help would be instantly forthcoming. The recent decline in the stock market, she claimed, caught her off guard, and her business manager, J.S. Rex Cole, had ordered her to watch every penny. From the beginning of her adult life, she had been a staunch Republican, and she lost no time in sidestepping Richard's request by insisting that Franklin Roosevelt's economic policies had put her and many like her in a precarious spot. "The country is in a panic with this administration and stock market," she said. "If it gets any worse there will be chaos, with no incentive to big business at all. If you haven't money, you worry about how to get it, and if you have, you worry about how to protect it. The latter seems the worst, just when you've worked yourself practically to the bone to accumulate it, the government with one fell swoop demolishes it, either with taxes or ruining the market. It's a great life, I suppose, if you can take it, but the riding is awfully rough."

Constance was not always such a cold-blooded businesswoman. She was also capable of unexpected bursts of generosity. At some point in the late 1930s, she received a hard-luck letter from a farmer in the Midwest who had been wiped out by the Depression. It was not uncommon for her to receive such letters, but something about this particular one touched her, and she sent the man a sizeable loan, which he faithfully repaid, a few dollars a month, for the next several years. She could also be sympathetic to the difficulties of those who worked for her. In 1938, her longtime maid, Dora Pinter, was diagnosed with terminal cancer. All Constance's servants were treated by her own physician, and when the doctor told Constance that Pinter would have to remain in the hospital under twenty-four-hour care, she immediately went to Pinter and asked her if she wouldn't be more comfortable at home. When Pinter said yes, Constance arranged for her bedroom to be outfitted with all the proper hospital equipment, permitting her a death with dignity at Carolwood Drive.

Perhaps Joan was the only one who wasn't surprised when her marriage to Gene Markey failed to go the distance. Outwardly, they seemed quite happy. They were young, bright, and attractive, and at the vortex of Hollywood social life. Diana continued to dote on Gene, and Melinda was a beautiful and healthy child. Privately, however, Joan knew the road she was on would eventually end. She had married Gene because she was in a vulnerable state, following her breakup with John Considine and the trauma of her horse-riding accident. But he had never been a great passion in her life, a truth that had been hammered home since she had met Walter Wanger. They were mismatched in other ways, too. Unlike Jack Fox and John Considine (and many of those who would follow), Gene was self-possessed and not emotionally dependent on Joan. Joan later observed that her marriage to Gene degenerated into a "dull, lusterless routine" that simply ran out of steam. But the real cause of their breakup was Wanger, and everyone close to her knew it.

At one point, Gene's parents moved into the guest room on Tower Road for an extended stay, and Gene slept on an extra bed in Diana's room—a sign, Diana recalled, "that he and Mother were not hitting it off at all." Arguments, many of them over Wanger, became more and more frequent. In the spring of 1936, Gene moved out. Melinda was too young to understand, but Diana was devastated: she had lost her favorite playmate and companion.

On June 3, 1937, Joan divorced Gene on the grounds of cruelty. Gene moved into an apartment in Los Angeles, and Joan was faithful about taking Diana and Melinda for regular visits. But the stress of balancing the affair with Wanger and her crumbling marriage to Gene had taken its toll. She sought distraction through work, and Wanger obliged by casting her in *I Met My Love Again*, a romantic drama costarring Henry Fonda. It didn't do well with critics or audiences, and Joan never thought much of it, although she is rather appealing in it—fresh and vibrant as a small-town girl yearning for a sexual awakening. When she finished shooting the film, no other acceptable roles were offered. She felt restless and pent-up, and wanted nothing more than a change of scenery.

She was in luck: Broadway producer Sam Harris was looking for a box-office name to head the national touring company of the George S. Kaufman–Edna Ferber hit comedy *Stage Door.* On Broadway, Margaret Sullavan had played the role of Terry Randall, the upper-crust girl who longs for a stage career and moves into the Footlights Club, a theatrical rooming house where she finds difficulty being accepted by her fellow struggling actresses. But Sullavan was pregnant, and a big movie name was sought to make the lengthy national tour pay off. Joan was reluctant at first. She had not appeared onstage since *The Pirate* in 1929, but she reasoned that a stage success might well boost her stock in Hollywood. A weekly salary of $2,000 was set, and in September she prepared to open at the Bushnell Memorial Theater in Hartford, Connecticut.

The *Stage Door* tour was well-timed for other reasons. Eager for a home of her own at last, Joan had purchased a substantial lot on Mapleton Drive, in Holmby Hills, not far from Constance's home on Carolwood Drive. She commissioned the noted architect Wallace Neff to design a grand-scale French Provincial house on the property. Joan took an active role in all stages of planning the house. For her decorator, Joan engaged Hazel Ray Davies. Unlike Constance, who left her decorator, William Haines, to his own devices and later criticized his choices, Joan was absorbed by the details of assembling her dream house, right up until the time she had to head east for the beginning of her *Stage Door* tour. She gave up the lease on Tower Road, put her belongings in storage, and registered Diana at her own alma mater, St. Margaret's Academy in Waterbury, Connecticut. Melinda and a nurse would travel with her for the duration of the tour.

Joan's return to the stage was far from a seamless transition. She felt ill at ease at first, accustomed as she was to minimizing her gestures and reactions for the camera, and she had difficulty projecting her personality into the larger arena of the theater. In the first act, she appeared tentative, but as the play progressed, she found the character of Terry and became more and more confident. The reviews were mixed, partly, it would seem, because of the snobbery that existed toward film actors who ventured into the theater. One reviewer felt that Joan's portrayal of Terry emphasized "the fact that there is no substitute for stage experience for one who would play stage roles." At the three-week engagement at Boston's Shubert Theater, one critic noted that what the play needed in the chief role was not necessarily a striking beauty, but an actress of Elisabeth Bergner's caliber. Despite the notices, the tour was an enormous success at the box office. It extended northward as far as Quebec City, where Joan and her daughters spent the Christmas holidays, then headed west, ending at Chicago's Grand Opera House in February. In Chicago, the entire four-week engagement was sold out and reviews were among the best on the tour. (One critic was happy that Chicago had experienced the pleasure of "Joan Bennett, acting like her father's daughter." Sam Harris begged her to extend the run, but she declined. She was exhausted, but more to the point, the house on Mapleton Drive was now finished and she couldn't wait to settle in.

The only blight on the Chicago run was the news about Richard and *On Borrowed Time*. In a letter to Mabel, Joan felt he was "really washed up this time and won't be able to get another job. So it's up to us to provide for him, and much as I'd like not to, it looks like we'll have to. I say 'we' because I hope Constance will help. He asked me to let him stay with me. I just couldn't bear that. I'd not only lose my mind but wouldn't be able to keep a servant in my house. . . ." She asked Mabel to appeal to Constance for help in providing Richard with some kind of consistent financial support. Her own position, taking into account her new income tax status as a single woman and the hefty mortgage taken out on the Mapleton Drive home, "wouldn't permit me to do it alone."

Once Joan saw the Mapleton house, she loved it even more than she had imagined she would. It was a magnificent creation: a fifteen-room French Provincial–style house of whitewashed brick, with twin chimney towers—a Wallace Neff trademark. The driveway curved its way up from Mapleton, and there were no security gates, which Joan found boorish. The outside shutters were painted Joan's favorite shade of peacock blue. Flowers abounded, window boxes spilling over with brilliant blooms. In back of the house was a great lawn, with flowerbeds hedged in with boxwood. This led to the pool, poolhouse, and outdoor dining area. There were immaculately designed cutting gardens, a greenhouse, and a great magnolia tree right outside Joan's bedroom window. Inside, four balconies hung over the elegant circular entrance hall, with a crystal chandelier, purchased in France, hanging from the two-storied ceiling. The living room was dominated by a hand-tufted blue-and-yellow rug, with a blue-and-white floral patterned couch—actually two couches put together—and a long, low coffee table with compartments at either end to hold bright pepper plants and miniature orange trees.

The dining room had a more masculine atmosphere, with its blue Chinese broadloom rug and an elaborate mural of hunting scenes, painted in autumnal tones, covering the walls. There was an oak-paneled library, and everywhere, from top to bottom, shelves to accommodate her vast collection of ornaments and miniatures brought back from Paris, Venice, New York, and New England. Upstairs were six bedrooms. For her own room, Joan had selected a sea-foam-and-peach color scheme, with a soft green rug, chintz-covered walls, and a great canopied bed. At last, Joan had become a member of Hollywood's "landed gentry." For the next fifteen years, 515 South Mapleton Drive would be one of her proudest accomplishments.

Once she was settled into a home of her own, Joan's domestic streak emerged more strongly than ever. She once described herself as "a compulsive housekeeper," a statement corroborated by those close to her. She had to keep a strict working schedule herself. When she was filming, she rose at 5:30 A.M., and in the pre–labor union days before World War II, the work week often extended to Saturday. On the set, she dictated memos to the household staff and planned the menus for the coming week. Once a day, her chauffeur arrived with shopping lists from the cook for her to approve and telephone messages from her secretary; Joan sent back detailed instructions for both. "Every place where Joan lived was kept up most fastidiously," remembered Victor Morrison.

No doubt Joan thought that her new domestic surroundings might prove alluring to Wanger. By now she was deeply in love with him, and, conventional as ever, she wanted to marry him. He seemed to her a superb catch: even though his films didn't always turn a profit, he was regarded in Hollywood as one of the brightest and most promising of independent producers—and one of the few with truly global interests. Earlier in 1938, at the peak of the Spanish Civil War, he had produced *Blockade,* which he intended to be a powerful antiwar statement but which was interpreted by the Spanish fascists as a piece of Loyalist propaganda. Walter incurred the wrath of General Franco, who saw to it that the picture was banned in Spain. Germany, Italy, Yugoslavia, Poland, and many other countries quickly followed suit. The film posted a net loss of more than $135,000 but earned Wanger the National Peace Conference citation.

With his understated elegance, and his strong belief in reading, education, and the importance of leading a socially productive life, Joan thought he would make a wonderful father figure for Diana and Melinda. Wanger, however, was not so sure that Joan's brand of domestic bliss was for him. He made it clear that he and Justine Johnston had had an open relationship, and that such a situation suited him perfectly. In 1938, he allowed Johnston to sue him for divorce on the ground of mental cruelty, but he pointed out that the dissolution of the marriage did not mean that he was immediately ready to settle down again.

Disappointed, Joan threw herself into work. On loan-out, she made two indifferent films: *The Texans,* with Randolph Scott, and *Artists and Models Abroad,* with Jack Benny. Her salary was now up to $7,000 per week, but she was treading water professionally, and Wanger knew it. Although he had given her small boosts with

Private Worlds and *Vogues of 1938,* he had yet to figure out a bold new direction for her career. The solution came with his next picture, *Trade Winds.* Earlier in 1938 he had produced a romantic drama, *Algiers,* starring Charles Boyer. Playing opposite him, in her American film debut, was Viennese actress Hedy Lamarr. Five years earlier, she had shocked audiences with her nude race through the woods in the German film *Extase.* By 1938, Hollywood's abiding fascination with sultry, exotic European beauties like Greta Garbo and Marlene Dietrich had receded but not vanished altogether. Lamarr, slimmed down and lighted and made up to meet Hollywood standards of beauty, became a star in *Algiers.* She wasn't much of an actress, but it hardly mattered. She was widely thought to be the most ravishing woman that the movies had yet discovered, and the publicity fanfare accompanying her appearance in *Algiers* was enormous.

The script for *Trade Winds,* being written by the husband-and-wife team of Dorothy Parker and Alan Campbell, was the story of a glamorous blonde socialite, Kay Kerrigan, who becomes a murder suspect and goes on the lam. The picture follows her around the world, as she changes her identity and dyes her hair black, only to be trailed by a detective (Fredric March) who falls in love with her. *Trade Winds* was the best script Joan had been assigned in some time, a lively mixture of suspense, romance, and travelogue, with plenty of trademark Parker zingers thrown in. Wanger felt that in a black wig Joan would be a dead ringer for Lamarr, and make-up tests confirmed his hunch. He ordered his crew to play up the resemblance as much as possible, and instructed Joan to drop her voice an octave. As she later recalled, "I positively smoldered all over the South Seas."

The color change triggered the emergence of a new and intriguing screen persona for Joan. On occasion, she had shown signs of a sly, funny streak, which had seemed somewhat at odds with her gentle, blonde, china-doll looks. In *Trade Winds,* she was transformed—tougher, sexier, more worldly. Critics voiced their approval. "Joan Bennett looks attractive and gives an unusually credible performance," wrote *Variety.* "She has much more animation than normally and she brings a new and appealing warmth to her emotional scenes." Years later, Pauline Kael wrote that the Lamarr takeoff had worked so well because Joan "had no trouble at all outacting her." (In truth, the new hair color caused her to resemble English star Margaret Lockwood more than Lamarr.) Joan was delighted with the results, claiming that the transformation made her feel "not a bit like a pig-tailed little sister, which I've always felt like before. Now I feel much more vivid, alive, daring—practically like a menace." The color change also had far-reaching results among her fans. Across America, blondes and redheads went brunette; it was one of the strongest fashion alerts Hollywood had issued in years.

Before *Trade Winds* was released, word of Joan's new image had gotten around town. One of those most intrigued was David Selznick, deep in the planning stages for the biggest production of his career, the screen version of Margaret Mitchell's best-seller, *Gone With the Wind.* He was by now two years into his search for the right actress to play the fiery heroine, Scarlett O'Hara, and he approached Joan about testing for the part. Dozens of established stars, including Joan Crawford, Norma Shearer, and Loretta Young, had been mentioned for the part, and dozens more actresses had been tested, both known (Paulette Goddard, Frances Dee, Anita Louise, Lana Turner) and unknown (Nancy Coleman, Linda Watkins, Edythe Marriner—who later became Susan Hayward). The film's director, George Cukor, had approached Joan in the fall of 1937 about testing for the part, but she had declined, partly because she was about to leave on her *Stage Door* tour, and partly because it was rumored that Paulette Goddard was as good as set for the role.

But Joan's new look had fueled her ambitions, and she agreed to make a test for Selznick. For a couple of weeks, she worked on the Southern accent with dialogue coach Will Price, and on December 20, 1938, she filmed the test in three scenes: Scarlett dressing for the Twelve Oaks barbecue, drunk in her room following her husband Frank Kennedy's death, and trying to persuade Ashley Wilkes to abandon the ruins of Tara and run away with her to

Mexico. Selznick judged her effort "magnificent," and Joan found herself on a list of four finalists for the role, along with Goddard, Jean Arthur, and a relatively unknown English actress named Vivien Leigh.

A look at the tests today makes us wonder that Joan came as close as she did to winning the part. Her test is a worthy effort, but she is not at all right for Scarlett. In the dressing scene, she cannot capture the young Scarlett's flightiness, and she seems not so much feisty as downright tough. In the scene with Ashley, she tries to show Scarlett near defeat, but her pacing is fatally slow, and she kills any chance of establishing a crisp rhythm to her performance. She was philosophical about losing the part to Leigh, whose performance she regarded as superb. Selznick offered Joan a consolation prize of sorts, by asking her permission to cast Diana as Scarlett's doomed daughter, Bonnie Blue Butler. "She absolutely turned it down," said Diana. "It was the last thing in the world she wanted me to do. Actually, it was the last thing *I* wanted to do."

Scarlett had eluded her, but coming so close to winning the role had boosted her stock in Hollywood. To Joan, there was a clear turning point in her career: "I switched from blonde to brunette," she said, "and all the parts were better after that." Not all, exactly. For producer Edward Small, who specialized in making modestly budgeted versions of literary classics, she appeared as Maria Theresa, Infanta of Spain, in a film of Alexandre Dumas's *The Man in the Iron Mask*. She looked beautiful in the period costumes, but the role required little of her. Neither did her next two pictures, *The Housekeeper's Daughter* and *Green Hell,* challenge her at all. The first was an inane comedy made for Hal Roach, significant in Joan's career only because she objected to the film's crude advertising campaign. Among the tag lines used to plug the picture were "The Housekeeper's Daughter did things she hadn't oughter" and "She couldn't cook, she couldn't sew, but O how she could so and so." Joan launched a campaign against the picture by writing to twenty-six hundred women's clubs across the country, asking for their support. The ladies of the clubs responded, threatening to boycott *The Housekeeper's Daughter* on the local level if such advertising were used. The incident got considerable play in the press, which served only to give the picture a boost at the box office.

Green Hell was even worse. A cliché-ridden adventure set in the South American jungles, it was filmed on Universal's un-air-conditioned sound stages in the dead of summer, and the actors constantly had to have cold packs applied to the backs of their necks. Joan found George Sanders one of the most disagreeable actors she ever worked with. "He was rude," remembered Carmen DiRigo, Joan's hairdresser. "He would sit in the director's chair and let the ladies stand up." In the end, it was hardly worth the trouble. The *Harvard Lampoon* listed it as one of the year's ten worst pictures.

With Henri still in Europe, Gilbert Roland had now moved in with Constance at Carolwood Drive, where they conducted a busy social life. There were frequent dinners and homecoming parties. One of Constance and Gilbert's favorite guests was Countess Dorothy Di Frasso, who was funny, lively, and loved to gamble. Lady Sylvia Ashley was also present at the house a good deal, as well as Gloria Morgan Vanderbilt and her twin sister, Thelma, and Sonny and Jock Whitney. A game of some sort, whether charades, cards, or tennis, was always in progress, and the press was beginning to drop strong hints that this was not appropriate behavior for one of the screen's leading actresses. Hollywood was still jittery about couples openly living together. Paulette Goddard's inability to offer legal proof of her marriage to Charlie Chaplin was one of the things that cost her the role of Scarlett O'Hara. The January 1939 issue of *Photoplay* ran an article called "Hollywood's Unmarried Husbands and Wives," naming Chaplin and Goddard, Barbara Stanwyck and Robert Taylor, Carole Lombard and Clark Gable, and Constance and Gilbert among the industry's wayward couples.

The Constance-Gilbert affair produced further complications in the spring of 1938, when another child entered Constance's life. Little is known about the circumstances surrounding the birth of Constance's daughter, Lorinda. Constance always claimed that the child was born in April 1938 in New York City, in the apartment where she was staying at the time. Once again, she claimed that she had not delivered the child in a hospital because she wanted to avoid the publicity that was sure to result. There is no birth certificate in existence for Lorinda, and it remains a mystery whether her father was Henri or Gilbert. It was widely known that Henri did not wish to have children and had been quite adamant with Constance on that point, but in his unpublished memoirs Gilbert makes no mention whatsoever of Lorinda's birth, while he does chronicle their later daughter Gyl's birth in some detail.

Lorinda was a healthy child with red hair and a robust temperament; Constance often joked that she was one of the homeliest babies she had ever seen. Over time, Constance became concerned because the child sucked her thumb obsessively. Determined that no child of hers should possess such a bad habit, even in infancy, Constance instructed the nurse to attach metal ball cups on the baby's hands so she couldn't suck her thumbs or fingers. She also put her in a crib outfitted with a sheet with a collar on it, so that Lorinda's arms were forced underneath the sheet and she was unable to touch herself on the face. It was the kind of treatment usually reserved for mental patients, and it sent Lorinda into uncontrollable rages, but Constance seemed certain she was doing the right thing.

Constance's ardor for Gilbert may have been bolstered by her mother's disapproval of him, and Gilbert cared no more for Mabel than she did for him. "My father didn't like my grandmother at all," said Lorinda Roland. "He found her rather uppity." In his memoirs, Gilbert asserted that Mabel perpetually interfered in his relationship with Constance, leaping to her daughter's defense every time the couple had an argument—which was often. Once, Mabel turned on Gilbert with such ferocity that he decided she was just a washed-up actress indulging in a bit of overacting, and told her to go to hell. Relations between them were chilly from that point. On the other hand, Gilbert liked Richard immensely—he admired his bravado and his literary interests, and encouraged his love of good cigars and liquor.

For several years, Constance had been an integral part of Hollywood's poker-playing elite, and once she had established herself at Carolwood Drive, she continued to indulge her passion for the game. The stakes were high. Several observers said that on the wildest nights, studios came close to changing hands. A few select women were admitted to the circle: Marion Davies, Countess Dorothy Di Frasso, and Kay Francis. (Constance always maintained that Francis supported her mother on her poker winnings.) Mostly, however, Constance played only with men: Sid Grauman, owner of Grauman's Chinese Theatre on Hollywood Boulevard, Benny Thau, Mervyn LeRoy, David O. Selznick, Joseph Schenck, Jack Warner, Darryl F. Zanuck, Samuel Goldwyn, William Goetz. The competition was stiff, but the practice was generally fair. If one player slipped too far into the hole, the game continued until he was able to reduce his debt to a reasonable amount.

Usually there was a set routine: the poker games were a postlude to dinner. Several of the studio heads and their wives would be invited in for a meal on Friday night. Around 9:30, the wives would say their good-byes and leave their husbands to face Constance around the poker table in the yellow music room. The games frequently lasted for twenty-four hours straight—or even longer. In the early morning hours, Constance would make coffee and scrambled eggs for the bleary-eyed holdouts. Frequently, Constance won, and won big, and her secret weapon was her inscrutable expression. "I came in a couple of times while they were playing," recalled Peter Plant, "and my mother would be sitting there looking at her cards, and she had an expression on her face like this plate without the cake on it. No expression. And I noticed that all the other people were always looking at each other. You looked at her—you didn't get anything. [Later] I understood that one of the reasons my mother was a successful card player was that she was the only actor or actress at the table, other than Gilbert, who wasn't a very good card player—and not a very good actor, either."

The poker winnings came in handy, because maintaining her lifestyle was becoming more of a challenge. In the late 1930s, she launched Constance Bennett Cosmetics, a line of beauty products she hoped would bolster her fortunes. The products were packaged in deep-rouge boxes with Constance's name running across the top in pink, just above a tiara symbol, and at first they were well received. Sales were good, if not spectacular. A few years later, however, she became bored with managing the project and made the mistake of granting a franchise to a competitor in the cosmetics industry. "He undercut the product," said Peter Plant. "What he did was proceed to fill the containers with nothing but scented lanolin. He wrecked the name." Constance was livid, and later sought to revive the product with new packaging, but it never got off the ground. Constance Bennett Cosmetics had lost its credibility in the marketplace, and would serve as a reminder—one of several over the next few years—that Constance's business drive often far outstripped her business acumen.

She also struggled with her investments. During the late 1930s and early 1940s, she sunk her money into a wide variety of enterprises, many of which failed to pay off. One missed opportunity came when Hal Roach tried to persuade both Constance and Gilbert to buy stock in the brand new Santa Anita Race Track for $5,000 a share. They laughed off his suggestion, unable to imagine why anyone would want to go all the way to Santa Anita to play the horses when there were other racetracks close by. In hindsight, it was a tactical error, since the Santa Anita Race Track became a huge success, and one $5,000 share would have netted them a fortune.

By early 1939, there were no decent offers of work, and Constance decided to take a sabbatical from Hollywood. She joined Henri at the Paris apartment and stayed on for much of the year. If one avoided reading the headlines, there would have been little indication, by the summer of 1939, that France was only months away from entering the war against Germany. The city's mood was more festive and electric than it had been in some time. American and English tourists flocked into Paris, and elegant costume balls and dinner parties abounded. It was the 150th anniversary of the French Revolution; that summer, for the first time, both English and French flags waved at the Bastille Day festivities.

What was to be the Falaises' last year in Paris had passed pleasantly: the chestnut trees had been in full flower that spring, and Peter had enjoyed his long walks up and down the Champs-Elysées, whiling away long, sunny afternoons watching sidewalk Punch and Judy shows. There were still frequent visits to the country, too, where Henri took the boy on fishing trips. But as the summer wore on, it became clear that Hitler would fail to abide by the terms of the Munich Agreement signed the previous year. The average French citizen had come to view the outbreak of war as a strong probability, and by August the government had put out the word: anyone capable of leaving Paris should do so immediately. Within days, it was common to see cars, stuffed with luggage and other belongings, jamming up the streets and highways. Many of the great museums were boarded up, their priceless treasures spirited off to the countryside for safekeeping. Air-raid sirens were tested daily, causing a jumpy public to believe that the hour they had long dreaded had finally arrived. Early in the morning of September 1, Hitler invaded Poland. That same day, Constance, Henri, and Peter fled Paris with all the belongings they could gather. The international scene was already so tense that their ship didn't stop at Liverpool or Southampton, as was customary. Instead, it went straight up to the North Sea, where icebergs prevented the German submarines from operating. The ship was blacked out for the entirety of its five-day crossing.

Back again on Carolwood Drive, Constance was disappointed to find that there were still no suitable movie offers. Worried about maintaining her cash flow, she decided to seek work in the theater. She had long delayed making her adult stage debut, partly because film work had always been more lucrative, but mostly because she was terrified by the thought of appearing before a live audience. In the end, she accepted a revival of Noël Coward's 1925 comedy, *Easy Virtue*. She enlisted Mabel's help in finding a playwright, John Crosby, to update it for her. The production opened on December 31, 1939, in Wilmington, Delaware. Constance had hoped to take it to Broadway, but the reviews didn't warrant a New York engagement: after the Wilmington opening, the *New York Times* praised her final scene, in which she "conferred an extra flavor of spontaneity to Coward's lines," but reported that overall her performance was marred by "an overemphasis on the debutante manner which she has so often affected on the screen." Nevertheless, the opportunity of seeing Constance Bennett live paid off at the box office, and *Easy Virtue* was a hit wherever it played.

Sometime after *Easy Virtue* had closed, Constance's marriage to Henri Falaise came to an end. She and Henri had long faced its imminent collapse, and with Gilbert now a steady presence in her life, there seemed little reason to go on pretending. Constance moved temporarily to Nevada in order to establish residence there, and on November 14, 1940, she became the ex–Marquise de la Falaise de la Coudraye. At the time, Henri was fighting for the French cause in Europe; in fact, he was one of the thousands evacuated from Dunkirk earlier that year. For the second time in his life, he demonstrated that he was a brave and rugged soldier, and he later recorded his experiences in a book, *Through Hell to Dunkirk*.

Many film historians regard 1939 as the high-water mark of Hollywood's creative achievements up to that time. The astounding success of *Gone With the Wind* had awakened the industry to new visions of what could be accomplished on film. Simultaneously, *The Wizard of Oz* demonstrated that wit, flair, and imagination could push the screen musical toward greatness. These two were the year's most significant releases, but there was no need for many of the others to stand in the shade. This was also the year of Frank Capra's *Mr. Smith Goes to Washington,* Greta Garbo's rebirth as a comedienne in *Ninotchka,* ditto Marlene Dietrich in *Destry Rides Again,* Charles Laughton's staggering Quasimodo in *The Hunchback of Notre Dame,* and Bette Davis's brilliant display of full-throttle emotionalism in *Dark Victory.*

In spite of this banner year of artistic achievement, Hollywood's financial future looked uncertain by early 1940. In 1938, the major studios had been hit with an antitrust suit, brought against them by the Justice Department. One of the results was that the practice of block booking—forcing independent exhibitors to take the low-grade "B" films along with the top-line products—came under much closer scrutiny. "B" films had long been crucial to the financial health of the studios, since they turned a substantial profit on a minimal investment. Now they began to do a slow fade—and the studios' budget sheets showed the results.

To pick up the slack, studio executives began to cut more and more deals with independent producers, while talents such as Frank Capra were cutting themselves loose from the major studios that had employed them and were striking out on their own as independents. It was advantageous to both sides: the studios provided financing and distribution and use of their soundstages for filming, and were rewarded with a healthy share of the profits. It was a sweet deal for the filmmakers, too: although studio control over the final product varied from deal to deal, it was inevitably diluted. Then, too, there was the beginning of war in Europe, which would seriously undercut foreign profits. By August 1940, Germany would ban all MGM pictures on the grounds that they contained anti-German sentiments.

It was during this shaky period that Walter Wanger embarked on his most rewarding era in the industry. His vintage years began in 1939, with John Ford's *Stagecoach*—the film that reshaped the entire Western genre by giving it the serious treatment it deserved—and continued through two of 1940's most critically praised pictures, Ford's *The Long Voyage Home* and Alfred Hitchcock's *Foreign Correspondent*. In 1939, Walter had been elected president of the Academy of Motion Picture Arts and Sciences, a position which further boosted his standing in Hollywood. All of this made him even more desirable to Joan. But even though Walter had divorced Justine Johnston in the spring of 1939, he continued to resist the idea of marriage. Accordingly, Joan had launched a persistent campaign to win him over. She had engaged in a string of high-profile romances, most of which seemed designed to rouse Walter into action. There were brief affairs with Errol Flynn and socialite Woolworth Donohue. "She tried everything to make Walter jealous," said Diana Anderson. "But he felt she was too young [for him] and he didn't want to be married. He had had a comfortable situation with his wife, Justine Johnston, because he could do anything he wanted."

Late on the evening of January 11, 1940, Wanger and Joan were talking on the telephone when, much to her shock, he proposed. The next day, accompanied by her publicist and friend Maggie Ettinger, they traveled to Phoenix, where they were married by Justice of the Peace Harry Westfall. Their busy schedules made a honeymoon impossible, and they returned immediately to Hollywood and settled in at Mapleton Drive. The children got along well with Walter, and soon began calling him by the affectionate nickname "Bossie." For Joan, it was the beginning of the most rewarding period of her life. "She was happiest, in the beginning, with Walter," said Diana. "She really believed in him."

Joan's marriage to Wanger coincided with a temporary break in their working relationship. After Wanger starred her opposite George Raft in a routine crime drama, *House Across the Bay* (1940), her personal contract with him came to an end. By mid-1940, the financial performance of Wanger's recent films could scarcely have inspired confidence in investors. Although 1939's *Stagecoach* had been a great success, all four of Wanger's 1940 releases—*Slightly Honorable, House Across the Bay, Foreign Correspondent,* and *The Long Voyage Home*—lost money, despite the critical praise lavished on the last two. In a cost-cutting effort, Wanger divested himself of most of his top contract stars, including Henry Fonda, Charles Boyer, and Joan. Although she preferred not to be bound by contracts with major studios—she liked the luxury of turning down unsuitable properties—Joan also felt the need to develop the new image that *Trade Winds* had given her. The most expedient way of doing that seemed to obtain a studio berth, which would also give her the financial security she craved. In mid-1940, she signed a nonexclusive contract with Twentieth Century–Fox.

Under Darryl F. Zanuck's leadership, Twentieth Century–Fox had grown from a struggling, undistinguished studio to one of the leaders of the industry—by 1940, second in profits only to MGM. Fox had made its mark specializing in nostalgia: both sentimental dramas, often with rural settings, such as the Shirley Temple vehicles, and musicals such as *Lillian Russell,* with Alice Faye singing away in period costume. While a studio such as MGM was noted for its excellence at building up its individual stars, Zanuck (the ex-writer) was more interested in properties than actors. By 1940, he had begun to fill out Fox's wholesome and homespun movie lineup with a string of socially conscious dramas; critic Ethan Mordden has astutely observed that this move marked a continuation of Zanuck's excellent track record producing "social problem" pictures during his tenure at Warners in the early 1930s. By 1940, Hollywood was stepping up its production of movies with war-related themes. One of these was Joan's first film under her new contract, *The Man I Married.*

On the surface, *The Man I Married* seemed inspired by confession magazine fiction; in fact, its original working title was *I Married a Nazi.* What made it a picture of minor significance was the swift direction of Irving Pichel, who maintained firm control of the film's potent anti-Nazi propaganda. The result was a picture that opened the public's eyes to the growing menace in Europe, but never degenerated into heavy-handed jingoism. Joan plays Carol Cabot, the art critic of a smart New York magazine who is persuaded by her German-born husband (Francis Lederer) to take a trip to Berlin. Since the picture is set in 1938, it asks a lot for us to believe that Carol is as naive about the rise of fascism as she appears to be. But the conceit of Oliver H.P. Garrett's script is that she is the vehicle for the audience's own unanswered questions. Her initial admiration for the Germans' efficiency in mobilizing their industry turns to disgust and horror when she witnesses the Nazis visiting humiliation on a group of Czech peasants. Encouraged by the American newspaper correspondent (Lloyd Nolan) who befriends her, she soon begins to voice her contempt for the Nazis. This enrages her husband, who, it turns out, has planned to make this a one-way trip, and intends to remain in Germany as a full-fledged member of the Nazi party.

One of the picture's key scenes involved a public rally at which Carol hears Hitler speak for the first time. Fox's publicity department got maximum mileage out of its claim that, with the spread of war in Europe, no actor could be persuaded to portray Hitler onscreen. (Character actor Jack Cooper was reportedly asked to make a test and refused, citing his loyalty to his native Britain.) In the end, the studio obtained permission to use an actual soundtrack of Hitler's speech from Berlin's Sportpalast, just prior to Germany's occupation of Czechoslovakia.

For audiences accustomed to reading in the morning headlines about Hitler's aggressive advances, *The Man I Married* had powerful resonance. The movie's big climactic scene belonged to Joan. Faced with the complete truth of her husband's betrayal, Carol denounces him: "What are you—a holy roller? Can any cheap demagogue make you roll over and froth at the mouth? . . . I can't stand being in the same room with you! I don't want to breathe the same air you breathe! Heil, heel!"

An incident at the film's Des Moines opening in mid-August reflects the public's rising emotional temperature where the Nazi movement was concerned. As a promotional stunt, the Tri-States Theatre Corporation outfitted a pair of teenagers in Nazi uniforms and marched them down the streets of downtown Des Moines. A near-riot ensued, and violence was avoided only when the crowd was persuaded that it was all a publicity gimmick.

With the American public's hostility toward German aggression heating up by the week, there was little doubt that *The Man I Married* would find its audience. Early box-office returns were excellent, and reviews were generally good. In the *New York Times,* Bosley Crowther admired the film's emotional restraint and factual accuracy, and praised it for picturing the Germans as "hypnotized zealots rather than congenital brutes." The only critical target was Joan, whose smooth, nonchalant style seemed at odds with the film's serious tone. Crowther felt that she "might have brought more vitality and internal conflict to her role; as it is, she does little more than model dresses and express incredulity."

For all of her progress during her eleven years in Hollywood, Joan had a long way to go as an actress, and she knew it. Her deep-rooted lack of confidence prevented her from seeing herself as much more than a poised and elegant glamour girl. As her daughter Stephanie Wanger Guest observed, "I don't think she saw acting as much more than her job. I don't think she really sat around and analyzed what it meant to be playing a certain role." But Joan's sense of her own possibilities was about to change. The next picture that Fox had in line for her was called *Man Hunt*. It was another anti-Nazi drama, but with a difference—it was to be directed by Fritz Lang.

In the summer of 1939, Richard was rescued from professional oblivion by his young friend St. John Terrell, who had played a minor role in the New York company of *Winterset*. Properly respectful, even worshipful, Terrell had quickly become a member of Richard's charmed circle. Terrell's ambitions extended beyond acting; he wanted to make a distinctive mark in the theater, and he did so in 1939, when—with money borrowed from friends—he opened the Bucks County Playhouse in picturesque New Hope, Pennsylvania. Bucks County by this time had become a fashionable retreat for New York celebrities who fancied themselves country squires. Among the writers who had migrated there in recent years were Dorothy Parker and Alan Campbell and S.J. Perelman. It struck Terrell as the ideal setting for a summer theater, and in July 1939 the Bucks County Playhouse began its long and distinguished history. Terrell engaged Richard to spend the summer coaching the young members of the theater's apprenticeship program in acting and stagecraft. Richard found that he had a great rapport with the young actors, and threw himself into the summer's activities with zeal, offering valuable insights on reading technique, interpretation, and voice placement. He returned to the Playhouse in subsequent summers, and it provided him with a stretch of activity to look forward to for the rest of the year.

Although there was always at least one woman in his life, Richard continued to cast Mabel as the great lost opportunity. To those closest to him, he pined away for her—but by this time Mabel had enough problems of her own. In March 1939, Eric Pinker was charged with having embezzled $10,000 worth of royalties from mystery writer E. Phillips Oppenheim. Pinker was arrested, and a full-length investigation revealed that he had misappropriated an additional $6,000 due Oppenheim. The affair was a shock to all concerned. Even Joan, whose resentment of Pinker was undiminished, admitted that "there had never been cause to doubt his honesty." The actual crime was not quite as black as the newspapers made it sound: his intent had not been to steal from Oppenheim or any of the firm's other authors, but to use the income due them to pay operating expenses, and simply postpone the payment of royalties to a more convenient date. Many businesses worked this way, but the New York County grand jury that indicted him took a dim view of it, and he was convicted of grand larceny in the first degree. He was sentenced to two and a half years in Sing-Sing Prison in Ossining, New York.

The reporters who covered the case seldom failed to mention that Pinker's wife and business partner was Adrienne Morrison, mother of the Bennett sisters. It was a major shock to Mabel, but Joan recalled that she shouldered the disaster quietly and without complaint. The scandal closed the doors on the Pinker-Morrison Literary Agency, and Mabel worried that no one in the publishing or theater world might ever trust her again. Initially, it seemed that she had indeed been blacklisted in literary circles, but later in 1939 a successful literary agent named Mary Leonard Pritchett offered her a partnership in her firm. For Mabel, the move was a financial lifesaver, and she settled in to the Pritchett-Morrison offices, bringing with her years of knowledge and expertise as a play broker.

At the time of the scandal, Constance, Barbara, and Joan had concocted a scheme to contribute $150 a month each for Mabel's support if she left New York and retired to the country home she shared with Pinker in Old Lyme. But the idea of inactivity didn't appeal to Mabel, and she declined her daughters' offer. In the spring of 1940, she surprised everyone by announcing that she would return to the theater in Hector Boiltho and Terrence Rattigan's psychological thriller *Grey Farm*. It told the story of an insanely possessive father (played by Oscar Homolka, in his U.S. debut) who is driven to murder by his son's impending marriage. Mabel was cast in the comic relief part of Lady Weaver, a feather-brained English lady who lives next door to the homicidal maniac. In an interview given shortly before the opening, she didn't seem to have much riding on her return to the stage: "I make an entrance down a flight of stairs," she said, "and here's hoping I don't fall into the set." She could have spared herself the worry, as *Grey Farm* had plenty of other problems. The critics found it slow-moving and unconvincing, and it closed before the month was out.

For some time, Mabel had suffered from hypertension, and no doubt the stress created by the Eric Pinker scandal had aggravated her condition. But if she felt unwell, she kept quiet about it. As the weeks went by, she worked dutifully at the agency office, and on visiting days made the trip to visit Pinker in Sing-Sing. On the morning of November 20, 1940, she rose at the usual time and began preparing for her day's work. A little before noon, her maid arrived at the East Sixty-sixth Street apartment. She found Mabel lying partially dressed on the bathroom floor. The maid, failing to rouse her, telephoned a nearby doctor, who pronounced Mabel dead. The cause was heart failure. She was fifty-seven.

Mary Pritchett was notified immediately, and it fell to her to break the news to Mabel's daughters, all of whom were in Los Angeles at the time. The next day, they flew to New York, accompanied by Walter, plus Constance's good friend Sylvia Ashley. A flock of newspaper reporters waited as the three sisters, dressed in black, solemnly descended from the plane and were met by Morton. The following day, they all drove to Connecticut for Mabel's funeral at the Old Lyme Congregational Church. She was buried in the Morrison family plot in Old Lyme's Pleasant View Cemetery.

Mabel had played many roles in her daughters' lives: Mother Isis, confessor, conscience—and most crucially, North Star. During their childhood, her calm, reassuring presence had provided an antidote to Richard's excesses and absences. Constance, Barbara, and Joan all possessed a strong emotional identification with Mabel, although none of them fully inherited her talent for constructing a sturdy fortress out of life. Joan, with her love of domestic tranquility, resembled her most. But Constance, with her brazen egocentricity and fickleness, and Barbara, with her emotional extremes, both owed more to Richard, whether they admitted it or not.

For much of their marriage, Mabel and Richard had disagreed about the direction their daughters would take in life. Both of them were pleased when success came to all three, and yet, they somehow failed to pass on to their children their intense passion for their profession. The life of the theater, with all its pleasures and hardships, was embraced wholeheartedly by Richard and Mabel. Their pride in being actors sustained them through high times and hard times. Looking back, they might question many of their choices and accomplishments, but never their devotion.

Constance and Joan were lucky: they entered the movie industry at just the right time, and after only a few years in Hollywood their own celebrity had overshadowed that of their parents. But the burning ambition that had propelled Richard and Mabel into the theater was for the most part alien to them. They would always be grateful when good scripts and directors came their way, but acting would never be a matter of life and death to them. It was a good way of making a living—nothing more, nothing less. Still, they respected the traditions of the acting profession and in many ways did their best to honor them. From now on, it would be up to them to keep the family flame alive. Over the years, it might flicker in the wind, but thanks to their determination, hard work, and inherited ability, it would never go out altogether.

Chapter Fourteen

1941–1943

With her retirement from acting and marriage to Morton Downey in 1929, Barbara had chosen her place out of the sun—seemingly, without regret. Her quiet life as a Connecticut housewife and mother had given her a distinction all her own: while Constance and Joan had each had three husbands by the time they turned thirty, the press delighted in pointing to Barbara as the stable member of the family, the exception to the rule of tempestuous Bennetts. The truth was that her marriage to Morton had been in rocky shape for some time. During his peak years on the radio in the 1930s, he had commanded $12,000 a week. His radio fame caused him to be in demand for concert tours, and he spent more and more time performing on the road, taking only occasional time out to check in with his rapidly growing family in Greenwich. At some point in the late 1930s, Barbara began to drink, moderately at first, but more heavily as time went on.

By now the Downey brood numbered five—Tony had been born in 1935, Kevin in 1938—and her life in Connecticut, managing the household and waiting for Morton to come home, left her feeling lonely and confined. She began to suffer bouts of severe depression, intensified by her drinking. The emotional instability of her youth, which had seemed a distant dream during the early years of her marriage to Morton, now returned. "She was so warm and friendly," remembered Morton's younger brother, Edward Downey. "When she started drinking, I couldn't understand it."

Diana Anderson remembered a visit to the Downey household in 1937, and being shocked at how despondent her aunt had become: "The children were all very subdued. I remember my Auntie Barbara just sitting in the corner not saying anything. It was kind of scary for a nine-year-old."

In late 1937, Barbara and Morton had arranged for someone to look after their Connecticut home and moved the family to Beverly Hills, into a house adjoining Jack Warner's property on Angelo Drive. Morton was getting a good deal of work on the West Coast, and the move was intended to be temporary. Shortly after the move, Barbara rekindled her friendship with Louise Brooks. Not long after their days at Denishawn, Louise had gone to Hollywood, where she had played leading roles in several silent films. But she achieved real distinction only when she traveled to Germany in 1928 to make two films for G.W. Pabst, *Pandora's Box* and *Diary of a Lost Girl.* Both the films and her performances in them were destined to become classics, but at the time, they were not well received. When she returned to Hollywood in the early 1930s, she was unable to find roles of comparable quality. She worked as a nightclub dancer and appeared in some worthless "B" films, and by 1937 her movie career had neared its end.

At the time she and Barbara had their reunion, Louise had a new man in her life, Addison "Jack" Randall, a dark-haired, good-looking actor in his early thirties who appeared in cheap cowboy pictures at Monogram Studios. Randall would never attain the success of his brother, Robert Livingston, who starred in Republic's Three Mesquiteers series, but Louise prized him for other reasons. Tall, with strong, broad shoulders and a good, firm jaw, Randall was an exciting lover—or so Louise told her friends. All too soon, however, she grew bored with his company, and at some point after she defected from Hollywood in 1938, Randall began seeing Barbara on the sly.

What began as an on-again, off-again affair picked up momentum over the next two years. Downey was constantly on the road and spent very little time at home, and during one of his prolonged absences Barbara temporarily moved Randall into the house.

Barbara's oldest son, Michael Downey, recalled that Randall was "on his best behavior with us. He was sort of—I don't know—almost in deference to us. A little overly friendly. You know: 'Anything you need?' That sort of thing. Tried to ingratiate himself a bit."

On January 14, 1941, Barbara informed the press that she and Morton were separating. Morton, appearing in a New Orleans hotel, claimed that her announcement had caught him off guard and vowed that he would fly to Hollywood to try to reason with her—as soon as his engagement had ended.

As Barbara began to follow up the separation with legal action, it seemed not to occur to her that she might lose any of the children. In her view, Morton had largely been an absent father, and she assumed he would give her little trouble over custody. But as the matter dragged out over the winter and spring of 1941, she found him a formidable adversary. He pointed out that she had branded herself an unfit mother with her drinking and infidelity. On February 27, Morton filed suit against her in Superior Court in Bridgeport, Connecticut, charging her with intolerable cruelty dating from January 1940. Barbara had temporarily surrendered the children to him, and he had returned with them to Connecticut, where he put them in the care of his sister Helen, still living in the house Morton had built for their parents on Long Hill Road in Wallingford.

The divorce proceedings continued to be deadlocked. Barbara, torn between her children and the hope of happiness with Addison Randall, saw no reason why she couldn't have both, but Morton set stiff terms: he would proceed with the divorce only if she signed over custody of all five children to him.

To Joan, it was unthinkable that Barbara would agree to such a harsh proposal. But to Michael Downey, it was her way of escaping a situation that had become too much for her to deal with. "I don't think she really realized what she was getting into when she had a family," he observed. Perhaps Morton simply was trying to force the reconciliation he claimed to want, but he underestimated Barbara's desire to be rid of him. She was backed into a corner, and she rashly agreed to Morton's terms. The divorce was final on June 4, 1941, and three days later Barbara and Addison Randall left Los Angeles and drove to Ensenada, Mexico, where they were married. Joan saw it as nothing more than "a gesture of defiance"—a pitiful attempt to save face and assert her own independence.

The divorce decree had carried a final stinger, courtesy of Morton: Barbara was not allowed to visit the children unless she remained completely sober, showed up unaccompanied, and handled herself "with propriety becoming a good mother." Morton himself was permitted to determine whether or not Barbara's conduct passed muster.

In the months following the divorce decree, Barbara grew extremely despondent, and her behavior became more bizarre than ever. In November 1942, she made arrangements to meet a friend, an agent named James Doane, for dinner at a Beverly Hills restaurant. But then she telephoned the Doanes and told them that she wouldn't be able to keep the date. She later checked herself into a private nursing home. Addison was frantic, and reported her missing after twenty-four hours—which Barbara discovered a few days later when she bought a newspaper and saw her named splattered across the headlines. She telephoned Addison right away and explained to him and to the press that she had simply been in need of a rest, and couldn't comprehend what the fuss had been about.

There is little evidence that these sad developments in Barbara's life distressed Constance at all. By this time, relations between the two were strained to the breaking point, mostly because of disagreements over who would support Richard. Then, too, Constance remained a teetotaler and had no patience with alcoholics. Barbara, as far as she was concerned, had had plenty of opportunity to see what drink had done to their father, and had clearly made her own choice in the matter. As it was, Constance felt Barbara deserved none of her sympathy.

Joan was altogether more understanding. She had never cared for Morton, whose demands seemed to her "a cruel bargain." She had guessed, correctly, that Barbara would almost immediately regret the decision to surrender her children. But what Joan, for all her good intentions, failed to understand was that for the acute alcoholic—which Barbara was well on her way to becoming—the desire to drink overpowers all else. The alcoholic lives to drink, more than she lives to work, enjoy sex, care for her children. In Addison Randall, Barbara had found not only romance but a drinking companion. In that sense, the "cruel bargain" was as much her doing as it was Morton's.

In any case, Michael Downey recalled that she almost completely failed to take advantage of her visitation rights, and remembered seeing her only a handful of times after the divorce. "She would come to visit occasionally," he said. "It was difficult—always a very tense situation. She didn't stay very long—maybe an hour."

The children were presumably being given proper care by Helen Downey, although Peter Plant, who visited the Downey household in Wallingford during the summer of 1943, wasn't so sure. Helen seemed at the end of her rope dealing with the children; she screamed at them all day long and never seemed to show them the slightest affection. As a result, the children were cowed and submissive, except for Lorelle, now eight, who was wild and unruly. That summer, there had been a tremendous outbreak of polio throughout the New England states, and eventually it reached Wallingford. Lorelle contracted a mild case of the disease, with the result that the entire family was quarantined for the period of Peter's visit. Peter remembered thinking that Lorelle's behavior was strange, even for a little girl who had fallen ill.

The picture that pushed Joan's career out of second gear was *Man Hunt.* It was based on Geoffrey Household's popular 1939 novel *Rogue Male,* which Twentieth Century–Fox had purchased and intended to give a deluxe big-screen treatment. It was the story of Roger Thorndike (played in the film by Walter Pidgeon), a free-spirited British big-game hunter. After the Nazis come to power, Thorndike tracks Hitler, just for the sport of it, but is apprehended just as he has literally gotten the Führer in his sights. Thorndike is tortured and nearly killed by the Nazis, who are convinced that he is part of a British plot against Germany. He escapes and makes his way back to England, but the Nazis are in hot pursuit and trail him all over London and, later, the English countryside. The idea that Germans could infiltrate England was guaranteed to unnerve readers in 1939. By the time filming began in the spring of 1941, the Battle of Britain had already dominated headlines throughout the previous summer and fall. At Fox, Darryl F. Zanuck was sure that *Man Hunt* would resonate with American audiences, who by now were wondering how long they could remain at arm's length from the war in Europe.

Had it been handed to one of Fox's journeyman directors, *Man Hunt* could easily have turned out to be just another run-of-the-mill wartime thriller. Fortunately, Zanuck assigned the picture to Fritz Lang, who had recently joined the studio's roster of contract directors. Lang's deal with Fox gave him a temporarily safe harbor, since the last ten years of his life had been riddled with adversities that might have defeated a less resilient man. Born in Vienna in 1890, Lang abandoned an architect's career early on and set out to make his mark as a screenwriter and director. During the 1920s, he had risen to become one of the masters of German expressionist cinema. His films, including *Dr. Mabuse der Spieler, Die Nibelungen,* and *Metropolis,* had represented triumphs of the visual imagination; Pauline Kael once commented that *Die Nibelungen* was such a visual orgy that it made the earlier expressionistic classic *The Cabinet of Dr. Caligari* (1919) seem as dull as a television sitcom. In 1931, Lang had made a brilliant transition to sound with *M,* a study of a pathetic child murderer who is apprehended only when the Berlin underworld becomes involved in hunting for him.

Throughout the early to mid-1930s, many of the top German acting and directing talents had emigrated to Hollywood. By early 1933, Joseph Goebbels, Hitler's minister of propaganda, had realized that the German film industry would have to be radically overhauled if the rest of the world was going to be persuaded that the Nazis were the instruments for positive change. Among Lang's recent films, he particularly admired *M,* choosing to interpret it not as a plea for tolerance but as a strong-minded endorsement of capital punishment. Lang's own relationship with the Nazis has been viewed by many as complicated and ambivalent. In his biography of the director, Patrick McGilligan quotes witnesses' claims that Lang flew a Nazi flag over his house early in the 1930s—a distinct possibility, given that his wife, screenwriter Thea von Harbou, was a fanatic nationalist who remained active in the Nazi-run film industry throughout the war.

For Lang to have stayed in Germany would have been potentially dangerous, since his mother had Jewish blood. Nevertheless, it seems likely that he mostly regarded the Nazis as a distraction from his work, and preferred to ignore them until it was no longer possible. Years later, in interviews, he claimed that Goebbels had invited him to helm a new agency overseeing all film production under the Nazi regime and that that very night he fled Berlin for Paris, carrying only a handful of jewelry, a gold cigarette case, and whatever cash he had in the house. Patrick McGilligan isn't so sure—he points out that there is no mention of a meeting with Lang in Goebbels's copiously detailed diaries. Nevertheless, leave he did. After an interlude in Paris, he came to Hollywood, where he made three films starring Sylvia Sidney: *Fury* (1936), *You Only Live Once* (1937), and *You and Me* (1938)—all box-office failures.

In Hollywood, Lang soon built a reputation as an obsessive perfectionist who would put his cast through dozens of takes until he had achieved exactly the effects he wanted. A director like George Stevens would also demand that his actors repeat a scene dozens of times until he was satisfied, but he offered little advice along the way. Lang was a martinet who tended to dictate every facet of an actor's performance, down to the exact moment at which he would lift a glass or turn his head. This method was anathema to an actor like Henry Fonda or Spencer Tracy, who prided themselves on naturalism and spontaneity, but others thrived on it. Sylvia Sidney, for one, was delighted by Lang's irascible and exacting personality and strove to please him. Jane Wyatt, who appeared in Lang's *The House by the River* (1950), remembered that the director demanded that his actors carefully monitor the way their performances were taking shape. "He always wanted you to see the rushes," she recalled. "A lot of big stars didn't want to do it. But Fritz Lang begged us and forced us to watch the rushes."

In Joan, Lang found an apt pupil, all too willing to do as she was told if it meant a good performance in the end. In *Man Hunt,* she was cast as Jerry Stokes, a Cockney streetwalker who helps Roger Thorndike dodge the Nazi agents who pursue him to London. Jerry was the invention of screenwriter Dudley Nichols, who felt that Geoffrey Household's novel was lacking in any sex angle and provided one in his script. Initially, Wanger advised her against doing it—Jerry was a vivid character role, quite unlike anything else she had ever done, and it seemed to call for a more high-energy breed of actress, an Ida Lupino or a Joan Blondell.

But Joan knew that Jerry was the best opportunity that had been handed to her, and she was determined to make the most of it. She set to work studying the accent with British character actress Queenie Leonard, who specialized in playing Cockney maids in Hollywood films. Once on the set, Joan found that everything she had heard about Lang's dictatorial style was true. At the time, most pictures weren't extensively rehearsed, but Lang put his cast through their paces before the cameras ever rolled. "It was the only movie I ever made in which I knew the entire script, like a play, beforehand," Joan remembered. Lang drilled her endlessly in the part, until Jerry's gamine toughness began to feel like second nature to her. For the first time since George Cukor, she had found a director who took her seriously. Lang was often abrasive, but the proof was in what wound up on film. As Jerry, she showed an earthy warmth and sensuality new to her.

Amazingly, the Hays Office worried that *Man Hunt* might be considered a "hate picture"—one that could be perceived as unfair in its portrayal of the Nazis' brutality. But it was the part of Jerry that turned out to be the film's most problematic aspect. Upon reviewing Nichols's script, the Hays Office ruled that Jerry could not be portrayed as an out-and-out streetwalker; they suggested that some reasonable occupation, such as waitress or dance-hall girl, be substituted. Lang was furious, but the Hays Office was too powerful even for him. In the end, the director ordered that a sewing machine be placed on the set depicting Jerry's apartment. It was prominently lit, asking the audience to conclude that Jerry was a seamstress. (Lang saw to it that Walter Pidgeon emphasized the sewing machine's presence by repeatedly standing next to it.)

There were other hurdles. The Hays Office insisted that Jerry must not be allowed to stand with her hand on her hip, her purse dangling from her wrist, because it would cue the audience that she was a prostitute. The censors also protested a scene in which Jerry is seen crying because Thorndike declines to sleep with her. But the biggest objections were reserved for a scene in which Jerry, helping Thorndike conceal his identity from a policeman, creates a diversion by pretending to be a prostitute on the make. Zanuck, fearing the censors' verdict, demanded that the scene be deleted. Lang outmaneuvered him by conspiring with crew members to shoot the scene on a pre-existing set, shrouding it entirely in fog and mist. The effect was visually stunning: Jerry, knowing she will never see Thorndike again, tearfully asks him to kiss her good-bye. Just as Thorndike is about to comply, a policeman interrupts them. Jerry creates a ruse by pretending to harass Thorndike, and the policeman hustles her away, cautioning Thorndike not to get "mixed up with these 'ere girls." As Jerry disappears into the fog, Thorndike surreptitiously blows her a kiss. The scene played so beautifully that Zanuck dropped his objections and it stayed in the picture.

As a director of suspense thrillers, Lang's greatest recurring handicap is a somewhat heavy hand—he tends to over-emphasize character and push his plots too hard. *Man Hunt* is a case in point. Although the film is marvelously atmospheric and benefits from Arthur Miller's superb photography, one can't help wishing that the plot twists could be less relentlessly driven, more subtly revealed. Even a master manipulator like Alfred Hitchcock gave his audience credit for a little imagination, and watching Lang's American films, one often wishes for a little of the distance that Hitchcock puts between himself and his subject, for some of his wicked playfulness and dispassionate wit.

In this respect, Joan's performance helps *Man Hunt* immeasurably. She created Jerry with the boldest strokes she had yet used as an actress. Her characterization of a Cockney tart seems more appropriate for a Broadway revue than a realistic movie thriller, but she gives the film a humor and buoyancy and sexiness that it sorely needs. Once Jerry is killed by the Nazi agents, the heart seems to go out of the picture, and what follows feels like aftermath.

When *Man Hunt* opened in June 1941, critics hailed it as one of the year's best thrillers, and a sure sign that Lang was back on track. Joan received her best notices to date. The *Hollywood Reporter* felt that she had "never been so appealing . . . she makes a real characterization of the London street waif." *Man Hunt* was one of the year's big hits, earning $1.4 million in domestic rentals alone.

Man Hunt looked like another turning point in Joan's career, and she was delighted when Zanuck announced that her next picture, *Confirm or Deny,* would also be directed by Lang. It was another British war drama, with Joan cast as a teletype operator in a wire service office that tries to carry on in the midst of the London blitz. From the outset, Lang was unenthusiastic about the project, feeling that he deserved better material after the success of *Man Hunt.* Two weeks into filming, he suffered a gallstone attack. Patrick McGilligan feels that he exaggerated its seriousness to get out of finishing the picture; in any event, *Confirm or Deny* was handed over to Archie Mayo. Joan recalled that on his first day of shooting, Mayo addressed the cast and crew: "I know I'm not Fritz Lang, but I'll do my best." Joan was warm and appealing in the film, but Mayo was right, he was no Lang, and her performance passed without much comment.

The year 1941 was a big money-earner for Joan. Her contract with Fox was nonexclusive, and she took advantage of the fact to sign another multi-picture deal with Columbia. Although it had come a long way from its poverty-row status in the early 1930s, Columbia still pursued a policy of making a couple of big, prestige pictures every year, and filling out the rest of its schedule with medium- and low-budget films. Joan's films there were a sorry lot, beginning with *She Knew All the Answers* (1941), a feeble comedy with Franchot Tone. But her Columbia salary rounded out her year's earnings nicely. Her 1941 income tax returns show that she made a total of $181,305.50—although her professional expenses were staggering—over $141,000 for such items as advertising and publicity, chauffeur and studio maid salaries, and management fees.

By 1940, the momentum that *Topper* had restored to Constance's career had been lost. She made no films at all during that year. In 1941, she was considered for two big pictures, *Adam Had Four Sons,* which went to Ingrid Bergman, and *The Great Lie,* which went to Mary Astor. From 1941 to 1942, she did appear in a half-dozen pictures, but except for the middling amount of income they brought her, she might well have saved herself the trouble. Efforts like *Submarine Zone* (1941) and *Law of the Tropics* (1941) were nothing but nails in the coffin of a once-spectacular career. The only movie of this period from which she benefited at all was MGM's *Two-Faced Woman* (1941), which has earned a niche in cinema history as Greta Garbo's swan song. That remains its only distinction, as *Two-Faced Woman* is a sorry mess of a comedy, intended to reinvent Garbo as a bright, sparkling comedienne along the lines of Rosalind Russell or Irene Dunne. She was cast as a woman who passes herself off as her twin sister in order to confound her husband (Melvyn Douglas). George Cukor, who directed, tried to keep the witless situations afloat, but the script is full of tedious, unplayable scenes, and Garbo, incessantly smiling over nothing, makes one wish for the gloomy heroine of *Grand Hotel* or *Anna Karenina.* Cukor, still loyal to Constance from the old days at RKO, tried to give her flagging career a boost by casting her as Garbo's rival. What little there is to steal, Constance steals; Cukor even provided the character with a few in-jokes about the Bennett nearsightedness. But it was poor compensation for having to accept below-the-title billing for the first time in years.

It was a difficult time for Constance. The most worrisome aspect of her run of bad films was the meager income they brought her. For *Wild Bill Hickok Rides,* a Western made at Warners in

1941, she was paid only $10,000. For two Universal pictures in 1942, *Sin Town* and *Madame Spy*, her total salary was below what she was paid for one week of filming *Bought!* eleven years earlier. Compared with Joan, married to a successful producer, supervising a smoothly running household, and earning more money and greater respect as an actress than ever before, Constance's situation looked dire. But the serenity and stability that Joan worked so hard to cultivate had always been alien to Constance.

Constance's machinations in 1941 offer ample evidence of her mercurial nature. In mid-1941, while working at Warner Bros., she met John Theron Coulter, an Army Air Corps colonel nine years her junior. A native of Nettleton, Mississippi, his great love of flying had taken him into Officer's Candidate School, after which he had risen quickly. Eventually he was stationed in Riverside, California. When war broke out, his commanding general gave him a choice of going overseas or remaining stateside, as a technical advisor on military pictures at Warner Bros. Since his wife, Martha, was in the hospital at the time, recovering from injuries sustained in a car accident, Coulter chose the Warners job, where he spent his days teaching Gary Cooper and Cary Grant the finer points of combat.

It was at a party at Warner Bros. that Coulter and Constance first met. The colonel came with his wife, a proper southern lady from Shreveport, Louisiana, who was still confined to a wheelchair but dressed in her most elegant suit. "He wheeled her in and she saw all these glorious stars," recalled Coulter's daughter, Patricia McElroy. "And all of a sudden this woman came out and draped herself in the doorway in this slinky Jean Harlow dress, and she took one look at Dad, and my mother knew it was the end."

It was. The Coulters were divorced, and Martha Coulter returned to Louisiana. With the country on the brink of war, Constance had gotten herself a military boyfriend, which she regarded as a personal coup, especially because she was unable to secure any good film roles. "Constance loved Dad because he was younger, and handsome in his uniform," said McElroy. "He was impressed by her fame in the beginning. He soon learned."

It was a recurrence of the standard Constance pattern of overlapping relationships, but in this case it was particularly striking. In April 1941, she had finally married Gilbert. They eloped to Yuma, Arizona, and at the end of that year a third child joined their household. Again, Constance took great care to obscure the circumstances of her child's birth, but Gilbert recorded in his unpublished autobiography that their daughter, Gyl Christina, was born at home on Carolwood Drive on December 9, 1941.

Gilbert's official entry into the household made little difference to Peter Plant one way or another. To Peter, Gilbert was his mother's cardboard lover—all show, little substance. They did forge one bond: Gilbert passed on to Peter his great love of classical music and opera. He had amassed an impressive collection of recordings, and after dinner Peter often joined Gilbert in the music room, where Gilbert would choose a particular work from his collection, tell Peter the composer's life story, then play the recording.

Mostly, however, Gilbert struck Peter as a poseur whose suave masculinity seemed nothing more than an extension of the tin soldier roles he played onscreen. He was fascinated by the works of Ernest Hemingway, which he reread obsessively throughout his life. Hemingway's masculine code of ethics resonated with Gilbert, and his own unpublished memoirs imitate the author's lean, elusive style. But by the end of 1941, Gilbert's fantasy life in Hollywood was interrupted by the United States' entry into the war. Shortly after Pearl Harbor, Gilbert was drafted into the army and sent to the Presidio in Monterey, California. From there, he was sent to the Army Signal Corps. Now that he was occupied with the military, Constance's affair with Coulter blossomed.

On some level, how can we not admire Constance's skill as a master puppeteer? She was Becky Sharp, Cousin Bette, Sister Carrie, and Holly Golightly all rolled into one. She manipulated husbands and lovers with the kind of sangfroid unimaginable to most of us, even in our most sordid fantasies. As she grew older, she never lost her youthful habit of playing the game for the sake of winning. Again, one thinks of F. Scott Fitzgerald's Jordan Baker, who observed that it takes two to make an accident. Constance played with people's lives so casually because she never imagined that she would meet another bad driver. And when her own duplicity was thrown back in her face, there were no tears or apologies. Whatever chaos and pain she left in her path derived from the unflinching tough-mindedness that once permeated American life, combined with a willingness to accept the consequences of her actions. Throughout her life, Mabel Morrison had exhibited formidable discipline, and she had tried her best to pass it on to her daughters. Barbara absorbed it not at all, but Constance and Joan—albeit in very different ways—achieved it to perfection.

And so, in 1942, Constance calmly enlisted Coulter's help in removing Gilbert even farther from the scene. With Constance's prodding, Coulter arranged for Gilbert to be sent to the Army Air Corps Officer Candidate School in Miami Beach. Unfortunately, Gilbert's sketchy education made it impossible for him to pass the rigorous examinations. "He was very embarrassed about the whole thing," said Peter Plant, "because he was being pushed into something, made into something, that he really was not suited for." In the end, Coulter pulled enough strings to ensure that Gilbert graduated from officer's training as a second lieutenant, even without passing marks. Subsequently, Coulter delivered the coup de grâce: he arranged for Gilbert to be assigned to an aerial mapping squadron that covered South America, photographing the country in order to prepare flight routes that would later be used by Pan American, then the United States' flag-carrier airline. Gilbert, who suffered from agoraphobia, was miserable with the assignment, but to Constance it mattered little. Once again, she had won a round.

Earlier, in 1939, Constance had turned her attention to Peter. He had grown into a bright and energetic boy, but Constance had begun to worry that it was unhealthy for him to be raised in a household filled with women. Soon she arranged to have him sent to Raenford, a military boarding school in the San Fernando Valley. Not surprisingly, Peter felt rejected. He had been happy at home and didn't understand what he had done to warrant his exile. After three years at Raenford, Constance began to give some thought to where he might continue his education. She was insistent that he not enter any of the big-name prep schools in the east, since she associated them with the snobbish eastern set—like the Plants. It would be better altogether, she felt, if Peter could attend a school where he might acquire a more wholesome set of values.

It was Wendell Willkie who helped her find the answer. In 1940, Constance, always a loyal Republican, had supported Willkie in his campaign for the presidency against incumbent Franklin Delano Roosevelt. (Willkie's appeal actually extended far beyond party lines, for many Democrats who were fed up with Roosevelt's New Deal politics also backed Willkie. Even Joan and Walter, normally staunch Democrats, were persuaded to move over to Willkie's side.)

One day, while Constance was having lunch with Willkie, the subject of Peter's schooling came up. Willkie suggested several possibilities, and Constance sent for the brochures and asked Peter to study them and make his choice. He selected Culver Military Academy in Culver, Indiana, partly because he was already an accomplished horseman and Culver was a noted riding school. In September 1942, Constance and Coulter drove him to Pasadena, where he caught a train to Indiana. Fortunately, he immediately took to Culver and the solid work ethic and sense of responsibility that the school sought to cultivate. In the end, he was probably happier there than he would have been at home, where John Coulter was by now a frequent presence. Peter found him, like Gilbert, a man of weak character—not at all malign, but somewhat vain and superficial—the sort of man who could not command his respect. As he looked back on the situation years later, it seemed to Peter that Coulter was just another inevitable installment in Constance's topically themed love life. She married the high-living Philip Plant during the high-living 1920s, and she discovered Gilbert during Hollywood's craze for all things Latin. Perhaps she reasoned that, with the country at war, only a military man would do.

Once the war effort got rolling, Constance was given plenty of opportunities to atone for her shabby treatment of Gilbert. Her record of wartime service was admirable by any standard. In 1940, she had become active in Bundles for Britain, an organization founded that January by socialite Natalie Wales Latham. Its purpose was to ship war-relief items to Britain, which Latham felt had been unjustly overlooked in the outpouring of public sympathy for France. Gloves, pullovers, caps, comforters, and socks were knitted by the band of volunteers that manned the organization's nearly three hundred coast-to-coast branches. Constance worked tirelessly for Bundles for Britain. She also donated much of her time to the International Rescue Committee, founded at Albert Einstein's instigation to assist those facing religious and racial persecution at the hands of the Nazis. "She was an effective organizer," recalled Peter Plant, who felt that her conviction sprang from a source unknown to most Hollywood stars, namely the years in Paris which had provided her with firsthand awareness of the plight of Europeans who had opposed Hitler.

Constance was also involved in the war effort as a performer. In 1940, she had appeared at Los Angeles's El Capitan Theater in a special, all-star production of Noël Coward's multipart play *Tonight at 8:30,* the proceeds of which went to British Relief. Constance, who appeared in the playlet *We Were Dancing,* was one of the few American-born stars in a cast that included Ida Lupino, Gladys Cooper, Joan Fontaine, Brian Aherne, Greer Garson, and Roland Young. She also participated in numerous bond-selling drives, including Stars Over America, organized by the U.S. Treasury Department, in which she traveled to dozens of cities in the company of other Hollywood personalities, such as Charles Laughton, Ann Rutherford, and Virginia Gilmore.

By early 1942, Hollywood had entered an era of unprecedented prosperity. The studios had been on shaky financial ground early in 1940, partly because the war had brought about a swift decline in European markets. But around six months later, a tremendous boom began that continued steadily throughout the war years and beyond. As the war in Europe grew in intensity, Americans hungered for an increasing number of pictures with war-related themes, and for newsreels, too. The Office of War Information persuaded Hollywood studios that they had a mission to inject wartime content into as many of their films as possible, and the studios were happy to do so, particularly when it meant hefty profits, which jumped from a little over $19 million in 1940 to $60 million in 1943.

American industry had now mobilized for the war effort, and employment at the nation's factories was booming. In large cities, it was common to see movie theaters staying open practically around the clock, with special advertisements of swing-shift showings. Movies no longer helped pass the leisure time—they filled it.

Constance did not benefit from the wartime boom. After *Madame Spy* in 1942, she would not make another picture for four years. When there was more work available than ever, why was she continually passed over? The answer is probably that the studios would no longer tolerate the temperamental behavior that had earned her a bad reputation at RKO in the early 1930s. By the 1940s, the various unions were entrenched at the studios. The 1930s had seen a tremendous growth in the number and influence of the technicians' union. They had been spurred on in part by liberal activist Upton Sinclair, whose 1934 campaign for state governor had been decidedly unpopular among the Hollywood moguls. In 1933, the Screen Actors Guild was established, and four years later the studios officially recognized it as the bargaining spokesman of the acting community. Similar deals followed with the Screen Directors Guild in 1939 and the Screenwriters Guild in 1940. By the time the new decade began, over one-third of all Hollywood motion picture industry employees were members of the International Alliance of Theatrical and Stage Employees (IATSE). In a tight-ship mentality, demanding stars of the 1930s, including Kay Francis, Miriam Hopkins, and Constance, had difficulty finding work, and with the spirit of patriotism flourishing, Constance seemed a relic from a hedonistic time. People still remembered her $30,000-a-week demands while the country was in ruins, and felt more than justified in turning their backs on her.

Since Constance couldn't earn enough money in the movies, she was determined to get it elsewhere. If a cosmetics business hadn't worked, perhaps a clothing line would. In the mid-1940s, she entered into an agreement with Fashion Frocks, Inc., a mail-order dress company based in Cincinnati. Constance's involvement was in the nature of an endorsement. She posed in a series of advertisements wearing simple shirtmaker-style dresses "designed by Constance Bennett," which she accessorized with elegant belts, shoes, and jewelry of her own. Unfortunately, Fashion Frocks didn't sell accessories, and without them the dresses didn't look anything like they appeared in the ads. Had they offered a complete line of goods, as Spiegel's later did, Fashion Frocks might have succeeded, but interest in the line quickly died. It was another sign that Constance's reputation as Hollywood's shrewdest businesswoman was exaggerated. In truth, she lacked the organized mind and command of detail that mark true business acumen. Her steamroller approach to doing business didn't allow for the need to step back and reassess situations when they weren't working. "I think she worked a lot with female intuition," said Peter Plant. "But her scope of knowledge? Quite limited. She had many good ideas, but she couldn't understand the constraints that had to be imposed if you chose to execute them. Consequently, she got in a lot of trouble and lost a lot of money."

In the summer of 1941, Constance was launched, by a roundabout means, on the path to recouping some of her losses. On June 18, Philip Plant, who had been living quietly in Connecticut for several years, died of a heart attack, just months before his fortieth birthday. In his last will and testament, there were to be only three bequests: $150,000 to his third wife, Marjorie Plant, $5,000 to his valet, Thomas McCarthy, with the rest, residues, and remainder of his property and estate to go to his mother, Mae Hayward.

When Morton Plant had died in 1918, Mrs. Hayward had inherited the bulk of his estate. But the Commodore had also made separate provisions for Philip—an outright bequest in the neighborhood of $150,000, plus a sizeable trust fund, to be distributed in quarter allotments when he reached the ages of twenty-five, thirty, thirty-five, and forty. If it could be proven that Philip died without issue before his fortieth birthday, the final payment—$550,000—would go directly to Mrs. Hayward. Over the next year, Philip's will was in probate. In October 1942, in the Probate Court of

Groton, Connecticut, Judge Arthur P. Anderson ruled that Philip had died childless, and that the remaining balance of the trust could be paid out in accordance with the Commodore's will. But the stakes concerning the final $550,000 were unusually high. Twelve years after Philip's divorce from Constance, he had done nothing to alter his profligate ways, and it appears that the $550,000 was nearly all he had left. After legal expenses and debts were taken care of, and payments were made to his widow, somewhere between $250,000 and $275,000 would remain, and all of it would go to Mrs. Hayward.

Shortly after Philip's death, Constance had been approached by Mrs. Hayward's attorneys with an unusual request: would she sign a statement affirming that Peter was adopted, and that neither she nor Peter would make any claim whatsoever against the Plant estate? But Mrs. Hayward's strategy backfired. Constance declined. She assured them that Peter really was Philip's child. Weren't his visits over the years and faithful remembrances of the boy on his birthday and Christmas proof of that?

Even in the best of times with Philip, there had never been love lost between Constance and Mrs. Hayward. But to Constance, this latest skirmish was an unforgivable insult. Mrs. Hayward's refusal to recognize Peter as her legitimate grandson had stirred her litigious streak. She consulted with her attorneys, certain that she could prove that Peter was really her son and that rumors of his adoption were spurious. If she played her cards right, she might even win him a share of Philip's estate.

In November 1943, Constance's appeal of Judge Anderson's ruling was heard in New London Superior Court, with Judge James R. Murphy presiding. Constance showed up in court tired and ill. She had been appearing in a grueling road tour of Philip Barry's comedy *Without Love,* and the hearing had been scheduled during a break before she took the play to Los Angeles. On the day she checked into the Mohican Hotel in New London, she was suffering from bronchitis and running a fever.

On November 16, the two opposing sides faced each other in court. The attorneys for the Morton and Philip Plant estates promised to prove that Constance had adopted Peter, and that his biological mother was an Irish girl, Sarah Savina Armstrong, now training as a nurse in a London hospital. Constance's representative, Francis F. McGuire, who had supplanted Rex Cole as Peter's guardian ad litem, told the judge that he would prove that Philip and Constance were Peter's natural parents.

Wrapped in a full-length mink coat and fighting a rattling bronchial cough, Constance waited in a court clerk's office, while a throng of giggling teenage girls crowded in the hallway. She indulged them by giving them all her autograph "with a smiling graciousness," one reporter noted. Confident that she would emerge triumphant, she explained to the press that, technically, neither she nor Peter had made any claim on the Plant fortune. Peter's involvement was involuntary simply because she refused to permit him to carry the stigma of being adopted.

Her high-minded approach played well in the press. But inside the courtroom, the attorneys for the Plant estate had gathered plenty of ammunition. One of their principal documents was a statement sworn out in London on February 24, 1942, by Sarah Armstrong. In it, Armstrong stated that her son, Dennis Arthur, had been born on January 21, 1929, and that in the fall of that year she had applied to the National Adoption Society. "On the ninth day of January 1930," she attested, "I entered into an agreement with Constance Bennett Plant who was at that time the wife of Philip M. Plant. This Agreement provided for the adoption of my said child by the said Constance Bennett Plant."

The veracity of Sarah Armstrong's statement was undermined by a deposition she gave in London at the U.S. Consul's office almost five months later, on July 15, 1942. In it, she gave a much less persuasive account of how the adoption had taken place. Could she recall meeting any other party connected with the adoption? "If I did, I cannot remember them," she replied. On what basis had she sworn that she "entered into an agreement with Constance Bennett Plant"? "For the simple reason that some years ago I read it in the paper that she had adopted the boy." Pressed further, Armstrong attempted to elaborate. She had read—she couldn't recall in which newspaper—that Constance Bennett the film star was adopting a boy named Peter Armstrong, whose parents had both been killed in an auto accident.

"Did you think that you had been killed in a motor accident?" asked Constance's attorney derisively.

"I do not know," Armstrong replied.

"Who informed you that at the time of this agreement Constance Bennett Plant was the wife of Philip M. Plant?"

"I suppose I must have read it. I do not know."

The questioning grew more heated. "I suggest to you, if you read any such thing in any paper, that it never for one moment suggested to your mind that it had anything to with any child of yours. It is true that in fact it did not suggest that to you?"

"No; I just thought the name was very familiar. That is all."

"It was the same name as your own?"

"Yes."

With Armstrong having failed to inspire confidence as a witness, other depositions were introduced from Armstrong's sister, Lillian Nicholson, Helen Blackburne, secretary of the National Adoption Society, and Constance's friend Rita Kaufman Lowe. In the end, Judge Murphy ruled that all the depositions taken in London were inadmissible on a technicality—a Connecticut statute requiring that the purpose of the deposition must be certified by the individual taking it. One deposition admitted as evidence was that of Barbara Bennett Randall, taken in Los Angeles in July 1942. Barbara had been ordered to appear two previous times and failed to show up. After the third subpoena, she did appear, but refused to say anything unless Addison Randall remained in the room with her.

It was well known that there had been bad blood between Constance and Barbara for some years; it was also well known that Randall had failed to be a steady provider and that Barbara was pressed for money. Randall did sit in on the deposition, and at one juncture he was reprimanded for cracking his knuckles, which was taken to be an unspoken cue of some sort to his wife.

There is no hard evidence to support the belief, held by many in the Bennett family, that Barbara was paid five hundred dollars by the Plant estate to give a deposition against Constance. But her testimony is an uncertain and confusing dance, and gives the distinct impression that she has been carefully coached not to perjure herself. She stated that she had believed Peter to be adopted, that Mabel had told her that Peter was "found up in Ireland." Asked how she first learned that Constance planned to assert a claim that Peter was really the child of Constance and Philip Plant, she replied that she had read it in the newspaper.

Had she communicated with anyone after reading the newspaper item? "With Marjorie King Plant, Phil Plant's widow."

"And when you communicated with Mrs. Marjorie King Plant, you told her, did you not, what you believed to be the fact: that Peter Bennett Plant was an adopted child?"

"Yes."

The questioning then turned to Barbara's relationship with Constance. "It has not been unfriendly," she answered. "We don't get along." Pressed for further details, she added, "It has not been one thing or the other; neither flesh, fish, nor fowl."

"In other words, you don't see each other?"

"I don't care."

"You don't care?"

"No."

Constance did not appear in the courtroom until the afternoon of November 18. One local reporter observed, "it was a dramatic moment as the actress looked up and saw her former mother-in-law. . . . Although Miss Bennett was hot from fever, the glance she gave Mrs. Hayward was cool enough." Once she took the stand, Constance held to her story: she had given birth to Peter in a house in the London suburbs. The only witnesses to attest to that fact—a Dr. Dawson, her mother, and her maid—were all dead. She had become pregnant in the final weeks before her separation from Philip, and she had concealed the pregnancy for fear that the Plant family would initiate custody proceedings. The adoption papers for Dennis Armstrong, introduced as evidence by the attorneys for the Plant estate, had been manufactured as part of her plan of concealment. In an attempt to carry out the plan, she later concocted the story that Peter was the illegitimate son of a distant cousin in England. Eventually, when concealment was no longer necessary, Philip had openly acknowledged the boy as his own—all of which corresponds with Peter's memories of Philip's visits to him in the intervening years.

Unfortunately, the only trace left of Constance's testimony exists in paraphrased newspaper accounts. There is no copy of her testimony in the case records, now housed in the Groton Superior Court House. Such a glaring omission leads to endless speculation: could Mrs. Hayward, with great local power and influence on her side, have succeeded in destroying these documents because of what they revealed?

Late in the day of November 18, a compromise agreement, which modified the lower courts' original ruling, was reached. Judge Murphy commented "that the proof is complicated and difficult, and it is for the best interest, well-being, and welfare of the minor that the pending approval from probate be compromised and settled." He then awarded Peter $150,000, from which $27,000 was to be paid in attorneys' fees.

Surely Constance had hoped to secure a larger amount for Peter, but she appeared upbeat about the decision. She told the press, "Today's outcome vindicates the position I took when the appeal was filed for my son Peter Bennett Plant." No matter that the settlement represented a compromise, and that the court had put aside the question of Peter's paternity; she claimed that the $150,000 award was sufficient refutation of the Plant estate's claim that Peter was adopted.

As the publicity surrounding the case faded, Peter continued his studies, secure in the knowledge that he would one day have a sizeable nest egg. Joan wasn't so sure. After the settlements were final, she told Diana, "Peter will never see that money."

The entire business was, as one newspaper commented, "one of the most bizarre cases in court annals." To this day, numerous unanswered questions remain. Did the attorneys for the Plant estate use money to induce the fractured testimony of Sarah Armstrong and Barbara Bennett Randall? Did something specific in Constance's testimony suddenly prompt the Plant estate to agree to a reasonable settlement? Why is there no court record of Constance's appearance on the witness stand?

What may be the most telling answer to these questions was provided Peter in the early 1950s by Francis McGuire, who represented him at trial, when he told him to drive to the courthouse and walk around the outside. Peter did. Near the entrance to the courthouse was a plaque marking it as a recent gift from Maisie Hayward.

Since the 1940s, Peter Plant has remained unswerving in his belief that he is the biological son of Philip Plant and Constance Bennett. What about Dennis Armstrong? There is no way of knowing, and speculation leads to many dead ends. Constance had a lifelong habit of embroiling herself in messy affairs, fully confident that she would be able to find her way out. Often she did not succeed—as events in the years ahead would prove.

In Tchaikovsky's opera *The Queen of Spades,* the impoverished soldier Gherman attempts to divine an elderly Countess's secret of winning at cards. But when he threatens her, she expires without revealing the truth. "She died," says Gherman, "and her secret died with her."

So it was with Constance. Like many stars of her time who were largely self-invented, she felt that she had been granted license to invent herself to the world. The questions surrounding the case will no doubt never be answered to anyone's satisfaction. The only thing that seems indisputable is a comment made by Barbara during the course of her deposition. "You must take into consideration," she remarked to one of the attorneys questioning her, "that this is a very peculiar family."

By the early 1940s, it seemed unlikely that Richard would ever act again. He had settled in Los Angeles, where he would live out the rest of his days. At one point, he moved in with Constance and Gilbert at Carolwood Drive. Gilbert nicknamed him Cicero and was delighted every morning when his father-in-law appeared in his dressing-gown and greeted the day with a fresh Shakespearean quotation. Later on, Richard lived in a series of rented houses, provided chiefly through Joan's generosity.

Now in his early seventies, he was an unmanageable as ever. Diana Anderson recalled an evening at Mapleton Drive when he became incensed by the hunting mural that decorated the dining room walls. "He started carrying on that the positions of the riders on the horses were all wrong," said Anderson. "He wouldn't stop. It was just awful." He was also antagonistic toward Walter, whom he did not consider the equal of Gene Markey, and made a number of anti-Semitic comments about him in Joan's presence.

He was no longer too proud to resist painting himself as a figure of pathos if he thought it served his needs. One person who was a perfect foil in this respect was Hollywood columnist Hedda Hopper, who was to become a particular nemesis of Joan's in later years. Hopper didn't hesitate to fawn over Richard. She did a special seventieth birthday tribute to him on her radio program, and frequently lamented his reduced state in her column. "I felt so badly about Dick Bennett and his daughters, I'm afraid, paid very little attention to him," Hopper scolded. "I remember going to a preview not long ago in which Joan appeared, and there was Dick on the sidewalk. He couldn't even get a ticket to see his own daughter on the screen. . . . The last time I heard of him, he had no will to live. He said, 'After all, nobody wants me and what do I want with this shell?'"

But one last memorable performance lay ahead. One member of the Hollywood community who did not regard Richard as a has-been was Orson Welles, who in 1941 had galvanized the film industry with his critically acclaimed *Citizen Kane*. Its portrait of megalomaniac newspaper tycoon Charles Foster Kane was a barely disguised portrait of William Randolph Hearst. When *Citizen Kane* was released, the vast Hearst newspaper chain had come out strongly against the picture, helping it post a $160,000 loss for RKO. Nevertheless, *Citizen Kane* did give the studio a boost in prestige, and RKO gave Welles the go-ahead for his next project, a screen version of Booth Tarkington's 1918 novel *The Magnificent Ambersons.*

In his youth, Welles had seen many of Richard's greatest stage performances. Welles felt that he had the greatest lyric power of any actor he had ever seen in the theater, and he was delighted to offer him the small but important role of Major Amberson, the aging patriarch of a prominent Indianapolis family that sees its way of life swept away by the automotive age. Richard was thrilled to be working again. "My good fortune has created a new spindrift in my current of existence," he wrote to Welles. "You have made me happy with sweet potentialities."

As filming got under way, Richard once again found it impossible to retain his lines. Welles was patient with him, doing everything possible to make him comfortable. Richard's most powerful scene in the picture was his last one, a monologue in which the Major, his spirit broken and mind clouded, prepares to meet death. It is one of the most emotionally naked moments in any of Welles's films: the Major's daughter Isabel has just died, and as the other relatives search for the deed to the house, the camera closes in on the Major, sitting before the fire. He stares blankly ahead as he readies himself to enter "an unknown country where he was not even sure of being recognized as an Amberson." He begins to ramble: "It must be the sun. There wasn't anything here but the sun in the first place. The sun . . . the earth came out of the sun . . . and we came out of the earth . . . So whatever we are . . ." and his face slowly fades out of the frame.

It was a brilliant turn, regrettably diminished by the studio's extensive cutting of the picture. The following year, Welles provided him with another vivid character role, as the Greek captain on a spy-laden ship in the thriller *Journey into Fear.* This time the director had a more creative solution to Richard's difficulty with lines: the captain spoke no English. It was Richard's final performance.

Barbara had not had an easy time of it since the divorce. Her guilt over her decision to surrender custody of the children haunted her, and she was drinking more than ever. "My mother's life sort of fell apart in stages," recalled Michael Downey. "I think when you look at the childhood they were brought up with, the Bennett sisters were all getting by on personality, charm, and acting ability. But getting along in the real sense—going to work and coping with life like the great unwashed—they just didn't know how to take care of themselves."

True, the Randalls had serious financial realities to face. Addison had endured a long dry spell in Hollywood, and with no money coming in, Barbara had to take work where she could get it. Suddenly, in the summer of 1943, she was offered a leading part in *Victory Belles,* a new Broadway farce by Alice Gerstenberg. She had no particular interest in returning to show business, but a job was a job—and when Addison was cast in a supporting part as a butler, she decided to go ahead with it.

Victory Belles was a disaster. When it opened at the Mansfield Theatre on October 26, 1943, many critics judged it the worst play of the season. The *New York Times* called it "as dull and dreary and ineptly written a script as has been foisted upon the public in many a sad moon." The *New York Post* noted that Barbara, playing one of a group of women coping with the wartime shortage of men, managed "now and then to get off some insufferable lines as if they were the latest bon mots."

Victory Belles closed almost immediately, too soon to bring the Randalls any real attention—but an event that took place several weeks later did. Around ten o'clock on the evening of December 14, they joined another couple for a visit to the fashionable nightclub El Morocco. An hour or so later, Walter and Joan wandered in and sat down at a nearby table, in the company of William Randolph Hearst Jr. and his wife, Lorelle, and Joan's good friends Muriel and Ben Finney. In a short while, Morton walked into the club, happened by the Wangers' table, and sat down to talk with them.

At first the two parties avoided each other. Randall and Barbara left the main room and got a table in the Champagne Room. On his way to the restroom, Randall, apparently reeling from too many drinks, tripped and fell. According to the story he gave the press, he rose to his feet to see the Wanger party laughing at him. He strode over to their table and challenged Morton to a fistfight. A scuffle ensued, with Finney and Hearst reportedly getting into the act, too, but it ended when a candelabrum was brought down on top of Randall's head, while the El Morocco's unflappable pianist played "Tales from the Vienna Woods." On coming to, Randall said to proprietor John Perona, "I take it that I am now barred from El Morocco"—and he was right.

Like Constance, Joan played a vital role in Hollywood's war effort. Her political interests had deepened under Walter's influence. In the late 1930s, she was one of fifty-seven industry leaders who signed a "Declaration of Democratic Independence," designed to pressure the Roosevelt administration into responding to the persecution of German Jews. With the U.S. entry into the war, Joan quickly became involved in the American Women's Volunteer Service, helping to arrange entertainment for servicemen across the country. David O. Selznick persuaded her to get involved in one of his pet causes, China Relief. In April 1943, a gala concert was given at the Hollywood Bowl to welcome Madame Chiang Kai-shek, and Joan was one of several star actresses who served on the benefit committee.

She was also a steady presence at the Hollywood Canteen, a restaurant and nightclub founded by Bette Davis and John Garfield for the purpose of giving the thousands of servicemen who passed through Los Angeles a glimpse of some authentic movie stars. Sponsored and endorsed by forty-two screen guilds and unions, the Canteen was a success from the outset, pulling in a crowd of thirty thousand on its opening night on October 3, 1942. Most of the major stars in Hollywood volunteered their services on a regular basis, performing, dancing with enlisted men, waiting on tables, washing dishes. Beginning on opening night, both Constance and Joan worked tirelessly for the Canteen, a fact that did not go unnoticed by the canteen's president; in later years, Bette Davis praised them both for their service to her pet wartime project.

In the spring of 1942, Joan was one of a large group of stars on the Hollywood Victory Caravan, a cross-country train tour organized by the Army-Navy Relief Fund to raise money for the widows and children of men killed in action. Some of Hollywood's finest boarded the seventeen-car train, among them, Bob Hope, Bing Crosby, James Cagney, Cary Grant, Claudette Colbert, Spencer Tracy, Olivia de Havilland, Charles Boyer, Groucho Marx, Bert Lahr, Charlotte Greenwood, Joan Blondell, Eleanor Powell, Merle Oberon, and Stan Laurel and Oliver Hardy. "Some of us would sing, and some of the comedians would do stand-up routines," recalled Metropolitan Opera mezzo-soprano Risë Stevens, who was also on the tour. "And stars such as Joan Bennett would sell kisses to the men, and raised quite a lot of money doing it." It was a memorable trip for Joan; Colbert, Oberon, and Tracy were all good friends of hers, and during the course of the trip she established a close bond with Joan Blondell, who remained a friend for life. For Joan, it was a chance to witness what the movies really meant to people in the heartland. The only hardship she faced on the tour was having to appear in public without her glasses. But she loved the high spirits, the camaraderie, and the parties that usually began about midnight, when all official duties had been performed. Once the Victory Caravan had returned to California, she and Joan Blondell sent out telegrams to everyone else on the tour that read: "ARE YOU GETTING MUCH?"

Later that year, in between making a string of indifferent movies for Twentieth Century–Fox and Columbia, Joan signed a contract with Alfred A. Knopf to write *How to Be Attractive,* a beauty book targeting busy American women in the workforce. There were sections on "Eight Steps for an Eight-Hour-Day Make-Up," "Tune Up Your Motor," and "Is This Any Time to Worry About Clothes?" The latter segment particularly captured the overall patriotic tone of the book. "This is one time when we must think about clothes—to buy wisely, to choose basically becoming, rather than fleetingly fashionable or downright dowdy clothes. Even if we could afford to buy, try, and discard a poor choice, our country can't afford the material and labor for this unwise buying. . . . Our men in the services and eventually the shivering, unclad men, women, and children of two thirds of the globe are going to need the fabric and the labor that a few of us once used so prodigally." In a chapter called "Time for Headwork," she advocated pursuit of the arts, reminding her readers that it was important to "vary your diet—swing music, cake, and comic strips are all perfectly good 'food.' But try to include a little Beethoven and Grant Wood even if they taste like spinach at first. You'll go right on liking dessert—but you'll find that this indigestible age needs the solid main course, too."

Early in 1943, Joan discovered she was pregnant again. She was thrilled to be having a child with Walter, and after being directed by Otto Preminger in *Margin for Error,* Twentieth Century–Fox's screen version of the Clare Boothe Luce stage hit, she made no other films that year. She busied herself organizing fifteen years' worth of press clippings and seeing that they were put into scrapbooks, and by late April the finishing touches were put on the baby's nursery.

Then on May 3, 1943—Mother's Day—she weathered one of the most devastating catastrophes of her life. Just after dawn, Rosalie Miller, one of the maids at Mapleton Drive, was awakened by the smell of smoke coming from the basement. She roused the family, who had all been upstairs asleep. Walter activated the fire alarm and quickly dressed in a coat, trousers, and slippers, while Joan, Diana, Melinda, and the servants barely had time to pull robes on over their nightclothes. By this time, smoke had filled the house, and seven fire companies answered the call as the family and most of the neighborhood stood outside on the lawn, watching the flames that had engulfed the upstairs and were now shooting through the roof.

The source of the fire, it turned out, was a badly wired hot water heater in the basement. The flames had begun smoldering in the walls and then shot upward with terrifying speed, missing most of the ground floor, which was damaged mostly by smoke and water. Firemen fought the blaze for several hours before it was extinguished. It was one of the only times Joan's children had seen her break down completely. She wept uncontrollably as the family trudged across the street to take shelter in the home of director Allan Dwan. "I can't bear to see it," she sobbed, "It's sickening."

The damage was estimated at around $200,000. The white brick exterior was unharmed, but the entire upstairs was effectively gutted. Much of the furniture and most of the family's clothes, including Joan's collection of valuable furs, were destroyed. A great many paintings and etchings, including a Grant Wood original, were also lost, and Walter's vast library of first editions sustained considerable damage. Because of the wartime shortage of materials, it was estimated that reconstruction might take as long as a year. The family moved temporarily to a hotel, then signed a year's lease on a semi-furnished house at 10451 Bellaggio Road, and attempted to put their lives back in order. A few weeks later, on June 26, Joan and Walter's first daughter, Stephanie, was born. Although Walter had resisted the idea of having children, Joan remembered that once Stephanie arrived, "he was the proudest of fathers."

Chapter Fifteen

1944

There is a scrap of dialogue in Robert Wise's 1947 thriller *Born to Kill* that might serve as an epitaph for the film noir genre as a whole. The picture concerns a divorcée, Helen Brent (Claire Trevor), who must confront her own corrupt nature when she falls for Sam Wilde (Lawrence Tierney) whom she knows to be a psychopathic killer. Helen discovers that Mrs. Kraft (Esther Howard), an elderly friend of one of Wilde's victims, has hired a private detective to find the killer and bring him to justice. Helen goes to see the old lady and warns her that unless she calls off the investigation, she will have her killed. Terrified, Mrs. Kraft agrees to Helen's terms. But as Helen is leaving, Mrs. Kraft demonstrates what she thinks of her by spitting on her back.

> HELEN (turning around): Bad cess to me?
> MRS. KRAFT: No need for me to say it. You carry your own curse. Inside of you.

This is the key to so many of the men and women who sauntered through the great noir films of the 1940s and early 1950s: they all carried their own curse. In film noir, even the most virtuous heroes and heroines are damaged goods, one way or another. They are the ones who can no longer believe in the complacent dreams that lie at the heart of American life, which is exactly what puts them in the path of danger. Because they no longer aspire to lead a nice, clean existence, they become susceptible to the stiff drink, the cheap thrill, the fast buck.

Film noir came along just when American audiences were ready for it. It seemed the ideal antidote to the noble, flag-waving films of World War II, such as David O. Selznick's *Since You Went Away* (1944), with its condescending portrait of the brave "little" people holding down the home front. Said actress Teresa Wright, who played a long string of fresh-faced heroines in the 1940s, "The girl next door wasn't really the girl next door. She was the girl next door to the movie star next door. There's something in all my early performances . . . I don't know how to describe it except to say that it's *so* 1940s. . . . It's not that I wasn't *thinking* the right thing. I was, but the thought is dressed in something prettier. We were all used to that technique. You were doing the real thing as that girl would do it *if she were perfect.*"

In truth, film noir was not necessarily more realistic than the scrubbed and wholesome wartime dramas. Strictly speaking, realism in the American cinema was still at least a decade away, and most film noir had a stylized language and grammar all its own that had little to do with the way real people spoke or behaved. Often, the press scorned these films—"so many of these murder operas are an insult to thinking people," sniffed Louella Parsons in 1944—and the actors who appeared in them often failed to recognize their significance. Audrey Totter, who starred in fine noir examples such as *The Lady in the Lake* (1946) and *Tension* (1949), said, "*Film noir* really wasn't regarded as anything important in the 1940s. It was the big color historical and musical movies that were highly thought of."

But to many in the audience, film noir presented an accurate picture of the world—or what the world had become. With the world split asunder by war, Americans suddenly saw darkness all around them, in a frightening and immediate way. Many in the audience sought escapism, but many others seemed to have developed a craving for brutality on film, as if the fantasy world of crime onscreen could help blot out the horrors taking place around the globe. In this respect, film noir belongs absolutely to the 1940s, but there were earlier influences. Among them were the Warner Bros. crime melodramas of the 1930s, although they were spare and artless, without all the striking lighting effects and camera angles associated with the noir style.

But what really presaged film noir was German expressionism—an embrace of the decadent side of human nature that had sprung up following Germany's defeat in World War I. The harsh terms of the armistice, and the humiliation and suffering that Germany endured in the years that followed, led to a nationwide malaise that was reflected on the screen in the works of such filmmakers as G.W. Pabst and F.W. Murnau. These films featured dark and often violent themes, sometimes with an element of the fantastic, surreal, or supernatural. Many of the principal noir directors—Michael Curtiz, Fritz Lang, Otto Preminger, Robert Siodmak, Edgar G. Ulmer, and Billy Wilder—had honed their talents in the Austrian-German film industry during the 1920s and early 1930s. Now, in the 1940s, they took many of the dramatic camera and lighting techniques that they had absorbed years earlier and adapted them to create a new genre in American cinema. In 1944, Lang, having already guided Joan to serious critical attention with *Man Hunt,* turned her into one of the screen's most striking femme fatales.

At the time, Joan probably wouldn't have known what to make of the term *film noir,* since it didn't come into wide use until later on. But she did know a good script when she saw one. In 1943, her good friend William Goetz left his post at Twentieth Century–Fox to form a new company, International Pictures. One of its first films was to be a suspense drama written by Nunnally Johnson and directed by Fritz Lang. In mid-1944, Joan wrote to Diana at school, "I am starting a picture in three weeks for Mr. Goetz called *The Woman in the Window.* I love the story and my part."

Since he and Joan had worked together in *Man Hunt,* Lang had parted company with Twentieth Century–Fox and made two pictures, *Hangmen Also Die* (1943) and *Ministry of Fear* (1944), both anti-Nazi thrillers. With *The Woman in the Window,* he returned to an American setting. The new picture was based on J.H. Wallis's 1942 novel *Once Off Guard,* about a married, middle-aged college professor who one night goes home with a woman of questionable virtue and winds up getting involved in murder.

Nunnally Johnson transformed the book into a beautifully structured screenplay, in which suspense was mingled with strong currents of sexuality and flashes of malicious humor. The plot of an ordinary man fatefully drawn into perilous circumstances was no doubt one Hitchcock would have found himself attracted to. The central character is Richard Wanley (played in the film by Edward G. Robinson), an assistant professor of criminal psychology at Manhattan's Gotham College. After sending his wife and children off on a holiday, Wanley spends an aimless evening at his club with two old friends, to whom he complains about sinking into middle age ("I hate this solidity, the stodginess I'm beginning to feel").

Later that night, on his way home, Wanley stops to gaze at an alluring female portrait in an art gallery window, and is astonished when the subject of the painting saunters up and strikes up a conversation. The woman, Alice Reed (Joan), persuades Wanley to take her out for a drink, then back to her Greenwich Village apartment for champagne. Their pleasant encounter is shattered when Alice's lover bursts in on them and flies into an uncontrollable rage. He tries to strangle Wanley, who manages to stab his attacker to death with a pair of scissors. Rather than face the police and certain ruin, Wanley and Alice make a pact to cover up the crime. At first they appear to have succeeded, but soon the dead man's bodyguard (Dan Duryea) shows up and blackmails them. Wanley and Alice contrive to poison the blackmailer, but Alice botches the job and the bodyguard holds out for even more money. Realizing that he is in too deep to find his way out, Wanley commits suicide.

The Woman in the Window succeeds as a suspense thriller and a cautionary tale (it probably made men as wary of getting picked up by strange women as *Fatal Attraction* would some forty years later.) But what really gives the film distinction is its penetrating depiction of what it is like to be trapped in a lie. After he hides the body, Wanley's world slowly caves in on him and he is forced to sit back and watch as his best friend, a district attorney (Raymond

Massey) fits the pieces of the case together. The details are flawless: Wanley sitting with his friends at their club, attempting to cover up a poison ivy rash he contracted while dumping the body; burning the dead man's hat in the fireplace just as a radio announcer divulges the victim's true identity; accompanying his D.A. friend to the murder scene and inadvertently walking right toward the spot where the body was found; the fatuous boy scout who discovers the corpse ("No, I was not scared. A boy scout is *never* scared."). Lang never overplays his hand; in none of his other American films would Lang surpass the sureness and subtlety he shows in *The Woman in the Window.* Small wonder that his biographer, Patrick McGilligan, calls *The Woman in the Window* the director's "chamberwork."

For the most part, the film follows the Wallis novel closely. But a number of significant changes occurred in translating it to the screen. The most controversial switch concerned the ending. In the film, Wanley commits suicide by drinking poison. There is a slow fade, and suddenly a waiter at his club is shaking him awake. It turns out that the whole thing has been a dream. Happy endings were an unusual occurrence in film noir, and this one—a concession, it seems to the Hays Office, which didn't approve of suicide—provided the one consistent caveat in the otherwise glowing reviews. And yet, it seems a sublimely logical stroke on Lang and Johnson's part, for it beautifully underlines the inexorable, dreamlike pull of the story.

But the most sweeping changes from novel to film involved the character of Alice Reed. In the book, she is as common as dirt. Wallis writes that Wanley "knew as surely as if the woman had told him that her life was sex. Her life was satisfying the desire of some man." In the film, Alice is moved up the social scale—she's a wealthy man's classy mistress. Joan's first appearance is one of the most memorable entrances in any 1940s film: her reflection appears in the window of the art gallery, superimposed over the portrait—an introduction of the idea of images intruding on reality. Alice is right out of a dream, a fantastic figure in a dark, glittering jacket with a matching cap that shoots out black feathers. She has a long cigarette holder, she blows smoke out her nose, and she has a rapacious, unnerving smile, as if she knows instantly that she has made her conquest for the night.

Joan's Alice is one of the most predatory of noir women. She doesn't lead the man on, like Barbara Stanwyck's Phyllis Dietrichson in *Double Indemnity.* Instead, she steers him up to her apartment with breathtaking confidence. There is a humorous element of role reversal here—the woman on the make invites the man up to the apartment to look at *her* etchings—that Lang seems not entirely to have grasped. Instead, he took great care to make the girl's apartment into a threatening sexual trap. There is the provocative dress she is wearing, the nude statue on the mantlepiece, the glimpse of her bedroom in the distance, the vase of phallic-looking canna on the coffee table.

Throughout the film, Lang keeps us at an intriguing distance from Alice, and we never quite figure her out. Our minds wander from the action to wonder if her role in the murder of her lover could have been premeditated. Alice is perhaps the most ambiguous of all noir's did-she-or-didn't-she seductresses, and Joan gives her an edge of malevolent wit, providing many of the dissonant grace notes in Lang's "chamber-work"—most memorably when Alice insists on taking the money off the corpse:

> WANLEY: You searched him?
> ALICE: It had to be done, didn't it?
> WANLEY [going through wallet]: Tomorrow, get on one of the ferries and drop it overboard. And be very careful that you aren't seen.
> ALICE: The money, too?

During filming, Joan found Lang as exacting as ever. He still fussed over every detail of her performance, still dictated many of her line readings. Nevertheless, she found both the film and her part more stimulating than anything she had done since *Man Hunt.* Her relationship with the other actors was congenial. She was fond of Edward G. Robinson, who looked in the rushes as if he would be superb, and felt at ease with Dan Duryea, whom she found an unusually serious-minded actor.

When it was previewed late in 1944, *The Woman in the Window* proved to be a triumph for everyone connected with it, with many reviewers hailing Joan's performance as her finest yet. "Joan Bennett was never lovelier than in the role of the artist's model," wrote the *Hollywood Reporter,* "nor has she ever given a more versatile performance." "Miss Bennett has not been seen to better advantage since she appeared in *Man Hunt* four years ago," observed the *New York Times.* In her letters to Diana at boarding school, Joan seldom mentioned her work, but it was clear that she was proud of her latest effort. "*The Woman in the Window* is doing a terrific business," she wrote to Diana early in 1945. "It broke the house record in New York and is being held over a third week here. They expect it to run six weeks in New York."

Unfortunately, Richard's deteriorating health prevented Joan from fully enjoying her success in the new film. Since he completed work on *Journey into Fear,* Richard's activity had ground to a halt. He lived quietly—as quietly as he was able—in the house Joan had rented for him in Santa Monica, growing weaker as the months passed, yet still insisting that he had given no thought to retirement. But all of those close to him knew he was long past accepting any offers of work. His breathing had grown labored, and it became difficult for him to walk for any distance at all. When Constance opened in Los Angeles in *Without Love,* he declined to attend any of the performances because he could not make it down the aisle unassisted.

In mid-October, he suffered a severe heart attack, and Joan admitted him to Los Angeles's Good Samaritan Hospital. He had reached the end, and he seemed to know it. At one point, as he grew increasingly disoriented, he cried out repeatedly for Mabel. After a little over a week, he lapsed into a coma. On October 22, 1944—Constance's fortieth birthday—Joan sent a telegram to Diana in the east:

DITTY DARLING: TRIED TO PHONE YOU BUT THERE IS A DELAY. I WANTED TO LET YOU KNOW IMMEDIATELY THAT GRAMPS PASSED AWAY AT 11:15 THIS MORNING. WE'RE HAVING THE SERVICES AT ALL SAINTS ON TUESDAY. DON'T FEEL TOO BADLY DARLING AS HE IS REALLY MUCH BETTER OFF. THE END WAS PEACEFUL. BOSSIE JOINS ME IN WORLDS OF LOVE, MUMMY.

On Tuesday, October 24, funeral services were held at All Saints' Episcopal Church in Beverly Hills. Dr. J. Herbert Smith officiated, reading the 23rd and 121st Psalms and scripture from Romans, chapter 8, and the Gospel of St. John, chapter 14. Flowers from friends and loved ones filled the church, but apart from Constance, Joan, and Melinda, only a select few were present. They included director Gregory Ratoff, character actor Frank Craven, and the honorary pallbearers: Walter, Gene, Victor Morrison, Al Woods, Burgess Meredith, Monroe Childs, Samuel Hoffenstein, Victor Wise, Jim Tully, and Lionel Barrymore.

Conspicuously absent was Barbara, who was in New York, unable to make the trip, she confessed to reporters, because she was flat broke. She also lost no time telling the press that her sisters had not informed her of Richard's death until twelve hours after the fact, and hadn't bothered to invite her to the funeral. This brought forth a response from both Constance and Joan. "I deeply regret," said Constance, "that even upon this sorrowful occasion, Barbara has once again placed me in the position where honesty demands my public repudiation of her irresponsible moments." Joan was slightly kinder: "It is regrettable that her recent bereavement did not allow her sufficient humility to at least let our father's death be a moment of dignity instead of one of dissension."

Richard would have had no reason to complain about the press coverage that his death received. Extensive obituaries appeared in all of the leading newspapers, and he no doubt would have been pleased by some of the descriptions that made their way into print. One notice called him "a truly colorful figure who wrote his own book of rules through his long years," while another observed that he was "laid to his final rest in ceremonies which in their quietness contrasted with the turbulence of his stage and screen career."

Would he have been pleased that the first paragraph in nearly all the obituaries identified him as the father of Constance, Barbara, and Joan Bennett? Certainly there is no question that he loved all three of his daughters deeply. He had relished their successes over the years just as often as he had fumed over their choice of men. Yet he had had to face one of the most painful and inevitable truths that ambush most parents: he had lived to see his daughters become independent of him, while he leaned on them more and more with the passing years.

For Constance, losing Richard was hideously painful. She had worshipped him more than Barbara or Joan had, and now she seemed to be following in his footsteps: a temperamental star left behind by a profession she had once ruled. Joan owed him the most, namely *Jarnegan* and the start of her career, which now looked as if it was going to go the distance. But they both knew what Richard had known: that they had surpassed him in celebrity, but not in talent.

Richard's body was placed in a temporary vault at Forest Lawn Memorial Park. Sometime later, it was shipped by train for burial in the Morrison family plot at Old Lyme. Joan traveled with his remains to ensure that they reached Old Lyme safely. On board, she ran into pianist Oscar Levant, widely known for his galloping neuroses, among them, an irrational fear of death.

"Are you traveling alone?" Levant asked her.

"No," replied Joan. "My father is with me."

"Well, where is he?"

"In the baggage car," smiled Joan. "He's dead."

Levant became so upset that he got off the train at the next stop. It was a story that Richard surely would have loved.

At the cemetery in Old Lyme, Richard's marker is all too appropriate: a great, tall, phallic-looking monument with the name "Bennett" carved in bold letters. It dwarfs an otherwise unassuming plot, and several of the Morrison clan found it in poor taste. "The girls, particularly Joan, wanted to bury him next to their mother," recalled Victor Morrison. "Which must have had her spinning in her grave! And my mother said, 'Every time you go out there, just lean on it a little bit. Eventually, maybe you'll knock it over.'"

Chapter Sixteen

1945–1947

The Woman in the Window signaled the beginning of Joan's most rewarding period as an actress. She always gave Lang all the credit for the fact that Hollywood suddenly began to take her more seriously. No matter that he obsessively dictated every detail of her performances. If being treated like a puppet was the price of doing quality work, then she was happy to pay it. Lang, for his part, had no illusions about her limitations. If Joan lacked the emotional range and imagination of a Barbara Stanwyck, she still brought plenty to the party, and Lang knew it. Not only did her name provide a box-office boost to the films he made, her brooding, sexy personality was perfectly suited to the shadows-and-fog atmosphere of his films. It was an ideal meeting of director and actress, and for the time being, everyone was happy.

So happy that they decided to go into business together. Independent productions were becoming a fixture in Hollywood by the time World War II neared its end. Initially the practice had appealed primarily to directors such as Frank Capra, who wanted to work without interference from the moguls. But as the 1940s progressed, independent production became equally attractive to actors. By this time, the studio system was beginning to crack around the edges. In a landmark case in 1944, Olivia de Havilland took Warner Bros. to court and won an important victory for all film actors. From that point on, studios could no longer tack extra time onto actors' contracts to cover periods when they had been placed on suspension. As a result, the studios' power over actors was weakened, and many of the top stars began to form independent companies. One of the earliest had been James Cagney, who launched Cagney Productions in 1942, but with war's end, Bette Davis, Humphrey Bogart, Joan Fontaine, and many others established companies of their own.

Walter had been at the forefront of independent production for years, and he was the first to point out that an independent producer was actually dependent on many entities: banks, the press, distributors, and most of all, the public. Nevertheless, through his association with Paramount and United Artists, he had achieved a status in Hollywood rare for an independent. In 1941, his arrangement with UA was canceled by mutual consent, and he began one of the most commercially rewarding periods of his career, in association with Universal Pictures. When the first film he brought them, *Eagle Squadron* (1942), turned out to be a hit, he signed a long-term deal to function essentially as an in-house independent. He came up with the properties and developed them, then saw them through production without studio interference. It was a lucrative deal for Walter, who was paid a weekly salary and received 50 percent of his pictures' net profits. Many of his Universal films, like *Gung Ho!* (1943) and *Ladies Courageous* (1944), featured war themes, and while they may have been routine entertainment, they pulled in big grosses. He also favored exotic escapist films set in the Middle East. One of his pictures, *Arabian Nights* (1942), the first of the studio's Technicolor Maria Montez vehicles, posted net profits of $1,851,921.

He was at his peak, but obviously, none of these films came close to satisfying his artistic ambitions. In the spring of 1945, while renewing his arrangement with Universal as an independent unit producer, he cut a separate deal with the studio that established an independent production company. The result, Diana Productions—named for Joan's daughter—would make pictures for Universal distribution. Although it was not stated, it was understood that Diana pictures would strive for a higher degree of quality than the gaudy crowd-pleasers Walter had been turning out for the studio.

His partners in the new venture were Fritz Lang and Joan; she provided one-third of the start-up money, and received a salary of $75,000. Because she wanted to maintain her upgraded status in Hollywood, her investment was as much emotional as it was financial. The same was true for Lang, who was eager for a situation that would allow him to be his own boss without intrusion from the studio heads; the contracts for Diana Productions spelled out that Walter was to handle all financial arrangements so Lang could be free to concentrate on creative matters.

Lang was fond of playing the misunderstood genius, and Joan was far more willing than Walter to indulge him. "I always thought that Fritz Lang and Joan Bennett had a rather strange relationship," recalled Lang's secretary Hilda Rolfe. "She was rather flirtatious with him. If Lang was in a bad mood, she would sort of try to tease him out of it, tweak him on the cheek. She'd say things like, 'Oh, Fritz, now, don't be a bad boy.' You would almost have thought that they had something going on between them, although I really don't think they did."

With Diana Productions, Walter and Lang formed an uneasy alliance. Although Walter had the utmost respect for Lang as an artist, the two men never particularly warmed to each other. Lang credited Walter with having a higher level of taste than the average producer, and was encouraged by Walter's reputation for not meddling in the director's work. In the end, however, their relationship never progressed much beyond polite tolerance, and Joan proved to be the ballast as Diana Productions prepared for its maiden voyage.

The idea for the first film came from Walter: a remake of Jean Renoir's 1931 drama *La Chienne* (The Bitch). It was based on a novel by Georges de la Fouchardiere about a meek cashier who picks up a shady young girl and sets her up in an apartment. When he learns that she is cheating on him with her pimp, he kills her, and eventually sinks into guilt-ridden despair. The story had been steamy stuff when it was filmed originally. Renoir recalled that when his bosses saw the finished version, they nearly ran him out of the studio. The property had been kicking around Hollywood for years; Ernst Lubitsch had planned a version for Paramount in the mid-1930s, to star Charles Laughton and Marlene Dietrich, but he never came up with a way of getting around the Production Code roadblock.

This was precisely the sort of challenge that stimulated Walter. Dudley Nichols was set to work constructing a viable script. When Nichols's work was submitted to the Hays Office, Joseph I. Breen's response was surprisingly agreeable. He did object to the high number of bedroom scenes, and requested that any inference that the girl is a prostitute be downplayed. Nichols was essentially faithful to the Renoir original, but relocated the story to Greenwich Village.

The central character in *Scarlet Street*, as the film was eventually called, is Christopher Cross, a timid and repressed cashier in a large clothing store. Trapped in a hopeless marriage, he has only one outlet: his Sunday painting, which his harridan wife will let him do only in the bathroom. One rainy night, Chris comes to the aid of a beautiful girl, Kitty March, who is getting beaten up by her boyfriend, Johnny Prince. Chris asks Kitty out for a late-night drink and becomes instantly entranced by her. Here, the two of them make fateful errors: Chris mistakes Kitty for an actress, while Kitty believes Chris to be a rich and famous painter. Egged on by Johnny, Kitty cons Chris into footing the bill for a Village apartment where she can live and he can paint. Chris embezzles money from his firm to pay for the apartment, and soon he is stealing more and more as Kitty's demands escalate. Eventually, Kitty sells Chris's paintings to an important Manhattan gallery by passing them off as her own. In one of the script's most painful scenes, Chris, having found out that she has sold the paintings, goes to the apartment to confront her; she tearfully explains that she did it only because she was desperate for money. Chris is pathetically delighted, and agrees to go on supplying paintings for her to sign. ("Why, it'll be just like we were married. Only I take your name.")

The paintings become an enormous success and Kitty is hailed as the art world's discovery of the year. When Chris discovers that she has been deceiving him with Johnny, he accuses her, she laughs in his face, and in a blind rage he stabs her to death with an ice pick. The police never discover Chris's connection to the crime and

Johnny is executed. His bank thefts having been discovered, Chris is fired from his job and wanders the streets, alone, broke, and guilt-ridden, tormented by the ghostly voices of Kitty and Johnny that fill his head.

The three leads of *The Woman in the Window* all took an encore in *Scarlet Street.* Edward G. Robinson was cast as Chris, Joan as Kitty, and Dan Duryea as Johnny. Lang worked in his usual meticulous manner, and filming stretched from July to October of 1945. Tensions arose among the Diana partners: Lang accused Walter of betraying him when the producer eliminated a handful of minor scenes from the final cut. But Lang was making much out of little—he had a fine film, and he knew it.

Given the censorship standards that existed at the time, *Scarlet Street* expresses an unusually adult point of view. Perhaps no other screen drama of the period took such a casual and frank look at sex. When Kitty tells Johnny, "I don't know why I'm so crazy about you," he replies, "Oh, yes, you do." There is a disturbing S and M undercurrent in Johnny's relationship with Kitty. During an argument, when Kitty snaps, "If I had any sense, I'd walk out on you," Johnny slaps her and growls, "You haven't *got* any sense." The most daring scene of all takes place in the apartment, with Kitty demanding that Chris paint her toenails. As he does so, she whispers with sexy malevolence, "They'll be masterpieces."

Surprisingly, for a film noir set in Manhattan, *Scarlet Street* shows us very little of New York—practically nothing of the city's gloomy, dingy streets. This may have been intentional. The private world in which the characters move is confined, closed-in and distorted—almost hallucinatory. Unlike the principals in *The Woman in the Window,* the characters in *Scarlet Street* seem to exist in a dark place of their own making; perhaps this is what critic David Thomsen meant when he called it "a film that seems to have very little to do with America."

For Joan, *Scarlet Street* marked a great personal success. Lang had drawn out of her the finest performance she had yet given. *The Woman in the Window* belongs to Edward G. Robinson, but *Scarlet Street* is all hers; she gives an all-out, carnal performance that

David Thomsen felt "made the official love goddesses of 1946 look downright reserved." Joan makes Kitty's rottenness sexy, almost lascivious, never hateful, since every duplicitous move she makes is calculated to please Johnny. One of the many pleasures of Joan's performance is her uncomprehending look when she thinks she has done something to make Johnny happy and he hauls off and slaps her anyway. Never before had Joan shown such a range of vocal expression: she speaks in a petulant, childish purr when trying to play up to Johnny, but when she bawls out Chris for bursting in on her unannounced, her tone is hard and spiteful and vicious. (Lang was almost entirely successful in getting her to drop her finishing school accent, which would have been all wrong for a lowlife like Kitty.)

When *Scarlet Street* was previewed just before Christmas 1945, Joan's work received warm reviews. The *New York Daily Mirror* asserted that Joan had "never turned in a finer performance," while the *Hollywood Reporter* found Joan "most attractive and sultry as the siren who leads the cashier to his ruin. It is a performance that ranks with her best, and she takes full advantage of the role." One of the best notices she received came from her old friend David Selznick: "I saw *Scarlet Street* last night and thought it extremely well made and an enormously interesting picture. I think your performance was superb and the best you have given to date, which is saying a great deal."

For a time early in 1946, after the picture had gone into general release, it appeared that there might not be a second effort from Diana Productions. Although the Production Code had passed *Scarlet Street,* and the Catholic Legion of Decency had let it slip by with a "B" rating (meaning "objectionable in part"), the New York State Board of Censors refused to give the film a license, denouncing it as "immoral, indecent, corrupt, and tending to incite crime.") The principal obstacles were Kitty and Johnny's lewd relationship and the fact that Chris is never brought to justice for murdering Kitty. Writing about the censors' verdict years later, Pauline Kael called it "a judgment that seemed off-the-wall even then." At the time, that was the view held by Bosley Crowther, the powerful film critic of the *New York Times*. Although he did not find *Scarlet*

Street a particularly persuasive drama, he devoted a column to attacking the censors. He wrote, "the dilemma is this: there are too many censor boards functioning with too confused concepts of morals." He went on to urge moviegoers to pressure the censors to modify their standards, "now, when so many minds are open to the true cultural influence of the screen."

In the end, the New York censors accepted a few nips and tucks in the film, and revoked the ban in late January 1946. One source of their objections was the number of times Chris stabs Kitty in her bed. Initially, in an almost coital frenzy, he had plunged the pick into her seven times, but in the final approved version the number of stabs was reduced to one. This inspired H.I. Philips of the *New York Sun* to compose a satirical poem:

> "We thought the picture was the sort
> That reeked with crime and vice,"
> The censor said quite boldly, "and
> We thought it wasn't nice;
> We banned this picture firmly;
> Now our okay we affix . . .
> For seven strokes of number have
> Been cut by five or six!"

Once the film was in general release, letters poured into the offices of Eric Johnston, head of the Motion Picture Association of America. One outraged mother from Fresno, California, complained that "It is by far the most obscene, vulgar, disgusting picture I have ever seen. . . . Our theatre was packed with teen agers who whistled, giggled, and made demonstrations at the most sensational scenes." In February, the censors in Milwaukee and Atlanta refused to permit the picture to be shown. In the *Atlanta Journal,* Wright Bryan wrote, "I felt I needed a bath when it ended. . . . The feminine lead has the most completely despicable role I have seen since Bette Davis appeared as Mildred in *Of Human Bondage.*"

Walter was incensed: "My wife is the mother of three children," he told Universal's southeastern representative, Harry Graham. "She would be the last person in the world to lend herself to any vehicle that might give impetus to the wave of delinquency, adult as well as juvenile, that is now sweeping the nation." Diana Productions and Universal brought suit against the city of Atlanta, and eventually a judge decreed that the film could be shown. But *Scarlet Street* would have made an excellent showing even without Atlanta. All across the country, it was pulling in moviegoers in huge numbers. After its first run was completed, it had grossed an impressive $2.5 million. Later that year, it did equally well abroad. The management of the Gaiety Theatre in Manchester, England, wired Walter excitedly: "*Scarlett* [*sic*] *Street* shattered every existing record for any premiere opening. . . . Queues lined up all day hundreds unable to gain admission."

Scarlet Street was one of the pictures that Joan's reputation later rested on, and for the remainder of her life, she always referred to it as one of her two or three favorites. At the time of its release, it gave her a much needed boost of confidence. Over the next few years, her inferiority complex about her acting would recede somewhat as she pursued her career more aggressively.

With 1946, the twilight years of Hollywood's golden age began—something that few people at the time could have predicted. A number of factors conspired to make 1946 the industry's all-time peak year so far. With America's veterans back from the war, dating resumed on a grand scale, and attendance at the movies soared. Another reason for the big profits was the reopening of the foreign markets that had been closed during wartime. Because its own film industry had declined sharply during the war, England in particular gave a warm welcome to the movies coming out of Hollywood. All told, studio profits for 1946 reached nearly $120 million.

For Joan, these were happy, successful years. With *Scarlet Street,* she had distinguished herself as both actress and executive, and the future seemed full of exciting possibilities. Over the years, her preparedness and high level of professionalism—she was widely known for seldom blowing a take—earned her the admiration of film crews. Diana Anderson discovered this years later, when she had embarked on a ten-year stint as an actress in television commercials. One night, as she was preparing to leave the studio, one of the gaffers approached her and said, "You're Joan Bennett's daughter." "That made me very uncomfortable," said Diana. "But he said, 'No, no. Don't feel badly. We just wondered whether you had your aunt's temperament or your mother's. Thank God you have your mother's.'"

Her domestic life was thriving, too. She had overseen the reconstruction of the Mapleton Drive house and the family had returned to it in mid-1944. She continued to entertain on a grand scale. Occasionally the Wangers threw enormous parties, often charity events for the war effort, but it was more customary for them to have formal sit-down parties for around twenty. At these gatherings, guests often benefited from Walter's unstinting intellectual curiosity; he would speak excitedly about a book he had just read, and a few days later his dinner partners would receive a copy of the book, with a note from him exhorting them to read it. Joan always supervised the menus and kept careful guest lists to ensure that no one ever ate the same thing at different parties. She often served roast beef or pheasant, with endive salad; favorite desserts were crème brûlée, chocolate mousse, and a molasses cookie stuffed with ice cream. Frequent guests included Claudette Colbert and Dr. Joel Pressman, Myrna Loy (who later turned up with Gene Markey, her husband from 1946 to 1950), Jane Greer and Edward Lasker, Edie and William Goetz, Irene and David Selznick, Marjorie and Alexander Hall, Alma and Alfred Hitchcock, Diana Lynn and Mortimer Hall, Joan Fontaine and William Dozier, Marge and Ed Maltby, Frances and Samuel Goldwyn, Maria Montez and Jean-Pierre Aumont, and Merle Oberon and Lucien Ballard. On Sunday, the cook's day off, there would either be a barbecue or Joan would take over the kitchen, turning out a fine roast chicken or leg of lamb.

Jane Greer, a close friend of Joan's during this period, remembered her as "a perfect woman, dressed beautifully and with a wonderfully funny sense of humor." She had only one significant handicap: her poor eyesight. "She told me about being on a set," recalled Greer, "and her scene was to sit in the garden and pick the flowers and put them in a basket. During the rehearsal she was wearing glasses and of course when they said, 'Let's take it,' she took her glasses off. She sat picking flowers and her eyes were two inches from them and the director finally said, 'Why are you getting so close?' And she said, 'I can't see them otherwise.'"

"She was appreciative and generous to a fault," remembered Carmen DiRigo, Joan's hair stylist on many films from the late 1930s to the mid-1940s. "I used to go quite a bit before her social gatherings to do her hair. Once I had an appointment to go to her house, and I did an intricate hairstyle around a hat. I got there early, and she hadn't had her bath yet, so with the hairstyle around the hat, Joanie got in the tub. It was really funny. She wouldn't take a shower because she didn't want to ruin my creation." She was generous to DiRigo in other ways, too. With wartime shortages, automobiles were hard to get. DiRigo lived in Burbank and had to take public transportation all the way to Holmby Hills. "So she got me a new car, an Oldsmobile," said DiRigo. "I almost fainted."

Now that she had reached the zenith of her career, Joan might have permitted herself to relax a bit, but her formidable discipline had not diminished in the least. When she was working on a film, she now rose at 5 A.M. and was usually in bed by 10 at night. Every day, she selected fresh flowers from the cutting gardens, and she still spent her free hours on the set monitoring the running of the house. She supervised the children's meals carefully: little fat, fish and liver once a week, always two vegetables at dinner, plenty of fruits, no rich desserts.

Joan tried her best to impress upon her children the importance of a disciplined life. In a letter from April 1946, written to Diana, who was then enrolled at the Ethel Walker School in Simsbury, Connecticut, she sounds like anybody's mother:

> I was happy to hear from you today but very sorry to hear of the loss of your cross. When you didn't return with it at Easter vacation I feared as much but hoped for the best. However, hoping for the best in a case of com-

> plete carelessness is too much to expect of the Good Lord. It's gone. . . . I had hoped you would have it to pass on to your own children (if you don't leave them in the park.)
>
> You say in your letter that you are afraid to have anything valuable around your room. Your wits will prove quite valuable to have around in years to come, so I wouldn't be defeatist about it, but rather make up your mind not to be so *non compus mentis* in the future. . . . I beg of you, Ditty, and pray for you at night to think, think, think. Take care of a situation as it presents itself. School and train your mind to be *orderly*. Get organized!

Another letter from the same period gives a clue as to the source of Joan's obsession with order and discipline. In it, she is remonstrating with Diana for her moodiness, irresponsibility, and resentment of criticism:

> I certainly don't expect you to be my counter-part. I am extremely interested (you'll forgive me—it's a mother's privilege) in your growing into the finest type of woman there is to be found. . . . I want to guide you in the right direction. Possibly you feel I am not. . . . Perhaps I have been over zealous in some respects, but it is only because I want to spare you unhappiness—unhappiness that I think could have been avoided if I had been brought up differently. You see, everyone in my family was self-centered—I didn't have a chance to be because I had you to think of—when most girls my age were thinking of boys—dancing and having fun—of my entire family, I would say I am the only one who found happiness, but it took me a long time to find it, and it was quite a struggle. You see, I was mixed up, due to my upbringing, for a great many years.

But by the mid-1940s, that chaotic time in Joan's life seemed very far away. As a wife, mother, star, and member of the community, she had achieved complete success and security.

For Constance, the end of the war signaled another change of partners. As early as 1944, Gilbert had known that his marriage was in serious trouble. By then, he had advanced in the Army Air Corps to the rank of first lieutenant. Late that year, following one of his aerial missions out of the country, he was granted a short leave and headed for Hollywood. Constance had recently returned to Carolwood Drive after a stint in New York, during which time she had rented the house to Clifton Webb and his mother.

For Gilbert, it was an unceremonious homecoming. Constance was out when he arrived. He went upstairs to his bedroom and found that Constance had disposed of nearly everything in his bedroom suite: clothes, shoes, personal items. He came downstairs to the game room, went to the bar, poured himself a drink, then went into the living room and dashed it against the large portrait of Constance that hung on the living room wall. Then he found a kitchen knife and slashed the canvas across the middle of her face.

In a short time, Constance had given the scoop to Hedda Hopper for the *Los Angeles Times*: "In order to remain friends," she told Hopper, "we have decided to make our separation permanent." In the spring of 1945, she filed suit for divorce, complaining of mental cruelty and grievous mental pain and suffering, calling Gilbert "insanely jealous and moody." The divorce was granted without delay, Judge Joseph W. Vickers having presided over a hearing in closed chambers, which Constance insisted on: her attorney, Harvey Silbert, recalled that she was terrified the public would find out that both Lorinda and Gyl were illegitimate.

Constance still found it impossible to scare up a decent job in the movies, and in time, she was forced to sell the Carolwood Drive house. Although it was a wrenching decision—she had owned it for barely six years—she didn't dwell on her slipping fortunes. She had known all along that the final decline in her career would come, and now here it was. As part of the divorce settlement, she agreed to purchase a small house for Gilbert, at 518 Roxbury Drive. He was to live in a small apartment and rent out the house until his film career got rolling again. The rental income would enable him to pay a modest monthly amount of child support, which he was bound to do because the court decision decreed that he acknowledge both Lorinda and Gyl as his daughters.

By now, Peter was sixteen, and still thriving at the Culver Academy. He had witnessed the changing of the guard in his mother's personal life so often that Gilbert's exit had little impact on him, but for Lorinda and Gyl it was a more difficult loss to bear. For the rest of his life, Gilbert would be faithful about remembering them at birthdays and Christmastime, but he would cease to be any kind of sustaining presence in their lives. He was not there as they matured into young women and had to make decisions about their education and careers, nor did he provide any financial assistance beyond court-ordered child support. Peter thought that his half-sisters received shabby treatment from Gilbert: "They would go to his house on all the holidays and it was 'Daddy, Daddy.' But he didn't behave like a daddy. He did not."

Gilbert continued to make pictures for more than thirty years; in 1977, he even appeared in an adaptation of one of his beloved Hemingway works, *Islands in the Stream*. In the 1950s, he married outside the industry to Guillermina Cantu, and remained with her until his death at age eighty-eight on May 15, 1994.

By 1945, Constance's film career had neared its end. That year, she made one picture, *Paris Underground,* a French resistance drama which she also produced. Although she was intriguingly paired with popular English star Gracie Fields, the film was unremarkable in all ways. After the Carolwood Drive house was sold, Constance and her daughters moved temporarily to Ocean Front in Santa Monica, and she cast about for work. Eventually, she swallowed her pride and went to Darryl Zanuck, who had remained a close ally. She admitted that she needed work and couldn't afford to be choosy. His response was to cast her in *Centennial Summer,* an original Jerome Kern musical made for Twentieth Century–Fox. Two of Twentieth's loveliest and most popular female stars at the time were Jeanne Crain and Linda Darnell. They played sisters in *Centennial Summer.* Constance played their aunt.

Centennial Summer wrapped on May 20, 1946, and on June 22 Constance married her fifth husband, John Coulter, at the Saint Francis Chapel of the Mission Inn in Riverside, California. Peter gave her away, Darryl Zanuck's wife, Virginia, was matron of honor, and Lorinda, Gyl, Joan, and Walter were also in attendance. Coming on the heels of her marriage to Gilbert, Constance's union with Coulter seemed downright serene. In her memoirs, Joan wrote, "At last, she'd met her match in a perfect husband who adored her but would not suffer her temperamental nonsense." This was far from the case. Although there was a tremendous sexual charge between Coulter and Constance, she was not transformed into a submissive, adoring wife. Coulter was no more successful at reining in Constance than any of her previous husbands had been, and she continued to do as she pleased with very little interference from him. "Nobody ever crossed her or said no to her," said her stepdaughter, Patricia Coulter McElroy. "And nobody—not even Dad—would interfere with any ultimatum she made."

Certainly Constance did not segue quietly into the role of officer's wife. At home, she was such an authority figure that the children would fight to push in her chair at dinner. Nobody could sit until she was seated, and Lorinda, Gyl, and Patricia were not allowed to speak unless they were spoken to first. She moved like a streak around the house, and Lorinda remembered that "You had to get out of her way when you saw her coming. If you didn't, she would knock you right down." As for Coulter, both Lorinda and Gyl considered him an ideal stepfather because he never interfered in their lives. It might have been better if he had, since both girls exhibited difficulties that Constance seemed ill-equipped to handle. Lorinda was an unruly, hot-tempered tomboy who loved to climb trees and ride horses. She hated dolls and dresses and longed to play with knives and cap pistols and electric trains. She showed a great tenderness for any and all animals, but had difficulty getting along with other children. Although she was a bright child, she was undisciplined in her studies and was constantly running into trouble in school. At home, most of her nurses and governesses either feared or despised her, and as she grew older, she frequently ran away from home for short periods. Yet Constance seems to have been somewhat taken with her daughter's rebellious nature, no doubt because she reminded her of herself as a child. In time, Lorinda became her favorite.

Gyl posed a different sort of challenge. She was sweet-natured and submissive, and while many mothers might have welcomed such a docile child, Constance appeared to resent her from the beginning. She had no patience whatsoever with Gyl's frequent crying fits, and failed to understand how she could have such an emotional daughter. The more timid and complacent Gyl became, the more she refused to fight back at home, the more she seemed to incur her mother's wrath. Constance held to her old pattern: once she had lost patience with something or someone, no amount of reasoning could bring her around, and she pushed harder than ever. She even made up a derisive name for Gyl, "Cloud Nine," and encouraged everyone else in the family to call her that in an attempt to jolt her out of her passivity.

To her credit, she was concerned that her children not become typical, lazy Hollywood brats, but that they grow up to be independent, strong-minded people with solid values. When it came time for Peter to think about college, she didn't attempt to influence him at all, but simply asked where he planned to go. He applied at Harvard, Dartmouth, and Stanford. Culver had served him well, as he was admitted to all three, and selected Dartmouth.

Constance also thought it was important that her children develop some sort of spiritual life, and encouraged them to attend a variety of churches in order to have a fully rounded religious education. Over the years, they would explore Presbyterianism, Episcopalianism, Roman Catholicism, and Christian Science. She was concerned that they understand the nature of responsibility and the importance of accepting it, and that they behave with integrity and concern for others. The fact that she did not always apply such rigorous standards to herself did not diminish her belief in them.

By mid-1945, Barbara and Addison Randall were living in the San Fernando Valley, struggling to make ends meet. Things looked up somewhat when Walter used his connections at Universal to get Randall a job in a cheap serial, *The Royal Mounted Ride Again.* On July 16, while on location at Canoga Park filming a chase scene, Randall lost his hat. Trying to retrieve it, he fell off his horse, struck a tree, and was killed instantly.

Barbara was paralyzed by grief. However unsettled her life with Randall had been, she had loved him and found in him the companionship and attention that had been missing in her marriage to Morton. She had given up custody of her children so she could be free to marry Addison. His presence in her life had been the only thing that helped assuage her guilt at having turned her back on her family. Now she had nothing at all.

She gave up the house in the Valley and moved into the servant's cottage that the Wangers had built at Mapleton Drive. Joan and Walter were both busy with *Scarlet Street,* and there was little to occupy Barbara during the day. She moved about the house like a sleepwalker, drinking quietly—and occasionally not so quietly. There were times when she appeared at dinner barely able to sit up in her chair.

Barbara in stormy weather often pushed Joan's patience to the breaking point. Joan was always there to help her sister, to do what had to be done to get her through the latest crisis. Inwardly, she was not quite as sympathetic as she appeared. Having had to work so hard from the beginning, having sacrificed some of the best part of her youth in her attempt to find stability, Joan had begun to resent Barbara's inability to cope with her own problems. Walter was more tender-hearted where Barbara was concerned, partly because he had not been subjected to her turbulent behavior for as long as Joan had; time and again, over the next several years, he would provide her with financial assistance, employment opportunities, shelter, and genuine sympathy.

After a few aimless months at Mapleton Drive, Joan and Walter decided that Barbara needed some sort of meaningful work that would make her feel she was making some kind of significant contribution. To that end, Walter engaged her to be his New York literary representative, at a salary of fifty dollars weekly. She moved to Manhattan and began her duties in the fall of 1945. Her principal task was to scout literary properties for Walter and report on their film potential. Walter set up an account for her at Brentano's Bookstore so she could purchase books as soon as they hit the shelves, but it was also important for her to get her hands on advance galley proofs before any other production company had a chance to option them. In particular, she was to search for appropriate material for Diana Productions (especially those that might make good vehicles for Joan) and for Walter Wanger Productions (with an eye toward finding suitable properties for Walter's contract star Susan Hayward).

In the beginning, Barbara was conscientious about her work, and recommended several novels that she thought had strong screen potential. She urged Walter to purchase the rights to Elizabeth Janeway's *Daisy Kenyon,* a love triangle with political overtones that she guessed would be "a perfect vehicle for Joanie." (It was bought by Twentieth Century–Fox, where it was turned into an imperfect vehicle for Joan Crawford.) She also encouraged him to consider Evelyn Waugh's *Brideshead Revisited.* In her report, she stated that the novel "deals delicately and sometimes humorously, principaly [*sic*] with the life of Sebastian, who is a homosexual but never gives in to his perverted desires." She thought it would be ideal for Susan Hayward and Hurd Hatfield, who had recently made a success in MGM's *The Picture of Dorian Gray,* but Walter found Waugh's subject matter too problematic. She enthused over the possibilities of Erich Maria Remarque's *Arch of Triumph,* but failed to notice in her weekly perusal of *Publishers Weekly,* the book industry's bible, that the novel already had been purchased by another company. This made her the recipient of a gentle rebuke from Walter: "So you see, Barbara, your judgment is very good, but in addition it is important to smell these things out long before anyone else does." A few weeks later, in early March 1946, he wrote to her. "You are becoming more and more adept at your work with each report." "Thank you very much for your encouraging letter," she responded, "I can't tell you how it raised my morale, because to date, I have felt that I was getting no place fast in the line of usefulness."

But feelings of inadequacy overwhelmed her once again. On March 13, she was admitted to City Hospital after taking an overdose of sleeping tablets. She had been found in her apartment by an unidentified man, who telephoned the police, telling them, "She's serious. Hurry." Her hospital confinement lasted only fourteen hours and she was released in good condition, but a hospital attendant notified the press that she had said that she didn't want "Joan and Constance to find out about this."

She went back to work with energy and concentration through much of 1946, but by year's end, her reports had come to a standstill. She pleaded illness, and by February 1947 Walter was concerned that she had fallen back in the habit of purchasing books from Brentano's that had already been snapped up by other studios or independent producers. "If you still have your typewriter," he wrote, "I wish you would get busy with it, because your reports are excellent and very helpful to me."

But Barbara already had begun a slow fade that was to continue for the next eleven years. Soon Joan was receiving word from a New York attorney that Barbara had failed to pay a doctor's bill. There were more travails in September, when Barbara set her heart on moving into the Lombardy, an exclusive Manhattan apartment house, and assured the management that Joan would guarantee her ability to make the monthly rent. Joan balked, and Walter fired off a telegram demanding that she drop the Lombardy deal and find less expensive living quarters. Barbara sent her own telegram back to California: "SIGNED LEASE ABOUT TWO MINUTES BEFORE RECEIVED WIRE NOW WHAT DO I DO BARBARA."

She was drinking again, and as always, when she was in a bad phase she proved incapable of taking responsibility for even the smallest things. She was clearly of no further use to Walter—her book reports had ground to a halt—yet she was unable to carry out as simple a task as returning her rented typewriter to the office machine supply company.

In the meantime, Walter's relations with Universal had become increasingly complicated. The studio had merged with International Pictures in 1946 and was now cutting tougher deals with all of its semi-independent producers. By the fall of 1947, Walter had made the decision to shut down all of his operations at Universal and move over to a new company, Eagle-Lion, that had designs on becoming a major player in the business. In October, Walter wrote to Barbara that since Eagle-Lion had its own literary department, he would no longer be in need of her services, but asked her to remain on the lookout for any promising talent or properties. "I have lots of confidence in your judgment," he wrote, "and will investigate very carefully any recommendations you make."

Barbara stayed on in New York, picking up miscellaneous jobs. She continued to drink a great deal. Peggy Sobel, who met her at Sherman Billingsley's Stork Club in the mid-1940s, recalled, "It was obvious that she was a drunk. Everybody knew it." Although Barbara did her best to keep up her rounds at the top night spots, privately she was haunted by the fact that she had let down the people who had believed in her and tried to help her. Over the years, she would continue to lean on the Wangers for occasional financial assistance. From Constance she received nothing—not advice, not sympathy, not support.

Joan's long-term association with Twentieth Century–Fox had ended when the inconsequential comedy *Colonel Effingham's Raid* wrapped early in 1945. Now she was back to freelancing full time, and, thanks to the success of *Scarlet Street,* a hot commodity. While she waited for Walter and Lang to come up with another appropriate vehicle for Diana Productions, she had time to peruse the numerous scripts sent her by other producers.

Early in 1946, it was announced that she would star in *Desirable Woman* at RKO. It was based on a popular suspense novel by Mitchell Wilson, *None So Blind.* Barbara had read the book while she was working for Walter and reported back to him, "Don't think anything like it has been done before—am sure Joanie with Fritz Lang could make something very outstanding out of it." Walter passed on it, but RKO bought the property and offered it to Joan.

She thought it was an intriguing story that would benefit from a strong director. She suggested Jean Renoir, the acclaimed filmmaker and son of the great Impressionist painter Pierre-August Renoir. He and Joan had known each other for several years, and when she wrote him a note asking him to take on the project, he accepted at once. The idea of making a film with her appealed to him, perhaps because her cool, slightly mysterious screen persona struck him as being more continental than American.

Renoir's work was quite familiar to Joan; his 1931 film *La Chienne,* after all, had been the basis for *Scarlet Street.* She and Walter had seen many of his later efforts: *Grand Illusion, La Bête Humaine,* and *La Règle du Jeu.* Stylistically, Renoir was always something of a maverick. Unlike Fritz Lang, his films did not unfold in sharp focus, driving home a particular idea or message. Renoir's work was considerably more complex, his intentions never precise or explicit. He never regarded the shooting script as a bible, and often used improvisatory techniques, with the result that the production process seemed to take on a life of its own, changing direction without warning.

Renoir had fled Paris in 1939, and landed in Hollywood two years later. But beginning with the disappointing *Swamp Water* (1941), his American career had proceeded in fits and starts. Part of the problem was that his methods were alien to those of the Hollywood studio system, and he never found a producer who would support him in ways that would permit him to do his best work. *This Land Is Mine* (1943) was a shrill and jumbled drama of Nazi occupation, and while *The Southerner* (1945), a study of a destitute family of migrant workers, was well received, a vehicle for Paulette Goddard, *Diary of a Chambermaid* (1946), was too fey for postwar audiences, and flopped. By the time he was approached by Joan, Hollywood seemed on the verge of writing him off altogether, but Renoir liked Los Angeles and wanted to stay. As filming began on *Desirable Woman,* everyone concerned knew he had a great deal riding on it.

As the title suggests, Renoir initially wanted the film to be a study of physical passion, a love affair, in his own words, "in which emotion played no part." Joan was again cast as a femme fatale, Peggy Butler, the sultry wife of a once-famous painter (Charles Bickford) who is now blind. One day, while gathering firewood on the beach, Peggy meets Scott Burnett (Robert Ryan), a Coast Guard lieutenant, whose experiences in the war have left him emotionally damaged. The two begin a heated affair, and Scott begs Peggy to leave her husband, but she claims she can't. She is bound to him by guilt, since it was she who had blinded him during a drunken brawl several years earlier. Butler appears to want to befriend his rival, but there is something malevolent and threatening in his manner that rouses Scott's suspicions. He begins to believe that Butler really isn't blind after all, and sets out to prove it. Before long, the three of them are locked in a sort of macabre dance, none of them knowing how it will end.

After the film—now retitled *The Woman on the Beach*—had been edited, Renoir was quite satisfied with it. He recognized that it was a tricky mood piece with a rather deliberate pace, and he wasn't at all sure that American audiences would respond to it, but he felt he had done what he set out to do. A preview was arranged in Santa Barbara, before an audience made up mostly of students. Their reaction was devastating—they didn't respond at all to Renoir's attempt to create an atmosphere of existential gloom. In a panic, he set about reshooting approximately one-third of the picture, mostly scenes between Peggy and Scott. He enlisted another writer to assist him and asked Walter for advice as well, since, as he later admitted, "It seemed to me at the time that I didn't have the right to take all the responsibility for the film by myself. I think, by the way, that I was wrong and that this fear didn't help the film."

The greatest pleasure that *The Woman on the Beach* gave him was the opportunity to work with Joan. She communicated with him throughout the filming in flawless French. He also was amused by the disparity between her onscreen and offscreen image. He wrote to Paul Cézanne, "Joan Bennett, who plays the desirable woman, is amazing for her complete lack of vanity. She talks about her false eyelashes, about the gadgets she puts in her mouth to make her teeth look more regular and shiny, about her wig, even about her age with bemused irony and a complete lack of shame. She spends the whole day knitting, and I find it really funny to think that this homey person is considered by the American moral groups to be the most dangerous sexpot on the screen today."

Unfortunately, by retreating from his original vision, Renoir doomed *The Woman on the Beach* to failure. What remains is certainly unusual, and much more intriguing than most of the films to come out of Hollywood in 1947. Working in a steady, adagio tempo, Renoir successfully creates a mood of emptiness and anxiety and sustains it. It turns out to be just the right rhythm for the film's lonely beach setting—this is a place where no hope exists at all. *The Woman on the Beach* seems less a study in physical passion than an extended tone poem about three people irrevocably bound to the past; Scott, Peggy, and Butler are all paralyzed by events that have taken place earlier in their lives. *The Woman on the Beach* is really a kind of modern ghost story: Scott is haunted by his wartime experience, just as Peggy is tormented by her guilt over causing Butler's blindness, and Butler by his glory days as a painter, which he cannot reconcile with his present circumstances.

It is easy to understand why critics and audiences in 1947 greeted the film with such hostility. Probably thanks to Renoir's cutting and reshooting, the film never really jells. The relationships develop in an odd, jarring manner; Scott and Peggy seem to know far too much about each other from the very beginning, and the scenes between Scott and his true-blue girlfriend (Nan Leslie) run on far too long. The climactic sequences, especially the one in which Scott takes Butler on a fishing expedition during a storm at sea with the plan of letting him drown, don't grow organically out of the story. In attempting to establish the right tone for their lost characters, Renoir and his co-scenarist Frank Davis came up with some unplayable dialogue, as in the scene in which Scott and Peggy first meet on the beach:

> SCOTT: The hard thing, I guess, is to know yourself.
> PEGGY: Yes, that is difficult. Anyway—what's the use?

When *The Woman on the Beach* was released in the spring of 1947, the reviews were almost all negative. *Cue* felt that most of the picture "should have been left on the cutting room floor." The *Hollywood Reporter* found the film a "strangely garbled" version of Mitchell Wilson's novel, and predicted that "for every person who will be pleased with the artiness of *The Woman on the Beach,* two people or more will find it empty and meaningless." Most critics agreed that Joan's sexy, melancholy presence held the picture together. The *New York Times* found the film "curiously foggy and stylized" but praised her for adding "another competent portrait of a sullen and seductive dame to an ever-growing gallery."

While *The Woman on the Beach* was still being filmed, producers Benedict Bogeaus and Casey Robinson signed Joan to play the treacherous wife in a screen adaptation of Ernest Hemingway's 1936 short story "The Short Happy Life of Francis Macomber." The producers had paid Hemingway $85,000 for the property, which they felt had enormous box-office potential despite the obvious censorship problems the story posed.

The Hemingway original chronicles the tensions that explode when a wealthy American couple, Francis and Margaret Macomber, hire Robert Wilson, a seasoned guide with a vaguely shady past, to lead them on a safari in British East Africa. The Macombers' marriage has been deteriorating for some time, and Francis has seized on the hunting expedition as a last-ditch attempt to salvage it. Everything goes awry. When he is charged by a lion, Francis panics, drops his gun, and runs. Margaret needles him mercilessly for his cowardice and completes her humiliation of him by sleeping with Wilson. In the end, Francis rallies and stands up to his wife, accusing her of having conditioned him to be a weakling, beginning his "short happy life" as a real man. But as Francis loses his fear, Margaret confronts hers, for she now realizes that her husband is through with her. The next day, Francis stands his ground against a charging buffalo, which he kills with a beautifully placed shot. Seconds later, another gun sounds: Margaret, unwilling to accept her husband as anything but a pathetic coward, has shot him in the back of the head.

Hemingway had been and was to remain a difficult proposition for Hollywood. The prose that seemed so tough, natural, and modern on the page did not translate particularly well to film, where it tended to sound self-conscious and artificial. Robinson's script was extremely faithful to the story, lifting chunks of dialogue verbatim. But the censors were not about to accept either the relationship between Wilson and Margaret or the original ending, where it is clear that Margaret has killed Francis intentionally. So Robinson was forced to compromise. In the screenplay, Wilson and Margaret sanctify their one night together by falling in love. Robinson also diluted Margaret's vitriol slightly by painting her as a woman once in love who has become disillusioned by her husband's behavior. She tells Wilson that she realized on their honeymoon that her husband was a weakling by the way he mistreated "little people." She's tried—God knows she's tried—but she hasn't been able to make it work. Thus Robinson purposely made her motives for killing Francis cloudy. When Wilson presses her for an answer on whether she intentionally pulled the trigger, she responds, "If there's such a thing as murder in the heart—there's your certain answer." The film ends with Margaret walking off to face the coroner's inquest; Wilson will be waiting for her, whatever the verdict.

Once the script was deemed censor-proof, Bogeaus and Robinson assembled their cast. For box-office insurance, Gregory Peck, then one of the most popular leading men in Hollywood, was signed to play Wilson. Joan was cast as Margaret, with Robert Preston as Francis. Zoltan Korda, the brother of British film giant Alexander Korda, was hired to direct. A camera crew was dispatched to Africa to film background material and the hunt scenes, using doubles for Peck, Preston, and Joan. A crew of 125 then headed for Mexico, where principal photography would be done outside a brewery town called Tecate. Unfortunately, the only adequate accommodations, at the Rosarita Beach Hotel, were forty-five miles away, which meant a lengthy commute each day to and from location. It was a happy company: "The picture is going wonderfully," Joan wrote to Diana. "Mr. Korda couldn't be nicer and is a wonderful director. Mr. Peck is as dreamy acting as he is looking, so all in all it's lots of fun." Peck and Preston often stayed out all night drinking cheap Mexican beer but were always letter-perfect before the cameras the next morning. Peck played in some local baseball games, while Joan performed matron-of-honor duties at a local wedding and was godmother at a christening when one of the Rosarita Beach Hotel's waiters named his daughter after her.

Apart from her hairdresser, Meryl Reeves, and a wardrobe assistant, Joan was the only woman on location, but she didn't mind. She was delighted with Korda's direction. Like Lang, he was exacting but imaginative, insisting on multiple takes until his actors had achieved exactly the desired effect. Joan always thrived under such conditions, and it showed in the results on film. Although Peck and Preston are both in excellent form, *The Macomber Affair* belongs to Joan. She captures Margaret's resentment and bitterness in a performance that is a model of economy. Joan never makes her into an out-and-out wicked lady, as some actresses might have. Instead, her Margaret is a sad, deeply disappointed woman. Sitting in the jeep as she watches her husband run to escape the charging lion, her face registers an unforgettable mixture of disgust, pity, and contempt. She uses the tone of asperity to drive home some of the script's most caustic lines. After the disastrous lion hunt, when Francis comments that the whole incident has made him red in the face, Margaret responds icily, "No—it's mine that's red today." She goads her husband relentlessly. When he takes out his frustration on one of the natives, she exclaims, "Francis! Is so much exercise good for you? You're simply not used to it." When she comes back to their sleeping tent after her liaison with Wilson, and Francis confronts her, she pushes him once again ("You awake? I thought you'd be getting your beauty sleep.") And toward the end, after he threatens to leave her, she hisses, "I hate you, Francis Macomber," with chilling malevolence.

Although it was filmed after *The Woman on the Beach, The Macomber Affair* was released two months before the Renoir film, to excellent reviews. The *Hollywood Reporter* wrote, "Joan Bennett has never excelled her work as the wife," while *Time* felt that "None of the three principal players could possibly be improved on." But the strongest praise came from the *New York Times*'s Bosley Crowther, who wrote, "Joan Bennett is completely hydrochloric as the peevish, deceitful dame, showing in every glance and gesture her corrosive concern for herself." Only the film's evasive ending came under attack: The *New Yorker* felt that Joan was "most convincing when she is being wicked. It is probably no fault of Miss Bennett's that she fails to establish herself as a domestic type toward the picture's end after she has worked so hard to portray an outdoor Messalina."

After this string of films with such distinguished directors, Joan had developed a tony image as an actress with a self-determining approach to her career. Walter believed that there was a great future in European distribution, and perhaps the fact that Joan had become a favorite of some of Europe's finest émigré talents was largely due to his influence, his own vision of what her career should be. But by the time 1947 drew to an end, it was clear that Joan was going to have to concentrate on something other than prestigious directors. By mid-1947, Hollywood had experienced a dismal economic downturn. The movies were now competing for Americans' leisure time in ways they hadn't before. As film historian Thomas Schatz has observed, "Moviegoers were growing more selective, and they also were opting for other activities as a wider range of amusements and diversions became available—from night baseball to bowling to night classes on the GI bill." The result was that movie attendance slipped dramatically in 1947, and by the following year, with the rising popularity of television, it would plummet. Tastes were changing, too. Some savvy producers realized it. In 1946, Samuel Goldwyn made a fortune with a downbeat drama about the problems of returning veterans, *The Best Years of Our Lives*. At Twentieth Century–Fox, Darryl F. Zanuck understood that audiences were ready for more mature fare, and gave it to them with such adult dramas as *Gentleman's Agreement* (1947), which explored the nature of anti-Semitism, *Boomerang* (1947), about an innocent man whom society is quick to condemn, and *The Snake Pit* (1948), a study of life in a mental institution. Other studios, however—notably MGM and Columbia—were slower to catch up with their audiences and mostly continued to produce upbeat musicals and bland comedies barely distinguishable from the ones they had turned out during the war. Audiences fell away; they had seen this kind of thing too many times before. And since production costs had been steadily rising throughout the war and showed no sign of slowing down, the dismal climate at the box office was indeed something to worry about.

By 1947, Joan had reached the peak of her career. What she really needed now in order to keep up with the changing audience was another big box-office hit. At Diana Productions, Walter and Fritz Lang were developing a new property for her, *Secret Beyond the Door.* Expectations were high. After all, Lang had never led her astray.

Chapter Seventeen

1948

On July 4, 1948, Joan and Walter's second daughter, Shelley, was born. To outsiders, the Wangers' lives seemed satisfying and complete: the independent producer, married to the independent star, both at the peak of their careers and respected members of the Hollywood establishment, at a time when much of the industry looked ahead to an uncertain future. Throughout 1948, box-office receipts continued to slide, but the moguls had even greater cause for worry, for it looked as if the government was about to take action that would divest the studios of their theater ownership. The trouble had begun in 1938, when the government had filed an antitrust suit against the major studios. *U.S. v. Paramount* charged that the studios were in violation of antitrust law by engaging in practices such as block booking—in which exhibitors were forced to take poor-quality films if they wanted the studio's top-line pictures. Two years later, the studios made minor concessions by signing the Paramount consent decree, which put certain restrictions on block booking and set up a system of checks and balances to monitor studio exhibition practices. But the war proved a splendid distraction from the antitrust issues that threatened the industry and, for the most part, it was business as usual until 1946, when the government once more began to pursue the issue aggressively. In 1948, the Supreme Court ruled that Paramount, Twentieth Century–Fox, Warners, MGM, and RKO had to give up their vast theater chains. The postwar years posed a serious challenge for independent producers, too. Production costs rose dramatically after the war, and this, combined with falling box-office attendance after the peak year of 1946, caused studios to cut much tougher deals with independent producers. But with the success of *Scarlet Street* and other recent pictures, Walter seemed to have less reason to worry than most of his colleagues. Confidence was high as work began on Diana Productions' second venture, *Secret Beyond the Door.* Once again, it was to be released by Universal, or as it was now called, Universal-International, having merged with International Pictures in the summer of 1946. The new management reserved the right to scrap its contracts with independent producers and start from scratch with terms that were considerably less attractive; still, in the beginning, most of the principals connected with *Secret Beyond the Door* seem to have believed that they had the makings of another quality hit. Instead, it turned out to be the most misbegotten venture of Joan's career, the most bizarre film noir of the decade.

Secret Beyond the Door began life as "Museum Piece No. 13," by Rufus King, a weird mystery with Freudian overtones serialized in *Redbook*. Lang engaged his current lover, Silvia Richards, to write the screenplay. Richards had written the script for Warner Bros.' *Possessed,* in which Joan Crawford played a neurotic nurse obsessed with winning the love of self-absorbed engineer Van Heflin. *Possessed* was an enormous success for the studio, earning Crawford some of the best reviews of her career and an Academy Award nomination. Once Richards was free of her Warner commitments, Diana Productions promptly signed her to work in an editorial capacity, and writing the screenplay for *Secret Beyond the Door* was one of her principal assignments.

To Walter, the Rufus King story may have seemed exactly the right property at the right time. When the film was released in 1948, many critics compared it (unfavorably) to Alfred Hitchcock's *Rebecca,* and it does have certain elements in common with that film: a heroine who moves into her husband's gloomy mansion and comes face to face with an assortment of mysterious characters, the husband's enigmatic behavior, a climactic fire. But it also has much in common with *Spellbound,* Hitchcock's 1945 thriller that cast Gregory Peck as an amnesiac thought to be guilty of the murder of a famous psychiatrist. That film's Salvador Dalí–designed Freudian dream sequence, which explored the amnesiac's tortured mind and provided a symbolic key to the mystery, was taken quite seriously in some quarters, and shortly, numerous films began to explore elements of Freudian psychology. Probably it was not a good idea to imitate any aspect of *Spellbound,* for it is hard to disagree with Irene Mayer Selznick's opinion that the film is nothing more than "a collection of gimmicks." But profitable it was.

A thriller told in textbook Freudian terms, *Secret Beyond the Door* wasn't much of a story. Silvia Richards seems to have been the first member of the creative team to have serious doubts about the viability of Lang's new project. She worked diligently, but she couldn't make the bizarre elements of the story cohere, and the script took months to finish. "I remember typing up the pages as they were handed to me," recalled Lang's secretary, Hilda Rolfe, "and I thought it was just awful. And I thought, 'Well, if I can see it, why can't *they*?'" Lang, still riding high from his success with *Scarlet Street,* was at his most insufferably arrogant, and paid no attention to the danger signs. He was confident that together he and Richards would turn out a masterpiece for Diana that would surpass the best work of Hitchcock.

Secret Beyond the Door opens in Mexico, where Celia Barrett, a beautiful young heiress on vacation, meets an enigmatic architect, Mark Lamphere. Celia, who has always avoided any serious emotional involvement, finds herself aroused by Mark in a way that is entirely new to her. Mark tells Celia that he sees in her "a twentieth-century Sleeping Beauty, a wealthy American girl, who's lived her life wrapped in cotton wool. But she wants to wake up. Maybe she can." After a whirlwind courtship, they get married and return to the United States, settling in at Mark's family estate. Soon Celia is troubled by her husband's behavior. His mood swings are violent and unpredictable. Strangest of all, he has an aversion to locked rooms and lilacs. Mark has a sinister hobby: he replicates rooms where unusual murders have taken place. His pet theory is that "the way a place is built determines what happens in it. . . . Certain rooms cause violence, even murder." He is particularly careful to keep one room locked at all times; when Celia discovers that it is a replica of her own bedroom, she naturally assumes that she is to be his next victim. Rather than merely wait to be disposed of, she helps Mark come to grips with the childhood trauma that is the root of all his problems, saving her life in the process.

Apart from its unwieldy script, the film was undone by a grievous casting mistake: Joan is far too cool, detached, and self-possessed to be convincing as the terrified Celia. Her particular brand of brooding assurance makes us confident that she will always succeed in staying several steps ahead of Mark, and she's not particularly good at registering distress, so the suspense never mounts. The singularly demanding part of Mark required an actor with a highly individual brand of intensity, someone from outside the usual Hollywood circle. When James Mason turned down the role, Michael Redgrave was brought over from England to shoot his first American film. The Wangers had met him in London in 1946 at a Royal Command performance, and he had accepted the role on the basis of seeing only a small part of the script. Once filming began, he immediately wondered if he had made a mistake. Lang was now a nightmare to work with, abusive to every member of the cast. Redgrave's insecurities began to shoot to the surface. "Michael Redgrave was a mess," remembered Diana Anderson. "I was on the set quite a bit, and I remember that he was nervous and uptight. Fritz was being very naughty. He was diabolical and cruel. Maybe he thought that he was going to get a performance that way. He had absolute confidence in his way of doing things."

Joan had never acquired that brand of confidence. Although she complained to Redgrave that Lang treated her like a puppet, she reminded herself that she had done some of her best work when he pulled her strings. The considerable strides she had made as an actress during the war years were entirely due to him, and she tried to tell herself that somehow Lang would manage to make a good film out of *Secret Beyond the Door.*

But Lang was out of control. He bullied Barbara O'Neil, who

was playing Mark's mysterious secretary, to the point where she was unable to deliver her lines. He tried the same tactics on Natalie Schafer, cast as Celia's silly socialite friend. Schafer called working with Lang the most difficult experience of her career. "He was a famous sadist, you know," the actress observed years later. "I remember that I had a scene in which I had to stand in front of a fireplace. The weather was about 110. And Lang had a real fire, and he said [sarcastically], 'Darling, I'm *so sorry* I had to do this to you.' I said, 'That's all right, Mr. Lang. I'm a masochist.'"

Joan was having her own troubles with Lang. For one thing, they had crossed swords over the choice of cameraman on the film. Lang wanted Milton Krasner, who had photographed *Scarlet Street,* but Joan insisted on Stanley Cortez, who had done landmark work in *The Magnificent Ambersons* and other films. It was a shrewd move on her part, because Cortez's contribution turned out to be the only thing in *Secret Beyond the Door*'s favor. He created an atmosphere of mood and tension that the script fails to deliver. Lang complained that Cortez worked at too slow a pace, but when she viewed the rushes, Joan was justly happy with Cortez's work. She is magnificently lit and photographed in *Secret Beyond the Door*; never in her career had she looked so beautiful onscreen.

But her greatest arguments with Lang involved the voice-over narration. Lang wanted to experiment with a new technique, using a different actress's voice to utter Joan's thoughts, thus making a bold distinction between the conscious and subconscious. It was a preposterous idea that ran the risk of further muddling a film that was already an incoherent mess, but Lang originally filmed it his way. Joan was not at all happy, and Lang was upset that his protégé had suddenly shown a rebellious streak.

For the scenes in which Celia is wandering through the darkened house, trying to discover the secret of the hidden room, Lang had lights strapped to Joan's arms in order to achieve the visual effect he wanted. It was painful for Joan, but Diana Anderson felt that "Fritz didn't care if she bled." Then there was the climactic fire sequence, for which Lang refused to use doubles for Joan and Redgrave. It was a demanding stunt, and Joan's poor eyesight only heightened her tension. In take after take, she and Redgrave ran, terrified, through flames that jumped out at them from all sides.

Because of his relationship with Richards, Lang refused to acknowledge the crippling flaws in the screenplay, and he objected violently to the efforts of Universal-International production chief William Goetz to cut *Secret* down to size. It seems that Lang honestly believed the project had merit, that he saw a profundity in Richards's screenplay that simply wasn't there. Walter, for his part, may well have thought they were making an important film, too; it's likely that the film's elusive nature and unconventional narrative structure appealed to him, reminding him of some of the European pictures he admired so much. In any case, he appears not to have interfered much in production. As stipulated in the original production agreement, Walter concentrated instead on the business end and left the creative aspect to Lang.

In the end, *Secret* was done in by its ridiculous, derivative plot and clouded character motivation. The writing is arch and pretentious, a combination of Freud 101 and awkward attempts to be literary. In the film's early scenes, when the couple meet in Mexico, Mark tells Celia, "There' s something in your face that I saw once before, in South Dakota. Wheat country. Cyclone weather. Just before the cyclone, the air has a stillness, a flat, gold, shimmering stillness. You have it in your face—the same hush before the storm." At the film's climax, as Celia is desperately trying to uncover the crippling secret in Mark's past, she implores him, "Search your mind, darling. There's something hidden in your mind so deep, hidden so far back, that you no longer knows it's there. You're keeping something locked up in your mind, Mark, for the same reason you're keeping this room locked up—because you don't want anybody to know what's in it." Joan, who always hated anything that smacked of pretense, was visibly uncomfortable delivering such dialogue.

After a disappointing preview in early September 1947, Universal-International panicked and took charge of the picture, recutting it substantially and re-recording the narration using Joan's voice. All of this enraged Lang, who considered filing a breach of contract suit against the studio but was eventually dissuaded from doing so by his attorney. Lang also felt that U-I's final version was so unrepresentative of his work that his name should be removed from the credits, which the studio refused to do because of the commercial value attached to it. Most of all, he was incensed at Joan's agreement to record the new narration at U-I's request. In a highly emotional board of directors meeting, he complained that she had purposely worked against the best interests of the picture, and accused her of acting under Walter's influence.

Released early in 1948, *Secret Beyond the Door* proved a disaster for Diana Productions. Bosley Crowther in the *New York Times* dismissed it as "a pretty silly yarn . . . played in a manner no less fatuous by the sundry members of the cast." It quickly died at the box office; in fact, it is listed in several sources as Universal-International's biggest money-loser of 1948. Lang was livid, blaming everyone but himself for the picture's crushing failure. U-I was eager to cancel its agreement with Diana, and since there was nothing but discord among the officers, the company was soon dissolved. Diana Anderson remembered that Lang was so furious with the Wangers that he refused to attend her May 1948 wedding to real-estate executive John Anderson. It would be years before Joan's relationship with her mentor was repaired.

Secret's failure increased the pressure for Joan's next film to be a good one. Unfortunately, it was followed by a weak film noir, *Hollow Triumph,* made at Eagle-Lion during Walter's tenure there. The movie cast Paul Henreid in a dual role as a hood on the run and a prominent psychoanalyst who is his exact look-alike; the hood murders the doctor and attempts to take his place. Joan gave a good account of the analyst's cynical secretary, and Henreid, who also directed the film, was delighted with her performance, but the movie got no attention whatsoever. She busied herself with radio appearances, supervising the household, and her two younger daughters, uncertain of her next career move.

On occasion over the next few years, Barbara continued to turn up for brief stays at Mapleton Drive. To Stephanie Wanger Guest, Barbara seemed the most real and natural of the three sisters. Stephanie recalled an evening at Mapleton when she refused to eat a vegetable dish that was being served, claiming she was allergic to it. Barbara gently remonstrated with her to try it. "I tried it and said I didn't like it," replied Stephanie. "And Barbara said, 'You're just saying that because you said you wouldn't try it. But I think you really like it.'" Her aunt had seen right through her, and Stephanie suddenly realized she was a shrewd, intuitive person. "She was sweet and down to earth, without pretense," said Stephanie. "I think she had less to lose, less to protect, than my mother and Aunt Constance. So she was a little more open."

Walter was almost always sympathetic to Barbara's weaknesses and failings. At one point in the late 1940s, while she was staying at Mapleton Drive, a bleeding ulcer that had plagued her for some time suddenly erupted. Joan was not at home, and Walter had to drive her to the hospital. "I thought he was going to have an accident," remembered Stephanie, "He was so upset. He wasn't the kind of person who had to deal with things like that."

Barbara's visits were quite different from those of Constance, who would occasionally descend on Mapleton Drive for dinner and take over in her usual flamboyant manner, parading about the house, waving her long cigarette holder and greeting everyone with "Hello, daaaahhling!" To her nieces, she seemed nothing but show and affectation, but they couldn't help noticing how she continued to play the domineering older sister. Joan consistently deferred to her, as if it were second nature to do so.

At the time, Constance was living the nomadic existence of an officer's wife. Occasionally, she commuted to join John at Hamilton Field, near San Francisco, where he was part of the first class at the Air Command and Staff School. She continued to scramble for work, but all she could find were roles in low-budget films. For Allied Artists, she played a tough attorney in *Smart Woman,* costarring Brian Aherne, who had appeared with her in *Merrily We Live.* At Republic, she costarred in a jungle drama called *Angel on the Amazon.* The film's leading lady, Vera Hruba Ralston, recalled her as "very charming and cooperative. And she was in a wonderful mood because she was very much in love with her husband."

In mid-1948, the *Hollywood Reporter* announced that Constance had made a deal with Republic to set up production facilities for a string of films in which she would also star. The first venture was supposed to commence filming in late 1948. But by then, John had completed his special training session in California and been assigned to duty at the Air Lift base in Fassberg, Germany—a small village east of Hamburg. Fassberg was divided into different zones—American, English, French, and German, and John had been appointed base commander of the American zone. Soon after he was settled, Constance and the children joined him there.

Fassberg was bleak, gray, and, to Constance, unspeakably depressing. There was no commercial center to speak of. It was a cold, wet winter, and on the shortest day of the season there was barely two hours of sunlight. But she had made the decision to be with John, and she slogged through the mud and rain, keeping her complaints to a minimum. She got the family settled into their new, spacious living quarters—a "double house," one building that had been forged out of two. Constance and John lived on one side, with the children and their governess on the other. She installed the girls in schools, and set about learning German herself.

One thing that she refused to do, according to Patricia Coulter McElroy, was to lead the existence of a model officer's wife. "She wouldn't live on the base," recalled McElroy. "She called them all 'tacky.' Everything was common and cheap as far as she was concerned. She never went to the officer's wives' teas and other functions. Dad would have been a general a lot sooner if she had played the game."

By 1948, Walter's reputation as one of Hollywood's leading independent producers was secure. But even though he had many distinctive and successful films, a lot of them had been second-rate escapist fare; for every *Stagecoach* and *Scarlet Street,* there had been an *Arabian Nights* or a *Salome Where She Danced.* More crucially, he had yet to produce a film that would provide the capstone of his career, securing his place in screen history once and for all. More than anything, he longed to make a career-defining film that would do for him what *Gone With the Wind* had done for David O. Selznick. Eventually he hit on a project that he felt would cement his reputation, a film version of the life of Joan of Arc, with Ingrid Bergman in the title role.

By the time World War II ended, Bergman was one of the world's most popular stars. Selznick had brought her to America in 1939 to star opposite Leslie Howard in *Intermezzo*. Shrewdly, she refused to let Hollywood make her over into its idea of a standard glamour star; in fact, on meeting her for the first time at a party given by David and Irene Selznick, Joan had cattily referred to her as a kitchen maid. But Bergman sensed that her unvarnished self might make her stand out in a sea of leading-lady mannequins, and she turned out to be right: the public instantly took to her natural beauty and simple, unaffected charm. She racked up one success after another: *Casablanca, For Whom the Bell Tolls, Gaslight, The Bells of St. Mary's, Saratoga Trunk, Spellbound, Notorious*. She was, along with Betty Grable and a handful of others, one star whose films seemed foolproof at the box office.

For years, Bergman had been intrigued by the possibility of playing Joan of Arc. She had read numerous accounts of the saint's life and closely studied the transcripts of the trials that led to Joan's execution. At a party in 1940, she met playwright Maxwell Anderson, whom she told of her fascination with the Maid of Orléans. On the spot, Anderson promised to write a play about Joan for her. Bergman probably didn't expect him to follow through; after all, when she had signed her long-term contract with Selznick, the producer had also promised to star her in a film about Joan. Later he reneged on his vow, claiming that with pro-British sentiment running so high in the early years of the war, it wouldn't do to make a movie that portrayed the British as the enemy. A more credible reason for Selznick's refusal to make the film was that such an elaborate production would cost a staggering amount of money. Better for one of the bigger studios, such as MGM or Twentieth Century–

Fox, to take on such a risky project. Then, if it failed, the losses would be offset by profits on their vast roster of other, less expensive films. This line of reasoning does not appear to have occurred to Walter, who became obsessed with making the film, and in the end risked everything he owned, and then some.

In the beginning, at least, it appeared that his gamble would pay off. Anderson made good on his promise to Bergman, and when she opened in the playwright's *Joan of Lorraine* at Broadway's Alvin Theater in November 1946, it quickly became one of the great successes of the season. The play had what was then an unusual framing device: Mary Grey, a young actress cast in a stage production about Joan of Arc, is battling with a hard-nosed director over the most honest way to interpret the character of Joan. The play shifts back and forth, contrasting Joan's struggles to lead the French to their rightful place in the world with Mary's attempts to portray Joan's spiritual core onstage. The idea Anderson weaves throughout the drama is the necessity of compromise to achieve the greatest results—both for Mary Grey, in her artistic quest, and for the historic Joan, in her spiritual and political journey.

Bergman's reviews were ecstatic. She won the Drama League and Tony Awards for Best Actress of the season, and the play enjoyed a 199-performance run, closing in May 1947. Not long after it opened, Victor Fleming, the director who had helped shape Bergman's acclaimed performance as the prostitute, Ivy, in *Dr. Jekyll and Mr. Hyde,* came backstage to tell her how much her performance had excited and inspired him. The production had convinced him that he had to direct a film about Joan, and that she must star in it. Bergman was elated; perhaps she would have the chance to bring her beloved Joan to the screen after all. Soon enough, the pieces of the project fell into place. Bergman, Fleming, and Walter formed an independent production company, Sierra Films. For Bergman, it looked like a highly lucrative arrangement: she and her husband, Petter Lindstrom, were to receive a salary of $175,000, plus a cut of the profits. Maxwell Anderson was contracted to write the screenplay, with Andrew Solt brought in late in the game, sharing screen credit with Anderson.

Three million dollars of the budget was advanced by Bankers Trust, New York. Initially, MGM had agreed to distribute the film, but in the uncertain climate of the postwar economy the company grew nervous and withdrew. Walter quickly locked in RKO as distributor, but the struggle to make up the balance dragged into the early stages of production. In the end, *Joan of Arc* would cost $4.5 million, making it the most expensive Hollywood movie up to that time; Walter's biographer, Matthew Bernstein, notes that it cost $200,000 more than *Gone With the Wind.* It would require a break-even of $8–9 million, a figure that only a handful of films had reached at that point.

Still, Walter was confident that his film was destined for greatness. So, for that matter, was much of the Hollywood community. As filming began on September 16, 1947, at the old Hal Roach Studios in Culver City, the buzz around town was that by securing Bergman for the film, Walter had scored the great coup of his career. It was predicted that *Joan of Arc* would be a colossal success and sweep the 1948 Academy Awards. For years, Walter's success as an independent filmmaker had made him the envy of many of his colleagues, but he had never been envied as much as he was now.

Only Joan had misgivings about Walter's big gamble. She had put some of her own money into the film, but she was always skeptical about big, ambitious projects, considering them pretentious. She also felt that Walter was capable of doing his best work on a medium-sized budget, and from the beginning she was uneasy about *Joan of Arc*'s chances. On the evening in 1946 when Walter had burst through the front door waving a fountain pen and proudly proclaimed, "This is the pen that closed the deal with Ingrid Bergman!" Joan had a strong premonition of disaster. She remembered looking around at the house that had been such a source of pleasure to her for so many years, and wondering how much longer she would be able to enjoy it. From that point on, she purposely distanced herself from *Joan of Arc,* refusing even to sit through a rough cut of the finished picture.

Joan of Arc's chief handicap was its leaden script. The theatrical setting of Anderson's original had been thrown out in favor of a straight historical approach to Joan's life. This seemed fair enough—but there was little electricity in Anderson and Solt's screenplay, which moved listlessly from one talky scene to another: Joan tells God that she feels unequal to the challenge of leading the French army, Joan tells the Dauphin that he must fulfill his destiny as king, Joan tells the French soldiers that they must behave as holy men, even on the battlefield, Joan defends herself on trial. Fleming did his best to punctuate these static scenes with elaborate battle sequences, but they run on excessively. Although Jose Ferrer received much acclaim and a Best Supporting Actor Academy Award nomination for his portrayal of the Dauphin, neither he nor anyone else in the large supporting cast quite comes into focus. The camera never seems to be in the right place, and a clumsy narrative further deadens the film. Throughout, *Joan of Arc* has an oddly lugubrious rhythm; at times, it feels more like an educational film aimed at elementary students than a major Hollywood production. Moreover, Victor Fleming had fallen in love with Bergman and thus was not able to step back and objectively pull the film into shape, as he had with *Gone With the Wind*. Had David O. Selznick been *Joan*'s producer, he would have been on the set, directing the director every day. But that had never been Walter's style.

Walter remained so confident that he had an instant classic on his hands that he decided to release *Joan of Arc* on a roadshow basis—playing it in select legitimate theaters for a strictly limited number of times a day, at escalated ticket prices (a high of $2.40 for Saturday and Sunday evening performances in its initial New York run). This was principally a means of tricking the public into believing that *Joan of Arc* was a prestigious cultural event that they would be foolish to miss. (Matthew Bernstein notes that Walter was probably inspired by the successful roadshow marketing, two years earlier, of Laurence Olivier's *Henry V.*)

Walter and Joan were in the audience when *Joan of Arc* opened at New York's Victoria Theater, at Broadway and Forty-sixth Street, on November 11, 1948. In his retelling of the night's events, Walter always claimed that his wife was restless throughout the showing, and during the climactic scenes of Joan at the stake muttered, "Burn, damn you, burn!" In an odd way, an audience reaction sometimes can affect a film as much as it can a play. In this case, it became obvious to most of those closely involved with *Joan of Arc* that the film was a dud.

Initially, it didn't seem that the quality of the film was going to hurt the box-office returns, since *Joan of Arc* took in $67,500 in its first week at the Victoria. Nor was it the across-the-board critical disaster that it was later portrayed as being. "The picture bespeaks class, size and scope all the way," enthused *Variety.* "A stunning super-spectacle," the *New York Daily Mirror* reported. "The picture is tremendous . . . an unbelievably great achievement." The *New York Daily News* felt it was destined to "become a classic of the screen." Other critics were less generous. "Awash in Technicolor," sniffed the *New Yorker,* which in the 1940s had a habit of panning nine out of ten pictures, "it staggers from one unlikely scene to another." In the *New York Times,* the frequently dismissive Bosley Crowther soft-pedaled his criticism, but pointed out that Fleming had "allowed this whole drama to be played in the wide frame of a pageant, with consequent lack of real insight and intimacy." (It was Fleming's final credit; he died of a heart attack in January 1949.)

"I remember going to the opening in Hollywood, at the Beverly Theater," said Diana Anderson. "My heart sank. I knew right away. I'd seen too many films by that time. I just knew that it was a really overweight production." Walter desperately tried to plug the film as a spiritual tonic, telling the press that the public craved something beyond material possessions—but the public wasn't fooled. In the end, the year's most eagerly anticipated movie had become the decade's most spectacular flop.

That Christmas was a grim one for the Wangers. In the weeks since its premiere in New York, *Joan of Arc* had limped along. Eventually, it would gross over $2 million—good for a film of that era, but a far cry from the amount needed to turn a profit. Walter slowly came to terms with the fact that his big gamble—which had never really struck him as much of a gamble at all—had failed. All of this, coupled with the dismal returns on *Secret Beyond the Door* and the dissolution of Diana Productions, meant that the future suddenly looked uncertain.

Within a short time, Walter found that his status in Hollywood had slipped considerably. He was no longer one of the movie industry's most daring and high-minded producers; he was just a foolhardy man who had made an enormous and costly flop. People found excuses not to meet with him, avoided catching his eye at parties, failed to return telephone calls. There was nothing left to do except pour his energy into more films. He planned three for release in 1949: *Tulsa,* his latest vehicle for Susan Hayward, *Reign of Terror,* a French Revolution drama starring Robert Cummings and Arlene Dahl, and a new vehicle for Joan, *The Reckless Moment.*

Coincidentally, Ingrid Bergman was entering a difficult professional period as well. Although her box-office power was thought to be infallible, she had run aground with *Arch of Triumph,* a critical and commercial disappointment released a few months before *Joan of Arc.* Her next film, Alfred Hitchcock's *Under Capricorn,* also turned out badly. Fed up with what she considered Hollywood's creative bankruptcy, she jumped at the chance to make a film with Roberto Rossellini, whose neorealist *Open City* and *Paisan* had moved her deeply. In the early spring of 1949 she flew to Italy to commence filming on Rossellini's latest project, *Stromboli,* which she hoped would bring her the artistic freedom she had sought for so long. *Stromboli* turned out to be far less important than many of the glossy Hollywood films that she professed to dislike, but it had its rewards: she fell in love with Rossellini, had a child by him, and left Petter Lindstrom and their daughter Pia behind to start a new and exciting life for herself.

The Hollywood press was outraged, and so were her fans. Quiet scandals were routine in Hollywood—for years, illegitimate babies, abortions, homosexual interludes, and statutory rape had figured in the lives of some of the industry's biggest stars. But studio watchdogs were always on the alert to make sure that little of this was leaked to the public, and for the most part they were successful. In many respects, Hollywood had prided itself on being a closed community, and now Bergman had flaunted her indiscretions publicly. The unspoken cause for alarm throughout the industry was that Bergman's adulterous behavior might fuel the notion that all Hollywood actresses were sluts offscreen and alienate a large segment of the moviegoing public. Newspapers called for audiences to boycott her movies; she was even denounced on the Senate floor. By the spring of 1949, when news of her involvement with Rossellini had broken, *Joan of Arc* was in general release. Business was bad, and Walter was quick to put the blame on Bergman's conduct. He even went so far as to send her a hostile (and hypocritical) telegram: "The malicious stories about your behavior need immediate contradiction from you. If you are not concerned about yourself and your family you should realize that because I believed in you and your honesty, I have made a huge investment endangering my future and that of my family which you are jeopardizing if you do not behave in a way which will disprove these ugly rumors broadcast over radio and press throughout the world."

Walter fell into a deep depression, and Joan kept an eye on the household finances. Over time, there were several ominous meetings with the Bank of America. It seemed entirely possible that the bank would foreclose on the house, which Walter put up as collateral when he took out a further loan of $528,500 to finance Columbia Pictures' *The Reckless Moment.* Joan began taking on more and more work: radio, product endorsements, anything she could find. But, realist and pragmatist that she was, she no doubt sensed that the decline had begun.

Chapter Eighteen

1949–1950

By 1949, Walter was again desperate for a hit, and he hoped *Tulsa* and *Reign of Terror* (also known as *The Black Book*) would change his luck. As always, he earned the respect of his colleagues by researching his films meticulously: no detail of the sets or costumes escaped his attention. But with the changes in Hollywood at the time, he was forced to keep a closer eye on the budget than he had in the past. *Reign of Terror*'s leading lady, Arlene Dahl, noted his insistence on keeping costs down. "I remember him getting together with [director] Tony Mann and the set decorator and cinematographer," she recalled, "looking to shoot in a way that would save them money. Usually, the set decorator would decorate whole rooms, but on this picture, he would decorate only two of the four walls, and would open it up to the camera, so they could shoot one wall for one part of the scene. It cut the expenses of set decorating in half, but it would still set the tone of the period." Unfortunately, both *Reign of Terror* and *Tulsa* failed, and Walter became more anxious than ever about the future.

In late 1949, the Berlin airlift reached its conclusion. The Fassberg air base was deactivated and the Coulters resettled in Wiesbaden. Coulter had been appointed deputy chief of staff for occupational Air Force headquarters. They moved into a home fit for a movie star: a great three-story house at 35 Rösselstrasse that once had been the residence of the Dutch consul. The estate was surrounded by magnificent gardens, including a glassed-in vegetable patch and a cherry orchard. The house was well staffed, and for Constance, the Wiesbaden years represented a sort of return to her glamorous peak years in Hollywood. The military officers and their wives took great pride in having a movie star in their midst, and Constance was the center of attention wherever she went. She was constantly in demand to perform a variety of duties, whether it was opening a new service club, organizing entertainment for the troops, or presenting a trophy to a star athlete. She also had lost none of her sympathy for the plight of European refugees. When she learned of a White Russian couple that had been on the run, constantly changing residences in order to avoid being captured and deported, she took pity on them and struck a deal: if they would tutor her in German, she would allow them to live in the apartment over the garage. Coulter's career might have been jeopardized had anyone in officialdom discovered her deception, but Constance made certain that they did not.

It was as a theatrical producer that Constance made her biggest impact in Germany. While still in Fassberg, it became obvious to her that the troops had little to relieve the tedium of occupation duty. Quickly, she set about arranging for a series of American companies to cross the Atlantic and entertain the troops. She wangled the use of military transport service to fly the actors to and from Germany, and oversaw all financial arrangements and creative decisions.

Because lifting the GIs' spirits was the main order of business, Constance selected light comedies only: *Over Twenty-One, Dear Ruth,* and *John Loves Mary.* In 1949, June Lockhart, fresh from a Tony Award–winning Broadway success in *For Love or Money,* appeared with her father, Gene Lockhart, in *John Loves Mary.* The company rehearsed for a few weeks in Los Angeles before being flown to Westover Field, Massachusetts. There they were briefed before flying overseas on Military Air Transport.

The companies toured bases all over Germany, flying from one city to the other, usually in DC-3s or DC-4s. Everywhere they went, the entertainment-starved soldiers greeted the plays with wild enthusiasm. Wiesbaden had not been hit as hard by Allied bombing as many German cities had, but in Berlin conditions were bleak. In each town the company played, Gene Lockhart, a Catholic, tried to find out where daily Mass was held; often, it was in a private home because many of the old churches were destroyed. The business districts had been all but wiped out, whole neighborhoods reduced to rubble. Old women spent their days picking up the bricks and stacking them up in an orderly way. "There would be an eight-story building totally bombed out," recalled June Lockhart. "You could look through a window and see the sky beyond it. And all the buildings were covered in ivy that was still growing. So you had this parasite growing on this dead edifice."

According to Lockhart, Constance was an energetic, hands-on producer who was present for rehearsals, presided over the opening, organized press coverage, and occasionally accompanied the actors on sightseeing trips. Lockhart remembered her as "cordial, charming, gracious, and very professional about the whole thing. Once, she gave a wonderful anniversary party for my parents, even though my mother wasn't there—she had stayed behind in the U.S. The big moment was a phone call in which my father was able to speak to her. Constance had tears in her eyes."

(1949-50)

During this period, Barbara struggled on, moving from odd jobs to lengthy stays with the Wangers. Despite the infrequency of her visits with her children, she was quite aware that there were serious difficulties with Lorelle. Bright and energetic, Lorelle was already a skilled and avid golfer by the time she reached her teens, but often she was seized by fits of uncontrollable rage. One day, while at school, Lorelle suffered a particularly violent outburst and had to be hospitalized for a lengthy period. When Barbara paid her a visit at the hospital, Lorelle appeared not to know her, and rushed at her angrily, scratching her across the arm. Morton, certain that his daughter was showing signs of extreme emotional disturbance, consulted various doctors. He also discussed the matter in some depth with his old friend Joseph Kennedy.

Morton was well acquainted with the difficulties that Kennedy had had with his second daughter, Rosemary. As an infant, she had exhibited a marked lack of physical coordination, and as she entered school, she had difficulty reading and writing. Her shaky academic performance was only part of the worry: she also threw wild tantrums, much like the ones that Lorelle had been suffering. In a family of athletes and overachievers like the Kennedys, Rosemary was quickly branded a failure. In 1941, after talking the matter over with a number of doctors, Joe Kennedy had decided to have Rosemary subjected to a prefrontal lobotomy.

The roots of the modern lobotomy stretch back to 1890, when a German scientist named Friedrich Golz performed a series of procedures on dogs. He found that by cutting away the temporal lobe of the neocortex, he could render the animals docile. Two years later, similar surgeries were performed on a group of human patients in a Swiss asylum. The procedure developed little until 1935, when scientists at Yale University formulated the lobotomy as it came to be known—an invasion of the frontal and prefrontal cortex with a sharp instrument. It was practiced on human patients by a Portuguese neuropsychiatrist, Dr. Antonio Egas Moniz, and the results were sufficiently encouraging to make many in the field believe that there might be hope for surgically alleviating certain extreme types of psychosis, such as schizophrenia, or affective disorders, such as obsessive-compulsive syndrome.

Moniz developed the procedure known as leucotomy, which involved drilling a number of tiny holes on either side of the brain and running a thin wire knife through the tissue. The results were mixed, but they proved fascinating to an American neurologist named Walter Freeman, who, with the help of a colleague, James Watts, introduced the procedure to the United States in the mid-1930s. The fact that most of their patients were transformed from agitated psychotics into complete vegetables does not appear to have dampened the enthusiasm of either doctor. Watts set about developing a method known as ice pick lobotomy, which involved placing an instrument that looked like an ordinary ice pick just above the eye and giving it a swift tap so that it could tear neatly through tissue and bone and be manipulated into a position to cut the prefrontal lobe. During the early 1940s, thousands of lobotomies were performed in the United States, promoted as a kind of cure-all for general aggressive behavior. By the early 1950s, the surgery had been exposed as the horror it was. But in the 1940s, when Morton consulted Joe Kennedy, it had yet to be thoroughly discredited in the medical profession.

Rosemary Kennedy's lobotomy (performed five years before Freeman and Watts had "improved" their technique by developing the ice pick instrument) was a crashing failure. In time, she regressed to an infantlike state and was barely able to converse at all. In 1941, she was sent off to be cared for at St. Coletta's School, a Roman Catholic institution for the developmentally disabled in Jefferson, Wisconsin, where she remains to this day. Whether Morton realized the extent of Rosemary's post-lobotomy deterioration is unknown. In any event, he agreed with his friend that Lorelle might benefit from a lobotomy. It is not known exactly where Lorelle's surgery was performed, although the close friendship between Morton and Kennedy suggests that it may have been done at George Washington University Hospital by James Watts, the surgeon who had operated on Rosemary. Wherever the surgery took place, the results were catastrophic. Lorelle regressed immediately, and soon was hospitalized in Central Islip, New York. She remained there for many years until she was moved to the Pennhurst State Hospital in southeastern Pennsylvania. In the 1970s Pennhurst was the subject of litigation, charging that its conditions were so bad that they violated state law. Lorelle died there in 1977, under circumstances never fully explained.

For Barbara, the incident was devastating, and she surely must have partly blamed herself for not being a presence in Lorelle's life. She took no solace in the knowledge that, according to the terms of the divorce decree, Morton had essentially rendered her powerless to help. Her failure to prevent her daughter's brutalization, and later confinement, would haunt her for the rest of her life.

One of the benefits of the growth of the film studies movement in the 1960s and 1970s was the rehabilitation, by both critics and fans, of so many worthy pictures that had failed in their original release. When a play flops, usually it is a flop forever, but for a failed film a second act is always a tantalizing possibility. When *The Reckless Moment* was released in the post-Christmas season of 1949, the press and public barely acknowledged its existence. Coming so soon on the heels of the epic pomp of *Joan of Arc*, this subdued but penetrating domestic drama, filmed on a modest budget (under $1 million), was dismissed as an unremarkable and oddly muted thriller. Its dissection of suburban American life appeals to us more now, with the distance of years, than it possibly could have at the time of its release. In its portrayal of a woman trying to hold on to her safe, domestic existence, *The Reckless Moment* is a startling time capsule, and a good example of Walter's imaginative instincts. It also contains the most probing performance of Joan's screen career.

The Reckless Moment marked a transition for Joan. In February 1949, she turned thirty-nine. (Later that year, she would receive an unusual burst of publicity as "Hollywood's most glamorous grandmother" when Diana gave birth to her first child, Amanda.) For most star actresses in Hollywood, their late thirties and early forties proved a difficult time. By the judgment of movie audiences (and moguls) at the time, they were no longer young. Many of the women who had ruled at the box office in the 1930s had been unable to reinvent themselves as tastes changed and they were required to reveal some new dimension in their personalities. Certainly it seems unlikely that Greta Garbo ever intended that *Two-Faced Woman* would be her final film, but as the years passed and public tastes began to shift dramatically, she became paralyzed by the thought of returning to the screen in a world that now seemed alien to her. Many of the elegant stars of the previous decade—Norma Shearer, Miriam Hopkins, Merle Oberon, Jeanette MacDonald, Constance—now seemed somewhat quaint; and they all ran aground as the 1940s wore on.

Joseph L. Mankiewicz once observed that when an actress

decides to play the mother of a teenager, she can usually forget about ever again being offered a romantic lead. Joan wasn't afraid. Having reinvented herself in both *Trade Winds* and *Man Hunt,* she now prepared for yet another career switch with *The Reckless Moment.* Walter felt it was time for her to take on a new sort of role, and since she had grown tired of playing femmes fatales, she welcomed the change. Cast as the mother of a rebellious seventeen-year-old girl, she cut her hair and chose a sensible wardrobe appropriate for the suburban matron she would be playing. Just the year before, in *Secret Beyond the Door,* she was at her high-glamour peak; now she looked decidedly middle-aged.

The Reckless Moment was based on a short novel by Elizabeth Sanxay Holding, *The Blank Wall,* published in the October 1947 issue of *Ladies' Home Journal,* and later brought out in hardcover by Simon and Schuster. Walter's keen interest in British cinema prompted him to buy the property for Joan. He wanted to make a film that depicted two lost and lonely people from different worlds who are thrown together by circumstance and almost, but never quite, have an affair. His inspiration was David Lean and Noël Coward's 1946 success *Brief Encounter,* in which two ordinary, married, middle-class Brits (Celia Johnson and Trevor Howard) consider committing adultery, then think better of it.

In *The Reckless Moment,* Joan plays Lucia Harper, a housewife living on Balboa Island, a pleasant coastal community near Los Angeles. Tom, her engineer husband, is away in Germany working on a building project, and she has been left in charge of a household that includes her seventeen-year-old daughter Bea (Geraldine Brooks), fifteen-year-old son David (David Bain), aged father-in-law (Henry O'Neill), and maid (Frances Williams). As the film opens, Lucia leaves her comfortable home and drives into a seedy section of Los Angeles to keep an appointment with Ted Darby, a shady character Bea has been seeing. Lucia has investigated Darby's background and orders him to leave her daughter alone, but he refuses to do so unless Lucia promises to back up her demand with money.

Late that night, Bea meets Darby in the family boathouse. They quarrel, and she hits him over the head with her flashlight, then runs back to the house without seeing Darby, reeling from the blow, crash through the railing and fall onto the beach below. The next morning, Lucia, unable to sleep, goes out for an early morning walk and discovers Darby's body (when he fell, he landed on the anchor belonging to the Harpers' motorboat). Frantic with fear that the body will be discovered, Lucia drags it into the boat, takes it out to the middle of the bay, and dumps it overboard.

Initially, Lucia seems to have succeeded in covering up for her daughter. But one evening, as she returns home from shopping for a Christmas tree, an Irishman named Martin Donnelly (James Mason) is waiting for her. He is a partner in a blackmail ring and informs her that he has a bundle of torrid letters that Bea wrote to Darby that, if discovered, will link her with the crime. Donnelly asks that Lucia come up with $5,000 in cash within a few days or he will turn the letters over to the police.

After deciding against contacting her husband in Germany, Lucia goes about dealing with the problem in her own determined, methodical way. She starts cutting down on household expenses, tries to secure a bank loan, pawns her jewelry. Along the way she comes face to face with all sorts of unsavory types that she would never have imagined meeting. Donnelly, watching Lucia's frantic and ultimately hopeless attempts to raise the money, is so moved by her devotion to her family that he finds himself falling in love with her.

The basic story outline sounded like standard suspense melodrama, but Walter was determined to give it a more personal point of view. He perceived it as a story of a repressed woman whose comfortable life is both a haven and a trap, whose true worth is seen not by the family she is devoted to, but by the man who is blackmailing her. Initially, Wanger felt that Jean Renoir was the right director for the project, but Renoir's asking price was too high, and so he turned to Max Ophuls, another distinguished director whose years in Hollywood had not been all he had hoped.

Ophuls's career had begun in his native Germany, where he worked extensively in the theater as both actor and director. After breaking into films as an assistant director for Anatole Litvak, he turned out a number of films of his own before fleeing Germany in 1933. He worked for a number of years in France and Switzerland, then emigrated to the United States in 1941. He did not direct a full-length Hollywood film until 1947, when he made *The Exile,* a Douglas Fairbanks Jr. swashbuckler. He was assigned two subsequent pictures, both for independent producers: *Letter From an Unknown Woman* (1948), a love story set in turn-of-the-century Vienna starring Joan Fontaine, and *Caught* (1949), a drama with noir overtones starring Robert Ryan. *The Reckless Moment* was quite different from anything he had attempted before, and he signed on with Walter enthusiastically.

The script for *The Reckless Moment* captured an aspect of American life that had not yet been widely represented on the screen—the repressive, complacent nature of American suburbia. With the end of the war, more and more people had deserted the city for the suburbs. This new, conformist culture was looked on with disdain by many leading European directors working in the United States. German-born Douglas Sirk, for one, spent much of the 1950s filming variations on the dark side of the prosperous, middle-class American family.

The movies reflected this social shift. As James Harvey has argued in his perceptive study *Movie Love in the Fifties,* the screen romances of the 1950s were in many respects much less daring than those of the 1940s. And *The Reckless Moment,* made just as one decade was giving way to another, is one of the few films of the period to take a sharp critical look at what was happening to American family life. Looking at it from the perspective of another century, it seems quite prescient about America in the 1950s.

The original script had been written in late 1947 by Robert E. Kent, whose work was judged awkward and unsatisfactory. The script was reworked by Mel Dinelli, but he had little sympathy for the subject and at one point asked to be taken off the project. Walter wasn't happy with Dinelli's results and engaged a pair of little-known writers, Robert Soderberg and Henry Garson, to rework Dinelli's screenplay. Their principal challenge was to warm up the script, to add sharper details of the Harpers' domestic life—to make it, in

Garson's words, "homey." Soderberg and Garson worked on the radio series *Junior Miss* in the mornings, then labored on the script in the afternoons. Walter was happy with their first draft, delivered early in 1949. Not only was it shrewdly observed—it showed the benefit of their frequent consultations with Ophuls, who had already mapped out how he was going to shoot the story.

Ophuls had long had a reputation as a director who loved a constantly restless, roving camera. Some of his critics found that his penchant for tracking shots and circular movement bordered on mannerism, but in truth few directors in history have known how to use the camera as a way of underlining character. One example: the moment in *Letter From an Unknown Woman* when the teenaged Lisa (Joan Fontaine) stands at the top of the staircase in her tenement, watching as Stefan (Louis Jourdan), the hedonistic pianist she is in love with, mounts the stairs with his conquest for the evening. Ophuls positions the camera behind Lisa, as she stares down at the whispering, laughing couple from the top landing; the slight movement of the back of her head tell us all we need to know about the depth of her despair.

In similar ways, *The Reckless Moment* is an intensely *personal* film, as Walter had intended. Ophuls ingeniously makes the audience feel Lucia's stifled existence. Her life has consisted of rules and order, to the point of being slightly obsessive—and now that order is being threatened by Donnelly's world, of which she knows nothing. Lucia always moves straight ahead, without veering to the left or right—it's the only way she knows. And Burnett Guffey's perpetually roving camera mimics her movements, following her up and down stairs, through doors, down streets. When Lucia ventures into the seedier sections of Los Angeles to visit Darby, and later to try to raise the money Donnelly has demanded, we feel we are in step with her, so that her jarring discovery of the dives and pawn shops has an immediacy rare in films of the period.

For Joan, *The Reckless Moment* was an ideal meeting of actress and role. She vividly portrays Lucia's determination to protect her comfortable lifestyle at any cost; perhaps without fully realizing it, she drew on her own compulsive need to maintain a safe and secure existence. Even though she is busy disposing of bodies and negotiating with blackmailers, she never forgets about her duties at home: she is constantly reminding her son not to take too much butter or to put on a shirt.

Joan builds Lucia's growing anxiety slowly and beautifully; she is always preoccupied, impatient, smoking one cigarette after another, not quite catching what one of the other characters has just said to her. We watch her going through her pitiful attempts to cut down on expenses by slashing the grocery budget and canceling a new suit she's ordered. We feel deeply for her when she is subjected to the barely veiled insults of Mrs. Loring, a condescending loan officer (memorably played by Kathryn Card). Lucia is at sea in this world, and Mrs. Loring lets her know it. When Lucia tries to raise money on a brooch, Mrs. Loring coolly informs her that they aren't allowed to lend money on jewelry because they don't have a pawnbroker's license. She adds primly, "It's, ahem, state law, you know." Ophuls brilliantly illustrates the contrast between the two women by showing Mrs. Loring from the back, rigid and upright, the figure of authority, while all we see of Lucia is her watery reflection in the window of the office door.

Part of *The Reckless Moment*'s unusual texture comes from the distance that we in the audience feel from Lucia. She is so intensely private that we almost feel guilty for being shown *this* much of her pain and suffering. Lucia is the embodiment of those Greatest Generation women whose entire lives were about simply getting on with it. She doesn't fall apart (until the very end) because she has never had the *luxury* of falling apart, there have always been household bills to pay or meals to supervise or marketing to do. Her only indulgence is her cigarettes. Her constant smoking seems an expression of both her anxiety and her strength. Near the end, as she is about to go off to the boathouse to deal with Donnelly's sinister partner (Roy Roberts), she lights a cigarette as if she's drawing a sword and marching into battle.

Lucia's life never permits her a moment's peace or privacy. When she drives into Los Angeles to deal with Darby, everyone wants an account of her whereabouts. When Donnelly shows up to make his blackmail overtures and she tries to rush him out of the house, her windbag father-in-law keeps inviting him to stay for dinner. When she and Donnelly are in his car, negotiating the blackmail terms, a local contractor pulls up next to them, rolls down his window, and tells her that he needs to start working on her roof soon. Lucia doesn't seem to object to any of this. It's all she knows, which is why Donnelly's growing fondness for her barely seems to register. He asks her if she ever gets away from her family. "No," she says sharply—and it sounds like equal parts gratitude and rebuke. She seems to contemplate saying something else, but instead she trails off into a heavy silence.

Much has been made of Lucia's close relationship with her maid, Sybil. It is true that Sybil is more astute and sophisticated than practically any of the black servant characters who cropped up in films of the period, and Frances Williams gives the character an intelligence and dignity that makes us notice her right away. Yet Lucia hardly seems any more responsive to Sybil than she does to anyone else around her. She is truly a woman alone.

In the picture's best scene, Lucia and Donnelly are taking a ferry from Balboa to the mainland. Lucia is explaining to him that she will need a few extra days to collect the money; she hasn't had the time to raise it. "You don't know how a family can surround you," she says quietly. "You're quite a prisoner, aren't you?" Donnelly says. "I don't feel like one," she responds, too quickly. By now Donnelly is entirely taken with her, and part of the reason is that she doesn't really seem to fear him. The tone of asperity in her voice indicates that she regards him almost as a nuisance, an affront—and he in turn senses her great reserves of strength. When he gently tells her that Bea is lucky to have a mother like her, she snaps, "Everyone has a mother like me. You probably had one, too."

But Lucia was not the sort of heroine audiences expected to find in film noir. When Columbia studio chief Harry Cohn viewed the finished film, he was dismayed. He felt that the entire picture was too low-key, that it needed at least one "Stanwyck scene" so that the audience could experience Lucia having a spectacular outburst. But such a scene would have violated Ophuls and the writers' conception of Lucia. Her only breakdown comes privately, behind closed doors, near the end of the film, in a scene almost shocking in its intimacy: the camera moves slowly across her darkened bedroom as she lies on the bed, sobbing hysterically. Soon, the telephone is ringing. It's Tom, calling from Germany. She gets up, wipes her eyes, and pulls herself together and goes downstairs to take the call. She would never dream of letting her family see her in such a state.

Ophuls and Walter had stuck to their vision, but they paid a price. In 1949, few appreciated the film's originality. Every first-run theater in New York screened it and rejected it, and it was forced to open in neighborhood theaters on a flat rental basis. The reviews were mostly downbeat, with scattered praise for Joan and James Mason. In late December, Walter wrote to Ophuls in Paris, "The film is suffering very much . . . the business is catastrophic and most disappointing." In Great Britain, *The Reckless Moment* fared better. The *Evening Standard* found it "a really first-class film," while the *Times of London* judged that "the film belongs to Miss Joan Bennett; her performance matches the intelligence of the direction."

Decades later, when Ophuls's work began to be re-evaluated in film societies and on college campuses, *The Reckless Moment*'s reputation began its slow ascendancy. Soon it was a favorite rarity in New York City revival houses. Joan, however, never wavered in her opinion of it, finding it "nothing exceptional . . . not like *The Woman in the Window* or *Scarlet Street.*" In the mid-1990s, the Los Angeles County Museum of Art showed *The Reckless Moment* as part of a Max Ophuls retrospective. Diana Anderson attended, and for her it was a highly emotional experience. "She was *exactly* like the role she played in the film," said Diana. "It's almost as if she wasn't acting."

Once *The Reckless Moment* was completed in May 1949, Walter pursued his next project. Undaunted by the failure of *Joan of Arc,* he took on the immense challenge of coaxing Greta Garbo out of retirement. The vehicle he settled on was Balzac's *La Duchesse de Langeais,* a Napoleonic-era love story which had already been filmed in France. Garbo was keen enough on the idea to submit to photographic screen tests. Max Ophuls was once again lined up to direct, as well as to work on the script, and James Mason was engaged as leading man.

But after *Joan of Arc,* Walter's status as a bad risk followed him, and he had to scramble to secure backing. The Wangers spent much of the summer and fall of 1949 in Paris and Rome, trying to arrange a consortium of investors. In September, Stephanie and Shelley, accompanied by their nurse, Catherine Ann "Randy" Randall, sailed on the *Queen Mary* to meet them. Happy as he was to get away from Hollywood, Walter was working under extreme pressure and was irritable and exhausted much of the time, and Joan had little patience with his mood swings. She knew that the most serious consequences of his *Joan of Arc* gamble lay ahead, and, aware that the security she had worked so hard to build up was in danger of being wiped out, she had become tense and sullen. Randall hated being away from Mapleton Drive for so long, Stephanie disliked her French school and detested French food, and Shelley became ill from drinking contaminated water.

The Garbo project proceeded in fits and starts. Walter worked out a shaky and complicated coalition involving RKO Studios and both American and Italian investors, but it was a house of cards that soon collapsed. Mason quit the project (seemingly at no cost to his friendship with the Wangers). Garbo, having lost confidence in Walter's ability to bring the whole thing off to her satisfaction, withdrew. All in all, it was a miserable autumn. Both girls were seriously run down when the family finally returned to California just before Christmas—Stephanie so much so that she had to be put on a regimen of beef tea and kept out of school for six weeks.

Another project that Walter pumped considerable energy and money into was a hoped-for film version of Rosamond Lehmann's best-selling novel *The Ballad and the Source.* Walter saw it as a vehicle for Joan, and once again wanted Ophuls to direct. The role of Sybil Jardine, a woman who defied social convention by pursuing a life both as a mother and an adulteress, did seem ideal for

Joan. But in the end, the book resisted all attempts to turn it into a censor-proof script.

The Wangers returned from Europe in time for Joan to begin preparations on her next film, *Father of the Bride,* at MGM. It was based on Edward Streeter's popular comic novel about the trials of an upper-middle-class man whose beautiful daughter has her heart set on a grand-scale wedding; tensions and expenses mount as the wedding day approaches. Because the script unfolded as a series of anecdotes, the picture would stand or fall based on who played the harassed father, Stanley Banks. Fortunately, MGM assigned the role to longtime contract star Spencer Tracy, who gave Stanley a warmth, depth, and irascible humor that gave the picture some needed substance. Vincente Minnelli was signed as director, and he showed tremendous skill at portraying the everyday details in the lives of an ordinary suburban family.

Joan was cast as Stanley's wife, Ellie, and MGM contract star Elizabeth Taylor played their daughter, Kay. Shooting proceeded smoothly. Since Joan's daughter, Diana, had had a proper church wedding à la Kay Banks, her wedding book was used as a touchstone by Minnelli and his crew. Joan was delighted to have the chance to act once more with Tracy, whom she found unchanged professionally from their old days at Fox. He still loved to tease her just as much as he had twenty years earlier, and he still stopped shooting promptly at five o'clock, regardless of the schedule. Joan always dismissed her role in the film ("I thought Spence was great, but I wasn't mad for *my* part"), but she was underestimating her contribution to the picture. She plays off Tracy with understated wit and charm, and together they create a lively performance rhythm; we really do believe that Stanley and Ellie have been married for twenty years. She is warm and affecting in the scene in which Ellie persuades the belligerent Stanley to let Kay have her big wedding. Elsewhere, she uses dry sarcasm to convey Ellie's exasperation with Stanley's excesses, notably in the sequence in which they go to visit the Dunstans, Kay's future in-laws (Billie Burke and Moroni Olsen). Stanley is nervous about the meeting, and tries to discredit the Dunstans before they even pull into the driveway. "I bet they won't even have a drink," he complains. "Well, what if they don't?" she snaps. "You're not an alcoholic, are you?" Joan knew that Tracy was supposed to be the picture's focal point, and merely allowed him to be. While Tracy stole nearly every picture he appeared in by underplaying everyone else, Joan shrewdly manages to underplay *him*.

Around the time *Father of the Bride* wrapped in February 1950, Joan crossed swords with columnist Hedda Hopper. Although she had always enjoyed a congenial relationship with Hopper's rival, Louella Parsons, Joan found Hopper vicious, shallow, and a right-wing hawk, and took great pains to avoid her. In early 1950, Hopper had taken a few jabs at Joan in print during the filming of *Father of the Bride*. She also wrote a column in which she accused Joan's friend Joan Fontaine of exhibitionism at a Hollywood party. When columnist Harry Crocker wrote a piece about the need for high standards in movie industry journalism without naming Hopper specifically, Joan took out full-page advertisements in the Hollywood trade papers around Valentine's Day. She ran Hopper's attack on Fontaine and Crocker's remarks next to each other, had them both outlined with Valentine's hearts, and splashed a large-point headline, "CAN THIS BE YOU, HEDDA?" across the top. But that wasn't enough: she had a live skunk sent to her with a typewritten note attached:

> Be my filthy Valentine
> Little peas in a pod, oh, how divine,
> For just like you, I am 'de trop'
> And also leave a horrible scent wherever I go.

It was considered risky for any star to take on Hopper, who immediately informed her readers that she had dubbed the skunk "Joan" and given it to James and Pamela Mason. Given the returns on *Joan of Arc,* Hopper was surprised that Joan and Walter could afford the ads.

Now that Joan had left her femme fatale period behind, suitable roles were harder to find. But she had heard that the hottest script in town was Joseph L. Mankiewicz's *All About Eve,* soon to be filmed at Twentieth Century–Fox. Joan, who had mostly put her career in the hands of others and never aggressively set her sights on a particular role, had her agent, Jennings Lang, get hold of a copy of the script. Once she read it, she fell in love with the part of Margo Channing, the egocentric stage star who finds her position threatened by an ambitious newcomer, Eve Harrington. Twentieth Century–Fox player Jeanne Crain, originally cast as Eve, had been Diana's matron of honor, and Joan urged Diana to use her influence with Jeanne to try to talk Mankiewicz into giving her the role. The brittle Margo seemed more appropriate for Constance than Joan, but in the end, of course, most appropriate for Bette Davis.

When *Father of the Bride* was released in June 1950, it became one of the popular hits of Joan's career. In July, *Box-Office Digest* reported that the picture had a "very strong" opening and was being held over in nearly every booking. Dorothy Manners, in the *Los Angeles Examiner,* found that Joan "couldn't be more charming in what stacks up as her best performance in several years," while the *Hollywood Citizen-News* wrote, "As the bride's mother, Joan Bennett fills the bill to perfection."

Joan's success in the film didn't do much to help matters at Mapleton Drive, where tensions were building by the week. Most Hollywood producers were constantly tempted by the beautiful women who surrounded them, and Walter was no exception. Shortly after their marriage, Joan had discovered that Walter was being unfaithful to her, but was persuaded by her mother to forgive him. From the start, Walter was grateful to Joan for providing him with a stable and happy home life and two beautiful daughters, but he loved to flirt with the women who crossed his path, and often the flirtations blossomed into casual affairs.

By now, the infidelities were not only on Walter's side. A few years earlier, Joan had become a client of the enormous Music Corporation of America agency, presided over by the shrewd and powerful Jules Stein. Her career had come under the personal direction of one of Stein's top men, Jennings Lang. Stein's faith in Lang was so great that he had put him in charge of MCA's television branch. Lang spent long hours with both Walter and Joan talking to them about the future of television. He was particularly concerned about getting Joan involved in the new medium, since he reasoned that most actresses of her generation could not expect their movie stardom to last long into the 1950s. But, Joan, like many of her contemporaries, was unimpressed with television, and was keen to delay the plunge onto the small screen for as long as possible.

In addition to taking charge of her career, Lang also took a great interest in her personally. His attentions came at a time when she felt she needed them. Walter was away from home a good deal, claiming to be attending production meetings, which frequently turned out to be assignations with other women. When he was on the scene at Mapleton Drive, his mood swings intensified. Having been a leading member of Hollywood's establishment for so long, he found that many in the community viewed him with equal degrees of pity and contempt.

In 1950, Walter turned fifty-six. While he remained in good physical condition, his hair had gone gray and he very much presented the image of a distinguished older man. (Joan was only forty and still extremely glamorous and youthful-looking.) Over the years, few producers had proved more in step with the times than Walter, but it was now clear that his age was working against him in the new Hollywood climate. He was seen by many in the industry as being the product of another era. His enemies continually pointed to *Joan of Arc* as a sign of how out of touch he was with the times. He did not ease gracefully into the role of a Hollywood also-ran, and he began to have outbursts of temper and frustration. As Melinda Markey noted, "He was not someone who wore his heart on his sleeve. Until it was being torn out. And then it was painfully obvious."

It was around the time of Walter's career decline that Joan began her romance with Jennings Lang. In her memoirs, she was discreet: "Suddenly, I was offered the sympathy and gentleness I found lacking at home, and I turned to Jennings more often . . . with feelings that went beyond our business relationship." In fact, they had regular rendezvous, and soon their romance had become a staple of Hollywood gossip. Frequently, Joan would show up at a Hollywood party with another couple; Jennings Lang would also be there, absent his wife, Pam. Before long, the two would make separate exits, presumably to spend the rest of the evening together. The rumors eventually reached Walter, who was enraged by them. It was enough for Joan to be unfaithful—but for her to be deceiving him with her agent seemed a symbol of how his own position had slipped in Hollywood. At Mapleton Drive, there were frequent arguments behind closed doors or at the breakfast table. As Joan later wrote in purple but nonetheless accurate terms, "Daily, the circle of discontent widened between us."

Chapter Nineteen

1951–1952

One of the sobering truths faced by many of the biggest stars of Hollywood's golden age was that their time at the top would not last very long without extraordinary luck or determination. The 1950s were particularly trying times for actresses. A few were lucky: Katharine Hepburn was able to continue finding scripts ideally suited to her eccentric personality. While she never had a good script throughout the 1950s, Joan Crawford was able to preserve the illusion of stardom by means of her legendary determination and hard work. But most came to grief. Except for one final burst of glory with *All About Eve* (1950), Bette Davis's vintage years paralleled the World War II years, 1938–1945. Greer Garson turned up in exhibitors' top-ten lists from 1942 to 1946, but after that, her career lost its momentum. Olivia de Havilland, having struggled to establish herself as a dramatic actress with *To Each His Own* (1946), *The Snake Pit* (1948), and *The Heiress* (1949), abruptly cut back on making films. Ida Lupino alternated movie roles with directing assignments, and Barbara Stanwyck slipped into a string of inferior melodramas and Westerns, while the screen careers of Irene Dunne, Claudette Colbert, and Jean Arthur all ground to a halt. The men were luckier: James Stewart, Humphrey Bogart, Cary Grant, and Spencer Tracy enjoyed some of their greatest successes in the 1950s. The kind of action thrillers and Westerns in which they excelled were not age-dependent genres. Also, audiences had no trouble accepting them opposite younger actresses. Grant benefited from being paired with Grace Kelly, and the same held true for Bogart with Audrey Hepburn, Ava Gardner, and June Allyson.

Hollywood was shedding its skin. By the 1950s, the decline of traditional glamour had begun, done in by the austerity of postwar studio production, and by creative influences such as Italian neorealism and Lee Strasberg's Actor's Studio in New York. The meeting of old and new was perhaps best represented by Stanley Kramer's 1950 drama *The Men,* in which Marlon Brando made his screen debut opposite Teresa Wright. "Brando was wonderful," Wright recalled. "He came across very well. But the film didn't do anything for me. I felt very dissatisfied with my work in it. There was a reality about Brando's performance that was absent from mine."

Late in 1950, Constance returned to Hollywood, again at Darryl Zanuck's invitation, to play a secondary role in the Twentieth Century–Fox comedy *As Young As You Feel.* Monty Woolley and Thelma Ritter headed the cast, but most of the press attention focused on Twentieth's rising young starlet Marilyn Monroe, cast as a dizzy secretary. One day during filming, after watching Monroe saunter across the set, Constance allegedly observed, "There's a broad with a future behind her." There were no offers after that, and she went back to Germany and her "second career" as an officer's wife. If Constance was privately troubled by the fact that Joan had gathered an impressive list of credits during the 1940s, while her own screen career languished, she tried her best never to show it. To her new circle of friends in Europe, she rarely mentioned her movie star past. To all appearances, she needed Hollywood no more than it needed her.

There was no question that she loved John Coulter, but it is probably also true that her marriage to him provided her with a kind of safety net. Given Constance's habit of changing husbands with changing times, Peter Plant found himself wondering if Constance would abandon Coulter after the war ended and marriage to a military officer was no longer fashionable. "If she hadn't stayed with him, I suppose she might have gone after someone with a position like Averell Harriman had—an adviser in the upper levels of government," said Peter. "That would seem to have made sense at that time. But she stayed with Coulter. I think age crept up on her a bit. I think she got stuck and couldn't move forward."

Joan seemed to be in a position of strength as the new decade began: *Father of the Bride* had been one of the top money-making films of 1950, and its 1951 sequel, *Father's Little Dividend,* was also a solid hit. There were plans at MGM for yet a third film, but it never got made, a cause of great relief for Spencer Tracy: "Spence said he didn't want to be another damned Judge Hardy," Joan laughed years later.

Now established as the ideal screen mother, Joan found herself playing mother onstage—to her own daughter. For some time, Melinda had expressed interest in pursuing an acting career. Joan had promised Melinda that as soon as she graduated from Los Angeles's Westlake School for Girls in May 1951, she would appear in a play with her. A few weeks after Melinda's graduation, she made good on her promise. Mother and daughter opened at the La Jolla Playhouse in Rachel Crothers's comedy *Susan and God.* The play had been a successful Broadway vehicle for Gertrude Lawrence in 1937, and now it was becoming a summer stock favorite of actresses looking for an acceptable star vehicle that did not make excessive demands of them. Joan played the vain, self-absorbed socialite Susan Trexel, whose sudden, superficial religious conversion provides her with an excuse for failing to confront the problems that are tearing apart her family. Melinda was cast as Susan's neglected daughter, Blossom. After breaking in the show in La Jolla, Joan and Melinda took it on a highly successful tour of the summer-theater circuit: Princeton, New Jersey; Marblehead, Massachusetts; Ivoryton, Connecticut; and Boston. Joan's weekly guaranteed percentage from the box-office take was $2,000, but in both Princeton and Marblehead she wound up walking away with $4,500. (In Ivoryton, where *Susan and God* broke house records, the following week brought Constance in a touring production of another old Gertrude Lawrence vehicle, *Skylark.*) At various points on the tour, Jennings Lang turned up to be with Joan. Melinda was quite aware that her mother was having a romance with her agent, and although the circumstances made her uncomfortable, Lang always treated her with warmth and affection.

Despite initial nervousness, Joan loved being back in the theater, and told reporters that she hoped to do a Broadway play soon. Buoyed by the success of *Susan and God,* Melinda quickly abandoned any thought of going on to college. She had set her sights on an acting career, and her initial reviews were encouraging. The *New York Post* wrote of the Princeton engagement that while *Susan and God* showed Melinda to be a promising talent, it failed to do much for Joan. The reviewer noted Joan's "ravishing beauty" and "handsome costumes," but said that "one may not always feel compelled to listen." Melinda, on the other hand, seemed "possessed with natural charm and instinctive talent."

The run of *Susan and God* was not a happy time for Joan. During the course of the play, Blossom went from ugly ducking to swan, a transformation that seemed to make Joan uneasy. Melinda had developed early and had already grown into a lovely young woman—one who bore a striking resemblance to the younger Joan. Melinda continued to be the most headstrong of her daughters, and since Joan still worried about her avid interest in boys, there were frequent quarrels. On the subject of sex, Diana Anderson felt, "Mother forgot to look at her own past."

Perhaps because Joan recalled how her father had taken over her life during rehearsals of *Jarnegan* back in 1928, she avoided trying to coach Melinda at home. The only stage wisdom she ever passed on to her daughter was to powder her eyelashes before she put on her mascara. After the *Susan and God* tour, Melinda returned with Joan to Mapleton Drive, but tensions between the two escalated. Eventually it was decided that Melinda would leave home to set out on her career in earnest. At seventeen, she left California for New York and the life of a struggling actress, searching for work in the theater while supporting herself by modeling and filming television commercials.

Each day, Joan had to confront the fact that she and Walter were swimming in debt. The financial independence that she had worked so hard to achieve was in jeopardy. Walter had been unable to repay $178,500 of the Bank of America's production loan on *The Reckless Moment.* Early in January 1951, the bank petitioned the U.S. district court, charging Walter with involuntary bankruptcy. Knowing that the taint of bankruptcy could truly finish him in Hollywood, Walter fought the action, but by August 1951, with no payments having been made, the Bank of America served notice that it would foreclose on the Mapleton Drive house. Because the bank's manager, Mario Giannini, was a personal friend of the Wangers, and a frequent dinner guest, the attempts to attach the house smacked of personal betrayal. (According to Matthew Bernstein, the bank chose to make an example of Walter in part because his liberal background seemed highly suspect as Hollywood's anti-Communist movement gathered steam.) The bank's threat was staved off, but the thought of losing the house hounded Joan throughout the fall.

With Walter bringing in very little money, Joan had to work twice as hard. It wasn't enough, now, to count on the income from two pictures a year. Besides the *Susan and God* tour, she made more and more radio appearances and did frequent product endorsements for newspapers and magazines. Then there was the booming industry of television. Joan didn't think much of the quick-and-dirty nature of television work. The tight production schedules and minimal rehearsals were alien to her; in later years, she would refer to television as "summer stock in an iron lung." Still, she realized that as a source of additional income, it was not to be dismissed. Throughout 1951, Joan appeared in such television programs as *Danger, Somerset Maugham TV Theatre,* and *Nash Airflyte Theatre.* Many of these contracts were negotiated by Jennings Lang.

In 1951, a cross-country coaxial cable did not exist, and most television programs were aired from New York City. As the Wangers' financial difficulties worsened, Lang suggested that a regular television series for Joan might alleviate their money worries. In January 1951, Joan and Walter flew to New York to discuss a proposed deal for a dramatic anthology series, Originals by Bennett. Lang's idea was that she would host and occasionally star in a different dramatic episode each week (this format soon became popular with a number of stars, notably Loretta Young and Jane Wyman). But once it became clear that *Originals by Bennett* would be filmed in New York, Walter flew into a rage. Aware of the rumors about Lang, he perceived the television project as an attempt to isolate Joan from him in New York, where she could pursue her affair more freely than in California. Walter railed and threatened, and negotiations for the series bogged down. Meanwhile, the debts continued to mount.

At this point, Joan was seeing Lang on a regular basis. Those closest to her knew that she never loved him, that he was merely a distraction. She had reached a point in her marriage where she felt vulnerable to outside attentions, and Lang, a seasoned ladies' man, knew how to capitalize on her feelings. By mid-1951, Joan and Lang were having weekly assignations at an apartment at South Bedford Drive in Beverly Hills. The lease on the apartment was held by one of Lang's associates at MCA, Jay Kantor, who was very popular with his agency cronies—he regularly lent the flat to them so they could arrange discreet encounters with a long string of girlfriends. Joan's meetings with Lang were not overly discreet. The apartment-house landlady, Rowena Nate, later recalled that their constant meetings were "the talk of the neighborhood." Later, Kantor's "buddy system" became immortalized on film when Billy Wilder and screenwriter I.A.L. Diamond made it the subject of their 1960 hit comedy, *The Apartment.*

The affair was now widely discussed in Hollywood. "Walter was in a state of denial," remembered Arlene Dahl. "I don't think many women had left him. He didn't particularly relish wearing horns. It became more and more talked about in social circles around Hollywood that he was planning to do something drastic about Jennings Lang, and had talked many times to Jules Stein about getting him fired from the agency."

At home, Walter's mood swings continued. At times he was despondent, unable to believe that after all his years as one of

Hollywood's most influential independent producers, he was suddenly a professional outcast. After Florabel Muir, a reporter for the *Los Angeles Mirror,* ran into him in a drugstore on LaCienega Boulevard in the late fall of 1951, she quoted him as saying, "Hollywood is a strange, cruel place. When you're down on your luck, you run out of friends." At other times, he erupted in rage, often directed at Joan and Lang.

With Walter paying out money on his projects in development and bringing in nothing to speak of, Joan could no longer afford to be at all discriminating when it came to accepting assignments. She snapped up jobs in radio and television as quickly as they were offered. The more money she brought into the household, the more Walter resented it, just as he resented having to rely on Joan for an allowance of five hundred dollars a week. After the Garbo film and *The Ballad and the Source* failed to materialize, several other projects in development fizzled out, and he had been forced to take a producing job at Monogram, one of Hollywood's poverty-row studios. (Its reputation was summed up by a quip Bob Hope made one year at an Academy Awards banquet in the 1940s. Surveying the crowd of Hollywood power brokers, Hope observed that while several of the major studios had a table, Monogram had a stool.) It was humiliating enough for Walter to be employed at Monogram, but to make matters worse, none of the properties he had struggled to develop, even in the studio's bargain-basement format, showed any sign of getting off the ground. At the time, Joan was in the wake of two of her biggest commercial hits, *Father of the Bride* and *Father's Little Dividend,* films that had nothing whatsoever to do with Walter. For fifteen years, he had been regarded as the mastermind behind her career. Now she seemed perfectly capable of going on without him.

On December 13, 1951, Joan drove her kelly green Cadillac convertible to the MCA building in Beverly Hills. There she met Jennings Lang, who drove her, in his car, to what she later referred to as a business lunch, but what was in all likelihood a rendezvous at the apartment. Unfortunately, Walter drove by around 2:30 and saw her car in the MCA lot. When he drove by the lot again one hour later, it was still there. He pulled in and waited for Joan and Lang to appear.

At some point between 5:00 and 5:30, Joan and Lang pulled into the MCA parking lot in Beverly Hills. It was dusk, possibly the reason that Lang and Joan did not see Walter approach them. Lang helped Joan into her car, and stood chatting with her for a few minutes before she started the engine. Suddenly, Joan looked up and saw Walter, "standing not more than a dozen feet away with a gun in his hand." A parking lot attendant, working nearby, later stated that Joan shouted, "Get away from here and leave us alone!" For a few seconds Lang attempted to reason with Walter. "Don't be silly, Walter, don't be silly," he pleaded, putting up his hands to protect himself. Walter fired two shots. The first went wild, grazing Lang's pant leg and bouncing off a fender of the Cadillac. The second ricocheted off the pavement and hit Lang in the groin. He collapsed to the pavement, doubled over in agony.

Walter dropped the gun—a .38-caliber pistol—which Joan picked up and threw in the back seat of her car. (Later, she would not even remember having touched it.) Walter seemed strangely calm, as if he had completed to his satisfaction an ordinary, everyday task. The parking lot attendant came running and immediately drove Joan and Lang to the offices of Lang's personal physician, Dr. Robert Riemer. The doctor immediately placed a call to Midway Hospital, where Lang was rushed into surgery.

Joan could barely absorb what had happened. Walter had always seemed a man of cool intellect and reason, the last person in the world to be governed by his emotions. Now he had degenerated into a gun-toting stalker. He did manage to recover himself quickly. While Joan and Lang were sped to the doctor's offices, Walter waited for the police to turn up and escort him to the police station, which happened to be located directly across the street. His explanation was calmly matter-of-fact: "I've just shot the sonofabitch who tried to break up my home." He was joined at the police station by two attorneys, his good friend Mendel Silberberg and Jerry Giesler, one of Hollywood's top legal minds. Walter was booked on charges of "assault with a deadly weapon with intent to commit murder," a charge that threatened a prison sentence of up to fourteen years. He wound up spending only a single night in jail, since Harold Mirisch, vice president of Monogram, appeared at the station, ready to post the $5,000 bail.

Joan placed a call to her old friend and publicist Maggie Ettinger, who drove immediately to Midway Hospital. C.H. Anderson, the Beverly Hills chief of police, escorted the two women to the police station, where Ettinger waited in the hall while Joan was subjected to aggressive questioning. Her detached and dignified responses baffled Chief Anderson. Joan recalled that after she answered several of Anderson's increasingly rude questions as calmly as she could, he snapped, "You're pretty cool about this, aren't you?" Joan remained stoic. "If Walter thinks there is any romance between us, he is wrong," she told Anderson. Puzzled that she had not broken down in hysterics, he kept pressing harder. But Joan was not about to engage in an emotional outburst for the sake of garnering sympathy, not for Chief Anderson, not for Assistant District Attorney S. Ernest Roll, who questioned her after Anderson had finished, and certainly not for the press, which by now had gathered at the police station, eager to pounce on the most sensational Hollywood scandal in years.

By the time Joan had completed her interview with Roll, reporters were blocking the sidewalk outside the station. Slowly, she made her way through an explosion of flashing cameras and a crowd of outstretched hands and went straight to Maggie Ettinger's house. By now she was showing signs of strain, and was placed under mild sedation. Soon Gene Markey and Ed Maltby, Marge Kelley's husband, arrived and escorted her home to Mapleton Drive.

Jennings Lang's wife, Pam, was notified of the incident while dining at Jane Wyman's house, and rushed to her husband's bedside at Midway Hospital. Diana Anderson was alerted and went immediately to Mapleton Drive. In the face of such a shocking incident, it was initially difficult for her to split her loyalty between her mother and Walter. She told Joan, "I love you both very much and I would walk naked down the street with you if that's what it takes."

For Melinda, in New York, the incident obliterated what should have been a joyous occasion: her television debut on dance star Arthur Murray's program, *The Arthur Murray Party.* After having spent the morning rehearsing for the program, she left for lunch. When she returned the set was swarming with reporters. Once she was informed of what happened, she told the press that she intended to proceed with her performance, but Arthur Murray did not want to have his show tainted by scandal and fired her on the spot.

Joan's sisters rallied. Constance, staying temporarily in New York, telephoned to say she would be there on the next available plane if Joan needed her, but Joan downplayed the scandal and told her there was no need for her to fly to the West Coast. On December 14, however, Barbara flew to Los Angeles from San Francisco, where she was now living, to stand by Joan.

Lang's surgery was successful and he was home recuperating a few days after the incident. Walter had already engaged the formidable Jerry Giesler as his attorney, and Joan realized she would need a representative of comparable stature—someone who had not been associated with the Wangers as a couple. At David O. Selznick's recommendation, she hired the wily Grant Cooper, whose highest-profile case would come in 1969, when he headed up the defense team for Robert Kennedy's assassin, Sirhan Sirhan. Cooper immediately orchestrated a campaign to protect Joan's status as one of Hollywood's leading citizens. He arranged for the press to be invited to a luncheon at her house, where, the rooms spilling over with brightly wrapped Christmas presents, she read a prepared statement:

> I hope that Walter will not be blamed too much. He has been very unhappy and upset for many months because of money worries and because of his present bankruptcy proceedings which threaten to wipe out every penny he ever made during his long and successful career as a producer.

> We have lived together in my Holmby Hills home for some eleven years, with our children who love Walter dearly. Jennings Lang has been my agent and close friend for a long time. Walter and I have been close friends of Jennings and his wife, Pam, and saw them often.
>
> I feel confident that Walter would never have given voice to the suspicions expressed by him in the newspapers were it not for the fact that he has been so mentally upset with the complexities of the financial burden he has been carrying for such a long time.
>
> Knowing Hollywood as I do, knowing how good, wholesome and sincere by far and away a majority of motion picture people are, I want to express my deep regret that this incident will add to the opinions entertained by so many.

Although she was willing to pose for newspaper photos, she declined a reporter's request that she press a lace handkerchief to her eye, and refused to offer any comment apart from the prepared statement.

Initially, it seemed that the scandal might die fairly soon, because Lang made a speedy recovery and chose not to press charges against Walter. But the newspapers were not about to let go of the incident, which was a front-page story across the country for weeks. Much to Joan's surprise, many reporters were eager to paint her as the villain of the piece. Suddenly, she was the adulterous wife who had driven her cuckolded husband to shoot his rival. Many in the film community saw it that way, too. The fact that Walter had pulled the trigger seemed immaterial, and there was an unexpected groundswell of sympathy for him from many of his colleagues. After he was indicted as charged on December 18, a group of important producers, including Walt Disney, Spyros Skouras, and Samuel Goldwyn, banded together to help him with legal expenses. There was no question about how they chose to delegate blame for the incident—Joan's place was by her husband, especially given the difficult time he had been having in the industry for the past few years. Hollywood was notorious for short memories and fleeting loyalties, and several of his staunchest defenders willingly forgot that only months before, they had been crossing the street to avoid him.

For a movie star embroiled in scandal, Joan had one overwhelming handicap: she was not a fresh, rising talent in whom producers had a hefty investment for the future. She was an actress over forty who had worked in films for twenty-two years. Had she been under contract to a major studio, she might have been guaranteed a certain amount of protection. But she was a freelance actress—the easiest kind to write off. Maggie Ettinger tried to help, but there was little she could do. In the best of times, Joan had maintained a guarded view of Hollywood reporters, but she was shocked by the ferocity with which they turned on her. In the days immediately following the shooting, a crowd of reporters waited to spring on anyone who stepped out the front door of Mapleton Drive. Day after day, the press rehashed her marital history, and even dredged up her tempestuous romance with John Considine. Several newspapers ran photos of Joan in *The Macomber Affair,* glaring contemptuously at Robert Preston as her cowed husband. The *Los Angeles Daily Mirror* stooped lowest when it reprinted a section from *How to Be Attractive* under the headline "Joan Bennett's Advice on Men." The newspapers mentioned nothing about Walter's reputation as a womanizer, and Joan kept quiet on the matter as well, since to raise it would have been viewed by many as reckless finger-pointing. Only a few members of the Hollywood press were objective or sympathetic, notably Louella Parsons, who wrote, "I think it so typical of Joan, whom I have known since she was a little girl, that she thought nothing of her own anguish in all this uncomfortable publicity. She was concerned only about Walter. . . ."

She did receive a good deal of personal support. One of the first to respond was Joan's Holmby Hills neighbor Lana Turner. Although the two women had never been close, Turner telephoned and asked if there was anything she could do to help. And her closest friends, Maggie Ettinger, Marge Kelley, Frances Brody, Muriel Finney, James and Pamela Mason, and Humphrey Bogart and Lauren Bacall, were there for her to lean on. But offers of work came to a halt. Joan waited and waited for an offer of a new film or television play, anything that would help distract her from the chaos that had suddenly overtaken her life, but the weeks rolled by and no offers were forthcoming. She was particularly concerned that her two youngest children be protected from the scandal. Early each morning, she ran out onto the lawn to collect the newspapers so Stephanie would not see them. She was able to rely on her own formidable self-discipline, and spent her days supervising the housekeeping, preparing for the Christmas holidays, trying to behave as if nothing had changed.

Walter was with the family for Christmas. "It could have been horrible," remembered Diana, "but Mother was so sweet to Walter. She was as tolerant and nice as she could be under the circumstances. But obviously, she was nervous. I remember that she had only half her lipstick on. She'd forgotten to put on the rest of it, and none of us wanted to say anything."

Christmas was one thing, but having Walter under the same roof permanently was another. He moved out of the house, staying for a time with their good friends Edward Lasker and Jane Greer. "He would come and sit in our parlor," recalled Greer, "and read the newspapers. He was a celebrity all over again. It was almost as if he were reading his own obituary. He used to get the papers and talk to us about them; he'd say, 'Look what they say here.'" Joan explained his absence to Stephanie and Shelley by telling them that Walter was ill and would be home when he recovered.

On December 18, after hearing two hours of evidence, a jury indicted Walter on a charge of assault with a deadly weapon with intent to commit murder. A few weeks later, on January 7, 1952, Giesler entered a double plea of not guilty and not guilty by reason of temporary insanity on Walter's behalf. A trial date was set in Santa Monica Superior Court for February 26, then postponed. Subsequently, Giesler persuaded Walter to waive the trial and plead guilty to a charge of "assault with a deadly weapon." (Giesler announced that Walter had decided against jury trial "first, because of his children and second, in consideration of the film industry.") On April 22, Joan listened in the courtroom as Judge Harry J. Borde of the Santa Monica Superior Court sentenced Walter to four months in the Wayside Honor Farm in Castaic, California, north of Los Angeles.

His prison sentence began on June 4. For most of his term, he served as head of the prison library. Joan did not visit him. She had a good excuse: Walter's sentence had coincided with an offer for her to succeed Rosalind Russell in the national company of John Van Druten's hit comedy *Bell, Book, and Candle.* She was to play Gillian Holroyd, a modern-day witch living in Greenwich Village with designs on an attractive publisher (played by Zachary Scott). After a few months of professional isolation, Joan's situation had grown desperate, and the offer was beautifully timed. Unlike radio and television, the stage had never been a merchant-controlled medium, and she would not have to face a sponsor who objected to her image as a dangerous woman.

Diana Anderson visited Walter at Wayside on two occasions. On her first trip, Walter refused to see her, but when she returned, accompanied by his great friend Dana Tasker, an editor at *Time,* she was given a tour of the facilities. To Diana, Walter looked elegant, even in his prison uniform.

After two months at Wayside, Walter appealed for parole, citing the financial hardship his incarceration was causing himself and others. On August 1, parole was denied. His prison term ended slightly ahead of schedule, on September 13. All told, he had been at Wayside for 102 days. On the day of his release, only his secretary, Rita O'Neil, was there to greet him. Immediately, he deflected queries about his reconciliation with Joan by railing against the U.S. penal system. "The public should start cleaning up corruption right here in the Los Angeles County Jail," he fumed, denouncing the prison system as "the nation's number one scandal."

In the wake of the failure of *Joan of Arc,* Walter had been generally regarded as an outcast, as an independent who had gambled far beyond his means, lost, and was not to be trusted with an important project. Now he had to wonder whether or not he faced complete professional oblivion.

The tour of *Bell, Book, and Candle* had provided Joan with a welcome opportunity to get out of town until the scandal had lost some momentum. A few weeks before the May 5 opening in Chicago, Diana Anderson and Walter had driven her to Los Angeles International Airport to see her off. A number of reporters had gathered. While being interviewed, Joan noticed a ladybug crawling up a reporter's coat and asked to have it. "It's good luck," she said. "I could use some."

By the time Joan and Zachary Scott joined the company of *Bell, Book, and Candle*, the play had already enjoyed several successful weeks in town at the Great Northern Theater, with Rosalind Russell and Dennis Price. With the cast change, the play moved to the more intimate Selwyn Theater. The Chicago critics came to see it again and gave it excellent notices. The box office picked up and it ran for eleven weeks. All in all, it was not a bad summer: the play's success gave her a much-needed boost, she got along well with Zachary Scott, and she was delighted to have Stephanie and Shelley with her for an extended period. They stayed at the luxurious Ambassador East Hotel, and Stephanie spent much of her time at Lake Shore Day Camp while Shelley was looked after by a nurse. On Stephanie's ninth birthday, Joan took her to Marshall Field and told her she could choose her own outfit, which turned out to be a purple checked blouse, purple skirt, and purple shoes. It was far from what Joan would have chosen for her, but she went along with it, and Stephanie remembered the shopping trip as a sign that her mother was beginning to relax a bit after the tremendous strain of the past few months.

On tour, Stephanie and Shelley's lives were as orderly as they had been in Los Angeles. They still had to rise at seven in the morning, brush their teeth, and keep to a strict daily schedule. Stephanie recalled that the experience of going on the road with *Bell, Book, and Candle* "filled me with an everlasting loathing for summer theater. But it was also a wonderful time. In Chicago, if people knew what had happened with the shooting, they didn't indicate that they did. One didn't have the sense that Mother was always having a wonderful time afterward. But she was taking a pragmatic view of what was going to be her life for a few years."

During the early weeks of the Chicago run, Joan experienced extreme stage fright, to the point that her hands would break out in tiny red spots. But she faced the nightly terror of a live audience with unyielding discipline. At one point, she came down with a severe cold. Her sore throat made it painful to speak, but she refused to cancel, and each evening a doctor was sent to her dressing room to paint her throat with gentian violet so she could get through the performance.

By the time Walter was released from Wayside, *Bell, Book, and Candle* had moved west. Soon after his release, she finished the play's run in Portland, Oregon, and returned briefly to Los Angeles before rejoining the company at the next stop. After a long, private talk with Walter, she agreed to let him stay on at Mapleton Drive until the tour had ended—but she made it clear that from her point of view, the marriage was all but finished.

For the girls, the scandal would have its repercussions for some years to come. Prior to the shooting, Stephanie had been enrolled in Los Angeles's exclusive Westlake School. When Joan returned to Los Angeles during the brief break in the tour, she was informed by the headmistress of Westlake that Stephanie would not be readmitted, since it would be unadvisable for the school to be connected in any way with the scandal. That fall, Joan enrolled Stephanie in the Arizona Desert School, and Shelley continued to tour with her. She was forced to cut back on the staff while Walter was staying on at Mapleton Drive.

On September 20, 1952, *Bell, Book, and Candle* opened its Los Angeles run at the Biltmore Theater. William Windom, who played the heroine's warlock brother, remembered, "Joan was terrified when we played L.A. She didn't want to do it at all." But he recalled her as a wonderful colleague. "Zachary Scott played the movie star too much to suit me. Joan did not. When Roz Russell and Dennis Price left, a little spark went out of the show, because

Roz was such a dynamo. But Joan had a darker quality, a more witchlike quality than Roz. If you want a witch, Joan did it better." (Joan's fears about the Los Angeles opening turned out to be justified, since receipts there were among the lowest on the tour.)

Work on *Bell, Book, and Candle* grew harder. After the company finished playing California in the fall of 1952, the tour schedule became heavily dotted with one-night stands. On October 22, while in Colorado Springs, on her way to the play's Denver opening, Joan was notified of the sudden death of Jennings Lang's wife, Pam. Mrs. Lang had suffered from angina and a thyroid condition for years, but her death still came as a shock to those who knew her. Asked for a comment by the press, Joan could say only, "I'm sorry. I'm so sorry."

Diana Anderson felt that privately, Joan suffered feelings of extreme guilt. She probably couldn't help but think back to the time, only a few years earlier, when her life with Walter had been filled with success and the promise of more. Now what had seemed unassailable was lost, her children's secure and comfortable lives disrupted. The only answer was to keep working and hope that someday she would be able to put the past behind her.

By 1951, Addison Randall had been dead for six years, and Barbara had drifted from one menial job to the next. Through Walter's connections, she did manage to find a position that she enjoyed, as reference librarian for radio station KCBS in San Francisco. It was a new start in a new city, but the loneliness that had haunted her in New York remained a force to contend with. In August 1951, she visited her fifteen-year-old son Anthony, who was attending a summer camp in Maine. Of all the children, Anthony had always been a particular favorite of hers, and when she arrived in Maine she was alarmed to find him ill and run-down. Convinced that he needed the care of a proper doctor, she removed him from the camp and took him to New York, where the two of them moved in temporarily with a friend of hers, Mrs. Charles C. Nash.

It took Morton very little time to intervene. The law was on his side, so Anthony was promptly returned to Helen Downey's care in Wallingford. But the brief period of contact with her son had left Barbara determined to make a serious stab at rehabilitating herself. That fall, she launched an attempt to gain partial custody of the four younger children. Joan provided financial support for the court battle, which she later recalled "did little to endear me to Morton."

The case was heard in a series of private sessions in Superior Court in Bridgeport, Connecticut. Judge John T. Cullinan threw out Morton's request that Barbara be held in contempt of court for stealing Anthony away from Maine during the previous summer. But he also denied her motion for shared custody on the grounds that the children had received "excellent care" from Helen Downey for the past ten years and that it would be unadvisable to disrupt the stability of the Wallingford household. Cullinan also felt that to grant Barbara any degree of custody ran the risk of provoking "a child-parent relationship marred by discord and strife." He commended Barbara for triumphing over her difficulties—perhaps Morton's side had not prepared a very effective case—and hoped the children would always treat her as their natural mother and spend as much time as possible with her. But the hoped-for outcome "must be accomplished through the free choice of the children rather than by judicial decree."

To anyone who asked her, Constance claimed not to miss Hollywood at all, and continued to be absorbed in her new role as an officer's wife. When she was out at dinner or a cocktail party, she could give the appearance of being quite submissive to John. But to those living under the same roof with her in Wiesbaden, her authority as head of the household was unquestioned. She never wavered in her conviction that she knew what was best for her children, no matter what the results were.

In *Mommie Dearest,* the 1981 screen version of Christina Crawford's scathing memoir of her mother, Joan Crawford, there is a scene of the young Christina sitting in her bedroom on her birthday, surrounded by lavish gifts, including an expensive-looking doll. "Christina, is that the present you like best?" her mother asks. When Christina says yes, her mother replies, "Then that is the one you can keep. We'll take the rest to the orphans who don't have anything."

There was a similar scene in the Coulter household during one Christmas in Wiesbaden. Patricia and Gyl had each been given a new scooter, a model that was exceptionally popular at the time. Once all the presents were opened, Constance turned to Patricia and asked her, "Well, Patricia, what is your favorite gift?" Patricia named the scooter. Not far from the house was an orphanage. "Well, that's going to go to the orphanage," Constance declared. When she posed the same question to Gyl, the child quickly named another toy. No doubt Constance was motivated by her concern that the children not grow up to become over-indulged show business brats. Years later, Gyl felt sure that Constance had heard about Joan Crawford's holiday ambush, and performed her own variation on it.

For a person who in most respects lived in the present, Constance showed great reluctance to accept the passage of time where her daughters were concerned. By 1951, Lorinda was thirteen, yet Constance continued to dress her in little-girl pinafores. Often she would have matching dresses made for herself, Lorinda, and Gyl. With Lorinda, she was candid about her reasons: "Lorrie," she once said, "watching you get older makes *me* feel old."

Yet given her strict ideas about parenting, Peter, Lorinda, and Gyl came, to varying degrees, to regard her toughness and sense of order and discipline as virtues. She constantly tried to teach them the importance of loyalty, integrity, and honesty. "My personal feeling is that Mummy should never have been a mother," said Lorinda. "But she was one hell of a woman. I am very happy that Mummy was this fantastic woman: intelligent, great sense of humor, full of all kinds of wonderful things. Someone I respected so much as a person. I much prefer that she was someone like that than a 'good mother.'"

By mid-1951, Coulter had completed his assignment in Germany and the family packed up and moved back to the States. For a brief time he was stationed in Montgomery, Alabama, then in Arlington, Virginia. Constance had been a remarkably good sport about her European jaunt, but she did worry that being away for so long had made the film industry forget about her altogether. As always, she did not miss Hollywood itself, but only the money it could provide.

Constance found life in suburban Virginia dull and stifling. The fawning attention of the other officer's wives, thrilled to have a movie star in their midst, had begun to irritate her. At home, she began to pressure John to get an assignment somewhere nearer the center of things.

In mid-1952, Peter Plant finished his tour of active duty with the Strategic Air Command and came home to California. He had been told that the money in his trust fund had been quietly appreciating, and he looked forward to using it to launch his new life. Already it had provided him with a first-class education at Dartmouth and the University of Neuchâtel. The remaining amount in his trust fund did not represent even a shadow of the Plant fortune, but it was a respectable nest egg—around $300,000—for a young man about to strike out on his own in the early 1950s.

He made an appointment to see Constance's business manager, Rex Cole, in Hollywood. Over the course of twenty minutes, he learned that the trust had been emptied and closed. He walked out, unable to speak. He returned to the small apartment he had rented and sat staring at the carpet. Suddenly he began to laugh—its color was the exact shade of green as that on the back side of a dollar bill. After a bit, he gathered himself and spent the evening planning his next move; his upbringing and education were about to come into play.

Peter's shock did not prevent him from absorbing the truth of the situation, that Constance and Coulter had been siphoning off his money for years. He contacted the law firm of Schwartz and Frohlich in Manhattan and demanded copies of all financial records relating to the trust. It was soon revealed that Constance and Coulter had used the money to pay off numerous personal obligations, but they had also lied outright about the purpose of a number of withdrawals from the account. Several sizeable checks were earmarked to pay for special tutoring sessions for Peter by Coulter's mother, Elonia Hobson, a simple Mississippi woman who lived with the family from time to time. The tutoring sessions, of course, had never taken place—Peter wasn't even in California at the time—but Coulter had stood by and allowed Constance to bleed the account dry year after year. Unable to persuade Constance that it was essential that they live within their limited means, Coulter took the easy way out and let her have her way.

Probably Constance, who made up her own rules as she went along, intended to replace the money in due time. In the 1940s, she had frantically tried to put together one production deal after another to reactivate her flagging career. But nothing worked, and by the time she left for Germany her days of screen stardom were permanently behind her. By the early 1950s, she had gone too far. Replacing the money was an impossibility, and she was forced to wait for Peter to discover her theft and see what his reaction would be. Probably she was able to delude herself into thinking that he would be understanding and forgiving. He was not, but he did not confront her angrily, either. Instead, he kept a cool head. Remembering her around the poker table at Carolwood Drive, he decided to borrow a trick out of her book and run a bluff.

He instructed his attorney, Ernest Zack, to draw up papers filing a multimillion-dollar lawsuit against Constance and Coulter. Accompanying the papers was a letter of transmittal, telling the Coulters that unless they signed over a deed to the Summit Drive house, he would proceed with the suit. In a short time, the Coulters complied, and ownership of the house passed to Peter—although it was small compensation for what he had lost.

Constance apparently felt no great degree of remorse over swindling her own son. Privately, she may well have been livid that Peter had managed to wrest the Summit Drive house away from her. Winning had been a way of life for Constance for so long that it was impossible for her to imagine any other. She couldn't bear to think that her own son had forced her hand, and she shut him out of her life. For the next several years, she would refer to Peter only as "Unmentionable."

Chapter Twenty

1953–1958

By early 1953, the Coulters had been transferred to Washington, D.C., where John was to work on the Armed Forces Special Weapons Project. They rented a three-story brick townhouse at 1513 Northwest Thirtieth Street in the affluent Georgetown neighborhood. After the years of relative isolation in Germany, Constance was thrilled to be living in Washington. Whatever her shortcomings as a mother, she had always had a gift for friendship, and in Washington she enjoyed a busy social life. One of her constant companions was Louise Gore, a bright, witty hotelier several years younger than Constance. Louise had been born into politics: although she was a first cousin of Albert Gore Sr., the Democratic senator from Tennessee, she was a staunch Republican who worked tirelessly for the party. Eventually, she would win a seat in the Maryland State Senate, serve as Richard M. Nixon's United Nations delegate to Paris, and run for Maryland governor in 1974. Once Louise discovered Constance's strong Republican ties, she called on her to appear at party functions. Constance's experience during World War II bond drives had made her a seasoned and effective public speaker, and she was often tapped to address the Federation of Republican Women.

After twenty years of the Democrats riding high, the Republican party had been launched on a remarkable comeback by Dwight D. Eisenhower's 1952 presidential victory. For the first time in years, Constance was on the winning side, and she reveled in it. Spurred on by Cold War tensions and Sen. Joseph McCarthy's anti-Communist crusade, a new wave of conservatism had engulfed the country. Constance and Louise had frequent discussions about "beating the bastards"—and the "bastards" they were talking about weren't the Democrats, but the liberal Republicans whom they felt were holding the party back from achieving its true potential.

Constance became a core member of a group of Washington conservatives that included Barry Goldwater, who in 1952 narrowly defeated Ernest W. MacFarland for Arizona's U.S. Senate post. In a few years, thanks to his vocal criticism of Eisenhower's budgetary practices, he would become one of the Senate's most articulate conservative voices. In 1960, Goldwater would publish *The Conscience of a Conservative,* a highly persuasive statement of conservative ideology. Louise Gore remembered Constance reading aloud from the book "in that great voice of hers. You could have heard a pin drop. First of all, it was her voice reading it. Secondly, it was what all of us wanted to hear. It gave all of us conservatives a new lease on life, the feeling that there was a place to go."

In Washington, Constance revived her passion for playing poker. Her new card-playing cronies included Louise Gore and her frequent escort, public-relations executive Jon Jonkel, Bazey Tankersley, publisher of the *Miami Times-Herald,* the *New York Daily News,* and other major newspapers, Idaho Republican senator Herman Welker, Larry and Charlotte Spivak, Barry and Peggy Goldwater, and Alice Roosevelt Longworth, the tart-tongued daughter of Theodore Roosevelt. Occasionally they would admit a neophyte like Louise's longtime friend socialite Anne Slater, who remembered Constance's patience in teaching her the fine points of poker. The entire group reveled in Constance's wit, energy, and high spirits. Constance relished her friendship with all of them, and had a particular fondness, bordering on hero worship, for Alice Longworth. Famous for her sharp wit and her ability to decimate those she deemed unworthy of her attention, Longworth earned Constance's everlasting respect. Lorinda remembered that Alice Longworth was the only person she could ever recall who visibly intimidated her mother.

Another prominent figure who became part of Constance's poker-playing set was Sen. Joseph McCarthy. Although Constance did not support many of his crude Red-baiting tactics—in fact, some of her own World War II charity work had caused her to be investigated by the FBI—her loyalty to the Republican party prevented her from criticizing him. She attended sessions of the House Committee on Un-American Activities but never commented publicly on McCarthy's methods. It was typical, thought Louise Gore, that "with Constance, the point was always to talk in favor." Nevertheless, many columnists and editorial page writers incurred her wrath. Most of them wrote for the *New York Times,* whose liberal outlook Constance despised. Gore recalled that once, when Constance was appearing in a summer stock production of Samuel Taylor's comedy *Sabrina Fair,* she came offstage, jumped instantly out of character, and began to rail about an editorial piece in that morning's *Times.*

By April 1953, Constance had gained enough experience touring on stage that she decided to take a gamble on Broadway. The thought of appearing on the New York stage had always filled her with dread, but once again money was her motive. Her vehicle was George Batson's *A Date with April,* a flimsy romantic comedy about a glamorous composer and concert pianist who engineers a scheme to marry her longtime lover, a Hemingway-style author and big-game hunter.

During the previous summer, Constance had successfully toured with the play (then titled *I Found April*) on the summer stock circuit. By the late 1940s, many of the sound era's fading stars had found a new lease on life by touring in stock. Often they found the conditions primitive, certainly compared to what they had been accustomed to in Hollywood. A national company tour, such as Joan's *Bell, Book, and Candle,* was deluxe compared to the average stock engagement.

But in other ways, a job in stock could be attractive to an actor who had lost his Hollywood contract. If they were able to arrange the right combination of salary and percentage of the box-office take, actors with Constance's kind of name value could do very well for themselves. The theaters themselves were often quite small, with under five hundred seats. Often they were converted barns, whose wood produced a flattering acoustic, and made the whole experience much less daunting for a film actor without proper stage technique. (Lillian Gish once joked, "They ran the cows out of the barn and then they let in the actors.") Audiences flocked to see their favorite stars, and reviewers were on the generous side: what most people wanted to see was how well Paulette Goddard or Joan Fontaine or Kay Francis were holding up after all their years in Hollywood.

A Date with April might have been acceptable summer-theater fare, but it was sadly out of place on Broadway. When it opened at the Royale Theater on April 15, 1953, the *New York Times* dismissed it as "one of those popular little comedies which, while meaning no offense to anyone, simply weighs itself down with dullness." In the *New Yorker,* Woolcott Gibbs observed, "Miss Bennett, who hadn't much to do, except change her clothes and pretend to be banging away at the piano, looked very handsome and self-possessed, and even gave some indication that she is quite capable of playing comedy, in the event that she ever gets the chance." After thirteen performances, Broadway broke its date with *April.*

The play's failure made Constance twice as determined to find something that would succeed. She may not have possessed a towering intellect, but she was blessed with an active mind and boundless energy. "She wasn't as active in films as she wanted to be," recalled her poker-playing chum Bazey Tankersley. "It was an awkward thing for her to be in Washington, because she was not much of a novelty in Washington. There were lots of important people, in government and diplomacy, and John was not that high up in the military for him to be important." Constance spent a good deal of time trying to influence military kingmakers to promote John to general, but no matter how hard she tried, his career seemed stalled. This may well have been, as Peter Plant believed, because John had chosen to remain stateside during the war rather than serve overseas. "He was offered a key position by Curtis LeMay, when LeMay was in charge of the Twentieth Air Force in the Pacific Theater. But

Constance with her attorney, Francis McGuire, in New London, Connecticut, during the hearing to determine her son Peter's claim to the Plant fortune. (International News Photos/ Photofest)

Peter Plant and Constance in happy times. (Diana Anderson Collection)

Richard in Welles's *Journey into Fear.* In this, his final role, he had no lines. (Photofest)

Constance, Joan, and Walter leaving Richard's funeral at the All Saints' Episcopal Church in Beverly Hills, October 24, 1944. (ACME/Photofest)

Joan as the enigmatic artist's model and Edward G. Robinson as the hapless professor in Fritz Lang's *The Woman in the Window* (1944). (Photofest)

Joan in the formal dining room at Mapleton Drive, 1947. (Universal-International/Photofest)

Above, 1945: Joan and Fritz Lang on the set of *Scarlet Street,* the high-water mark of their partnership. (Photofest) *Below,* 1947: A tense moment during *Secret Beyond the Door,* the disaster that ended their working relationship. (Photofest)

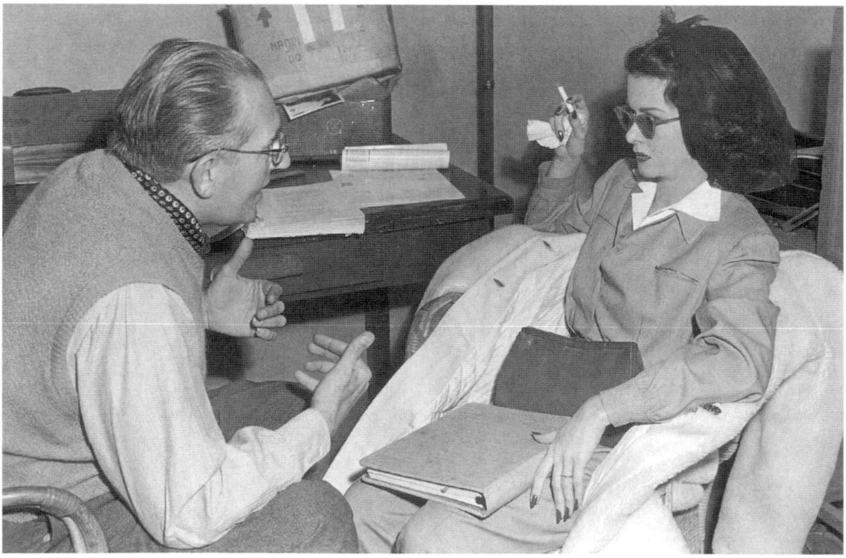

Above, Constance with Peter Plant at his 1947 graduation from Culver Military Academy. (Courtesy of Peter Bennett Plant) *Below,* Lorinda and Gyl Roland, mid-1940s. (Courtesy of Lorinda Roland)

Joan with Diana, Stephanie, and Melinda in 1947. (Universal-International/Photofest)

Joan as the duplicitous Margot in *The Macomber Affair* (1947), with Robert Preston and Gregory Peck. (Wisconsin Center for Film and Theater Research, Image WCFTR-2299)

Joan's finest screen performance—Lucia Harper in Max Ophuls's *The Reckless Moment* (1949). (Author's collection)

Mother's Day on the set of *Father of the Bride* (1950): Joan, Shelley, and Stephanie. (International News Photos/ Photofest)

Joan leaving the Beverly Hills police station after Walter's arrest for the shooting of Jennings Lang—the biggest Hollywood scandal of the early 1950s. (ACME/ Photofest)

Joan's return to the stage in *Bell, Book, and Candle,* with Zachary Scott. (Wisconsin Center for Film and Theater Research, Image WCFTR-2293)

Joan with Stephanie and Shelley in the early 1950s. (Diana Anderson Collection/John Engstead)

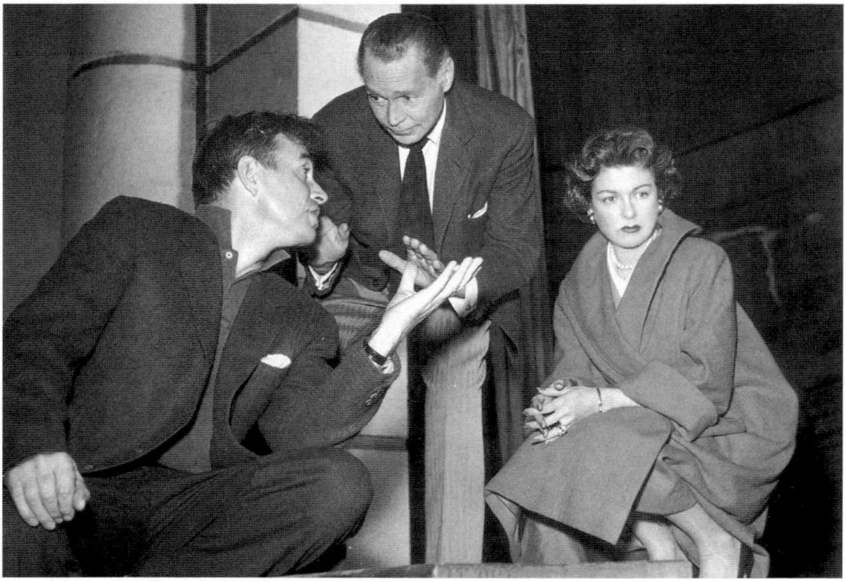

James Mason, Franchot Tone, and Joan rehearsing for *Playhouse 90*'s "The Thundering Wave," directed by John Frankenheimer. (CBS Television/Photofest)

Constance, on the road in *Auntie Mame*. (Wisconsin Center for Film and Theater Research, Image WCFTR-2297)

Above, Joan with Donald Cook in the 1958 Broadway comedy *Love Me Little*; she later told friends that its failure left her "bloody but unbowed." (Friedman-Abeles/Photofest) *Below,* Hollywood reunion: Constance at a party with Myrna Loy (left) and Bette Davis (center) in the early 1960s. (Friedman-Abeles/John Springer Collection)

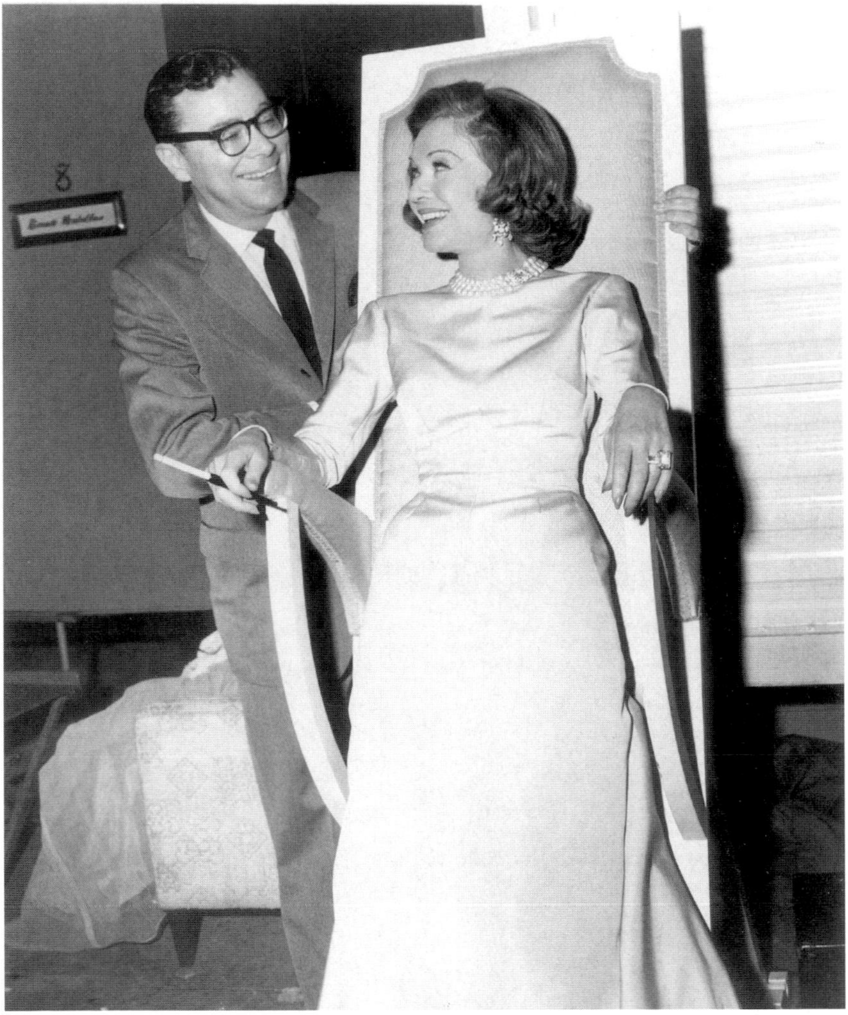

Constance with producer Ross Hunter on the set of her last film, *Madame X* (1966). (Universal/Photofest)

Constance and her fifth husband, John Coulter, shortly before her death in 1965. (Photofest)

Melinda, Joan, and Diana, 1960s. (Diana Anderson Collection)

Joan as Judith Collins, one of several roles she played in ABC-TV's *Dark Shadows.* (Courtesy of Dan Curtis Productions)

Joan with her fourth husband, David Wilde (left), and film historian Ronald L. Bowers at the first annual D.W. Griffith Awards, New York City, 1980. (Susan Frelinghuysen/Courtesy of Ronald L. Bowers)

he preferred to stay in the United States, taking an assignment setting up reserve units for after the war, so he could live in Beverly Hills with my mother. An officer cannot decline combat and expect promotions in the future."

If Constance couldn't propel John forward in the military, she had just as much difficulty developing a substantial outlet for her own talents. For a time, she thought she had found it in the Carter-Barron Amphitheater, a four thousand–seat outdoor arena in Washington's Rock Creek Park. The theater, owned by the Department of the Interior, had not been used for some time, and Constance and Tankersley hatched the idea that it would make an ideal venue for summer musical productions. They leased it from the government and assembled a consortium of investors, including several of their close friends. Constance served as the principal hands-on producer, and busied herself lining up the talent from New York and elsewhere. Her maiden season was ambitious: *The Merry Widow, Show Boat, Carousel, Of Thee I Sing,* and *Kiss Me Kate.*

Constance didn't appear onstage, but she was a star presence nonetheless. The distinguished actor and director Charles Nelson Reilly recalled an incident that took place at a stage rehearsal just hours before the opening of *The Merry Widow,* starring Irra Pettina. That summer, Reilly was in the early stages of his career, playing small parts in each of the Carter-Barron productions. At *The Merry Widow* rehearsal, Reilly suddenly spotted Constance approaching from the back of the arena. "She was walking slowly toward us," he remembered, "wearing a knee-length dress that was unbelievable. Gorgeous. And it mesmerized the eighty or ninety people in the cast standing on the stage. We all watched her move toward us, this dress swinging back and forth like a bell. And she got up on the stage and she said one word: 'Mainbocher.'"

The Carter-Barron turned out to be another disaster. Washington had its rainiest summer in years, and night after night, performances had to be canceled. Constance and Tankersley had roped Louise Gore into serving as an officer in their newly formed company, and several times a week Gore had the unenviable task of driving from her Washington home to Rock Creek Park to post the night's closing notice. Sometimes the rain would let up enough for the performance to begin, only to return full force, and the show would have to be abandoned halfway through. Often, when Gore walked onstage to announce a cancellation, the audience booed and threw things at her. Soon she grew so disgusted with this part of her duties that she refused to continue, and insisted that Constance take her place. This appeased the audience somewhat—at least they got to see an authentic movie star deliver the bad news. But after a couple of shaky seasons, the Carter-Barron was a part of Constance's past.

At home, she kept as close an eye on her daughters as possible. Gyl's academic performance had not improved over the years, and Constance was forever out of patience with her. Unable to tolerate weakness in anyone, she could not understand how any daughter of hers could be making such a poor showing in school. "I was a terrible student," admitted Gyl. "*Terrible.* I was thoroughly convinced that I was stupid, and I think she was convinced that I was, too. I don't think that she ever thought that she had anything to do with that. She probably thought that I was some throwback to the Gilbert side, or something." She was much more at ease around Lorinda, who in recent years had discovered what would turn out to be her life's work. It had begun one day around the pool at the home of Louise Gore's parents in Potomac, Maryland. Some of Louise's nieces and nephews had been playing with some clay, and left it behind. Lorinda sat down and began to work the clay into the shape of a bird, then a tree. Lorinda had always been a bright but undisciplined student; soon she was studying art with an earnestness and dedication that amazed Constance. In the years to come, as Lorinda settled down to become a serious artist, her relationship with her mother grew more loving and serene than ever.

Patricia Coulter continued to divide her time between her father and Constance and her mother in Louisiana. Constance continued to be as strict with Patricia as if she were her own child, constantly monitoring her appearance and social graces. "I remember Mother sending me some party dresses," Patricia recalled, "and Constance took me down to the furnace in Washington and made me throw the dresses in. She said they were common and cheap." When Patricia complained to her mother about the treatment she received from Constance, Mrs. Coulter said, "Think of the places you will go and the people you will meet. You will thank me later on."

Privately, Constance fretted over her estrangement from Peter, anxious that the situation had spun so far out of control. She did not blame herself entirely; in her view, the blame largely rested at the feet of the foolish movie producers who refused to hire such a capable and reliable actress. But Constance was also making some effort to change. She had always been hard-working and energetic, but over the past decade her fading fortunes had wreaked havoc on her nerves. No longer a soignée movie star who exerted her will casually and recklessly, with no thought of the consequences, she was now an over-the-hill actress, worried about the limitations that age would impose. Occasionally, her nervous condition led her to seek medical attention. One doctor in Washington recommended a drink at night, which she hated—possibly because she feared the streak of alcoholism that ran in the family. "Her idea of a hard drink was a grasshopper—crème de cacao and crème de menthe," Lorinda laughed. "I would mix a drink for her—say grapefruit juice and vodka, and she would say, 'That's enough! That's enough!' She didn't even want an *ounce* of vodka." In time, she grew concerned that her recurring anxiety had made her too negative-minded, and she began a deeper exploration of Christian Science. She never became a fanatic about it; rather, she seems to have used the religion as a kind of twelve-step program for overcoming some of her fears.

Constance's principal show business activity in 1954 was limited to a tour of solo dramatic readings on the college circuit and a cameo appearance as herself in her old friend George Cukor's screen comedy *It Should Happen to You,* starring Judy Holliday. Late the following year, the Coulters left Georgetown for New York, where they took up residence in a rambling, ten-room apartment at 1155 Park Avenue. Patricia Coulter was living with them, and both she and Gyl were enrolled at Miss Hewitt's, an exclusive private school on Manhattan's Upper East Side. By now Lorinda had entered Wheaton College in Norton, Massachusetts, as an art major. All of this was expensive, and Coulter worried how they would be able to continue. Peter's money was no longer there to be relied on, and their substantial investment in the Carter-Barron Amphitheater was gone forever, but Constance seemed unwilling to live within their means.

Patricia and Gyl, now in their teens, were still dressed in pinafores and Mary Janes, while all their friends were wearing poodle skirts and bobby sox. Constance continued to dodge the subject of her own age whenever possible. Patricia remembered a shopping trip to Bloomingdale's, when a clerk requested identification and Constance haughtily replied, "My dear, my *face* is my identification."

Occasionally, Coulter's mother, Elonia Hobson, made the trip north from Nettleton, Mississippi, to stay with the family, often to look after the girls while Coulter and Constance were away. From the beginning, there had been little love lost between Constance and her mother-in-law, a genteel, conservative, deeply religious woman from Mississippi with decidedly mixed feelings about her son having married an actress. Mrs. Hobson was particularly out of her element in New York, which she regarded as the most sinful of cities, and seldom ventured out of the apartment for any length of time. Constance had never been particularly fond of southerners to begin with—she regarded most of them as common and backward—and she delighted in making fun of Mrs. Hobson behind her back and just out of her hearing.

During the summer of 1955, Constance toured in *Sabrina Fair.* Lorinda, who had served as her mother's dresser during the tour of *I Found April,* repeated her duties and found that her mother showed her no special treatment. Quite the contrary—if there was ever a slip, she could be verbally brutal. By now, Constance had come to like the feel of the stage and, despite a normal degree of nervousness, looked forward to each summer's tour. Louise Gore found her more natural and incandescent onstage than she ever was on the screen. Louise caught a performance of that summer's *Sabrina Fair* and remembered her as "marvelous. Onscreen, I died for her. But onstage, I applauded."

Because of their busy schedules, Constance and Joan were only sporadically in touch during this period, but Louise Gore recalled one encounter that she felt spoke volumes about both their relationship and their upbringing. In 1954, Melinda Markey had married Donald Hayden, an up-and-coming television actor featured on the popular comedy series *My Little Margie*. The marriage was not a notable success—Hayden had a serious drinking problem—and at one of its low points, it generated some messy headlines in the tabloids, one of which was spotted by Louise one evening in New York while she was on her way to Constance's apartment. Louise bought a copy of the newspaper and left it for Constance, who glanced at it and said nothing. Over dinner, the two women exchanged various pieces of gossip. Once the meal was finished, Constance said quietly, "I guess I'd better telephone Joan." Louise was sitting in the room while Constance made the call; at no point in the conversation with Joan did she refer to Melinda's predicament.

Professionally, Constance still seemed to be trying to find her bearings. In June 1956, she did a tour of dramatic readings, *The World of John Steinbeck*. It seemed calculated to help audiences expand their image of her, since the denizens of Steinbeck's Salinas Valley were as far removed as possible from the sophisticates Constance normally played. Lorinda, who ran lines with her, remembered that she threw herself into the work with as much intensity as ever. Although she was determined that physically she would not try to resemble the earthy, *Tortilla Flat* type of woman Steinbeck often created, she did her best to capture the character in vocal terms.

That September, she underwent the most surprising reinvention of her career—as a nightclub singer. For years, the club scene had been home to many "voiceless wonders"—singers whose dramatic intent and instinct for projecting a lyric and inflecting a phrase far outweighed their vocal skill. These artists knew how to put a song over in an intimate room, making each person in the audience feel that the words were being sung to him alone. In particular, Mabel Mercer's performances in the 1940s, at the Manhattan nightclub Tony's West Side, made many fine singers, notably Frank Sinatra and Eileen Farrell, rethink the way popular songs should be sung.

Constance's entry into the nightclub scene owed a great deal to the emergence of Marlene Dietrich as a chic cabaret star. After years of entertaining the troops during World War II, Dietrich had opened at Las Vegas's Hotel Sahara in 1953 and launched herself on a second career as a nightclub chanteuse. Like Dietrich, who was comfortable only in one-and-a-half octaves, Constance had her musical limitations—she had a range from A-flat below middle C to A-flat above middle C—but she set out to employ them as a strength rather than a drawback. Her goal would be to capture the audience's attention despite her vocal imperfections.

After trying out her act in Miami Beach, Constance opened at the Cotillion Room of Manhattan's Hotel Pierre. Her act was staged by Herbert Ross, a talented choreographer who went on to become the director of Hollywood successes such as *The Turning Point* and *The Goodbye Girl,* and she was backed up by a young dancing and singing couple, Jean Carrons and Joe Ross. Her numbers included "Down with Love," "What's She Gonna Do?," "Happiness Is a Thing Called Money," "What Is a Friend For?," and, best of all, the song she had introduced more than twenty years earlier in *Moulin Rouge,* "Boulevard of Broken Dreams." But the real showstopper came at the end, when she came out in a shirt with the tail hanging out and a pair of blue jeans patched with sequins to sing a thirteen-minute string of rock-and-roll numbers, including "A Teen-Age Prayer" and "Lipstick, Candy, and Rubber-Soled Shoes."

Her pianist was Donald Pippin, who had just made a splash with Broadway star Lisa Kirk's *Live at the Plaza* recording. The notices were positive, and Constance was invited to open for Tony Bennett at the Sands Hotel in Las Vegas. Pippin recalled that she wasn't at her best with up-tempo numbers like Irving Berlin's "You're Just in Love," because she didn't know how to relax the beat. But in the ballads, she was comfortable, confident, and at ease. For Las Vegas, Pippin worked up a new arrangement of the classic French song "Parlez-moi d'amour," which never failed to mesmerize the audience. Often she fell back on some of her old movie techniques. Pippin remembered that when the orchestra was playing and she was not singing, she would focus her eyes and hold the stage for measure after measure. During the Las Vegas engagement, Constance received a call from Peter in Los Angeles, who asked to come see her. "I wouldn't bother if I were you," she replied, and hung up on him.

According to Pippin, one of those most impressed with Constance's presence as a club singer was Tony Bennett, who often stood offstage watching the show. Like most of the top recording artists of the time, he had always concentrated on the melody and paid minimal attention to the words. After watching Constance's effect on the audience, he began to talk to her about the way she sang. She explained to him how to act a song, how to pause for effect, find the subtext, create the proper mood. In time, Tony Bennett would carve out a second career for himself as a master stylist who learned how to give song lyrics their due.

Word had gotten out that Constance's act was a success, and General Donald Neville Wilding, manager of London's renowned Café de Paris, notified her that he was interested in offering her an engagement. He made arrangements to see her while he was visiting New York, and Constance knew why: he wanted to see if she looked good enough to warrant a booking at the Café de Paris. She roped Donald Pippin into a scheme that she hoped would shame Wilding into signing her. She borrowed a wheelchair from a neighbor, and on the day that Wilding visited her Park Avenue apartment, she asked Pippin to come over. Beautifully made up and dressed, Constance seated herself in the wheelchair and wrapped a worn shawl around her head and shoulders. On cue, Pippin wheeled her out to greet Wilding. In a cracked old-lady's voice, she said, "Oh, it's so nice that you would come to see me, all the way from London." Wilding was visibly horrified until Constance leaped out of the wheelchair, threw off her shawl, and revealed herself in all her glamour. Wilding immediately signed her for the Café de Paris, where she enjoyed a successful run in 1957.

During her nightclub stints, her agent, Geoffrey Barr, kept an eye out for suitable film and television roles. One day, while working with Pippin, she received a telegram from NBC offering her the starring role in a new situation comedy that the network was developing. A script had been sent along, too, and she became enraged when she read it and realized she was being asked to play a maid. "Oh, Constance, do it," said Pippin, naively. "It will make you a star again." Constance replied coolly, "I *am* a star." Pippin didn't bring up the subject again. The script was for *Hazel,* in which Shirley Booth went on to become one of television's most popular domestics.

Occasionally Constance received a telephone call from Barbara. Time after time, Constance hung up on her. "She's an alcoholic," she would tell Pippin. "She's impossible, a lost cause. I will have nothing more to do with her. Even the doctor says the less I have to do with her, the better she'll help herself." A difficult position to take, Pippin thought, but for Constance it seemed all too easy.

In October 1957, Constance began a lengthy cross-country tour of *Auntie Mame,* Jerome Lawrence and Robert E. Lee's hit stage adaptation of Patrick Dennis's best-selling novel. The play had opened on Broadway in October 1956, with Rosalind Russell as the freewheeling aristocrat who shows her timid nephew how life is meant to be lived. Russell had such a triumph that a slew of aging actresses began lining up to take their turn at playing Mame. Some accented her zaniness, some her brittleness, some her vulnerability. Greer Garson succeeded Russell on Broadway, and successful road companies featured Eve Arden and Sylvia Sidney (whose performance was thought by many to be the closest to Patrick Dennis's conception of the character.)

Shortly before she signed to do the tour, Constance met with producer Charles Bowden of Bowden, Barr and Bullock, who was concerned about her reputation for being difficult. "I'm not the world's greatest actress," she admitted right up front. "I have to look right and I have to feel that I've been properly presented. I come out there, and most people don't know if I've been well-directed or not. All they see is me. Surround me with brilliance, and I don't have anything to be upset about. I just need a lot of money." Bowden saw to it that she was provided with the best. Scenic design was by the brilliant Oliver Smith, who had created the sets for the Broadway production, and her gowns—she had fourteen costume changes—were made by Travis Banton, who had created movie wardrobes for both Constance and Joan.

Bowden's widow, the distinguished Broadway actress Paula Laurence, recalled that Constance brought tremendous style to *Auntie Mame.* Apart from that, her scenes with young Patrick had a tremendous emotional pull. "You really believed that she loved him," remembered Laurence, "which made the whole thing more than a lot of gags and jokes." In rehearsals, no one worked harder than Constance: anyone caught performing at less than maximum potential was likely to feel her wrath. If she was hard on the other actors, it was only because she was carrying the show on her back and knew that everything possible had to be done to show her off to the best advantage. Her hard work paid off. *Auntie Mame* opened at the Hanna Theater in Cleveland on October 30, 1957, and grossed $1.5 million in the first nine months of the tour. Constance felt that the reasons for its success were obvious: "Never again," she told one interviewer, "will the people be satisfied with anything but the best in entertainment. . . . The day of the sleazy, second-rate road show has passed."

Many agreed that the high point of Constance's performance came in her last-act denunciation of the grown-up Patrick. Instead of becoming the free spirit she had hoped, he has grown into a shallow social climber. Patrick tells Mame that his fiancée, debutante Gloria Upson, comes from a conservative family and "doesn't have to know about a lot of things that ordinary mortals simply don't have to know about." Time seemed suspended when Constance's Mame, in low, grave tones, replied, "Should she know that I think you've turned into one of the most beastly, bourgeois, Babbitty little snobs on the Eastern seaboard? Or will you be able to make that quite clear without any help from me?" To Lorinda, sitting backstage, it was a reminder that few actresses knew how to play anger as effectively as her mother.

By now, Barbara's personal crises had become a steady if unwelcome presence in Joan's life, but she was no longer able to provide Barbara with the same level of financial assistance that she had in the past. Joan was out of town when the next flare-up occurred. On July 17, 1953, shortly before noon, Barbara was discovered sitting with a male companion in a Cadillac, parked in front of a market on a Beverly Hills street swigging vodka out of a bottle. The two were taken to the Beverly Hills police station, where they were booked on a charge of drunk in auto. At the station, it was revealed that Barbara's companion was Robert Livingston, brother of Addison Randall. Although Livingston had earned a measure of fame as a cowboy star in the 1930s and early 1940s, he was now relegated to playing occasional supporting roles. Neither was able to come up with bail money—$25 for Barbara and $100 for Livingston—until a telephone call was placed to Livingston's mother, Mrs. Clarence Meyers. But there was more startling news to come: Barbara announced that three days earlier, she had married Livingston in Las Vegas. On July 20, both appeared in Municipal Court, where Livingston paid a $50 fine. Barbara asked for a continuance until August 3, when she paid an identical amount. At the hearing, she failed to hide her gaunt and haggard appearance behind a large pair of sunglasses. Although just shy of her forty-seventh birthday, she looked much older. Reporters noted that the marriage already seemed strained, and that Barbara gave her address as 515 South Mapleton Drive.

Nothing further is known about the marriage of Barbara Bennett and Robert Livingston, but it appears to have lasted no more than a couple of months. Barbara stayed on in California for a time, but her health was failing fast. She had long been plagued by asthma, and in recent years it had grown progressively worse, and she had developed severe stomach ulcers, aggravated by her drinking.

Eventually, Barbara drifted back to New York, where she picked up a few odd jobs. At some point in 1954, she met a dark-haired, burly French-Canadian journalist named Laurent Surprenant. Again, she had made a regrettable choice, since, like so many of the men she was drawn to, Surprenant was a heavy drinker. Often he was physically abusive. At the time, Melinda Markey was living in New York, pursuing an acting career, and she saw her aunt fairly often. Sometimes Barbara would show up with bruises on her arms and face. She would vaguely admit that Surprenant had laid hands on her, but she seemed to show no real interest in leaving him, probably because no better opportunity had presented itself.

Joan met Surprenant only once, and later described him as "another disaster" in Barbara's life. But in 1954, the couple moved to Montreal and were soon married. From this point, Joan and Barbara would see little of each other. Even had Joan not been occupied with her stage tours, Barbara had pushed her younger sister's patience to the breaking point.

On March 14, 1953, Joan's tour of *Bell, Book, and Candle* reached its end at Philadelphia's Locust Theatre. It was time: while the play had hefty returns on most of its tour, the profits for the final weeks had been disappointing. The play's engagement at Washington, D.C.'s National Theater had provided Joan with an opportunity to visit Constance. She was a guest at the Coulters' Georgetown house for the duration of the run, and all the children basked in her warm, maternal presence. She treated them like adults, listened to them discuss their problems at school, and every night climbed upstairs to their third-floor bedrooms to tell them good-night. As compulsively organized as ever, even on tour, she helped Constance balance her checkbook and straighten out her household accounts—much to John Coulter's relief.

Back in Hollywood, Joan found no worthwhile offers of film work. So in the summer of 1953, she went back to the theater, appearing with Debbie Reynolds and Alice Pearce in a production of the popular Hugh Martin–Ralph Blane musical *Best Foot Forward* at the Dallas State Fair. Joan sang "That's How I Love the Blues," "The Guy Who Brought Me Can't Send Me," and "Ev'ry Time," and joined the company for the show's hit number, "Buckle

Down, Winsocki." She had always had a secret ambition to do a stage musical, found Reynolds a highly professional colleague, and enjoyed herself immensely. When she returned to the West Coast, she filmed a low-budget quickie, *Highway Dragnet,* from a story by Roger Corman. It was a miserable location shoot in Indio, California, and the picture was of "B"-minus proportions. Still, she did her work without complaining and did not transmit her low state of mind to her coworkers. Veteran character actress Iris Adrian, who played a supporting part as a waitress, remembered, "Joan Bennett was wonderful. I'd done pictures with her several years earlier, and she came up to me on the set and said, 'Hello, Iris!' I didn't even know she remembered me!"

In Hollywood, changes were coming so quickly that Joan could barely take them in. The kind of beautifully mounted pictures the studios had once turned out for glamour stars of her breed were dwindling. The screen embraced realism more fully with each passing year, and Joan had difficulty conceiving how she could fit into the new Hollywood.

Even Fritz Lang had moved ahead. His latest film, *The Big Heat* (1953), was a brutal gangster drama. In it, Gloria Grahame played the girlfriend of mobster Lee Marvin. Grahame was Lang's 1950s-style femme fatale—tough, crude, aggressively sexual. In *The Big Heat,* when Grahame makes a play for cop Glenn Ford, Marvin evens the score with her by throwing a pot of scalding hot coffee in her face, permanently scarring her. It had been only eight years since audiences had been horrified by the ice pick murder of Kitty March in *Scarlet Street.* But it seemed much longer.

Although Joan and Walter's relationship continued to be distant at best, they abided by their decision to stay together for the girls' sake. But by the spring of 1954, it had become clear that the Mapleton Drive house would have to be sold. With both Joan's and Walter's film careers stalled, there was precious little money coming in. During Joan's *Bell, Book, and Candle* tour, the household staff had been sharply cut back, so that only the girls' governess, Catherine Randall, and the cook, Elizabeth Finnerty, remained. Still, the Wangers faced enormous expenses, including the repayment of Walter's debts and the education of both Stephanie and Shelley. In the end, Joan arranged to sell the house to producer Hal B. Wallis and his wife, actress Louise Fazenda. It was a heartbreaking decision, for the Mapleton house had been more than just a happy home—it had been a symbol of the order and stability she had always pursued, and it served to remind her, always, that she had overcome the chaos of her early years. Now she had no safe harbor. Like Constance and Barbara, she faced a future that offered no guarantees.

She wasn't ready to give up on Hollywood altogether, so she purchased a smaller home at 1421 Stone Canyon. Designed by California architect Burton Scott, it seemed quite modern after the French Provincial formality of Mapleton Drive. It had several special features: a lanai, a bricked-in terrace surrounded by camellia bushes, and an attractive Japanese garden, tended by a gardener who was constantly adding decorative touches, such as stone pathways. It also had the advantage of being a one-story home, which was now a necessity. For some time, Walter's heart had been giving him trouble, and he was to avoid stairs whenever possible. There were lots of children in the neighborhood for Stephanie and Shelley to play with, and the Wangers settled in, all doing their best to adjust to their new life. Joan continued to keep a close eye on household expenses, and often accompanied Elizabeth the cook to Ralph's Supermarket, where onlookers were treated to the sight of a glamorous movie star hunting for the best bargains and carefully checking items off her shopping list.

Joan busied herself with product endorsements and occasional television appearances, but no more film roles came her way until the spring of 1954, when she was assigned a supporting role in Paramount's *We're No Angels.* It was based on *My Three Angels,* the 1953 Broadway hit comedy by Bella and Samuel Spewack, and Joan landed the role only through the intervention of the film's star, her loyal friend and ex-neighbor, Humphrey Bogart. Aware of Joan's precarious situation in Hollywood, Bogart demanded that she be cast in the film. Paramount relented, but played down her presence by giving her below-the-title billing—her first since *Little*

Women. Directed by Michael Curtiz, it was a labored, listless comedy about three convicts who came to the aid of an impoverished storekeeper (Leo G. Carroll) and his wife (Joan). She was paid $5,000 a week with a five-week guarantee for playing a rather colorless role. She did get to sing a Frederick Hollander song, "Sentimental Moments," and when the film was released in 1955 she received generally warm notices, but it was hardly an auspicious return to the screen.

It did, however, demonstrate that she was still eager to work in films, and a brief spurt of activity followed. For Allied Artists (formerly Monogram), Walter had gotten hold of a property he thought might be suitable for Joan: Tats Blain's novel, *Mother-Sir!,* about the wife of a naval officer who tries to liberate a community of tradition-bound Japanese women. Filmed on a tiny budget, its title was changed to *Navy Wife,* and it came and went quickly on the second half of double bills.

Her next film, Douglas Sirk's *There's Always Tomorrow,* also faded fast, but like *The Reckless Moment,* its reputation has grown. Like Ophuls, Sirk's European background helped him develop a perceptive eye for the tensions of modern American life. Beginning in the mid-1950s, Sirk turned out a series of romantic dramas for Universal that were scorned by most critics as glossy, artificial throwbacks to the Hollywood soap operas of the 1940s. What reviewers failed to see at the time was the peculiar, unsettling texture of Sirk's pictures. Underneath the studio-bred formality, the careful lighting, the meticulously composed shots, Sirk's best films were startling studies of people trapped by life's conventions, the expectations of friends and family, and their own yearnings and limitations. In a way, their effect is not unlike that of Edward Hopper's paintings: the familiarity of what we are shown fails to reassure us—instead, it disturbs us.

Like Sirk's earlier film, *All That Heaven Allows* (1955), *There's Always Tomorrow* centers on a character who has done everything that might have been expected of him—only to be left deeply unfulfilled. Clifford Groves (Fred MacMurray) is a successful toy manufacturer living in an upscale Los Angeles suburb with his wife,

Marion (Joan), and three children. But Clifford has come to feel hemmed in by his routine existence. Marion is wrapped up in the children, who are wrapped up in themselves. Even the housekeeper (Jane Darwell) appears to take him for granted. Clifford is a deeply sensitive man, and as the film opens, we see that he is growing increasingly hurt by his family's neglect. When he tries to persuade Marion that they need to spend more time alone together, she insists that the children need her more.

Then, by chance, Cliff receives a visit from an old business associate, Norma Vail (Barbara Stanwyck). A single career woman who lives in New York, Norma is in Los Angeles to open a high-end women's clothing store. The two spend a weekend together in Palm Desert; Norma shows him the affection and attention he has been missing for so many years, and he feels a reawakening of life's possibilities. When the two older children discover his friendship with Norma, they refuse to consider the possible reasons for it, and treat her with contempt. In the end, Norma decides that she is not cut out to be a home wrecker and returns to New York. It's a bitter ending on two counts, for Norma thinks she is acting in Cliff's best interests; she has not grasped the fact that he is deeply lonely within the family. Although Cliff resigns himself to returning to Marion, there is no indication that anything will change between them; the marriage will most likely continue on Marion's terms. The final scene offers a typically Sirkian comment on the ambushes of family life: as Cliff and Marion walk off arm in arm, the youngest daughter gushes, "They make a handsome couple, don't they?" Harmony has been restored for the children—and they are the only ones who matter.

When Joan first read the script, Marion must not have struck her as much of a role. But under Sirk's assured, detailed direction, she gave a fine account of a smug housewife whose complacency has an edge of cruelty. Marion is enormously self-protective, and a thread of steel runs underneath her charming veneer. The picture's most painful and memorable scene takes place between Cliff and Marion on the balcony of their bedroom. Earlier that evening, Norma has been the Groves's guest for dinner, and the children have treated her with hostility. Cliff is angry with them, but Marion defends them. Desperate that Marion should understand the reasons for his unhappiness, Cliff tries one last time to explain it to her. With maddening calm, Marion blocks him at every turn, appearing to have no idea what he is talking about. As he becomes more emotional, she becomes more immovable. "Oh, Marion," Cliff pleads, "When we were younger, we shared so many things together. We had fun. No two days were alike. Life was an adventure. But now—" And Marion responds coolly, "Darling, if life were always an adventure, it would be *very* exhausting." Then she goes inside, worrying about the next day's marketing, warning him not to stay outside and catch cold. By refusing to embrace her husband's pain and loneliness, Marion has won. And that is a big part of what makes this quietly remarkable film one of the screen's finest studies of the constricted nature of 1950s suburbia.

Unfortunately, in 1956, most critics saw it as an ordinary domestic drama with three aging stars. Nothing else turned up in Hollywood, and in September 1956, Joan returned to the stage in the national touring company of Carolyn Green's hit Broadway comedy *Janus,* produced by Alfred DiLiagre. She played Jessica, the wife of a Seattle shipping magnate who spends her summers in New York, collaborating with Denny, an Andover professor, on a string of sexy historical novels. The partnership is a secret: they write under the *nom de plume* "Janus," and no one suspects anything until Jessica's husband, Gil, unexpectedly turns up in New York. The rest of the play turns on Jessica's attempt to persuade Gil that she needs both men in her life. A free spirit who lives "the way other people dream," Jessica has always wanted to be "indoors and outdoors at the same time." As she pleads with Gil for understanding, she says, "Do you think I was just in love with Denny? I'm in love with the horse that pulls the flower wagon! I'm in love with the Italian that sells the flowers! I'm in love with living and breathing and running upstairs and opening packages and riding trolley cars!" She has loved Gil more, she explains, because she has also loved Denny, and she sees no reason to change now.

There wasn't much real wit in *Janus*—it was the sort of 1950s comedy most often described as "bright"—but it did offer three lively leading roles. Joan was given casting approval, and at her suggestion, DiLiagre engaged Donald Cook to play Gil. Her decision, as it turned out, was her next important step in her development as an actress.

Born in 1900 into a banking family in Portland, Oregon, Donald Cook had appeared on the Broadway stage in the late 1920s, then headed for Hollywood, where he made numerous films, including James Whale's 1936 version of *Show Boat.* But his greatest successes came with his return to the stage in the 1940s, when he demonstrated his skill as a light comedian in hits such as *Skylark* (1939) with Gertrude Lawrence, *Claudia* (1941) with Dorothy McGuire, and *The Moon Is Blue* (1951). In the mid-1940s, he weathered three years of touring as Elyot Chase in Noël Coward's *Private Lives,* opposite the Amanda of Tallulah Bankhead, who became his lover. (About Bankhead, Cook once observed, "Her idea of a good night's sleep runs between a half hour and forty-five minutes.")

Cook's theatrical pedigree was the exact reason Joan had selected him to be her leading man in *Janus.* By now she had faced the fact that the bulk of her future employment would be in the theater. Although she had made a big hit in *Bell, Book, and Candle,* she had begun to regret that she had not had proper theatrical training, as actors in the British repertory system did. For *Janus,* she wanted her costar to be someone from whom she could learn a thing or two about stage technique. Unfortunately, her initial meeting with Cook did not augur well for their association. She greeted him with "Hello, Donald," and he coolly replied, "How do you do, Miss Bennett?" In fact, neither of them remembered that they had appeared together in a film, *The Trial of Vivienne Ware,* in 1932.

Cook did possess an air of weary eminence, and coworkers often found him distant and withdrawn. But shortly after rehearsals for *Janus* got under way, he began to warm up to Joan. She studied him minute by minute, amazed by his impeccable comic timing. Joan, who always claimed that she learned by osmosis, quickly began to absorb many of the finer points of pacing a lengthy speech and holding for a laugh. Gradually, the spirit of ensemble acting was being revealed to her.

In his youth, Donald Cook had been strikingly handsome, but in his mid-fifties, he looked like a matinee idol gone to seed. His more-than-moderate drinking had given him a rather sallow complexion, and his eyes were a bit like an aging bloodhound's. Nevertheless, he was warm and kind and witty, and Joan was deeply drawn to him. *Janus* opened on September 27, 1956, at the Auditorium in Rochester, New York. Soon after, Donald and Joan were spending nearly all their free time together.

Walter may have heard rumors about Joan's growing attachment to her costar, but back in Hollywood, he was occupied with professional matters. Things were going considerably better for him. After his release from Wayside Honor Farm in the summer of 1952, Walter had made a number of statements to the press about the deplorable conditions that existed in the nation's prisons. He longed to make a film on the subject, and in 1954 he produced *Riot in Cell Block 11,* a low-budget exposé that received good notices and made a strong showing at the box office. Operating on a slightly higher budget, he produced a CinemaScope film, *The Adventures of Haiji Baba* (1954), starring John Derek. It was reminiscent of some of the films he had produced at Universal in the mid-1940s (*Arabian Nights, A Night in Paradise*), and did well with family audiences. Perhaps as a conciliatory gesture toward Joan, Walter cast Melinda in a small role in the film.

Two years later, Walter had another highly praised low-budget film on his hands with the science fiction thriller *Invasion of the Body Snatchers.* Starring Kevin McCarthy and Dana Wynter, it depicted the takeover of a small California community by "pod people"—exact clones who take the place of the town's citizens while they are sleeping. Walter had never before gravitated toward science fiction as a subject, but *Invasion of the Body Snatchers* was something more than the average horror movie. Its allusions to the bland conformity of the 1950s as the source of the pod people's takeover gave the film added dimension.

One particular exchange in the script, between McCarthy's Dr. Miles Bennell and Wynter's Becky Driscoll, may have reminded Walter of his own recent experiences in Hollywood:

> MILES: In my practice, I've seen how people have allowed their humanity to drain away. Only it happened slowly, instead of all at once. And they didn't seem to mind.
> BECKY: Just some people, Miles.
> MILES: All of us, a little bit. We harden our hearts, grow callous. Only when we have to fight to stay human do we realize how precious it is to us. How dear.

Invasion of the Body Snatchers received good reviews. Although Matthew Bernstein notes that the film was "slow to recover its costs," it has enjoyed a long life as a cult film, becoming a favorite of college audiences in the 1960s and 1970s. In 1978, it was remade by director Phil Kaufman, but the original is the one that the public still affectionately remembers.

After its Rochester opening, *Janus* moved on to Cleveland. "This is a gruesome city," Joan wrote to Diana. "The only thing that makes me feel in touch with civilization is Bonwit Teller across the street." On opening night in Cleveland, she was as nervous as she had been in Rochester, but she was cheered by the enthusiastic audiences, good notices, and brisk box office. "It really is a cute play full of laughs," she told Diana. "After I have played it another week I'll start having fun."

Still, she was pleased to be on the road, away from California, because her romance with Donald Cook was now in full sail. Donald drank a great deal, and Joan joined him. Although cocktails before dinner had been part of her routine through all her years in Hollywood, she now drank to keep Donald company. At first, her level of intake was not heavy, but in time it gradually increased. Still, it never interfered with her work, and her professional reputation remained intact.

She missed Stephanie and Shelley and wrote to them often, but she was delighted to have been granted a lengthy sabbatical from her deteriorating marriage. With Donald in the picture, her feelings toward Walter became more hostile. In a letter to Diana while on tour, she couldn't resist jabbing her housebound husband: "Poor Papa. I don't think he is enjoying his role of mother and housekeeper." The *Janus* tour wound on, through Detroit, San Francisco, Los Angeles (where, as with *Bell, Book, and Candle,* she particularly dreaded the audience's reaction), Cincinnati, and Chicago, closing on March 16, 1957, at Baltimore's Ford Theater. Joan returned to Stone Canyon for a couple of months, but relations with Walter were more tense than ever. She was relieved to leave home again in the late spring, this time for a tour of *Janus* on the summer-theater circuit. Again Donald was her costar, and he also took over as director. Audiences were just as responsive as they had been on the national tour, and the notices were excellent. When *Janus* played at the Cape Playhouse in Dennis, Massachusetts, the *Cape Cod Standard-Times* found Joan "remarkably fresh and vital in her part." With Donald as her constant companion, the summer passed pleasantly.

Her intense work on the *Janus* tour turned out to be ideal preparation for her next major project, Robert Alan Aurthur's drama "The Thundering Wave," telecast on CBS's acclaimed dramatic anthology series *Playhouse 90.* The script's parallels to her own life were striking: she played Victoria Maxwell, a forty-five-year-old screen actress who returns to the stage after a long absence, playing opposite her estranged husband, Allen Grant (Franchot Tone). At first, Victoria appears the confident, glamorous star, but in reality she is terrified of facing a live audience in a serious acting challenge. During the out-of-town tryout, she seems incapable of the hard, concentrated work required to pull the play into shape. She throws fits, feigns illness, and does whatever she can to undermine its chances of success. The playwright, Lew Downs (Jack Klugman) is alternately frantic and depressed, but the director, Sidney Lowe (James Mason) keeps trying to break through her defenses, as the play's future looks increasingly doomed.

The director of "The Thundering Wave" was twenty-seven-year-old John Frankenheimer, who in the preceding years had made a name for himself directing many live television dramas. On *Playhouse 90,* he was known for pushing some of Hollywood's biggest names to explore levels of dramatic truth they had never imagined. The part of Victoria Maxwell was unlike anything Joan had ever attempted. The script called for one emotional outburst after another, and she was not used to performing at such a highly sustained level of energy. At first, rehearsals began to mirror the situation depicted in the script. Joan was giving a surface reading of the part, and Frankenheimer lost no time letting her know that he was unhappy with her performance. He came to Stone Canyon several times to coach her; not since Fritz Lang had she encountered such a ruthless director. He hammered away at her to invest more of herself emotionally in the role, bluntly pointing out the parallels between the character and her own life. Jack Klugman recalled that the rehearsal period lasted for seventeen days. He recalled feeling sorry for Joan, because "Frankenheimer was cruel to her—a bully. There was no need for that kind of treatment."

Joan had always been suspicious of Method acting and other similar techniques that required working from the inside out. "She would always say, 'You don't have to probe. That's not the way *we* did it,'" recalled Stephanie Guest. "But I think that she couldn't *afford* to do that. If you think about what she had to cope with—even if some of it was because of what she had created—it was a lot to have to deal with. I think the way she got through it was just to be very disciplined and live in the moment."

Despite her initial resistance to Frankenheimer's methods, Joan did her best to give him what he asked. When he left the house after a particularly grueling rehearsal, Joan said to Diana, "That young man is a very fine director." When "The Thundering Wave" was telecast on December 12, 1957, she had to admit it had been worth the effort. She gave a deeply felt study of an actress terrified that she lacks the resources to face the advancing years. "I was doing all right in Hollywood!" Victoria exclaims. "I was a star. Why did I have to learn to act?" She is particularly fine in the scene at the Boston opening in which Sidney Lowe tells Victoria that she is ruining the play, just minutes before she makes her entrance: "You've been stinking up the theater! You're rotten! You're lousy! When are you going to show me something?" Without saying a word, Joan eloquently expresses Victoria's fear of failing—and the near certainty that she will.

The reviews for "The Thundering Wave" were excellent. Jack O'Brian wrote in the *New York Journal-American,* "Joan Bennett delivered a better acting performance than any we've witnessed her in through the considerable seasons. . . . always we'd seen her as an actress who'd sort of chugged along on glamor through the years. . . . Now talent is plainly apparent."

The next few months passed uneventfully. She and Walter were seen around town from time to time, and inevitably, Hollywood columnists suggested that perhaps their marital difficulties were behind them. But although they didn't parade the conflicts between them and behaved with the utmost civility whenever the occasion demanded it, their relationship was finished. Joan had been much quicker than Walter to realize this. Although he had initially resisted the idea of marrying her and having children, he had quickly grown accustomed to the comfort and security of their life together. Now that Joan had taught him the pleasures of domestic life, he was reluctant to give it up.

No doubt additional tensions rose from the fact that her film career remained at a standstill while his was on the upswing again. *Riot in Cell Block 11* and *Invasion of the Body Snatchers* had done well enough that he had been able to get a major "A" project off the ground: *I Want to Live!,* starring his former contract star Susan Hayward as convicted murderess Barbara Graham, the first woman in California to be sent to the gas chamber. *I Want to Live!* took on an issue of great personal concern to Walter, the inhumanity of capital punishment. Walter insisted that the film wasn't "a treatise against capital punishment. This is a treatise against the whole social system which we are so apathetic about." The film, which ended with a terrifying depiction of Graham's execution, was a tremendous critical and commercial success when it was released in November 1958, and earned Hayward the Academy Award for Best Actress. When reporters expressed surprise that he had managed to climb back to the top of the heap in Hollywood, Walter replied, "This is my fourteenth career. What people here don't realize is that I'm the perennial man-who-came-back."

Ever since she had toured in *Susan and God,* Joan had toyed with the idea of returning to Broadway. She did not want to go in a revival, since she felt that only a new play would present a worthy challenge. Early in 1958, producer Alexander H. Cohen offered her a role in John G. Fuller's *Love Me Little.* It was a slender comedy about a seventeen-year-old girl's efforts to lose her virginity. It aimed to be smart and sophisticated, but succeeded in being merely strained. The girl was played by Susan Kohner, daughter of Hollywood agent Paul Kohner. Joan and Donald Cook were cast as her knowing and worldly parents, who communicate chiefly in wisecracks. Joan had no illusions about the size of her part or the quality of the play, but it was a chance to be near Donald for an extended period. The director was the talented Alfred Drake, and she held out hope that perhaps the play could be reworked, during its out-of-town tryout, into a Broadway success.

At first it seemed possible that she might get her wish. When *Love Me Little* opened at the Shubert Theatre in New Haven, Connecticut, on March 6, 1958, the notices were better than Joan had expected. Most of the critics agreed that if the choppy first and third acts could be brought up to the level of the bright and funny second act, the play might have a good future. The *Hartford Times* found it "a compact, sometimes wonderfully droll commentary on contemporary affairs." Predictably, Susan Kohner stole the reviews, but the *Hartford Times* critic allowed that Joan did "manage, whenever stage center, to add substantially to the proceedings at hand."

The play moved on to Boston's Wilbur Theater, where hopes soared higher. The venerable Elliot Norton of the *Boston Globe* found *Love Me Little* "gay and amiable and, after its own fashion, rather impressively wise." Like the New Haven critics, he urged Fuller and director Alfred Drake to bring the rest of the play up to the most "uproariously funny" scenes. Again, most of the reviewers' space was devoted to praising Susan Kohner's performance.

Rewriting took place on a nightly basis. Kohner recalled Cook as highly professional, but somewhat distant and stuffy, and Joan as pleasant and charming, although "She was probably a bit apprehensive, because of being thrown new stuff daily." The two of them spent most of their time together and didn't mix a great deal with the rest of the cast, and Kohner remembered being quite aware that they were an item.

On April 14, 1958, *Love Me Little* opened at the Helen Hayes Theatre in New York, to a frozen critical reception. Calling it "a sadly belabored discourse on a pitifully small theme," the *New York Journal-American* found it "deplorable that Joan Bennett should return to the stage in New York with this shabby charade, because she is wonderfully decorative and appealing in her role." The *New York Daily Mirror* found the play "as slick as a new deck of cards" populated by "caricatures rather than characters, types rather than human beings," but admitted that "Joan Bennett stands out as the adolescent's practical mother." Walter Kerr, in the *New York Herald-Tribune,* observed that Joan "folds her arms, looks wise, and does nicely by anything workable that is thrown her way." *Love Me Little* closed after eight performances. The only one to benefit from the experience was Susan Kohner, as film producer Ross Hunter came to the play's opening night in New York and promptly signed her for his next film, *Imitation of Life* (1959).

After the play folded, Joan lingered on in New York for several weeks, pondering her predicament. She had promised Walter that she would return to California if *Love Me Little* closed, hoping all the time that it would enjoy a long run. Now she was torn. She wanted to be with Donald, yet she missed Stephanie and Shelley desperately. She didn't quite see the point of living full-time in California, where the only work she was likely to turn up was the occasional guest appearance on television. Now that Walter was on firmer ground professionally, she thought he might be more open to discussing a divorce. One night, she brought up the idea over the telephone. Walter replied that if she tried to get Stephanie and Shelley in a divorce action, he would create a front-page scandal. In a rare moment of letting her guard down, Joan poured our her frustrations to Diana in a letter dated April 29, 1958:

I miss the children so much I ache. I want them with me. I don't want to uproot them—I don't want to sit across the table from Pops's grumpy face and make phony conversation for the benefit of the children. I don't want to deprive the children of their father or he of them. I'm sick of living a lie with him. I'm sick of living a lie period. I am thoroughly miserable and don't know what to do about it, which is a fine predicament to be in. There isn't an hour day or night, for that matter in my dreams, that I am not trying to work things out.

Darling, you were an angel to write and ask me what you should say. I honestly don't know because I don't know what to say myself. What a mess. What a life. Why can't people live and let live? Pop has always had his cake and eaten it too yet that's what he accuses me of wanting. He makes me feel like a wanton, wicked, neglectful mother, a harpy, a bitch, and everything awful.

Unwilling to return to Stone Canyon for any length of time, Joan accepted another stock tour offer for the summer of 1958. While she was on the road, she received a letter from Barbara in Montreal. Barbara told her that she had reached an impasse in her marriage to Laurent Surprenant. On top of that, the chilly climate aggravated her ever-worsening asthma, and she asked Joan for the money to get herself to California, where she might enjoy a good, long rest in a warm setting.

Before Joan was able to respond, Barbara died in her home on August 9, 1958. Reeling under the toll of her heavy drinking, her body had simply given out.

Even if Constance had been moved to attend Barbara's funeral, it was impossible for her to do so. She was committed to the *Auntie Mame* tour. Joan also was busy onstage. Of Barbara's children, only Michael and Kevin made the trip to Canada to attend the services. There, they were given a hostile reception by Laurent Surprenant. "At the funeral, it was unconscionable the way he carried on," remembered Michael. "He kept saying that he had no responsibility to take care of any of the funeral arrangements. No interest at all."

Barbara was buried in the Burtonville Union Cemetery in the town of Lacolle, Quebec. A memorial service was held at the Church of the Good Shepherd in Beverly Hills. Attendance was sparse, and Melinda Markey and Stephanie Wanger were the only family members present.

For the rest of her life, Joan would remain tight-lipped about the circumstances of Barbara's death, causing many to speculate that she had committed suicide. In a sense, perhaps that is just what she did, over a period of years. Certainly she seemed to will her own self-destruction. As the poet Anne Sexton once wrote, those who want to die "have a special language. / Like carpenters they want to know *which tools.* / They never ask *why build.*"

In the end, Barbara's life was a study in failure. Early on, she lacked the strong core that sustained her sisters in their pursuit of careers in show business. She apparently showed some promise as a dancer, but was quick to give it up, which is probably just as well—someone so emotionally fragile and easily wounded is best discouraged from a performing career. The collapse of her marriage and family life seemed to confirm her view of herself as an outsider, and her life's pattern became set. Her continual drinking isolated her further, and failure became a way of life—something she was accustomed to and almost comfortable with—a known quantity.

But the saddest fact of Barbara's death is that it was a solitary one. When Diana Anderson telephoned her mother to commiserate, Joan's reply was devastating in its honesty: "For me, she died a long time ago."

Chapter Twenty-One

1959–1965

Following the demise of *Love Me Little,* Joan began taking serious steps toward getting out of California altogether. The only Hollywood offers she received were occasional guest shots on television—hardly reason enough to stay. There was plenty of reason to relocate to New York: the difficulties of the past few years seemed more remote there, and she could enjoy the company of good friends, such as Muriel and Ben Finney and Zachary Scott and Ruth Ford. By now, much of her stage work was centered in the northeast, and she reasoned that she might be able to pick up a regular job on one of the popular television panel shows aired from New York. Most of all, she could be near Donald, with whom she was now deeply in love.

At home in Stone Canyon, the tension between Joan and Walter showed no sign of diminishing. Generally, they managed to avoid heated arguments in front of the children and household staff, but more and more their conversation was peppered with sarcasm and mean-spirited barbs. At Stephanie's graduation from the Ethel Walker School, the hostility between them was palpable.

Joan's frustration may partly have stemmed from the fact that things in Hollywood were going rather well for Walter. By the fall of 1958, *I Want to Live!* was awaiting release, with excellent advance word-of-mouth. In October, Walter became a major player once more when he signed a contract with Twentieth Century–Fox. Since 1956, when Darryl Zanuck had vacated the studio to go into independent production, Twentieth had gone into steep decline. Its new production chief, Spyros Skouras, began aggressively recruiting more and more big prestige products to help pull the studio out of its doldrums, and signed Walter, despite the view of many in the industry that he was a relic from another era. The project that dominated Walter's thoughts at the time was a color spectacle, *Cleopatra.* It is difficult to conceive how he could have risked taking on such a complex and expensive project after the *Joan of Arc* debacle. But he was determined that *Cleopatra* would be one of the great pictures of its time. What Twentieth had initially envisioned as a relatively modest effort with contract player Joan Collins in the title role escalated, over the next several years, into a $37 million extravaganza starring Elizabeth Taylor and Richard Burton. In 1958 and 1959, it was only in its planning stages, but it claimed most of Walter's time and energy. It seemed the perfect time for Joan to take her leave.

When she first arrived in New York, she lived like a gypsy in a string of undistinguished apartments: Diana recalled a first-floor flat on Third Avenue where the living room wall shook each time someone slammed the building's entry door. In the winter of 1959, Joan toured in Harry Kurnitz's comedy *Once More with Feeling,* playing the free-spirited wife of a tempestuous orchestra conductor. In May, she and Donald starred in a summer-replacement comedy series for NBC-TV, *Too Young to Go Steady.* It was filmed live, presented Joan as the distinctly middle-aged mother of a pair of restless teenagers, and disappeared after six weeks.

Onstage and off, Joan was deeply happy with Donald. Although he had been a loner for much of his life, Joan managed to create a domestic haven for him, just as she had with Walter. She also looked up to Donald, as she had to Walter years earlier, for she considered him one of the finest actors she ever worked with, and an incomparable teacher. He was a fixture in her various New York apartments, a somewhat cool and remote presence who sat chain-smoking and sipping endless glasses of Pernod. Eleven-year-old Shelley was with Joan in New York for several months, but for much of 1960 and 1961 she joined Walter in London, where he was supervising the early stages of *Cleopatra*'s production at Pinewood Studios. The older girls were all doing well. Diana's husband, Jack Anderson, had developed some serious health problems, which necessitated Diana's going to work as a model and actress in television commercials. She had matured into a tall, striking blonde, and secured steady employment in a long line of product endorsements for more than a decade. Melinda had struggled along as an actress for much of the 1950s, appearing in small parts in a number of Hollywood films, and playing a supporting role in a Broadway revival of *On Borrowed Time,* the play that had proven to be Richard's Waterloo. After divorcing Donald Hayden in 1957, she met Joseph Bena, a handsome and outgoing man who had no connection to show business. In October 1960, she married him, settled down in Los Angeles, and seemed content to raise her family and turn her back on show business. To her friends, Joan registered no disappointment that Melinda did not turn out to lead the sixth generation of the family into the acting profession; instead, she seemed equally proud of Melinda's accomplishments as "a devoted mother and compulsive housekeeper." Stephanie entered Barnard College, which made Walter very proud; both Stephanie and Shelley remembered that he was always concerned that they receive a first-class university education. Joan, Stephanie observed, "sort of drew the line at college."

More than anything, Joan wanted to marry Donald, but Walter still refused to consider a divorce. Joan considered it "sheer perverseness" on his part, but Walter had grown accustomed to family life and was reluctant to give it up without a fight. While Walter was occupied with *Cleopatra,* Joan kept busy with jobs in winter and summer stock. In December 1959, Joan and Donald were again teamed onstage when they replaced Cornelia Otis Skinner and Cyril Ritchard in the national tour of *The Pleasure of His Company,* a long-running Broadway hit by Samuel Taylor and Skinner. This droll comedy, about a middle-aged man who turns up for the wedding of the daughter he barely knows, thereby infuriating his newly remarried ex-wife, had good parts for both Joan and Donald. While Skinner and Ritchard took a four-week vacation, they led the play on a tour through Toronto, Louisville, Cincinnati, and St. Louis. Not long after, a bus-and-truck version of the play was put together under the auspices of Guber, Gross, and Ford. Once more, Joan and Donald were paged to play the leads, and they took off on a grueling cross-country tour that occupied them for much of 1960.

Some years earlier, bus-and-truck productions had revolutionized theatrical touring: sets were designed so that they could be broken down easily and transported from one city to another, while the actors and other company members traveled by bus. Since bus-and-truck schedules were dotted with split weeks and one-night stands, there was usually not much opportunity to get familiar with local surroundings; restaurants and hotel rooms all began to look alike after several weeks. As the play's stars, Joan and Donald often flew from one destination to the next, but when the distance was short, they rode the bus with the other actors. Sometimes, when the schedule was especially tight, Joan would have to apply her make-up en route. Occasionally, she even slept in the back of the bus. Throughout it, she seldom complained. Being with Donald, even under these conditions, was what she wanted most.

By now, she had absorbed many of Donald's acting lessons and exhibited considerable confidence onstage. She had developed a sense of rhythm and pacing, and a positive reaction from the audience could always give her a rush of pleasure. Diana remembered seeing *The Pleasure of His Company* on its stop in Santa Barbara. "There wasn't an empty seat in the house," she said. "And after they struck the set and were packed up to go, I said, 'Golly, Mamma, you were wonderful!' And she said, 'Well, you don't have to sound so surprised.' I think we underestimated her."

In the summer of 1960, during a break in the tour, Joan went to Baton Rouge for a few weeks' work on a film called *Desire in the Dust*. It was a heavy-breathing melodrama about a corrupt southern family, with Joan playing a woman who retreats into a fantasy world following the death of her young son. The script was poor, her role small, and the locations hot and humid. The experience afforded her little pleasure.

In 1961, after *The Pleasure of His Company* completed its tour, Joan returned to New York, where she rented a three-bedroom penthouse apartment at 8 East Ninety-sixth Street, between Fifth and Madison. It had a spacious living room, decorated in the blues and yellows she had favored at Mapleton Drive, a separate dining room, and a good-sized terrace, where she maintained an extensive garden. With its abundance of greenery and bright colors, the new apartment was a pleasant reminder of her happy days in California.

She still held out hope that one day she would be free to marry Donald, who in the late summer of 1961 had gone into rehearsals for a Broadway-bound comedy, *A Shot in the Dark,* starring Julie Harris. On September 30, Joan received a paralyzing shock: news reached her that Donald had collapsed of a massive heart attack in New Haven, where the play was being tried out. He died the following day. The composure and self-discipline that had carried Joan through so many tense situations temporarily deserted her. She stayed up all night, sobbing uncontrollably and drinking heavily, while Diana, who was working in New York at the time, did her best to comfort her. Not since the fire at Mapleton Drive had Diana seen her mother come apart this way; she remembered wondering if Joan could possibly withstand the loss.

In the weeks that followed, Joan did her best to conceal her grief and go about her daily business. Eventually, her humor returned, as is evidenced in a letter she wrote to Diana in November 1961: "Shelley's been dying to see snow, but apparently watching it makes her feel dizzy. . . . Maybe I'll drown her in the water tomorrow on the terrace. I took her shopping on Saturday for snow boots, mittens, golashes and a fitting for a new dress. She took *Great Expectations* with her, on which she had to make a book report over the weekend and she actually read it as we were walking on the street. Give me a happy go lucky dunce anytime."

Without Donald, Joan was not sure that she would have the courage to appear onstage again. But in 1962, she returned to Chicago's Drury Lane Theatre in William Douglas Home's comedy *The Reluctant Debutante.* Her costar was John Emery, a fifty-seven-year-old veteran of dozens of Broadway plays and films. A polished player of well-bred men of distinction, Emery also had a colorful offstage life that included a brief period as the husband of Tallulah Bankhead. His profile and vocal delivery were astonishingly like those of John Barrymore; in fact, there was a persistent rumor—later thought to be untrue—that Emery was Barrymore's illegitimate son. Joan was apprehensive about appearing opposite a leading man she had never worked with before, but her uneasiness abated somewhat when she found that Emery had once been a good friend of Donald's. (In fact, he had followed Donald on Broadway in *Skylark* and *The Moon Is Blue.*) Each night, when *The Reluctant Debutante* ended, Joan and John would go to a restaurant or nightclub and spend hours talking about Donald. Their friendship helped Joan immeasurably in coping with her grief. But she could not be without a man for long, and soon John had become a romantic substitute for Donald. (That made two men from Bankhead's past that Joan had inherited.) Joan's social circle widened; John had a good many close friends, including John Steinbeck and his wife, Elaine, formerly a successful stage manager who had worked on many important plays, including the original production of *Oklahoma!* in 1943. Both the Steinbecks were intrigued by Joan, whom they found direct, no-nonsense, and unpretentious, quite unlike any other movie star they had ever known. Elaine and Joan quickly became close friends and were to remain so for nearly twenty years.

In a short time, John Emery had moved into the apartment on East Ninety-sixth Street. Warmer and more high-spirited than Donald, John quickly made friends with Stephanie, and took an interest in her studies. But Joan observed that Shelley, still skeptical about anyone who might supplant her father, was slower to warm to him.

Although she was not as serious about John as she had been about Donald, Joan continued to press Walter for a divorce. Walter hedged for weeks, citing his precarious financial situation. In mid-1962, he had been fired by Twentieth Century–Fox as producer of *Cleopatra.* It was a crippling blow to his ego and prestige, but the studio showed him no mercy, citing mismanagement and huge cost overruns as the principal reasons for his dismissal. Later that year, when Twentieth's board of directors ousted Spyros Skouras and brought back Darryl Zanuck as president, Walter thought there might be some hope that his connection to *Cleopatra* could be salvaged. But Zanuck, appalled at the film's condition, denied Walter any access to the project during its final stages of production. Walter was desperate: "This picture has been my life," he pleaded in a memorandum to Zanuck—to no avail. At sixty-eight, he was once again washed up in the industry.

At the moment, Walter insisted to Joan, a divorce was out of the question. He was in no position to commit to regular monthly support payments, while she argued that he had done nothing to curb his expensive tastes: he lived in a lavish, $1,000-a-month suite at Manhattan's Stanhope Hotel, and dined regularly at "21" and The Four Seasons. There was some comfort in the fact that he liked John Emery and didn't seem to regard him as the same kind of threat that he had Donald; "at least he isn't playing the role of the green-eyed monster," Joan wrote to Diana.

In New York, Joan busied herself supervising the household—in order to keep expenses down, she did the marketing herself, just as she had in Los Angeles—and cast around for a job in the theater. She picked up occasional work on television, guesting on dramatic and panel shows. Then, in mid-1963, she received an offer to star at Miami Beach's Coconut Grove Playhouse in a production of Arthur Sumner Long's popular comedy *Never Too Late*. It was the story of Harry and Edith Lambert, an upper-middle-class couple well into middle age, who discover that they are about to become parents again. It was really more of an expanded one-joke television sitcom than appropriate Broadway fare, but the performances of Paul Ford and Maureen O'Sullivan had carried it to enormous success, and it would be a consistent moneymaker in summer stock for years to come. There was talk, if the Miami performances went well, of taking the production to London.

In the cast was Mary Cooper, a veteran of Broadway productions such as *The Doughgirls*, *Winged Victory*, and *Harvey*, who quickly became a member of Joan's inner circle. Joan's sardonic wit often surfaced during rehearsals; once, when she received a telephone call offering her a stock tour of *Sabrina Fair,* she replied, "Well, I'm really too old for it. Why don't you call my sister Constance?" John Emery was present for the Miami run. One night he confided to Mary Cooper that he had been coughing up blood. "Don't tell Joan," he begged her. "I don't want her to worry."

When *Never Too Late* opened at the Coconut Grove, it was a hit, and London's Prince of Wales Theatre was booked for a September opening. Joan was thrilled with the prospect of making her London debut: stock tours were one thing, but here was the chance to have the kind of prestigious stage success that had eluded her on Broadway. The production would also reunite her with George Abbott, who had worked with her in *Jarnegan* thirty-five years earlier, and had since become one of the most important and successful directors in the business.

First, though, was a major family event that required her attention. Stephanie, who turned twenty in June 1963, had announced her engagement to Manhattan investment banker Frederick Edward Guest. The announcement sparked considerable interest nationwide, for it represented a meeting of the theatrical and social worlds, one to rival Constance's marriage to Philip Plant. Frederick Guest belonged to one of New York's most prominent families. His father was society polo player Winston F.G. Guest; he was a cousin of Sir Winston Churchill, and he was the great-grandson of both Frank Winfield Woolworth, founder of the chain of five-and-dime stores, and steel tycoon and noted philanthropist Henry Phipps. Joan had mixed feelings about the marriage. She was fond of Guest and pleased that he seemed to have a bright future, but she thought that Stephanie was too young to marry.

The wedding took place at St. James' Episcopal Church on Madison Avenue and Seventy-first Street, on August 21, 1963. Shelley served as her sister's maid of honor, Diana and Melinda were among the other attendants, and Joan, Walter, and Constance all were present. The couple sailed for Europe on an extended honeymoon, and the following day Joan flew to London to begin rehearsals for *Never Too Late.*

Joan's costar was Fred Clark, a character comedian and veteran of numerous movies (*Sunset Boulevard, Auntie Mame*) and television series (*The George Burns and Gracie Allen Show*). Because Clark's role was central to the play, Joan insisted that he receive first billing. Rehearsals were trying, since Clark indulged in the kind of exaggerated, frenzied mugging that had long since helped give American farce a bad name in England. His acting struck Joan as coarse and vulgar, especially compared to Donald's dryly elegant comic style. Patiently, she tried to remember all the things that Donald had taught her, trying to get her laughs by smoothly underplaying the situations.

Still, when *Never Too Late* opened at the Prince of Wales Theatre on September 26, 1963, Clark stole most of the notices, while the play was attacked for being loud, broad, and witless—"just the job for the coach party trade," sniffed Philip Hope-Wallace in the *Guardian.* Joan received polite notices for her portrayal of resigned, middle-aged motherhood, although the *Times of London* pitied her for having to "utter lines of such nitwit improbability that I fear she will put the cause of the all-American mom back by twenty years."

"She was very good in the part of Edith," recalled film biographer Roy Moseley. "A cozy actress with great beauty, and very real." Despite the harsh reviews, Joan's name brought in the customers, and the play settled in for what looked like a long run. Having a London success made her very proud, and she was delighted that John was able to be with her throughout the run. After a night's performance, they often went to the Savoy Grill for dinner, where she graciously signed autographs. She also enjoyed shopping in Bond Street and being invited to dine at Buckingham Palace. In interviews, she admitted, "I didn't give up films—they gave me up. The parts got more and more ghastly and I didn't even bother to see the last I made four years ago."

A run of 150 performances at the Prince of Wales Theatre was considered a solid success, and by January 1964, *Never Too Late* had surpassed that goal. But Joan's hopes for a year's run were cut short by a personal crisis. A short time earlier, John had been diagnosed with terminal cancer, and needed to be near his doctors in

New York. Although the management pleaded with Joan to remain with the play, she refused; her commitment to John outweighed any other concerns. She returned to New York to be with him, and *Never Too Late* closed after a respectable 191-performance run.

For most of 1964, Joan accepted no offers of work that would take her away from John. By the fall, the cancer had metastasized to his bones, and he underwent surgery to have an arm amputated. On his return from the hospital, he went into swift decline, requiring oxygen twenty-four hours a day. Although she had engaged nurses around the clock, Joan stayed at home with him all day long. "I don't think he can last much longer," she wrote to Diana in early November 1964, "and I hope for his sake he doesn't."

Mary Cooper felt sorry for Joan, being confined to the apartment with no distractions. "So I called her and said, 'Joanie, would you like me to come and stay with you?' And she said, 'Oh, would you?' I don't think she ever would have asked me." Cooper joined her at East Ninety-sixth Street for a week or so. On the afternoon of November 16, 1964, John Emery died, with Joan and Mary Cooper standing in the doorway of his room. "Joan, as long as I knew her," said Cooper, "never had a drink before 6:00. And about a quarter to six that day, she said, 'I think it would be a good idea if we had a drink.' She was very disciplined that way. She could have had one at 2:00 for all I cared."

On November 18, funeral services were held for John Emery at Frank M. Campbell Funeral Home at Madison Avenue and Eighty-first Street. John Steinbeck wrote the eulogy, read by Zachary Scott. Tallulah Bankhead attended the services, and Cooper remembered noting the study in contrast: Bankhead, playing the role of the grieving ex-wife to the hilt, and Joan, sitting nearby, quiet and dignified.

Nearly one year after John's death, Joan finally obtained a divorce from Walter. As early as January 1962, she had announced to the press that she and Walter had agreed to the terms of a divorce, but a number of complications had arisen to delay any final action—

namely his struggles on the *Cleopatra* production. By the time their marriage was finally dissolved, Joan no longer had a man in her life, while Walter had fallen in love with Aileen Mehle, the lovely blonde gossip columnist who wrote for the *New York Mirror* and *Journal-American* under the byline "Suzy."

Joan had obtained the divorce in Juarez, Mexico, in September 1965. She appeared in Civil Court, heard the judge grant the decree on the grounds of incompatibility, then returned to her hotel across the border in El Paso, Texas. She was fifty-five, Walter seventy-one.

In later years, Joan often referred to Donald Cook as the love of her life. But many people close to her felt that her great love, at least in the beginning, had been Walter. Certainly they had enjoyed a closer bond than many other, more celebrated Hollywood couples. They differed from one another in many respects: Walter's passion was for the world of art and ideas, Joan's for order and security; Walter was committed to the cause of education and advancing oneself, Joan to hard work and harmonious family life. In the end, they helped each other. He challenged her to explore a greater range of possibilities as an actress than she had ever imagined, while she taught him the importance of basic, honest values and the pleasures of parenthood. Most important of all was what they had in common, an independent spirit that permitted them to go their own way and prevented them from becoming too embroiled in the insular machinations of Hollywood.

In an industry where one's prime years often seem to have ended as soon almost as they had begun, both Walter and Joan flourished for a remarkably long period. For two people who achieved so much, who kept evolving and honestly believed in the value of what they were doing, there is something elegiac about the decline of their marriage. As one of Hollywood's golden couples, it may have surprised even them how suddenly it all seemed to go wrong. But what they gave each other, in the end, made for a kind of lasting legacy. Perhaps, even when things between them were at their worst, they were able to recognize that.

Constance had good reason to be pleased with herself when her tour of *Auntie Mame* ended in early 1959. It had earned her excellent notices and restored some degree of financial stability to her life. After that, she occupied herself with a string of stock engagements, including *Call Me Madam, The Marriage Go-Round,* and *September Tide.* At the best summer theaters, such as Chicago's Drury Lane, where she was frequently a guest artist, the money was good: $5,000 a week. But she was concerned that the summer-theater circuit was facing difficult times ahead. "The main thing wrong with the road today," she told a reporter during the summer of 1959, "is that people aren't sending out enough shows to enable owners to keep up theaters properly and to keep the public in the habit."

Her frequent touring meant long separations from John Coulter, who had been moving from one post to another, frozen in the rank of colonel. Several friends recalled that Constance never stopped campaigning in top military circles on her husband's behalf, and eventually he was rewarded with a promotion to brigadier general. Constance was not too proud of him to boast to her closest friends that she had engineered it. Patricia Coulter McElroy remembers it differently: "She refused to play the game at all. The only thing she would do was pose for publicity pictures."

Constance's stage outings had consisted almost entirely of light comedies and musicals. Now her manager, Geoffrey Barr, thought she might have better luck in a wider market if she appeared in a serious play. His solution, in late 1961, was to get her a job in the national touring company of what was to be Lillian Hellman's last successful play, *Toys in the Attic.* It was thought by many to be Hellman's bid at writing a Tennessee Williamsesque drama, and certainly it was over-embroidered with Gothic touches in the Williams manner. Set in New Orleans, *Toys in the Attic* is the story of two spinster sisters, Anna and Carrie Berniers, and their wandering wastrel brother, Julian. As the play opens, Julian comes home, bringing along his young bride, Lily. It is soon revealed that Lily is deeply emotionally disturbed. The play hurls itself toward a bleak conclusion—there are references to incest—and its plot is dense even by Hellman's standards.

Constance was cast as Albertine Prine, the wealthy mother of Julian's bride who may well have paid Julian $10,000 to get her daughter to the altar. Albertine prides herself on keeping the rest of the world at a steady distance: she sleeps by day and comes out only at night, accompanied by her black lover, Henry, who at his own insistence poses as her chauffeur. From the beginning, Constance loathed both the part and the play. Although she recognized Hellman's talent, she found *Toys in the Attic* a degrading and depressing play into which no light shone. She had never sympathized with or understood the southern mentality, and now she was forced to confront it on a nightly basis. During rehearsals in New York, before the play traveled to Wilmington, Delaware, for its November opening, she requested a release from her contract, but the producer, Kermit Bloomgarden, refused to consider it until he found an adequate replacement for her.

Her unhappiness was all too clear to director Adrian Hall and to her fellow actors (including Anne Revere, Patricia Jessel, and Scott MacKay). Penny Fuller, then a young and inexperienced actress, played Lily, and remembered that working with Constance helped her develop "a very valuable technique—how to act with my back to the audience. She was always upstage, which was not exactly the blocking." Constance managed to get through the Wilmington engagement, and the play moved on to Washington, D.C. During the run there, Bloomgarden notified company manager Clayton Coots that he was going to attend the Washington opening. He urged Coots not to tell Constance that he was coming, since he wanted to observe her performance without her knowing about it. When Bloomgarden came backstage after the performance, Constance, realizing that Coots had been in on the deception, let it be known that she was displeased. That night, Bloomgarden took the entire cast to the Jockey Club for dinner, where Constance kept darting combative, I'm-going-to-get-even-with-you glances across the table at Coots. Scott MacKay ordered steak tartare, and when it arrived, he asked if anyone else would like to try some. Constance asked for some for her apricot-colored poodle, Bijou, who occupied the chair next to hers, but the dog refused to touch it. Just then

Clayton Coots said, "I'd like to try some." "Would you?" replied Constance sweetly, and hurled Bijou's steak tartare across the table at Coots. "I'd never seen anything like this," remembered Fuller. "I mean, this really was another generation!"

Toys in the Attic moved on to Chicago's Blackstone Theater. The *Chicago Tribune*'s formidable drama critic Claudia Cassidy called it "a curious, oddly fascinating play . . . rather like an overcrowded Chekhovian *Streetcar,* and not one you would willingly leave until the end of the line. And it could scarcely have chosen a stranger night than Christmas to come to the Blackstone, for its toys are ugly, festered longings and its attic a Freudian nightmare." Cassidy found the role of Albertine underwritten, and noted that "Constance Bennett does not mar the sketch of the rich one, nor does she develop it."

During the run in Chicago, Constance made a move that most actors would never have dared. During an interview on Irv Kupcinet's WBBM television program *At Random,* she was asked how she got through a part that she was known to find unsympathetic. "My manager, Geoffrey Barr, in New York, decided that I should change my image," she answered. "I'm going to change his when I get back." When Kupcinet pressed her for her opinion of the play, she admitted that she found Hellman "a very powerful and very wonderful writer." But she added that she found *Toys in the Attic* an example of "sick" theater, "because I think that the theme is sick and there's so much sickness in the world I don't think that it should be forced on people as entertainment." She went on to castigate Tennessee Williams for writing "neurotic plays," and Harold Clurman for being "a neurotic director." She also hoped that someday Hellman might turn her "talent into something happy."

Bloomgarden was furious and launched a counterattack on her in *Variety,* while he contemplated taking legal action against her via Actors' Equity. In the end, Constance bowed out of the play after the Chicago run. *Toys in the Attic* had one more stop, at Los Angeles's Biltmore Theater, where her understudy, Ann Shropshire, took over the part. Constance was delighted when the Los Angeles press gave it a middling reception, and in a letter to the editor in *Variety,* she wondered where Bloomgarden would place the blame now.

At this point, Constance's daughters were faring better than they ever had. Lorinda was thriving, still living on her own in New York and working toward her dream of becoming a sculptor. Academics had remained a struggle for Gyl, but in her teens she discovered that she had a natural aptitude for the stage. She appeared in several school productions, and Constance, who had constantly fretted that her younger daughter wasn't good at much of anything, was relieved that she seemed finally to have discovered where her true talents lay. Gyl had enrolled in the American Academy of Dramatic Art, and was happier than she had been at any time in her life. Late in 1962, both Constance and Gyl appeared at Chicago's Drury Lane Theatre in a production of Noël Coward's *Hay Fever.* The engagement was to be a family reunion in more ways than one.

Except for the brief telephone conversation in Las Vegas, Peter and Constance had not had any contact whatsoever since he had pressured her to sign the Summit Drive house over to him in 1952. To Constance, he continued to be known as "Unmentionable." Now he decided to chance a face-to-face meeting.

On December 16, 1962, Peter flew to Chicago and took a room at the luxurious Drake Hotel, where he wrote his mother a short note, explaining that their differences should be reconciled before time denied them the choice. On Sunday afternoon, he and his good friend Don Feather, a former instructor of Peter's at Culver, drove out to the Drury Lane. Peter asked that the letter be delivered to Constance, who was staying in an apartment, reserved for the visiting stars, that adjoined the theater. Shortly after, Peter and Don Feather returned to the Drake. When the telephone rang, Peter was certain that it was his mother. Preferring to face her in person, he asked Don to take it, and if it was Constance, to tell her he was not in. Don picked up the phone, and heard Constance's imperious voice come over the line: "I'm expecting my son this evening," she said. "Please remind him that Sunday evening curtain is an hour earlier."

Peter and Don had drinks and dinner at the Drake, then drove out to the theater around the time the play was scheduled to end. After a wait of about half an hour, Peter climbed the stairs and knocked on the apartment door. Constance answered. She had not seen her son in a decade, had no idea of the kind of man he had become, knew nothing about him whatsoever. For once, she was at a complete loss. Her anxiety was acute; to Peter, she seemed completely glacial. Doing her best to recover herself, she simply said, "Let's not talk about it."

"And I wasn't going to," Peter remembered, years later. "She really didn't know what a good job she did in bringing me up. She didn't realize that she had brought me up along the lines that she had in mind, and that I would have different values and a different sense of responsibility than she had. And when life started evolving between us, she would play her part as she always had, and I would play my part based on how she had instructed me to behave."

Their visit was brief, but it was not their last. Constance had been relieved of the enormous burden of guilt and anxiety she had carried around for years. Both John Coulter and some of Constance's closest friends would later tell Peter that she had suffered terribly during their long estrangement, and that their reconciliation provided her with a new lease on life. Now, she had been granted absolution by her own son.

In December 1961, John had been named deputy commandant of the NATO Defense College in Paris. Constance was with him at certain intervals, but continued to make New York her home base. By this time, Lorinda was living on the Lower East Side, and Patricia was grown up and on her own, so the Coulters gave up the Park Avenue apartment and took a smaller one at 405 East Fifty-fourth Street, between First Avenue and Sutton Place South. The building was known as "Four out of five," because of the rumor that four out of five tenants were gay. Constance, who loved the company of gay men, was delighted with the new living quarters, even though she did not occupy its regal penthouse—that belonged to actress Hermione Gingold. Constance and Gyl lived here whenever Constance wasn't in Paris with John or on the road in a play.

In February 1963, John flew from Paris to the States to give

Patricia away at her wedding to Michael Roger Neal McDonnell. Constance was not present, having gone to Switzerland for a brief skiing vacation. On the morning of the wedding, a person-to-person transatlantic telephone call was placed to John. Martha Coulter, who was helping her daughter get dressed, took the call. She listened for a moment, then said, "Sorry—no understand. Upstairs maid," and hung up. Then she looked at Patricia and said, "Serves her right. She broke her leg." Eventually John was told the specifics: Constance had fallen on the ski slopes while completing a complicated run. She sustained a triple fracture in one leg. She was confined to bed for some time, and it was a few months before she was able to walk without crutches.

By August 1963, John was once again stateside, as commander of the New York Air Defense Sector at New Jersey's McGuire Air Force Base. The Coulters lived on the base part of the time, while maintaining the East Fifty-fourth Street apartment. Since Constance hadn't earned any big money since the *Auntie Mame* tour ended early in 1959, the Coulters' bank account was again running low. While John was stationed at McGuire, Constance tried to keep up appearances. They drove a rather beaten-up 1957 cream-colored Ford Thunderbird with the stuffing spilling out of the seat covers, but whenever they had to make an official appearance, Constance insisted that they use the shiny new Cadillac sedan owned by one of John's aides. "Everywhere they went he wore his uniform," Peter recalled. "That was the only presentation that they were comfortable with."

Privately, Constance tried to economize. The East Fifty-fourth Street apartment was less expensive than living on Park Avenue, and she saved a considerable amount by shopping at McGuire's PX. At McGuire, she gamely played the role of officer's wife. "The wives of the other officers seemed quite thrilled to have her in their midst," remembered Anne Slater. "They would come up and say 'Hello, Miss Bennett,' and you could practically see the stars in their eyes. And she was very nice to them."

Constance was in touch with Peter on a regular basis, and always he honored her request that they not discuss the past. By this point, Peter had begun what would become a thirty-seven-year career with Farmers Insurance Group at its headquarters in Los Angeles. Constance took special pride in Lorinda, who was still living in New York, her sculpting career boosted by a Guggenheim fellowship she received in 1963. Gyl was also off and running in her professional life. In 1963, with her boyfriend, fellow actor Hank Sgrosso, she had opened a tiny eight-table restaurant, The Red Rug, on the corner of Twenty-eighth Street and Third Avenue. On one occasion, Constance came for dinner, and Gyl remembered thinking that her mother was mildly impressed to see her twenty-year-old daughter turning out filet mignon and sauce bordelaise. After Gyl graduated from the American Academy of Dramatic Art, she was signed to a seven-year contract by Twentieth Century–Fox television. She got a good break in 1964, when she was cast as Selena Cross in the pilot for a proposed series based on Grace Metalious's sensationalistic study of small-town life, *Peyton Place,* for ABC-TV. But by the time the network picked up the series for its fall schedule, Gyl's part had been written out. She stayed on in New York, pursuing acting and modeling jobs.

The long, slow process of recovering from her broken leg kept Constance away from acting for some time, but by the fall of 1964 she was well enough to make a guest appearance on an episode of the CBS television dramatic series *The Reporter.* Around the same time, an unexpected movie offer came along from producer Ross Hunter at Universal. A former actor, Hunter had turned to producing in the early 1950s. Blithely ignoring the industry's shift toward contemporary themes, he made a string of romantic dramas and glossy comedies which, despite being rather retrograde, earned a lot of money. Hunter had a particular weakness for aging actresses from the 1930s and 1940s: he hired Jane Wyman for *Magnificent Obsession* and *All That Heaven Allows,* Barbara Stanwyck and Joan for *There's Always Tomorrow,* and Lana Turner for *Imitation of Life* and *Portrait in Black.* Now he was putting together a new vehicle for Turner, except that it was actually a very old one—a big-budget, Technicolor remake of the tearjerker *Madame X,* which had previously served as a vehicle for Pauline Frederick, Ruth

Chatterton, and Gladys George. With Turner set for the title role, Hunter turned his attention to casting a key supporting part, that of the heroine's cruel mother-in-law. After receiving turndowns from Kay Francis and Myrna Loy, he sent the script to Constance, who accepted at once. She delighted in telling friends that she would be "costarring with Lana Turner," even though her part was definitely a subordinate one.

Madame X is the story of Holly Anderson (Turner), the neglected wife of socially prominent politician Clay Anderson (John Forsythe). When Holly accidentally causes the death of her playboy lover (Ricardo Montalban), she is persuaded by Clay's manipulative mother, Estelle (Constance), that the ensuing scandal will ruin Clay's political future, as well as the future of their son, Clay Jr. Estelle arranges for Holly to fake her own death and leave the country under an assumed name. Years later, Holly, now a broken-down alcoholic, murders the blackmailer (Burgess Meredith) who has discovered her true identity, and winds up going on trial, where she is defended by the grown-up Clay Jr. (Keir Dullea)—who has no idea that his client is really his mother.

In 1965, a year that included such strikingly modern films as *A Patch of Blue, The Pawnbroker,* and *Darling,* it seemed a bit hard to believe that Hunter was going to undertake a dated, melodramatic soap opera like *Madame X*. But Turner had drawn very well for him in her previous star vehicles, and he was hoping that lightning would strike once again.

Even in preproduction there were intimations of trouble. When the film's costume designer, Jean Louis, had flown to New York to discuss the wardrobe with Constance, he was stunned to find her looking marvelous—the result of a recent face-lift. When he returned to Hollywood, Jean Louis told Hunter that he was concerned that Constance did not look old enough to play Lana Turner's mother-in-law. After Constance arrived to begin filming, Hunter told her that in the interest of dramatic credibility, they would have to add a few wrinkles, a few gray hairs, perhaps a little padding. "You're not going to *touch* me!" Constance snapped. "This is exactly what I want and how I want to look."

There was some bravado in all of this; as filming progressed, Constance was feeling far from her best. For several weeks she had been plagued by bouts of dizziness. In late December 1964, when she had flown to Hollywood to begin work on *Madame X,* Lorinda had met her at Los Angeles International Airport. As Constance stepped onto the escalator, she lost her balance and staggered. Lorinda was alarmed and asked if her mother was feeling all right, but Constance quickly brushed it aside.

Constance seemed pleased to be back in Hollywood. Eva Gabor lent her her house for the duration of the filming, and Peter visited her frequently. She caught up with several of her old cronies, and on Valentine's Day Gilbert Roland turned up, bearing a huge satin heart. They had not seen each other in some time, and Constance was delighted by his surprise appearance. Being on the set of *Madame X* was less pleasant; director David Lowell Rich had little trouble conveying the tension between Holly and her mother-in-law, since Turner and Constance loathed each other almost from the start. Turner was tense to begin with, since *Madame X* presented her with a much more emotional role than she usually played. But there were other difficulties as well: Turner had put on some weight and Jean Louis's lavish wardrobe did not flatter her. On the other hand, Constance, sixteen years older than Turner, looked almost alarmingly youthful—more like an older sister than a mother-in-law. Turner was acutely aware of this, and became increasingly hostile toward Constance. Anne Slater, who visited the set, recalled that "Constance looked wonderful in the clothes and moved like a dream, and I'm afraid that Lana just didn't like that at all. She would come out and watch Constance rehearsing a scene, and she would stand and watch her for a few minutes, and then just sort of glare at her, turn, and walk off to her dressing room."

One particularly harsh exchange took place over a choice of wardrobe for a montage sequence: both women wanted to wear a sable coat, but Turner insisted that Constance wear chinchilla, because, according to Jean Louis, "it was more like an old lady." (In the end, Constance got the sable, while Turner settled for white mink.)

As production went on, Constance continued to feel unwell, but she was determined to give the public its money's worth. Perhaps she simply tried too hard, for her performance in the finished film is downright strident. She declaims most of her lines so briskly and loudly that the rest of the cast seems almost catatonic. There is no question that it's a star turn, but her performance at times seems like a routine by a seasoned drag queen.

When Constance had completed her scenes in the film, she continued to feel dizzy and fatigued, and arranged for a thorough medical examination. The news was grim: X-rays revealed a large tumor in her left lung. Through John's military connections, arrangements were made for surgery to be performed at Walter Reed Army Medical Center in Washington, D.C. The tumor was malignant and advanced, causing the surgeons to fear that the cancer might already have metastasized. Right away, she underwent surgery to have the affected lung removed. Her recovery was remarkably swift, and John was there to see that she did everything she was supposed to do. Gyl remembered him marching her around the apartment, military-style, to be sure that she had the requisite exercise.

What John did not know was that further tests had revealed another tumor, the size of a golf ball, at the base of Constance's skull. It was inoperable, and the doctors told her that she might have only a few months left. She was adamant that John not discover the truth. Frequently she lost her balance and fell, and always she pleaded with her maid, Clemencia, "Don't tell the General about this."

Apart from Clemencia, the only person Constance told about her illness was Joan. Stunned and upset by the gruesome treatments Constance was receiving, Joan called Diana and confided in her—but no one else was told the truth. For the past few years, Joan and Constance had been only sporadically in touch, but now they were in constant contact. Joan was committed to appear in a stock tour of *Never Too Late* that summer, but she promised to check in as often as possible.

During Constance's hospitalization at Walter Reed, Joan was

preparing for a stock tour of Noël Coward's *Fallen Angels*. Once again, her costar was Mary Cooper. One afternoon, the two of them were rehearsing at Cooper's home when Joan suddenly broke off and said, "May I call Constance?" She and Constance had a brief conversation, which ended with Joan saying quietly, "I love you too, Constance." She hung up, waited a few moments, and said to Cooper, "That's the first time in our lives that we've ever said that to each other."

By midsummer, Constance's condition seemed outwardly stable. One evening in mid-July, she suddenly collapsed, and John rushed her to the nearby Fort Dix Hospital. There he was finally made aware of the gravity of her illness. There was some discussion of flying her to Walter Reed, but the doctors were concerned that the flight would be too risky, so she was left at Fort Dix. Constance was quite unresponsive as she was wheeled in to the admitting desk. John began helping the nurse on duty fill out the entrance forms, but when the nurse asked Constance's age, a clear, strong voice called out from behind them, "I was born in 1914"—cleanly shaving off ten years.

On the afternoon of July 24, 1965, John telephoned Lorinda and told her, "Lorrie, your mother has only a few hours to live." Lorinda, who had assumed Constance's hospitalization was related to her lung surgery of a few months earlier, was numb with shock. Later that day, when Joan was onstage in Philadelphia in a summer stock production of *Never Too Late,* she received a call backstage from Stephanie, who told her that Constance had died that evening at Fort Dix Hospital. The official cause of death was a cerebral hemorrhage.

The following evening, Joan's *Never Too Late* tour took her to Laconia, New Hampshire. She opened there that night, then was flown in a private plane by a local man named James Tyler to New York's La Guardia Airport so that she could attend Constance's services at Frank Campbell's Funeral Home on Madison Avenue and Eighty-first Street.

Peter flew to New York from California, and Gyl was on hand, but it was Lorinda who took charge of the funeral details. With Stephanie's assistance, she arranged for all the flowers and the music.

Although some thought it might be appropriate for a few of Constance's favorite songs to be played, Lorinda insisted on an all-Bach program. While the family members debated whether to have an open- or closed-casket service, John asked Anne Slater to go around to Campbell's to make sure that Constance had been properly attended to by the staff. Slater was shocked at what she found: Constance was made up like a Dresden doll, with round, rosy cheeks, pasty lips, and curled hair. She hardly resembled her true self at all. "Would it be all right if I re-did it?" Slater asked. Somewhat taken aback, the funeral home staff agreed. Slater went to work and painstakingly restored her friend's trademark pageboy, and fixed her makeup. When she had finished, Constance looked like Constance.

In the end, the decision was made to have a closed-casket service. A large crowd attended the funeral at Campbell's on July 28. After the service, James Tyler flew Joan back to New Hampshire for the second night of her run there in *Never Too Late*. Joan told a reporter, "When you are a show business family for 100 years as we are, the cliché about 'The show must go on' is not really a cliché but a way of life."

To Lorinda, it made sense, in a strange way, that Constance died prematurely. "I always felt that Mummy died because she was being forced to live her life over again," said Lorinda. Despite the fact that she had always lived in the present, Constance probably had little to look forward to professionally. Had she taken direction as well as Joan did, she might have been able to reshape her screen persona to suit changing tastes and standards. But the debacle with *Toys in the Attic* had been a kind of warning bell that she seemed unable to bend with the times. For someone whose greatest pleasure in life had been having her own way—from her tantrums as a child to her adolescent rebellions to her outrageous demands in Hollywood to her perpetual delight in manipulating the men in her life—Constance was surely not a woman who would have dealt easily with the concessions and limitations that come with old age. Perhaps it was a gift, in a way, that she died when she did. Probably she would not have found the world a welcoming place for much longer.

On July 29, 1965, at 11:00 in the morning, Constance was buried in Arlington National Cemetery, in keeping with her status as a general's wife. At her request, only the date of her death appears on her tombstone.

Chapter Twenty-Two

1966–1971

Late in 1965, Joan left Ninety-sixth Street for a new apartment at 150 East Seventy-second Street, just east of Lexington Avenue. With the help of interior designer Airey Mays, she turned it into another bright and colorful reminder of her years in California. The foyer sported white-and-green wallpaper in a kind of trellis pattern, with lots of plants scattered about. The living room and library were both painted lemon yellow—Joan called the color her therapy—while her large bedroom was done in her favorite combination of pink and green. A second bedroom, brightened up with lots of chintz, was occupied by Shelley, by now a serious-minded student at Vassar College.

The political interests that Walter had ignited in Joan continued to burn steadily throughout the turbulent 1960s. In 1966, she campaigned vigorously for John V. Lindsay, then running for mayor of New York City. Her grandson, Timothy Anderson, remembered visiting her in New York and attending a Lindsay fund-raising event at a West Village rock and roll club called The Cheetah. Joan gave a speech on Lindsay's behalf, sharing the stage with the Maharishi Mahesh Yogi. It was a strange pairing—elegant Hollywood legend and 1960s counter-culture hero—but Joan behaved as if it were the most natural thing in the world. "It was late at night," recalled Anderson, "and the place was packed inside and out. I was so impressed with how in control of everything she was. Very much a presence. At the end, she just marched out into the street—by this time, it was two or three in the morning—to hail a cab back to her apartment. I recall trying to take her arm, thinking that I was a young man with his grandmother, in a very rough neighborhood, and that I should reveal some authority here—but she just plunged right ahead."

With John Emery dead, work once again consumed Joan's attention. More than anything, she wanted to do another Broadway play. Her agent, Tom Korman, was unable to turn up anything appropriate, but he did stumble across something that he thought might benefit her. It was a bizarre project, quite unlike anything she had done before: a five-day-a-week half-hour serial produced by ABC television. The idea of appearing in a soap opera struck Joan as depressing: she had hardly spent thirty-eight years in the profession to wind up emoting on the small screen for an audience of bored housewives. But this wasn't an ordinary soap about unfaithful husbands and long-suffering wives. This was a Gothic-style mystery, set in a gloomy mansion on the coast of Maine. The idea had been dreamed up by independent producer Dan Curtis, whose experience was mostly limited to sports broadcasting (including *The CBS Golf Classic*). Curtis was looking for someone with a distinctive brand of elegance and authority to play the leading female part, and he felt that Joan had just the right qualities.

The name of the series was *Dark Shadows,* and Korman urged her to take the job—the idea was just offbeat enough that it might succeed. But Joan still said no. It was practically unheard of for an actress of her stature to appear on daytime television. She had never watched a single episode of a soap opera, and was sure that the actors who appeared in them must all be third-rate. She was also apprehensive about the intensive workload: rehearsing and taping the show by day, and learning lines for the next episode by night. Still, she needed some sort of steady income, since she had not worked regularly since leaving the London company of *Never Too Late*. In the end, she told Korman that she would give it a try. She consoled herself with the likelihood that the series would run no more than several weeks, and signed on for a salary of $333 an episode with a guarantee of three episodes per week.

The concept of *Dark Shadows* may have been original, but its content was not. Over its five-year run, its plotlines would borrow heavily from the works of several famous authors, from Bram Stoker to Shirley Jackson to the Brontë sisters. The very first episode, telecast on June 27, 1966, was reminiscent of *Jane Eyre*: the young and innocent Victoria Winters (Alexandra Moltke) comes to Collinwood, a perpetually fog-shrouded Maine estate presided over by an enigmatic recluse named Elizabeth Collins Stoddard (Joan). Victoria has been engaged as governess to Elizabeth's troubled nephew David (David Henesy), and soon finds herself embroiled in the daily turmoil of a bizarre household that includes David's aristocratic father (Louis Edmonds) and Elizabeth's high-strung daughter (Nancy Barrett). Victoria soon discovers that the nearby town, Collinsport, is no ordinary, peaceful fishing village, but a place where eerie legends abound, where nearly everyone seems to have a hidden past.

The *Dark Shadows* cast performed energetically and with desperately straight faces. In time, the series would be regarded as a classic piece of high camp, perhaps best illustrated by Louis Edmonds playing stuffy Roger Collins as if he were in a whodunit put on by a British repertory company. Each episode opened with a florid voice-over from one of the characters. An example: "A desperate secret, long held, has finally been revealed at Collinwood. And the truth, cutting back across time, has seared the heart and stunned the mind, opening ancient wounds that seem beyond the cure of time and truth."

At first, Joan's apprehensions about doing the series seemed validated. The wild, melodramatic plotlines did not capture a sizable audience, and the work was the most grueling she had ever known. Cast members arrived at ABC's Studio 2 at 24 West Sixty-seventh Street around 8 A.M.; blocking rehearsal began one-half hour later. At 10:30, there was an early lunch break, during which the actors also went into make-up and hair styling. At 11:30, the cast was given its places for the camera blocking, which was followed by another run-through with camera, then a dress rehearsal at 2:00. After the director had given notes to the cast, the show was taped from 3:00 to 3:30. Although *Dark Shadows* was not live, the taping was done as if it were; there were even pauses, timed down to the last second, for the commercial inserts. Frequently, there were mishaps: an actor would stumble over a line or accidentally back into a boom; occasionally, a stagehand was glimpsed. One day during rehearsal, Joan was supposed to fling open a set of French doors and utter the line, "Welcome to Collinwood," which unfortunately came out, "Welcome to Hollywood." Sometimes there were last-minute script additions, which required the actors to keep their eyes glued on the teleprompter. But there were hardly ever any do-overs, because the budget didn't allow for them. Early on, a couple of goofs were so glaring that a physical tape edit was called for, but it required the approval of one of ABC's top executives; the network was still several years away from using electronic editing on two-inch video. But the actors' workday didn't finish with the taping. From 4:00 to 6:30, there was always a rough reading of the script for the next day's episode.

Joan was not pleased with her new assignment. The pace was faster and rougher than anything she had been accustomed to, and because of her poor eyesight, she was unable to rely on the teleprompter, so each night she had to commit her lines to memory. (In one sense, work on *Dark Shadows* was similar to her early movie work in Hollywood, when most films were shot in long takes.) "It was clear to me from the first scenes I had with her," remembered Nancy Barrett, "that she was terrified. She had these incredible eyes, and they were sparkling—she looked scared to death. Therefore, I found her one of the most courageous actresses I ever met. It was a stunningly difficult thing for her to do."

Joan had never objected to hard work, but she was concerned most of all about the quality of the series. The scripts were preposterous—not unlike those of the cheap horror serials of the 1930s—and, as with all daytime soaps, the action moved at an extremely slow pace. One plot strand, involving blackmailer Jason McGuire (Dennis Patrick) and his attempts to force Elizabeth Stoddard to marry him—took nearly an entire season to unfold. Production values were low; in the early episodes, shot in black and white, the lighting was dim and crude. One day, during the first weeks of taping, Walter visited the set, immediately noticed the lighting deficiencies, and suggested that a series of small lights be attached to the camera that would produce a kind of footlight effect.

Joan was not at all sure what to make of Dan Curtis. "Dan does have genius," said Kathryn Leigh Scott, who played Maggie Evans, the Collinsport waitress who eventually moves to Collinwood to work as David's governess after Victoria Winters departs. "But for Joan, coming from the background she had, to work with a producer who had never done anything but the golf classic . . . well . . . Dan had to prove himself. I think she looked at him in horror, because he had rough edges."

Joan's worries about the series were intensified by the lukewarm reviews and Nielsen ratings. After *Dark Shadows* had been on the air for one month, it had succeeded in capturing only a 17.8 share of the viewing audience—around 9 million viewers by the week. Not bad, certainly, but not enough to survive in the competitive world of daytime programming. Surprisingly, ABC seemed willing to give the series a fighting chance. At the end of August 1966, the *Dark Shadows* production unit moved to a studio of its own, a renovated loft at 433 West Fifty-third Street.

No matter how much the series' no-frills, one-take system rankled, Joan tried her best never to let on to her coworkers. "She was used to working like a trouper," remembered Kathryn Leigh Scott. "And she had to know that her colleagues—people like Lillian Gish, Myrna Loy, Joan Fontaine—were tuning in at home to watch. With her sense of professionalism, she wanted to be good for them." Marie Wallace, who played a variety of character roles on the series, was also impressed with her dedication. "At the end of the day, when we were supposed to read the next day's script until around 6:30—well, we all tried to get out of it. We would say that we had an audition or use whatever excuse we could find. But Joan never once tried to get out of it. She would always go until the end of the day."

As the months rolled by, Joan realized that she had underestimated the quality of the actors she would be working with; many of them, over time, became close friends. She grew quite attached to Louis Edmonds, whose résumé boasted numerous Restoration comedies and Shakespearean plays, including a television production of *Richard II* with Maurice Evans. Grayson Hall, who joined the cast as Dr. Julia Hoffman in 1967, had lengthy experience on stage and had received an Academy Award nomination for her performance in the 1964 film version of Tennessee Williams's *The Night of the Iguana.* Joan was especially fond of two of the younger cast members, Kathryn Leigh Scott and Alexandra Moltke, to whom she gave a photograph of herself inscribed, "To Alexandra—my fifth daughter." Years later, Alexandra Moltke Iles recalled Joan as a woman of sardonic wit as well as great sweetness and warmth. Iles frequently had dinner with Joan, and remembered that "she never dominated. She would reminisce about the old days in Hollywood if you asked her, but she would never go out of her way to tell funny stories, and she would never cut someone off in conversation." Scott concurred: "Joan somehow managed to create the perfect aura of star status without acting like a star. We enjoyed looking up to her."

Occasionally, she imparted advice to the younger actresses. She didn't think much of the fashion trends of the late 1960s, and once, when Scott came to rehearsal wearing a long skirt and rimless Granny glasses, Joan said, "Kathryn, you're pretty. Why do that? Leave that to the others." From time to time, she cautioned Scott against overemoting for the camera, knowing that it would read too "big" on film. "You're using your face too much," she would warn, "Pull back or you won't have anywhere to go as the scene builds." Once, when Nancy Barrett was contemplating cutting her long blonde hair, Joan warned her not to do it. "She said to me, 'Nancy, don't you realize that your hair is your crowning glory?'" Barrett remembered. "She didn't mean that I couldn't act or had nothing else going for me—she just told the truth. So I didn't cut it." Seldom did Joan make a derogatory observation about any of her fellow cast members, young or old. Yet occasionally, her summing up of people could be quite blunt. Of Roger Davis, the actor who played Maggie Evans's love interest, Jeff Clark, she observed privately, "He thinks he's Henry Fonda—except that he has no talent."

Not long after *Dark Shadows* began its run, its future was endangered by a thirteen-day strike launched by the American Federation of Television and Radio Artists. Enough episodes had been taped to cover the period of the strike, so no break in the series occurred. But in October 1967, the technicians' union, the National Association of Broadcast Employees and Technicians, launched a strike of its own. Initially, members of the *Dark Shadows* cast honored a request from AFTRA not to cross picket lines, even though most felt that NABET was asking for too much. But as the strike became more contentious, AFTRA's request turned into a demand: a statement was issued ordering all members not to cross the picket lines. The bullying tone of AFTRA's order offended many actors, but it hit a particularly raw nerve with the *Dark Shadows* cast members, who were concerned that their series had not yet found its audience and was too vulnerable to withstand a prolonged strike. Joan and most of the other actors had had enough. Despite threats of penalties and legal action, they returned to work. The dispute finally was settled, and Joan's reward for taking a stand was a $5,400 fine from AFTRA.

By the spring of 1967, *Dark Shadows* was still flailing about, trying to find its audience. Certain that ABC would cancel the series unless something changed drastically, Curtis rolled the dice by ordering his writing staff to introduce a vampire into the storyline. In April, on the series' 210th episode, the character of Barnabas Collins made his first appearance. Barnabas was not the ordinary savage monster; he was an elegant and civilized man whose vampirism was the result of a curse placed on him in 1797 by his beautiful nemesis, a witch known as Angelique (Lara Parker). Barnabas was portrayed by Jonathan Frid, a Canadian actor with a long list of Shakespearean credits. Children loved the show's new supernatural elements, and Barnabas had tremendous appeal to women: he was a vampire who was horrified by his own condition and longed to reform. His charms were summed up in a letter from a viewer from Hattiesburg, Mississippi: "If it takes blood to keep him alive, he can have some of mine." The series also attracted many celebrity viewers, among them Joanne Woodward, who developed a "Joan Bennett scream" that she used in one of her movies. The ratings shot up. By June 1968, a little over a year after the introduction of Barnabas, *Dark Shadows* claimed a 28.8 share, making it one of the most-watched daytime series. ABC executives were elated. *Dark Shadows* merchandise suddenly popped up everywhere: paperback novel tie-ins, lunch boxes, posters, board games, bubble-gum cards. Now Joan could enjoy all the benefits of being in a hit television series—she was once again the frequent subject of magazine and newspaper interviews, and she often made guest appearances on television's top talk shows. Suddenly she had an army of teenage fans who had never heard of *The Woman in the Window* or *Scarlet Street*—at the end of her working day, many of them were waiting for her outside the studio stage door, hoping for an autograph. In the summer of 1968, while narrating a fashion show in the Midwest, she was mobbed by teenagers, and told a reporter, "I felt positively like a Beatle."

But Joan's busy schedule had not diminished her need to have a man in her life. Whenever she was appearing in a play in summer stock, she often dated one of the actors in the company, but she had not really had a steady escort since John Emery. During *Dark Shadows*'s second season, Joan received an invitation to a party given by Donald Farber, a New York theatrical attorney, and his wife, Anne. There she met an old friend of the Farbers named David Wilde. In a short time, they were seeing a good deal of each other.

David Wilde was quite unlike anyone else Joan had ever dated. A short, attractive man with gunmetal blue eyes, he seemed charming and down-to-earth. Comfortably well off from birth, he had a degree from Yale in English literature, two daughters from a previous marriage, and a rather checkered work history. For several years beginning in 1949, he published *The Record,* a weekly newspaper in the Westchester County village of Bedford; later on, he had worked in public relations; and soon after he met Joan he was publishing a magazine called *Girl Talk,* distributed free in beauty parlors across the country. A lifelong movie and theater buff, he was delighted with his new life as a steady escort of Joan Bennett.

But David was not quite the regular weave that he appeared

to be. While still a child, he had discovered that he received a great sensual release, an inexplicable thrill, from dressing in women's clothes. As an adult, it became his great passion, one that caused considerable complications for a married man with two children. Like many cross-dressers, David was resolutely heterosexual. He was, in fact, not always comfortable in the presence of homosexuals, and considered transsexuality hideously extreme and unnatural. He established a separate cross-dressing identity for himself, and many who knew "Gail" found her gentler and easier to take than David as David. In time, he was an integral part of a vast network of male cross-dressers; like David, they were mostly white-collar, upper-middle-class men who found complete freedom only in their female identities.

When David confessed his complicated past to Joan, she was dismayed. He assured her that he was not currently in a cross-dressing phase, and that he had no intention of returning to it as long as their relationship continued. After the initial shock that greeted David's confession, Joan seemed to accept his fetish quite calmly. Too calmly, thought David, and he summoned a friend, Dr. Harry Benjamin, to offer his professional insights on the cross-dressing phenomenon. Again, she seemed unperturbed.

Although David's cross-dressing was kept out of sight, there were other thorny aspects to his relationship with Joan. While he plainly adored her, his devotion could be too much. Early on in their relationship, he appointed himself Joan's guardian and protector. Both stubborn and opinionated, he did not shy away from confrontations, particularly whenever he felt that Joan's position or presence had been overlooked or slighted. "He seemed kind of doting," said Alexandra Moltke, "but he didn't strike me as being worthy of her." Many found his connection to Joan like that of a devoted fan to a star. "He thought he knew a great deal about the theater," said Joan's friend, actor Robert Wallsten. "And he was always trying to tell everybody all about it. And the fact was he knew nothing."

Yet to others, David was a positive force in Joan's life. He insisted that she keep up socially and attend all the latest movies and plays; given her quiet nature, Joan, left to her own devices, might simply have faded from the scene. Most of all, David provided the two things she desired most at this point in her life: steady companionship and financial stability. David's independent income meant that she would not have to be a burden on any of her children as she aged and professional opportunities inevitably narrowed. She also had seen enough of her colleagues from the old days in Hollywood dependent on professional escorts for social activity. David's secure position seemed a good enough reason to stay with him as she neared sixty, still the self-reliant woman that she had been in 1929, when she had left New York for Hollywood.

During this period, there were numerous changes in the lives of Joan's children. Melinda and Joe Bena left California and moved east to a comfortable home in Chappaqua, New York. Diana's life was far more chaotic. Her marriage to Jack Anderson had been troubled from the beginning. Although they had had four children, Diana never felt certain that she could depend on him. "There was an elusive quality about him that I couldn't put my finger on," she recalled. "He just was not made out to be a family man." During the early 1960s, she made the acquaintance of the Austrian-born actor Oskar Werner. They saw each other, platonically, off and on for several years. In 1965, the year that Werner made a great success in Stanley Kramer's film *Ship of Fools,* he and Diana became romantically involved. Her close friend, soprano Irmgard Seefried, begged her to give up Werner, telling Diana that the actor had ruined every life he had ever touched. But Diana, deeply in love, ignored Seefried's advice. Soon enough, she discovered that she was pregnant. Joan was shocked and tried to persuade her to have an abortion, but Diana separated from Anderson and in 1966 gave birth to Felix Florian Werner. The relationship with Werner was over within another two years, but Diana had no regrets: the union had given her a fine, healthy son—Joan's eighth grandchild.

In the years since the *Cleopatra* debacle, Walter Wanger had tried perpetually to launch another film project. But nothing quite worked. Either the ideas fizzled or he wound up selling them to other producers who saw them to fruition. Even on his strictly limited income, he led a very comfortable life in New York. Still, without his work, he felt only half the man he had once been. In 1968, he found a novel that he liked, John Reese's crime drama *The Looters,* and set about trying to turn it into a movie.

The Looters would eventually reach the screen, in 1973, as *Charley Varrick,* directed by Walter's old colleague Don Siegel. But it was made without Walter's participation. On November 17, 1968, he suffered a fatal heart attack in his apartment at 444 East Fifty-seventh Street. On November 21, funeral services were held at Frank Campbell's in Manhattan. Joan, escorted by David, was in attendance.

From 1968 through 1970, *Dark Shadows* rode high as one of daytime television's most popular programs. The fact that Jonathan Frid's Barnabas Collins character had become the series' focal point did not bother Joan in the least. As the seasons rolled on, and the plotlines unfolded in other historical time periods, she was given acting opportunities that were meatier than the perennially tense and nervous Elizabeth Collins Stoddard. When *Dark Shadows* began airing flashbacks to 1795, Joan portrayed Barnabas's mother, the long-suffering Naomi Collins, who commits suicide when she learns that her son is afflicted with vampirism. In a long sequence of episodes set in the Collinwood of 1897, she played Judith Collins, an iron-willed Regina Giddens–type matriarch who marries the obsessive, witch-hunting minister Reverend Trask, then kills him by walling him up in the old house. In a plot strand set in 1840, she played the slightly addled Flora Collins, author of frilly romance novels and a devotee of astrology. Whenever Joan needed time off, the writers wrote in a coma or nervous breakdown for her character—once, she was even buried alive.

With *Dark Shadows* doing so well, Joan was approached by the New York publishing firm Holt, Rinehart, and Winston to write her autobiography. Intrigued by the idea, she interviewed a number of possible collaborators before settling on Lois Kibbee, an actress and director who had previously collaborated on the autobiography of Christine Jorgensen, the celebrated transsexual. Like Joan, Kibbee came from a distinguished theatrical family—her uncle was the noted character actor Guy Kibbee. Otherwise, they made an odd pair: Kibbee, strong and forthright, with a bawdy sense of humor; Joan, reserved and elegant.

Initially, Joan's book was to be a straightforward autobiography, but as Kibbee undertook the interviewing process, she found Joan to be less than forthcoming. "Mother really led poor Lois a merry chase," said Diana Anderson. "She just wouldn't tell her anything revealing." Desperate to make something out of the book, Kibbee was forced to rethink it as a family history, dating back to Joan's great-grandfather, William F. Wood, and progressing through the various generations of Woods and Morrisons. Exhaustively researched by Kibbee, it did provide a good deal of useful historical data for theater buffs; the trouble was, according to Kibbee's close friend, actress Patricia O'Connell, "Joan couldn't have cared less about the theatrical side of her family. Lois said that she didn't seem to give a damn about it."

Kibbee did an excellent job of capturing Joan's voice, but personal information was generally glossed over: Constance's machinations involving the Plant family were strictly off-limits, as was any direct discussion of Joan's relationship with Jennings Lang. Overall, the tone of the book was one of reticence. Speaking of Barbara's arrest in the mid-1950s, Joan describes it as "a messy, if minor incident."

The title was a cause of some concern. Initially it was called *Joan Bennett and Company.* David Wilde at one point insisted that it be called *The Tree and Me*—as in family tree—a suggestion Kibbee quietly vetoed. Ultimately, everyone agreed on a compromise: *The Bennett Playbill,* slightly misleading since the bulk of the book dealt with Adrienne Morrison's side of the family. It was published in the fall of 1970, and although it received generally respectful press, sales were disappointing. Joan later admitted to friends that the book would have sold much better if she had chosen to be completely open—but she never regretted her decision to err on the side of discretion.

Dark Shadows's success enabled Joan to return to feature filmmaking for the first time in ten years. In 1970, with the series still enormously popular, Dan Curtis launched a movie spin-off called *House of Dark Shadows*, which told—or rather retold—the story of Barnabas's discovery in the family crypt, of his murderous rampage in Collinsport, and of Dr. Julia Hoffman's attempts to cure him. *House of Dark Shadows* was filmed at the palatial Lyndhurst estate in Tarrytown, New York. Shooting the film posed a thankless chore for Joan. Despite special billing, her role was small and confined to the sidelines. In addition, she lost patience with Curtis's working methods, which she considered inefficient; while she was able to accept television's low standards, she expected more of film. "Once, Joan and I drove out to the location at Lyndhurst," remembered Kathryn Leigh Scott. "And she said, 'My entire career, people have told me that I would be a great second unit man or assistant director.' In other words, she was so organized herself that she could look at a call sheet and tell what was going to work and what wouldn't. She would go out at some ungodly hour and look at the call sheet and know she was going to sit around half the day." One morning on location, the sink drains in the hair-dressing rooms were plugged, and it was impossible to do anyone's hair. Scott recalled Joan sitting in her makeup chair with a scowl on her face. When a plumber came to fix the drains, he did a double take and said, "Aren't you Joan Bennett?" "I used to be," she muttered.

Distributed by MGM, *House of Dark Shadows* was a sizeable hit when it was released in the fall of 1970, grossing $2.5 million. But by early 1971, the series' television ratings had begun to slip. Most put the blame on the increasingly convoluted plotlines that called for the characters to enter parallel time, where they led very different lives. "We were all so confused," said Nancy Barrett. "At that point, I was doing three different characters, and I didn't know what time period I was in, what my hair was supposed to be, what clothes I should be wearing." In any case, Curtis was not enthusiastic about continuing the run for much longer—he wanted to go to Hollywood to make feature films—and several of the cast members were eager for new challenges. On April 2, 1971, *Dark Shad-*

ows aired its 1,245th and final episode. Ironically, in the series' final months, the ratings had once again been on the upswing.

For Joan, *Dark Shadows*'s cancellation meant that she could finally have more time to relax, to enjoy her family and friends. In a way, however, the show's demise seemed like a little death. Although the steady income it provided had been a godsend, she had been most grateful of all for the opportunity to work. Suddenly, without the demanding routine of each week's taping to organize her life around, she felt at loose ends. She missed the daily contact with her coworkers and the feeling of satisfaction that she was still active in the industry, while so many of her contemporaries seemed to have retired.

Unfortunately for her, the demise of *Dark Shadows* coincided with an aggressive campaign by David to leave the city for the suburbs. Joan loved New York and had no desire to move, but David was insistent. He preferred the quiet life—he was eager to recapture some of the peace and happiness he had known during his years in Bedford—and he was certain that Joan would like it, too, once she got used to it.

Initially they looked around Bedford, but Joan found it too isolated. Eventually, they compromised on Scarsdale, an upper-middle-class suburb twenty miles northwest of New York. The house they purchased was a comfortable, three-bedroom white Colonial at 67 Chase Road North, a quiet cul-de-sac backed by a wooded area. Joan gave up the lease on her Seventy-second Street apartment, and had her furniture—much of it left over from the years on Mapleton Drive—moved to Scarsdale. Paul Clemons's portrait from *The Woman in the Window* was given pride of place in the foyer. It seemed the only visible reminder that this newly transplanted Westchester County matron had once been an important Hollywood star.

Chapter Twenty-Three

1972–1990

"Scarsdale," said Diana Anderson, "is where you go to die." Joan would not have assessed it so harshly; nonetheless, it was clear to many friends and family members that moving to Westchester County was not the easiest transition for her to make. "She was not cut out to be a suburban housewife," said Melinda Markey. "Not at all." Still, since David was dead-set against living in the city, she did her best to adjust. Certainly there were many things about the house that she liked: breakfast and lunch were served in a glassed-in, plant-filled morning room. David set to work turning the sloping back yard into an elaborately designed garden, complete with a small brook, stone paths, and a little terrace. He also turned the basement into a playroom, painted in Joan's favorite kelly green, and decorated with framed posters from her film and stage career. In one corner he created a cozy space for their frequent bridge games. She also relished the elegant meals served by their devoted cook-housekeeper, Carmen Guillem. On Carmen's day off, Joan often took over the kitchen to prepare her specialty dish, chicken Kiev.

Joan was not completely isolated. Two or three times a week, she and David drove into Manhattan to attend plays or movie screenings, have dinner with friends, or participate in a tribute to one of Joan's former colleagues. David enjoyed their round of theater- and movie-going more than Joan, who was shocked by the new era of permissiveness in films. She detested anything that emphasized violence; journalist-film historian Ronald Bowers, whom she befriended when he published a profile of her in *Films in Review,* remembered that she would often walk out on a screening if the film featured gratuitous gore. (She was particularly appalled by Roman Polanski's 1974 *Chinatown,* which her daughters had urged her to see.) Although the 1970s was a fertile, thrilling period in both films and theater, Joan was discouraged by the preponderance of depressing themes and graphic language.

She seemed to enjoy night life as much or more than the theater itself. Ronald Bowers remembered that at intermission, Joan never ordered drinks from the theater bar, because they were too weak. Instead, she insisted on crossing Eighth Avenue to one of the dive bars in the West Forties and ordering a stiff Chivas Regal. "She would breeze into one of these places in her mink coat, and step right up to the bar," said Bowers. "Believe me, we always got served." Joan felt no compulsion to stay to the end if the play's first act didn't appeal to her. Often she would take a book along, and spend the second and third acts reading and smoking in the ladies' lounge.

One of Joan's great pleasures during the 1970s was the opportunity to travel. After *Dark Shadows* went off the air, she was frequently invited to be a guest on luxury cruises around the world. Many aging stars found this to be a pleasant way of keeping their names before the public and enjoying a first-class holiday at no expense to themselves. Normally, their names would be used in advertisements promoting the cruise as inducement for older movie fans to sign up. Joan's only real commitment was to appear at a screening of one or two of her pictures and at the question-and-answer session that followed. These voyages took Joan and David coast to coast by way of the Panama Canal, along the Mississippi River, to Mexico, Alaska, and often to Europe.

Much as Joan relished these and other travel opportunities, she was not ready to retire from acting. Even in her mid-sixties, she thrived on work. To her daughters, she always seemed somewhat restless and disgruntled whenever she was between projects. By this point, most of her offers came from dinner theaters and summer and winter stock companies. The plays were mostly light fare:

Janus, Jane, The Reluctant Debutante, The Man Who Came to Dinner, Barefoot in the Park—but always she approached her work with her old discipline and professionalism. She also liked to have fun, and as time went on, she enjoyed going out for rounds of drinks after the show. Mary Cooper recalled a tour of *The Man Who Came to Dinner* in the early 1970s which also featured character actress Margaret Hamilton. "After the Saturday night performance, we would always go from one town to another," recalled Cooper. "And I remember sitting up until four in the morning once when we got to a new town—Maggie, Joan, and myself. I had to go to bed, but Maggie and Joan both said, 'Oh, come on, stay a little bit!'"

The play that Joan acted in most frequently throughout the 1970s was Leonard Gershe's *Butterflies Are Free,* a romantic comedy about a blind boy, living on his own in Greenwich Village, who falls in love with a free-spirited actress. It had been a hit on Broadway during the 1969–1970 season, and since then numerous touring companies had cropped up around the country. *Butterflies Are Free* offered an unusually good role for an older actress: Mrs. Banks, the blind boy's overprotective mother from Westchester County. On Broadway, Mrs. Banks was created by Eileen Heckart, who played her as tough and sarcastic. Arthur Whitelaw, director of the Broadway version, had plenty of opportunity to observe a wide range of actresses in the part, including Heckart's Broadway replacement, Gloria Swanson, who played Mrs. Banks in the grand manner of an old-time movie star, Eve Arden, who played her as Eve Arden, and Vivian Vance, Virginia Graham, and Maureen O'Sullivan. Joan played Mrs. Banks for the first time in 1972 at the Cherry County Playhouse in Traverse City, Michigan, and soon she was being asked to reprise the role in dinner theaters and summer stock companies all over the country. For Whitelaw, she brought a warmth and reality to the part that many of her predecessors had missed. James Graves, who appeared with her in a production of the play at Tidewater Dinner Theater of the Stars in Virginia Beach, Virginia, agreed: "She was a little bit gentler than most actresses who played it. The character was from Scarsdale, and she was living in Scarsdale, so she knew how to do that Westchester matron thing. She had a lovely warm quality onstage: she could be haughty and all the things the character needed to be, but she was also lovable." Until the end of the decade, Joan played Mrs. Banks at least once a year. David often traveled to see her in the play. At the end of the performance, in the scene in which Mrs. Banks understands that she must let her son go, David found that Joan invariably moved him to tears.

One of the great friends Joan met during her years in summer stock and dinner theater was a handsome young actor-dancer named Richard Stack. David also got along well with Richard, who was frequently a guest at Chase Road, playing bridge until well into the night. "Joan liked to entertain rather formally," said Stack. "Once, on New Year's Eve, she wanted the men to come in black tie. And she walked into the room wearing a beautiful white gown with a matching white turban. Suddenly, it was the 1930s!" At Joan and David's parties, the liquor flowed freely, and accordingly, Joan's drinking escalated somewhat. As a result, they sometimes got in arguments in front of their guests. Ronald Bowers recalled several occasions when he met Joan and David for after-theater supper at Joe Allen's on West Forty-sixth Street. Whenever her glass of Scotch ran low, she would tap David on the wrist, which was his cue to summon the waiter to bring another drink.

After *Dark Shadows*'s cancellation, Joan still made occasional television appearances. Actor Peter Haskell appeared with her in a 1972 movie for ABC-TV, *The Eyes of Charles Sand,* a supernatural thriller, and a pilot for a series that ABC ultimately did not pick up. Haskell recalled that Joan was rather apprehensive about the project—much as she had been with *Dark Shadows.* "This is an industry of youth and fantasy and all the rest of it," Haskell observed. "I think when you're that old, you're apprehensive because you wonder: am I going to disappoint the people who saw me do what I used to do?' I think that was in her psyche at that point. But she was prepared and professional and without attitude. Of the people I worked with who came out of that era—Edward G. Robinson, Barbara Stanwyck, Miss Bennett—in every single case, it was just another actor coming to work."

In 1976, quite unexpectedly, she received another offer to do a feature film. It was called *Suspiria,* and it was yet another thriller, this one about a German ballet school that is actually a front for a deadly coven of witches. Given Joan's objections to violence in the movies, it is surprising that she accepted a part in the film, which featured several gruesome murders—the first in the opening scenes. The script was chaotic and didn't make much sense, and her role as the headmistress of the ballet school was not large, but David urged her to accept it. The director was Dario Argento, whose 1970 film *The Bird with the Crystal Plumage* David had admired; besides, *Suspiria* meant an all-expenses-paid trip for two to Italy.

Once she arrived in Rome, where principal photography was to take place, Joan almost immediately regretted that she had said yes to the project. The Italian methods of filming were slow and disorganized. One day, in preparation for filming a scene in which she had a single line, she reported to the studio, had her makeup and hair done, and got into her costume by 12:30 P.M. Five hours later, the scene was finally shot. One consolation was the chance to get to know veteran Italian actress Alida Valli, cast in the film as a sadistic ballet instructor. Valli, who had enjoyed a brief Hollywood vogue in the 1940s with Alfred Hitchcock's *The Paradine Case* and Orson Welles's *The Third Man,* befriended Joan and David and introduced them to several of the excellent, little-known local restaurants. On days off from filming, Joan and David traveled to Venice—scene of her honeymoon with Jack Fox in 1926—and Florence. On the whole, however, the trip was not a success. "I'm fed up with Italy and Italians," Joan wrote to Diana toward the end of filming. "It has changed a lot. . . . Venice has become very noisy because now they have water taxis that blow their damned horns constantly. Before, there were only gondolas. I have only three more scenes to do in the picture and I wish they would do them and let me out of here."

When *Suspiria* received its premiere in sixteen major Italian cities in February 1977, it turned out to be a surprise success, grossing 220 million lire in its opening days. It did less well in its U.S. release that September. Although some critics made note of Argento's undeniable visual flair and the film's chilling soundtrack, most reviews were downbeat. Joan received the most appalling notices of her career. *Cue*'s William Wolf admitted that he "didn't know whether to laugh or weep at the embarrassing sight of Bennett, looking dowdy and walking and talking like a programmed grandmother doll." The *London Sunday Times* likened her to a "waxwork Princess Margaret." John Simon, in *New York Magazine,* wrote that he had always liked Joan in the past; in *Suspiria,* however, he felt that she revealed "a totally synthetic personality and zero acting ability, which she and her directors have previously managed very tactfully to conceal." In time, however, *Suspiria* acquired the reputation of a cult classic and became a popular item on videocassette; it is unlikely that Joan knew or cared.

Joan had no particular desire to marry again, but David had other ideas. Frequently, when he and Joan were at a party or on a cruise, someone would ask whether he was her agent or business manager. This irritated him so much that he began to press Joan to marry him. Always she said no, that she was afraid of ruining their relationship. But by the late 1970s, she was growing increasingly frail and had to face the fact that her stage work could not continue indefinitely. She began to reconsider David's frequent proposals, and finally said yes. On February 14, 1978, David became Joan's fourth husband, in a private civil ceremony in White Plains, New York. The judge who performed the marriage, Anthony Cerrato, happened to live in the Park Hill house that had been home to Richard, Mabel, and their daughters more than sixty years earlier. David was ecstatic about the marriage, but to Richard Stack Joan admitted, "I just got tired of saying no."

The wedding was dutifully noted in the local newspapers and many of the leading national magazines. Only a few weeks later, on March 24, 1978, the Wildes were awakened just before dawn by a burst of orange flame outside their bedroom window. David jumped out of bed to investigate, and found that a huge fire was burning at the back of the house and had already consumed a good part of the morning room. Terrified, David and Joan escaped out the front door. Since the telephone and electricity had already been knocked out, David had to call the fire department from a neighbor's home. After the fire was put out, most of the house remained structurally intact, but the smoke and water damage was extensive. The basement that David had so carefully decorated now held a foot of standing water. It seemed a clear case of arson—in fact, the insurance company, as well as the local police, suspected David of having set the fire himself. In the end, the culprits were never found. David and Joan moved into a series of temporary quarters for a period of several months while the house was being repaired.

The renovations completed, the Wildes settled back in at Chase Road North. Their life in Scarsdale continued in the pleasant routine that had long been established: each morning, David worked the *New York Times* crossword puzzle while Joan did the one in the *Daily News*. There were frequent weekend parties, with marathon sessions of bridge and charades, during which Carmen turned out a succession of superb meals for guests that included Drew Dudley, Ronald Bowers, Richard Stack, Mary Cooper, Arthur Whitelaw, Maureen Stapleton, Robert Wallsten, Elaine Steinbeck, and Richard Rodgers's widow, Dorothy Rodgers. Yet in time, David noticed that Joan seemed somewhat different. Although she had always been reserved, she now appeared downright withdrawn. More and more, David had to coax her into going out to dinner or to the theater. Often when they were alone, she spoke hardly at all.

There were family tensions as well. None of Joan's daughters had ever fully accepted David—Diana was the most tolerant of his moodiness and argumentative nature—but his relations with Melinda had grown quite strained. With the death of Gene Markey in 1978, Melinda had come into a sizeable share of her father's estate. After years of struggling financially, she was suddenly comfortably well off, and proceeded to upgrade her lifestyle accordingly. David, however, seemed to resent Melinda's newfound security, and constantly made snide comments about what he considered her acquisitive nature. One Easter weekend, the Wildes and Muriel Finney were dinner guests of Melinda and her husband, Joe Bena. In recent years, David's mistrust of Melinda had intensified, largely because he didn't feel she was properly attentive to Joan.

Often he enjoyed baiting her. On this particular evening, he made a hostile comment about the Catholic Church. The Benas, both of whom had been baptized as Catholics, were incensed. A bitter quarrel ensued, climaxed by Joe Bena's demand that David leave his house and not return. Joan calmly accepted the incident and said little about it. She had always had a more contentious relationship with Melinda than with any of her other daughters, but now a great distance developed between them. In the years that followed, Joan would see Melinda only sporadically.

Increasingly, Joan's activity was limited to appearances at industry functions. Always she was witty and gracious. At the National Board of Review's first-ever David Wark Griffith Awards, at Luchow's in 1980, she presented the award for outstanding foreign film to Marcello Dannon, producer of the French comedy *La Cage aux Folles,* the hit French comedy about a middle-aged gay couple. "My, how movieland has changed since I made *Little Women,*" she wryly observed. "Or has it?" Occasionally, she herself was the subject of a tribute. In September 1981, Westchester Community College held a Joan Bennett Festival to inaugurate its new Academic/Arts Center. September 21 was proclaimed Joan Bennett Day by Westchester County Executive Alfred Del Bello. At the college's festivities, Chuck Scarborough hosted a banquet where the guests included family members and many of Joan's close friends, including Lillian Gish, opera baritone Robert Merrill, Elaine Steinbeck, and Myrna Loy, who was heard to comment, "This is the first time I've ever sat on the dais when they used paper plates."

On December 18, 1981, the Carnegie Hall Cinema presented a two-day Joan Bennett film festival, consisting of *The Woman in the Window, Scarlet Street, The Reckless Moment,* and *We're No Angels.* Joan appeared at a question-and-answer session, offering rather vague and taciturn responses to the audience's queries. Her opinion of *The Reckless Moment* had not changed in the intervening years. Out in the lobby, following the picture's screening, Ronald Bowers overheard her murmur to David, "Well, that wasn't much."

In 1982, Joan was one of seven actresses honored with the George Eastman Award for Distinguished Contributions to the Art of Film. The ceremony was held at the Eastman Theater in Rochester, New York, and Joan and David were in attendance along with three of the other recipients, Luise Rainer, Maureen O'Sullivan, and Sylvia Sidney. (Dolores Del Rio, Myrna Loy, and Rochester resident Louise Brooks were unable to attend.) While in town, Joan visited Brooks, now seventy-five and quite ill, whom she had not seen since their early days in New York.

By the early 1980s, Joan looked shockingly frail and gaunt. Her eyesight had grown worse, and she had undergone both cataract surgery and a procedure for a detached retina, all of which made her more unsure of herself than ever before. Still, she summoned the energy to appear in the occasional made-for-television movie. In 1981, she played a character part, as a demented rag lady, in a supernatural thriller called *This House Possessed.* The following year, she turned up in the cast of one of the season's most critically praised teleplays, *Divorce Wars: A Love Story,* starring Tom Selleck and Jane Curtin. She appeared in only two brief scenes, her alarming physical decline obvious. Her face looked almost skeletal: her hair, boldly black as ever, was thinning badly in front; her lips were done in a garish bright red bow; and she was poorly lit. She rattled off her lines with little feeling or sense of timing, as if she no longer cared about acting at all. Later in 1982, she made a guest appearance as herself in a segment of ABC's popular daytime serial *The Guiding Light.* It was her last performance.

Visitors to Chase Road North encountered a wan and diminished Joan. She had grown almost preternaturally quiet and aloof. She still enjoyed reminiscing with friends and family, but she never dwelled on any of the hard times of the past. Once, however, she did express a certain regret to Richard Stack. "I should have been more of a bitch," she told him. And after a moment, she added, with a smile, "I should have been more like Constance."

Interviewers who turned up often had their questions greeted with a slightly confused smile and very little in the way of a detailed answer. Pressed for an opinion on a former costar, Joan would often reply, "Cary Grant was very sweet," or "Don Ameche couldn't have been nicer," but she seemed unable to come up with any specific anecdotes. Still, despite her faulty memory, she invariably exhibited great charm and humor, treating journalists with courtesy and respect.

In the early 1980s, James Watters, onetime entertainment editor of *Life,* began a collaboration with the celebrated photographer Horst on a coffee-table book of photographs called *Return Engagements.* The idea was to run vintage photographs of a vast array of female stars next to a new portrait of the star in old age, accompanied by a concise block of text by Watters. The stars photographed and interviewed for the book included Katharine Hepburn, Bette Davis, Barbara Stanwyck, Pola Negri, Lillian Gish, Olivia de Havilland, Gloria Swanson, Mary Astor, and dozens of others. Eventually, Watters and Horst made their way to Chase Road North, where they were greeted by a frail and retiring Joan. It was one of their more problematic photo sessions: Joan's thinning hair posed a problem, and when the shot was agreed on—Joan sitting at her dining room table holding a pair of roses up to her cheeks—she had difficulty maintaining the pose for any length of time. After several painful hours, Horst got the best shots he could, but when *Return Engagements* was published in 1985, Watters described Joan as "a study in slow motion."

In the mid-1980s, there was one final movie offer. Ron Howard was preparing *Cocoon,* a comedy-fantasy about a group of senior citizens miraculously rejuvenated by the arrival on Earth of a delegation of friendly aliens. Howard thought Joan would be perfect for one of the leading female roles, and was intrigued that the picture would also provide a reunion with her old leading man, Don Ameche, who had already been cast. When the script arrived at Chase Road North, Joan gave it to David to read. He promptly vetoed the idea, claiming that it was an imitation of Walter's old hit, *Invasion of the Body Snatchers,* and that she was not up to the physical demands of the role. Joan turned it down, claiming that she was tired of working, and the part went to Gwen Verdon. Both Diana and Melinda felt that rejecting the part was a grave mistake, particularly when *Cocoon* became one of the box-office hits of 1985, winning a Best Supporting Actor Academy Award for Ameche.

Although relations with Melinda and Joe Bena continued to be strained, Joan saw as much of her other children and their families as their schedules would permit. Diana came from California for annual visits, and both Stephanie and Shelley were close by, in New York. By this time, Stephanie's marriage to Frederick Guest had ended, and she had launched on a new phase in her life by opening two popular restaurants on Manhattan's East Side, The Brighton Grill and Stephanie's. Since her graduation from Sarah Lawrence College in 1970, Shelley had embarked on a successful career in publishing. She had gotten her start at the *New York Review of Books* and later became Articles Editor of *House and Garden,* then editor-in-chief of *Interview*—where many felt she raised the magazine to an editorial level it had not previously attained. After a new owner took control of *Interview,* Shelley became a senior editor at the prestigious publishing house of Alfred A. Knopf. In her private life, she became the wife of David Mortimer—like Frederick Guest, a member of a prominent old New York family. Joan was quietly proud of her daughters' accomplishments, and always claimed that she was not at all disappointed that none of them had decided to devote themselves to an acting career.

By now, Joan had a total of thirteen grandchildren, and she remembered their birthdays religiously. Some of her grandchildren, such as Diana's eldest, Amanda Anderson, regarded her as a rather formal and distant presence, but both Timothy and Lisa Anderson found her warm and affectionate. "There was a limit, perhaps, to what you could say to her," said Timothy. "I don't think she was an intellectual, and I certainly didn't talk to her about books or anything like that—but I always felt that she was very interested in what I was doing."

Joan's physical decline continued. She stopped appearing on the celebrity cruises, partly because her memory had faded so badly that David needed to prompt her during the question-and-answer sessions. Although she had always had a reputation for being able to match her friends drink for drink, she now lost her capacity to handle alcohol, and was permitted only a miniature carafe of white wine at dinner. Various family members pleaded with her to give up cigarettes, but she lost none of her zeal for chain smoking. But there were other worries: On occasion, she would slip into peculiar bouts of physical and mental fatigue and depression, until she was put on a round of medication that helped her regain her balance.

Still, there were many things she enjoyed: watching *Jeopardy!* every night, answering the ceaseless supply of fan mail, which she organized in files with her usual efficiency, granting the occasional interview, going out for dinner and gossip with close friends like Drew Dudley and Ronald Bowers, and participating in several of the annual *Dark Shadows* fan club reunions. Jim Pierson, an associate of Dan Curtis's, recalled Joan sitting patiently at the reunions for hours, signing autographs for up to a thousand fans. She also continued to attend the theater regularly, although the direction in which Broadway had gone continued to upset her. Two productions of the 1980s that she particularly despised were Marsha Norman's *'Night, Mother,* about a middle-aged woman who decides to commit suicide, and Tennessee Williams's *Orpheus Descending,* which director Peter Hall revived as a vehicle for Vanessa Redgrave in 1989. She was stunned to see Redgrave—daughter of her old *Secret Beyond the Door* costar—drop her clothes near the end of the first act. "That was shocking," she confided to an interviewer. "And I didn't think she had much of a figure."

In the fall of 1990, while Diana was visiting Joan at Chase Road North, she received news that her ex-husband, John Anderson, had died of a heart attack, and immediately flew back to Los Angeles to attend to the details of the services. Joan was saddened by the news. She had always been fond of her former son-in-law, and was pleased when, following the dissolution of Diana's 1974 marriage to film and television producer Ivan Tors, Anderson had returned to Diana's home to live with her on a platonic basis. Anderson had been seventy-two when he died, nearly as old as Joan, who had celebrated her eightieth birthday the previous February.

With Diana back in California, Joan's life settled once more into a comfortable routine. The Christmas holidays approached. On the night of December 6, as she was preparing for bed, Joan complained of mild chest pains. David told her that if they weren't better in a few days, she should see their doctor. She promised that she would.

The following day, Friday, December 7, 1990, Joan and David drove into Manhattan for their last shopping trip before Christmas. They went their own ways to buy gifts for each other, and agreed to meet in the late afternoon at the St. Regis Hotel, where they were joined by Richard Stack. Together, they all drove out to Scarsdale for a weekend of bridge.

At the house, they unloaded their packages and enjoyed a cocktail before sitting down to dinner. They had had the soup course and were finishing off the salmon when Richard called out David's name in alarm. Joan had slumped forward, her head dropped onto her chest. David called 911 and then their personal physician, Robert Pearson, who instructed them to lay her down on the floor. Richard knew immediately that Joan was dead, but David refused to face it at first. The ambulance arrived, and the paramedics attempted artificial respiration, to no avail. Joan was taken to White Plains Hospital, where she was declared dead on arrival. David, sobbing uncontrollably, returned to the house with Richard. After he composed himself, he began to make the necessary telephone calls to Joan's daughters, and to Muriel Finney, Elaine Steinbeck, and other friends.

On Sunday, December 9, the *New York Times* ran a half-page obituary headlined, "Joan Bennett, Whose Roles Ripened From Sweet to Siren, Dies at Eighty." Other publications devoted ample space to her passing. In the *Hollywood Reporter,* Robert Osborne noted that she had enjoyed several significant lives: as screen actress, Hollywood social leader, wife, mother, stage performer, and finally, daytime television star. For *People* magazine, Katharine Hepburn provided a touching tribute to her *Little Women* costar: "She was an angel, and she will be missed by everyone. She was a joy, which is a rare quality."

On Thursday, December 13, at 10:30 A.M., funeral services were held for Joan at Manhattan's St. James' Episcopal Church on Madison Avenue and Seventy-first Street, with the Reverends James N. Lodwick and Kenneth W. Mann officiating. A selection of traditional hymns was offered, including "Rock of Ages" and "Amazing Grace," and Joan's old friend Robert Wagner read from the Twenty-third Psalm.

With Joan's death came the break in the chain of five generations of actors. None of the children of the three Bennett sisters went on to make acting their life's work. Melinda Markey came the closest, although she gave it up after she met Joe Bena, to whom she remained married until his death in 1990. Subsequently, she married Thierry Van Dyck and relocated to South Carolina. Gyl Roland, too, initially seemed determined to carry on the family tradition, and was still appearing in television commercials and in bit parts in films well into the 1970s. Eventually, however, she eased out of the business to become a Los Angeles–based image consultant. And while Morton Downey Jr. was a singer who later became a popular (if controversial) television talk show host, he never pursued a legitimate acting career. However, three of Joan's grandchildren have ventured into working behind the camera. Diana's youngest son, Felix Werner, has established his own production company, Werner Film, which in 2003 produced its first feature, *The Failures,* and two of Stephanie's children have entered the business—Andrew Guest as a film editor and Vanessa Guest as an aspiring producer.

It is hard to escape the feeling that the beginning of the story of Richard Bennett and his three acting daughters, set in the rough-and-tumble stock theaters of the Midwest, is intoxicating, while its ending, on a quiet street in Scarsdale, is a little sad. For a tradition is a living tradition only as long as the talent and drive exist to propel it forward.

There is little doubt that Richard believed what he told a reporter in the 1930s—that he was one of a handful of America's greatest living actors. In the end, he failed to pass on that particular brand of bravado to his daughters. A pair of quotes tell the story. Shortly before she died, Constance was contacted by film writer Gene Ringgold, who had been assigned to write an account of her career for *Films in Review*. She wrote back to him, "I'm flattered that you want to write about me. But if you do, keep it light. And be truthful about my film work. After all, I was no Sarah Bernhardt. Good luck."

And in 1986, when Joan was interviewed in Scarsdale by show-business historian Richard Lamparski, she confessed, "I don't think much of most of the films I made, but being a movie star was something I liked very much."

The youngest of Richard's daughters was laid to rest in the Morrison family plot at Pleasant View Cemetery in Lyme, Connecticut. Victor Morrison's mother never got her wish: the towering column marking Richard's grave still stands proud, overshadowing everything around it, which is surely the only way he would have had it.

Feature Films

Richard Bennett

Damaged Goods (American Mutual, 1914)
Directors: Richard Bennett, Thomas Ricketts
Writer: Harry A. Pollard
Camera: Thomas B. Middleton
Cast: Adrienne Morrison, Maud Milton, Olive Templeton, Josephine Ditt, Lewis Bennison

The Sable Blessing (American Mutual, 1916)
Director: George L. Sargent
Writer: Anthony Coldeway
Cast: Alfred Hollingsworth, Rhea Mitchell, Adrienne Morrison

Philip Holden—Waster (American Mutual, 1916)
Director: George L. Sargent
Writer: Kenneth B. Clarke
Cast: George Periolat, Adrienne Morrison, Rhea Mitchell, Clarence Burton

And the Law Says (American Mutual, 1916)
Director: Richard Bennett
Cast: George Periolat, Adrienne Morrison, Alan Forrest, William Carroll

The Valley of Decision (American Mutual, 1916)
Director: Rea Berger
Writers: Richard Bennett, Clifford Howard
Cast: Adrienne Morrison, Rhoda Lewis

The Gilded Youth (American Film Co., 1917)
Director: George L. Sargent

Writer: Anthony Coldeway
Cast: Rhea Mitchell, Adrienne Morrison, George Periolat, Alfred Hollingsworth

The End of the Road (War Department Commission Training Camp Activities, 1919)
Director: Edward H. Griffith
Writers: Katharine Bement Davis, Edward H. Griffith
Cast: Claire Adams, Joyce Fair, Raymond McKee, Maude Hill

The Eternal City (Madison, 1923)
Producer: Samuel Goldwyn
Director: George Fitzmaurice
Writer: Ouida Bergere
Camera: Arthur Miller
Cast: Barbara LaMarr, Lionel Barrymore, Bert Lytell

Youth for Sale (C.C. Burr, 1924)
Director: W.C. Cabanne
Writer: Raymond S. Harris, from a story by Izola Forrester
Cast: May Allison, Sigrid Homquist, Charles E. Mack

Lying Wives (Ivan Players, 1925)
Producer-director-writer: Ivan Abramson
Cast: Clara Kimball Young, Madge Kennedy, Edna Murphy

The Home Towners (Warner Bros., 1928)
Director: Bryan Foy
Writers: Bryan Foy, Addison Burkhart, Murray Roth, from a play by George Cohan
Camera: Barney McGill
Cast: Doris Kenyon, Robert McWade, Robert Edeson, Gladys Brockwell

Five and Ten (MGM, 1931)
Director: Robert Z. Leonard
Writer: A.P. Younger
Camera: George Barnes
Cast: Marion Davies, Leslie Howard, Irene Rich, Kent Douglass

Bought! (Warner Bros., 1931)
Director: Archie Mayo
Writers: Charles Kenyon, Raymond Griffith, from a novel by Harriet Henry

Camera: Ray June
Cast: Constance Bennett, Ben Lyon, Dorothy Peterson, Ray Milland

Arrowsmith (Goldwyn, 1931)
Producer: Samuel Goldwyn
Director: John Ford
Writer: Sidney Howard, from the novel by Sinclair Lewis
Camera: Ray June
Cast: Ronald Colman, Helen Hayes, A.E. Anson, Clarence Brooks, Myrna Loy

This Reckless Age (Paramount, 1932)
Director: Frank Tuttle
Writers: Joseph L. Mankiewicz, Frank Tuttle
Camera: Henry Sharp
Cast: Charles "Buddy" Rogers, Peggy Shannon, Charles Ruggles, Frances Dee

No Greater Love (Columbia, 1932)
Director: Lewis Seiler
Writers: Isadore Bernstein, Lou Breslow
Camera: William C. Thompson
Cast: Mischa Auer, Hobart Bosworth, Alexander Carr, Beryl Mercer, Betty Jane Graham

Madame Racketeer (Paramount, 1932)
Directors: Alexander Hall, Harry Wagstaff Gribble
Writers: Malcolm Stuart, Stuart Boylan, Harvey Gates
Cast: Alison Skipworth, George Raft, Robert McWade

Strange Justice (King, 1932)
Producer: J.G. Bachmann
Director: Victor Schertzinger
Writer: William A. Drake
Camera: Merritt B. Gerstad
Cast: Marian Marsh, Reginald Denny, Norman Foster, Irving Pichel, Nydia Westman

If I Had a Million (Paramount, 1932)
Directors: Ernst Lubitsch, Norman Taurog, Stephen Roberts, Lothar Mendes, Norman Z. McLeod, Stephen Roberts, William A. Seiter, H. Bruce Humberstone, James Cruze
Writers: Claude Binyon, Whitney Bolton, Malcolm Stuart Boylan, John Bright, Sidney Buchman, Lester Cole, Isabel Dawn, Boyce DeGaw,

Walter DeLeon, Oliver H.P. Garrett, Harvey Gates, Grover Jones, Ernst Lubitsch, Lawton Mackall, Joseph L. Mankiewicz, William Slavens McNutt, Seton I. Miller, Robert Sparks
Cast: Gary Cooper, Charles Laughton, George Raft, Alison Skipworth, May Robson, Mary Boland, Charles Ruggles, W.C. Fields, Gene Raymond, Wynne Gibson, Jack Oakie, Frances Dee, Roscoe Karns

Big Executive (Paramount, 1933)
Director: Erle C. Kenton
Writer: Laurence Stallings
Camera: Harry Fischbeck
Cast: Ricardo Cortez, Elisabeth Young, Sharon Lynn

Nana (Goldwyn, 1934)
Producer: Samuel Goldwyn
Directors: Dorothy Arzner, George Fitzmaurice
Writers: Harry Wagstaff Gribble, Willard Mack
Camera: Gregg Toland
Cast: Anna Sten, Lionel Atwill, Mae Clarke, Phillips Holmes, Reginald Owen, Jessie Ralph

This Woman Is Mine (Allied, 1935)
Producer: Gregory Ratoff
Director: Monty Banks
Writer: Frederick A. Thompson
Camera: Geoffrey Faithfull
Cast: Gregory Ratoff, John Loder, Benita Hume, Kathryn Servaga

The Magnificent Ambersons (RKO, 1942)
Producer-director-writer: Orson Welles
Camera: Stanley Cortez
Cast: Tim Holt, Joseph Cotten, Dolores Costello, Agnes Moorehead, Ray Collins, Anne Baxter

Journey into Fear (RKO, 1943)
Director: Norman Foster
Writers: Orson Welles, Richard Collins, Joseph Cotten, from a novel by Eric Ambler
Camera: Karl Struss
Cast: Joseph Cotten, Dolores Del Rio, Ruth Warrick, Agnes Moorehead, Everett Sloane

Constance Bennett

The Valley of Decision (American Mutual, 1916)
Director: Rea Berger
Writers: Richard Bennett, Clifford Howard
Cast: Richard Bennett, Adrienne Morrison, Rhoda Lewis

Reckless Youth (Select, 1922)
Producer: Lewis J. Selznick
Director: Ralph Ince
Writer: Edward J. Montagne, from a story by Cosmo Hamilton
Camera: Jules Cronjager
Cast: Elaine Hammerstein, Niles Welch, Myrtle Stedman

Evidence (Select, 1922)
Producer: Lewis J. Selznick
Director: George Archainbaud
Camera: Jack Brown
Writer: Edward J. Montagne

What's Wrong with the Women? (Equity, 1922)
Producer: Daniel Carson Goodman
Director: Roy William Neill
Writer: Daniel Carson Goodman
Camera: George Folsey
Cast: Wilton Lackaye, Montagu Love, Rod LaRocque

Cytherea (Associated First National, 1924)
Producer: Samuel Goldwyn
Director: George Fitzmaurice
Writer: Frances Marion, from a novel by Joseph Hergesheimer
Camera: Arthur Miller
Cast: Lewis Stone, Irene Rich, Norman Kerry

Into the Net (Pathé, 1924, serial)
Director: George B. Seitz
Writer: Frank Leon Smith
Cast: Edna Murphy, Jack Mulhall

The Goose Hangs High (Paramount, 1925)
Producers: Alfred Zukor, Jesse L. Lasky
Director: James Cruze

Writer: Walter Woods
Cast: Myrtle Stedman, George Irving, Esther Ralston

Married? (Herman Jans, 1925)
Director: George Terwilliger
Writer: Marjorie Benton Cooke
Cast: Owen Moore, Evangeline Russell, Julia Hurley

Code of the West (Paramount, 1925)
Producers: Adolph Zukor, Jesse L. Lasky
Director: William K. Howard
Writer: Lucien Hubbard, from a novel by Zane Grey
Camera: Lucien Andriot
Cast: Owen Moore, Mabel Ballin, Charles Ogle, George Bancroft

Wandering Fires (Arrow, 1925)
Producer-director: Maurice Campbell
Writer: Warner Fabian
Camera: Harry Stradling
Cast: George Hackathorne, Wallace MacDonald, Effie Shannon

My Son (First National, 1925)
Producer-director: Edwin Carewe
Writer: Finis Fox, from a play by Martha M. Stanley
Camera: L.W. O'Connell
Cast: Alla Nazimova, Jack Pickford, Hobart Bosworth

The Goose Woman (Universal, 1925)
Producer: Carl Laemmle
Director: Clarence Brown
Writer: Melville Brown, from a story by Rex Beach
Camera: Milton Moore
Cast: Louise Dresser, Jack Pickford, James O. Barrows

Sally, Irene and Mary (MGM, 1925)
Director: Edmond Goulding
Writer: Edmond Goulding, from a play by Edward Dowling and Cyrus Wood
Camera: John Arnold
Cast: Joan Crawford, Sally O'Neil, William Haines, Henry Kolker

The Pinch Hitter (Associated Exhibitors, 1925)
Director: Joseph Henabery

Camera: C. Gardner Sullivan
Camera: Jules Cronjager

This Thing Called Love (Pathé, 1929)
Associate producer: Ralph Block
Director: Paul L. Stein
Writer: Horace Jackson, from a play by Edwin Burke
Camera: Norbert Brodine
Cast: Edmund Lowe, Roscoe Karns, ZaSu Pitts, Stuart Erwin

Rich People (Pathé, 1929)
Associate producer: Ralph Block
Director: Edward H. Griffith
Camera: Norbert Brodine
Cast: Regis Toomey, Robert Ames, Ilka Chase

Son of the Gods (First National, 1930)
Director: Frank Lloyd
Writer: Bradley King, from a story by Rex Beach
Camera: Ernest Haller
Cast: Richard Barthelmess, Dorothy Mathews, James Eagles

Common Clay (Fox, 1930)
Producer: William Fox
Director: Victor Fleming
Writer: Jules Furthman, from a novel by Cleves Kincaid
Camera: Glen MacWilliams
Cast: Lew Ayres, Tully Marshall, Matty Kemp, Hale Hamilton

Three Faces East (Warner Bros., 1930)
Producer: Darryl F. Zanuck
Director: Roy Del Ruth
Writer: Oliver H.P. Garrett, from a play by Anthony Paul Kelly
Camera: Chick McGill
Cast: Erich von Stroheim, Anthony Bushell

Sin Takes a Holiday (Pathé, 1930)
Producer: E.B. Derr
Director: Paul L. Stein
Writer: Horace Jackson, from a story by Robert Milton
Camera: John Mescall
Cast: Kenneth MacKenna, Basil Rathbone

Feature Films

The Easiest Way (MGM, 1931)
Director: Jack Conway
Writer: Edith Ellis, from a play by Eugene Walter
Camera: John Mescall
Cast: Adolphe Menjou, Robert Montgomery, Anita Page, Marjorie Rambeau, Clark Gable

Born to Love (RKO-Pathé, 1931)
Director: Paul L. Stein
Writer: Ernest Pascal
Camera: John Mescall
Cast: Joel McCrea, Paul Cavanagh, Anthony Bushell

The Common Law (RKO-Pathé, 1931)
Producer: Charles R. Rogers
Director: Paul L. Stein
Writer: John Farrow, from a novel by Robert W. Chambers
Camera: Hal Mohr
Cast: Joel McCrea, Lew Cody, Robert Williams, Hedda Hopper

Bought! (Warner Bros., 1931)
Director: Archie Mayo
Writers: Charles Kenyon, Raymond Griffith, from a novel by Harriet Henry
Camera: Ray June
Cast: Ben Lyon, Richard Bennett, Dorothy Peterson, Ray Milland

Lady with a Past (RKO-Pathé, 1932)
Producer: Charles R. Rogers
Director: Edward H. Griffith
Writer: Horace Jackson, from a novel by Harriet Henry
Camera: Hal Mohr
Cast: Ben Lyon, David Manners, Don Alvarado

What Price Hollywood? (RKO-Pathé, 1932)
Executive producer: David O. Selznick
Associate producer: Pandro S. Berman
Director: George Cukor
Writers: Jane Murfin, Ben Markson, from a story by Adela Rogers St. John
Camera: Charles Rosher
Cast: Lowell Sherman, Neil Hamilton, Gregory Ratoff

Two Against the World (Warner Bros., 1932)
Producer: Lucien Hubbard
Director: Archie Mayo
Writer: Sheridan Bigney, from a novel by Marion Dix
Camera: Charles Rosher
Cast: Neil Hamilton, Helen Vinson, Allen Vincent, Gavin Gordon, Clara Blandick

Rockabye (RKO-Pathé, 1932)
Executive producer: David O. Selznick
Director: George Cukor
Writers: Jane Murfin, Kubec Glasmon, from a play by Lucia Bronder
Camera: Charles Rosher
Cast: Joel McCrea, Paul Lukas, Walter Pidgeon, Jobyna Howland

Our Betters (RKO, 1933)
Executive producer: David O. Selznick
Director: George Cukor
Writer: Jane Murfin, from the play by W. Somerset Maugham
Camera: Charles Rosher
Cast: Violet Kemble-Cooper, Phoebe Foster, Charles Starrett

Bed of Roses (RKO, 1933)
Producer: Merian C. Cooper
Associate producer: Pandro S. Berman
Director: Gregory LaCava
Writers: Wanda Tuchok, Eugene Thackrey
Camera: Charles Rosher
Cast: Joel McCrea, Pert Kelton, John Halliday

After Tonight (RKO, 1933)
Producer: Merian C. Cooper
Director: George Archainbaud
Writer: Jane Murfin
Camera: Charles Rosher
Cast: Gilbert Roland, Edward Ellis, Sam Godfrey, Mischa Auer

Moulin Rouge (United Artists, 1934)
Producer: Darryl F. Zanuck
Director: Sidney Lanfield
Writers: Nunnally Johnson, Henry Lehrman, from a play by Lyon de Bri
Camera: Charles Rosher

The Affairs of Cellini (United Artists, 1934)
Producer: Darryl F. Zanuck
Director: Gregory LaCava
Writer: Bess Meredyth, from a play by Edwin Justus Mayer
Camera: Charles Rosher
Cast: Fredric March, Frank Morgan, Fay Wray, Jessie Ralph, Vince Barnett

Outcast Lady (MGM, 1934)
Producer-director: Robert Z. Leonard
Writer: Zoe Akins, from a novel by Michael Arlen
Camera: Charles Rosher
Cast: Herbert Marshall, Mrs. Patrick Campbell, Elizabeth Allan, Hugh Williams

After Office Hours (MGM, 1935)
Producer: Bernard F. Hyman
Director: Robert Z. Leonard
Writer: Herman J. Mankiewicz
Camera: Charles Rosher
Cast: Clark Gable, Stuart Erwin, Billie Burke

Everything Is Thunder (Gaumont-British, 1936)
Producer: S.C. Balcon
Director: Milton Rosmer
Writers: Marion Dix, John Orton, from a novel by J.B. Hardy
Camera: Günther Krampf
Cast: Douglass Montgomery, Oscar Homolka

Ladies in Love (Twentieth Century–Fox, 1936)
Producer: B.G. DeSylva
Director: Edward H. Griffith
Writer: Melville Baker, from a play by Ladislaus Bus-Fekete
Camera: Hal Mohr
Cast: Janet Gaynor, Loretta Young, Paul Lukas, Simone Simon, Don Ameche, Tyrone Power

Topper (MGM, 1937)
Producer: Hal Roach
Director: Norman Z. McLeod
Writers: Jack Jevne, Eric Hatch, Eddie Moran, from a novel by Thorne Smith
Camera: Norbert Brodine
Cast: Cary Grant, Roland Young, Billie Burke, Eugene Pallette, Alan Mowbray

Merrily We Live (MGM, 1938)
Executive producer: Milton H. Bren
Producer: Hal Roach
Director: Norman Z. McLeod
Writers: Eddie Moran, Jack Jevne
Camera: Norbert Brodine
Cast: Brian Aherne, Billie Burke, Clarence Kolb, Tom Brown, Bonita Granville, Patsy Kelly

Service de Luxe (Universal, 1938)
Associate producer: Edmond Grainger
Director: Rowland V. Lee
Writers: Gertrude Purcell, Leonard Spiegelglass
Camera: George Robinson
Cast: Vincent Price, Helen Broderick, Charles Ruggles, Mischa Auer

Topper Takes a Trip (United Artists, 1939)
Producer: Hal Roach
Director: Norman Z. McLeod
Writers: Eddie Moran, Jack Jevne, Corey Ford, from a novel by Thorne Smith
Camera: Norbert Brodine
Cast: Roland Young, Billie Burke, Alan Mowbray, Verree Teasdale

Tail Spin (Twentieth Century–Fox, 1939)
Producer: Darryl F. Zanuck
Director: Roy Del Ruth
Writer: Frank Wead
Camera: Karl Freund
Cast: Alice Faye, Nancy Kelly, Joan Davis, Jane Wyman, Charles Farrell

Submarine Zone (Columbia, 1941)
Producer: Sam Bischoff
Director: John Brahm
Writer: Frederic Frank
Camera: P.J. Wolfson
Cast: Pat O'Brien, John Halliday, Alan Baxter, Melville Cooper

Law of the Tropics (Warner Bros., 1941)
Producer: Bryan Foy
Director: Ray Enright
Writer: Charles Grayson, from a novel by Alice Tisdale Hobart

Camera: Sid Hickox
Cast: Jeffrey Lynn, Regis Toomey, Mona Maris

Two-Faced Woman (MGM, 1941)
Producer: Gottfried Reinhardt
Director: George Cukor
Writers: Sidney H. Behrman, Salka Viertel, George Oppenheimer, from a play by Ludwig Fulda
Camera: Joseph Ruttenberg
Cast: Greta Garbo, Melvyn Douglas, Roland Young, Ruth Gordon, Robert Sterling

Wild Bill Hickok Rides (Warner Bros., 1941)
Producer: Edmund Grainger
Director: Ray Enright
Writers: Charles Grayson, Paul Girard Smith, Raymond Schrock
Camera: Ted McCord
Cast: Bruce Cabot, Warren William, Walter Catlett, Howard da Silva

Sin Town (Universal, 1942)
Producer: George Waggner
Director: Ray Enright
Writers: W. Scott Darling, Gerald Geraghty
Camera: George Robinson
Cast: Broderick Crawford, Anne Gwynne, Patrick Knowles, Andy Devine

Madame Spy (Universal, 1942)
Associate producer: Marshall Grant
Director: Roy William Neill
Writer: Lynn Riggs
Camera: George Robinson
Cast: Don Porter, John Litel, Edward Brophy

Paris Underground (United Artists, 1945)
Executive producer: Constance Bennett
Director: Gregory Ratoff
Writers: Boris Ingster, Gertrude Purcell, from a novel by Etta Shiber
Camera: Lee Garmes
Cast: Gracie Fields, George Rigaud, Kurt Kreuger

Centennial Summer (Twentieth Century–Fox, 1946)
Producer-director: Otto Preminger

Writer: Michael Kanin, from a novel by Albert E. Idell
Camera: Ernest Palmer
Cast: Jeanne Crain, Cornel Wilde, Linda Darnell, William Eythe, Dorothy Gish

The Unsuspected (Warner Bros., 1947)
Producer: Charles Hoffman
Director: Michael Curtiz
Writer: Ranald MacDougall
Camera: Woody Bredell
Cast: Claude Rains, Audrey Totter, Joan Caulfield, Hurd Hatfield

Smart Woman (Monogram, 1948)
Producer: Hal E. Chester
Director: Edward A. Blatt
Writers: Alvah Bessie, Louise Morheim, Herbert Margolis
Camera: Stanley Cortez
Cast: Brian Aherne, Barry Sullivan, Michael O'Shea, Otto Kruger, Isobel Elsom, Iris Adrian

Angel on the Amazon (Republic, 1948)
Associate producer-director: John H. Auer
Writer: Lawrence Kimble
Camera: Reggie Lanning
Cast: George Brent, Vera Ralston, Brian Aherne

As Young As You Feel (Twentieth Century–Fox, 1951)
Producer: Lamar Trotti
Director: Harmon Jones
Writer: Lamar Trotti
Camera: Joe MacDonald
Cast: Monty Woolley, Thelma Ritter, Jean Peters, David Wayne, Marilyn Monroe

It Should Happen to You (Columbia, 1954)
Producer: Fred Kohlmar
Director: George Cukor
Writer: Garson Kanin
Camera: Charles Lang
Cast: Judy Holliday, Jack Lemmon, Peter Lawford, Michael O'Shea, Connie Gilchrist

Madame X (Universal, 1966)
Producer: Ross Hunter

Director: David Lowell Rich
Writer: Jean Holloway, from a play by Alexander Bisson
Camera: Russell Metty
Cast: Lana Turner, John Forsythe, Burgess Meredith, Keir Dullea, Ricardo Montalban

Barbara Bennett

The Valley of Decision (American-Mutual, 1916)
Director: Rea Berger
Writers: Richard Bennett, Clifford Howard
Cast: Richard Bennett, Adrienne Morrison, Rhoda Lewis

Syncopation (RKO, 1929)
Executive producer: Joseph I. Schnitzer
Producer: Robert Kane
Director: Bert Glennon
Writer: Frances Agnew, from a novel by Gene Markey
Camera: Dal Clawson, Frank Landi, George Webber
Cast: Bobby Watson, Morton Downey, Dorothy Lee, Fred Waring and his orchestra

Mother's Boy (Pathé, 1929)
Producer: Robert Kane
Director: Bradley Barker
Writer: Gene Markey
Camera: Harry Stradling, Walter Strenge, Philip Tannura
Cast: Morton Downey, Beryl Mercer, Helen Chandler, Brian Donlevy, Osgood Perkins

Love Among the Millionaires (Paramount, 1930)
Director: Frank Tuttle
Writer: Herman J. Mankiewicz
Camera: Allen G. Siegler
Cast: Clara Bow, Stanley Smith, Skeets Gallagher, Stuart Erwin, Mitzi Green

Joan Bennett

The Valley of Decision (American-Mutual, 1916)
Director: Rea Berger

Writers: Richard Bennett, Clifford Howard
Cast: Richard Bennett, Adrienne Morrison, Rhoda Lewis

The Eternal City (Associated First National, 1923)
Producer: Samuel Goldwyn
Director: George Fitzmaurice
Writer: Ouida Bergere
Camera: Arthur Miller
Cast: Barbara LaMarr, Lionel Barrymore, Bert Lytell, Richard Bennett

Power (Pathé, 1928)
Producer: Ralph Block
Director: Howard Higgins
Writer: Tay Garnett
Camera: Peverell Marley
Cast: William Boyd, Alan Hale, Jacqueline Logan, Carole Lombard

Bulldog Drummond (United Artists, 1929)
Producer: Samuel Goldwyn
Producer-director: F. Richard Jones
Writers: Wallace Smith, Sidney Howard
Camera: George Barnes, Gregg Toland
Cast: Ronald Colman, Montagu Love, Lilyan Tashman, Lawrence Grant

Three Live Ghosts (United Artists, 1929)
Producer: Max Marcin
Director: Thornton Freeland
Writers: Helen Hallett, Max Marcin
Camera: Robert H. Planck
Cast: Beryl Mercer, Hilda Vaughan, Robert Montgomery, Harry Stubbs

Disraeli (Warner Bros., 1929)
Director: Alfred E. Green
Writer: Julien Josephson, from a play by Louis Napoleon Parker
Camera: Lee Garmes
Cast: George Arliss, Florence Arliss, Anthony Bushell, Doris Lloyd

The Mississippi Gambler (Universal, 1929)
Producer: Carl Laemmle
Director: Reginald Barker
Writers: Edward T. Lowe, Winifred Reeve, H.H. Van Loan

Camera: Gilbert Warrenton
Cast: Joseph Schildkraut, Carmelita Geraghty, Alec B. Francis

Puttin' on the Ritz (United Artists, 1930)
Producers: Joseph M. Schenck, John W. Considine
Director: Edward Sloman
Writers: John Considine Jr., William K. Wells
Camera: Ray June
Cast: Harry Richman, James Gleason, Aileen Pringle, Lilyan Tashman

Crazy That Way (Fox, 1930)
Producer: William Fox
Director: Hamilton MacFadden
Writers: Hamilton MacFadden, Marion Orth, from a play by Vincent Lawrence
Camera: Joseph Valentine
Cast: Kenneth MacKenna, Regis Toomey, Jason Robards

Moby Dick (Warner Bros., 1930)
Director: Lloyd Bacon
Writer: J. Grubb Alexander, from the novel by Herman Melville
Camera: Robert Kurrle
Cast: John Barrymore, Lloyd Hughes, Noble Johnson, Walter Long

Maybe It's Love (Warner Bros., 1930)
Director: William Wellman
Writer: Joseph Jackson
Camera: Robert Kurrle
Cast: Joe E. Brown, James Hall, The All-American Football Team

Scotland Yard (Fox, 1930)
Producer: William Fox
Director: William K. Howard
Writer: Garrett Fort, from a play by Denison Clift
Camera: George Schneiderman
Cast: Edmund Lowe, Donald Crisp, George Renavent

Doctors' Wives (Fox, 1931)
Producer: John W. Considine Jr.
Director: Frank Borzage
Writer: Maurine Dallas Watkins, from a novel by Sylvia and Henry Lieferant
Camera: Arthur Edeson
Cast: Warner Baxter, Victor Varconi, Helen Millard

Many a Slip (Universal, 1931)
Producer: Carl Laemmle Jr.
Director: Vin Moore
Writer: Gladys Lehman, from a play by Edith Fitzgerald and Robert Riskin
Camera: Jerome Ash
Cast: Lew Ayres, Slim Summerville, Ben Alexander, Roscoe Karns

Hush Money (Fox, 1931)
Director: Sidney Lanfield
Writers: Sidney Lanfield, Dudley Nichols, Courtney Terrett, Philip Klein
Camera: John Seitz
Cast: Hardie Albright, Owen Moore, Myrna Loy

She Wanted a Millionaire (Fox, 1932)
Producer: William Fox
Director: John Blystone
Writers: William Anthony McGuire, William Collier Sr.
Camera: John Seitz
Cast: Spencer Tracy, Una Merkel, James Kirkwood, Dorothy Peterson

Careless Lady (Fox, 1932)
Director: Kenneth MacKenna
Writer: Guy Bolton
Camera: John Seitz
Cast: John Boles, Minna Gombell, Weldon Heyburn

The Trial of Vivienne Ware (Fox, 1932)
Director: William K. Howard
Writers: Philip Klein, Barry Conners
Camera: Ernest Palmer
Cast: Donald Cook, Richard "Skeets" Gallagher, ZaSu Pitts

Week-Ends Only (Fox, 1932)
Director: Alan Crosland
Writers: William Conselman, Warner Fabian, from a novel by Fabian
Camera: Hal Mohr
Cast: John Halliday, Ben Lyon, Halliwell Hobbes

Wild Girl (Fox, 1932)
Director: Raoul Walsh
Writers: Doris Anderson, Edwin Justus Mayer, from a story by Bret Harte and a play by Paul Armstrong

Camera: Arthur Miller
Cast: Charles Farrell, Eugene Pallette, Ralph Bellamy

Me and My Gal (Fox, 1932)
Director: Raoul Walsh
Writer: Arthur Kober
Camera: Arthur Miller
Cast: Spencer Tracy, Marion Burns, J. Farrell MacDonald, Henry B. Walthall

Arizona to Broadway (Fox, 1933)
Director: James Tinling
Writers: William Conselman, Henry Johnson
Camera: George Schneiderman
Cast: James Dunn, Herbert Mundin, Sammy Cohen, J. Carroll Naish

Little Women (RKO, 1933)
Executive producer: Merian C. Cooper
Director: George Cukor
Writers: Sarah Y. Mason, Victor Heerman, from the novel by Louisa May Alcott
Camera: Henry Gerrard
Cast: Katharine Hepburn, Frances Dee, Jean Parker, Spring Byington, Paul Lukas

The Pursuit of Happiness (Paramount, 1934)
Producer: Arthur Hornblow Jr.
Director: Alexander Hall
Writers: Stephen Morehouse Avery, Jack Cunningham, J.P. McEvoy, Virginia Van Upp, from a play by Lawrence Langner and Armina Marshall
Camera: Karl Struss
Cast: Francis Lederer, Charles Ruggles, Mary Boland, Minor Watson

The Man Who Reclaimed His Head (Universal, 1934)
Producer: Carl Laemmle
Director: Edward Ludwig
Writers: Jean Bart, Samuel Ornitz, from a play by Bart
Camera: Merritt B. Gerstad
Cast: Claude Rains, Lionel Atwill, Juanita Quigley

Private Worlds (Paramount, 1935)
Producer: Walter Wanger

Director: Gregory LaCava
Writer: Lynn Starling, from a novel by Phyllis Bottome
Camera: Leon Shamroy
Cast: Claudette Colbert, Charles Boyer, Joel McCrea, Helen Vinson, Esther Dale

Mississippi (Paramount, 1935)
Producer: Arthur Hornblow Jr.
Director: A. Edward Sutherland
Writers: Francis Martin, Jack Cunningham, from a play by Booth Tarkington
Camera: Charles Lang
Cast: Bing Crosby, W.C. Fields, Gail Patrick, Queenie Smith

Two for Tonight (Paramount, 1935)
Producer: Douglas MacLean
Director: Frank Tuttle
Writer: George Marion Jr.
Camera: Karl Struss
Cast: Bing Crosby, Mary Boland, Lynne Overman, Thelma Todd

She Couldn't Take It (Columbia, 1935)
Producer: B.P. Schulberg
Director: Tay Garnett
Writers: Oliver H.P. Garrett, Gene Towne
Camera: Leon Shamroy
Cast: George Raft, Walter Connolly, Billie Burke, Lloyd Nolan

The Man Who Broke the Bank at Monte Carlo (Twentieth Century–Fox, 1935)
Associate producer: Nunnally Johnson
Director: Stephen Roberts
Writers: Nunnally Johnson, Howard Smith, from a play by Illa Sugutchoff
Camera: Ernest Palmer
Cast: Ronald Colman, Colin Clive, Nigel Bruce, Montagu Love

Thirteen Hours by Air (Paramount, 1936)
Producer: E. Lloyd Sheldon
Director: Mitchell Leisen
Writer: Bogart Rogers, from his own story
Camera: Theodore Sparkuhl
Cast: Fred MacMurray, ZaSu Pitts, Alan Baxter, Brian Donlevy

Big Brown Eyes (Paramount, 1936)
Producer: Walter Wanger
Director: Raoul Walsh
Writers: Raoul Walsh, Bert Hanlon, from stories by James Edward Grant
Camera: George Clemens
Cast: Cary Grant, Walter Pidgeon, Lloyd Nolan, Alan Baxter, Isabel Jewell

Two in a Crowd (Universal, 1936)
Executive producer: Charles R. Rogers
Director: Alfred E. Green
Writers: Lewis R. Foster, Dorris Malloy, Earle Snell
Camera: Joseph Valentine
Cast: Joel McCrea, Henry Armetta, Alison Skipworth, Reginald Denny

Wedding Present (Paramount, 1936)
Producer: B.P. Schulberg
Director: Richard Wallace
Writer: Joseph Anthony
Camera: Leon Shamroy
Cast: Cary Grant, George Bancroft, Conrad Nagel, Gene Lockhart

Vogues of 1938 (United Artists, 1937)
Producer: Walter Wanger
Director: Irving Cummings
Writers: Bella and Samuel Spewack
Camera: Ray Rennahan
Cast: Warner Baxter, Helen Vinson, Mischa Auer, Alan Mowbray, Marjorie Gateson

I Met My Love Again (United Artists, 1938)
Producer: Walter Wanger
Directors: Arthur Ripley, Joshua Logan
Writer: David Hertz, from a novel by Allene Corliss
Camera: Hal Mohr
Cast: Henry Fonda, Alan Marshal, Dame May Whitty, Louise Platt

The Texans (Paramount, 1938)
Producer: Lucien Hubbard
Director: James Hogan
Writers: Bertram Millhauser, Paul Sloane, William W. Haines
Camera: Theodor Sparkuhl
Cast: Randolph Scott, May Robson, Walter Brennan, Robert Cummings

Artists and Models Abroad (Paramount, 1938)
Producer: Arthur Hornblow Jr.
Director: Mitchell Leisen
Writers: Howard Lindsay, Russel Crouse, Ken Englund
Camera: Ted Tetzlaff
Cast: Jack Benny, Mary Boland, Charley Grapewin, The Yacht Club Boys

Trade Winds (United Artists, 1938)
Producer: Walter Wanger
Director: Tay Garnett
Writers: Dorothy Parker, Alan Campbell, Frank R. Adams
Camera: Rudolph Mate
Cast: Fredric March, Ralph Bellamy, Ann Sothern, Sidney Blackmer

The Man in the Iron Mask (United Artists, 1939)
Producer: Edward Small
Director: James Whale
Writer: George Bruce, from the novel by Alexandre Dumas
Camera: Robert Planck
Cast: Louis Hayward, Warren William, Joseph Schildkraut, Alan Hale

The Housekeeper's Daughter (United Artists, 1939)
Producer-director: Hal Roach
Writers: Rian James, Gordon Douglas
Camera: Norbert Brodine
Cast: Adolphe Menjou, John Hubbard, William Gargan, Peggy Wood, Victor Mature

Green Hell (Universal, 1940)
Producer: Harry Edington
Director: James Whale
Writer: Frances Marion
Camera: Karl Freund
Cast: Douglas Fairbanks Jr., George Sanders, Vincent Price, Alan Hale

The House Across the Bay (United Artists, 1940)
Producer: Walter Wanger
Director: Archie Mayo
Writer: Kathryn Scola
Camera: Merritt Gerstad
Cast: George Raft, Lloyd Nolan, Walter Pidgeon, Gladys George

The Man I Married (Twentieth Century–Fox, 1940)
Associate producer: Raymond Griffith
Director: Irving Pichel
Writer: Oliver H.P. Garrett, from a novel by Oscar Schisgall
Camera: Peverell Marley
Cast: Francis Lederer, Lloyd Nolan, Anna Sten, Otto Kruger, Maria Ouspenskaya

The Son of Monte Cristo (United Artists, 1940)
Producer: Edward Small
Director: Rowland V. Lee
Writer: George Bruce
Camera: George Robinson
Cast: Louis Hayward, George Sanders, Florence Bates, Ian MacWolfe

Man Hunt (Twentieth Century–Fox, 1941)
Associate producer: Kenneth Macgowan
Director: Fritz Lang
Writer: Dudley Nichols, from a novel by Geoffrey Household
Camera: Arthur Miller
Cast: Walter Pidgeon, George Sanders, Roddy McDowall, John Carradine

She Knew All the Answers (Columbia, 1941)
Producer: Charles R. Rogers
Director: Richard Wallace
Writers: Harry Segall, Kenneth Earl, Curtis Kenyon
Camera: Henry Freulich
Cast: Franchot Tone, John Hubbard, Eve Arden

Wild Geese Calling (Twentieth Century–Fox, 1941)
Producer: Harry Joe Brown
Director: John Brahm
Writer: Horace McCoy, from a novel by Stewart Edward White
Camera: Lucien Ballard
Cast: Henry Fonda, Warren William, Ona Munson, Barton MacLane, Iris Adrian

Confirm or Deny (Twentieth Century–Fox, 1941)
Producer: Len Hammond
Director: Archie Mayo
Writer: Jo Swerling
Camera: Leon Shamroy
Cast: Don Ameche, Roddy McDowall, John Loder

Twin Beds (United Artists, 1942)
Producer: Edward Small
Director: Tim Whelan
Writers: Curtis Kenyon, Kenneth Earl, E. Edwin Moran, from a story by Margaret Mayo and Edward Salisbury Field
Camera: Hal Mohr
Cast: George Brent, Mischa Auer, Una Merkel, Glenda Farrell, Margaret Hamilton

The Wife Takes a Flyer (Columbia, 1942)
Producer: B.P. Schulberg
Director: Richard Wallace
Writers: Gina Kaus, Jay Dratler
Camera: Franz Planer
Cast: Franchot Tone, Allyn Joslyn, Cecil Cunningham

Girl Trouble (Twentieth Century–Fox, 1942)
Producer: Robert Bassler
Director: Harold Schuster
Writers: Ladislas Fodor, Robert Riley Crutcher
Camera: Edward Cronjager
Cast: Don Ameche, Billie Burke, Frank Craven, Helene Reynolds

Margin for Error (Twentieth Century–Fox, 1943)
Producer: Ralph Dietrich
Director: Otto Preminger
Writer: Lillie Hayward, from a play by Clare Boothe
Camera: Edward Cronjager
Cast: Milton Berle, Otto Preminger, Carl Esmond

The Woman in the Window (RKO, 1944)
Producer: Nunnally Johnson
Director: Fritz Lang
Writer: Nunnally Johnson
Camera: Milton Krasner
Cast: Edward G. Robinson, Dan Duryea, Raymond Massey, Edmond Breon

Nob Hill (Twentieth Century–Fox, 1945)
Producer: André Daven
Director: Henry Hathaway
Writers: Wanda Tuchock, Norman Reilly Raine
Camera: Edward Cronjager
Cast: George Raft, Vivian Blaine, Peggy Ann Garner, Alan Reed

Scarlet Street (Universal, 1945)
Executive producer: Walter Wanger
Producer-director: Fritz Lang
Writer: Dudley Nichols, from a novel and play by George de la Fouchardiere
Camera: Milton Krasner
Cast: Edward G. Robinson, Dan Duryea, Margaret Lindsay, Rosalind Ivan, Jess Barker

Colonel Effingham's Raid (Twentieth Century–Fox, 1946)
Producer: Lamar Trotti
Director: Irving Pichel
Writer: Kathryn Scola, from a novel by Berry Fleming
Camera: Edward Cronjager
Cast: Charles Coburn, William Eythe, Elizabeth Patterson, Frank Craven

The Macomber Affair (United Artists, 1947)
Producers: Benedict Bogeaus, Casey Robinson
Director: Zoltan Korda
Writer: Casey Robinson, from a story by Ernest Hemingway
Camera: Karl Struss
Cast: Gregory Peck, Robert Preston, Reginald Denny, Jean Gillie

The Woman on the Beach (RKO, 1947)
Executive producer: Jack J. Gross
Director: Jean Renoir
Writers: Frank Davis, Jean Renoir, from a novel by Mitchell Wilson
Camera: Leo Tover, Harry Wild
Cast: Robert Ryan, Charles Bickford, Nan Leslie, Irene Ryan

Secret Beyond the Door (Universal, 1948)
Producer-director: Fritz Lang
Writer: Silvia Richards, from a story by Rufus King
Camera: Stanley Cortez
Cast: Michael Redgrave, Anne Revere, Barbara O'Neil, Natalie Schafer, Mark Dennis

The Scar (originally released as *Hollow Triumph,* Eagle-Lion, 1948)
Executive producer: Bryan Foy
Producer: Paul Henreid
Director: Steve Sekely
Writer: Daniel Fuchs, from a novel by Murray Forbes

Camera: John Alton
Cast: Paul Henreid, Eduard Franz, Leslie Brooks

The Reckless Moment (Columbia, 1949)
Producer: Walter Wanger
Director: Max Ophuls
Writers: Henry Garson, Robert W. Soderberg, Mel Dinelli, from a novel by Elizabeth Sanxay Holding
Camera: Burnett Guffey
Cast: James Mason, Geraldine Brooks, Shepperd Strudwick, Frances Williams

Father of the Bride (MGM, 1950)
Producer: Pandro S. Berman
Director: Vincente Minnelli
Writers: Frances Goodrich, Albert Hackett, from a novel by Edward Streeter
Camera: John Alton
Cast: Spencer Tracy, Elizabeth Taylor, Don Taylor, Billie Burke, Moroni Olsen

For Heaven's Sake (Twentieth Century–Fox, 1950)
Producer: William Perlberg
Director: George Seaton
Writer: George Seaton, from a play by Harry and Dorothy Segall
Camera: Lloyd Ahern
Cast: Clifton Webb, Robert Cummings, Edmund Gwenn, Joan Blondell

Father's Little Dividend (MGM, 1951)
Producer: Pandro S. Berman
Director: Vincente Minnelli
Writers: Frances Goodrich, Albert Hackett, from characters created by Edward Streeter
Camera: John Alton
Cast: Spencer Tracy, Elizabeth Taylor, Don Taylor, Billie Burke, Moroni Olsen

The Guy Who Came Back (Twentieth Century–Fox, 1951)
Producer: Julian Blaustein
Director: Joseph Newman
Writer: Allan Scott, from a story by William Fay
Camera: Joseph La Shelle
Cast: Paul Douglas, Linda Darnell, Don DeFore, Billy Gray

Highway Dragnet (Allied Artists, 1954)
Executive producer: William F. Broidy
Producer: Jack Jungmeyer
Director: Nathan Juran
Writers: U.S. Anderson, Roger Corman
Cast: Richard Conte, Wanda Hendrix, Mary Beth Hughes, Iris Adrian

We're No Angels (Paramount, 1955)
Producer: Pat Duggan
Director: Michael Curtiz
Writer: Ranald MacDougall, from a play by Albert Husson
Camera: Loyal Griggs
Cast: Humphrey Bogart, Aldo Ray, Peter Ustinov, Basil Rathbone, Leo G. Carroll

Navy Wife (Allied Artists, 1956)
Producer: Walter Wanger
Director: Edward L. Bernds
Writer: Kay Lenard, from a novel by Tats Blain
Camera: Wilfrid Cline
Cast: Gary Merrill, Judy Nugent, Shirley Yamaguchi

There's Always Tomorrow (Universal, 1956)
Producer: Ross Hunter
Director: Douglas Sirk
Writer: Bernard C. Schoenfeld, from a story by Ursula Parrott
Camera: Russell Metty
Cast: Fred MacMurray, Barbara Stanwyck, William Reynolds, Pat Crowley

Desire in the Dust (Twentieth Century–Fox, 1960)
Producer-director: William F. Claxton
Writer: Charles Lang, from a novel by Harry Whittington
Camera: Lucien Ballard
Cast: Raymond Burr, Martha Hyer, Brett Halsey, Ken Scott, Irene Ryan

House of Dark Shadows (MGM, 1970)
Producer-director: Dan Curtis
Writers: Sam Hall, Gordon Russell
Camera: Arthur Ornitz
Cast: Jonathan Frid, Grayson Hall, Kathryn Leigh Scott, Nancy Barrett, John Karlen

Feature Films

Suspiria (International Classics, 1977)
Executive producer: Salvatore Argento
Producer: Dario Argento
Writers: Dario Argento, Daria Nicolodi
Camera: Luciano Tovoli
Cast: Jessica Harper, Stefania Casini, Alida Valli, Flavio Bucci, Barbara Magnolfi

Selected Television Appearances

Constance Bennett

Guest Appearances

The Jack Carter Show (NBC), 1951
Your Show of Shows (NBC), 1951
Cameo Theatre (NBC), ep. "Avalanche," 1951
Faith Baldwin Theater of Romance (ABC), ep. "Love Letters," 1951
Betty Crocker Star Matinee (ABC), ep. "Eastward in Eden," 1951
Somerset Maugham TV Theatre (CBS), ep. "Home and Beauty," 1951
Robert Montgomery Presents (NBC), ep. "Senora Isobel," 1952
Broadway Television Theatre (CBS), ep. "Twentieth Century," 1953
Suspense (CBS), ep. "Mr. Nobody," 1953
Philip Morris Playhouse (CBS), ep. "Kitty Doone," 1954
Toast of the Town (CBS), 1956
Matinee Theatre (NBC), ep. "One Hundred Red Convertibles," 1956
Robert Montgomery Presents (NBC), ep. "Onions in the Stew," 1956
The Ann Sothern Show (CBS), ep. "Always April," 1961
The Reporter, ep. "The Man Behind the Badge," 1964

Joan Bennett

Continuing Roles

Too Young to Go Steady (NBC), May 14, 1959–June 25, 1959
Dark Shadows (ABC), June 27, 1966–April 2, 1971

Guest Appearances

Nash Airflyte Theatre (CBS), ep. "Peggy," 1951
What's My Line? (CBS), 1951

Selected Television Appearances

Somerset Maugham TV Theatre (CBS), ep. "The Dream," 1951
Your Show of Shows (NBC), 1951
Danger (CBS), ep. "A Clear Case of Suicide," 1951
General Electric Theater (CBS), ep. "You're Only Young Once," 1951
Somerset Maugham TV Theatre (CBS), ep. "Smith Serves," 1951
This Is Show Business (CBS), 1953
The Best of Broadway (CBS), ep. "The Man Who Came to Dinner," 1954
Ford Theater (NBC), ep. "Letters Marked Personal," 1955
Shower of Stars (CBS), ep. "The Dark Fleece," 1955
Ford Theater (NBC), ep. "Dear Diane," 1956
Climax! (CBS), ep. "The Louella Parsons Story," 1956
Playhouse 90 (CBS), ep. "The Thundering Wave," 1957
DuPont Show of the Month (NBC), ep. "Junior Miss," 1957
To Tell the Truth (CBS), 1958
Pursuit (CBS), ep. "Epitaph for a Golden Girl," 1959
Mr. Broadway (CBS), ep. "Don't Mention My Name in Sheboygan," 1964
Burke's Law (ABC), ep. "Who Killed Mr. Colby in Ladies' Lingerie?," 1965
The Mike Douglas Show (syndicated), 1967
The Merv Griffin Show (syndicated), 1967
The Governor and J.J. (CBS), 1970
The Mike Douglas Show (syndicated), 1970
The Movie Game (syndicated), 1970
Love, American Style (ABC), ep. "Love and the Second Time," 1971
The Mike Douglas Show (syndicated), 1977
The Guiding Light (ABC), 1982

Made-for-Television Movies

Gidget Gets Married (ABC, 1972)
Executive producer: Harry Ackerman
Producer-director: E.W. Swackhamer
Writer: John McGreevey
Camera: Joseph F. Biroc
Cast: Monie Ellis, Michael Burns, Don Ameche, Macdonald Carey, Paul Lynde

The Eyes of Charles Sand (ABC, 1972)
Producer: Hugh Benson
Director: Roza Badiyi
Writer: Henry Farrell
Camera: Ben Colman
Cast: Peter Haskell, Barbara Rush, Sharon Farrell, Bradford Dillman, Adam West
Suddenly, Love (NBC, 1978)

Producers: Ross Hunter, Jacque Mapes
Director: Stuart Margolin
Writer: Katherine Coker
Camera: Robert B. Hauser
Cast: Cindy Williams, Paul Shenar, Eileen Heckart, Lew Ayres

This House Possessed (ABC, 1981)
Producer-writer: David Levinson
Director: William Wiard
Camera: Thomas Del Ruth
Cast: Parker Stevenson, Lisa Eilbacher, Slim Pickens, K Callan

Divorce Wars: A Love Story (ABC, 1982)
Producer: Sam Manners
Director: Donald Wrye
Writers: Linda Elstad, Donald Wrye
Cast: Tom Selleck, Jane Curtin, Viveca Lindfors, Charles Haid

Notes

Abbreviations

BP *The Bennett Playbill,* by Joan Bennett and Lois Kibbee (New York: Holt, Rinehart, and Winston, 1970).

RB Richard Bennett's unpublished memoirs, quoted with the permission of Diana Anderson.

WW *Walter Wanger: Hollywood Independent,* by Matthew Bernstein (Berkeley and Los Angeles: Univ. of California Press, 1994).

Prologue

1 "There are only three great actors": *BP,* p. 216.
2 "could have recited the alphabet": Joseph Jefferson, RB, p. 123.
3 "count on five fingers": ibid., p. 124.
4 "noble experiment": *BP,* p. 229.
4 "My God, the day may come": ibid., p. 92.
4 "I wouldn't give up": ibid., p. 216.

Chapter One: 1870–1900

8 "Bennett's switch, which is located near Kokomo and Logansport": *BP,* p. 239.
9 "meanest boy in town": RB, p. 23.
10 "make a man": ibid., p. 15.
11 "We got to learn you to keep your temper": ibid., p. 34.
13 "an act of Divine Providence": ibid., p. 127.
15 "A property man": ibid., p. 144.
16 "From the time you first cast": ibid., p. 189.
17 "I want to be an actor": ibid., p. 209.
18 "Here I was again": ibid., p. 214.

19 "had a double responsibility": author interview with Helen Hayes, June 1990.

20 "A play that has vitality": *New York Times,* August 9, 1909.

21 "After each act I had to call her": author interview with Marta Eggerth, June 30, 2000.

OTHER SOURCES

1870 Census, Howard County, Indiana.

Ned Booher and Linda Ferries, *Kokomo: A Pictorial History* (St. Louis: G. Bradley, 1989).

Thomas B. Helm, *History of Cass County, Indiana* (Chicago: Brant and Fuller, 1886).

Dr. Jehu Z. Powell, *History of Cass County, Indiana* (Chicago/New York: Lewis, 1913).

Indiana State Gazettes & Business Directory, 1880–1881.

Kokomo Dispatch, September 22 and 29, 1881.

Chapter Two: 1900–1904

25 "like a flag flying": *New York Times,* April 30, 1922.

25 "Born in the theater and of it": RB, p. 224.

25 ". . . with a definite leaning toward": ibid.

25 "You are the first person I've ever met": ibid., p. 225.

26 "I'm glad to meet you, Mr. Morrison": ibid., p. 226.

26 "I had never seen anything so beautiful": ibid., p. 229.

26 "Here I was, hooked high and dry": ibid., p. 230.

27 "If all you married my daughter for": ibid., p. 232.

28 "PUT MORRISON IN DE WOLFE'S PART . . . . FROHMAN": ibid., p. 236.

28 "Liar!": ibid.

28 "All I ask of you": ibid., p. 237.

28 "It's no use, Dick": ibid., p. 239.

28 "I will not say that I do not": ibid.

29 "PLEASE COME TO FLAT B": ibid., p. 243.

29 "I knew you'd want a boy": ibid., p. 246.

29 "She is her father's own daughter": ibid., p. 247.

Chapter Three: 1904–1914

32 "never burlesque, even in the comedy scenes": *New York Times,* October 24, 1905.

33 "You always want to take into consideration": RB, p. 254.

33 "a new kind of play": Charles W. Collins, *Chicago Tribune,* 1905.
34 "Mr. Richard Bennett, in the rather thankless part": *Times of London,* May 24, 1906.
35 "Richard Bennett merits more praise": *New York Times,* August 31, 1906.
36 "with the affection of a cockroach": RB, p. 259.
37 "silly-assed Englishman": ibid., p. 260.
38 "It was worse than army drill": ibid., p. 265.
38 "A small-town, midwest country boy": ibid., p. 268.
39 "Probably it is true": *Hampton Magazine,* September 1916.
39 "What is charm, exactly, Maggie?": *The Plays of James M. Barrie* (New York: Scribner's, 1950), p. 326.
40 "The triumph of the night": *New York Times,* December 24, 1908.
42 "She was lying in her baby carriage": RB, p. 273.
42 "I CONGRATULATE YOU": *BP,* p. 35.
42 "a very much overrated actress": ibid., p. 34.
42 "a rather lively, moving melodrama": ibid., p. 276.
43 "My idea is very simple": *New York Times,* October 19, 1913.
44 "stupid people": George Bernard Shaw, Preface to Eugene Brieux's *Damaged Goods* (New York: Brentano, 1910).
44 "When asked, 'What then . . .'": ibid.
45 "All that is needed": Brieux, *Damaged Goods.*
47 "For once": *BP,* p. 45.
48 "I think you are doing something worthwhile": RB, p. 290.
48 "no scene to provoke scandal": Fulton Theatre Playbill, *Damaged Goods,* 1914.
49 "as much a sermon on imbecility": *Chicago Tribune,* January 1914.
49 "I do not feel that I am an inspired or divine Messiah": *BP,* p. 47.
49 "The more we have of *Damaged Goods*": Fulton Theatre Playbill, *Damaged Goods,* 1914.
50 "It is not too much to say": ibid.
50 "I had fought": RB, p. 292.

Chapter Four: 1914–1920

52 "with anything but polite tolerance and contempt": *BP,* p. 52.
52 "a ray of hope": *Variety,* July 15, 1915.
52 "like refugees from a number three company": *BP,* p. 53.
53 "Won't you come over": James Robert Parish, *The RKO Gals* (New Rochelle: Arlington House, 1974), p. 67.
54 "Father at home": *BP,* p. 53.
55 "rocking gently and talking gently": James Agee, "Knoxville: Summer of 1915" (1949).

56 "patronized by those who spend freely": *Who's Who in the Private Schools,* 1925 ed.
57 "like a Roman senator": *BP,* p. 55.
57 "like a hot wind": ibid., p. 9.
57 "a long patch of shaded green": ibid., p. 58.
58 "the grandest, squarest Jew in the theater": RB, p. 241.
59 "They always sat in the front seat": author interview with Jane Wyatt, October 13, 1997.
60 "skillfully motivated and constructed": *New York Times,* September 16, 1918.
60 "a real triumph": ibid.
60 "surpasses in ingenuity": *Smart Set,* September 1918.
68 "Do you like absinthe?": Travis R. Bogard and Jackson R. Bryer, eds., *Selected Letters of Eugene O'Neill* (New Haven: Yale Univ. Press, 1988), p. 104.
68 "there was not a line changed": RB, p. 305.
68 "I'm sick of *Beyond*": *Selected Letters of Eugene O'Neill,* p. 107.
69 "Let's have a few more fights": ibid.
69 "the fare available for the New York theatergoer": *New York Times,* February 4, 1920.
69 "as the homebound wanderer": ibid.
69 "Richard Bennett realizes the hapless dreamer": *New York Evening World,* February 4, 1920.

Chapter Five: 1920–1924

71 "a cause for relief on both sides": *BP,* p. 74.
72 "Catholic communities are": *Boston Herald,* February 17, 1921.
73 "The shiftiest manipulator in pictures": RB, p. 310.
73 "the greatest, gaudiest spree in history": F. Scott Fitzgerald, *The Far Side of Paradise.*
77 "It is a drama marked by astonishing courage": *New York Evening Telegram,* September 6, 1921.
77 "an uncommonly nourishing play": *New York Times,* September 6, 1921.
77 "When I see a man trying Shakespeare": RB, p. 123.
78 "Life has withdrawn itself": *Theater,* March 1924.
79 "What do you care?": RB, p. 314.
79 "a great play": ibid., p. 315.
80 "That was the way he saw it": Theresa Helburn, *A Wayward Quest* (Boston: Little, Brown, 1960), p. 187.
80 "Don't worry, children": ibid.
80 "the Theatre Guild emerged, flushed and triumphant": *New York Times,* January 4, 1922.

80 "the biggest hit since Eva LeGallienne": RB, p. 315.
80 "much more successful than it had any right to be": *A Wayward Quest,* p. 188.
81 "a Russian fairy": *BP,* p. 79.
81 "That poor girl": author interview with James Fraser, November 25, 2002.
83 "intense and sincere": *BP,* p. 313.
84 "as trained and responsive as": Lillian Gish, *The Movies, Mr. Griffith, and Me* (New York: Prentice Hall, 1969), p. 100.
84 "In Fairy Town": Louise Brooks, *Lulu in Hollywood* (New York: Alfred A. Knopf, 1982), p. 12.
85 "worn and unhappy": ibid., p. 13.
85 "a wonderful success": *BP,* p. 5.
85 "Mr. Bennett, you see, is a genius": *New York Herald Tribune,* November 1940.
86 "a coherent and finely articulated play": *New York Times,* October 18, 1923.
87 "the beau ideal of the twentieth century": *New York Times,* July 3, 1945.
87 "Truly . . . ours was a heartless racket": *Lulu in Hollywood,* p. 15.
88 "that barmaid": Brooke Hayward, *Haywire* (New York: Random House, 1978), p. 101.
91 "the honest, God-fearing, thrifty people": *New York World,* December 7, 1924.
91 "never points a moral": unidentified publication.
91 "belongs among the best": *New York World,* November 25, 1924.
91 "a cheerful, intuitive, understanding contribution": *New York Sun,* November 25, 1924.
92 "magnificent": *New York World,* November 25, 1924.
92 "by turns comic and pathetic": *Theatre,* February 1925.
93 "Who owns Tony's pants, Dick?": *New York Post,* June 23, 1925.

Other Sources

Records from the Probate Court of Groton, Connecticut.

Chapter Six: 1925–1927

98 "kicked and Charlestoned all over my floor": *Collier's* Magazine, August 1927.
101 "There was something cold and forbidding about it": *BP,* p. 96.
102 "pompous": ibid., p. 99.
102 "overbearing": ibid.

102 "He treated Auntie Mab like a queen": author interview with Victor Morrison, March 11, 2000.
103 "one find not stolen by Cupid": *Collier's* Magazine, August 1927.
105 "scared stiff": *BP,* p. 103.
106 "life was serene and happy again": ibid., p. 104.

Chapter Seven: 1927–1929

107 "the Western distributors for Babbitry": *BP,* p. 106.
109 "She was beautiful and full of enthusiasm": author interview with Victor Morrison, March 11, 2000.
109 "the most disastrous thing of my life": RB, p. 316.
110 "more of an endurance test": ibid., p. 333.
111 "waving a gun and threatening to shoot": *BP,* p. 117.
112 "Mr. Hards": RB, p. 348.
113 "The girl's the best thing in the show—build up her part": author interview with Joan Bennett, September 29, 1989.
113 "Don't hamstring it with a lot of fool ideas": RB, p. 349.
113 "completely nerveless, and just too inexperienced": *BP,* p. 119.
114 "In his playing he achieved the externals of an excellent performance": *New York Times,* September 25, 1928.
114 "His daughter, Joan": ibid.
114 "immense technical difficulties . . . cannot engage our attention": *New York World,* September 25, 1928.
114 "took a difficult part": *New York American,* September 25, 1928.
114 "Joan made the grade—and how!": RB, p. 351.
115 "very sweet": *BP,* p. 122.
116 "I figured that if a studio wanted an actress": ibid.
116 "good but not gorgeous": RB, p. 352.
117 "It wasn't a particularly ego-building time": *BP,* p. 203.
118 "That one didn't win me any acting awards either": ibid.
118 "defeated her natural pulchritude": *New York Times,* April 21, 1929.
119 "I wouldn't play that damn place": *New York Herald-Tribune,* June 10, 1929.
119 "Joan Bennett, who must get tired of hearing it": *New York Herald-Tribune,* September 10, 1929.
119 "consisted of twitching watery eyes to express cuteness": David Shipman, *The Story of Cinema* (New York: St. Martin's Press, 1982), p. 238.

Chapter Eight: 1929–1930

123 "every inch the aristocrat": Gloria Swanson, *Swanson on Swanson* (New York: Random House, 1980), p. 224.

124 "If French officialdom fell in love with me": ibid., p. 227.
125 "a classic example of that person in the arts": ibid., p. 397.
126 "The fire has burnt": ibid., p. 399.
127 "agreeable, easy manner of talking": *New York Times,* December 14, 1929.
130 "made every chorus girl in every chorus line": Ronald Kessler, *The Sins of the Father: Joseph P. Kennedy and the Dynasty He Founded* (New York: Warner Books, 1996), p. 43.
130 "a typical, old-fashioned Irishman": author interview with Victor Morrison, March 11, 2000.
131 "Here's what I ask 'em": *New Movie Magazine,* March 1931.
131 "very pleasant, warm, and friendly": author interview with Edward Downey, July 6, 2002.
131 "I'll not be satisfied until I have nine children": *Los Angeles Times,* April 8, 1952.

Chapter Nine: 1930–1931

133 "like the year of a comet": Eudora Welty lecture, Ninety-second Street YMHA, New York City, April 22, 1985.
135 "Progress. Bah!": Lawton Campbell, *Solid South* (New York: Samuel French, 1930), p. 31.
135 "So!": Bette Davis and Sandford Dody, *The Lonely Life* (New York: G.P. Putnam's Sons, 1962), p. 98.
136 "enough mountbankery": Brooks Atkinson, *New York Times,* October 15, 1930.
136 "It is amusing stuff, much of it": Burns Mantle, *New York Daily News,* October 15, 1930.
136 "Mr. Bennett makes the Major a likeable old duffer": *New Yorker,* October 20, 1930.
136 "excessive actoralities": *New Republic,* October 29, 1930.
136 "I predict that ere his Lyceum engagement ends": *New York Herald Tribune,* October 15, 1930.
136 "a surprise and a tantrum": Davis, *The Lonely Life,* p. 100.
143 "They want to press their noses": Michael Korda, "Wasn't She Great?" *New Yorker,* August 15, 1995.
145 "She was supposed to be a bitch": John Kobal, *People Will Talk* (New York: Alfred A. Knopf, 1985), p. 309.
148 "That the business of suffering": Elinor Hughes, *Boston Herald,* May 5, 1931.
150 "sterling": *Motion Picture Herald,* November 21, 1931.
151 "an authentic one": *BP,* p. 220.

152 "to earn a million dollars": *Time,* December 20, 1929.
152 "Among the Hollywood detestables": Brooks, *Lulu in Hollywood,* p. 14.

OTHER SOURCES

"Warner Bros. Film Grosses, 1921–1951," *Historical Journal of Film, Radio, and Television* 15, no. 1 (1995).

Chapter Ten: 1931–1932

159 "studied painting and learned nothing": "Boulevardier," *Esquire,* October 1964, p. 162.
160 "He was my playmate": author interview with Diana Anderson, August 10, 2000.
161 "Well, I thought she was much better than I was": author interview with Joan Bennett, September 30, 1989.
161 "Bore, bore, bore": interview with Joan Bennett, *Spencer Tracy: An Actor's Legacy,* PBS television, 1986.
161 "a sheer delight": Parish, *The RKO Gals,* p. 49.
161 "[She] has seldom been better than she is here": ibid.
164 "bright and entertaining": *New York Times,* February 22, 1932.
164 "excellent": ibid.
164 "From the way you are starting": David Chierichetti, *Hollywood Costume Design* (New York: Harmony Books, 1976), p. 139.
165 "adopted": files at Groton Probate Court, Groton, Connecticut.
170 "the story was frankly rather crappy to begin with": Robert Emmet Long, ed., *George Cukor: Interviews* (Jackson: Univ. Press of Mississippi, 2001), p. 39.

Chapter Eleven: 1933–1935

174 "one of the finest boys in the world": RB, p. 360.
175 "Come on, you little bitches!": author interview with Joan Bennett, September 30, 1989.
176 "She looks like a child": *New York Daily News,* November 16, 1933.
176 "Joan Bennett's Amy is so far beyond anything": *New York American,* November 17, 1933.
176 "She took me to the studio to see the picture": author interview with Diana Anderson, August 13, 2000.
177 "much more interesting": *New York Times,* June 30, 1933.
179 "One story that spread like wildfire": Colleen Moore, *Silent Star* (New York: Doubleday, 1968), pp. 140–41.

179 "He was not a bad man—not at all": author interview with Peter Plant, August 12, 2000.
179 "My mother was attracted to elegance, number one": author interview with Gyl Roland, March 18, 2001.
183 "a definite connotation of gross vulgarity": report from J.I. Breen, January 18, 1934, on file at Margaret Herrick Library, Academy of Motion Picture Arts and Sciences.
183 "libidinous persons who engage in promiscuous sexuality": ibid.
185 "The gallantry of Iris March": *New York Times,* November 3, 1934.
186 ". . . beauty, great acting ability": Brooks, *Lulu in Hollywood,* p. 13.

Chapter Twelve: 1934–1937

188 "seven years have proved conclusively": *Los Angeles Examiner,* date unknown.
188 "a case of nerves": unidentified publication.
189 "RICHARD BENNETT BEAT HER, HIS SECOND WIFE CHARGES": *Los Angeles Times,* April 11, 1934.
189 "DARLING. CAN'T YOU FIND SOME PLACE IN YOUR HEART": *Los Angeles Examiner,* May 7, 1934.
189 "I'd rather pay the President's salary": ibid.
190 "We never had any idea where Michael came from": author interview with Edward Downey, July 6, 2002.
191 "Conka–I've had a hell of a time": letter from Richard Bennett to Constance Bennett, March 23, 1935.
191 "Did you get in touch with Neil?": letter from Richard Bennett to Constance Bennett, April 18, 1935.
192 "no matter how large a fortune one is supposed to have": letter from Constance Bennett to Richard Bennett, June 29, 1935.
193 "He knows damned well": letter from Barbara Bennett to Joan Bennett, undated.
193 "Dear Joan, Do your cheeks turn red . . . ?": letter from Richard Bennett to Joan Bennett, August 22, 1935.
193 "Believe it or not": letter from Constance Bennett to Richard Bennett, August 27, 1935.
194 "a religious institution": *New York Times,* October 17, 1937.
195 "to embark on the troubled waters": RB, p. 266.
195 "Awake and sing! The hour has come!": Burgess Meredith, *So Far So Good* (Boston: Little, Brown, 1994), p. 2.
195 "But then, he found the pace, the rhythm, the center of meaning": ibid., p. 5.
196 "a brilliant work of art": *New York Times,* September 26, 1935.

196 "All right, gentlemen, I'll go with you": *Boston Globe,* date unknown.
198 "refused to buckle down to the discipline of the ordinary student": *WW,* p. 13.
198 "cracked up the first five planes assigned to him": *BP,* p. 257.
199 "the appeal of the movies to the city's social elite": *WW,* p. 50.
201 "the first really challenging and the most dramatic role": *BP,* p. 234.
201 "of almost no assistance": *New York Times,* March 28, 1935.
202 "at her dramatic best": *Variety,* March 28, 1935.
202 "the terrifying climax to the drama": *New York American,* March 28, 1935.
202 "nothing short of amazing in her work": *Hollywood Reporter,* March 29, 1935.
202 "That picture was a big help": Kobal, *People Will Talk,* p. 294.
206 "Love was in the air": author interview with Penny Singleton, June 10, 2001.

Chapter Thirteen: 1937–1940

210 "For those who don't know": Pauline Kael, *5001 Nights at the Movies* (New York: Holt, Rinehart, and Winston, 1985), p. 781.
211 "the most exhilarating light comedy of the season": *New York Daily Mirror,* March 17, 1938.
211 "Constance Bennett, who proved to be a top-notch comedienne": *New York Daily News,* March 18, 1938.
211 "There was a scene where she had to slap me": author interview with Alice Faye, September 10, 1997.
213 "very realistically, even off the stage": *Los Angeles Examiner,* April 10, 1934.
214 "One at a time! One at a time!": *BP,* p. 265.
214 "vitally touching, virile and funny": Joshua Logan, *Josh: My Up and Down, and In and Out Life* (New York: Delacorte Press, 1976), p. 114.
215 "one of the best performances of his career": *New Yorker,* February 12, 1938.
215 "I want a return of some of that bread": letter from Richard Bennett to Constance Bennett, March 6, 1938.
215 "How are you going to feel at the age of sixty-seven": letter from Richard Bennett to Constance Bennett, March 26, 1938.
216 "The country is in a panic with this administration and stock market": letter from Constance Bennett to Richard Bennett, March 6, 1938.
217 "dull, lusterless routine": *BP,* p. 253.
217 "that he and Mother were not hitting it off at all": author interview with Diana Anderson, August 12, 2000.

219 "the fact that there is no substitute for stage experience": *Hartford Times,* October 11, 1937.

219 "Joan Bennett, acting like her father's daughter": *The Best Plays of 1937–38,* ed. Burns Mantle (New York: Dodd, Mead, 1942), p. 18.

219 "really washed up this time": letter from Joan Bennett to Adrienne Morrison, February 1938.

219 "wouldn't permit me to do it alone": letter from Joan Bennett to Adrienne Morrison, February 1938.

220 "landed gentry": *BP,* p. 256.

220 "a compulsive housekeeper": ibid., p. 298.

221 "Every place where Joan lived": author interview with Victor Morrison, March 11, 2000.

222 "I positively smoldered all over the South Seas": *BP,* p. 262.

222 "Joan Bennett looks attractive": *Variety,* December 10, 1938.

223 "had no trouble at all outacting her": Kael, *5001 Nights at the Movies,* p. 786.

223 "not a bit like a pig-tailed little sister": Erma Taylor, "Give Us Two Hedys–And They Did!" King Features Syndicate, 1939.

224 "magnificent": *BP,* p. 263.

224 "She absolutely turned it down": author interview with Diana Anderson, October 25, 1991.

224 "I switched from blonde to brunette": author interview with Joan Bennett, September 30, 1989.

224 "The Housekeeper's Daughter did things she hadn't oughter": Hollywood Museum Collection (Hal Roach material), on file at the University of Southern California.

225 "He was rude": author interview with Carmen DiRigo, March 18, 2001.

226 "My father didn't like my grandmother at all": author interview with Lorinda Roland, July 20, 2001.

227 "I came in a couple of times while they were playing": author interview with Peter Plant, August 13, 2000.

228 "He undercut the product": ibid.

230 "conferred an extra flavor of spontaneity": *New York Times,* December 31, 1939.

231 "She tried everything to make Walter jealous": author interview with Diana Anderson, August 14, 2000.

232 "She was happiest, in the beginning": ibid.

234 "hypnotized zealots": *New York Times,* August 3, 1940.

235 "I don't think she saw acting as much more than her job": author interview with Stephanie (Wanger) Guest, April 24, 2001.

236 "there had never been cause to doubt his honesty": *BP,* p. 270.

237 "I make an entrance down a flight of stairs": *New York Times,* May 1, 1940.

Chapter Fourteen: 1941–1943

239 "She was so warm and friendly": author interview with Edward Downey, July 6, 2002.

240 "The children were all very subdued": author interview with Diana Anderson, November 13, 1997.

241 "on his best behavior with us": author interview with Michael Downey, September 12, 2002.

241 "I don't think she really realized what she was getting into": ibid.

242 "a gesture of defiance": *BP,* p. 278.

242 "with propriety becoming a good mother": ibid.

242 "a cruel bargain": ibid.

243 "She would come to visit occasionally": author interview with Michael Downey, September 12, 2002.

246 "He always wanted you to see the rushes": author interview with Jane Wyatt, April 10, 2002.

246 "It was the only movie I ever made": *BP,* p. 283.

248 "never been so appealing": *Hollywood Reporter,* June 1941.

248 "I know I'm not Fritz Lang, but I'll do my best": *Films in Review,* July 1977.

250 "He wheeled her in and she saw all these glorious stars": author interview with Patricia Coulter McElroy, June 20, 2001.

250 "Constance loved Dad because he was younger": ibid.

252 "He was very embarrassed about the whole thing": author interview with Peter Plant, August 15, 2000.

254 "She was an effective organizer": author interview with Peter Plant, August 15, 2000.

256 "I think she worked a lot with female intuition": ibid.

258 "with a smiling graciousness": *New London Evening Day,* November 17, 1943.

258 "On the ninth day of January, 1930": deposition of Sarah Savina Armstrong, July 15, 1942, on file at Groton Probate Court, Groton, Connecticut.

258 "If I did, I cannot remember them": ibid.

258 "For the simple reason": ibid.

260 "found up in Ireland": deposition of Barbara Bennett Randall, July 1942, Los Angeles, on file at Groton Probate Court, Groton, Connecticut.

260 "it was a dramatic moment as the actress looked up": *New London Evening Day,* November 18, 1943.

261 "that the proof is complicated and difficult": ibid.

261 "Today's outcome vindicates the position I took": *New London Evening Day,* November 19, 1943.

261 "Peter will never see that money": author interview with Diana Anderson, August 11, 2000.

261 "one of the most bizarre cases in court annals": *New London Evening Day,* November 19, 1943.

262 "You must take into consideration that this is a very peculiar family": deposition of Barbara Bennett Randall, July 1942, Los Angeles, on file at Groton Probate Court, Groton, Connecticut.

263 "He started carrying on that the positions of the riders": author interview with Diana Anderson, March 18, 2001.

263 "I felt so badly about Dick Bennett and his daughters": from Hedda Hopper Collection, on file at Academy of Motion Picture Arts and Sciences, undated.

264 "My good fortune": letter from Richard Bennett to Orson Welles, on file at Lilly Library, Indiana University, Bloomington, Indiana.

265 "My mother's life sort of fell apart in stages": author interview with Michael Downey, September 12, 2002.

265 "as dull and dreary and ineptly written": *New York Times,* October 27, 1943.

265 "now and then to get off some insufferable lines": *New York Post,* October 27, 1943.

266 "I take it that I am now barred from El Morocco": *New York Daily News,* December 15, 1943.

267 "Some of us would sing": author interview with Risë Stevens, February 10, 2002.

267 "ARE YOU GETTING MUCH?": John Lahr, *Notes on a Cowardly Lion* (New York: Alfred A. Knopf, 1969), p. 219.

267 "This is one time when we must think about clothes": Joan Bennett, *How to Be Attractive* (New York: Alfred A. Knopf, 1943), p. 88.

268 "vary your diet": ibid., pp. 121–22.

269 "I can't bear to see it—it's sickening": *Los Angeles Times,* May 3, 1943.

269 "he was the proudest of fathers": *BP,* p. 286.

Chapter Fifteen: 1944

272 "The girl next door wasn't really the girl next door": author interview with Teresa Wright, March 18, 1990.

272 "so many of these murder operas": *Los Angeles Examiner,* January 20, 1945.

272 "*Film noir* really wasn't regarded as anything": author interview with Audrey Totter, November 8, 1999.

273 "I am starting a picture in three weeks": letter from Joan Bennett to Diana Anderson, 1944.

275 "chamberwork": Patrick McGilligan, *Fritz Lang: The Nature of the Beast* (New York: St. Martin's Press, 1997), p. 326.
277 "Joan Bennett was never lovelier": *Hollywood Reporter,* October 10, 1944.
277 "Miss Bennett has not been seen": *New York Times,* January 26, 1945.
277 "*The Woman in the Window* is doing terrific business": letter from Joan Bennett to Diana Anderson, 1945.
278 "DITTY DARLING: TRIED TO PHONE": telegram from Joan Bennett to Diana Anderson, October 22, 1944.
278 "I deeply regret": *Los Angeles Herald-Express,* April 5, 1952.
278 "It is regrettable": ibid.
278 "a truly colorful figure": *Los Angeles Examiner,* October 24, 1944.
278 "laid to his final rest in ceremonies which in their quietness": ibid.
279 "Are you traveling alone?": author interview with Diana Anderson, August 14, 2000.
279 "The girls, particularly Joan, wanted to bury him next to their mother": author interview with Victor Morrison, March 11, 2000.

Chapter Sixteen: 1945–1947

283 "I always thought that Fritz Lang and Joan Bennett": author interview with Hilda Rolfe, October 13, 2000.
285 "a film that seems to have very little to do with America": David Thomson, *Biographical Dictionary of Film* (New York: William Morrow, 1981), p. 43.
286 "made the official love goddesses": ibid.
286 "never turned in a finer performance": *New York Daily Mirror,* February 15, 1946.
286 "most attractive and sultry": *Hollywood Reporter,* December 13, 1945.
286 "I saw *Scarlet Street* the other night": letter from David O. Selznick to Joan Bennett, March 5, 1946.
286 "immoral, indecent, corrupt, and tending to incite crime": Kael, *5001 Nights at the Movies,* p. 659.
286 "a judgment that seemed off-the-wall even then": ibid.
287 "the dilemma is this": *New York Times,* January 13, 1946.
287 "We thought the picture was the sort": *New York Sun,* January 30, 1946.
287 "It is by far the most obscene": letter from Mrs. W.F. Scott to Eric Johnson, Director of Censorship, Motion Picture Industry, date unknown.
287 "I felt I needed a bath when it ended": *Atlanta Journal,* January 16, 1946.
287 "My wife is the mother of three children": *Los Angeles Times,* February 9, 1946.

288 "*Scarlett* [*sic*] *Street*": telegram from Harry Buxton, Manchester, England, June 3, 1946.
289 ". . . That made me very uncomfortable": author interview with Diana Anderson, August 14, 2000.
289 "a perfect woman": author interview with Jane Greer, April 3, 2001.
290 "She was appreciative and generous": author interview with Carmen DiRigo, March 23, 2001.
290 "I was happy to hear from you today": letter from Joan Bennett to Diana Anderson, 1944.
291 "I certainly don't expect you to be my counter-part": letter from Joan Bennett to Diana Anderson, 1944.
292 "In order to remain friends": *Los Angeles Times,* June 1945.
292 "insanely jealous and moody": *Los Angeles Times,* June 15, 1945.
293 "They would go to his house": author interview with Peter Plant, August 16, 2000.
294 "At last, she'd met her match": *BP,* p. 293.
294 "Nobody ever crossed her": author interview with Patricia Coulter McElroy, June 20, 2001.
294 "You had to get out of her way": author interview with Lorinda Roland, July 20, 2001.
297 "a perfect vehicle for Joanie": memo from Barbara Bennett to Walter Wanger, November 24, 1945.
297 "deals delicately and sometimes humorously": memo from Barbara Bennett to Walter Wanger, February 9, 1946.
297 "So you see, Barbara": letter from Walter Wanger to Barbara Bennett, February 22, 1946.
297 "You are becoming more and more adept": letter from Walter Wanger to Barbara Bennett, March 6, 1946.
297 "Thank you very much": letter from Barbara Bennett to Walter Wanger, March 8, 1946.
298 "She's serious. Hurry": *New York Times,* March 15, 1946.
298 "Joan and Constance to find about this": ibid.
298 "If you still have your typewriter": letter from Walter Wanger to Barbara Bennett, February 14, 1947.
298 "SIGNED LEASE ABOUT TWO MINUTES": telegram from Barbara Bennett to Walter Wanger, September 23, 1947.
299 "I have lots of confidence": letter from Walter Wanger to Barbara Bennett, October 10, 1947.
299 "It was obvious that she was a drunk": author interview with Peggy Sobel, March 11, 2002.
299 "Don't think anything like it": memo from Barbara Bennett to Walter Wanger, December 8, 1945.

300 "in which emotion played no part": Jean Renoir, *Renoir on Renoir,* trans. by Carol Volk (New York/Cambridge: Cambridge Univ. Press, 1989), p. 147.
301 "It seemed to me": ibid.
301 "Joan Bennett, who plays the desirable woman": Celia Bertin, *Jean Renoir—A Life in Pictures* (Johns Hopkins Univ. Press, 1991), p. 213.
303 "should have been left on the cutting room floor": *Cue,* June 6, 1947.
303 "strangely garbled . . . for every person": *Hollywood Reporter,* May 14, 1947.
303 "curiously foggy and stylized": *New York Times,* June 9, 1947.
304 "The picture is going wonderfully": letter from Joan Bennett to Diana Anderson, undated.
305 "Joan Bennett has never": *Hollywood Reporter,* January 17, 1947.
305 "None of the three principal players": *Time,* April 7, 1947.
306 "Joan Bennett is completely hydrochloric": *New York Times,* April 21, 1947.
306 "most convincing when she is being wicked": *New Yorker,* April 26, 1947.
306 "Moviegoers were growing more selective": Thomas Schatz, *Boom and Bust: American Cinema in the 1940s* (Berkeley: Univ. of California Press, 1997), p. 295.

Chapter Seventeen: 1948

311 "a collection of gimmicks": David Thomson, *Showman: The Life of David O. Selznick* (New York: Alfred A. Knopf, 1992), p. 427.
311 "I remember typing up the pages": author interview with Hilda Rolfe, October 13, 2000.
312 "Michael Redgrave was a mess": author interview with Diana Anderson, August 10, 2000.
313 "He was a famous sadist, you know": author interview with Natalie Schafer, April 28, 1990.
313 "Fritz didn't care if she bled": author interview with Diana Anderson, October 25, 1991.
315 "a pretty silly yarn": Bosley Crowther, *New York Times,* January 16, 1948.
316 "I tried it and I said I didn't like it": author interview with Stephanie Wanger Guest, March 29, 2001.
316 "I thought he was going to have a car accident": ibid.
316 "Hello, daaaahhling!": ibid.
317 "very charming and cooperative": author interview with Vera Hruba Ralston, November 10, 1999.

317 "double house": author interview with Lorinda Roland, July 20, 2001.
317 "She wouldn't live on the base": author interview with Patricia Coulter McElroy, June 21, 2004.
320 "This is the pen that closed the deal with Ingrid Bergman!": *BP,* p. 295.
322 "Burn, damn you, burn!": *BP,* p. 296.
322 "The picture bespeaks class": *Variety,* November 12, 1948.
322 "A stunning super-spectacle": *New York Daily Mirror,* November 12, 1948.
322 "become a classic of the screen": *New York Daily News,* November 12, 1948.
322 "Awash in Technicolor": *New Yorker,* November 17, 1948.
322 "allowed this whole drama": *New York Times,* November 12, 1948.
322 "I remember going to the opening": author interview with Diana Anderson, August 12, 2000.
324 "The malicious stories": Ingrid Bergman and Alan Burgess, *Ingrid Bergman: My Story* (New York: Delacorte, 1972), p. 227.

Chapter Eighteen: 1949–1950

325 "I remember him getting together with Tony Mann": author interview with Arlene Dahl, March 10, 2001.
327 "There would be an eight-story building totally bombed out": author interview with June Lockhart, December 29, 2001.
327 "cordial, charming, gracious": ibid.
330 "Hollywood's most glamorous grandmother": *BP,* p. 295.
334 "homey": author interview with Henry Garson, July 8, 2001.
336 "Stanwyck scene": *Max Ophuls in the Hollywood Studios,* p. 308.
337 "The film is suffering very much": letter from Walter Wanger to Max Ophuls, December 28, 1949, housed at Wisconsin Center for Film and Theater Research.
337 "a really first-class film": *Evening Standard,* January 6, 1950.
337 "the film belongs to Miss Joan Bennett": *Times of London,* January 7, 1950.
337 "nothing exceptional . . . not like *The Woman in the Window* or *Scarlet Street*": author interview with Joan Bennett, September 29, 1989.
337 "She was *exactly* like the role she played in the film": author interview with Diana Anderson, November 25, 1991.
339 "I thought Spence was great, but I wasn't mad for *my* part": author interview with Joan Bennett, September 30, 1989.
340 "Be my filthy Valentine": card from Joan Bennett to Hedda Hopper, February 14, 1950, on file in Hedda Hopper Collection, Academy of Motion Picture Arts and Sciences.

341 "very strong": *Box-Office Digest,* July 1950.
341 "couldn't be more charming": *Los Angeles Examiner,* June 11, 1950.
341 "As the bride's mother, Joan Bennett fills the bill to perfection": *Hollywood Citizen-News,* June 12, 1950.
342 "He was not someone who wore his heart": author interview with Melinda Markey, February 23, 2001.
342 "Suddenly, I was offered the sympathy": *BP,* p. 298.
343 "Daily the circle of discontent widened between us": ibid., p. 299.

Chapter Nineteen: 1951–1952

346 "Brando was wonderful": author interview with Teresa Wright, February 20, 1990.
346 "There's a broad with a future behind her": Parish, *The RKO Gals,* p. 96.
346 "If she hadn't stayed with him": author interview with Peter Plant, March 23, 2001.
347 "Spence said he didn't want to be another damned Judge Hardy": author interview with Joan Bennett, September 29, 1989.
348 "ravishing beauty": *New York Post,* July 12, 1951.
348 "Mother forgot to look at her own past": author interview with Diana Anderson, August 10, 2001.
349 "summer stock in an iron lung": *Films in Review,* July 1977.
350 "the talk of the neighborhood": *Los Angeles Herald and Express,* December 21, 1951.
350 "Walter was in a state of denial": author interview with Arlene Dahl, March 10, 2001.
351 "Hollywood is a strange, cruel place": *Los Angeles Mirror,* December 1951.
352 "standing not more than a dozen feet away": *BP,* p. 300.
352 "Get away from here": *WW,* p. 275.
352 "I've just shot the sonofabitch who tried to break up my home": ibid.
353 "assault with a deadly weapon": ibid.
353 "You're pretty cool about this, aren't you?": *BP,* p. 302.
353 "If Walter thinks there is any romance between us": unidentified publication, December 1951.
353 "I love you both very much": author interview with Diana Anderson, August 10, 2000.
354 "I hope that Walter": *BP,* p. 304.
356 "I think it so typical of Joan": *Los Angeles Examiner,* December 14, 1951.
357 "It could have been horrible": author interview with Diana Anderson, August 11, 2000.

357 "He would come and sit in our parlor": author interview with Jane Greer, April 3, 2001.

358 "first, because of his children and second, in consideration of the film industry": *Los Angeles Herald and Express,* April 15, 1952.

358 "The public should start cleaning up": unidentified publication, 1952.

359 "It's good luck . . . I could use some": *Los Angeles Herald and Express,* May 9, 1952.

359 "filled me with an everlasting loathing for summer theater": author interview with Stephanie Wanger Guest, February 10, 1990.

360 "Joan was terrified when we played L.A.": author interview with William Windom, October 9, 2001.

361 "I'm sorry. I'm so sorry": unidentified publication.

362 "did little to endear me to Morton": *BP,* p. 279.

362 "excellent care": *Los Angeles Evening Herald and Express,* October 12, 1951.

362 "a child-parent relationship": ibid.

362 "must be accomplished through the free choice of the children": *Los Angeles Evening Herald and Express,* October 12, 1951.

363 "Well, Patricia, what is your favorite gift?": author interview with Gyl Roland, August 13, 2000.

363 "Lorrie, watching you get older makes *me* feel old": author interview with Lorinda Roland, July 20, 2001.

363 "My personal feeling": ibid.

366 "Unmentionable": author interview with Gyl Roland, August 13, 2000.

Chapter Twenty: 1953–1958

368 "beating the bastards": author interview with Louise Gore, June 26, 2001.

368 "in that great voice of hers": ibid.

369 "with Constance, the point was": ibid.

370 "They ran the cows out of the barn": author interview with James Fraser, November 25, 2002.

370 "one of those popular little comedies": *New York Times,* April 16, 1953.

370 "Miss Bennett, who hadn't much to do": *New Yorker,* April 25, 1953.

370 "She wasn't as active": author interview with Bazey Tankersley, December 17, 2001.

370 "He was offered a key position": author interview with Peter Plant, August 15, 2000.

371 "She was walking slowly toward us": author interview with Charles Nelson Reilly, May 10, 2003.

372 "I was a terrible student": author interview with Gyl Roland, March 18, 2001.

372 "I remember Mother sending me some party dresses": author interview with Patricia Coulter McElroy, June 20, 2001.
373 "Think of the places you will go": ibid.
373 "Her idea of hard liquor was a grasshopper": author interview with Lorinda Roland, July 20, 2001.
374 "My dear, my *face* is my identification": author interview with Patricia Coulter McElroy, June 20, 2001.
374 "marvelous. Onscreen, I died for her": author interview with Louise Gore, June 26, 2001.
375 "I guess I'd better telephone Joan": ibid.
377 "I wouldn't bother if I were you": author interview with Peter Plant, March 23, 2001.
377 "Oh, it's so nice that you would come to see me": author interview with Donald Pippin, March 6, 2002.
378 "Oh, Constance do it": ibid.
378 "She's an alcoholic": ibid.
378 "I'm not the world's greatest actress": author interview with Paula Laurence, October 5, 2002.
379 "You really believed that she loved him": ibid.
379 "Never again": *New York Journal-American,* August 15, 1958.
381 "another disaster": *BP,* p. 294.
382 "Joan Bennett was wonderful": author interview with Iris Adrian, November 16, 1990.
387 "Her idea of a good night's sleep": *New York Daily News,* March 11, 1951.
387 "Hello, Donald": *BP,* p. 311.
389 "slow to recover its cost": *WW,* p. 314.
389 "This is a gruesome city": letter from Joan Bennett to Diana Anderson, undated.
389 "It really is a cute play full of laughs": letter from Joan Bennett to Diana Anderson, 1956.
390 "Poor Papa": letter from Joan Bennett to Diana Anderson, 1957.
390 "remarkably fresh and vital in her part": *Cape Cod Standard-Times,* July 2, 1957.
391 "Frankenheimer was cruel to her–a bully": author interview with Jack Klugman, August 5, 2003.
391 "She would always say, 'You don't have to probe'": author interview with Stephanie Wanger Guest, September 4, 2001.
391 "That young man is a very fine director": author interview with Diana Anderson, August 12, 2000.
392 "Joan Bennett delivered a better acting performance": *New York Journal-American,* December 13, 1957.

392 "a treatise against capital punishment": *WW,* p. 339.
393 "This is my fourteenth career": ibid.
393 "a compact, sometimes wonderfully droll commentary on contemporary affairs": *Hartford Times,* March 7, 1958.
393 "gay and amiable and, after its own fashion": *Boston Globe,* March 16, 1958.
394 "She was probably a bit apprehensive": author interview with Susan Kohner, December 11, 2000.
394 "a sadly belabored discourse": *New York Journal-American,* April 15, 1958.
394 "as slick as a new deck of cards": *New York Daily Mirror,* April 15, 1958.
394 "folds her arms, looks wise, and does nicely": *New York Herald-Tribune,* April 15, 1958.
395 "I miss the children so much I ache": letter from Joan Bennett to Diana Anderson, April 29, 1958.
395 "At the funeral, it was unconscionable": author interview with Michael Downey, September 12, 2002.
396 "have a special language": Anne Sexton, "Wanting to Die," *The Complete Poems* (Boston: Houghton Mifflin, 1981), p. 142.
396 "For me, she died a long time ago": author interview with Diana Anderson, August 11, 2000.

Chapter Twenty-One: 1959–1965

399 "a devoted mother and compulsive housekeeper": *BP,* p. 298.
399 "sort of drew the line at college": author interview with Stephanie Wanger Guest, April 24, 2001.
399 "sheer perverseness": *BP,* p. 309.
400 "There wasn't an empty seat in the house": author interview with Diana Anderson, October 25, 1991.
401 "Shelley's been dying to see snow": letter from Joan Bennett to Diana Anderson, November, 1961.
403 "This picture has been my life": *WW,* p. 373.
403 "at least he isn't playing the role of the green-eyed monster": letter from Joan Bennett to Diana Anderson, undated.
404 "Well, I'm really too old for it": author interview with Charles Hollerith, May 8, 2003.
404 "Don't tell Joan": author interview with Mary Cooper, July 9, 2001.
405 "just the job for the coach-party trade": Philip Hope-Wallace, *Guardian,* September 27, 1963.
405 "utter lines of such nitwit improbability": *Times of London,* September 27, 1963.

405 "She was very good in the part of Edith": author interview with Roy Moseley, June 16, 2002.
405 "I didn't give up films—they gave me up": unidentified publication, September 10, 1963.
406 "I don't think he can last much longer": letter from Joan Bennett to Diana Anderson, November 4, 1964.
406 "So I called her": author interview with Mary Cooper, July 9, 2001.
406 "Joan, as I long as I knew her": ibid.
408 "The main thing": Associated Press, August 16, 1959.
408 "She refused to play the game": author interview with Patricia Coulter McElroy, June 21, 2004.
409 "a very valuable technique—how to act with my back to the audience": author interview with Penny Fuller, January 26, 2003.
410 "I'd never seen anything like this": ibid.
410 "a curious, oddly fascinating play": *Chicago Tribune*, December 26, 1961.
410 "My manager, Geoffrey Barr, in New York, decided": *Variety*, January 3, 1962.
411 "I'm expecting my son": author interview with Peter Plant, March 23, 2001.
412 "Let's not talk about it": ibid.
412 "And I wasn't going to": ibid.
413 "Everywhere they went he wore his uniform": author interview with Peter Plant, March 6, 2000.
413 "The wives of the other officers": author interview with Anne Slater, May 24, 2001.
415 "costarring with Lana Turner": author interview with Donald Pippin, March 6, 2002.
415 "You're not going to *touch* me!": Kobal, *People Will Talk*, p. 445.
416 "Constance looked wonderful in the clothes": author interview with Anne Slater, May 24, 2001.
416 "it was more like an old lady": Kobal, *People Will Talk*, p. 445.
417 "Don't tell the General about this": author interview with Lorinda Roland, March 21, 2003.
418 "May I call Constance? . . . That's the first time in our lives": author interview with Mary Cooper, July 9, 2001.
418 "I was born in 1914": author interview with Lorinda Roland, March 21, 2003.
418 "Lorrie, your mother has three hours to live": author interview with Lorinda Roland, July 20, 2001.
419 "Would it be all right if I re-did it?": author interview with Anne Slater, May 24, 2001.

419 "When you are a show business family": James Robert Parish, *The RKO Gals* (New Rochelle, N.Y.: Arlington House, 1974), p. 98.

419 "I always felt": author interview with Lorinda Roland, July 20, 2001.

Chapter Twenty-Two: 1966–1971

421 "It was late at night": author interview with Timothy Anderson, April 30, 2003.

424 "It was clear to me": author interview with Nancy Barrett, March 18, 2003.

425 "Dan does have genius": author interview with Kathryn Leigh Scott, June 7, 2001.

425 "She was used to working like a trouper": ibid.

425 "And she had to know": author interview with Kathryn Leigh Scott, March 14, 1990.

425 "At the end of the day": author interview with Marie Wallace, April 30, 2003.

426 "she never dominated": author interview with Alexandra Moltke, March 8, 2003.

426 "Joan somehow managed": author interview with Kathryn Leigh Scott, June 7, 2001.

426 "Kathryn, you're pretty": ibid.

426 "You're using your face too much": ibid.

426 "She said to me, 'Nancy, don't you realize'": author interview with Nancy Barrett, March 18, 2003.

426 "He thinks he's Henry Fonda": ibid.

427 "If it takes blood to keep him alive": *Saturday Evening Post,* November 30, 1968.

428 "Joan Bennett scream": Rex Reed, *People Are Crazy Here* (New York: Delacorte Press, 1973), p. 220.

428 "I felt positively like a Beatle": ibid.

429 "He seemed kind of doting": author interview with Alexandra Moltke, March 8, 2003.

429 "He thought he knew a great deal about the theater": author interview with Robert Wallsten, March 18, 2003.

430 "There was an elusive quality about him": author interview with Diana Anderson, August 14, 2000.

432 "Mother really led poor Lois a merry chase": author interview with Diana Anderson, August 12, 2000.

432 "Joan couldn't have cared less about the theatrical side": author interview with Patricia O'Connell, April 30, 2003.

432 "messy, if minor incident": *BP,* p. 294.

433 "Once, Joan and I drove out to the location": author interview with Kathryn Leigh Scott, June 7, 2001.

433 "We were all so confused": author interview with Nancy Barrett, March 18, 2003.

Chapter Twenty-Three: 1972–1990

435 "Scarsdale is where you go to die": author interview with Diana Anderson, August 14, 2001.

435 "She was not cut out to be a suburban housewife": author interview with Melinda Markey, February 23, 2001.

436 "She would breeze into one of these places": author interview with Ronald Bowers, April 24, 2002.

437 "After the Saturday night performance": author interview with Mary Cooper, July 9, 2001.

437 "She was a little bit gentler": author interview with James Graves, February 16, 2001.

438 "Joan liked to entertain rather formally": author interview with Richard Stack, May 6, 2001.

438 "This is an industry of youth": author interview with Peter Haskell, September 26, 2001.

439 "I'm fed up with Italy and Italians": letter from Joan Bennett to Diana Anderson, undated.

440 "didn't know whether to laugh or weep": *Cue,* September 3, 1977.

440 "a waxwork Princess Margaret": *London Sunday Times,* October 9, 1977.

440 "a totally synthetic personality": *New York Magazine,* September 12, 1977.

440 "I just got tired of saying no": author interview with Richard Stack, May 6, 2001.

442 "My, how movieland": author interview with Ronald Bowers, June 10, 2002.

442 "This is the first time": author interview with James Fraser, November 25, 2002.

442 "Well, that wasn't much": author interview with Ronald Bowers, June 10, 2002.

443 "I should have been more of a bitch": author interview with Richard Stack, May 6, 2001.

444 "a study in slow motion": James Watters and Horst, *Return Engagements* (New York: Potter, 1985), p. 141.

445 "There was a limit, perhaps": author interview with Timothy Anderson, April 30, 2003.

446 "That was shocking": author interview with Joan Bennett, September 30, 1989.

447 "She was an angel": *People,* January 1991.

448 "I'm flattered that you want to write about me": *Films in Review,* October 1965, p. 490.

449 "I don't think much of most of the films I made": Richard Lamparski, *Whatever Became Of . . . ?,* 11th ser. (New York: Crown, 1989), p. 14.

Selected Bibliography

Aherne, Brian. *A Proper Job*. Boston: Houghton-Mifflin, 1969.

Allen, Frederick L. *Only Yesterday: An Informal History of the 1920s*. New York: John Wiley and Sons, 1997.

Atkinson, Brooks. *Broadway*. New York: Macmillan, 1970.

Bacher, Lutz. *Max Ophuls in the Hollywood Studios*. New Brunswick: Rutgers Univ. Press, 1996.

Basinger, Jeanine. *A Woman's View: How Hollywood Spoke to Women,* 1930–1960. New York: Alfred A. Knopf, 1993.

Behlmer, Rudy, ed. and annotator. *Memo from Darryl F. Zanuck: The Golden Years at Twentieth Century–Fox*. New York: Grove Press, 1993.

Bennett, Joan. *How to Be Attractive*. New York: Alfred A. Knopf, 1943.

Bennett, Joan, and Lois Kibbee. *The Bennett Playbill*. New York: Holt, Rinehart, and Winston, 1970.

Bennett, Richard. "Memoirs" (unpublished).

Berg, A. Scott. *Goldwyn*. New York: Alfred A. Knopf, 1989.

Bergman, Ingrid, and Alan Burgess. *Ingrid Bergman: My Story*. New York: Delacorte Press, 1980.

Bertin, Celia. *Jean Renoir—A Life in Pictures*. Baltimore: Johns Hopkins Univ. Press, 1991.

Bernstein, Matthew. *Walter Wanger: Hollywood Independent*. Berkeley and Los Angeles: Univ. of California Press, 1994.

Binns, Arthur. *Mrs. Fiske and the American Theatre*. New York: Crown, 1955.

Bogard, Travis, and Jackson Bryer, eds. *Selected Letters of Eugene O'Neill*. New Haven: Yale Univ. Press, 1988.

Booher, Ned, and Linda Ferries. *Kokomo: A Pictorial History*. St. Louis: G. Bradley, 1989.

Brady, Frank. *Citizen Welles*. New York: Anchor Books, 1989.

Brandt, Allan W. *No Magic Bullet: A Social History of Venereal Disease in the U.S. Since 1880*. New York/Oxford: Oxford Univ. Press, 1985.

Brooks, Louise. *Lulu in Hollywood*. New York: Alfred A. Knopf, 1982.

Brown, Gene. *Movie Time*. New York: Macmillan, 1995.

Cerf, Bennett A., and Van H. Cartmell. *Sixteen Famous American Plays*. New York: Modern Library, 1941.
Chalmers, David M. *Hooded Americanism: The History of the Ku Klux Klan*. New York: Franklin Watts, 1981.
Chierichetti, David. *Hollywood Costume Design*. New York: Harmony Books, 1976.
Clark, Barrett H., and George Freedley. *A History of Modern Drama*. New York and London: D. Appleton-Century, 1947.
Davis, Bette, and Sandford Dody. *The Lonely Life*. New York: G.P. Putnam and Sons, 1962.
Douglas, Ann. *Terrible Honesty: Mongrel Manhattan in the 1920s*. New York: Farrar Straus Giroux, 1995.
Durgnat, Raymond. *Jean Renoir*. Berkeley and Los Angeles: Univ. of California Press, 1974.
Flanner, Janet. *Janet Flanner's World—Uncollected Writings 1932–75*, edited by Irving Drutman. New York: Harcourt Brace Jovanovich, 1979.
Fonda, Henry, and Howard Teichmann. *Fonda: My Life*. New York: NAL, 1981.
Fontaine, Joan. *No Bed of Roses*. New York: William Morrow, 1978.
Friedrich, Otto. *City of Nets: A Portrait of Hollywood in the 1940s*. Berkeley and Los Angeles: Univ. of California Press, 1986.
Gagey, Edmond M. *Revolution in American Drama*. New York: Columbia Univ. Press, 1947.
Gelb, Arthur, and Barbara Gelb. *O'Neill*. New York: Harper and Brothers, 1962.
Gilbert, Martin. *The Second World War*. New York: Henry Holt, 1989.
Gish, Lillian, and Ann Pinchot. *The Movies, Mr. Griffith, and Me*. Englewood Cliffs, N.J.: Prentice-Hall, 1969.
Goodman, Ezra. *The Fifty-Year Decline and Fall of Hollywood*. New York: Simon and Schuster, 1961.
Harris, Leon. *Upton Sinclair: American Rebel*. New York: Thomas Crowell, 1975.
Harvey, James. *Movie Love in the Fifties*. New York: Alfred A. Knopf, 2001.
Hayward, Brooke. *Haywire*. New York: Random House, 1978.
Helburn, Theresa. *A Wayward Quest*. Boston: Little, Brown, 1960.
Helm, Thomas B. *History of Cass County, Indiana*. Chicago: Brant and Fuller, 1886.
Hepburn, Katharine. *Me*. New York: Alfred A. Knopf, 1991.
Higham, Charles. *Orson Welles: The Rise and Fall of an American Genius*. New York: St. Martin's Press, 1985.
Hirschhorn, Clive. *The Columbia Story*. London: Octopus, 1999.
Hoopes, Roy. *When the Stars Went to War*. New York: Random House, 1994.

Jackson, Kenneth T. *The Encyclopedia of New York City.* New Haven: Yale Univ. Press, 1995.
Jewell, Richard P., and Vernon Harbin. *The RKO Story.* New York: Arlington House, 1982.
Kael, Pauline. *5001 Nights at the Movies.* New York: Holt, Rinehart, and Winston, 1985.
———. *When the Lights Go Down.* New York: Holt, Rinehart, and Winston, 1980.
Kendall, Elizabeth. *The Runaway Bride: Hollywood Romantic Comedy of the 1930s.* New York: Alfred A. Knopf, 1990.
Kessler, Ronald. *The Sins of the Father: Joseph P. Kennedy and the Dynasty He Founded.* New York: Warner Books, 1996.
Kidd, Charles. *DeBrett Goes to Hollywood.* New York: St. Martin's Press, 1987.
Kobal, John. *People Will Talk.* New York: Alfred A. Knopf, 1985.
LaGuardia, Robert, and Gene Areri. *Red: The Tempestuous Life of Susan Hayward.* New York: Macmillan, 1985.
Lahr, John. *Notes on a Cowardly Lion.* New York: Alfred A. Knopf, 1969.
Lamparski, Richard. *Whatever Became Of . . . ?* 11th ser. New York: Crown, 1989.
Leff, Leonard J., and Jerrold Simmons. *The Dame in the Kimono.* New York: Grove Weidenfeld, 1990.
Lewis, Judy. *Uncommon Knowledge.* New York: Pocket Books, 1994.
Logan, Joshua. *Josh: My Up and Down, In and Out Life.* New York: Delacorte Press, 1976.
Long, Robert Emmet, ed. *George Cukor Interviews.* Jackson: Univ. Press of Mississippi, 2001.
Loos, Anita. *Kiss Hollywood Good-by.* New York: Viking, 1974.
Madsen, Axel. *Gloria and Joe.* New York: William Morrow, 1988.
Mailer, Norman. *Marilyn.* New York: Warner, 1975.
Mann, William J. *Wisecracker: The Life of William Haines, Hollywood's First Openly Gay Star.* New York: Viking, 1998.
Mantle, Burns, ed. *The Best Plays of 1937–38.* New York: Dodd, Mead, 1942.
McGilligan, Patrick. *Fritz Lang: The Nature of the Beast.* New York: St. Martin's Press, 1997.
———. *George Cukor: A Double Life.* New York: HarperCollins, 1991.
Meredith, Burgess. *So Far So Good.* Boston: Little, Brown, 1994.
Meyer, Michael. *Ibsen.* New York: Doubleday, 1971.
Moore, Colleen. *Silent Star.* New York: Doubleday, 1968.
Mordden, Ethan. *The Hollywood Studios.* New York: Simon and Schuster, 1988.
Mosel, Tad, and Gertrude Macy. *Leading Lady: The World and Theatre of Katharine Cornell.* Boston: Atlantic Monthly Press–Little, Brown, 1978.

Mosley, Leonard. *Zanuck: The Rise and Fall of Hollywood's Last Tycoon.* Boston: Little, Brown, 1984.
Muller, Eddie. *Dark City: The Lost World of Film Noir.* New York: St. Martin's Press, 1998.
Paris, Barry. *Garbo: A Biography.* New York: Alfred A. Knopf, 1995.
———. *Louise Brooks.* New York: Alfred A. Knopf, 1989.
Parish, James Robert. *The Glamour Girls.* New Rochelle, N.Y.: Arlington House, 1975.
———. *The RKO Gals.* New Rochelle, N.Y.: Arlington House, 1974.
Peters, Margot. *The House of Barrymore.* New York: Alfred A. Knopf, 1990.
Powell, Dr. Jehu Z. *History of Cass County, Indiana.* Chicago/New York: Lewis, 1913.
Redgrave, Michael. *In My Mind's Eye: An Actor's Autobiography.* New York: Viking, 1983.
Reed, Rex. *People Are Crazy Here.* New York: Delacorte Press, 1973.
Renoir, Jean. *My Life and My Films.* New York: Atheneum, 1974.
———. *Renoir on Renoir.* Translated by Carol Volk. New York and Cambridge, Eng.: Cambridge Univ. Press, 1989.
Schatz, Thomas. *Boom and Bust: American Cinema in the 1940s.* Berkeley and Los Angeles: Univ. of California Press, 1999.
———. *The Genius of the System: Hollywood Filmmaking in the Studio Era.* New York: Henry Holt, 1988.
Scott, Kathryn Leigh. *Lobby Cards—The Classic Films.* Los Angeles: Pomegranate Press, 1988.
Scott, Kathryn Leigh, and Jim Pierson. *Dark Shadows Almanac: Millennium Edition.* Los Angeles: Pomegranate Press, 2000.
Sexton, Anne. *The Complete Poems.* Boston: Houghton Mifflin, 1981.
Shipman, David, *The Great Movie Stars: The Golden Years.* New York: Crown, 1970.
———. *The Story of Cinema.* New York: St. Martin's Press, 1982.
Shivers, Alfred S. *The Life of Maxwell Anderson.* New York: Stein and Day, 1983.
Simon, John. *Reverse Angle: A Decade of American Film.* New York: Crown, 1983.
Solomon, Aubrey. *Twentieth Century–Fox: A Corporate and Financial History.* Boston: Scarecrow Press, 1988.
Spoto, Donald. *Notorious: The Life of Ingrid Bergman.* New York: HarperCollins, 1997.
Swanson, Gloria. *Swanson on Swanson.* New York: Random House, 1980.
Tapert, Annette, and Ellen Horan. *The Power of Glamour: The Women Who Defined the Magic of Stardom.* New York: Crown, 1998.
Thomas, Bob. *Joan Crawford.* New York: Simon and Schuster, 1978.
———. *Selznick.* New York: Doubleday, 1970.

Thomson, David. *The Biographical Dictionary of Film.* New York: William Morrow, 1981.

———. *Showman: The Life of David O. Selznick.* New York: Alfred A. Knopf, 1992.

Waldau, Ray S. *Vintage Years of the Theatre Guild, 1928–1939.* Cleveland: Case Western Reserve Univ. Press, 1972.

Watters, James, and Horst. *Return Engagements.* New York: Potter, 1985.

Wright, William. *Lillian Hellman: The Image, The Woman.* New York: Simon and Schuster, 1986.

Zieger, Robert H. *America's Great War: World War I and the American Experience.* Lanham, Md.: Rowman and Littlefield, 2000.

Index

Index

Index

Index